2019-2020
SEPTEMBER–AUGUST

NIV®

Standard
COMMENTARY

NEW INTERNATIONAL VERSION®

EDITORIAL TEAM

RONALD L. NICKELSON
Senior Editor

JANE ANN KENNEY

MARGARET K. WILLIAMS

with
JEFF GERKE

Volume 26

Standard®
PUBLISHING
part of the David C Cook family

IN THIS VOLUME

INDEX OF PRINTED TEXTS

The printed texts for 2019–2020 are arranged here in the order in which they appear in the Bible.

Get the eCommentary for the **Logos Basic Library** or **Wordsearch Starter Engine!**

The Standard Lesson eCommentary®, for either PC or Mac, is included with purchase of a Deluxe Edition. Instructions for activating the eCommentary for the Deluxe Edition are printed on the inside cover. If you do not have a Deluxe Edition, you can purchase the SLeC separately at www.logos.com and www.wordsearchbible.com.

...and don't forget the visuals!

The thumbnail visuals in the lessons are small reproductions of 18″ x 24″ full-color posters that are included in the *Adult Resources* packet for each quarter. Order numbers 1629119 (fall 2019), 2629120 (winter 2019–2020), 3629120 (spring 2020), and 4629120 (summer 2020) from either your supplier, by calling 1.800.323.7543, or at www.standardlesson.com.

CUMULATIVE INDEX

A cumulative index for Scripture passages used in the STANDARD LESSON COMMENTARY
for September 2016–August 2020 (of the 2016–2022 cycle) is provided below.

✞

Notes

_____

_____

_____

Get the Most from Every Lesson!

Training for Service

For over 100 years Training for Service has equipped more than 1 million volunteers for Bible teaching. This 26-session Bible overview—designed to equip lay leaders to serve as elders, Sunday school teachers, small group facilitators, and in other positions of service in the church—can be completed as a group study or a self-study.

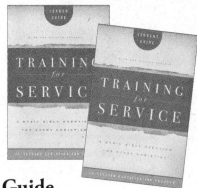

The Pocket Pronunciation Guide to Bible People, Places, and Things

Every Bible teacher knows the feeling of reading a Scripture passage out loud and getting to a hard-to-pronounce word. Now you can have at your fingertips information on how to pronounce hundreds of commonly mispronounced words in the Bible.

Standard Bible Atlas

Small group leaders, Bible teachers, and Bible students can use these satellite maps, reproducible maps, charts, chronologies, and time lines to enrich learning.

Standard Bible Dictionary

This Bible dictionary includes more than 2,000 entries with a popular how-to-say-it pronunciation guide as well as definitions to enhance teaching and personal Bible study.

Standard PUBLISHING
part of the David C Cook family

Standard Lesson Resources

Whether you use Standard Lesson Commentary® or Standard Lesson Quarterly®, you'll find a wealth of additional helps in the Standard Lesson Resources® line. These printed and digital products provide the most comprehensive resources for teaching the *ISSL/Uniform Series* available anywhere!

Adult Resources

This pack provides 12 full-color visuals to illustrate the lesson each week. Also included is a Presentation Tools CD that includes digital images of all the visuals and a PowerPoint® presentation for each lesson.

In the World

This online feature draws from a current event— something your students are probably talking about that very week— and helps you use it to illustrate the lesson theme.

Devotions®

Reflect on each Sunday's lesson outside of the classroom. Devotions® supplements the daily Bible readings recommended in Standard Lesson to challenge you to experience personal growth in Christ.

Standard®
P U B L I S H I N G
part of the David C Cook family

Explore these resources and more at:
https://www.standardlesson.com/standard-lesson-resources/

RESPONDING TO
GOD'S GRACE

Special Features

Lessons
Unit 1: God Is Faithful

Unit 2: Responses to God's Faithfulness

Unit 3: Faith Leads to Holy Living

QUARTERLY QUIZ

Use these questions as a pretest or as a review. The answers are on page iv of This Quarter in the Word.

Lesson 1

1. Lot fled from Sodom to _____. *Genesis 19:23*

2. Due to his promise to Jacob, God delivered Lot. T/F. *Genesis 19:29*

Lesson 2

1. Eli mistakenly thought Hannah was drunk. T/F. *1 Samuel 1:14*

2. Hannah named her son _____. *1 Samuel 1:20*

Lesson 3

1. God's people were frustrated, wishing he had killed them in Egypt. T/F. *Exodus 16:3*

2. God provided his people manna and _____ to eat in the desert. *Exodus 16:13*

Lesson 4

1. The 12 spies returned after searching out the land of Canaan for _____ days. *Numbers 13:25*

2. Joshua and Caleb were so upset with the Israelites for not trusting God that they fell on their faces. T/F. *Numbers 14:6*

Lesson 5

1. God considered destroying Israel and creating a new nation under Moses. T/F. *Numbers 14:12*

2. God guided Israel through the wilderness with miraculous signs. T/F. *Numbers 14:14*

Lesson 6

1. What did God say would set his people apart from other nations? (their armies, God's laws, their rich culture?) *Deuteronomy 4:8*

2. God revealed himself out of fire to deliver the Ten Commandments. T/F. *Deuteronomy 4:12*

Lesson 7

1. God used a wealthy matron to hide Elijah from King Ahab. T/F. *1 Kings 17:9, 12*

2. What provisions miraculously didn't run out for the impoverished family? (pick two: oil, firewood, flour?) *1 Kings 17:14*

Lesson 8

1. Jesus healed the centurion's son. T/F. *Luke 7:2*

2. Jesus said he didn't find faith as great as the centurion's in _____. *Luke 7:9*

Lesson 9

1. The sinful woman washed Jesus' feet with what? (pick two: tears, myrrh, her hair?) *Luke 7:38*

2. Jesus said, "Whoever has been forgiven little loves _____." *Luke 7:47*

Lesson 10

1. Paul stated his intent to make which visit to the church in Corinth? (second, third, fourth?) *2 Corinthians 13:1*

2. Some Corinthians doubted that _____ spoke through Paul. *2 Corinthians 13:3*

Lesson 11

1. Paul's team remembered which three characteristics of the Thessalonians? (faith, perseverance, strength, love, hope?) *1 Thessalonians 1:2, 3*

2. The Thessalonians' response to the gospel was so complete that they became _____ to those in Macedonia and Achaia. *1 Thessalonians 1:7*

Lesson 12

1. Peter told his congregation to imitate God's joy. T/F. *1 Peter 1:15, 16*

2. Christians are _____ by the precious blood of Christ. *1 Peter 1:18, 19*

Lesson 13

1. Peter said that God has given us _____ so we can participate in the divine nature. *2 Peter 1:4*

2. Peter knew that he would die soon. T/F. *2 Peter 1:13, 14*

QUARTER AT A GLANCE

by Larry Shallenberger

OUR TIMES are marked by dramatic changes in how we relate to each other, both as individuals and as communities. The days of tight-knit neighborhoods are a distant memory in many parts of the world. Families transplant themselves cross-country. A single mouse-click can dissolve an online friendship. Marriages often don't last. The new normal frequently comes at the price of loyalty and permanence, qualities the authors of the Scriptures might have referred to as "faithfulness."

A God Worth Knowing

The word faithfulness simply doesn't have much currency in our time. Before we fault cultural shifts for our fragile relationships, we should recall the opening pages of Scripture. Sin's curse disrupted all relationships, especially our relationship with God. Alienated from God, humanity hatched countless false religions throughout the world, each searching for truth about the Creator.

Against that backdrop of confusion, alienation, and idolatry, God revealed himself and his desire to enter into a faithful relationship with the people he created.

Unfaithful people struggle to trust others, so God's first task was to establish himself as worthy of humanity's confidence. God reveals himself throughout history as one whose faithfulness never fails. We see God keep a promise to Abraham by blessing his nephew (Genesis 19:29). We watch God lead his people out of slavery to the border of the promised land, only to see them prove unfaithful. God forgave their betrayal and kept his word (Numbers 14:20-25). God consistently demonstrates his loyalty to his people, no matter how many times they fail him.

Faithfulness Demands Faithfulness

God unilaterally reveals himself as true, the God to whom we can take the risk of attaching our hopes. But the invitation requires that we begin to take steps to reciprocate that loyalty. Those steps don't make us worthy of his faithfulness, but they show that we trust his faithfulness.

God's expects his people to practice faithfulness in our relationships with him. Moses uses the metaphor of a contract between a king and his people to show what the give-and-take of a faithful relationship between God and his people looks like (Deuteronomy 4:1-8, 12, 13). Later, a fugitive prophet and a starving widow are brought together by God (1 Kings 17:8-16). Together they learn to demonstrate faithfulness to God.

Faithfulness Transforms Character

We can't sustain faithfulness toward God on our own. The Old Testament witnesses to cycles of God's people violating the terms of the covenant, God's imposing judgment, people's repentance, and restoration. The prophets longed for the day when God would equip his people with a new heart that would allow them to sustain a steadfast relationship with their God. The third unit in this quarter focuses on four New Testament accounts that show this prophecy coming to pass. Christlike character was being formed in his people.

> *God reveals himself throughout history as one whose faithfulness never fails.*

Paul tells the people to examine themselves to see whether this transformation was actually occurring (2 Corinthians 13:1-9). Meanwhile, Paul's colleague Peter taught his congregations that a faithful relationship with God required holy living and goodness (2 Peter 1:1-15).

As we work through this quarter, may we be encouraged that our faithful God chooses to enter into a relationship with us that makes us more like him.

GET THE SETTING

by Ronald L. Nickelson

CULTURAL EXPECTATIONS suggest (or dictate) how we should respond when others are gracious to us. Whether that graciousness takes the form of extending a courtesy, offering hospitality, or overlooking an indiscretion, a response of appreciation is in order. And so it is with God. The manner and type of graciousness extended to us has a lot to do with the nature of what our response should be. God has expectations in this regard—expectations we dare not overlook!

Concepts from Contexts

Behind the translations "grace," "gracious," and similar renderings in the New Testament is a Greek word group whose members are also translated variously as "favor" (Luke 1:28, 30), "gift" (Romans 1:11), "commendable" (1 Peter 2:19), "benefit" (2 Corinthians 1:15), etc. This wide range of translation results rightly from the complicated grammatical rules of Greek. At the most basic level, *charis* (pronounced *kar-is*) is the Greek noun behind the English translation "grace."

The word charis was not a new word to the writers of the New Testament. It is attested as far back as the poet Homer (800–701 BC?). In Greek mythology, Charis was one of the goddesses of charm and beauty. But words change in their range of meanings over time. For example, the English word *charisma* is easily recognized as a transliterated variation of the Greek *charis*. A modern dictionary entry for *charisma* as "a special magnetic charm or appeal" does not match how that word is used in the New Testament. There its regular translation is "gift(s)" (example: Romans 1:11).

For the word group involving *charis*, a shift in range of meaning is seen in how a Greek historian of the fourth century BC used a verb form of that word in a context of appeasing the gods by offering sacrifices. Much later, a historian of the first century BC reflected a new shade of meaning as he used a form of charis in a context of overlook-

ing enmity in the interest of friendship. This signaled a shift toward the idea of "to forgive."

Much caution is therefore advised with regard to reading back modern usages of a word into Scripture, or vice versa. The writers of the Bible were much more likely to draw on the prevailing range of meanings for any given word rather than feeling bound to follow usage by, say, Homer. To have used words in ways that no longer prevailed was to risk misunderstanding.

Frequent usages of members of the *charis* word-group in the Greek Old Testament (the Septuagint) are in contexts of a weaker person finding favor in the eyes of a stronger person (examples: Genesis 39:4, 21). Noun, verb, and adjectival forms of *charis* occur more than 200 times in the New Testament. Contexts range from those of unique blessings bestowed on particular individuals only once in their lives for one-time earthly purposes (examples: Luke 1:11-17, 30) to the vital doctrinal fact of God's saving grace that is available to all for eternity (examples: Romans 3:24-27; Ephesians 2:5-8). Both kinds of God's graciousness, and every kind in between, call for a response.

Gratitude from Grace

Bestowals of grace by fictitious pagan deities called for adherents to offer sacrifices (compare Acts 14:11-13). First-century Judaism, having rejected the concept of grace available through Christ while clinging to that of Exodus 34:6, was left with a grace response based in human merit and law keeping. The ultimate result of this kind of view is self-congratulatory thankfulness such as seen in Luke 18:9-12.

We are to be grateful to God as our Creator. But a deeper reason for our thankfulness is the fact that God is also our Redeemer. In line with 2 Corinthians 4:15; Ephesians 4:32; etc., may we exhibit a thankfulness consistent with having been saved by means other than our own.

THIS QUARTER IN THE WORD

Answers to the Quarterly Quiz on page 2

Lesson 1—1. Zoar. 2. false. Lesson 2—1. true. 2. Samuel. Lesson 3—1. true. 2. quail. Lesson 4—1. 40. 2. false. Lesson 5—1. true. 2. true. Lesson 6—1. God's laws. 2. true. Lesson 7—1. false. 2. oil, flour. Lesson 8—1. false. 2. Israel. Lesson 9—1. tears, her hair. 2. little. Lesson 10—1. third. 2. Christ. Lesson 11—1. faith, love, hope. 2. models. Lesson 12—1. false. 2. redeemed. Lesson 13—1. promises. 2. true.

LESSON CYCLE CHART

International Sunday School Lesson Cycle, September 2016–August 2022

Year	Fall Quarter (Sep, Oct, Nov)	Winter Quarter (Dec, Jan, Feb)	Spring Quarter (Mar, Apr, May)	Summer Quarter (Jun, Jul, Aug)
2016–2017	**The Sovereignty of God** (Isaiah, Matthew, Hebrews, Revelation)	**Creation: A Divine Cycle** (Psalms, Luke, Galatians)	**God Loves Us** (Psalms, Joel, Jonah, John, Romans, Ephesians, 1 Peter, 1 John)	**God's Urgent Call** (Exodus, Judges, Prophets, Acts)
2017–2018	**Covenant with God** (Pentateuch, 1 & 2 Samuel, Nehemiah, Jeremiah, Ezekiel, 1 Corinthians, Hebrews)	**Faith in Action** (Daniel, Matthew, Acts, Ephesians, 1 Timothy, James)	**Acknowledging God** (Pentateuch, 2 Chronicles, Psalms, Luke, John, 2 Corinthians, Hebrews, Revelation)	**Justice in the New Testament** (Matthew, Luke, Romans, 2 Corinthians, Colossians)
2018–2019	**God's World and God's People** (Genesis)	**Our Love for God** (Deuteronomy, Joshua, Psalms, Matthew, Luke, Epistles)	**Discipleship and Mission** (Matthew, Mark, Luke, Acts, Romans)	**Covenant in God** (Ruth, 1 Samuel, Matthew, Mark, Ephesians, Colossians, Hebrews)
2019–2020	**Responding to God's Grace** (Pentateuch, 1 Samuel, 1 Kings, Luke, Epistles)	**Honoring God** (1 Kings, 1 Chronicles, Matthew, Luke)	**Justice and the Prophets** (Esther, Prophets, 1 Corinthians)	**Many Faces of Wisdom** (Proverbs, Ecclesiastes, Gospels, James)
2020–2021	**Love for One Another** (Genesis, 1 Samuel, Luke, John, Acts, Epistles)	**Call in the New Testament** (Gospels, Acts, Romans, 1 Corinthians, Hebrews)	**Prophets Faithful to God's Covenant** (Deuteronomy, Joshua, 1 & 2 Kings, Ezra, Nehemiah, Lamentations, Prophets)	**Confident Hope** (Leviticus, Matthew, Luke, Romans, 2 Corinthians, Hebrews, 1 John)
2021–2022	**Celebrating God** (Exodus, 2 Samuel, Psalms, Mark, Acts, Revelation)	**Justice, Law, History** (Pentateuch, 2 Samuel, Ezra, Job, Isaiah, Nahum)	**God Frees and Redeems** (Deuteronomy, Ezra, Matthew, John, Romans, Galatians)	**Partners in a New Creation** (Isaiah, John, Revelation)

A CREATION FOUNDATION

Teacher Tips by Jim Eichenberger

MARY, MAYNARD, and Manuel are active in their church. They support ministries, pray, and read the Bible. But Mary expressed a view about abortion that was contrary to the views of most others in her class. Maynard spoke words of support for a political movement that class members saw as dangerous. Manuel announced that he and his girlfriend will be moving in together. Arguments broke out, many resting on isolated Bible verses. The question repeated over and over was, "How can you call yourself a Christian and believe *that*?"

Church members are known to share Christian practices yet still disagree on important issues. That's because the Christian worldview they think they have in common varies in certain ways. The purpose of this article and the following three is to help clarify a Christian worldview to guide us to greater unity in our teaching.

For centuries, Christian believers have accepted four basic premises that compose a Christian worldview. These four planks have created the foundation for faithful congregations. But in past decades, these crucial ideas have been challenged, and many have accepted alternatives blindly.

The first of those premises is *creatio ex nihilo*— "creation out of nothing." Simply said, the universe has been designed by a rational architect who did not use preexisting building materials. This first plank of a Christian worldview is the foundation for the other three.

The Uncreated God

The proposal that matter randomly evolved into a universe with rationality or morality is based in Western naturalism. This is an ancient idea that has become more prevalent in the past two centuries. The different proposal that the material universe is an illusion projected from a higher reality is from Eastern pantheism, equally ancient. The notion is that everything from poison to prime rib is equally part of God. But what fits reality is that an uncreated God *made stuff* that *makes sense*.

The Creative God

The Creator is distinct from creation, which consists of both material and nonmaterial realities. An uncreated Creator is the author of the material world as well as that which has no mass and is invisible to any physical measurement. Love, courage, and goodness are just as real as a rock, a tree, or a person. Matter, spiritual values, and sentient spiritual beings all exist in fact.

The Sustaining God

Since everything that is not-God has been called into existence by a Creator who is distinct from creation, two things are true. First, the God who created the universe is powerful enough to sustain it. Second, he also has the power to destroy it. One would expect an all-powerful, rational Creator to have a plan for the universe and to be able to intervene to keep that plan on track.

Teach the principle of *creatio ex nihilo* by pointing out in nearly every lesson that this is how the God of the Bible is presented. He is the rational being who explained his plans to Abraham and Moses (lessons 1–5). He can break into the material universe to demonstrate his power—even to those outside of the ethnic group that accepted his existence—as he did with a widow in Zarephath and a Roman centurion in Galilee (lessons 7, 8). Because he created everything, even nonmaterial values such as faith, love, and hope are realities and not societal standards that change from culture to culture (lesson 11).

Making it clear that Christians affirm that the world was created and is sustained by a personal God will not solve all conflicts with your Mary, Maynard, or Manuel. But once the plank of God's power and nature is set, we are ready to understand who we are as human beings.

FAITHFUL DURING DISTRESS

DEVOTIONAL READING: Luke 17:22, 26-37
BACKGROUND SCRIPTURE: Genesis 18:16–19:29

GENESIS 19:1, 4, 5, 15-26, 29

¹ The two angels arrived at Sodom in the evening, and Lot was sitting in the gateway of the city. When he saw them, he got up to meet them and bowed down with his face to the ground.

. . . .

⁴ Before they had gone to bed, all the men from every part of the city of Sodom—both young and old—surrounded the house. ⁵ They called to Lot, "Where are the men who came to you tonight? Bring them out to us so that we can have sex with them.

. . . .

¹⁵ With the coming of dawn, the angels urged Lot, saying, "Hurry! Take your wife and your two daughters who are here, or you will be swept away when the city is punished."

¹⁶ When he hesitated, the men grasped his hand and the hands of his wife and of his two daughters and led them safely out of the city, for the LORD was merciful to them. ¹⁷ As soon as they had brought them out, one of them said, "Flee for your lives! Don't look back, and don't stop anywhere in the plain! Flee to the mountains or you will be swept away!"

¹⁸ But Lot said to them, "No, my lords, please! ¹⁹ Your servant has found favor in your eyes, and you have shown great kindness to me in sparing my life. But I can't flee to the mountains; this disaster will overtake me, and I'll die. ²⁰ Look, here is a town near enough to run to, and it is small. Let me flee to it—it is very small, isn't it? Then my life will be spared."

²¹ He said to him, "Very well, I will grant this request too; I will not overthrow the town you speak of. ²² But flee there quickly, because I cannot do anything until you reach it." (That is why the town was called Zoar.)

²³ By the time Lot reached Zoar, the sun had risen over the land. ²⁴ Then the LORD rained down burning sulfur on Sodom and Gomorrah —from the LORD out of the heavens. ²⁵ Thus he overthrew those cities and the entire plain, destroying all those living in the cities—and also the vegetation in the land. ²⁶ But Lot's wife looked back, and she became a pillar of salt.

. . . .

²⁹ So when God destroyed the cities of the plain, he remembered Abraham, and he brought Lot out of the catastrophe that overthrew the cities where Lot had lived.

KEY VERSE

When God destroyed the cities of the plain, he remembered Abraham, and he brought Lot out of the catastrophe that overthrew the cities where Lot had lived. —Genesis 19:29

RESPONDING TO GOD'S GRACE

Unit 1: God Is Faithful

LESSONS 1–5

LESSON AIMS

After participating in this lesson, each learner will be able to:

1. List the salient points of Lot's flight from Sodom.

2. Explain how this account demonstrates both the judgment and the mercy of God.

3. Prepare an explanation (one that could be presented to an unbeliever) of how God's judgment and mercy are displayed through the message of the gospel.

LESSON OUTLINE

Introduction
  A. No "Fair Weather" God
  B. Lesson Context
I. God's Warnings (GENESIS 19:1, 4, 5, 15-23)
  A. Angelic Visitation (vv. 1, 4, 5, 15-17)
  B. Lot's Hesitation (vv. 18-20)
    The Small-Town Ideal?
  C. Angelic Determination (vv. 21-23)
II. God's Judgment (GENESIS 19:24-26)
  A. Upon Sodom and Gomorrah (vv. 24, 25)
  B. Upon Lot's Wife (v. 26)
    Part of the Landscape
III. God's Mercy (GENESIS 19:29)
  A. Remembering Abraham (v. 29a)
  B. Rescuing Lot (v. 29b)
Conclusion
  A. Mercy in Judgment
  B. Prayer
  C. Thought to Remember

Introduction

A. No "Fair Weather" God

A farmer built a new barn on his property, and on the roof he placed a weather vane. Below the weather vane he attached a sign that read "God Is Love." On more than one occasion, someone passing by would see the weather vane and ask the farmer, "Are you saying that God's love changes with the wind?"

"Oh no," replied the farmer. "I'm saying that no matter which way the wind blows, God is love."

A similar statement can be made regarding many of God's qualities, including his faithfulness. He is always faithful, regardless of which way life's winds may blow. God is faithful not only in displaying his grace but also in carrying out his judgment on humanity's sin.

B. Lesson Context

Lot was a nephew of the great patriarch Abraham. Lot is first mentioned in the Bible in the genealogy of Abraham's brother (Genesis 11:27). Lot accompanied Abraham and his household when they journeyed from Ur to Canaan (11:31). Following a brief time in Egypt, the family returned to an area south of where the tribe of Judah eventually settles centuries later (13:1, 3). When land disputes broke out, Abraham allowed his nephew to choose the land he wanted for pasture (13:8, 9). Lot saw that the territory in the vicinity of Sodom and Gomorrah was especially desirable, so he settled nearby (13:10, 11).

The exact location of Sodom and Gomorrah is uncertain; some scholars place them within what later came to be the territory of Moab (Isaiah 15:5; Jeremiah 48:33, 34). Along with Zoar, Sodom and Gomorrah are listed as cities located on the Jordan plain (Genesis 13:10-12; see also 14:2, 8). Genesis 13:13 offers an ominous assessment: "The people of Sodom were wicked and were sinning greatly against the Lord."

Lot is a puzzling figure in the Bible. He perhaps understood from his uncle Abraham something of the Lord's righteous standards. Indeed, the New Testament depicts Lot as someone deeply troubled over the wickedness in Sodom. Second Peter 2:7

says that the Lord "rescued Lot, a righteous man, who was distressed by the depraved conduct of the lawless." Verse 8 describes Lot as a "righteous man," who "was tormented in his righteous soul by the lawless deeds he saw and heard." However, Lot also seems to have become attached to life in Sodom despite the tension between his righteousness and the wickedness of the city.

Genesis 18 begins with an account of the Lord's visit with Abraham. He was one of three "men" who came to Abraham (Genesis 18:2). After confirming the Lord's promise that Sarah would conceive and bear a son (18:10), the three "looked down toward Sodom" (18:16). The Lord told Abraham of his intention to discover more about the extent of the sin within both Sodom and Gomorrah (18:20, 21). Verse 22 records that "the men turned away and went toward Sodom, but Abraham remained standing before the Lord." At that point the exchange between the Lord and Abraham about sparing the righteous in Sodom occurred. Because the sins of Sodom and Gomorrah became "so grievous" in the Lord's sight (18:20), he determined that judgment must be carried out on them. Despite Abraham's intercession and God's willingness to relent from judgment, both cities would be destroyed for lack of 10 righteous people (18:22-33).

I. God's Warnings
(GENESIS 19:1, 4, 5, 15-23)

A. Angelic Visitation (vv. 1, 4, 5, 15-17)

1a. The two angels arrived at Sodom in the evening,

The *two angels* are generally taken to be two of the three men who had visited Abraham (Genesis 18:2). The third of those three "men" is thought to have been the Lord in temporary human form (18:33). This may imply that the Lord is not directly present with Lot in the ensuing discussion.

HOW TO SAY IT

Gomorrah	Guh-*more*-uh.
Sodom	*Sod*-um.
Zoar	*Zo*-er.

1b. and Lot was sitting in the gateway of the city.

That *Lot* sits *in the gateway of the city* may indicate that he holds a leadership position in Sodom. The gateway or gates of a city is the place where important decisions are made (Deuteronomy 16:18; 21:18-21) and business is transacted (example: Ruth 4:1-11). Given the reaction of the men of the town (Genesis 19:9), Lot is more likely there on business.

1c. When he saw them, he got up to meet them and bowed down with his face to the ground.

Lot greets his two guests in a manner similar to how Abraham greeted his three guests (Genesis 18:2). In the verses not in today's text (19:2, 3), Lot eagerly invites the two visitors to spend the night at his house. At first they decline, saying that they will spend the night in the street. But Lot, aware of the wickedness that permeates the city (see the Lesson Context), convinces them.

4, 5. Before they had gone to bed, all the men from every part of the city of Sodom—both young and old—surrounded the house. They called to Lot, "Where are the men who came to you tonight? Bring them out to us so that we can have sex with them.

If this is what happens when innocent people are behind locked doors, imagine what would have happened if the visitors were still out in the street! Two intended sins are in view: those of homosexual behavior and rape (compare Romans 1:24-27).

In the intervening verses not in today's lesson text (Genesis 19:6-14), Lot tries to dissuade those who surround *the house*, even offering his two daughters instead. The reply he receives promises that he too will be abused. At this, the two angelic guests pull Lot back into the house and strike the hostile crowd with blindness. The pair then plead with Lot to leave the city in order to avoid the judgment that is imminent. Lot begs his two sons-in-law to flee, but they treat his words as a joke.

15. With the coming of dawn, the angels urged Lot, saying, "Hurry! Take your wife and your two daughters who are here, or you will be swept away when the city is punished."

As dawn approaches, the urgency of the angels' appeal intensifies. Note that the terms *angels* and *men* are used interchangeably of the two individuals throughout this account (Genesis 19:1, 10, 15, 16). The likely speaks both to their appearance as men and their function as messengers, a common usage of the word in both Old and New Testaments. Note that the word translated "angels" here is rendered "messengers" in Genesis 32:3, 6; likewise in the New Testament, see Matthew 11:10 and 2 Corinthians 12:7.

16. When he hesitated, the men grasped his hand and the hands of his wife and of his two daughters and led them safely out of the city, for the LORD was merciful to them.

We are not told why Lot resists leaving Sodom. Is he hesitant to leave the wealth he has accumulated? Is he unsure about where he will live next? Later he will try to negotiate with one of the angels as to where he should go (see commentary on 19:18-20).

Whatever the reason, the angels know they cannot wait any longer for Lot to act. They take the foursome by their hands and lead them out of Sodom. The reason for their deliverance is stated plainly: the Lord is being *merciful* (compare Revelation 18:4, 5). The word translated *merciful* is rare in the Old Testament, occurring only here and in Isaiah 63:9.

> *What Do You Think?*
> In what ways can we encourage and help people to escape when they're trapped in sinful or challenging environments?
> *Digging Deeper*
> What does biblical encouragement include that secular viewpoints might not?

17. As soon as they had brought them out, one of them said, "Flee for your lives! Don't look back, and don't stop anywhere in the plain! Flee to the mountains or you will be swept away!"

The reason for the instruction *Don't look back* isn't entirely clear. Perhaps it is meant to prevent those fleeing from getting caught in the shock wave since looking back implies slowing down

to do so. Another possibility is that looking back would signal a desire to remain in the sinful environment of Sodom (compare Luke 9:62). Another possibility is that those fleeing are not to stop to engage in any smug satisfaction or gloating that those who may have troubled Lot's family are "getting theirs" (compare Proverbs 24:17). In any case, what will be descriptive when Jeremiah 46:5 is written later is prescriptive at the moment.

The Hebrew word translated *mountains* is actually singular; but since the singular can refer to "hill country" in general (Numbers 14:45), a specific mountain may not be intended. Of primary importance is that Lot and his family move a safe distance away from the judgment that is about to be poured out on two wicked cities.

B. Lot's Hesitation (vv. 18-20)

18. But Lot said to them, "No, my lords, please!

As Lot addresses the angels, he uses the same terminology as when he first encountered them at the gate of Sodom (Genesis 19:2). It is a term of respect and does not necessarily imply an acknowledgment of divinity.

19. "Your servant has found favor in your eyes, and you have shown great kindness to me in sparing my life. But I can't flee to the mountains; this disaster will overtake me, and I'll die.

Lot's response to the angels' urgent plea leaves a reader baffled. Three times he has been warned about the destruction coming on Sodom (Genesis 19:13, 15, 17), and Lot himself has urged his sons-in-law to leave the city (19:14). Lot readily admits that he has been the recipient of *favor* and *great kindness*, yet he fears going *to the mountains* (see commentary on 19:17, above) lest this disaster *overtake* him!

Consider the irony: Lot is more fearful of a disaster that *could* happen than of one that is clearly going to happen—and soon! Thus Lot reveals his lack of confidence in God's deliverance. How can Lot think God is rescuing him from Sodom only to allow him to die before reaching safety?

20. "Look, here is a town near enough to run to, and it is small. Let me flee to it—it is very small, isn't it? Then my life will be spared."

Lot suggests an alternative as a place of refuge. The name of the town is not given yet given (see commentary on verse 22, below), but Lot twice makes a point of the fact that the town is *small*. Perhaps his attitude is that a small place cannot be a sin-filled place, or perhaps that a small sinful place can be overlooked by the Lord.

Abraham's negotiation with God regarding Sodom has already been noted (Genesis 18:22-33; see Lesson Context). Lot is now engaging in his own brand of negotiation. But the motivation of Abraham and Lot could not be more different. Abraham was concerned that others be spared from judgment. Lot, in contrast with Genesis 19:14, seems interested only in self-preservation. He uses the pronouns *me* and *my* but says nothing about his wife or his daughters. That the three women in his life should also be spared is an afterthought, if any thought at all.

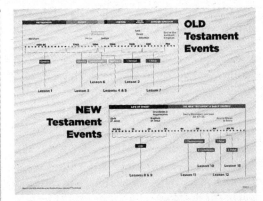

Visual for Lesson 1. *Keep this time line posted throughout the quarter to give participants a chronological perspective.*

ing in Sodom, Lot asked his angelic benefactors to allow him to relocate to a diminutive town. Tragically, Lot ended up discovering that his problems were personal, not geographical. When you're running *from* sin, be sure you're also running *toward* righteousness!   —J. E.

C. Angelic Determination (vv. 21-23)

21. He said to him, "Very well, I will grant this request too; I will not overthrow the town you speak of.

The angel agrees to Lot's request; Lot is granted permission to flee to *the town*. That the angel promises not to *overthrow* it implies that the town was intended to be included in the impending judgment. Now it will be spared so Lot and family can take refuge there.

22. "But flee there quickly, because I cannot do anything until you reach it." (That is why the town was called Zoar.)

Once more the angel urges haste. The promised judgment will not occur until Lot has reached *the town* to which he has asked to flee. The name of the town, *Zoar*, comes from a Hebrew word that can indicate small size or insignificance (Judges 6:15; Zechariah 13:7). Perhaps today we would call it something like Smallville.

Ironically, Lot and his daughters will later leave Zoar and live "in the mountains," where the angels had first commanded him to go (Genesis 19:30).

> *What Do You Think?*
> Under what circumstances, if any, is it proper to attempt to bargain with God?
> *Digging Deeper*
> How can we ensure that our motives are pure when we are tempted to bargain with God?

❧ THE SMALL-TOWN IDEAL? ❧

Small-town America is frequently used as an image of utopia. Fictional towns like Bedford Falls, Lake Wobegon, and Mayberry evoke images of peaceful lives of communal harmony, where any problem can be resolved.

While small towns have much to offer, they are not the Edens of our dreams. Children growing up in small towns are connected to the same internet, watch the same TV shows, and listen to the same music as those in cities and suburbs. Small-town couples go through divorces. Small towns have their share of crime and injustice. Changing one's location cannot guarantee that one will avoid the ravages of sin.

When escaping the corruption of big-city liv-

23. By the time Lot reached Zoar, the sun had risen over the land.

Dawn was approaching when the angels urged Lot to leave Sodom (Genesis 19:15). Now *the sun is fully up* as Lot enters his city of refuge, *Zoar*.

II. God's Judgment
(GENESIS 19:24-26)

A. Upon Sodom and Gomorrah (vv. 24, 25)

24. Then the LORD rained down burning sulfur on Sodom and Gomorrah—from the LORD out of the heavens.

The promised destruction of both *Sodom and Gomorrah* begins as *burning sulfur* rains down *from the Lord* on the thoroughly corrupt cities (compare Job 18:15; Psalm 11:6; Isaiah 30:33; 34:9; Ezekiel 38:22). The names of Sodom and its twin city Gomorrah became synonymous with human depravity and the outpouring of God's wrath as a result (Jeremiah 23:14; Zephaniah 2:9; Jude 7).

25. Thus he overthrew those cities and the entire plain, destroying all those living in the cities—and also the vegetation in the land.

When Lot first viewed Sodom and its territory, he had found "the *plain* of Jordan" to be "well watered, like the garden of the Lord" (Genesis 13:10). Now nothing is spared from the wrath of divine judgment; the *cities*, their inhabitants, and all plant life is gone.

> *What Do You Think?*
>   How can we use biblical accounts like that of
>   Sodom and Gomorrah to communicate the
>   nature of God to unbelievers?
> *Digging Deeper*
>   How do Matthew 11:23; Romans 9:29; 2 Peter
>   2:4-10; Jude 7; and Revelation 11:8 inform
>   your answer?

B. Upon Lot's Wife (v. 26)

26. But Lot's wife looked back, and she became a pillar of salt.

To this point in the record, little has been said regarding *Lot's wife*. When she has been mentioned previously, their daughters have been included as well (Genesis 19:15, 16). Now this woman looks *back*, perhaps out of a wistful longing to gaze one more time on the city where she has resided. Or, more distressingly, maybe she desires to return. The result of such disobedience of a clear command from the angel (19:17) is immediate: she is turned into *a pillar of salt*.

Some have noted the presence of salt formations found along the shores of the Dead Sea, near which Sodom and Gomorrah were likely located. Lot's wife thus becomes a kind of monument to the high price of disobeying God. Unlike other monuments, however, she blends in with the surrounding territory and is lost; not even her name is remembered.

Centuries later, Jesus will allude to this incident in warning people to be prepared for his return. The verse is short: "Remember Lot's wife!" (Luke 17:32). This suggests that Lot's wife lost her life because she was unprepared to accept the mercy extended to her (17:28-31). The folly of Lot's wife illustrates other teachings of Jesus, including trying to save one's life and losing it (Matthew 16:25; Luke 17:33) and his warning not to put one's hand to the plow and look back (Luke 9:62).

> *What Do You Think?*
>   What steps can we take to protect ourselves
>   from the temptation to "look back" in
>   unhealthy ways (Luke 9:62)?
> *Digging Deeper*
>   How do Ezekiel 16:43; 1 Corinthians 6:9-11;
>   1 Peter 1:18, 19; 2:10, 25 speak to healthy
>   ways of looking back?

❧ PART OF THE LANDSCAPE ❧

The Dead Sea earns its name. Though fed by the Jordan River, the sea has no outlet streams. Water escapes only through evaporation; any minerals swept in stay put. The high salt content—nearly nine times that of the oceans—prevents almost all organisms from surviving there. Tourists are routinely warned to seek medical attention should they accidentally swallow the water.

Like the Dead Sea, Sodom and Gomorrah became depositories for whatever "washed in." As wickedness accumulated, the cities became more lethal. As salts make the Dead Sea toxic to most life, so sinfulness in Sodom and Gomorrah choked out righteous living.

We surmise that Lot's wife may have been comfortable in Sodom's sinful environment. As a consequence of looking back, she received a permanent home on the shore of the Dead Sea. What sins tempt your heart to look back in longing? —J. E.

III. God's Mercy
(Genesis 19:29)
A. Remembering Abraham (v. 29a)

29a. So when God destroyed the cities of the plain, he remembered Abraham,

When God is said to remember, it signifies that he is committed to acting on a person's or group's behalf in fulfillment of his word. Previously, God remembered Noah and protected him and his family from the flood (Genesis 8:1). Later, God will remember his covenant with Abraham, Isaac, and Jacob (Exodus 2:24) and provide deliverance for his suffering people. This same sense is intended when God's people are commanded to remember his acts or laws (Exodus 20:8; Numbers 15:39, 40; Deuteronomy 7:18; 16:12; etc.). Lot's deliverance is attributed not to anything he did but to Abraham.

> **What Do You Think?**
> How can we best use "God remembered" passages such as Genesis 8:1; 30:22; Exodus 2:24; and Revelation 18:5 to comfort the disturbed and disturb the comfortable?
> **Digging Deeper**
> Considering Isaiah 43:25; Jeremiah 31:34; and Hebrews 10:15-17, what are some wrong ways to use "God remembered" passages?

B. Rescuing Lot (v. 29b)

29b. and he brought Lot out of the catastrophe that overthrew the cities where Lot had lived.

The implication is that Abraham's intercession in Genesis 18:16-33 results in Lot's rescue. The Lord didn't find 10 righteous people there, such as would spare the city 918:32). But he did find one.

Conclusion
A. Mercy in Judgment

On hearing the names Sodom and Gomorrah, most people think immediately of God's wrathful, fiery judgment that befell those cities. God's mercy, however, is also evident when we read of Lot's rescue. Lot acknowledged that he had been shown grace and kindness in being spared. Even so, he still wanted to negotiate regarding the place to which he could flee (Genesis 19:19). Rather than losing patience with Lot, the angel granted his request.

The flaws in Lot's character seen in this account should not draw our attention away from the strength of God's character. Lot's behavior may puzzle us, but God's behavior shouldn't. The goodness of his mercy and the terror of his judgment both stand out. We are to be genuinely grateful that on the cross Jesus took the judgment that we deserved so that God could display his mercy to us.

Like Lot, we too may be disturbed by the godless trends of our culture (compare 2 Peter 2:6-10) and the increasing contempt we see for the Bible and for Christian faith. But we can also become very attached to the pleasures of this world, which, as Jesus noted in the parable of the sower, can choke the spiritual life from us (Luke 8:14).

B. Prayer

Father, both your judgment and your mercy are revealed, not only in this account but throughout your Word. May we give thanks that in the cross of Jesus "mercy triumphs over judgment" (James 2:13). We pray in Jesus' name. Amen.

C. Thought to Remember
What happened to Sodom illustrates God's mercy even in judgment.

VISUALS FOR THESE LESSONS

The visual pictured in each lesson (example: page 13) is a small reproduction of a large, full-color poster included in the *Adult Resources* packet for the fall quarter. That packet also contains the very useful *Presentation Tools* CD for teacher use. Order No. 1629119 from your supplier.

INVOLVEMENT LEARNING

Enhance your lesson with NIV Bible Student *(from your curriculum supplier) and the reproducible activity page (at www.standardlesson.com or in the back of the* NIV Standard Lesson Commentary Deluxe Edition*).*

Into the Lesson

On the board write these words:

Godparent / Mentor / Counselor / Guru

Ask the class to tell how these words overlap in meaning. (*Expected response:* They refer to those who advise and otherwise look out for the best interest of someone else.)

Stimulate discussion by posing one or more of these questions: 1–If you have one or more godparents, what function have they served in your life? 2–In what ways has a mentor benefitted you? 3–What qualifies a person to be considered a guru (a spiritual instructor)?

Alternative. Distribute copies of the "Celebrity Godparents" exercise from the activity page, which you can download. Have students work individually for no more than a minute or in pairs for a few minutes to complete as indicated.

After either activity say, "It is not unusual for people, even after they become adults, to have an older and wiser adult looking out for their best interests. In the Bible, we find a similar situation concerning Abraham and his nephew Lot. Let's take a look."

Into the Word

Divide the class into three groups, giving each group a handout (you prepare) according to the following: **Lot Group:** Genesis 19:1, 15-22; 2 Peter 2:5-10 / **Wife and Sons-in-law Group:** Genesis 19:12-14, 23-26 / **Abraham Group:** Genesis 18:22-33; 19:29.

Ask groups to read their assigned Scripture passages and be prepared to answer the following interview questions as they take the role of the person or persons after which their groups are named.

1–What was life in Sodom like?
2–What would have been your long-term plans for living in Sodom?

3–How did you hear that disaster was about to come to Sodom? What was your reaction to that news?
4–What was your life, if any, like during and after the destruction of Sodom?

After 10–15 minutes, reassemble the class. Act as the interviewer while groups respond to your interview questions.

Alternative. Distribute copies of the "Surprising or Expected?" exercise from the activity page. Have students work in small groups to complete as indicated.

After either activity, make a transition to the Into Life section by saying, "Note that the people in today's lesson had varying degrees of faith as connected with their self-interest. Let's think about how we can use today's lesson effectively in our interactions with those who are less mature in the faith—newer believers who need to be aware of the tension between God's holy judgment and his gracious mercy."

Into Life

Have learners pair up and give each a handout (you prepare) of the text of 2 Timothy 2:11-13. Instruct pairs to prepare an explanation of the tension between God's holy judgment and his gracious mercy by summarizing the account of Sodom (Genesis 19) and comparing it with 2 Timothy 2:11-13, which is an early song of the church. After several minutes of work, encourage presentations as time permits.

Option. Include on the handout this question for deeper discussion:

1–Is *tension* the best word to use to describe how God's divine attributes of gracious mercy and holy judgment relate to one another? Why, or why not?
2–What word might you pick instead? Why?
(Be prepared to discuss proposals such as *balance*, *symmetry*, and *correlation*.)

Faithful During Grief

DEVOTIONAL READING: Psalm 99
BACKGROUND SCRIPTURE: 1 Samuel 1:1–2:10

1 Samuel 1:9-20

9 Once when they had finished eating and drinking in Shiloh, Hannah stood up. Now Eli the priest was sitting on his chair by the doorpost of the LORD's house. 10 In her deep anguish Hannah prayed to the LORD, weeping bitterly. 11 And she made a vow, saying, "LORD Almighty, if you will only look on your servant's misery and remember me, and not forget your servant but give her a son, then I will give him to the LORD for all the days of his life, and no razor will ever be used on his head."

12 As she kept on praying to the LORD, Eli observed her mouth. 13 Hannah was praying

in her heart, and her lips were moving but her voice was not heard. Eli thought she was drunk 14 and said to her, "How long are you going to stay drunk? Put away your wine."

15 "Not so, my lord," Hannah replied, "I am a woman who is deeply troubled. I have not been drinking wine or beer; I was pouring out my soul to the LORD. 16 Do not take your servant for a wicked woman; I have been praying here out of my great anguish and grief."

17 Eli answered, "Go in peace, and may the God of Israel grant you what you have asked of him."

18 She said, "May your servant find favor in your eyes." Then she went her way and ate something, and her face was no longer downcast.

19 Early the next morning they arose and worshiped before the LORD and then went back to their home at Ramah. Elkanah made love to his wife Hannah, and the LORD remembered her. 20 So in the course of time Hannah became pregnant and gave birth to a son. She named him Samuel, saying, "Because I asked the LORD for him."

KEY VERSE

Eli answered, "Go in peace, and may the God of Israel grant you what you have asked of him."
—1 Samuel 1:17

RESPONDING TO GOD'S GRACE

Unit 1: God Is Faithful

LESSONS 1–5

LESSON AIMS

After participating in this lesson, each learner will be able to:

1. Summarize the account of Hannah's desperate plea for a son.

2. Tell why prayer is a vital resource in times of grief and sorrow.

3. Provide examples of individuals who have demonstrated trust in God during times of grief.

LESSON OUTLINE

Introduction

A. A Hymn Written Through Tears

Many well-known and well-loved hymns celebrate God's faithfulness and provide a sense of comfort and peace to the grieving. In many cases, the hymns themselves were produced in the aftermath of great sorrow on the part of the writer. One of these is "What a Friend We Have in Jesus."

Joseph Scriven (1819–1886) wrote the words that were later set to music. He was living a very contented life in his native Ireland. Then, on the night before his wedding was to take place, his fiancée drowned. Not long after this, Scriven moved to Port Hope, Canada, determined to devote his life to helping others in need. When his mother became ill in Ireland, he wrote a letter to comfort her and included in it the words to "What a Friend We Have in Jesus." Sometime later, when Scriven himself fell ill, a friend who came to visit him happened to see a copy of the words scribbled on a piece of paper near his bed. The friend asked who wrote them. Scriven replied, "The Lord and I did it between us."

Through the years, the Lord has provided comfort to the disheartened and the grieving. He has done so sometimes through words of hymns or poems, sometimes through the words of Scripture, sometimes through the simple caring presence of concerned Christian friends, and through other means at other times. And while we often associate grieving with death, in a world broken by the curse of sin there are many other circumstances in which genuine grief can occur. One of these is seen in our Scripture text for today. A childless woman became so distraught over her condition that she determined she would "take it to the Lord in prayer."

B. Lesson Context

The events in the early chapters of 1 Samuel occur toward the end of the period when the judges provided leadership for the nation of Israel. The book of Judges is filled with turmoil and chaos due to Israel's pattern of disobedience and rebellion against God. This trend continues into 1 Samuel with a misbehaving priestly family (see commentary on 1 Samuel 1:14).

Hannah's turmoil is of a different kind: the strife that exists within a family and the heartbreak of a barren woman in that family. Hers was the grief of a hope unfulfilled, a desire for the joys of motherhood that she could see other women experiencing but which had been denied her. Hannah felt cruelly separated from those women and in some cases was likely ostracized by them. In a society in which a woman's primary vocation was to be a mother, infertility was often taken as a sign of God's displeasure and resulted in a loss of status. Hannah experienced the disdain of society and likely wondered whether the Lord saw her in a similar light.

Aside from the societal stigma attached to barrenness in biblical times, the surroundings in Hannah's home made her condition even more excruciating. Elkanah, Hannah's husband, had another wife besides Hannah, named Peninnah. Not only did Peninnah have children, but she taunted Hannah mercilessly for her inability to bear children (1 Samuel 1:6, 7). Peninnah was downright cruel in reminding Hannah of her barren condition. It is hard to imagine how deeply Hannah was hurt by such malicious words from a woman she could not simply cut out of her life.

Elkanah was a well-intentioned man and sympathetic toward Hannah, but he did not grasp fully the extent of her anguish. When Hannah would become so upset during their annual sacrifice that she refused to eat (1 Samuel 1:3, 7),

HOW TO SAY IT

Belial	*Bee*-li-ul.
Eli	*Ee*-lye.
Elkanah	*El*-kuh-nuh or El-*kay*-nuh.
Ephraim	*Ee*-fray-im.
Hophni	*Hoff*-nye.
Nazirite	*Naz*-uh-rite.
Peninnah	Peh-*nin*-uh.
Phinehas	*Fin*-ee-us.
Ramah	*Ray*-muh.
Shiloh	*Shy*-low.

Elkanah would say to her, "Hannah, why are you weeping? Why don't you eat? Why are you downhearted? Don't I mean more to you than ten sons?" (1:8). In truth, being a mother of just one son would have satisfied Hannah, so great was her grief at being childless.

I. Hannah's Sorrow
(1 SAMUEL 1:9-11)
A. Annual Visit (v. 9)

9a. Once when they had finished eating and drinking in Shiloh, Hannah stood up.

Shiloh is where the tabernacle was set up once Joshua and the Israelites had taken control of the promised land (Joshua 18:1). Shiloh is situated within the tribal territory of Ephraim and centrally located in relation to the rest of the land. Thus it is a fitting location for the tabernacle (see also Joshua 18:8-10; 19:51; Judges 21:19).

Each year Elkanah takes his family to worship and perform a sacrifice at the tabernacle at Shiloh. This may be at a national festival such as Passover, but the text does not specify. It appears that families can plan special gatherings of worship together, perhaps along the line of family reunions (1 Samuel 20:6, 28, 29).

Apparently a fellowship meal shared by Elkanah's family follows the time of sacrifice. This is meant to be a joyous time. But it was certainly not joyful for Hannah since her "rival" Peninnah constantly ridicules her barrenness (1 Samuel 1:6). On this occasion, the fact that Hannah is said to rise *when they had finished eating* the fellowship meal may mean that she herself has not eaten anything because she is so upset (see the Lesson Context).

9b. Now Eli the priest was sitting on his chair by the doorpost of the LORD's house.

The Hebrew word translated *house* is used in the Old Testament to describe a number of structures. These include the house of the Lord, or tabernacle (here and in 1 Samuel 3:3), a king's palace (1 Kings 21:1; 2 Kings 20:18), Solomon's temple in Jerusalem (18:16), and the Lord's heavenly temple (Micah 1:2). Virtually nothing is said about the tabernacle in the book of Judges, probably because the spiritual condition of the nation of Israel is so poor at the time. Thus, the tabernacle is not a priority because God is not often prioritized by the people.

But the tabernacle is still revered as a sacred place to those who seek to maintain a true relationship with the Lord. To his credit, Hannah's husband, Elkanah, is one of those individuals who desires to raise his family to honor the Lord.

Eli's two sons, Hophni and Phinehas, are mentioned as priests of the Lord in 1 Samuel 1:3, but nothing is said about Eli's service until the present verse. It is generally assumed that Eli is serving as high priest in Shiloh at this time. Perhaps this is why he is stationed *on his chair by the doorpost* of the tabernacle. People can come and bring their concerns to Eli or seek his counsel.

B. Desperate Prayer (vv. 10 11)

10, 11a. In her deep anguish Hannah prayed to the LORD, weeping bitterly. And she made a vow, saying,

Hannah's prayer likely includes more than the words recorded in the lines that follow. But this segment contains the most significant part of her prayer: the *vow* that she makes before the Lord.

11b. "LORD Almighty, if you will only look on your servant's misery and remember me, and not forget your servant but give her a son,

Two times Hannah refers to herself as the Lord's *servant*, a polite way of speaking of herself and emphasizing her lowly status in presenting her request. Hannah uses the words *remember* and *not forget*, which, as noted in the previous lesson, imply God's action to fulfill his word—in this case, to act in answer to a prayer.

Her repetition emphasizes how desperately she hopes the *Lord Almighty* will hear her and honor her prayer.

What Do You Think?
  What are some good habits to form to increase your patience in prayer?
Digging Deeper
  Why is it important to continue to worship God even when waiting for answers to prayer?

11c. then I will give him to the LORD for all the days of his life, and no razor will ever be used on his head."

The latter declaration sets her son's dedication apart from that of all firstborn sons to the Lord (see Exodus 13:2; Leviticus 27:26). These words reflect Hannah's awareness of the Nazirite vow, the regulations of which are explained in Numbers 6. Either a man or a woman can make such a vow. It includes not only abstaining from cutting one's hair but also from both fruit and drink from the vine and from going near any corpse (Numbers 6:1-8).

Normally the Nazirite vow is voluntary and is taken for a limited period of time (see Numbers 6:13-20). Hannah, however, is placing her son under this vow for life, even before he is conceived. The Lord placed Samson under a similar vow, also before he was conceived (see Judges 13:2-5).

What Do You Think?
  How can we determine when it might be appropriate to make an oath to God, if ever?
Digging Deeper
  How do you harmonize the following passages in this regard: Deuteronomy 6:13; Ruth 1:16-18; Jeremiah 4:1, 2; Matthew 5:33-37; 23:16-22; Hebrews 6:16; 7:20-22; James 5:12?

❧ BABY DEDICATION? ❧

Christian parents know that children are a gift from God. Parents know that they are charged with teaching their children to follow Jesus. But what is the best way to make this commitment publicly?

Some churches have "baby dedication Sunday." Even so, very few parents would presume that babies can be "dedicated" to specific service of the Lord as Hannah dedicated her future son. To recognize this fact, some churches have "baby introduction Sunday" where the attending adults—particularly the parents—dedicate themselves to instructing the child in the Christian faith. The result is more of a "parent dedication Sunday."

But what happens next? How do we daily demonstrate in concrete ways our dedication to raising children in the fear of the Lord?   —J. E.

II. Eli's Suspicion
(1 Samuel 1:12-16)
A. His Doubts (vv. 12-14)

12, 13. As she kept on praying to the LORD, Eli observed her mouth. Hannah was praying in her heart, and her lips were moving but her voice was not heard. Eli thought she was drunk

Hannah continues *praying in her heart*, or silently. Eli observes the movements of *her mouth*. Had Eli heard her speaking, he may have prepared a response to Hannah's vow, possibly to question the validity of it. Regulations for vows state that if a wife makes a vow and her husband hears it, he can forbid her from keeping the vow and nullify it (Numbers 30:6-8, 10-15). Nothing is said about what happens if a priest should hear the vow.

Then Eli notices that her lips are moving, but she is not speaking aloud. He assumes, mistakenly, that Hannah is drunk. This suggests she also made her vow silently.

> **What Do You Think?**
> What are some ways to avoid inaccurate conclusions from the actions of others?
> *Digging Deeper*
> What Scripture supports your ideas?

14. and said to her, "How long are going to stay drunk? Put away your wine."

Eli's accusation of drunkenness on Hannah's part and his inability to recognize her genuinely deep sorrow may say something about his spiritual sensitivity or lack of such (compare Eli's ignorance in 1 Samuel 3). It may also reflect the sad state of spiritual life at the tabernacle, something that unfortunately Eli has seen demonstrated all too often in the conduct of his own sons, Hophni and Phinehas.

These two men, priests though they are, have become widely known for their scandalous behavior within the sacred space of the taberna-

cle (1 Samuel 2:12-17, 22-25). While Eli rebukes Hannah for what he views as shameful behavior, it is Eli who will receive the Lord's rebuke and judgment from Hannah's son Samuel for his own shameful behavior regarding the conduct of his sons (1 Samuel 3:10-18; compare 2:27-36; 4:4, 11-18).

B. Her Denial (vv. 15, 16)

15. "Not so, my lord," Hannah replied, "I am a woman who is deeply troubled. I have not been drinking wine or beer; I was pouring out my soul to the LORD.

Hannah is quick to counter Eli's accusation of drunkenness. Her agitated state is not the result of hard liquor but of a hard life. She has not poured wine or beer into her body; instead she has been *pouring out* her distressed *soul to the Lord*.

16. "Do not take your servant for a wicked woman; I have been praying here out of my great anguish and grief."

The term *wicked* can take a range of meaning from "worthless" to "evil." Ironically (and sadly) this word is later translated "scoundrels" and is attached to the sons of Eli (1 Samuel 2:12). Paul transliterates this Hebrew word *Belial* to speak of Satan in 2 Corinthians 6:15. Hannah is no such person. *Out* of her *soul* comes the anguished, earnest prayer she has just prayed and the vow she has made.

III. Eli's Pronouncement
(1 Samuel 1:17, 18)
A. Declaring a Blessing (v. 17)

17. Eli answered, "Go in peace, and may the God of Israel grant you what you have asked of him."

Eli is satisfied with Hannah's explanation. To send her away *in peace* suggests that Eli hopes Hannah will find wholeness and healing from her distress. He declares a blessing on Hannah: *the God of Israel grant you what you have asked of him*. Whether Eli's words constitute a promise or merely a hope is difficult to say. The latter seems preferable given his spiritual weakness. This blessing may also be the standard way for a priest to respond to a request offered by any worshipper in prayer.

B. Departing in Peace (v. 18)

18a. She said, "May your servant find favor in your eyes."

Hannah concludes her exchange with Eli by asking that she *find favor in* his *eyes*—a reversal of the scornful attitude that he had previously displayed toward her. The presence of both *peace* (see commentary on 1 Samuel 1:17) and *favor* in this verse form a strong contrast to the "deep anguish" with which Hannah had approached the tabernacle (1:10).

18b. Then she went her way and ate something, and her face was no longer downcast.

With her spirit at peace, Hannah is now in a better frame of mind to eat. No longer is she "downhearted" (1 Samuel 1:8). *Her face* also reflects her state of contentment and her trust that her barren condition will be reversed through the Lord's intervention.

IV. The Lord's Provision
(1 SAMUEL 1:19, 20)
A. Remembering Hannah (v. 19)

19a. Early the next morning they arose and worshiped before the LORD and then went back to their home at Ramah.

Because *Ramah* could be one of several different locations, the trip from Shiloh could be anywhere from 3 to 13 miles. Samuel continued to live in Ramah after he became a recognized leader and judge among the Israelites (1 Samuel 7:15-17).

One can only imagine how different Hannah's worship is following the events of the previous day and whether Elkanah or Peninnah notice any-

thing different about her. Her prayer on her next visit to Shiloh might be some indication of her change of heart (see 1 Samuel 2:1-10).

19b. Elkanah made love to his wife Hannah, and the LORD remembered her.

At some point after the return home, *Elkanah* and *Hannah* become intimate. The Lord remembers Hannah, thus answering her earlier request (see commentary on 1 Samuel 1:11).

B. Responding to Her Prayer (v. 20)

20. So in the course of time Hannah became pregnant and gave birth to a son. She named him Samuel, saying, "Because I asked the LORD for him."

The result of the Lord's remembrance of *Hannah* is the birth of *a son*, whom Hannah names *Samuel*. She states her reason for doing so: *because I asked the Lord for him*. The name Samuel has been understood to mean "asked of God" or "name of God." Either meaning emphasizes the Lord's provision in answering Hannah's prayer.

❧ THE NAME GAME ❧

How do parents choose and reject names for their children? In the United States, there are very few laws in this regard. Other countries have very restrictive laws. The naming law in Sweden, for example, prevents families from giving their children nobility titles—no king, queen, or duke. The law has been expanded to exclude "names which for some obvious reason are not suitable as a first name."

Denmark, for its part, has a list of about 7,000 preapproved baby names. Names must indicate gender, and a last name is not suitable as a first name. Parents can submit names for approval, but about one-fifth of them are rejected each year. In Germany, names must be approved by the local registration office. That office consults a list of first names as well as foreign embassies for foreign names.

When selecting a name for her son, Hannah did not try to be novel or try to gain the approval of others. She chose a name that would remind her son that his very existence came about because Hannah was heard by God. How does your name remind you that you are God's creation?   —J. E.

God gives us *comfort*

Visual for Lesson 2. *Use with the first discussion question. Ask for examples of times when God has comforted participants in answer to their prayers.*

Conclusion

A. Grace for the Grieving

Women today have different means available for dealing with matters of infertility, means not known in Hannah's time. Still, infertility treatments are not always within the financial means of the would-be mother or even within the possibilities of medicine. The sorrow of infertility remains a particularly burdensome form of grief. A woman's heart is broken; her despair is immeasurable. She can relate to the words in today's Scripture such as "deep anguish," "misery," "deeply troubled," and "great anguish and grief." She feels she has been denied one of life's most precious experiences. *Why?* she asks repeatedly. *Why me?*

Hannah's barrenness became so excruciating for her that she finally vowed to the Lord that if he gave her a son, she would then give him right back to the Lord. The making of vows is something more in keeping with Old Testament law and practice than with New Testament practice (contrast Matthew 5:37). Prayer, however, continues to provide a means for anyone with a bitter soul or a sorrowful spirit to lay bare their grievance before the Lord as Hannah did.

The God to whom Hannah poured out her soul in her anguish is the God who hears our prayers today. He remains our rock, our fortress, our deliverer (Psalm 18:2), our strength and shield (28:7), our hiding place (32:7), our shepherd (23:1; John 10:11). He is the God of all comfort (2 Corinthians 1:3), and the God who will never leave or forsake us (Hebrews 13:5). What Paul advises in Philippians 4:6 still applies, and he was under arrest when he wrote it: "In every situation, by prayer and petition, with thanksgiving, present your requests to God."

Hannah demonstrated her faithfulness long before Paul wrote. She did so by taking her deepest hurt to the Lord. He, in turn, demonstrated his faithfulness by taking away her pain by providing the blessing she desired.

We keep in mind, however, that we are not guaranteed to receive what we ask of God. And his answer of yes, no, or wait always is in line with his bigger plans. In Hannah's case, her son became a pivotal figure in being the last of the judges and the first of the prophets (Acts 3:24; 13:20). We don't know the future and neither did Hannah. But with her we can say, "My heart rejoices in the Lord . . . There is no one holy like the Lord; there is no one besides you; there is no Rock like our God" (1 Samuel 2:1, 2).

B. Prayer

Father, we see that "deep anguish" abounds every night on the news. It abounds everywhere. Empower each of us to bring your grace, peace, and hope to people around us who need comfort from Heaven amidst their brokenness. We pray in Jesus' name. Amen.

C. Thought to Remember

God listens to our prayers
because he loves us.

INVOLVEMENT LEARNING

Enhance your lesson with NIV Bible Student *(from your curriculum supplier) and the reproducible activity page (at www.standardlesson.com or in the back of the* NIV Standard Lesson Commentary Deluxe Edition*).*

Into the Lesson

Write this quote on the board:

I am alone; I am always alone no matter what.
—Marilyn Monroe

Generate discussion with these questions and prompts: 1–How does this quote make you feel? 2–What might have caused the actress to say this? 3–What do you know about this actress and her death? 4–How does what you know make this quote even more tragic? 5–Tell about a time when you felt all alone and that no one seemed to care about what you needed or how you felt. 6–List some ways people deal with those types of feelings.

Lead into Bible study by saying, "We all have times when we feel alone and wonder if our deepest desires will ever be met. Believers are taught that we are never alone—we have someone who always hears. Such was the case with a woman named Hannah."

Into the Word

Divide the class into three groups, assigning each group one of the following statements and related section of today's Bible text: **Vow Group**—Big girls don't cry (1 Samuel 1:9-11). **Sober Group**—A shoulder to cry on is always nearby (1 Samuel 1:12-16). **Worship Group**—Don't expect change to happen overnight (1 Samuel 1:17-20). Ask groups to read their assigned Scripture passages and be prepared to refute the statement they are given with evidence from the text. Responses might be like these:

Vow Group—Big girls (and boys!) do cry! Even devout believers like Hannah experience and express real grief. Hannah's tears were real, but she knew she would be heard by God. She promised to be thankful when her prayers were answered.

Sober Group—We may find that those who should comfort us are quick to judge and offer useless advice instead. That was the case with Eli, who accused Hannah of being drunk. Even so we can find those who will listen and offer encouragement.

Worship Group—Hannah's request was not fulfilled immediately. God could have overruled human biology and allowed Hannah to become pregnant and bear a child in moments, but he does not usually act that way! Hannah did wait for her child, but some results of her prayers were immediate. She left with lifted spirits and renewed hope.

After 10–15 minutes, allow groups to share their conclusions.

Alternative. Distribute copies of the "Putting It Together" exercise from the activity page, which you can download. Have students work in groups to complete it as indicated.

After either activity, move to the final section of the lesson by saying, "Hannah's situation reminds us that life is messy. Her prayer was answered yes only after bitter tears. In the end, her burden was relieved. Let's see what we can learn from other believers who have turned to God in prayer."

Into Life

Divide the class into small groups. Ask each group to think of historical figures or people they know who have demonstrated reliance on prayer in times of trouble. Have each group come up with a Prayer Warrior All-Star Team of three believers.

Next, have groups compare and contrast the constituents of their teams with a view to adding two more members per team as groups try to convince each other whom to add. Use this to launch a discussion regarding which all-stars should be included on all teams and why.

Alternative. Distribute copies of the "A Prayer That Changed the World" exercise from the activity page to be completed and discussed as indicated.

FAITHFUL DURING UNCERTAINTY

DEVOTIONAL READING: 2 Corinthians 8:9-15
BACKGROUND SCRIPTURE: Exodus 16

EXODUS 16:1-15

¹ The whole Israelite community set out from Elim and came to the Desert of Sin, which is between Elim and Sinai, on the fifteenth day of the second month after they had come out of Egypt. ² In the desert the whole community grumbled against Moses and Aaron. ³ The Israelites said to them, "If only we had died by the LORD's hand in Egypt! There we sat around pots of meat and ate all the food we wanted, but you have brought us out into this desert to starve this entire assembly to death."

⁴ Then the LORD said to Moses, "I will rain down bread from heaven for you. The people are to go out each day and gather enough for that day. In this way I will test them and see whether they will follow my instructions. ⁵ On the sixth day they are to prepare what they bring in, and that is to be twice as much as they gather on the other days."

⁶ So Moses and Aaron said to all the Israelites, "In the evening you will know that it was the LORD who brought you out of Egypt, ⁷ and in the morning you will see the glory of the LORD, because he has heard your grumbling against him. Who are we, that you should grumble against us?" ⁸ Moses also said, "You

will know that it was the LORD when he gives you meat to eat in the evening and all the bread you want in the morning, because he has heard your grumbling against him. Who are we? You are not grumbling against us, but against the LORD."

⁹ Then Moses told Aaron, "Say to the entire Israelite community, 'Come before the LORD, for he has heard your grumbling.'"

¹⁰ While Aaron was speaking to the whole Israelite community, they looked toward the desert, and there was the glory of the LORD appearing in the cloud.

¹¹ The LORD said to Moses, ¹² "I have heard the grumbling of the Israelites. Tell them, 'At twilight you will eat meat, and in the morning you will be filled with bread. Then you will know that I am the LORD your God.'"

¹³ That evening quail came and covered the camp, and in the morning there was a layer of dew around the camp. ¹⁴ When the dew was gone, thin flakes like frost on the ground appeared on the desert floor. ¹⁵ When the Israelites saw it, they said to each other, "What is it?" For they did not know what it was.

Moses said to them, "It is the bread the LORD has given you to eat."

KEY VERSE

When the Israelites saw it, they said to each other, "What is it?" For they did not know what it was. Moses said to them, "It is the bread the LORD has given you to eat." —Exodus 16:15

RESPONDING TO
GOD'S GRACE

Unit 1: God Is Faithful

LESSONS 1–5

LESSON AIMS

After participating in this lesson, each learner will be able to:

1. Tell why the Israelites grumbled against Moses and Aaron and how the Lord addressed their discontent.

2. Compare and contrast the Israelites' grumbling with those of previous incidents of the same.

3. Keep a prayer journal to record one's spiritual journey.

LESSON OUTLINE

Introduction

A. Held from Heaven

A group of botanists traveled to the Alps to search for rare specimens of flowers. At one point they came across a beautiful flower down on a rock ledge that they could not reach. They saw a shepherd boy not far away, so they called him over and offered him some money if he would allow himself to be let down by them with a rope in order to get the flower.

The boy wanted very much to earn the money. He looked down at the ledge. Then he looked at the strange men—and he said no. They offered him a little more money, and he was tempted to say yes.

Still, he wasn't sure about trusting those strangers. Then all of a sudden his eyes lit up. "Wait here," he told them and ran off. About 10 minutes later he was back with another man. "I will get the flower for you," he told the men, "if you will let my father hold the rope."

In times of uncertainty and doubt, when we feel as if we are "at the end of our rope," we need the assurance that someone is holding the rope—or better still, holding us! David expressed his own confidence in the Lord that no matter where he might travel, on earth or in realms beyond the earth, "even there your hand will guide me, your right hand will hold me fast" (Psalm 139:10).

B. Lesson Context

After the Lord had brought forth the Israelites from 400 years of bondage in Egypt, Moses told the people, "Commemorate this day, the day you came out of Egypt, out of the land of slavery, because the Lord brought you out of it with a mighty hand" (Exodus 13:3). That "mighty hand" had been displayed in a series of plagues that provided clear and dramatic evidence that the Lord was superior to any of the gods of the Egyptians (chapters 7–11).

But after leaving Egypt, the Israelites forgot the Lord's "mighty hand." When they were camped by the Red Sea and saw Pharaoh and his horsemen and chariots approaching, immediately they panicked. They accused Moses of bringing them out into the wilderness to die (Exodus 14:10-13).

Moses spoke words of faith and assurance to the people, "The Lord will fight for you" (Exodus 14:14), and then proceeded to back up his words with the miraculous parting of the Red Sea (14:15-18, 21, 22). The Israelites safely crossed on dry land, after which the waters were brought back onto the Egyptians when they tried to give chase (14:23-28). Exodus 14 concludes with the statement that "the people feared the Lord and put their trust in him and in Moses his servant" (14:31).

But that trust was also short-lived. As the people came to the Desert of Shur, just east of where they had crossed the Red Sea, they traveled for three days and could find no water. When they finally did find water at Marah, they could not drink it because it was bitter. The people once more complained to Moses, whereupon the Lord once more provided for his people's needs (Exodus 15:22-25).

As they moved down the western edge of the Sinai Peninsula, the people's travels brought them to a place called Elim, where they came upon an oasis consisting of 12 wells of water and 70 palm trees (Exodus 15:27). The lesson text begins with the people's departure from Elim.

I. The People's Accusation
(Exodus 16:1-3)
A. Between Elim and Sinai (v. 1)

1. The whole Israelite community set out from Elim and came to the Desert of Sin, which is between Elim and Sinai, on the fifteenth day of the second month after they had come out of Egypt.

It is probably difficult for the Israelites to leave a place like *Elim* with its abundance of water and beautiful scenery. This is especially so given that their journey brings them *to the Desert of Sin*, located *between Elim and Sinai*. For the first time in the Bible, the name Sinai appears. It can refer to both the mountain where God will reveal himself to Israel and to the surrounding region (beginning in Exodus 19).

The names *Sin* and *Sinai* may come from the same Hebrew root, though the exact meaning of the word is uncertain. This designation Sin has nothing to do with sin as a violation of God's command, nor should it be confused with the Desert of Zin, which is an open, uncultivated region south of Palestine (Numbers 13:21; 20:1; Joshua 15:1).

Also noted is the people's arrival *on the fifteenth day of the second month* after the exodus. The exodus, along with all the miraculous demonstrations of the Lord's power both before and after it, should still be fresh in the people's minds.

B. Against Moses and Aaron (vv. 2, 3)

2. In the desert the whole community grumbled against Moses and Aaron.

The Israelites had *grumbled against* Moses previously at the Red Sea and at Marah (see Lesson Context; compare Exodus 16:7-9, 11, 12). Now they begin to grumble against both Moses and his brother, Aaron (see 4:14-17; 12:1, 28).

3. The Israelites said to them, "If only we had died by the LORD's hand in Egypt! There we sat around pots of meat and ate all the food we wanted, but you have brought us out into this desert to starve this entire assembly to death."

One should contrast the words of the people here with the description of how they "groaned in their slavery and cried out, and their cry for help . . . went up to God" (Exodus 2:23). Now, faced with the hardships of journeying through the wilderness, they see their past bondage in a whole new light: "Life was so much better in *Egypt*; we had all the food we could eat!" *Pots of*

HOW TO SAY IT

Aaron	*Air*-un.
Elim	*Ee*-lim.
manna	man-uh.
Moses	*Mo*-zes or *Mo*-zez.
Pharaoh	*Fair*-o or *Fay*-roe.
quail	kwayle.
Shur	Shur.
Sinai	*Sigh*-nye or *Sigh*-nay-eye.

meat now seem very appealing to a discontented people whose thinking has become distorted by unbelief.

The Israelites' grumblings, however, come close to blasphemy when they express the wish that they *had died by the Lord's hand in Egypt*. That same hand had performed wonders and signs that brought the Egyptians to their knees and made them beg the Israelites to leave Egypt (Exodus 3:20; 7:5; 12:33; 13:9, 14).

Ironically, not long before this murmuring, the people had sung praises to the Lord for what the power of his "right hand" had accomplished on their behalf (Exodus 15:12). They had proclaimed that "terror and dread" would fall on other nations when they heard of the Lord's mighty works (15:16). But now fear and dread fall on God's own people as they allow their circumstances to control their faith instead of trusting the Lord to continue to care for them as he has promised.

> **What Do You Think?**
> How can we discern when or to what extent it is appropriate to express dissatisfaction with our circumstances?
> **Digging Deeper**
> In addition to Exodus 2:23, 24; Numbers 11:1; Psalm 142:1, 2; Job 1:13-22; Jonah 4:1-11; Matthew 6:28-34; and 1 Peter 5:7, which passages most influence your perspective?

❧ THE GOOD OLD DAYS ❧

For 30 years, British families tuned in to *The Good Old Days*. The entertainment program recreated the music hall variety shows popular in the late 1800s and early 1900s. Entertainers performed onstage in Edwardian costume. Though the series ended, the original venue still presents live events. One could accurately say that the good old days are still alive in England!

The desire to return to a familiar past is called nostalgia. One need not have literally experienced an event or time to feel nostalgic. Dreaming of returning to a past that one never really knew, like British television viewers mentioned here, is referred to as vicarious nostalgia.

The Israelites also felt vicarious nostalgia for the "good old days" in Egypt—not the real days of slavery, but an imagined time of feasting and plenty! This nostalgia stunted their spiritual growth as they looked to the past instead of God's promises in the future. How does nostalgia impede your faithfulness today?   —J. E.

II. The Lord's Answer
(EXODUS 16:4-8)
A. Revealed to Moses (vv. 4, 5)

4. Then the LORD said to Moses, "I will rain down bread from heaven for you. The people are to go out each day and gather enough for that day. In this way I will test them and see whether they will follow my instructions.

Previously the Lord had responded to the people's cries of dissatisfaction by guiding Moses to perform a miracle that provided what the people needed (Exodus 14:15-18; 15:22-25). Here the Lord describes to Moses something that the Lord himself will do, without the need for an intercessor. The Lord will provide a response for his people in order to refute their claims that they were filled with *food* in Egypt and left to die since leaving. Bread will be given to the people, but not from wheat harvested from the ground; instead, it will come *down . . . from heaven*.

The instructions for this gathering will constitute a test for the Israelites, to reveal how faithfully they will adhere to what the Lord commands them to do. The people will be responsible for going out and gathering the bread *each day*.

> **What Do You Think?**
> What are some ways our church can become a vehicle for revealing the Lord's glory to those who are in difficult circumstances?
> **Digging Deeper**
> Why is it important to do so?

5. "On the sixth day they are to prepare what they bring in, and that is to be twice as much as they gather on the other days."

Here is a specific requirement that will test the people's willingness to obey the Lord. Nothing is said at this point about the significance of the seventh day as a sabbath day; that will come later (Exodus 16:23, 25, 26, 29). Perhaps the test of the people is in whether they will obey the Lord's instructions even when no reason is given for those instructions. Will they trust the Lord's authority enough simply to do what he says?

B. Relayed to the People (vv. 6-8)

6. So Moses and Aaron said to all the Israelites, "In the evening you will know that it was the LORD who brought you out of Egypt,

Nothing is said specifically about what *the evening* will bring that will cause the people to *know* that the Lord has *brought* them *out of Egypt*. The context suggests some form of miraculous provision. The people will learn that the Lord has not brought them out to kill them, as they claimed previously (Exodus 16:3), but to care for them throughout their travels.

7a. "and in the morning you will see the glory of the LORD,

Though no one can see God and live (Exodus 33:20; contrast 1 John 3:2), he chooses to reveal his glory in various ways to give his people confidence. This is the first specific reference in Exodus to *the glory of the Lord* appearing to the people, though they have certainly witnessed manifestations of the Lord's power and glory through events such as the plagues and the deliverance at the Red Sea.

The Lord's glory will be more dramatically and intensely manifested at Mount Sinai when he establishes his covenant with the Israelites and calls Moses to come to him on the mountain (Exodus 19:16-19; 20:18-21; 24:15-18). God's glory will also fill the tabernacle when it is completed (40:34, 35).

> **What Do You Think?**
> What steps can we take to prepare ourselves to see God's glory in situations when we feel abandoned by him?
> *Digging Deeper*
> What may happen if we fail to do so?

7b. "because he has heard your grumbling

against him. Who are we, that you should grumble against us?"

Even though this *grumbling* has been voiced to Moses and Aaron, in truth it is ultimately *against* the Lord. Moses and Aaron have not brought the people out of Egypt; that is God's doing (Exodus 16:6). Moses and Aaron are only the human tools in his hands.

8. Moses also said, "You will know that it was the LORD when he gives you meat to eat in the evening and all the bread you want in the morning, because he has heard your grumbling against him. Who are we? You are not grumbling against us, but against the LORD."

All the bread you want is a similar phrase to what the people previously used to describe how abundantly they had been fed in Egypt (Exodus 16:3). God assures his people that no one will go hungry when he feeds them.

Once again Moses points out that the people's complaints is directed *against the Lord*, not Moses and Aaron. Though the people think they are witnessing a failure of human leadership, Israel cannot see that the Lord is leading Moses and Aaron and has never left his people.

III. The Lord's Presence
(EXODUS 16:9-12)
A. The People Look (vv. 9, 10)

9. Then Moses told Aaron, "Say to the entire Israelite community, 'Come before the LORD, for he has heard your grumbling.'"

At this point, Moses instructs Aaron to have the people gather *before the Lord*. This will prepare the people for his response to their *grumbling*.

10. While Aaron was speaking to the whole Israelite community, they looked toward the desert, and there was the glory of the LORD appearing in the cloud.

The people have seen the Lord's presence in a *cloud* previously, guiding them when they left Egypt (Exodus 13:21, 22) and protecting them from the Egyptians at the Red Sea (14:19, 20). Given their earlier complaining, it seems they have assumed that the Lord has abandoned them in *the desert*. They are wrong.

B. Moses Listens (vv. 11, 12)

11, 12. The Lord said to Moses, "I have heard the grumbling of the Israelites. Tell them, 'At twilight you will eat meat, and in the morning you will be filled with bread. Then you will know that I am the Lord your God.'"

Now the directions previously given by Moses and Aaron to the people are backed up with divine authority (Exodus 16:4, 8). Once again the people's *grumbling* is cited. The Lord's providing food for the people is intended to impart the knowledge that *the Lord* is Israel's *God*. Similar words were used previously in Exodus to highlight the impact of the Lord's deliverance of his people on both the Israelites themselves (6:6, 7) and the Egyptians (7:5), specifically Pharaoh (7:14-17; 8:8-10). This is the same God who has brought the Israelites out of their bondage; he has not changed, and he will not abandon his people in this wilderness.

> **What Do You Think?**
> How can we ensure that any concerns about our leaders do not become complaints about God's provision?
>
> **Digging Deeper**
> How should the command to pray for and love our enemies (Matthew 5:43-48; Luke 6:27-36) change our hearts toward leaders we find ourselves disagreeing with consistently?

IV. The Lord's Provisions
(Exodus 16:13-15)
A. Meat for the People (v. 13)

13. That evening quail came and covered the camp, and in the morning there was a layer of dew around the camp.

Here the meat promised earlier by Moses (Exodus 16:8) and by the Lord (16:12) is provided in the form of *quail* (see Numbers 11:31; Psalm 78:27, 28; 105:40). The fact that the birds are found throughout *the camp* clearly indicates that there is a sufficient amount to feed the people.

Apparently, the quail come early enough in the evening that the people have time to prepare them for consumption. God has promised the people that there will be bread *in the morning* (Exodus 16:12), but when they awaken all they see is *a layer of dew* that normally appears on the ground.

B. Manna for the People (vv. 14, 15)

14, 15. When the dew was gone, thin flakes like frost on the ground appeared on the desert floor. When the Israelites saw it, they said to each other, "What is it?" For they did not know what it was.

Moses said to them, "It is the bread the Lord has given you to eat."

The people have never seen anything like this! And being in a desert environment, we wonder when was the last time they saw *frost*. They are at a loss for what to name the *thin flakes* because they are completely new to them. The name they finally give it, *manna*, signals this confusion since the word is from a Hebrew phrase meaning *What is it?*

Even so, there is no question regarding who provides it: only *the Lord* can distribute bread from Heaven. Later its taste is likened to "wafers made with honey" (Exodus 16:31). Perhaps the people are uncertain regarding what they are to do with this substance until Moses says, *It is the bread the Lord has given you to eat.* Psalm 78:24, 25 characterizes it as "the grain of heaven" and "the bread of angels."

> **What Do You Think?**
> What are some ways to prepare ourselves to recognize God's blessings when they come in unexpected forms?
>
> **Digging Deeper**
> Considering passages such as Matthew 17:12 and Luke 10:10-15; 13:34, what dangers can there be in failing to do so?

❧ *Spunyarn and Spindrift* ❧

The nineteenth-century novel *Spunyarn and Spindrift: A Sailor Boy's Log of a Voyage Out and*

Home in a China Tea-Clipper is not considered great. It is not considered required reading for lovers of English literature. Yet Robert Brown's maritime book printed a now-common English word for the very first time: "If the exact name of anything [the sailors] want happens to slip from their memory, they call it a chicken-fixing, or a gadjet, or a gill-guy, or a timmey-noggy, or a wim-wom."

Gadjet, or as we spell it today, *gadget*, was used by sailors of the day as a placeholder name—a word to employ when one has forgotten (or has never known) the correct name of something. Such placeholder names are common and include words like *thingamajig, thingumabob, gizmo,* or *doodad.*

When looking at the strange, edible wafers, the Israelites had no idea what they were. They simply asked, "Manna? What is it?" And the placeholder name stuck! What new thing about God have you learned that passes your previous understanding?

—J. E.

Conclusion

A. Faith for Times Like These

As the children of Israel entered a desolate territory following their exodus from Egypt, they became insecure about their food supply. Despite their collective discontent and grumbling, the Lord provided unmistakable visual aids to show that he would supply for their needs. He had not "let go of the rope"—or of them.

In truth, humanity has always lived in uncertain times. Every generation has viewed its times as unsettled or perilous in one way or another. One has only to read from the words of a passage like Psalm 74 to get a sense of the author's personal anguish and frustration with God over why he does not act more quickly to rescue his people from the desperate times that surround them: "O God, why have you rejected us forever? Why does your anger smolder against the sheep of your pasture?" (Psalm 74:1). "How long," he pleads, "will the enemy mock you, God? Will the foe revile your name forever?" (74:10). The psalmist's times were very uncertain!

Visual for Lesson 3. *Point to the visual as you ask, "In what ways have you found God's provision as surprising as encountering snow in a desert?"*

Our times are no different; there is an abundance of turmoil in so many areas of life. We frequently express our anxiety over uncertainty much as the Israelites did: through murmurings against leadership, from the local to the national level.

The response to living in such times is to return to the truth that is the focus of today's lesson title: God remains faithful, even during times of uncertainty. His promises remain true; his Word provides the assurance that we need—that when human hands are weak and untrustworthy, God's hands remain strong. The aforementioned psalmist, who was so distraught by the chaos around him, came back to this truth himself: "But God is my King from long ago; he brings salvation on the earth" (74:12).

David acknowledged, "My times are in your hands" (Psalm 31:15). So are ours.

B. Prayer

Father, in troubled and uncertain times, may we turn ever and only to you. We thank you that you remain our rock and our refuge—help us remember that! May our hearts be untroubled and find peace from this assurance. We pray in Jesus' name. Amen.

C. Thought to Remember

In uncertain times, God certainly remembers his promises.

INVOLVEMENT LEARNING

Enhance your lesson with NIV Bible Student *(from your curriculum supplier) and the reproducible activity page (at www.standardlesson.com or in the back of the* NIV Standard Lesson Commentary Deluxe Edition*).*

Into the Lesson

Say, "In 2005, two citizens of Finland had an intriguing idea. Instead of just complaining to each other, why not turn their protests into performance? That year, the first 'complaints choir' was organized in Birmingham, England. Soon groups from all over the world began singing about their gripes. Here's an example."

Play a clip of one of these performances from a video-sharing site. Have class members discuss the validity of these sung complaints.

Alternative. Distribute copies of the "Decode the Title" exercise from the activity page, which you can download. Have students work individually for no more than one minute or in small groups for up to three minutes to complete as indicated.

Lead into Bible study by saying, "We can't seem to help ourselves! We complain about the weather, high prices, long lines, and so much more. But this is nothing new. Although the Israelites were rescued from slavery, they found reasons to complain. Let's see how that happened and what resulted."

Into the Word

Divide the class into three groups, giving each group handouts (you create) of one of the following three assignments. **Remonstration Group**—Israel complained about their situation (Exodus 16:1-3). **Response Group**—God answered Israel's grumbling (Exodus 16:4-9). **Results Group**—God made it clear that he cared, by words and actions (Exodus 16:10-15).

Instruct groups to read their assigned Scripture passage and to create at least three questions about the passage for the other groups to answer. Anticipate the questions created to be similar to these:

Remonstration Group: 1–What event had happened just a month and a half before the complaining started? 2–Why does that make the complaining hard to understand? 3–How many people were complaining? 4–How does this dem-

onstrate a mob mentality? 5–How accurate was the Israelites' memory of conditions in Egypt?

Response Group: 1–Why did the Lord see the provision of food as a test of faithfulness for Israel? 2–In what way was the provision of food evidence for Israel of God's continued presence? 3–Against whom were the complaints truly directed? Why does that make a difference?

Results Group: 1–What role did Aaron (and his descendants) play in Israel? Why does it make sense that he would deliver a message from God? 2–How did God appear to the people? At what other times did he appear that way? 3–Why would it be accurate to call the feeding of the Israelites "miracle meals"?

As group discussion dies down, have one group at a time pose its questions to the other groups.

Alternative. Distribute copies of the "Here We Go Again!" exercise from the activity page. Have students work in small groups or as a class to complete it as indicated.

After either activity, make a transition to the Into Life section by saying, "A lifestyle of grumbling results from failing to be grateful for what one has and a failure to recognize the source of those blessings. Like Israel, we start listening to our desires and the influences around us. We can find ourselves believing that we are *victims* of God rather than *victors* enjoying victories won by God. Let's look at how we can avoid that trap and, instead, live in trust that our God will provide for us."

Into Life

Remind the class of whichever Into the Lesson activity you used and ask them to list their own common complaints. Have each learner choose one area in which he or she finds it is especially hard to have faith that God will provide. Encourage free discussion. Further encourage learners to keep a journal in which they record times in which God meets their concerns as they arise.

FAITHFUL DESPITE UNFAITHFULNESS

DEVOTIONAL READING: Psalm 106:1-12, 48
BACKGROUND SCRIPTURE: Numbers 13:1–14:10a

NUMBERS 13:1, 2, 17, 18, 25-28

¹ The LORD said to Moses, ² "Send some men to explore the land of Canaan, which I am giving to the Israelites. From each ancestral tribe send one of its leaders."

. . . .

¹⁷ When Moses sent them to explore Canaan, he said, "Go up through the Negev and on into the hill country. ¹⁸ See what the land is like and whether the people who live there are strong or weak, few or many."

. . . .

²⁵ At the end of forty days they returned from exploring the land.
²⁶ They came back to Moses and Aaron and the whole Israelite community at Kadesh in the Desert of Paran. There they reported to them and to the whole assembly and showed them the fruit of the land.
²⁷ They gave Moses this account: "We went into the land to which you sent us, and it does flow with milk and honey! Here is its fruit.
²⁸ But the people who live there are powerful, and the cities are fortified and very large. We even saw descendants of Anak there."

NUMBERS 14:1, 2, 5-10A

¹ That night all the members of the community raised their voices and wept aloud. ² All the Israelites grumbled against Moses and Aaron, and the whole assembly said to them, "If only we had died in Egypt! Or in this wilderness!"

. . . .

⁵ Then Moses and Aaron fell facedown in front of the whole Israelite assembly gathered there. ⁶ Joshua son of Nun and Caleb son of Jephunneh, who were among those who had explored the land, tore their clothes ⁷ and said to the entire Israelite assembly, "The land we passed through and explored is exceedingly good. ⁸ If the LORD is pleased with us, he will lead us into that land, a land flowing with milk and honey, and will give it to us. ⁹ Only do not rebel against the LORD. And do not be afraid of the people of the land, because we will devour them. Their protection is gone, but the LORD is with us. Do not be afraid of them."
¹⁰ᵃ But the whole assembly talked about stoning them.

KEY VERSE

If the LORD is pleased with us, he will lead us into that land, a land flowing with milk and honey, and will give it to us. —**Numbers 14:8**

RESPONDING TO
GOD'S GRACE

Unit 1: God Is Faithful
LESSONS 1–5

LESSON AIMS

After participating in this lesson, each learner will be able to:

1. Relate the events surrounding the sending out of the spies into Canaan and the Israelites' response.

2. Explain the consequences that could accompany taking a stand based on faith in the Lord in Moses' day.

3. Evaluate personal and communal fears that make walking by faith especially challenging, and consider ways to address these fears.

LESSON OUTLINE

Introduction
A. What Do You See?

Dale Carnegie (1888–1955) is probably best known for his self-help book entitled *How to Win Friends and Influence People.* Carnegie authored another book of the same style; its title is *How to Stop Worrying and Start Living.* In it he included this brief but thought-provoking illustration: "Two men looked out from prison bars / One saw the mud, the other saw the stars." Two individuals can be in the same challenging, perhaps even desperate, situation and see it quite differently.

The children of Israel faced the challenge of conquering the promised land. Two outlooks emerged on whether this feat was possible. This was not a matter of mud vs. stars; it was a matter of unbelief vs. faith.

B. Lesson Context

The previous study covered an incident that occurred on the fifteenth day of the second month after the Israelites' exodus from Egypt (Exodus 16:1; see lesson 3). On the first day of the third month, the Israelites entered the Desert of Sinai (19:1). There they camped before the mountain where the Lord established his covenant with the Israelites and gave his Ten Commandments and other laws to them.

The Israelites stayed at Mount Sinai for a little less than a year (comparing Exodus 19:1 with Numbers 10:11), in what should have been a sacred time of dedicating themselves to be God's covenant people. But the attitude of rebellion and discontent that we saw demonstrated in last week's lesson (Exodus 16:2, 3) reappeared at the foot of the mountain. Sadly, while Moses was on the mountain receiving God's laws, the people were breaking them (specifically the first two of the Ten Commandments) by building a golden calf and attributing God's mighty act of deliverance from bondage to the gods the calf represented (32:1-4).

Thus, perhaps it should come as no surprise that as the people traveled from Mount Sinai toward the promised land, their grumbling and discontent were right by their side. Once the Lord sent a fire to burn among the people, which consumed the fringes of the camp. Moses interceded on the people's behalf, and the fire died down (Numbers 11:1-3). Then the "rabble" (11:4; likely comprised of non-Israelites who had chosen to journey with the Israelites; compare Exodus 12:38) initiated a complaint about growing tired of the manna provided by God. They claimed as they had done previously that living in Egypt was so much better than journeying through the desert (11:5).

At this point, Moses became extremely frustrated with the people's behavior and voiced his frustration to the Lord. The Lord provided 70 men from among the elders of Israel to assist Moses with leading the people for a time (Numbers 11:25). The Lord also responded to the people's complaint with a provision of quail (11:31, 32), similar to what he had done in the Desert of Sin (Exodus 16:1, 12, 13).

Still, the grumbling did not end. Moses' brother Aaron and sister Miriam lodged their own protests against Moses, expressing an envy of Moses' position of authority (Numbers 12:2). The Lord responded by afflicting Miriam with leprosy. She was quarantined for seven days, during which time the people paused their travels. When their journey resumed, they reached the Desert of Paran (12:16) and specifically Kadesh Barnea (Deuteronomy 1:19), where today's lesson text begins.

I. Responsibility
(NUMBERS 13:1, 2, 17, 18)

A. The Lord's Command (vv. 1, 2)

1, 2a. The LORD said to Moses, "Send some men to explore the land of Canaan, which I am giving to the Israelites.

The Israelites are on the verge of a great turning point in their history. The time has come for preparing to enter *the land of Canaan,* which God had promised centuries before to give to Abraham's descendants (Genesis 13:14-17; 15:18-21). The land as a gift from God is emphasized throughout the history of God's dealings with the Israelites (Exodus 6:4, 8; Leviticus 23:9, 10; 25:38; Numbers 10:29; Deuteronomy 6:23; 28:11; etc.).

The people themselves have certainly done nothing to earn such a gift, but *the Lord* is committed to fulfilling his promise to Abraham. As with any gift, the giver sets the terms of how and when it will be given. In this case, the Lord determines how and when his people will receive the inheritance of land he has promised to give them.

2b. "From each ancestral tribe send one of its leaders."

The Lord tells Moses to *send . . . leaders,* one for each of the 12 tribes, who will search out the land of Canaan prior to the nation's entry. Each man is to be someone who is trusted and respected by his *tribe.*

When Moses refers to this process later while speaking to the second generation of Israelites, he will say that the Israelites came to him and suggested sending men to spy out the land (Deuteronomy 1:22). But this should not be seen as a contradiction of the account in Numbers. Most likely the people offer their proposal, then the Lord gives his approval to what they have suggested. Numbers 13:3-16, not in the printed text, lists the 12 men who are chosen for this task.

B. Moses' Counsel (vv. 17, 18)

17. When Moses sent them to explore Canaan, he said, "Go up through the Negev and on into the hill country.

When one examines a map of this territory, it shows that *Moses* sends the spies north from Kadesh Barnea, where the people are currently camped. The spies are to explore *the Negev,* the Hebrew word that means "south." This indicates

HOW TO SAY IT

Anak	*Ay*-nak.
Anakites	*An*-a-kites.
Canaan	*Kay*-nun.
Hamath	*Hay*-muth.
Hebron	*Hee*-brun or *Heb*-run.
Jephunneh	Jih-*fun*-eh.
Kadesh Barnea	*Kay*-desh *Bar*-nee-uh.
Negev	*Neg*-ev.
Paran	*Pair*-un.
Sinai	*Sigh*-nye or *Sigh*-nay-eye.

the territory south of that which will eventually make up the land possessed by Israel. Moses also instructs the 12 men to go *into the hill country*. The instruction to explore the Negev and the hill country will result in the spies' exploring the entire land.

18. "See what the land is like and whether the people who live there are strong or weak, few or many.

Moses specifies what the 12 men are to look for as they carry out their mission. They are to examine the terrain. Then they are to observe *the people who live there*. Are they *strong or weak, few or many*? Though God has allowed their proposed espionage mission (see commentary on Numbers 13:2b), 20/20 hindsight indicates that it would be better for the people to trust God to give them the land without their scouting it out, given the fear their mission ultimately causes (see commentary on Numbers 13:28; 14:1, 2, 9, 10).

Numbers 13:19, 20 (not in our printed text) records additional instructions to the spies, concluding with the exhortation, "Do your best to bring back some of the fruit of the land" (Numbers 13:20). Verses 21-24 record the itinerary of the group, noting that they gathered some of the fruit of the land (grapes, pomegranates, and figs). Their travels took them as far north as Lebo Hamath (13:21), which eventually became the northern boundary of the promised land (34:8).

What Do You Think?

What factors should we consider before setting out to fulfill something we sense God has called us to do? Why?

Digging Deeper

What evidence should we require when reevaluating work we think God called us to do? How is this process different from secular models of decision-making?

II. Report

(NUMBERS 13:25-28)

A. Produce of the Land (vv. 25-27)

25. At the end of forty days they returned from exploring the land.

Moses has not specified how long the spies' journey is to take. He is probably more concerned that the land be searched carefully and thoroughly than he is with a specific timeline. Given the territory the spies have covered (from Kadesh Barnea north to Lebo Hamath is approximately 250 miles), a time of *forty days* is reasonable.

The number 40 often indicates the significance of a period of time (see Genesis 7:4, 12, 17; 8:6; Jonah 3:4; Matthew 4:1, 2; Acts 1:3; etc.). The story of the exodus contains three good examples. Moses' life is broken into 40-year increments (Exodus 7:7; Deuteronomy 34:7), and he fasts for 40 days (Exodus 24:18; 34:28; Deuteronomy 9:9, 18). Including the years before the spy mission, the people wander for 40 years, the time given for a generation to pass away (Numbers 14:34; 32:13).

26. They came back to Moses and Aaron and the whole Israelite community at Kadesh in the Desert of Paran. There they reported to them and to the whole assembly and showed them the fruit of the land.

The 12 display their sample of *the fruit of the land*, including a single cluster of grapes so large that it requires two people to carry it on a staff (Numbers 13:23). The initial reaction of the people must have been one of wide-eyed amazement and anticipation, especially after all the time spent in *the Desert of Paran*, where comparatively little grew.

27. They gave Moses this account: "We went into the land to which you sent us, and it does flow with milk and honey! Here is its fruit.

The spies report back to *Moses*, who had given them their instructions. He had told the spies to report on essentially two items: *the land* and the people.

The phrase *flow with milk and honey* signifies an abundance of good things. When the Lord first called Moses to lead the Israelites out of bondage, he told him that the land was "flowing with milk and honey" (Exodus 3:8). Moses gave that same description to the people as they departed from Egypt (13:3-5). The people can see for themselves, judging from the *fruit* before them, that the words are no exaggeration.

B. People of the Land (v. 28)

28. "But the people who live there are powerful, and the cities are fortified and very large. We even saw descendants of Anak there.

While the land offers much to be desired, *the people who live there* are another matter altogether. They are powerful, and *their cities are . . . very large* and well-defended. The *descendants of Anak*—called Anakites—are a people group known for being exceptionally "strong and tall" (Deuteronomy 9:2).

The spies who do not believe the land can be taken will refer to them as "Nephilim," or giants (Numbers 13:33). These are the very people whom courageous Caleb, one of the 12 spies, will drive out of Hebron 40 years later so that he can possess that portion of the promised land (Joshua 15:13). In fact, the three sons of Anak named in Numbers 13:22 are the ones Caleb will defeat (Joshua 15:14)!

In Numbers 13:30 (not covered in today's text), Caleb responds to the claims about the formidable inhabitants of Canaan. He remains confident that the Lord will defeat these foes. But Caleb quickly finds himself in a minority; out of the 12 spies, only he and Joshua (not noted as part of the minority until Numbers 14:6, below) believe that the Lord will keep his promise. Their faithful voices are outweighed by the other 10 spies, who are intimidated rather than inspired (Numbers 13:31-33).

Visual for Lesson 4. *Point to this visual as you ask how both the wild and the cultivated natural worlds witness to God's enduring faithfulness.*

> **What Do You Think?**
> How should we prepare for opportunities and obstacles as we set out to fulfill God's calling to complete a task?
> *Digging Deeper*
> Considering especially Proverbs 3:5, 6; 15:22; Matthew 6:25-34; and Luke 14:28-33, how do we know at what point a fact-finding mission is really just a failure to trust?

❧ *Bitcoin* ❧

As the end of 2017 neared, investors were asking two questions: "Should I invest in Bitcoin?" and "What is Bitcoin?" As the name suggests, Bitcoin is a type of currency. Unlike others, this worldwide currency works without a central bank or single administrator. Instead, it operates through computer coding that verifies transactions and prevents counterfeiting.

The value of Bitcoin fluctuates wildly. In 2011, the value of one Bitcoin rose from about $0.30 to $32, then fell to $2. On December 12, 2017, a single Bitcoin was valued at $17,749 before plummeting again. The volatility of Bitcoin can cause an speculator to lose hundreds of thousands of dollars in a very short time.

All investors struggle to balance risk and reward. The Israelites on the way to Canaan didn't know whether to risk an investment in Canaan. But Joshua and Caleb knew that, unlike Bitcoin, the promise of God came with a guarantee.

—J. E.

III. Response
(NUMBERS 14:1, 2, 5-10a)
A. Cries of Anguish (vv. 1, 2)

1. That night all the members of the community raised their voices and wept aloud.

It does not take long at all for the negative outlook of the 10 spies to dampen the enthusiasm of the entire *community*. Cries of despair are heard that very *night* throughout the Israelite camp.

2. All the Israelites grumbled against Moses and Aaron, and the whole assembly said to

them, "**If only we had died in Egypt! Or in this wilderness!**"

As they did in last week's study, the people begin to grumble *against Moses and Aaron* (compare Exodus 16:1, 2). They also voice their wish that God had taken their lives, either *in Egypt or in this wilderness* (compare Exodus 16:3; Numbers 14:22-24). It is sobering to consider how the nation has managed to push out of their collective memory the mighty works that God has done for them in their own experience, going back to the 10 plagues in Egypt. To claim that the Lord has brought them into the promised land to die is utter blasphemy.

What Do You Think?
▶ Under what circumstances, if any, is it appropriate to express concern publicly over the actions of leaders or members of the congregation?

Digging Deeper
How do passages such Acts 18:12-16; 21:27-36; 1 Corinthians 6:1-4; and 14:40 help you answer this question in terms of issues within the church vs. violations of secular law?

B. Concerned Leaders (v. 5)

5. Then Moses and Aaron fell facedown in front of the whole Israelite assembly gathered there.

In Numbers 14:4 (not in today's printed text), the people propose that they mutiny against the leadership of *Moses and Aaron* and return to Egypt. Moses and Aaron sense the gravity of the people's demand and fall *facedown*. Perhaps this reflects a combination of emotions: fear of the Lord, alarm at the possible outpouring of his wrath against the people, and shock at such a brazen act of defiance.

C. Courageous Leaders (vv. 6-9)

6. Joshua son of Nun and Caleb son of Jephunneh, who were among those who had explored the land, tore their clothes

The two courageous, faith-inspired spies, *Joshua* and *Caleb*, express their anguish at what the people are doing: turning against Moses and Aaron and ultimately against the Lord.

7. and said to the entire Israelite assembly, "The land we passed through and explored is exceedingly good.

The other 10 spies have caused the people's attention to dwell on and be discouraged by the residents of Canaan and the size of their cities. Joshua and Caleb now remind the people of the *exceedingly good land* that lies within their grasp.

What Do You Think?
▶ What can a church do to ensure that no one is denied having his or her voice heard while also ensuring that a spirit of divisiveness does not result (Titus 3:10)?

Digging Deeper
How would the fact that divisiveness is coming from the biggest financial givers change the approach, if at all? Why?

---

8. "If the LORD is pleased with us, he will lead us into that land, a land flowing with milk and honey, and will give it to us.

Joshua and Caleb highlight the most important factor in taking the *land: the Lord*. He has not brought the Israelites this far to let them die (contrast Numbers 14:3). He *is pleased* with them; he has made a covenant with them; he has shown them his favor on repeated occasions (Exodus 12:1-13; 14:21-29; 16:4, 5; 17:5-7; etc.). He will lead them into that land and *give it* to them.

The emphasis on the promised land as God's gift to the people is clear (see commentary on Numbers 13:1, 2a). The giver will not desert his people or break his promise to them. Joshua and Caleb also remind the people again of the exceptional abundance of the land (see commentary on 13:27, above).

9. "Only do not rebel against the LORD. And do not be afraid of the people of the land, because we will devour them. Their protection is gone, but the LORD is with us. Do not be afraid of them."

Joshua and Caleb plead with the people not to *rebel* or *be afraid*. The people have grumbled, murmured, and rebelled against *the Lord*, testing his mercy and patience. Joshua and Caleb likely sense that judgment will follow if the people do not repent.

Joshua and Caleb describe the residents of the promised land as something to be devoured. The expression means that the Israelites can easily defeat them, or "have them for lunch." Their size, the strength of their cities, and whatever weaponry or defenses they possess are non-factors. All of that is totally worthless when the Lord *is with* his people. If he is, and there is no question of that for Joshua and Caleb, then there is no need to fear the inhabitants of the land (compare Isaiah 8:12, 13).

D. Cries of Anger (v. 10a)

10a. But the whole assembly talked about stoning them.

One would hope that the Israelites would take heart from Joshua and Caleb's challenging words. Their response, however, is the very opposite; they prepare to stone the two men. The nation's contempt for the faithful men's message is so great that they would rather silence the messengers than listen any longer. But the people's real offense is committed against the Lord.

> **What Do You Think?**
> When leaders within a congregation disagree, what are some productive ways to deal with extreme reactions by church members?
> *Digging Deeper*
> Considering that Jesus, John the Baptist, Paul, and others could rightly be called extremists, under what conditions would extreme reactions be appropriate?

❧ *MUTINY!* ❧

In 1610, British navigator Henry Hudson and the crew of his ship *Discovery* ventured into modern-day Canada trying to find a northwest passage from Europe to Asia. The voyagers succeeded in locating a large bay—later named the Hudson Bay. *Discovery* became lodged in ice, forcing voyagers to spend winter ashore with very limited provisions. The crew's morale eroded. Starving and desperate for home, many of the crew convinced themselves that Hudson was hoarding food.

By the time the ice had finally cleared, the men refused to continue searching for the passage. Instead they revolted, commandeered the ship, and abandoned Hudson, his son, and seven others. A later expedition looking for Hudson found a small shelter that they may have built. Their bodies were never recovered.

Some mutinies are justifiable, and that against Henry Hudson may have been one such. But mutinies in Christian contexts are especially fraught with danger, lest we discover too late that we are opposing God himself!   —J. E.

Conclusion

A. Words Printed in Yellow

Some Bibles print Jesus' words in red so that they stand out to the reader. Perhaps today's lesson text should be printed in yellow, a cautionary signal. The Israelites rebelled against God and his chosen leaders, refusing to trust that the Lord would lead them into the promised land. When Paul recounts the examples of the Israelites' disobedience, he emphasizes that these incidents are not just ancient history: "These things happened to them as examples and were written down as warnings for us" (1 Corinthians 10:11).

We can easily read an account like the one in today's text, shake our heads, and wonder how the Israelites could have forgotten so quickly all that the Lord had done for them. Instead of becoming haughty, reading today's account should humble us (see 1 Corinthians 10:12). We can learn much from the Israelites' negative examples. We should not treat their failures lightly as we journey toward our own "promised land."

B. Prayer

Father, examine, convict, and strengthen us so that we do not become guilty of faithlessness. We pray in Jesus' name. Amen.

C. Thought to Remember

In the midst of unfaithfulness,
God remains faithful.

INVOLVEMENT LEARNING

Enhance your lesson with NIV Bible Student *(from your curriculum supplier) and the reproducible activity page (at www.standardlesson.com or in the back of the* NIV Standard Lesson Commentary Deluxe Edition*).*

Into the Lesson

Before class, search the internet for free motivational posters. Download about 10 such posters. Print them out and display them around your classroom. (*Option*. Using digital files to create a slide show instead.)

As class members arrive, have them to move around the room and look at the posters. (If you choose the slide-show option, have it on a continuous loop.) Ask for volunteers to tell which posters are their favorites. Discuss the value of having such posters at a school, in the office, or even at home. Ask what kinds of situations discourage us more than others.

Alternative. Distribute copies of the "Motivation" exercise from the activity page, which you can download. Have students work individually for no more than one minute or in pairs for a few minutes to complete it as indicated.

Lead into Bible study by saying, "When life puts obstacles in our paths, why contributes to our ending up discouraged easily?" Discuss. Make a transition by noting that two Israelite spies believed that God could lead Israel to possess the promised land. But their inability to overcome human nature has something to teach us today.

Into the Word

Have some of your good oral readers take turns reading the text aloud. Then divide the class into groups of three to five. Distribute handouts (you create) to learners with identical instructions to create a military-style report for "Operation Homeland," the spy mission described in the lesson text. The report is to include the objective of the mission, personnel involved, observations from the mission, and recommendations.

After an appropriate amount of time, reassemble the class. Allow groups to read and explain their reports on Operation Homeland, which should be something like this:

Objective of Operation Homeland: *To scout the hill country and report on its natural resources, population, and state of military preparedness.*

Personnel Involved: *Twelve leaders, one from each tribe, to serve as a reconnaissance team.*

Observations: *The land has abundant resources and is very desirable. But the cities are well fortified, and the people are numerous. The warriors appear to be quite strong..*

Recommendations: *While the land is more than adequate to support the people of Israel, the majority concludes that the risk of defeat in mounting an invasion far outweighs the possible rewards. Those who object to this plan are few but vocal; they and those who agree with them must be punished for their presumption and silenced.*

After discussion, make a transition by asking, "Taking to heart the power of a negative committee report, as evidenced by the power of 10 spies to sway the people, let's discuss how we can strengthen our faith in such a way that we conquer our fears."

Into Life

On the board, write the words FEARS and FAITH vertically columns. Work with the class to create two acrostics that identify the danger of being ruled by fear and the power of faith to motivate us to accept challenges. Here is an example of a completed FEARS acrostics:

Facing situations and
Events that are threatening
Are likely to keep us from
Reaping the benefits we
Should be enjoying.

Alternative. Distribute copies of the "Counseling Session" exercise from the activity page. Have students work in small groups or as a whole class to complete it as indicated.

FAITHFUL IN
CONSEQUENCES

DEVOTIONAL READING: Psalm 103:1-14
BACKGROUND SCRIPTURE: Numbers 14:10b-23

NUMBERS 14:10B-20

¹⁰ᵇ Then the glory of the LORD appeared at the tent of meeting to all the Israelites. ¹¹ The LORD said to Moses, "How long will these people treat me with contempt? How long will they refuse to believe in me, in spite of all the signs I have performed among them? ¹² I will strike them down with a plague and destroy them, but I will make you into a nation greater and stronger than they."

¹³ Moses said to the LORD, "Then the Egyptians will hear about it! By your power you brought these people up from among them. ¹⁴ And they will tell the inhabitants of this land about it. They have already heard that you, LORD, are with these people and that you, LORD, have been seen face to face, that your cloud stays over them, and that you go before them in a pillar of cloud by day and a pillar of fire by night. ¹⁵ If you put all these people to death, leaving none alive, the nations who have heard this report about you will say, ¹⁶ 'The LORD was not able to bring these people into the land he promised them on oath, so he slaughtered them in the wilderness.'

¹⁷ "Now may the Lord's strength be displayed, just as you have declared: ¹⁸ 'The LORD is slow to anger, abounding in love and forgiving sin and rebellion. Yet he does not leave the guilty unpunished; he punishes the children for the sin of the parents to the third and fourth generation.' ¹⁹ In accordance with your great love, forgive the sin of these people, just as you have pardoned them from the time they left Egypt until now."

²⁰ The LORD replied, "I have forgiven them, as you asked."

KEY VERSE

In accordance with your great love, forgive the sin of these people, just as you have pardoned them from the time they left Egypt until now. —**Numbers 14:19**

Responding to
God's Grace

Unit 1: God Is Faithful
Lessons 1–5

Lesson Aims

After participating in this lesson, each learner will be able to:

1. List key factors regarding Moses' intercession on behalf of the rebellious Israelites.

2. Explain the importance of intercessory prayer.

3. Initiate a personal prayer ministry of intercession.

Lesson Outline

Introduction
  A. The Great and Powerful God
  B. Lesson Context
I. God's Intention (Numbers 14:10b-12)
  A. Glorious Presence (v. 10b)
  B. Destructive Plan (vv. 11, 12)
    Inoculated Against Facts
II. Moses' Mediation (Numbers 14:13-20)
  A. Example Before the Nations (vv. 13-16)
  B. Plea to Show Mercy (vv. 17-19)
  C. Plan to Pardon Israel (v. 20)
    Pardon!
Conclusion
  A. The Importance of Intercession
  B. Prayer
  C. Thought to Remember

Introduction
A. The Great and Powerful God

In the classic movie *The Wizard of Oz*, the wizard is reputed to be "the great and powerful Oz," who causes fear and trembling within those who dare to approach him. When Dorothy and her three friends (along with her dog Toto) come before the wizard, they react in the same way. But when Toto pulls back a curtain, the friends find an older man who is making himself appear by means of trickery to be "the great and powerful Oz." In reality, he is anything but great and powerful, and certainly no one to approach with fear and trembling.

Many have a view of God as a kind, grandfatherly figure who wouldn't hurt a flea. It follows, then, that we humans don't really need to take him seriously—when all is said and done, he will be merciful and simply overlook whatever sins we may have committed. But as the Israelites discovered at Kadesh Barnea, reality doesn't support this position. The God of Israel is truly "great and powerful," and his judgment of human sin and rebellion dare not be taken lightly. The writer of Hebrews reminds us of a truth that stands rock solid throughout both the Old Testament and the New Testament and remains just as trustworthy today: "It is a dreadful thing to fall into the hands of the living God" (Hebrews 10:31).

B. Lesson Context

Today's text follows immediately on the heels of last week's. The discouragement brought about by the 10 spies' report grew into a rebellion against Moses and Aaron. The text concluded with the congregation's desiring to stone Caleb and Joshua (Numbers 14:10a). Today's text begins with words even more ominous, as God comes in judgment to a people blinded by unbelief.

I. God's Intention
(Numbers 14:10b-12)
A. Glorious Presence (v. 10b)

10b. Then the glory of the Lord appeared at the tent of meeting to all the Israelites.

God's *glory* is referenced directly for the first time in the book of Numbers in this verse. The Israelites have already witnessed the glory *of the Lord* when he provided manna from Heaven to feed them in the wilderness (Exodus 16:7, 8; see lesson 3 commentary). His glory had appeared like a "consuming fire" on Mount Sinai (24:17) and filled the tabernacle upon its completion (40:33, 34).

One can only surmise how the people react when they see the glory approach, given how defiantly they have expressed their rebellion against the Lord and against his appointed leaders. However, their reaction after days of preparation suggests that nothing less than abject fear would be the response now (compare Exodus 20:18, 19).

> *What Do You Think?*
> What are some ways to detect the presence of God's glory? Why is it important to do so?
> *Digging Deeper*
> How will 2 Corinthians 4 influence your search for God's glory?

B. Destructive Plan (vv. 11, 12)

11. The LORD said to Moses, "How long will these people treat me with contempt? How long will they refuse to believe in me, in spite of all the signs I have performed among them?

The questions raised by *the Lord* in this verse reveal his anger. *The signs* that he has displayed among the Israelites have been numerous, going back to the plagues that were brought upon Egypt (Exodus 7:14–12:30). These signs were followed by the parting of the Red Sea's waters for Israel's safe passage and bringing the waters back upon the Egyptians (14:21-28).

God further gave signs in the form of provision for his people in the desert (Exodus 15:22–16:15). The Israelites "saw [his] glory and the signs [he] performed in Egypt and in the wilderness" (Numbers 14:22). They have been granted the truly sacred privilege of witnessing mighty works from the hand of the Lord. Yet they still react faithlessly to his promise that he will carry out another mighty work by bringing them safely into the promised land.

Furthermore, likely only a few weeks have passed since the display of divine majesty on Mount Sinai (Exodus 19:16-19). At that time, the voice of the Lord had been so terrifying that the people begged Moses to speak as the Lord's intermediary (20:18, 19). Though their fear is meant to teach them to trust and obey the Lord, they still *refuse to believe.*

> *What Do You Think?*
> What are some ways to help a doubtful person identify ways that the Lord has been active in his or her life?
> *Digging Deeper*
> In what ways will lessons learned during your own periods of doubt apply to others, and in what ways will they not? Why?

❧ INOCULATED AGAINST FACTS ❧

In the 1960s, psychologist Peter Wason demonstrated that people tend to seek information that confirms their existing beliefs. In the process, information that would disprove the belief is ignored. Wason called this phenomenon "confirmation bias."

Such bias is seen in many issues of today. One example is the debate on advances or supposed advances in vaccinations. Persistent questions linger regarding their safety and efficacy. For some folks on the side of the fence who reject vaccination, no amount of scientific study will ever be enough to convince them otherwise. For some folks on the other side of the fence, the barest hint of a breakthrough vaccine causes them to be the first to rush to get it for themselves or a family member. Those on either extreme of various issues often end up being inoculated against the facts (or lack thereof).

Israelites opposing Joshua and Caleb exhibited confirmation bias. The evidence of God's faithfulness should have led to fear being squashed. Instead, a bias toward fear led to the opposite. The choice they made is ours to make as well. Will faith (which is belief based on evidence; John 14:11) overcome a bias toward fear, or will you let the opposite happen?   —J. E.

12. "I will strike them down with a plague and destroy them, but I will make you into a nation greater and stronger than they."

The people gathered before the Lord are in an extremely precarious position: the God who has promised to give them the land now determines to *destroy them*. Is his patience finally at an end? When the Israelites built a golden calf while God gave Moses the law on Mount Sinai (Exodus 32), the Lord told Moses that he planned to do just what he is proposing here: destroy the people and create "a great nation" out of Moses instead (32:10).

The threatened destruction is specified to come about by *plague*. Such a severe punishment had been promised previously by the Lord should the people continue to turn from his ways (Leviticus 26:21-25); it would be included as one possible consequence for disobedience and unfaithfulness once they were living in the land (Deuteronomy 28:21).

II. Moses' Mediation
(NUMBERS 14:13-20)

A. Example Before the Nations (vv. 13-16)

13. Moses said to the LORD, "Then the Egyptians will hear about it! By your power you brought these people up from among them.

When *the Lord* stated his intention to destroy the Israelites for their rebellion at Mount Sinai, Moses interceded to the Lord on their behalf (Exodus 32:11-14). He noted at that time that if the Lord should carry out such an act, *the Egyptians* would question the Lord's motivation for delivering his people from Egypt. They would conclude that he had brought them out from Egypt for the express purpose of destroying them (32:11, 12).

Moses then went on to cite the promise God had made to Abraham, Isaac, and Jacob concerning their descendants. Destroying the people instead of multiplying them and blessing them would make God look faithless. As a result of Moses' intercession, the Lord held back his judgment of the people (Exodus 32:13, 14).

Moses now makes a similar appeal before the Lord, serving once again as the Israelites' intercessor. Even though Moses has become displeased at the people's pattern of rebellion (Numbers 11:10-15), he cannot bear to see them suffer such a devastating punishment as the Lord proposes. But Moses knows that the Lord's reputation is more important still.

> *What Do You Think?*
> What will unbelievers see in your refusing to hope for others to fail even when such failure would benefit you?
> *Digging Deeper*
> On a scale from 1 (lowest) to 5 (highest), how well do you follow Matthew 5:43-48 and Luke 6:27-36 in this regard now? How can you improve?

14a. "And they will tell the inhabitants of this land about it.

If the Lord completely destroys the Israelite nation, the Egyptians will not keep such news to themselves. The Egyptians will not know that Israel's rebellion is the reason for the Lord's destruction of his people. According to their misunderstanding of the spiritual world and their views of gods, a nation's destruction or loss in battle reflects the weakness or apathy of the god or gods of that nation. Those gods are thought to come to the aid of their worshippers if the gods possess power to defend their own reputations.

14b. "They have already heard that you, LORD, are with these people and that you, LORD, have been seen face to face, that your cloud stays over them, and that you go before them in a pillar of cloud by day and a pillar of fire by night.

The Lord's reputation as the God of Israel has already been established. He is known for his presence *with* his *people*, for having *been seen face to face*, and for his special protection of his people by means of *a pillar of cloud by day and a pillar of fire by night*.

The report that God has been seen face to face is noteworthy in light of God's having forbidden Moses to see his face (Exodus 33:19-23; compare John 1:18). At the same time, Moses was allowed to see a portion of God's glory (Exodus 33:21, 22; 34:4-6), and others besides Moses are described as having seen God (24:9, 10). The expression "face to face" is used of how the Lord spoke to all the Israelites (Deuteronomy 5:4) and of the special relationship that existed between the Lord and Moses (34:10). Thus, the phrase "face to face" is a way of describing the manner in which God reveals himself to his people at the time. His revelations occur strictly on his terms and are unlike anything that any other so-called god is able to do for their people.

15, 16. "If you put all these people to death, leaving none alive, the nations who have heard this report about you will say, 'The LORD was not able to bring these people into the land he promised them on oath, so he slaughtered them in the wilderness.'

News of such a massive destruction of the Israelites will quickly get around to the surrounding *nations*. Whatever reputation for power and glory *the Lord* has established for himself will be harmed, Moses asserts, if God proceeds to wipe his *people* from the face of the earth.

The Egyptians in particular, who experienced the pain of losing their firstborn sons (Exodus 12:29, 30), would no doubt take great pleasure in hearing of the demise of these people. The Egyptians will not see this as an expression of God's righteous wrath and judgment; they will interpret it as a sign that he is unable to follow through on his intention to bring them into their own land.

Moreover, peoples such as those residing in Canaan will hear of this and reach the same conclusion. They too hear of the Lord's great power and mighty acts, as Rahab in Jericho will later confess (Joshua 2:10, 11). Rahab will inform the two Israelite spies of this fact and how, because of who the Lord is and all he has done, "great fear of you has fallen on us" (2:9) and "our hearts melted in fear" (2:11). The witness of God's people dying *in the wilderness* will give the nations the false idea that God is inept and callous.

B. Plea to Show Mercy (vv. 17-19)

17, 18a. "Now may the Lord's strength be displayed, just as you have declared: 'The LORD is slow to anger, abounding in love and forgiving sin and rebellion.

Instead of God's demonstrating the greatness of his *strength* by judging the Israelites for their unbelief and disobedience, Moses now pleads with the Lord to manifest his strength by *abounding in love and forgiving sin and rebellion*. In so doing, Moses cites the Lord's self-description at Mount Sinai (compare Exodus 34:6, 7). To ask that the Lord be merciful to a very wayward people is indeed a bold request! Moses' intercessory pleading is reminiscent of Abraham's concern for Sodom and Gomorrah (noted in lesson 1).

> **What Do You Think?**
> What points can you use to speak in God's defense when others characterize him as being harsh, judgmental, and/or unfaithful?
> *Digging Deeper*
> How important will the distinction between *restorative justice* and *retributive justice* be in your response? Cite biblical examples of each.

18b. "Yet he does not leave the guilty unpunished; he punishes the children for the sin of the parents to the third and fourth generation.'

At the same time, Moses acknowledges the reality of God's judgment upon *the guilty*. The impact of one generation's *sin* on *the children . . . to the third and fourth generation* is found within the second commandment (Exodus 20:4, 5). There it is contrasted with God's mercy being displayed "to a thousand generations of those who love me and keep my commandments" (20:6).

Here at Kadesh Barnea, the mercy of God will actually be shown to the very next generation, to the children of those who have rebelled against the Lord and against Moses and Aaron. That next generation will be permitted to enter the promised land (Numbers 14:31).

19. "In accordance with your great love, forgive the sin of these people, just as you have pardoned them from the time they left Egypt until now."

Moses now comes to the gist of his intercession for the Israelites. He notes that the Lord has had a lot of experience pardoning them already; he did *forgive the sin of these people* again and again, from the moment *they left Egypt* up to the present. An early example of this forgiveness was when God responded to the Israelites' complaints about lack of food—not by punishing them but instead by providing them with quail and manna (Exodus 16:9-12; see commentary in lesson 3).

> **What Do You Think?**
> In what situations will you and will you not pray for God to be merciful toward another person?
> **Digging Deeper**
> In what ways, if at all, do Jeremiah 7:16; 11:14; 14:11; Luke 6:28; 1 Timothy 1:20; 2 Timothy 4:4; John 17:9; Ephesians 6:18; James 5:16; and 1 John 5:16 cause you to modify your response?

C. Plan to Pardon Israel (v. 20)

20. The LORD replied, "I have forgiven them, as you asked.

The Lord responds favorably to Moses' intercession. Yet stern consequences will follow. Pardon does not mean the removal of all consequences resulting from the people's unbelief and disobedience. Yes, the nation will be spared the immediate destruction that the Lord intended to bring upon them. But the unbelieving generation, consisting of those individuals who have constantly grumbled against the Lord, will not be allowed to enter the promised land (Numbers 14:21-23).

The people had "tested" God 10 times (Numbers 14:22), which may be a way of saying that the number of times the Israelites had refused to trust God's guidance and provision is completed. He will wait no longer to judge the unfaithful nation. That generation will be commanded to turn back and travel toward the Red Sea, from which their journey toward Canaan had begun (14:25). Eventually all of them, age 20 and older, will perish in the wilderness (14:29, 30). Only Caleb and Joshua will be spared to experience the thrill and the blessing of entering the promised land (14:30; contrast 20:7-12).

In place of that faithless generation, their children will enter the promised land. Ironically, these were the individuals whom the unbelieving ones claim would die in the wilderness (Numbers 14:3).

Instead, the Lord brings their own words back to haunt them: "As for your children that you said would be taken as plunder, I will bring them in to enjoy the land you have rejected" (14:31).

As a final solemn affirmation of the Lord's judgment, the 10 spies who had spread the "bad report" among their fellow Israelites (13:32) "died of a plague before the Lord" (14:37). What should have been an occasion for celebration and triumph becomes a day of great sorrow.

❧ PARDON! ❧

The U.S. president has nearly unchecked power to issue official pardons. This makes the pardon one of the most controversial presidential powers. Though this presidential power can be divisive, in some instances it has been used to heal wounds.

One of the most controversial presidential pardons was issued by President Gerald Ford. Richard Nixon, Ford's predecessor, resigned from office in August 1974 amid accusations of criminal behavior. After that resignation, Nixon could have been prosecuted and even jailed. Yet weeks later, President Ford pardoned the former president of any federal crimes he had "committed or may have committed or taken part in" during his terms in office.

Today many agree that Ford's pardon was necessary to help the nation move forward from an era of scandal and abuse of power.

Pardons are not justice. Rather, they are acts of undeserved mercy. When the treasonous Israelites rebelled against God, they deserved an outpouring of his wrath. Moses, acting as a defense attorney for his people, convinced pleaded for

HOW TO SAY IT

Canaan	*Kay*-nun.
Gomorrah	Guh-*more*-uh.
Jericho	*Jair*-ih-co.
Kadesh Barnea	kay-desh-***bar***-nee-uh.
Rahab	*Ray*-hab.
Sinai	*Sigh*-nye or *Sigh*-nay-eye.
Sodom	*Sod*-um.
tabernacle	***tab***-burr-*nah*-kul.
Thessalonians	*Thess*-uh-***lo***-nee-unz.

and received mercy. Ultimately, God's forgiveness of sin is based on the fact that Christ has made forgiveness possible because he took our penalty upon himself at the cross. What difference does God's pardon make in your life?   —J. E.

Conclusion

A. The Importance of Intercession

From cover to cover, the Bible reveals the devastating consequences of sin. When God placed Adam and Eve in the Garden of Eden, he clearly told them, "You are free to eat from any tree in the garden; but you must not eat from the tree of the knowledge of good and evil, for when you eat from it you will certainly die" (Genesis 2:16, 17). Many are familiar with Paul's declaration in Romans 6:23: "The wages of sin is death." The climax of that death sentence is specified in Revelation. According to Revelation 22:15, sinners will be outside of the holy city, the New Jerusalem, much as the Israelites were left outside of the promised land because of their unbelief.

Consider this tragic irony: the 12 spies brought back samples of the fruit of the promised land, fruit that could have been enjoyed by them and their fellow Israelites had they possessed the faith that God would give them victory over the land's inhabitants. But they rejected that fruit and ate instead the bitter fruit that results from choosing a path of unbelief and disobedience.

Intercessory prayer for the sins of others, such as that which Moses offered on behalf of the rebellious Israelites, remains a vital ministry for Christians today. The person who prays for another stands between Heaven and earth, calling on the Lord to intervene on behalf of a person in need of his mercy.

When the prophet Samuel gave what amounted to his farewell address, he said, "As for me, far be it from me that I should sin against the Lord by failing to pray for you" (1 Samuel 12:23). Though his leadership role was changing, Samuel's ministry of intercession for God's people remained the same. The apostle Paul also wrote of the importance of intercessory prayer: "I urge then, first of all, that petitions, prayers, intercession and thanksgiving

Visual for Lesson 5. *Point to this visual to launch a discussion regarding the relationship between forgiveness and intercessory requests for mercy.*

be made for all people" (1 Timothy 2:1). Paul then urged this to be done particularly for those in positions of authority (2:2). But intercessions can and ought to be carried out on behalf of anyone (possible exception: 1 John 5:16).

How many times have we heard someone describe a problem or a crisis that the person (or someone he or she knows) is going through and we respond by promising to pray for that individual in need? How many times have we then failed to follow through on that promise? To pray for another is one of the most sacred privileges a follower of Jesus has. We must keep our promise to pray!

There is so much in our hurting, broken world that needs to be covered by the prayers of faithful Christians. Instead of ceasing to pray, may we "pray continually" (1 Thessalonians 5:17).

B. Prayer

Father, forgive us for the times when we take the privilege of prayer for granted. Our world, our nation, and our cities and communities need our prayers as much as they ever have. Stir us to be a people of prayer—as individuals, as families, and as churches. We pray this in the name of the one who modeled prayer for us: Jesus. Amen.

C. Thought to Remember

Let us pray
—now as never before!

INVOLVEMENT LEARNING

Enhance your lesson with NIV Bible Student (from your curriculum supplier) and the reproducible activity page (at www.standardlesson.com or in the back of the NIV Standard Lesson Commentary Deluxe Edition).

Into the Lesson

Read the following to the class:

The name Merv Rettenmund may not be familiar to many. As a Major League Baseball player, Rettenmund had a career spanning 13 seasons playing for four teams—the Baltimore Orioles (1968–73), the Cincinnati Reds (1974–75), the San Diego Padres (1976–77), and the California Angels (1978–80). Rettenmund is not in the Hall of Fame; he won no batting titles, and he was never a part of an all-star team. Nevertheless, Rettenmund has made a mark in baseball for being one of baseball's best pinch hitters.

Being a pinch hitter is an underrated role in baseball. Pinch hitters must always be ready, both physically and mentally, to take the place of another player at bat and try to get on base. During his career, Rettenmund got on base more than 4 out of every 10 times he stepped into the batter's box for a teammate (a .422 on-base percentage). That made him a welcome replacement for another batter when a game was on the line.

Discuss these observations by asking what we mean when we say that someone "went to bat" for another. Ask, "In what other ways do people stand in the place of another?"

Alternative. Distribute copies of the "In Place Of" exercise from the activity page, which you can download. Have students work individually for no more than one minute (or in small groups for several minutes) to complete as indicated.

After either activity, lead into Bible study by saying, "There are times when all of us need someone to 'go to bat' for us. We need someone to stand up or to stand in, to be a broker or a backer, to support us in some way. When the people of Israel angered the Lord by their rebellion, they had an intercessor. His name was Moses."

Into the Word

Divide the class into three groups, assigning each group a different section of today's text:

Offer Group: Numbers 14:10b-12
Objection Group: Numbers 14:13-16
Counteroffer Group: Numbers 14:17-20

Each group should consider these questions that you can give them on a handout (you create) or write on the board: 1–What is the motivation of the speaker? 2–What consequences would follow after this proposed course of action? 3–What characteristics of the Lord are on display?

After 10 minutes, reassemble the class and have learners share their conclusions.

Alternative. Distribute copies of the "Substituting Subtext" exercise from the activity page. Have students work in small groups to complete as indicated.

After either activity, move to the final section of the lesson by saying, "The Lord's anger against Israel was certainly justified. But another theme is intercession. Ultimately, the intercessor who stands up for us is God's own Son! Let's look for ways we can be intercessors for our brothers and sisters in Christ."

Into Life

Divide the class into small groups, giving each group a Bible concordance. Allow groups five minutes to find commands given to believers to pray for one another. For each passage, students should be able to identify the people being prayed for and the reason for the prayer. Have groups share their findings.

Examples of possible responses are Matthew 5:44 (praying for enemies, that we may love them despite their actions toward us); Ephesians 6:18-20 (praying for other believers that they may effectively share the gospel); and 1 Timothy 2:1, 2 (praying for governing authorities so that the church will have a peaceful existence).

OBEDIENT
FAITH

DEVOTIONAL READING: Hebrews 8:1-12
BACKGROUND SCRIPTURE: Deuteronomy 4:1-14; 5:1-21

DEUTERONOMY 4:1-8, 12, 13

¹ Now, Israel, hear the decrees and laws I am about to teach you. Follow them so that you may live and may go in and take possession of the land the LORD, the God of your ancestors, is giving you. ² Do not add to what I command you and do not subtract from it, but keep the commands of the LORD your God that I give you.

³ You saw with your own eyes what the LORD did at Baal Peor. The LORD your God destroyed from among you everyone who followed the Baal of Peor, ⁴ but all of you who held fast to the LORD your God are still alive today.

⁵ See, I have taught you decrees and laws as the LORD my God commanded me, so that you may follow them in the land you are entering to take possession of it. ⁶ Observe them carefully, for this will show your wisdom and understanding to the nations, who will hear about all these decrees and say, "Surely this great nation is a wise and understanding people." ⁷ What other nation is so great as to have their gods near them the way the LORD our God is near us whenever we pray to him? ⁸ And what other nation is so great as to have such righteous decrees and laws as this body of laws I am setting before you today?

. . . .

¹² Then the LORD spoke to you out of the fire. You heard the sound of words but saw no form; there was only a voice. ¹³ He declared to you his covenant, the Ten Commandments, which he commanded you to follow and then wrote them on two stone tablets.

KEY VERSE

Keep the commands of the LORD your God that I give you. —Deuteronomy 4:2b

RESPONDING TO GOD'S GRACE

Unit 2: Responses to God's Faithfulness

LESSONS 6–9

LESSON AIMS

After participating in this lesson, each learner will be able to:

1. List Moses' reasons for obeying God's commandments.

2. Explain the importance of the Ten Commandments for the New Testament era.

3. Plan one way to obey God more fully in the week ahead.

LESSON OUTLINE

Introduction

A. Damaging Rule-Givers

Trauma-based research has discovered that when children are exposed to chronic distress, their developing brains adapt by becoming more alert to deal with future threats. The brain constructs new neural pathways to allow the child to consistently scan his or her environment for impending danger. The amygdala, the part of the brain that manages the fight-or-flight response, is placed on permanent high alert.

One of the prices of this self-protection is a decreased attention span. Focusing on a teacher's lesson or a book becomes difficult. This problem becomes semipermanent, tending to last into adulthood.

Our heavenly Father is nothing like a dangerous parent who changes rules randomly on a whim. Scripture says there are no "shifting shadows" with God (James 1:17). Our history with God provides us with confidence in his current dealings with us. And through the gift of his Word, we are given clear instruction on how we can please him. We face many anxious moments, but living with a capricious God is not one of them.

B. Lesson Context

During their 400 years of slavery (Genesis 15:13), Abraham's offspring must have felt like spiritual orphans. Israel had been exposed to a myriad of deities, none of whom cared for them. These so-called gods were vested only in the fortunes of the Egyptians.

Spiritual anxiety wasn't unique to these slaves. The ancient Near East was crowded with deities, each with his or her own temperament and character flaws. Sharing a world with unpredictable gods was a source of stress for those who seemed to be suffering without reason. For instance, an ancient Sumerian had fallen on dark days. In his desperate prayer, found by archaeologists, he pleads to know how he had offended which god and what could be done to appease the god.

The book of Deuteronomy contains none of that cosmic angst. Moses wrote the majority of the book toward the end of his life, decades after

God's character was revealed to Israel. The book is an anthology of Moses' sermons meant to remind the next generation of their history with God and what God expected of them. Moses alternated between narrative passages and exhortations that outline how Israel should respond to God in light of his faithfulness.

One of the devices that Moses uses in his sermons is borrowing from the legal language of "suzerainty treaties." In the ancient Near East, a king would enter into a covenant (treaty) with his people by first outlining examples of his greatness. The king would then outline the terms of the treaty. He would offer the people his continuing protection and just rule. In return, the people would offer their loyalty, which was expressed through their obedience to the king's laws. Moses uses these treaties to teach Israel about the type of covenant loyalty God wanted with Israel.

In Deuteronomy 1, Moses picked up Israel's history at a point of catastrophic failure: Israel refused to trust God and take the land, despite God's faithfulness to deliver them from Egypt. Moses then recounted the wilderness years, in which God's people wandered the desert until the disobedient generation passed away. He transitioned from recounting Israel's history (Deuteronomy 1–3) into an exhortation regarding the importance of Israel's keeping the terms of God's covenant (chapter 4). It's against the backdrop of Israel's continual struggle to trust God that Moses charges them to obey the covenant.

I. Obedient History

(Deuteronomy 4:1-4)

A. Brings Blessings (v. 1)

1. Now, Israel, hear the decrees and laws I am about to teach you. Follow them so that you may live and may go in and take possession of the land the LORD, the God of your ancestors, is giving you.

Now connects Moses' first exhortation to Deuteronomy 1–3. He prescribes a course for Israel's current behavior based on God's past history with his people. Israel's 40 years of wandering in the wilderness were the direct result of not trusting

God to keep his promise to give Abraham land for the people to dwell in (Genesis 12:1-3; Deuteronomy 1:32-36; 2:14, 15; 3:21-29). This distrust festered until it became overt rebellion (1:26-46). Yet God's actions toward Israel demonstrate his fidelity to the covenant with Abraham (7:8) even when the people were unfaithful.

In light of their blemished history, Moses implores Israel to listen. This is not in the passive sense of merely taking in information but in the active sense of becoming aware of God's will and then responding to it with obedience (Leviticus 18:4, 5; Romans 10:5).

Decrees are statutes are given by a king to prescribe boundaries for his subjects to observe. Such decrees order society, outlining how the people should function together. *Laws* are more like what we call "case law" today in referring to historical precedent. Moses pairs these two concepts frequently in Deuteronomy. He does so to refer to the totality of God's revelation to Israel since the time of the exodus until God spoke to them at Kadesh Barnea (Deuteronomy 4:1, 5, 8, 14, 45; 5:1, 31; 6:1, 20, 21; 7:11; 11:32; 12:1; 26:16, 17).

Moses identifies himself as the teacher of the law and not its originator because the law was given by God. Israel will enjoy the benefits of covenant obedience if they heed Moses' instructions, namely enjoying the promised *land* that God pledged to Abraham (Deuteronomy 30:15-20).

> *What Do You Think?*
> How will you go about identifying some personal areas where greater trust in God's directions could lead to a life more abundant?
> *Digging Deeper*
> Should you be concerned that greater trust in God might look like a step backward to an unbeliever? Why, or why not?

B. Brings Standards (v. 2)

2. Do not add to what I command you and do not subtract from it, but keep the commands of the LORD your God that I give you.

Deuteronomy 4:2 can be considered Moses' tamper-proof clause regarding the law (compare

Joshua 1:7; Jeremiah 26:2). The non-tampering clause is a common feature of suzerainty treaties that inform how Moses composes his sermons (see Introduction). A king uses a non-tamper clause to remind the masses that he alone sets the terms of the covenant. There is no negotiation or collaboration. In the same way, *God* alone sets the terms of the covenant.

Moses is God's sole interpreter of the law at this time. No other explanation of God's law but Moses' is to be considered normative in Israel. Moses isn't selfishly consolidating his power; he merely mediates God's terms to Israel as he was called to do.

When Aaron and Miriam challenged Moses' position as God's spokesperson (Numbers 12), Moses didn't speak in his own defense. Instead, Moses spoke to intercede on behalf of his rebellious family members. Thus, Moses reiterates the goal of his instruction again: the Israelites are to *keep the commands* of God. Consequences will follow when they do not.

While it's true that this no-tamper clause is specific to God's covenant with ancient Israel (see Deuteronomy 12:32; Proverbs 30:6), we find a similar clause in Revelation 22:18, 19. The new covenant, revealed by God through his Son, renews the non-tamper clause. Jesus is Lord and sets the terms of the covenant. It's up to us as his people to keep obeying the covenant as it was offered to us, not as we see fit.

What Do You Think?
What safeguards can we adopt to ensure that we honor God's Word in situations that the Bible does not specifically address?
Digging Deeper
Would you adopt different safeguards depending on whether the situation involved unbelievers? Why, or why not?

❧ AMENDING THE LAW ❧

In 1787, delegates met in Philadelphia to create a framework for the U.S. government that would replace the Articles of Confederation. As satisfactory as this manuscript appeared, members of the Constitutional Convention recognized that the document would have to change over time. Therefore, they needed a provision for amending the U.S. Constitution.

Article V of their document did just that with one very long sentence. It reads, in part,

> The Congress . . . shall propose Amendments to this Constitution, or . . . shall call a Convention for proposing Amendments, which, in either Case, shall be valid to all Intents and Purposes, as Part of this Constitution.

Since it came into force in 1789, more than 11,000 amendments to the U.S. Constitution have been proposed. Only 27 of these have been ratified. The U.S. Constitution is a human document and needs to be altered on occasion. The Law of Moses, being of divine origin, is rightly forbidden any amendments (compare Revelation 22:18, 19). How do you resist the urge to do so?

—J. E.

C. Brings Consequences (vv. 3, 4)

3. You saw with your own eyes what the LORD did at Baal Peor. The LORD your God destroyed from among you everyone who followed the Baal of Peor,

Next, Moses refers to the nation's most recent failure when they sojourned at Shittim (Numbers 25:1-9; Psalm 106:28). Several Israelites indulged in sexual immorality with the women of neighboring Moab. These immoral relationships led to worship of and sacrifices to the false gods of the Moabites. God responded by ordering the execution of all those who knelt before *the Baal of Peor*, a regional god the Israelites were wrongly worshipping.

4. but all of you who held fast to the LORD your God are still alive today.

Everyone who maintained their covenant fidelity to *God,* while others ran after Moabite women and their gods, is still standing and listening to Moses' voice. Even before the blessings and curses are presented in Deuteronomy 28–31, the premium that God places on covenant obedience is evident. God rewards obedience and judges rebellion.

Moses views the Shittim event as a template for

the nation to use to interpret their future choices. Soon they will be entering Canaan and again face the temptation of being corrupted by their idol-worshipping neighbors. Obedience will yield life; disobedience, death.

II. Obedient Future
(Deuteronomy 4:5-8)
A. Invites Blessings (vv. 5, 6)

5. See, I have taught you decrees and laws as the Lord my God commanded me, so that you may follow them in the land you are entering to take possession of it.

Moses opens his second argument as to why the congregation should obey God's law by reiterating the information covered in Deuteronomy 4:1, above. *God* has *commanded* Moses to teach the nation the scope of these *decrees and laws* so the Israelites will obey God. Obedience makes them eligible to enjoy the blessing of the covenant: the promised *land*.

The effect of this repetition is to emphasize how vitally important it is for Israel to obey God's covenant. In Deuteronomy 4:1-4, this necessity is expressed by reminding Israel of God's justice. He honors covenant faithfulness, but judges those who break their treaty with him. In the verse at hand, obedience will lead the faithful to inhabit the land just as God has promised.

6. Observe them carefully, for this will show your wisdom and understanding to the nations, who will hear about all these decrees and say, "Surely this great nation is a wise and understanding people."

Moses begins to lay out his second rationale for the Israelites' future obedience to God's covenant: they will become an object of curiosity among the surrounding *nations*. Those people will observe

HOW TO SAY IT

Baal Peor	Bay-al *Pe*-or.
Kadesh Barnea	*Kay*-desh **Bar**-nee-uh.
Moabite	*Mo*-ub-ite.
Shittim	Shih-*teem*.
Sumerian	Sue-*mer*-ee-un.

Israel's being governed by God and notice their wisdom and *understanding*. Israel's neighbors will see God's people prosper, begin to inquire as to the cause of their well-being, and become aware of the source of Israel's strength: adherence to God's *decrees*. The impact of obedience will transcend Israel's borders.

What Do You Think?
> What are some practical ways to be an example of one who keeps God's Word in situations it specifically addresses?

Digging Deeper
> In what ways do passages such as John 13:1-17; Romans 2:17-24; and 2 Corinthians 6:3-10 shape your response?

B. Indicates Intimacy (v. 7)

7. What other nation is so great as to have their gods near them the way the Lord our God is near us whenever we pray to him?

Moses develops his second appeal: God's nearness is the source of their greatness in comparison to any *other nation* (see Exodus 19:5, 6; 1 Peter 2:9, 10). Centuries later, when Elijah challenges the prophets of Baal at Mount Carmel, he will taunt them by suggesting that their god is out of the country on business (1 Kings 18:27). None of the other so-called gods offer the gift of closeness as does Yahweh with his people. As mentioned in the lesson Introduction, this lack of connection between a deity and the worshipper could become a source of spiritual anxiety, as demonstrated by the reaction of the prophets of Baal to Elijah's mockery (vv. 28, 29).

God's dealings with his people after Egyptian bondage emphasize his closeness to Israel. The cloud and pillar of fire were symbols of God's personal leadership in guiding Israel through the wilderness (Exodus 13:21, 22). However, for Moses the gift of the law and its accessibility is another lasting sign of God's nearness to his people. Moses will later argue the importance of God's revealing his will through his commandments (Deuteronomy 30:15, 16). His law isn't hidden in the heavens or beyond the sea (30:12, 13). Instead, God reveals his will so it will be continually in the Israelites' speech and hearts (Deuteronomy 6:5-9; compare Ezekiel 36:26; Jeremiah 31:33; Hebrews 8:10). The closeness of God, as demonstrated through the accessibility of his commandments, should provoke Israel to obedience (Deuteronomy 30:14).

C. Invokes Praise (v. 8)

8. And what other nation is so great as to have such righteous decrees and laws as this body of laws I am setting before you today?

These words could easily come from the mouth of the Queen of Sheba when she visits King Solomon to test his wisdom (1 Kings 10:1-13). The queen will test Solomon's wisdom by confronting him with a battery of riddles. Unable to stump him, she will acknowledge the source of his wisdom: the Lord God. God will give Solomon this wisdom so that the king can discern good from evil and lead his people in God's ways (3:1-14).

So according to Moses, Israel's international fame will not be found in the size of the nation's armies or in great wealth but in the *body of laws* found within the covenant God enacted. Why? Because those laws are supernaturally received from the one true God (Exodus 19, 20). As such, each law is perfect and just. Conforming to these rules leads the people into a harmonious relationship with God and each other. No *other nation* can boast the same origin of their laws, nor can they boast that their laws are of equal benefit. God's laws will make Israel unique among all nations, but only if Israel obeys.

❧ SIGNS FOR SAFETY ❧

The Angels on Track Foundation (AOTF) is an organization promoting railroad safety. In a 2006 report, the AOTF argued that the installation of automated gates equipped with flashing lights has been the predominant reason that casualties at railroad crossings have steadily declined over the years. Yet only 26 percent of the nation's public crossings had been equipped with gates at the time of the report.

The AOTF blamed the shortfall on the fact that racing to beat a train is obviously dangerous, so motorists are to blame for the vast majority of incidents. Why spend the money to save those who engage in self-destructive behavior?

While laws are often viewed as bothersome restrictions, the Bible presents a different view. Like flashing lights and crossing gates at railroad crossings, the law of God is a blessing for humankind. His clear statement of divine morality is an undeniable act of grace. How will you celebrate God's laws?

—J. E.

> **What Do You Think?**
> Without quoting Scripture, how would you respond to someone who views God's rules as oppressive, unfair, and/or irrelevant to modern life?
> **Digging Deeper**
> How will your response to a sincere seeker of truth differ from your response to someone who merely wants to argue?

III. Reasons to Obey
(DEUTERONOMY 4:12, 13)
A. Divine Voice (v. 12)

12. Then the LORD spoke to you out of the fire. You heard the sound of words but saw no form; there was only a voice.

Moses presents the grounds for his final appeal as to why Israel should obey the covenant: God himself initiates and authors the covenant. He rescued the Israelites from Egypt (Exodus 2:23-25; 3:7-10). He led them to Mount Sinai, where he ignited *the fire* from which he proclaimed the terms of the treaty (19:18). Since God revealed himself in fire as *a voice* and not through the *form* of a human agent (19:19), there can be no confusion regarding the origin of the law.

B. Divine Hand (v. 13)

13a. He declared to you his covenant, the Ten Commandments, which he commanded you to follow

Moses describes in more specific terms how the covenant was received. He associates the *covenant* with *the Ten Commandments* that God revealed to Israel in Exodus 20. These commandments serve as the basis against which all other laws in Israel must be measured. They serve as the bedrock principles that outline covenant living, which other laws will expand on. In fact, most of the civil laws found in Deuteronomy should be viewed as case laws that apply these 10 commandments to precedents that will come to be in the life of the nation.

13b. and then wrote them on two stone tablets.

Moses closes his argument regarding the covenant's divine authorship: not only did God speak the terms of the covenant, but he also engraved them in *stone*. In the ancient Near East, it was customary for two copies of a covenant to be given to each party to remind them of the terms of the agreement (Esther 3:14; 8:13; Jeremiah 32:11). Deuteronomy 10:1-5 notes that both copies of the Ten Commandments are stored in the ark of the covenant. These *two* sets of *tablets* are a permanent reminder that God initiated the covenant. By implication, the only proper response is obedience.

Visual for Lesson 6. *Have this visual on display as you pose the discussion question that is associated with Deuteronomy 4:2.*

> *What Do You Think?*
> In what ways might your faith-walk improve, were you to focus a week's devotional reflection on God's power?
> *Digging Deeper*
> How can we balance time spent reflecting on God's power, love, grace, etc.?

Conclusion

A. Perfect Rule-Giver

The three arguments that Moses made to persuade his people to obey the covenant apply to God's people today. First, Moses reminded Israel that God blesses obedience and punishes disobedience (see Deuteronomy 30:15-20). Similarly, Jesus described himself as the true vine. Believers who keep his commandments (John 14:15) are like fruitful branches, while those who will not abide in him are like dry branches that are torn off and thrown into the fire (15:1-17). While obedience doesn't secure our salvation, it is evidence that we are redeemed (James 2:14-26).

Moses' second argument was that obedience to the covenant made Israel special among the nations. The nations would see the way Israel prospered and discover that it was because of the righteous and just laws that God provided them. We all are familiar with personal testimonies of friends who were won over to Christianity because they observed a believer living with the conviction that God is real and that he has a knowable will. Conversely, we're all too familiar with stories of ministers whose actions have brought contempt to the name of Christ. It's vitally important that we keep God's law. By observing God's good laws, we draw attention to the author of those laws.

Finally, we share Moses' conviction that we should obey God's laws because the are of divine origin (compare 2 Peter 1:20, 21). Because the commandments were authored by a holy and loving God, given to us for our benefit, our only faithful response is to bow our knees and submit to the gracious terms of the covenant that God has provided.

B. Prayer

God, thank you for your perfect commandments! May we submit ourselves to them as your Son, Jesus, would have us to. We pray this in his name. Amen.

C. Thought to Remember

The nature of God's law compels obedience.

INVOLVEMENT LEARNING

Enhance your lesson with NIV Bible Student *(from your curriculum supplier) and the reproducible activity page (at www.standardlesson.com or in the back of the* NIV Standard Lesson Commentary Deluxe Edition*).*

Into the Lesson

Write *Why obey?* on the board. Ask class members to think of rules they've been asked to follow in various situations. (Some possible contexts are at work, in college dorms, in an apartment building, regarding a homeowners' association, in a foreign country, on an airplane.) Jot responses on the board.

Then ask half the class to think of a rule that seemed arbitrary; ask the other half to think of a rule that was obviously necessary. Ask volunteers from the first half to share their arbitrary rules. After each proposal, ask for reasons to follow the rule.

Then ask volunteers from the second half to share their necessary rules. Ask class members whether they agree or disagree with the necessity of the rule. Ask whether anyone will admit to breaking a necessary rule, such as "No Running!" at a public swimming pool.

Lead into Bible study by telling students that today's text records a speech by a leader who told his people why they should obey God's laws.

Into the Word

Provide each class member with a copy of today's printed text, or ask students to turn to Deuteronomy 4. Read aloud, or have a class member read, the text in three sections: verses 1-4, verses 5-8, and verses 12 and 13. (Note: verses 9-11 are not included in the printed text but may also be included in the study.) Before the readings, challenge class members to underline phrases that answer the "Why obey?" question as they listen.

Pause after each reading to allow learners to share phrases they've underlined. Then, as a class, agree on one sentence that summarizes that section's answer to the question. Write the summaries on the board underneath the "Why obey?" question. Responses should complement or come close to the following:

1–God blesses obedience and punishes disobedience (vv. 1-4).

2–Obedience distinguishes God's followers from those who do not worship him (vv. 5-8).

3–We obey because the laws came from God, not from a human (vv. 12, 13).

Into Life

Divide the class into three or more groups. Give each group one of the following sets of questions to discuss. After five minutes, call time and have the groups exchange their assignment with that given to another group. Each group will discuss at least two of the following sets:

1–Since God punishes disobedience and blesses obedience, what are we to make of the financial success of so many today who have come into their wealth through means that do not honor God's laws? What does it mean that honest people struggle in poverty?

2–In what areas of life are Christians tempted most to disobedience that makes them look and act like non-Christians? How does such disobedience reflect on God?

3–What can a Christian do to strengthen his or her resolve to obey God? How should that Christian react to his or her own disobedience?

Allow time for class members to share during whole-class discussion.

Tell class members you will give them 30 seconds of silence to consider how they can obey at least one Bible command this week. If you have time, ask volunteers to share their responses. (Be prepared to share your own.)

Alternative. Distribute to study pairs copies of the "Why Obey?" exercise from the activity page, which you can download. Have pairs complete it as indicated.

After either activity, close with a prayer of gratitude for God's laws and for opportunities in the coming days to obey them.

ACTIVE
FAITH

DEVOTIONAL READING: Proverbs 3:1-10
BACKGROUND SCRIPTURE: 1 Kings 17:1-24

1 KINGS 17:8-16

8 Then the word of the LORD came to him:
9 "Go at once to Zarephath in the region of
Sidon and stay there. I have directed a widow
there to supply you with food." 10 So he went
to Zarephath. When he came to the town gate,
a widow was there gathering sticks. He called
to her and asked, "Would you bring me a little
water in a jar so I may have a drink?" 11 As she
was going to get it, he called, "And bring me,
please, a piece of bread."

12 "As surely as the LORD your God lives," she
replied, "I don't have any bread—only a handful of flour in a jar and a little olive oil in a jug.
I am gathering a few sticks to take home and
make a meal for myself and my son, that we
may eat it—and die."

13 Elijah said to her, "Don't be afraid. Go
home and do as you have said. But first make a
small loaf of bread for me from what you have
and bring it to me, and then make something
for yourself and your son. 14 For this is what the
LORD, the God of Israel, says: 'The jar of flour
will not be used up and the jug of oil will not
run dry until the day the LORD sends rain on
the land.'"

15 She went away and did as Elijah had told
her. So there was food every day for Elijah and
for the woman and her family. 16 For the jar of
flour was not used up and the jug of oil did not
run dry, in keeping with the word of the LORD
spoken by Elijah.

KEY VERSE

The jar of flour was not used up and the jug of oil did not run dry, in keeping with the word of the LORD spoken by Elijah. —**1 Kings 17:16**

RESPONDING TO
GOD'S GRACE

Unit 2: Responses to God's Faithfulness

LESSONS 6–9

LESSON AIMS

After participating in this lesson, each learner will be able to:

1. Cite the risks that Elijah and the widow of Zarephath took to obey God.

2. Explain the relationship between behavior and confidence in God's willingness to reward.

3. Identify one way that his or her behavior betrays a lack of faith in God and formulate a plan to correct it.

LESSON OUTLINE

Introduction

A. The Need to Reward Good Work

Ralph Waldo Emerson famously said that "the reward of a thing well done is having done it." Emerson, it should be noted, did not work in a human resources office. Today's hiring managers know that relying on intrinsic motivators—like the satisfaction of doing a good job—is not often successful for recruiting and retaining talent.

Fortune 500 companies were studied to discover how they incentivized their employees in ways other than increasing salaries. The lengths that these large companies went to in order to reward their best employees are mind-boggling. Google, the internet giant, offered free food and outdoor workout facilities to employees. The Mayo Clinic offered free massages and mental health services to employees at its Arizona site. Aflac hosted an annual employee appreciation week complete with trips to theme parks, movie screenings, and prize drawings. Most employers can't bankroll such ambitious employee incentive programs. However, smaller employers also see the value of incentives and offer extra time off, gift cards, etc.

God offers incentives for obedience to him (see Leviticus 26:3-12; Psalm 19:7-11; etc.), but his motivation isn't to jockey with other deities for the loyalty of a committed work base. Instead, God's rewards flow from his just character (Romans 2:6; Hebrews 11:6). God's justice not only punishes the wicked but rewards those who faithfully obey him (Revelation 22:11, 12), especially when they do so in the face of adversity.

B. Lesson Context: Literary

Most scholars believe that the books of 1 and 2 Kings, originally a single book, were written after the fall of both halves of the divided kingdom of Israel but before Judah returned from Babylonian exile in about 539 BC. The author of these books, whom some believe to be Jeremiah or one of his contemporaries, drew on hundreds of years of historical sources. He viewed Israel's history through the lens of God's covenant with his people as described in Deuteronomy. The author of

1 and 2 Kings meticulously organized Israel's history to make it obvious to his fellow Israelites that they were suffering exile and humiliation because of their lack of faithfulness to God's covenant.

Throughout the books of 1 and 2 Kings, the Lord honored the faith of individuals—whether kings, prophets, or the lowly—who remained true to the God of Israel. The exiles who first read 1 and 2 Kings struggled to understand why God allowed them to be handed over to their enemies and how they might find forgiveness and restoration. The history served in part to assure them that God would honor their faith, no matter where the people found themselves.

C. Lesson Context: Historical

Our narrative is set in the northern kingdom of Israel during the reign of King Ahab (874–853 BC). The details of his reign reveal the king's unwillingness to trust God to reward the northern kingdom if they would remain faithful to the terms of the Mosaic covenant (1 Kings 16:30-33). God initiated a covenant with his people that was similar to political treaties that earthly kings entered into with a newly conquered population (see Lesson 6). As king, Ahab had been charged with the task of being a steward of the covenant, just like every king before him (Deuteronomy 17:14-20).

The blessings and curses of the covenant should have provided every incentive needed for Ahab to lead his people into a season of covenant renewal. However, his contempt for the covenant and the Lord could not have been clearer. Ahab placed no stock in God's sovereignty or in his ability to reward the faithful or judge the wicked.

HOW TO SAY IT

Ahab	*Ay*-hab.
Baal	*Bay*-ul.
Canaanites	*Kay*-nun-ites.
Jericho	*Jair*-ih-co.
Jezebel	*Jez*-uh-bel.
Phoenicia	Fuh-*nish*-uh.
Sidon	*Sigh*-dun.
Tyre	Tire.
Zarephath	*Zair*-uh-fath.

Instead of trusting God, Ahab cemented a political alliance with the Zidonians by marrying Jezebel, a princess from the coastal city Sidon. This alliance incited Ahab to disregard God's covenant. Jezebel turned Ahab's heart to the Canaanite god Baal and away from the Lord (1 Kings 16:31). Ahab in turn promoted Baal worship in the northern kingdom by constructing an altar in his honor (16:32). Ahab also allowed for the rebuilding of the city of Jericho (16:34), even though Joshua had placed a curse on anyone who attempted such folly (Joshua 6:26).

The author of 1 Kings draws parallels between Moses (the original prophet of the covenant) and Elijah (the ninth-century BC prophet who called the nation back to covenant loyalty). Both Moses and Elijah challenged rulers who defied God (Exodus 5:1; 7:10, 20; 1 Kings 18:17, 18). Both prophets hid from evil kings (Exodus 2:11-15; 1 Kings 17:1-7). Both confronted the false gods of their day (Exodus 32:19-35; 1 Kings 18:20-40). Both experienced the presence of God in a unique way (Exodus 33:17-23; 1 Kings 19:9-18). These parallel narratives suggest to the reader that Elijah has inherited Moses' authoritative role to call the people to covenant faithfulness.

The narrative of Elijah's ministry stretches from 1 Kings 17 through 2 Kings 2. First Kings 17 opens with Elijah defying King Ahab's chosen deity, Baal. Baal was thought to control the dew and rain, concerning himself with the fertility of the earth. Because the Canaanites were an agricultural society, Baal was one of the predominate gods in that land.

Elijah sought to make known to all God's people Ahab's foolishness in revering Baal. Elijah invoked the name of God and declared that there would be no more rain until the Lord permitted it (1 Kings 17:1). God protected Elijah from Ahab's retaliation by leading him to a hidden place near a brook. Every morning and evening, God sent ravens to Elijah with food (17:2-6).

Jesus noted that the drought lasted three and a half years (Luke 4:25). Sometime during that period, the brook dried up. When it did, Elijah lost his source of drinking water (1 Kings 17:7). This brings us to today's text.

I. Sent to Zarephath

(1 KINGS 17:8-10a)

A. The Lord's Command (vv. 8, 9)

8, 9a. Then the word of the LORD came to him: "Go at once to Zarephath in the region of Sidon and stay there.

The drying of the brook (see Lesson Context) forces Elijah out of his hiding spot. But God doesn't leave Elijah to his own devices to find a new source of food and water. God provides, but the new hiding spot may surprise his prophet. God leads Elijah to *Zarephath*, seaport in *Sidon* (later Phoenicia). The city lies approximately 22 miles north of Tyre with which it is often associated (Ezra 3:7; Jeremiah 25:22; Matthew 11:21, 22; etc.). This puts Elijah squarely in evil Queen Jezebel's homeland (1 Kings 16:31)—surprise!

9b. "I have directed a widow there to supply you with food."

God's second surprising choice regarding Elijah's hiding is to choose *a widow* to serve as the prophet's patroness. Widows in particular are economically vulnerable within a patriarchal society where men control the mechanisms of commerce. Without a living husband or other adult men in their families, widows and their children often find themselves destitute (compare Exodus 22:22).

The prospect of God's burdening a widow with the task of caring for Elijah must be disorienting to the prophet. Ordinarily, he would be tasked

Visual for Lesson 7. *Start a discussion by pointing to this visual as you ask, "Under what circumstances will action increase faith to act further? Why?"*

with caring for widows, not the other way around. God charges his people to care for the widow and the fatherless (Deuteronomy 10:18; 14:29; 24:19-21; 26:12, 13, 19; etc.). David later writes that God is the defender of both (Psalm 68:5; see also 146:9). Yet the Lord chooses instead to *sustain* Elijah through a widow.

> *What Do You Think?*
> How can we discern whether a seemingly unattractive opportunity might be God's opening a door for our protection or blessing?
> *Digging Deeper*
> How will you know if such an opportunity is optional for you to accept or reject vs. being a divine directive?

B. Elijah's Obedience (v. 10a)

10a. So he went to Zarephath.

The Scripture doesn't detail any internal struggle that Elijah may have over complying with God's counterintuitive plans. Instead, the narrative simply states that Elijah does as God directs. Elijah thus becomes an expatriate and remains separated from the comforts of home.

Perhaps part of God's purpose in sending Elijah out of Israel is to make it hard for Ahab and Jezebel to find him (1 Kings 18:10). After all, Jezebel will react to the Lord's prophets who reject Baal by ordering their slaughter (18:4, 13). She will gladly have Elijah killed along with all the others (19:2). Elijah needs to be kept safe until it is time for him to expose Baal for the false god he is (18:16-40).

II. Meeting at the Gate

(1 KINGS 17:10b-12)

A. Elijah's Request (vv. 10b, 11)

10b. When he came to the town gate, a widow was there gathering sticks. He called to her and asked, "Would you bring me a little water in a jar so I may have a drink?"

The town gate is a highly trafficked area. The comings and goings of people create such a steady flow of witnesses in the vicinity of the gate that the judges of the city often settle court disputes there (Genesis 34:20-24; Deuteronomy 17:5; 21:18-21; Ruth 4:1-12; etc.). The narrative doesn't reveal how Elijah picks the *widow* out of the crowd. Somehow God prompts the prophet.

The task of drawing daily *water* from the well customarily falls to women. (Genesis 24:11 provides an early example.) They draw the water for their households in the evening or early morning when the harsh Middle Eastern sun isn't beating down on the world (contrast John 4:6, 7). However, instead of coming to the gate to gather water, this woman is intent on *gathering sticks* to build her fire. The prophet's request is an interruption to her agenda.

11. As she was going to get it, he called, "And bring me, please, a piece of bread."

The widow complies with Elijah's request. As she goes *to get* the water, Elijah interrupts her to add a second. God has revealed his command to Elijah that the widow is to sustain him (see above on 1 Kings 17:9). But even with that knowledge, Elijah asks in incremental steps to have his needs met: first water, [then pause], then *a piece of bread*.

The text doesn't reveal the cause of Elijah's tentativeness. Perhaps his thirst is greater than his hunger when he first meets the widow. More likely, the prophet recognizes the widow's precarious economic situation. Even as he imposes on her for food, he only asks for a morsel of bread, not an entire meal.

B. Widow's Response (v. 12)

12. "As surely as the LORD your God lives," she replied, "I don't have any bread—only a handful of flour in a jar and a little olive oil in a jug. I am gathering a few sticks to take home and make a meal for myself and my son, that we may eat it—and die."

The widow's reply *as the Lord your God lives* is a strong oath. It swears truthfully that she is unable to honor the prophet's request (compare 1 Kings 1:29, 30; 22:14; Jeremiah 5:2; etc.). Unlike Ahab (see Lesson Context), the widow isn't resisting the request out of brazen disobedience. Rather, she speaks honestly about the reality of her situation. Her status as a widow and the impact of the

drought combine to make her destitute. She has no hope of generating a sustainable income. She has enough *oil* and *flour* left only to make one final loaf of bread for herself and her *son* before they *die* in their poverty, which she recognizes will not take long. The plan reveals her despair and resignation.

> **What Do You Think?**
> How can we challenge those who don't believe they are able to give much, so that they may be blessed to do more than they realize?
> **Digging Deeper**
> In what contexts of the question above would it be appropriate and inappropriate to point out this account of the poor widow? Why?

III. Faith in a Foreign Land
(1 KINGS 17:13-16)
A. Elijah's Confidence (vv. 13, 14)

13a. Elijah said to her, "Don't be afraid.

Refusing to *be afraid* emboldens individuals to trust God, especially when circumstances suggest that conformity to God's will isn't the safest or wisest course of action (compare Mark 5:36). The command not to fear is found throughout the Old Testament, often paired with a reminder of God's presence (Genesis 15:1; Joshua 10:25; Isaiah 43:5; Zechariah 8:13; etc.). The frequency with which God and/or his prophets repeat this concise command underscores its importance.

13b. "Go home and do as you have said. But first make a small loaf of bread for me from what you have and bring it to me, and then make something for yourself and your son.

Notice the sequence: the widow is to prepare Elijah's food *first* and *bring it to* Elijah. Only then may she prepare food for herself and her *son*. What faith this will require!

14. "For this is what the LORD, the God of Israel, says: 'The jar of flour will not be used up and the jug of oil will not run dry until the day the LORD sends rain on the land.'"

In identifying the source of his request as *the God of Israel*, the prophet assures the widow that her need will not go unmet, no matter how long the drought lasts. *The Lord* is at war with fictitious Baal for the purpose of provoking King Ahab and the people of Israel to return their affections to him (see Lesson Context).

God knows that faithful people are also adversely affected by the drought, to the point that obedience might look foolish and even life-threatening. But here we see that God is capable of caring for his prophet and the widow while simultaneously commanding the attention of his unfaithful king. Through Elijah, God assures the widow that her modest pantry will not be depleted until God again allows the *rain* to nourish the now barren *land*.

Elijah's confidence in God's provision reinforces what the drought suggests: God's power is not limited to a certain geopolitical area (contrast 1 Kings 20:23-25). He can withhold rain not just in the land of his own people but wherever he chooses. God can rescue a widow in Sidon as easily as he can rescue a widow within the confines of the promised land.

> *What Do You Think?*
> What are some ways to encourage the hesitant to trust God to provide?
> *Digging Deeper*
> What role should your personal example serve in answering the above question?

❧ PROMISE OF PLENTY ❧

Twice the offices of a well-known a "health and wealth" TV evangelist have been raided by government investigators. Part of what prompted the investigation were questions about whether millions of dollars in donations were used as promised. Ultimately, no charges of fraud or tax evasion were brought.

Yet many Christians still have questions about this person's ministry. Health and wealth preachers teach that Christians are meant to prosper, especially if they tithe their income to the evangelist's ministry. They propose that every Christian should be healed of sickness. Those who promote themselves as conduits of such healing are surely open to criticism when promises go unfulfilled.

Elijah also had been investigated by his government. But in his case he had been found guilty as charged. So he fled, eventually finding refuge in a widow's home. God promised the woman that her food supply would never diminish as long as she provided for Elijah, and God kept his word. How do you demonstrate trust in God, no matter your circumstances? See Luke 7:23.   —C. R. B.

B. The Widow's Obedience (v. 15a)

15a. She went away and did as Elijah had told her.

The widow listens to Elijah and abandons her original, hopeless plan. Perhaps Elijah's exhortation fills her with faith. Maybe she complies out of love for her son, even though she is not fully convinced that God will provide (compare Matthew 17:20). Either way, her faith allows her to act where King Ahab is unwilling: she puts her trust in the one true God and places her future in his hands.

C. The Lord's Provision (vv. 15b, 16)

15b. So there was food every day for Elijah and for the woman and her family.

The result of the widow's faithful action is exactly as Elijah says. Rather than consuming a final meal with her son, everyone in *her family* can eat for much longer than her provisions would have lasted naturally. The Lord's work through her obedience sustains everyone involved.

16. For the jar of flour was not used up and the jug of oil did not run dry, in keeping with the word of the LORD spoken by Elijah.

In the Old Testament, the formula *the word of the Lord* frequently attends a prophecy from God (1 Kings 17:2; 2 Kings 20:16; Jeremiah 33:19; Zechariah 7:4, 8; etc.). The repetition in these two verses of the fact that the widow's *flour* and *oil* fed the family for many days emphasizes God's work on behalf of these obedient people.

God has braided together the fates of the prophet Elijah, the unnamed widow, and the widow's son. The latter two, at least, would not have survived the drought otherwise. Because the widow welcomed the prophet, she shares in his reward (compare Matthew 10:41, 42).

My family and I served as missionaries in an African country for a time. An employer there was a foreign mining company that was extracting the country's iron ore deposits. The company was a joint venture of American and Swedish corporate interests that cooperated with the national government to create wealth for each party.

While we were there, the workers went on strike for a raise of a few cents to 25 cents per hour. The corporations were willing to grant the raise, but the government refused. Many speculated that the government didn't want to cut into the profits the officials were believed to be skimming.

Elijah and the widow of Zarephath were involved in a joint venture of faith. At the outset, the widow's point of view was that no "profit" was at stake—only the break-even prospect of staying alive. But through active faith she may have indeed reaped a unanticipated spiritual profit. What might that profit have been?   —C. R. B.

> **What Do You Think?**
> How will you respond to those who say they cannot believe in God because so many in the world lack the basics for having their physical needs met?
>
> **Digging Deeper**
> How will your response differ, if at all, due to the attitude and agenda of the one making the observation?

Conclusion

A. The God Who Rewards Generously

Due to the nation's apostasy under King Ahab, God-honoring faith was almost absent in Israel (compare 1 Kings 19:18). So God called an unlikely widow—a foreigner familiar with God only by reputation—to put her trust in him. Her faith in God was shown through her in obedience, feeding Elijah before providing for her son and herself. She responded to God in faith even though she was not among God's covenant people.

In Jesus' first public appearance after his temptation, he saw fit to mention the widow as an example of faith. He had returned to Nazareth to worship in the synagogue. After reading a prophecy from the book of Isaiah concerning the anointed one, Jesus proclaimed himself to be the fulfillment of that Scripture (Luke 4:14-30; compare Mark 7:24-30). Though the congregation spoke well of him momentarily, Jesus' response to their marveling at a hometown hero infuriated them. He reminded his audience that God hadn't sent Elijah to any of the widows within the confines of Israel. God had chosen an outsider who would demonstrate obedient faith.

The exiles who read these accounts in 1 Kings (see Lesson Context) were reminded as we are that God's influence is not limited to one group of people or one piece of land. God had not entered into a covenant with the widow's people. He had not revealed himself to them through the law. But God favored her modest faith by blessing her obedience. God still honors faithful obedience, no matter how tentative those attempts initially are.

> **What Do You Think?**
> Under what circumstances, if any, would liberal giving change from being an act of faith to an act of foolish failure to plan for the needs of oneself and one's own household? Explain.
>
> **Digging Deeper**
> Which of the following passages cause you most to reevaluate your response to the question above: Leviticus 5:6, 7; 14:21, 22, 30-32; Matthew 6:34; Luke 14:28-30; 18:22; 21:1-4; 2 Corinthians 8:1-5; 1 Thessalonians 2:9; 1 Timothy 5:8, 16?

B. Prayer

God, we desire to obey you, but sometimes our hearts are rebellious, and sometimes we are simply discouraged. We know that you honor those who strive to obey you. May this knowledge strengthen us. We pray in Jesus' name. Amen.

C. Thought to Remember

God honors the faithful.
Always has, always will.

INVOLVEMENT LEARNING

Enhance your lesson with NIV Bible Student *(from your curriculum supplier) and the reproducible activity page (at www.standardlesson.com or in the back of the* NIV Standard Lesson Commentary Deluxe Edition*).*

Into the Lesson

Ask students to tell a story about themselves with the title "It Didn't Make Sense, but I Did It Anyhow." Divide students into pairs or groups of three, and give each student about one minute to tell his or her story. Call time after each minute, and instruct the next student to tell a story.

Ask volunteers to share a story they heard in their groups. (Limit this to one or two stories—don't let it drag out.) Then have a show of hands, using these prompts: 1–Raise your hand if your choice to do something that didn't make sense turned out well. 2–Raise your hand if your choice did not turn out well. 3–Raise your hand if your choice was because you were depending on yourself. 4–Raise your hand if your choice was because you were depending on God.

Lead into Bible study by saying that today's lesson looks at two people who obeyed God even though it didn't seem to make sense to do so.

Into the Word

Explain the background for today's story, using material from the Lesson Context section. If possible, recruit a class member to present a three-minute lecture based on this material to set the stage for today's Bible study.

Alternative. Distribute copies of the "Obeying God with Confidence" exercise from the activity page, which you can download. These can be completed individually as indicated; the time limit is one minute.

Distribute copies of a chart (you create) featuring five columns with these headers, one each: *The Person / The Problem / God's Solution / The Surprise / The Result.* In the first column enter the name "Elijah" and the description "Widow of Zarephath" to begin separate rows.

Have students form or remain in the pairs or triads from the first activity. Read the lesson text while students look at the chart and listen for answers to complete it. Then ask students to talk with their partners to agree on what should go in the chart's blanks. (*Option.* To save time you may wish to assign half of the groups the task of answering for "Elijah" and the other half for the "widow of Zarephath.") After a few minutes, alternate between the groups and ask them to share their answers with the class. You may need to help them with some blanks, especially those under the heading *The Surprise.*

Here are some possible responses. **Elijah:** (Problem) nothing to eat or drink; (God's solution) find a widow in Zarephath and ask her for food and drink; (Surprise) God sent him to a foreign, pagan land for help from a vulnerable widow, not a person of power or influence. (Result) The widow was willing to share the little she had; God provided miraculously for the widow, her household, and Elijah. **Widow of Zarephath:** (Problem) almost nothing to eat or drink; (God's solution) God promised that her flour and oil would not run out. (Surprise) She, the person Elijah asked for help, was destitute and preparing to die; further, she was not an Israelite believer. (Result) The widow, her household, and Elijah had enough to eat for the duration of the famine.

Into Life

Send students back to the same pairs or triads to discuss at least one of these challenges: 1–Tell about a time when God surprised you with his answer to your prayer. 2–Share a serious prayer request you have been lifting to God for more than one week.

After about six minutes, challenge them to pray with faith, continuing in obedience, and be willing to receive a surprise from God. End with a prayer for God to respond to the faithfulness of your class members.

Alternative. Distribute copies of the "What Jesus Said" activity on the activity page. Discuss the questions as a class.

HUMBLE
FAITH

DEVOTIONAL READING: James 5:13-18
BACKGROUND SCRIPTURE: Luke 7:1-10

LUKE 7:1-10

¹ When Jesus had finished saying all this to the people who were listening, he entered Capernaum. ² There a centurion's servant, whom his master valued highly, was sick and about to die. ³ The centurion heard of Jesus and sent some elders of the Jews to him, asking him to come and heal his servant. ⁴ When they came to Jesus, they pleaded earnestly with him, "This man deserves to have you do this, ⁵ because he loves our nation and has built our synagogue." ⁶ So Jesus went with them.

He was not far from the house when the centurion sent friends to say to him: "Lord, don't trouble yourself, for I do not deserve to have you come under my roof. ⁷ That is why I did not even consider myself worthy to come to you. But say the word, and my servant will be healed. ⁸ For I myself am a man under authority, with soldiers under me. I tell this one, 'Go,' and he goes; and that one, 'Come,' and he comes. I say to my servant, 'Do this,' and he does it."

⁹ When Jesus heard this, he was amazed at him, and turning to the crowd following him, he said, "I tell you, I have not found such great faith even in Israel." ¹⁰ Then the men who had been sent returned to the house and found the servant well.

KEY VERSE

I did not even consider myself worthy to come to you. But say the word, and my servant will be healed.
—Luke 7:7

Responding to God's Grace

GOD'S GRACE

Unit 2: Responses to God's Faithfulness

LESSON AIMS

After participating in this lesson, each learner will be able to:

1. List elements of surprise in the healing of the centurion's servant.

2. Explain how humility strengthens faith.

3. Demonstrate humble faith in a way that may surprise others.

LESSON OUTLINE

Introduction

A. A Twist Ending

Bob Newhart starred in two popular television series. In *The Bob Newhart Show* (1972–1978), he played a Chicago psychologist, Dr. Robert Hartley. In the later series, *Newhart* (1982–1990), he played Dick Loudon, a New York author who moves to the country to operate an inn.

The second series is memorable for its twist ending. In the finale, viewers are shown what looks like Dr. Hartley's Chicago bedroom. Bob Newhart sits up in bed and says, "Honey, wake up! You won't believe the dream I just had!" Suddenly, we learn that the entire eight-year series has been nothing more than Dr. Hartley's dream.

Twists in television are great entertainment. Similar surprises in real life can be much less delightful. Sometimes we set ourselves up for unpleasant surprises with preconceived ideas about other people. When a stereotype gets debunked, we feel ashamed because of our newly revealed prejudice. We learn that this person is a unique and complicated human being—just like ourselves.

Stereotypes abounded in first-century Israel. Jews had their stereotypes of the Romans, and Romans had their stereotypes of the Jews. But occasionally, someone broke out of the mold. Broken stereotypes change the whole story, just like a twist in a television show.

B. Lesson Context

Matthew 8:5-13 contains another record of the healing of the centurion's servant found in Luke. The context for the parallel accounts in Matthew and Luke is nearly identical; in Luke it comes directly after Jesus' Sermon on the Plain (Luke 6:17-49), and in Matthew it is shortly after the Sermon on the Mount (Matthew 5–7).

The text of the sermon in Luke is shorter than in Matthew, but the two share a great deal of material (compare Matthew 5:3-12 with Luke 6:20-23; Matthew 5:38-42 with Luke 6:29, 30; Matthew 5:43-48 with Luke 6:27, 28, 32-36; etc.). For this reason, scholars tend to treat the sermons as two accounts of the same event. The seeming contradiction between the setting for the sermon on a "mountainside" (Matthew 5:1; 8:1) and a "level place," or plain (Luke 6:17) is easily resolved: Jesus found a wide, flat place on the mountainside from which to deliver his sermon.

This sermon helps us place this healing within a time line of Jesus' ministry. Assuming that Jesus' crucifixion occurred in AD 30, scholars work back to place the Sermon on the Plain in the fall of AD 28 during Jesus' ministry in Galilee. Though this was early in his ministry, Jesus' reputation was already solidifying as both a teacher and a miracle worker (Luke 4:36, 37, 42-44; 5:15).

The placement of the healing of Peter's mother-in-law poses a momentary chronological difficulty. In Matthew, her healing comes immediately after the healing of the centurion's servant (Matthew 8:14, 15), but Luke places her healing prior to Jesus' sermon and, consequently, also the healing of the servant (Luke 4:38, 39). It appears that Matthew made the rhetorical decision to place the healing of Peter's mother-in-law, as well as other miracles in Capernaum, after the centurion's story as a topical connection with Capernaum. The event likely happened before the sermon, as in Luke.

A similar account regarding the long-distance healing of a nobleman's son in Capernaum is unrelated to this story, though it may contribute to general knowledge about Jesus that was circulating in Capernaum prior to the centurion's request (see John 4:46-54). Such a healing in a reputable family would not have gone unnoticed by a centurion posted in the city. Taken with other events recorded in the first three Gospels, the groundwork for faith had certainly been laid in Capernaum (Mark 1:23-34; Luke 4:33-35).

I. Request

(LUKE 7:1-5)

A. Jesus' Arrival (v. 1)

1. When Jesus had finished saying all this to the people who were listening, he entered Capernaum.

Jesus' Sermon on the Plain comprises the sayings that he *finished* just before going to *Capernaum* (see Lesson Context). The location for the sermon was probably somewhere near the city. To say Jesus *entered* Capernaum rather than "traveled to" or similar suggests he was just outside of town.

Capernaum has become Jesus' residence and the headquarters for his ministry (Matthew 4:13; Mark 2:1). The precise location of the ancient city is unknown. From Matthew's description, scholars conclude that it would have been situated on the northwest coast of the Sea of Galilee.

B. The Centurion's Need (v. 2)

2. There a centurion's servant, whom his master valued highly, was sick and about to die.

We are not told the *centurion's* name or regiment (contrast Acts 10:1). His title reveals him to be the leader of a group of Roman soldiers. The term implies that the group numbers 100, though it may in fact be somewhat less than that.

Still, he is a person of status and rank. He has charge of both servants and soldiers to do his bidding. Other centurions mentioned in the Gospels and Acts point to the potential for righteousness and faith in Gentiles, an important theme in the New Testament (see Matthew 27:54; Mark 15:39; Luke 23:47; Acts 10; compare Acts 11; Romans 9:30, 31; Galatians 3:8, 14; etc.).

Romans can legally treat a *servant* as nothing more than a tool. Many servants suffer gravely because of this legislation. However, a servant of great merit can be treated quite well. Though the centurion might also feel some affection for the servant, the primary bond between them exists because of the servant's good work. Given that the servant is *valued highly* (elsewhere translated "precious"; see 1 Peter 2:4, 6), the servant probably has a specific set of skills that the centurion greatly appreciates.

Luke uses a general term for servant in this account, but Matthew uses a different word that

HOW TO SAY IT

Capernaum	Kuh-*per*-nay-um.
centurion	sen-*ture*-ee-un.
Galilee	*Gal*-uh-lee.
synagogue	*sin*-uh-gog.

can be translated "child." Children are not cherished in Jesus' day as they are today (see Matthew 19:13-15). Though the centurion can certainly care for a young servant, more likely the value of the servant points to his being an adult.

Luke's account mentions the severity of the illness but not a specific diagnosis. Matthew's account notes that the servant is paralyzed in some way (Matthew 8:6). This same ailment afflicted the man who was carried by his four friends to Jesus (Matthew 9:2; see also 4:24; John 5:3; Acts 8:7). Outside of divine intervention, paralysis is untreatable and incurable in the centurion's time.

> **What Do You Think?**
> What can we do to extend godly concern and care to those in positions of power?
> **Digging Deeper**
> In so doing, how do we avoid the appearance of trying to curry favor?

C. Jewish Emissaries (vv. 3-5)

3. The centurion heard of Jesus and sent some elders of the Jews to him, asking him to come and heal his servant.

The statement that *the centurion heard of Jesus* likely means when the centurion hears that Jesus has returned to Capernaum, not when he first heard of Jesus at all (see commentary on Luke 7:1). The centurion seizes the opportunity to find relief for *his servant.*

Some elders refers to the leaders of the Jewish community in Capernaum. Israel has depended on elders for leadership since the time of Moses (Exodus 3:16; Ruth 4:1-12; 1 Samuel 30:26; 2 Kings 10:5; Ezra 10:16; etc.). In spite of the centurion's role as a leader among the occupational force dominating Judea and given the animosity common between *Jews* and Gentiles in Judea, these elders are on friendly terms with the Roman centurion.

4a. When they came to Jesus, they pleaded earnestly with him,

Here is another surprise in the story: the elders come *to Jesus* and seek his help. This is the first mention of "elders" in Luke, but elders will later be listed among those who oppose Jesus, even seeking his death (see Luke 9:22; 20:1, 2; 22:52, 66-71). Jesus has already been criticized by other Jewish leaders, including scribes and Pharisees (see 5:21, 30). In contrast, these elders appear to have great respect for Jesus.

As though that were not surprising enough, the elders approach Jesus on behalf of a Gentile. The term translated *earnestly* is elsewhere translated "[search] hard" and "do everything you can" (see 2 Timothy 1:17; Titus 3:13). Contrary to the duplicitous behavior of the Jewish leaders who later seek to trick or trap Jesus (Luke 10:25), these elders are sincere in their request. From beginning to end, the elders' actions seem out of character with that of most other Jewish leaders.

> **What Do You Think?**
> What are some ways our church can act as a go-between in connecting resources to those in need?
> **Digging Deeper**
> In so doing, what safeguards could be put in place to avoid wrong appearances and actions?

4b. "This man deserves to have you do this,

The elders' earnest plea shows their high regard for the centurion. In their opinion, the centurion's acts mean he *deserves* not only to ask Jesus for healing but also to receive it (see next).

5a. "because he loves our nation

The centurion is not merely a successful diplomat who maintains a good relationship with the leaders of the subjugated nation. In yet another surprise, he genuinely *loves* the *nation.* Luke gives no insight into why the centurion loves Israel. His affection suggests that he is a God-fearing Gentile. A God fearer comes from a pagan background but believes in the one true God. Often God fearers are attracted to the high moral code evident in Jewish law. However, they live outside of Judaism because they do not choose to go through all the rituals that are necessary to be fully incorporated into the nation (contrast "God-fearing Greeks" in Acts 17:4, 17 with "convert[s] to Judaism" in Acts 6:5; 13:43).

5b. "and has built our synagogue."

As a tangible expression of his love for the nation of Israel, this centurion has *built* a *synagogue*, presumably in Capernaum. This does not mean he personally erected the structure. Instead, he financed the project, paying for the construction out of his own resources.

II. Protest
(LUKE 7:6-8)
A. On Worthiness (vv. 6, 7)

6a. So Jesus went with them.

Apparently, Jesus gives some kind of affirmative answer to the elders and begins walking toward the centurion's home.

6b. He was not far from the house when the centurion sent friends to say to him:

The second delegation to meet Jesus is called *friends*, and no mention is made of their nationality or ethnicity. One might suppose these friends are also Jewish. If so, the fact that they are with *the centurion* at home emphasizes the very special and unusual bond he has with the Jewish community (contrast Acts 10).

6c. "Lord, don't trouble yourself, for I do not deserve to have you come under my roof.

The friends deliver the centurion's message faithfully. The centurion refutes the elders' witness about him, saying that he himself does *not deserve* to have Jesus visit him. The centurion may be sensitive to the Jewish law cited by Peter: that it is unlawful for Jews to enter Gentiles' homes (Acts 10:28). If the centurion is sensitive to Jesus' becoming unclean by entering his home, then he may be unaware of Jesus' earlier actions of touching the unclean to effect healing (Luke 4:40; 5:12, 13).

> **What Do You Think?**
> ► How do we help a person who hesitates to turn to God because of self-acknowledged personal sinfulness and/or unworthiness?
> **Digging Deeper**
> How do passages such as Luke 5:8 and 1 Corinthians 15:8-11 help frame your answer?

❧ MAN OF THE CENTURY ❧

Was Sir Winston Churchill the greatest man of the twentieth century? Charles Krauthammer, a political commentator, argues that "without Churchill the world today would be unrecognizable—dark, impoverished, tortured." Churchill recognized early on that totalitarianism could destroy the world. A gifted wordsmith, his speeches gave the British people the backbone to resist Nazism at a time when no other nation could or would.

However, Churchill was not a humble man, and his rhetoric could also skewer his opposition. On one occasion, he was criticizing Clement Attlee, a political enemy. A friend interjected, "You must admit that Mr. Attlee is a humble man." Churchill responded, "He's a humble man, but then he has much to be humble about!"

The centurion had accomplished much for which he could be proud as witnessed by the fact that he commanded a cadre of Roman soldiers. Yet, unlike Churchill, he was a humble man. He recognized he wasn't worthy to host Jesus. May we demonstrate the same humble attitude!

—C. R. B.

7a. "That is why I did not even consider myself worthy to come to you.

The centurion's surprisingly humble message continues. Not only is he unworthy for Jesus to come to him, he considers himself to be *not worthy to come to* Jesus. This statement suggests that the centurion was not primarily worried about imparting uncleanness to Jesus if he visits the centurion's home. Instead, the centurion recognizes Jesus' greatness and power and concludes that his own accolades are paltry by comparison. In his own opinion, he does not deserve an audience with Jesus.

This verse emphasizes different details between Matthew and Luke in retelling this story. In Matthew's account, there is no delegation of elders or friends; the centurion himself presents the request to Jesus (Matthew 8:5). When Jesus consents to come, the centurion expresses in person his faith that Jesus need not be physically present to heal the servant (8:7-9). The easiest and best reconciliation

Faithful people are

HUMBLE & GRATEFUL

Visual for Lessons 8 & 9. *Allow the class to focus on this statement for a few moments before closing with prayer.*

of this seeming contradiction is that Matthew simply condenses the account. Having the centurion act and speak for himself cuts out the middlemen and takes the story from beginning to end quickly.

The different emphases of these accounts may also help explain the difference between them. The theme of whether or not the centurion is worthy to host Jesus or even meet him is not entirely absent from the shorter account (Matthew 8:8). Matthew emphasizes instead the centurion's status as an outsider of great faith (8:10-12). Luke highlights the humility of the centurion's faith by revealing that the centurion's friends and the elders speak on his behalf.

7b. "But say the word, and my servant will be healed.

Even more surprising than the centurion's humility is the faith that is coupled with it. He believes in Jesus' power to heal by a *word*. Perhaps he has heard of the nobleman's son (John 4:46-54; see Lesson Context). If so, he does not mention it. But just as he knows he needs only to speak a command for his soldiers or servants to obey, so the centurion has confidence that Jesus needs only to speak for his will to be accomplished.

B. On Authority (v. 8)

8. "For I myself am a man under authority, with soldiers under me. I tell this one, 'Go,' and he goes; and that one, 'Come,' and he comes. I say to my servant, 'Do this,' and he does it."

The centurion knows about *authority* from personal experience. He accomplishes his will not by personally attending to every detail but by giving orders. Rather, he commands *soldiers* and servants alike, and they do his bidding. He does not question his own authority over the soldiers; in the same way, he assumes Jesus' authority over the servant's sickness.

> **What Do You Think?**
> What distinctive of your occupation can you use in your witness of faith?
> **Digging Deeper**
> How do we guard against "too much of a stretch" in doing so?

Most of Jesus' healings take place with the sick or possessed person before him (just one chapter in Mark contains many examples; see Mark 1:25, 26, 30-34, 40-42). The centurion remains confident that Jesus can give the word to effect his servant's healing. The centurion has grasped something that many in Israel never will: Jesus has the authority and the power to heal whomever he chooses as he ushers in God's kingdom on earth (see Luke 4:18-21).

III. Impressed
(LUKE 7:9, 10)
A. Great Faith (v. 9)

9. When Jesus heard this, he was amazed at him, and turning to the crowd following him, he said, "I tell you, I have not found such great faith even in Israel."

Strictly speaking, to be *amazed* at someone or something does not require expressing surprise but only recognizing that person or thing as being worthy of admiration: "amazing." We too may marvel at the centurion's *great faith*. It is a thing of wonder, even though it does not surprise us after many readings.

Jesus frequently draws a crowd wherever he goes. Now he simply turns to the elders and *the crowd following him*. Jesus points out the irony of the Gentile's faith in the face of Jewish unbelief (compare Acts 13:46, 47). This dovetails with rejection Jesus has already faced (Luke 5:21, 30; 6:7, 11) and is yet to face in the months ahead (7:30; 9:22; 11:53, 54; 15:2; 16:14; 22:52).

These elders, for their part, act unlike most other elders in response to Jesus' ministry. So Jesus may commend the elders for their faith as well. Approaching Jesus shows that they too believe that he can heal the servant. This serves to highlight as well the centurion's faith that Jesus need not even be present in order to heal the servant.

> **What Do You Think?**
> What steps can we take to increase our faith in
>   God before we see him act?
> *Digging Deeper*
> How do cautionary admonishments, such as
>   that of Luke 12:22-34, help you form your
>   answer?

❧ *MARVELOUS MODELS* ❧

My wife, Pat, suffered for decades from debilitating back pain. One day, she surprised me by showing me her "suicide diary." It was a series of notations in Joyce Landorf Heatherley's *Silent September*, which tells of the author's suicidal thoughts as she struggled with relentless pain. Pat was a model of Christian perseverance, dying of cancer a quarter-century after I became aware of her "diary."

A year after Pat's death, I preached at our church on suicide. Three years later, I was amazed once more at the influence of Pat's model of faith. A woman told me one Sunday, "I struggle with a painful chronic disease. I recently stood with opioids in my hand and thought, 'I don't have to live with this anymore.' Then I thought of your sermon, and I felt God reassuring me that he would help me."

Jesus was amazed by the centurion's faith. The centurion's example created a perfect opportunity for Jesus to work a miracle. Does your model of faith cause others to marvel?   —C. R. B.

B. Good Health (v. 10)

10. Then the men who had been sent returned to the house and found the servant well.

No mention is made in Luke's Gospel of Jesus' dismissing the group or of assuring them that their mission has been successful. In Matthew's account there is such a word: "Go! Let it be done just as you believed it would" (Matthew 8:13). Jesus accomplishes precisely what the centurion anticipates: he makes *the servant well*. Does Jesus even have to speak in order to heal the servant? The centurion would not be surprised to hear that Jesus never spoke a word after commending his faith.

Conclusion
A. Simply Marvelous

Faith can be found in surprising places. When my oldest son was critically injured in an automobile accident, he was flown by helicopter to a university hospital. I had taken classes at that university several years before and had my faith questioned. I chalked it up to the way things are in secular universities. With my son in the hospital associated with that university, I assumed his caregivers would be secular in their approach. But I marveled at the doctor when I overheard him say something to the effect of, "I simply could not do this job without faith."

As a leader of the occupational force in Judea, the centurion faced hatred and resentment from the Jewish people who didn't know him. The easy and typical response would be to return the sentiment. But this centurion loved the Jewish nation. He trusted Jesus before and better than many in Israel ever would. His life experiences made him humble in the face of the true authority he recognized in Jesus. For this reason, his faith was simply marvelous.

B. Prayer

O God, make us humble in our faith. Help us to expect you to work in our world even when we cannot see you. Give us confidence that you make all things whole. We pray in Jesus' name. Amen.

C. Thought to Remember

Humility sets the stage
for great faith.

INVOLVEMENT LEARNING

Enhance your lesson with NIV Bible Student *(from your curriculum supplier) and the reproducible activity page (at www.standardlesson.com or in the back of the* NIV Standard Lesson Commentary Deluxe Edition*).*

Into the Lesson

Before class begins, distribute the crossword puzzle "What's Faith Like?" on the activity page, which you can download, to each class member as a take-home activity.

Hand students two slips of paper. On the first they are to complete this sentence: "The best surprise I ever received was . . ." After no more than one minute, collect the slips. Then ask students to complete this sentence on the second slip: "The worst surprise I ever received was . . ." Collect these slips also after no more than one minute. Read several slips from each set to the class.

Lead into Bible study by telling students that real faith is often surprising to those who witness it, as will be seen in this week's account of a man with great faith and great humility.

Into the Word

Write the following list of sentences on the board, or distribute them on a handout (you prepare). Have students work in pairs or groups of three to compare and contrast the list with the account in Luke 7:1-10. They are to (1) identify any statements that are false, then (2) eliminate items that are not a part of the story, and finally (3) write a replacement sentence that is accurate.

1–The centurion sent Jewish elders to ask Jesus if he would come heal the centurion's servant.

2–The Jewish elders were afraid of the centurion because of his harsh actions.

3–Jesus went with them and approached the centurion's house.

4–The centurion sent friends to Jesus to say, "I'm not healthy enough to come to you."

5–The centurion understood authority, and he understood that Jesus had authority to heal.

6–Jesus was displeased by the centurion's attitude.

7–Jesus knew the Jewish leaders had greater faith than the centurion's.

The incorrect sentences are 2, 4, 6, and 7. Allow several minutes for students to identify and correct the wrong sentences. Then agree on the right version of the list during whole-class discussion.

Pose the following questions for whole-class discussion. Reveal only one question and let the discussion run its course before revealing the next question. Anticipated responses are given in italics.

1–What does the reaction of the Jewish leaders to the centurion tell us about the man? (*He acted honorably and generously toward the Jews.*)

2–What does the centurion's statement to Jesus tell us about the centurion? (*He understood that Jesus had authority and power to heal.*)

3–What is remarkable about the centurion's attitude? (*Despite his authority, he was humble. Despite his Roman background, he had faith in Jesus.*)

4–What does Jesus' assessment of the centurion tell us about the centurion? (*He had a remarkable level of faith in Jesus' power to heal.*)

Into the Life

Continue the discussion with these questions:

A–Why is humility such a vital precursor to or element in faith?

B–How common is humility among people you know or the voices you hear from media or in the entertainment or sports worlds?

C–How common is faith in these groups?

D–When we see humble faith in the lives of people around us, how do we react?

Remind students of the closing discussion in last week's lesson (in which they reflected on surprising answers to prayer and shared a longtime prayer request). Ask students if they have any answers to prayer to share. Has God surprised them this week?

Alternative. Distribute copies of the "My Faith Looks Up to Thee" exercise from the activity page (download) to be completed as indicated. Discuss as time permits.

GRATEFUL FAITH

DEVOTIONAL READING: John 13:3-11
BACKGROUND SCRIPTURE: Luke 7:36-50

LUKE 7:37-48

[37] A woman in that town who lived a sinful life learned that Jesus was eating at the Pharisee's house, so she came there with an alabaster jar of perfume. [38] As she stood behind him at his feet weeping, she began to wet his feet with her tears. Then she wiped them with her hair, kissed them and poured perfume on them.

[39] When the Pharisee who had invited him saw this, he said to himself, "If this man were a prophet, he would know who is touching him and what kind of woman she is—that she is a sinner."

[40] Jesus answered him, "Simon, I have something to tell you."

"Tell me, teacher," he said.

[41] "Two people owed money to a certain moneylender. One owed him five hundred denarii, and the other fifty. [42] Neither of them had the money to pay him back, so he forgave the debts of both. Now which of them will love him more?"

[43] Simon replied, "I suppose the one who had the bigger debt forgiven."

"You have judged correctly," Jesus said. [44] Then he turned toward the woman and said to Simon, "Do you see this woman? I came into your house. You did not give me any water for my feet, but she wet my feet with her tears and wiped them with her hair. [45] You did not give me a kiss, but this woman, from the time I entered, has not stopped kissing my feet. [46] You did not put oil on my head, but she has poured perfume on my feet. [47] Therefore, I tell you, her many sins have been forgiven—as her great love has shown. But whoever has been forgiven little loves little."

[48] Then Jesus said to her, "Your sins are forgiven."

KEY VERSE

As she stood behind him at his feet weeping, she began to wet his feet with her tears. Then she wiped them with her hair, kissed them and poured perfume on them. —**Luke 7:38**

• 73

RESPONDING TO GOD'S GRACE

Unit 2: Responses to God's Faithfulness

LESSONS 6–9

LESSON AIMS

1. Summarize the account of Jesus' anointing by the woman of Luke 7.

2. Contrast the grateful behavior of the admittedly sinful woman with the ingratitude of the self-righteous Pharisee.

3. Suggest a specific action he or she can take in the coming week to display gratitude for forgiveness.

LESSON OUTLINE

Introduction
    A. Saying "Thank You"
    B. Lesson Context
 I. The Sinful Woman (LUKE 7:37, 38)
    A. Arrival (v. 37)
    B. Breakdown (v. 38)
II. The Host and His Guest (LUKE 7:39-43)
    A. Pharisee's Thought (v. 39)
      An Unexpected Answer
    B. Jesus' Parable (vv. 40-42)
    C. Simon's Response (v. 43)
III. The Guest (LUKE 7:44-48)
    A. On Hospitality (vv. 44-46)
      Blindsided
    B. On Forgiveness (vv. 47, 48)
Conclusion
    A. Showing Gratitude
    B. Prayer
    C. Thought to Remember

Introduction

A. Saying "Thank You"

Why is it so hard to say "thank you"? If you think it is not, then you are not the parent of a high school graduate who has received gifts of congratulations. If you are such a parent, you probably recall begging, pleading, cajoling—perhaps even threatening—to get the appropriate thank-you notes written!

Some people see a distinction between nongratitude and ingratitude. Robert Emmons, for example, makes a distinction between two attitudes that do not say thank you. Nongratitude is mere forgetfulness, but ingratitude is actively negative and meant to punish another. Others like Gina Barreca, however, see no gray areas: a person who is thankful says so, and one who isn't, doesn't. She considers laziness in saying "thank you" a symptom not of forgetfulness but of a lack of thankfulness. This in turn reveals deeper character flaws.

This debate can go on, but there is no question that showing gratitude is a virtue that befits the disciple of Jesus. When Jesus healed 10 men with leprosy, he was disturbed that 9 of them never thanked him (Luke 17:11-19). Jesus' obvious implication was that all 10 should have given thanks. So who is more likely to thank Jesus for his work: a religious leader or a notorious sinner?

B. Lesson Context

Jesus was invited to dine in the home of a Pharisee (Luke 7:36). The Pharisee's motive for this invitation is not given immediately (see commentary on 7:40). He may have wanted a time of quiet conversation with Jesus (compare the Pharisee Nicodemus in John 3). More likely, the Pharisee had less than honorable intentions. By this time in Jesus' ministry, the Pharisees have already shown themselves to be hostile to Jesus' work. Luke 6:1-11 records two events in which they opposed Jesus. We might be surprised that Jesus accepted the invitation in the first place knowing the potential hostility of his host. If so, we'll be even more surprised to learn that he went on to accept at least one more such invitation (Luke 11:37).

The Pharisee's invitation in today's lesson does not mention any other guests, not even whether Jesus' disciples were invited. But apparently others were included in the invitation, perhaps additional Pharisees, since "the other guests" judged what they saw and heard while eating (Luke 7:49). Their presence as well as their attitude adds to our suspicion that Jesus was invited to this dinner as an occasion to mock or question him in some way (see on Luke 7:44b, below).

This dinner party occurred not long after the centurion's servant was healed (see lesson 8). The location is not stated; it could have been in Capernaum since that city was something of a headquarters for Jesus' ministry (Matthew 4:13; Mark 2:1). While the healing of the centurion's servant did occur in Capernaum (Luke 7:1-10), we know Jesus left there and was in Nain, where he raised a dead man to life (7:11-17). The dinner in the Pharisee's home happens sometime after those events (7:36). Following today's text, Jesus toured "from one town and village to another" in Galilee (8:1), so the anointing in the Pharisee's home could have been in nearly any of them.

Each of the Gospels reports on an anointing of Jesus by a woman while Jesus was attending a dinner. As a result, some believe each reports on the same event. While showing some similarities, the anointing recorded in the other Gospels (see Matthew 26:6-13; Mark 14:3-9; John 12:1-8) is almost certainly a separate, later event (see John 12:1). Each of the other accounts locates the event in Bethany in Judea (Matthew 26:6; Mark 14:3; John 12:1), while Luke's account belongs to the Galilean ministry (Luke 4:14–9:51). John specifically identifies the woman as Mary of Bethany, whose reputation is certainly not that of a notorious sinner (compare Luke 7:37 with John 11:1-5, 28-32).

HOW TO SAY IT

alabaster	*al*-uh-*bas*-ter.
Bethany	*Beth*-uh-nee.
Capernaum	Kuh-*per*-nay-um.
Judea	Joo-*dee*-uh.
Nain	*Nay*-in.
Pharisees	*Fair*-ih-seez.

I. The Sinful Woman
(LUKE 7:37, 38)
A. Arrival (v. 37)

37. A woman in that town who lived a sinful life learned that Jesus was eating at the Pharisee's house, so she came there with an alabaster jar of perfume.

Dinner parties, often hosted in a courtyard, frequently include people the host has specifically invited and others who come to listen to or see a guest of honor. Uninvited people are allowed to come and participate as spectators. This custom emboldens the *woman* to come to the dinner, even though she is known as leading *a sinful life*. This suggests that she is a prostitute or adulteress. Likely there are several uninvited guests, and she is able to slip in unnoticed. She does not come out of curiosity or boredom; she comes on a mission to see *Jesus*.

The woman who anointed Jesus in Bethany (see the Lesson Context) also had *an alabaster jar* (Matthew 26:7; Mark 14:3). This is one of the similarities that has led to the confusion of one event with the other. Such containers are appropriate containers for various oils, though other materials are also used.

Mark 14:3-5 establishes both the nature and value of the *perfume* in the other account. But no such specifics are noted in the scene before us. Even so, this may be a great sacrifice on her part.

Host and guests adopt a posture of reclining while sharing a meal, the custom of the day. Low tables require that guests lie on their sides, leaning on their elbows and eating with their right hands. The significance of these facts is seen in the next verse.

B. Breakdown (v. 38)

38a. As she stood behind him at his feet weeping,

Because the guests are reclining around the table, the woman has an opportunity to stand *behind* Jesus *at his feet*. The reason for her emotion is not readily known (see commentary on Luke 7:47, below). But her reaction to Jesus' presence is obvious to everyone in attendance as she stands *weeping*.

38b. she began to wet his feet with her tears.

After an unspecified length of time, the unnamed woman changes posture from standing to kneeling near Jesus. That's the only way for her to be able to be in a position to *wet his feet with her tears.*

38c. Then she wiped them with her hair,

There's more than meets the eye here as the woman uses *her hair* as a washcloth. Women's hair of this era is meant to be bound up. Therefore this woman's letting her hair down is quite a departure from propriety. This act further suggests that she is lost in the moment with Jesus. She does not consider what anyone else might see or think.

38d. kissed them and poured perfume on them.

Perhaps the woman has come intending to anoint Jesus' head (compare Matthew 26:7; Mark 14:3). But for reasons unknown she does not do so. Instead, she anoints his feet, as Mary also will do (John 12:3; see Lesson Context).

This act of anointing Jesus recalls the definition of *Messiah*—"anointed one." Priests, prophets, and kings experienced anointing in Israel. Jesus fulfills all these roles (Matthew 21:11; 27:11, 37; John 4:44; 18:37; Hebrews 7:23-28). Thus this anointing is more appropriate than anyone in the room (other than Jesus) realizes!

> **What Do You Think?**
> What are some tangible, visible ways we can express gratitude to God?
> **Digging Deeper**
> What expressions of such gratitude are best kept private, if any? Why?

II. The Host and His Guest
(LUKE 7:39-43)
A. Pharisee's Thought (v. 39)

39. When the Pharisee who had invited him saw this, he said to himself, "If this man were a prophet, he would know who is touching him and what kind of woman she is—that she is a sinner."

The Pharisees frown on associations between "good" and "bad" people. A frequent complaint of theirs about Jesus is that he spends time with sinners. That was the issue after the calling of Matthew/Levi earlier (Luke 5:29, 30; compare 15:1, 2; 19:1-7). Shortly before this event in the Pharisee's home, Jesus himself confirmed that he has a reputation as "a friend of tax collectors and sinners" (7:34).

The host (whose name is Simon, per the next verse below) makes a mental note of Jesus' "failure." Likely Simon wants to discuss it with his Pharisee friends later, though all other Pharisees in attendance no doubt have noticed as well.

This criticizing thought betrays the Pharisee's ulterior motive for inviting Jesus: Simon doesn't want to learn; he wants to find fault. Perhaps Jesus' *Pharisee* host was not present at the time when Jesus acknowledged being friends with sinners. Otherwise, Simon would know that Jesus does indeed spend time with sinners, even eating with them.

Because Jesus allows this woman to touch his feet and anoint him, the Pharisee thinks that Jesus must not realize that this woman *is a sinner.* Since Jesus does not know her character, so Simon's thinking goes, then he cannot be *a prophet.* A prophet would know such things! But Simon the Pharisee operates from a false premise: he cannot establish what Jesus knows or does not know about the woman because Jesus has already demonstrated a willingness to associate with sinners (see on Luke 7:47, below).

> **What Do You Think?**
> How should we respond, if at all, when others question our associating with certain people?
> **Digging Deeper**
> In what circumstances should we heed the challenge of other believers about such associations?

❧ AN UNEXPECTED ANSWER ❧

I began my Christian college teaching career at a small college in the Midwest. In those days, Christians tended to see moral issues in more black-and-white terms than today. For example, in regard to alcohol, the consensus among most Christians was that it absolutely should be avoided.

In this cultural setting, someone hypothetically asked the president of the college, "Would the school accept a million-dollar gift from the brewery down the road?" The president answered, "If the brewery wanted to give the school a million dollars, we'd baptize it and use it for God's glory!" His answer was tongue-in-cheek, but it didn't sit well with the questioner.

The Pharisee expected Jesus to confirm his prejudice against others and affirm his black-and-white view of the world. The Lord looks a bit deeper into human hearts than we can! What assumptions do you hold that Jesus might call into question?
—C. R. B.

B. Jesus' Parable (vv. 40-42)

40. Jesus answered him, "Simon, I have something to tell you."

"Tell me, teacher," he said.

The name of the Pharisee is delayed until this point. In other Gospel accounts of an anointing, the host is also named Simon (Matthew 26:6; Mark 14:3; contrast John 12:1, 2). Though this could lead to the conclusion that these are the same events, one very significant detail sets Luke's account apart from those of Matthew and Mark. In the latter two accounts, Simon is referred to as a "leper," not a Pharisee. The fact that he is called a leper and yet is able to host a social occasion suggests he has been healed by Jesus. Such a person would be unlikely to treat Jesus as will the host of this dinner (see on Luke 7:44-46, below).

Jesus' attention-getting *Simon, I have something to tell you* serves to rouse the man from his faulty chain of thinking. Jesus wants the man's full attention, and he gets it.

41. "Two people owed money to a certain moneylender. One owed him five hundred denarii, and the other fifty.

One denarius represents a day's pay for a common laborer (see Matthew 20:2). *Five hundred denarii*, then, represents about a year and a half's wages. Even so, the lesser debt is still significant.

To repay the debt, either borrower would have to make substantial sacrifices. The one owing *fifty*

denarii could perhaps make enough such sacrifices to repay the debt. The other borrower, however, is certainly beyond his ability to repay; he will never scrimp and save enough.

42a. "Neither of them had the money to pay him back, so he forgave the debts of both.

The parable ends with a dramatic surprise. For one borrower, this goodwill produces a convenience: he no longer has to worry about being extra frugal for a few months to save up the 50 denarii he owes. For the other, it is lifesaving. Hopelessly in debt, he and his family faced the specter of being sold into forced servitude to repay the debt (see Matthew 18:25).

> *What Do You Think?*
> What modern metaphors or analogies might we use to help someone understand the depth of God's grace and forgiveness?
> *Digging Deeper*
> What are some dangers in using such a technique?

42b. "Now which of them will love him more?"

The lender shows love to both borrowers by forgiving the debt. Such generosity expects a response of *love* in return. The question assumes that one or the other will feel greater love.

C. Simon's Response (v. 43)

43. Simon replied, "I suppose the one who had the bigger debt forgiven."

"You have judged correctly," Jesus said.

Simon recognizes that greater forgiveness inspires greater love. He may not yet see that he is about to be rebuked for his own evil thinking in regard to *Jesus* (see commentary on Luke 7:39, 47).

III. The Guest
(LUKE 7:44-48)
A. On Hospitality (vv. 44-46)

44a. Then he turned toward the woman and said to Simon, "Do you see this woman?

Of course *Simon* sees the *woman*! He has just been regarding her with contempt (see Luke 7:39).

Simon might realize now that Jesus is about to turn the tables.

44b. "I came into your house. You did not give me any water for my feet, but she wet my feet with her tears and wiped them with her hair.

Jesus calls attention to Simon's own failures as a host. He has not accorded his guest the usual comforts demanded by cultural mores of hospitality. The host must provide *water* and a servant to wash his guests' *feet*. Simon has not done that, at least not for Jesus. (One wonders whether the others at the table have received this kindness.) Jesus' feet would have remained dirty and dusty were it not for the actions of the woman.

The Pharisee's failure to extend the usual courtesies of a host to a guest gives credence to the idea that the host has no intention of honoring Jesus. In contrast, the sinful woman has corrected Simon's inhospitable reception by honoring Jesus in a most humbling way.

45. "You did not give me a kiss, but this woman, from the time I entered, has not stopped kissing my feet.

Customary hospitality includes a greeting with *a kiss*. It shows a measure of affection, as one would expect from a well-intentioned host to his guests.

Once again, the *woman* has supplied what was lacking on Simon's part. *Kissing* Jesus' *feet* and not his cheek demonstrates her humility and devotion.

> *What Do You Think?*
> What additional hospitality can our church provide to ensure that all visitors feel welcome?
> *Digging Deeper*
> To what extent, if at all, should worship services be planned to benefit unbelievers? Why?

---

46. "You did not put oil on my head, but she has poured perfume on my feet.

To *put oil* on another's *head* goes beyond the normal treatment of a guest. It is reserved for very close friends or someone whom a host especially wants to honor (compare Psalm 23:5.) This contrast demonstrates the point of the parable. The woman has supplied not just what is lacking in the

treatment of Simon's guest. She has added a special blessing that shows great love. She is not able to anoint Jesus' head, but she has done what she could with the resources she has.

❧ *BLINDSIDED* ❧

"I sure didn't see that coming!"

According to those who keep track of the changes in the English language, the term blindside was first employed as a verb as early as 1960. It was used to describe a situation in a football game when, for example, a member of the defense came up from behind the quarterback or a receiver and tackled him before the target was aware of the tackler's presence.

The term has come to have many uses since its sports-related beginning. We've all been in situations where news blindsided us. It could have been news of a loved one's death, or it might be the sudden, unexplained breakdown of our heretofore perfectly running automobile.

We could say that Jesus sometimes used his parables to blindside his listener. He told Simon a story that seemed to come out of thin air. By the time Jesus finished, however, there was no way Simon could escape the conviction of Jesus' words.

Do you need to be blindsided by Jesus for him to get your attention?   —C. R. B.

B. On Forgiveness (vv. 47, 48)

47. "Therefore, I tell you, her many sins have been forgiven—as her great love has shown. But whoever has been forgiven little loves little."

Jesus here proves that he knows exactly what kind of woman has been attending him. She has *many sins*, to be sure. But she shows a great measure of love that suggests she knows she has been *forgiven*.

Jesus' declaration refutes Simon's unspoken thought that Jesus does not possess the divinely given awareness of a prophet (see commentary on Luke 7:39, above). Jesus' parable serves as a rebuke to Simon's objection that Jesus should not allow a "sinner" to touch him. Simon never voices that contention aloud, so how does Jesus know that Simon objects to Jesus' allowing a "sinner" to touch him? Jesus shows he not only knows who the woman is; he knows what Simon is thinking!

Just as likely is that the woman has come in faith. Her gracious acts of anointing and kissing Jesus' feet are done with some manner of expectation on her part. Simon, on the other hand, feels no need for anything from Jesus, least of all forgiveness. Simon believes himself to be righteous—more righteous than most people. Thus he *loves little*.

48. Then Jesus said to her, "Your sins are forgiven."

Jesus not only accepts her gift; he stands up for her. He exonerates her before the scorning crowd. He sends her home with a blessing!

What Do You Think?
What can we do to help fellow believers who have difficulty accepting the fact that God has forgiven them?
Digging Deeper
How will we know when sharing Scripture passages is not working and we need to supplement with a different witness?

One wonders whether Jesus says this as much for the benefit of the others at the table as for the woman. We can only guess what the woman feels as she leaves Simon's house. She must have come with considerable fear and trepidation. But her awareness of her need had driven her to seek out Jesus personally (compare Matthew 9:20). She must have known that she would be scorned by the Pharisee and many, if not all, of his other guests. To be able to honor Jesus is enough for her to face them all.

Luke 7:49 (not in our lesson text) records the reaction of those guests. It's along the lines of, "Who does this Jesus think he is?" This is the second time Jesus has declared forgiveness of sins for someone (see Luke 5:20). The witnesses' response is the same both times (5:21).

On the earlier occasion, Jesus defended his authority to forgive sins (Luke 5:22-26). Here he seems to ignore the critics. It's the woman

who is important. He turns back to the woman and says, "Your faith has saved you; go in peace" (Luke 7:50).

Conclusion

A. Showing Gratitude

How do we say "thank you" to Jesus? Today's text suggests we do so by acts of kindness. Of course, we cannot minister directly to Jesus, as the grateful woman did at Simon's house. But we can minister to our peers. We express our gratitude to God by kind acts to others (Luke 10:25-37; James 1:27; 1 John 4:20, 21). At least, we do if we are truly grateful! If God's grace and forgiveness toward us have produced in us the kind of love they produced in this woman, then that love will show in our treatment of other people. We will show our gratitude by being gracious.

B. Prayer

O God, thank you for forgiving our many sins. May we show our love and gratitude by our loving treatment of one another. We pray in Jesus' name. Amen.

C. Thought to Remember

Thankfulness may consist merely of words.
Gratitude is shown in acts.
—Henri-Frédéric Amiel (1821–1881)

Faithful people are
HUMBLE & GRATEFUL

Visual for Lessons 8 & 9. *Use this visual to introduce the Into Life section (next page) and/or as a backdrop to the closing prayer.*

INVOLVEMENT LEARNING

Enhance your lesson with NIV Bible Student (from your curriculum supplier) and the reproducible activity page (at www.standardlesson.com or in the back of the NIV Standard Lesson Commentary Deluxe Edition).

Into the Lesson

Write the following sentence on the board:

The greater the gift, the greater the gratitude.

Ask volunteers to tell stories from their past that illustrate how this sentence was true for them. Tell students that today's Bible story shows the gratitude of a woman who had been forgiven much by Jesus.

Into the Word

Read, or ask a volunteer to read, today's Bible story aloud. Ensure that the reader stops at verse 48 in order not to introduce other elements—as important as they are—that might overshadow the point of today's lesson.

Distribute handouts (you prepare) with the following multiple-choice sentences. Ask students to work in pairs or groups to agree on answers. Then read the sentences aloud to the class, asking for responses and discussing why students chose differently. (For many of these, there is not one correct answer. The lesson commentary provides information and background to help you respond to class members' choices.)

1–The Pharisee invited Jesus to his home because he wanted to (a) honor Jesus (b) trick Jesus (c) know more about Jesus.
2–The woman came to see Jesus because she (a) was a curious member of the crowd (b) was grateful that Jesus had forgiven her for her sins (c) wanted to do something good for a holy man.
3–The woman washed Jesus' feet because (a) his feet were dirty since the host had not provided a servant to wash his feet (b) her tears wet his feet, so she decided to finish the job with the ointment she had brought (c) she wanted to make a sacrificial gift of gratitude or worship.
4–The host was unhappy because (a) the woman was a person of ill repute (b) he assumed Jesus wasn't the prophet he claimed to be (c) the woman's outburst interrupted the meal.

5–Jesus told the parable of the two debts because he wanted (a) the Pharisee to learn about forgiveness (b) the woman to learn about forgiveness (c) the crowd to learn about gratitude.
6–Jesus rebuked the Pharisee because the man (a) had a wrong attitude (b) needed to discover that Jesus had read his mind (c) needed forgiveness as much as the sinful woman.
7–Jesus contrasted the woman with the Pharisee because he wanted to (a) shame the Pharisee (b) praise the woman (c) make a point about the connection between gratitude and forgiveness.
8–Jesus told the woman her sins were forgiven because he wanted (a) her to know that (b) the Pharisee to grapple with this claim to be deity (c) those in the crowd to think about their own need for forgiveness.

Alternative. Distribute copies of the "Reflecting on God's Forgiveness" activity on the activity page, which you can download, to be completed in pairs or groups. After several minutes, discuss with the whole class.

Into Life

Brainstorm with the class, asking them to answer this question: How can we feel and demonstrate more gratitude to God for his forgiveness? Ask class members to shout out as many answers as you can write on the board in 90 seconds. Then go back and circle the answers the class believes are most significant. Close with a prayer for class members to act on the ideas they have listed.

Alternative. Distribute copies of the "A Graph of My Gratitude" exercise from the activity page. Ask students to complete it in one minute. If learners cannot pinpoint a gratitude level for each line on the graph, ask them to mark the time in their lives when they were most grateful to God. Then discuss with them the questions on the activity as indicated.

FAITH THAT IS TESTED

DEVOTIONAL READING: James 1:12-18
BACKGROUND SCRIPTURE: 2 Corinthians 13:1-11

2 CORINTHIANS 13:1-11

1 This will be my third visit to you. "Every matter must be established by the testimony of two or three witnesses." 2 I already gave you a warning when I was with you the second time. I now repeat it while absent: On my return I will not spare those who sinned earlier or any of the others, 3 since you are demanding proof that Christ is speaking through me. He is not weak in dealing with you, but is powerful among you. 4 For to be sure, he was crucified in weakness, yet he lives by God's power. Likewise, we are weak in him, yet by God's power we will live with him in our dealing with you.

5 Examine yourselves to see whether you are in the faith; test yourselves. Do you not realize that Christ Jesus is in you—unless, of course, you fail the test? 6 And I trust that you will discover that we have not failed the test. 7 Now we pray to God that you will not do anything wrong—not so that people will see that we have stood the test but so that you will do what is right even though we may seem to have failed. 8 For we cannot do anything against the truth, but only for the truth. 9 We are glad whenever we are weak but you are strong; and our prayer is that you may be fully restored. 10 This is why I write these things when I am absent, that when I come I may not have to be harsh in my use of authority—the authority the Lord gave me for building you up, not for tearing you down.

11 Finally, brothers and sisters, rejoice! Strive for full restoration, encourage one another, be of one mind, live in peace. And the God of love and peace will be with you.

KEY VERSE

Examine yourselves to see whether you are in the faith; test yourselves. Do you not realize that Christ Jesus is in you—unless, of course, you fail the test? —**2 Corinthians 13:5**

RESPONDING TO
GOD'S GRACE

Unit 3: Faith Leads to Holy Living
LESSONS 10–13

LESSON AIMS

After participating in this lesson, each learner will be able to:

1. Summarize the history between Paul and the Corinthian church.

2. Explain the seeming paradox of "strength in weakness."

3. Ask self-examining questions to gauge his or her level of being "in the faith."

LESSON OUTLINE

Introduction

A. Restoration Risks

Close personal relationships bring us great joy, but they bring pain also. The stronger the emotional connection, the more we care. The closer and more longstanding the relationship, the greater its capacity for causing sorrow or creating happiness.

Because of the high stakes, it takes great courage to confront a close friend who is causing pain. We want to think that time will erase any relationship rift, but this is often not the case. As with an infection, sometimes the wound must be reopened before it will heal. When restoration is achieved, the relationship may emerge even stronger than before, but we know this does not always happen. When we find ourselves at odds with a friend, confrontation presents a risk because it could end the relationship altogether.

B. Lesson Context

Paul's first visit to Corinth occurred on his second missionary journey (Acts 18). He arrived between AD 52 and 54 after visiting Philippi (16:11-40), Thessalonica (17:1), and Berea (17:10), as well as Athens (17:16-34).

Corinth was the second-largest city in Greece, about 50 miles west of Athens, but the two cities were very different. Athens represented learning, culture, and the grand traditions of the Greeks. Corinth, on the other hand, thrived as a Roman commercial and transportation hub. Scholars were made in Athens; fortunes were made in Corinth.

Paul spent about 18 months ministering in the city of Corinth (Acts 18:11). His initial stay resulted in a church that included Jewish and Gentile believers (18:1-8). Mixing those two groups was not easy, for each had a sense of cultural superiority over the other (compare 1 Corinthians 1:20-22). The Greeks remembered the glory of their philosophers and the military exploits of Alexander the Great and his successors, dating back to 334 BC. It was they who brought Greek culture (Hellenism) to much of the Mediterranean world.

The Jews, for their part, identified themselves as God's chosen people, with an ancient law given to them by God himself (compare Romans 2:17-29). Yet Paul argued persuasively that they had a new, common identity as the body of Christ (1 Corinthians 12:12, 13, 27), united under a common Lord and Savior (1:2).

After Paul's departure in AD 54, outsiders arrived whom Paul sarcastically calls "super-apostles" for their claim of authority greater than his own or that of any other apostle (2 Corinthians 11:5; 12:11). These "apostles" tried to discredit Paul (11:5-15; 12:11, 12). Paul was deeply hurt by the Corinthians' acceptance of false teaching, which signaled to be a betrayal of friendship. Before writing 2 Corinthians, he traveled to Corinth to correct this false teaching, to clear his name, and to restore his relationships. The book of Acts does not tell us of this visit, but Paul refers to it as a "painful visit" (2 Corinthians 2:1).

The setting for the writing of 2 Corinthians is quite different from the setting for his writing of 1 Corinthians. In the first letter, likely written about AD 56, Paul draws on his relationship with the Corinthians to give authoritative directions concerning many problematic issues in the congregation (see 1 Corinthians 1:10-17; 5:1–6:20; 7:1–14:40). He does this with confidence, believing their love and respect for him will allow his voice to be heard even when he is not there (see 5:3-5).

By the time Paul wrote 2 Corinthians in AD 57, the impact of the false apostles had poisoned Paul's relationship with his friends. Because of this, Paul had some bold, harsh words for the Corinthians, words designed to put their relationship to rights. His response came in the form of a harsh, sorrowful letter (2 Corinthians 2:4). Paul saw more than a friendship at risk. He feared that a church he loved would turn to false teaching in ways that endangered their faith (11:1-15).

> *What Do You Think?*
> What steps can we take to ensure that a painful confrontation with friends or relatives is productive rather than destructive?
> *Digging Deeper*
> What biblical texts offer wisdom or cautionary tales for handling confrontation?

I. Examination
(2 CORINTHIANS 13:1-6)
A. Paul's Warning (vv. 1, 2)

1. This will be my third visit to you. "Every matter must be established by the testimony of two or three witnesses."

Paul uses this letter to prepare the way for his *third visit* (see 2 Corinthians 12:14). He emphasizes the decisive nature of this visit by citing an ancient Jewish tradition: *two or three witnesses* are required to uphold an accusation of wrongdoing (Deuteronomy 19:15). One theory is that Paul includes this quotation because he expects to be vindicated during this visit. He believes that not even two or three people will be willing to testify against him. The Corinthians know him and respect him too much to give false witness about his ministry.

Another theory is that the witnesses do not refer to people at all. For Paul, it is a matter of his refuting three times the accusations against him. These witnesses can be taken as his three visits during which the Corinthians have seen what they need to know in order to establish Paul's integrity in his ministry. This underlines the seriousness of this situation for Paul. He is devoting much time and effort to come to a good resolution of the frayed situation.

> *What Do You Think?*
> What forms might the principle of "multiple witnesses" take when someone must be confronted?
> *Digging Deeper*
> Considering Matthew 18:15, 16, in what kinds of circumstances might it be best not to bring others into a disagreement?

❧ *NO POTEMKIN CHURCH* ❧

As the story goes, Grigory Potemkin was just a Russian nobleman trying to win the favor of Catherine the Great. In 1783, Potemkin wanted to impress Catherine with the quality of her new Crimean possessions. Before her tour of the region, he ordered pleasant village façades to be built to impress her during her tour of the area. Peasants were dressed to look much wealthier than they were to give a false impression of prosperity. Today the phrase "Potemkin village" refers to a façade that is intended to deceive.

Paul warned the Corinthians that he was planning a visit. Previous visits had not solved the problem of the false teachers' influence. It would not suffice for the Corinthians to "make things pretty" for this visit. They had to face the underlying issues that were threatening the church's well-being. On a personal level, what do you need to do to be prepared for the Lord's next visit?   —C. R. B.

2. I already gave you a warning when I was with you the second time. I now repeat it while absent: On my return I will not spare those who sinned earlier or any of the others,

Paul plans to put an end to the influence of the "super-apostles" and their followers once and for all and *will not spare* them (2 Corinthians 11:5; 12:11). Sufficient warnings have been issued; if Paul sees that the Corinthians need discipline on his next visit, he will not hesitate to use the authority he has to administer it.

His warning specifically targets *those who sinned earlier.* He is already worried that he will find this group involved in unholy activities (2 Corinthians 12:20, 21). This may suggest that the false teachers have either turned a blind eye to these outrageous behaviors or even encouraged them, perhaps through their own participation.

> **What Do You Think?**
> How can we determine whether a confrontation calls for the approach in Matthew 10:34-36 or for the one in Romans 12:18 and 14:19?
>
> **Digging Deeper**
> How do passages such as Psalm 120:7; Ecclesiastes 3:8; and/or Micah 3:5 help frame your answer, if at all?

B. God's Power (vv. 3, 4)

3. since you are demanding proof that Christ is speaking through me. He is not weak in dealing with you, but is powerful among you.

This verse seems to challenge the false apostles directly. Their presentation and demeanor are brash and confident. This contrasts starkly with Paul's usual gentleness and patience (see 2 Corinthians 10:1). The opponents apparently claim that they speak with the very voice and authority of Christ. In so doing, they dismiss Paul's claim to speak for the Lord because he is unassuming in his presentation. The strategy of the other "apostles" is not so much to justify their own teachings through logical presentation as it is to undermine Paul's authority and thereby discredit him altogether.

Paul uses irony to make his counterpoint, seemingly agreeing that Christ speaks through him in a lesser way in comparison to how Christ speaks through the opponents. The real irony is that while they think highly of the power and authority of the false apostles, those fall short of Paul's power and authority. This points to his paradoxical argument that what appears to be weakness is sometimes a display of great strength (see 2 Corinthians 4:7-12; 13:4). Thus Paul is able to insist that his message to the Corinthians *is not weak.*

4a. For to be sure, he was crucified in weakness, yet he lives by God's power.

Paul's immediate example of strength despite seeming *weakness* is Christ himself. Jesus' crucifixion showed him *in weakness,* not resisting his accusers or executors. Although he could have called angels to deliver him (Psalm 91:11, 12; Matthew 26:53), Jesus submitted to an unjust death sentence. This self-imposed weakness (Philippians 2:6-8) was shown to be temporary and even illusory by his resurrection, a display of God's power unlike anything ever witnessed (2:9-11). The shame of the cross was replaced by Jesus' triumph over death to life *by God's power.*

4b. Likewise, we are weak in him, yet by God's power we will live with him in our dealing with you.

Paul's litany of the physical trials and perils he has suffered in his missionary endeavors demonstrates his own experience (see 2 Corinthians 11:23-28). His many troubles help him identify with Christ's own weakness in the cross. Rather than identifying with Christ's glorification, Paul points to persecutions as the mark of a true apostle.

Paul is confident, though, that his personal weaknesses will not determine the outcome of his dealings with his opponents. Instead, just as Christ lives by the resurrection power of God, so Paul *will live* in fellowship with Christ and in Jesus' power in confronting the issues at Corinth.

C. Know Yourself (v. 5)

5a. Examine yourselves to see whether you are in the faith; test yourselves.

Paul now shifts the focus from himself and the false accusations that have been made against him. He exhorts the Corinthians to *examine* and *test* themselves, to look at their own lives.

5b. Do you not realize that Christ Jesus is in you—unless, of course, you fail the test?

The Corinthian believers have questioned the Spirit-inspired nature of Paul's authority (2 Corinthians 13:3); now he questions them. Do they actually *realize that Christ Jesus* lives in them? If not, Paul contends, they *fail the test* of spiritual self-examination, thus disqualifying themselves from judging true spirituality and relationship to Christ.

Though the question is framed as being primarily about the spiritual condition of the Corinthians, it also serves as a test of Paul's apostleship. If they find that they are truly in the faith, then must not Paul also be in the faith? After all, Paul "planted the seed, Apollos watered it, but God has been making it grow" (1 Corinthians 3:6).

HOW TO SAY IT

Athens	*Ath*-unz.
Berea	Buh-*ree*-uh.
Corinth	*Kor*-inth.
Corinthians	Ko-*rin*-thee-unz (*th* as in *thin*).
Ecclesiastes	Ik-*leez*-ee-*as*-teez.
Ephesus	*Ef*-uh-sus.
Hellenism	*Heh*-leh-nih-zim.
Mediterranean	*Med*-uh-tuh-*ray*-nee-un.
Philippi	Fih-*lip*-pie or *Fil*-ih-pie.
Thessalonica	*Thess*-uh-lo-*nye*-kuh (*th* as in *thin*).

Contrary to his detractors' accusations, Paul indicates that the root cause of their problematic relationship is not the apostle sitting in Ephesus writing the letter. Instead he suggests that the false apostles rampaging in Corinth are the problems as they besmirch his reputation and gain a following. It is not so much that Paul is saying the Corinthians must be on his side, but that they should be sure they are on the Lord's side.

D. Know Us (v. 6)

6. And I trust that you will discover that we have not failed the test.

Paul's underlying confidence in his Corinthian brothers and sisters shines through here. Paul knows that he and his associates *have not failed the test*. He is also confident that, upon reflection, the Corinthians will agree.

II. Exhortations
(2 Corinthians 13:7-11)

A. Be True (vv. 7-9)

7. Now we pray to God that you will not do anything wrong—not so that people will see that we have stood the test but so that you will do what is right even though we may seem to have failed.

This is the focal point of the great decision the Corinthians must make. They must *not do anything wrong* but make the *right* choice by rejecting the false claims of Paul's critics who have painted him and his associates as lacking true spiritual qualifications. Given Paul's assertion that Christ does truly live in them, this momentous decision in Paul's favor should be obvious.

Furthermore, the Corinthians should do what is right even if it seems that Paul and his companions are in the wrong. He wants them to choose correctly not for his sake but because it is right. The fact that what is right will vindicate Paul is a side benefit to the apostle.

8. For we cannot do anything against the truth, but only for the truth.

Paul now expands his *we* to include the Corinthians. *Truth* must be the guide. The Corinthians must not be driven by self-interest or the charisma of a false teacher, but by a higher standard: truth detached from personal considerations. Rejecting truth will be met with the consequences of God's wrath (Romans 2:8). Paul would rather be shown false than to impede the journey of the gospel.

9. We are glad whenever we are weak but you are strong; and our prayer is that you may be fully restored.

Despite the frustrations he has expressed, Paul's great love for the Corinthians comes out at the end of this section. Paul is *weak* in many ways, not the least of which is his position of weakness due to his absence from Corinth. In this verse, he refers to his humble and unassuming demeanor he exhibits when he's with the Corinthians.

Paul's admission of weakness is not his primary interest. He wants the Corinthians to be *strong*. If they are strong in the faith in the ways they believe they are, then Paul has no reason to be strong in his own authority to reprimand them. He can be "weak" as he desires. Paul wishes for them to *be fully restored*, a goal that cannot be achieved following Paul. They must be guided and controlled by Christ, the Savior whom Paul has preached to them faithfully (1 Corinthians 15:1-8).

❧ *Where Is Our Strength?* ❧

Kraft durch Freude (KdF) was a movement in Nazi Germany in the 1930s. Translated into English, it means "strength through joy." KdF's stated intent was to provide leisure activities to the German working class in the belief that happy people create a strong nation.

However, the real purpose of KdF was to control every moment of the German worker's time and thus prevent anti-government sentiments and movements from developing. Nazi spies took part in KdF-sponsored cruises, day trips, athletic competitions, library visits, and theater events to make sure no dissent from Nazi ideology was expressed by participants.

Paul wanted the Corinthians' spiritual strength to be based on their bond with Christ, nothing else. Strength through Christ is available to everyone, regardless of status in this world. How does Jesus' strength shine through your weakness?

—C. R. B.

B. Be Perfectly Restored (v. 10)

10. This is why I write these things when I am absent, that when I come I may not have to be harsh in my use of authority—the authority the Lord gave me for building you up, not for tearing you down.

The picture we have of the apostle Paul from the New Testament is of a man who cherishes his relationships. Because of this, Paul recognizes the personal advantages of not being in Corinth at this time. His frustration and desire for corrective action could result in being *harsh*—the unpleasant exercise of the valid *authority the Lord* has given to him.

Paul does not take his God-given authority lightly. He wants to use it *for building [them] up, not for tearing [them] down* (see 2 Corinthians 13:9). His great hope is that this letter will prepare the way for his next visit. He wants to engage in church building, not church discipline. He does not want to take them back to the most basic elements of following Christ. Instead, Paul wants the Corinthians to ready their hearts to move forward in their quest for spiritual maturity (compare 1 Corinthians 3:2).

C. Be with God (v. 11)

11a. Finally, brothers and sisters, rejoice! Strive for full restoration, encourage one another, be of one mind, live in peace.

Paul ends the letter with five commands that summarize his desired outcomes for this corrective letter. First, is *rejoice*. Despite strained relationship, the Corinthians have much in common about which to be joyful (compare 2 Corinthians 1:24).

Second, the Corinthians should *strive for full restoration*. They should be guided by truth, living and making choices that reflect this "guide star." In this way they can attain "the whole measure of the fullness of Christ" (Ephesians 4:13).

Third, they should *encourage one another*. Paul is confident that this current rough spot in their relationship is nearing its conclusion and that good days are ahead.

Fourth, the Corinthians should be unified. This is very important for a congregation with a history of factionalism (see 1 Corinthians 1:12). Paul's goal in writing this letter will not have been accomplished if some people side with the false apostles and some side with him.

Finally, they should *live in peace*. never letting disagreements fester to the point of divisiveness and church-splitting passions. This is not a matter of sacrificing the truth (see 2 Corinthians 13:8 above). Rather, it is about laying down bombastic and disrespectful treatment of those with whom one disagrees. Paul will not be satisfied with winning back the confidence and affections of a majority of the Corinthians. He wants them all to respect him and each other.

11b. And the God of love and peace will be with you.

Two understandings of this phrase are possible. One possibility is that the presence of *God* with his *love and peace* is how the Corinthians will accomplish the tasks commanded above. The other is that God's love and peace will be a felt result of obedience in those tasks. It's not clear which Paul means. The ambiguity may suggest that Paul wants the Corinthians to assume both: God will help them in their quest for maturity, and they will experience his presence all the more as they strive toward that goal.

Visual for Lesson 10. *Ask the class what kinds of tests they can put to their faith to evaluate their strength in Christ.*

Conclusion

A. Strength in Weakness

The Old Testament offers many accounts in which followers of God found victory despite being in positions of weakness (see Exodus 14:26-28; Judges 7; 1 Samuel 17; 2 Chronicles 32:9, 16-21; Isaiah 37:36, 37). All have one thing in common: the God who wins the victory. Even in weakness, God's people are strong because of him.

We have this dynamic working for us too. We often think that success in the Christian life is a matter of trying harder. Our efforts are important, but we will never be fully mature in our Christian walk through our own efforts. In fact, self-focused striving may block the work of the Holy Spirit in our lives.

Think of your own life. Are you satisfied with your progress as a Christian believer? Are you weak like Christ or strong in your own wisdom? Maybe it is time to "let go and let God," giving him the glory along with your obedience.

B. Prayer

Father, we are weak in many ways and need your power in our lives. Strengthen us in obedience and love for you and for our brothers and sisters in Christ. We pray in Jesus' name. Amen.

C. Thought to Remember

We gain strength by trusting in God.

INVOLVEMENT LEARNING

Enhance your lesson with NIV Bible Student *(from your curriculum supplier) and the reproducible activity page (at www.standardlesson.com or in the back of the* NIV Standard Lesson Commentary Deluxe Edition*).*

Into the Lesson

Ask class members with smartphones to look up "false religions" on the internet. Other possibilities: "false prophets," "counterfeit Christianity," "false teachers," or "false churches." Allow several to share findings. Ask, "How big is the problem of truth in religion today?"

Alternative. Ask class members to share examples of contemporary false teachers from their experience and memory.

Tell class members that the ancient Corinthian church was plagued with false teachers, a problem the apostle Paul was forced to address. Tell them that today's Scripture text was written in the midst of that problem.

Into the Word

During the week before class, arrange for one or two participants each to deliver a two- or three-minute mini-lecture explaining the background and context for the lesson. As they do so, have them write the following headings on the board. (*Option.* You can put these on handouts.)

• Paul's visits with the Corinthians
• Paul's challenges to the Corinthians
• Paul's relationship with the Corinthians
• Paul's letters to the Corinthians

After the reading of the text, divide the class in groups to read the text again in their groups to discover *the why* and *the how* that each column heading suggests. Students should come to the board and record under the heading their discoveries as they occur. (If you use handouts, learners can record their discoveries there instead of coming to the board.

After an appropriate amount to time, fill in gaps during the ensuing whole-class discussion.

As time permits, use this discussion to offer information or insights from the lesson commentary to complete learners' understanding or correct misunderstanding.

Alternative. Distribute copies of the exercise "A Difficult Letter" on the activity page, which you can download. Divide the class into at least four groups, one to consider each of the headings listed. After several minutes of group work, have groups share their decisions during whole-class discussion.

Into Life

Ask class members to brainstorm answers to this question: "How do I know a person is 'in the faith'?" After 60 seconds in which they call out answers you write on the board, ask class members if everyone agrees with each item suggested. If you have time, decide as a class which of the items is most important. Number them in order, or circle three or four. (Do not hesitate to add items to the list if you think it is incomplete.)

Read aloud the first two paragraphs under "Strength in Weakness" in the Conclusion to the lesson commentary. Ask class members to think of other biblical examples. Discuss the following questions with the class or hand them to four groups that are each assigned a different question from the list below. (In that case, reconvene after a few minutes to discuss as a class.)

1–What makes the notion of "strength in weakness" difficult for us to understand or put into practice? 2–Who or what are examples of people or incidents in history or your own life when this principle played out? (Or perhaps you can name times when the opposite was true: a person or nation promoted strength only to be undone or put down.) 3–How might the principle of strength in weakness improve interpersonal relationships? 4–Why is this principle vital if we are to have a rich relationship with God?

Alternative. Distribute to pairs copies of the "Strength Through Weakness" exercise on the activity page to be completed as indicated. Ask volunteers to share what they've written.

FAITH THAT SETS AN EXAMPLE

DEVOTIONAL READING: 2 Corinthians 5:1-10
BACKGROUND SCRIPTURE: 1 Thessalonians 1:2-10

1 THESSALONIANS 1:2-10

2 We always thank God for all of you and continually mention you in our prayers. 3 We remember before our God and Father your work produced by faith, your labor prompted by love, and your endurance inspired by hope in our Lord Jesus Christ.

4 For we know, brothers and sisters loved by God, that he has chosen you, 5 because our gospel came to you not simply with words but also with power, with the Holy Spirit and deep conviction. You know how we lived among you for your sake. 6 You became imitators of us and of the Lord, for you welcomed the message in the midst of severe suffering with the joy given by the Holy Spirit. 7 And so you became a model to all the believers in Macedonia and Achaia. 8 The Lord's message rang out from you not only in Macedonia and Achaia—your faith in God has become known everywhere. Therefore we do not need to say anything about it, 9 for they themselves report what kind of reception you gave us. They tell how you turned to God from idols to serve the living and true God, 10 and to wait for his Son from heaven, whom he raised from the dead—Jesus, who rescues us from the coming wrath.

KEY VERSES

You became a model to all the believers in Macedonia and Achaia. The Lord's message rang out from you not only in Macedonia and Achaia—your faith in God has become known everywhere.

—1 Thessalonians 1:7, 8a

Responding to God's Grace

Unit 3: Faith Leads to Holy Living

LESSONS 10–13

LESSON AIMS

After participating in this lesson, each learner will be able to:

1. List salient points of the history between Paul and the Thessalonian church.

2. Explain the value of a good reputation for a Christian.

3. Identify an idolatrous trend in his or her life and make a plan to eliminate it.

LESSON OUTLINE

Introduction

A. Loving the Work

"Plan the work, then work the plan." This advice helps clarify the logistics needed to get a job done. Plans are futile if the workers fail to do the needed work. Working can be futile when there is no goal in sight.

We often speak of our Christian works as labors of love. What if we said we loved the work and worked our love? What if we found better motivation and more energy to transform talk about acts of love into actions of service, deeply motivated by our love for others? When we do things motivated by our love for Christ and for others, we are not seeking to earn anything. We are working out the love in our hearts in tangible and helpful ways. We are loving the work and working our love. As Paul wrote, the things that really count are seen in "faith expressing itself through love" (Galatians 5:6).

B. Lesson Context

The historical background concerning Paul's time in Thessalonica comes primarily from Acts 17:1-9. Paul set out on his second journey of missionary work with his new companion, Silas (see Lesson Context of lesson 13), in AD 52 (Acts 15:40). Paul wanted to return to churches he had planted on the first missionary expedition. After that, he decided to press on into new territory with the gospel.

Paul eventually came to the city of Thessalonica (Acts 17:1), about 100 miles west of Philippi. Situated on the Via Egnatia, Thessalonica served as a link between the eastern and western parts of the Roman Empire. It was a center of commerce where both land and sea routes met. If Christianity could find a foothold in Thessalonica, the faith would be set to explode westward.

Paul began his ministry in Thessalonica in the synagogue (Acts 17:2), though not to the exclusion of welcoming Gentiles (17:4). This caused Jews of Thessalonica to become jealous of Paul's success (17:5). A riotous mob formed. Christians were rounded up and jailed; only after posting bail were they allowed to return home (17:5-9). Paul and Silas left town under cover of darkness (17:10).

Paul spent less than four weeks in Thessalonica ("three Sabbath days"; see Acts 17:2). This short time for preaching and teaching combined with the agitation from Jewish opponents (17:11, 13) left the young Thessalonian congregation in a tenuous position. Would their faith hold? Would they continue to trust Paul and, more importantly, Christ?

While Paul stayed in Corinth for about 18 months (Acts 18:11), such questions undoubtedly troubled him. So he sent Timothy to Thessalonica to minister to the believers there (1 Thessalonians 3:2). Timothy returned with a report that the Thessalonians had remained faithful (3:6).

Paul's two letters that are called 1 and 2 Thessalonians in our Bibles addressed doctrinal questions that arose in the congregation. The questions especially concerned the resurrection and the second coming of Jesus. These two letters were written within a few months of each other in AD 52.

The greeting of 1 Thessalonians 1:1 lists Paul, Silas, and Timothy, the trio who had begun the good work in this city just a few months earlier. Whenever Paul refers to "we" or "us," he likely has at least these two other men in mind.

I. Encouragement
(1 THESSALONIANS 1:2, 3)
A. Prayer of Constant Thanks (v. 2)
2. We always thank God for all of you and continually mention you in our prayers.

Paul expresses warm feelings and concern for the Thessalonian Christians immediately by assuring them of their place in his *prayers*. Paul's letters give evidence of a deep, consistent, daily prayer life. He frequently tells the recipients of his letters of his constant prayer for them, a claim he can truthfully make only with a systematic and deliberate approach to his prayer life (see Romans 1:9, 10; Ephesians 1:15, 16; Philippians 1:3, 4; Colossians 1:3; 2 Timothy 1:3).

Paul is not alone in these prayers (see Lesson Context). Though the Thessalonians may have felt abandoned by Paul's understandably hasty departure, he assures them that he and his fellow evangelists have not forgotten them.

B. Remembrance of Loving Labor (v. 3)
3a. We remember before our God and Father your work produced by faith,

The content of Paul's prayerful remembrance *before our God and Father* is threefold. The first of the three concerns the Thessalonians' *faith*. Theirs is an active faith, as indeed all faith is meant to be (see James 2:26). Faith in Christ propels the Thessalonians to do good things for each other and for their community.

3b. your labor prompted by love,

The Thessalonian believers have not only an active faith, they also have the right motive for it. There is a big difference in staying power and end result when motivations other than *love* undergird a Christian's work.

What Do You Think?
▶ What self-tests can we conduct to ensure that our works of faith are done in a spirit of love, rather than from a sense of obligation or a desire to impress?

Digging Deeper
Under what circumstances would having an accountability partner be wise in this regard?

3c. and your endurance inspired by hope in our Lord Jesus Christ.

Third, Paul recognizes the Thessalonians' willingness to persevere because of what they hold dear. Their work, which is "produced by faith" and "prompted by love," finds staying power in long-term *hope*. Christian hope consists not of vague wishes that everything will work out well. Instead, Christian hope is the confident expectation that God will do as he has promised and that his work will be a blessing to his people (compare Hebrews 11:1). The Thessalonians anticipate the return of Jesus, and they work in the present with an eye on that future reality (see on 1 Thessalonians 1:10, below).

Faith, hope, and love form Paul's famous triad (see Romans 5:1-5; 1 Corinthians 13:13; Galatians 5:5, 6; Ephesians 4:2-5; Colossians 1:4, 5; 1 Thessalonians 5:8). Pondering how those three are evident among the Thessalonians encourages Paul greatly.

Vilfredo Pareto was an economist who found that 80 percent of Italy's income went to 20 percent of the population. The general "Pareto Rule" was the result of his research. It says that 80 percent of the effects in an organization are the result of 20 percent of the causes.

The Pareto Rule applies in congregations too. Eighty percent of the work is often the result of the involvement of 20 percent of its members. Such a study might be helpful in determining how your church could more effectively carry out its mission. Look at your membership roll and the list of non-member regular attenders. Examine how service activity roles are distributed among them.

The point of this exercise should be to make real in your church's life the characteristics for which Paul gave thanks in Thessalonica—works of faith and labors of love. What would change if 100 percent of your church invested in works of faith?   —C. R. B.

II. Election
(1 Thessalonians 1:4-6)
A. God's Choosing (vv. 4, 5)

4. For we know, brothers and sisters loved by God, that he has chosen you,

Paul goes to a deeper level to explain why he anticipates that the Thessalonians will remain faithful. He knows that they are both *chosen* and *loved by God*. To have been chosen means that because the Thessalonians have accepted Christ, they are the ones God grants eternal life. God's love is the framework for that choice. This should cause the Thessalonians to look forward to Christ's return with hope and anticipation, not with dread and fear.

God chooses according to his foreknowledge (Romans 8:29; 1 Peter 1:1, 2). We become believers by our freewill choice, and those whom God already knows will do so he predestines to receive eternal life (see 2 Thessalonians 2:13). God's chosen ones do not believe because they are chosen; rather, they are chosen because they believe (see Acts 10:43). God has known of our belief from eternity past (see Ephesians 1:4, 5). That's how he

can decide in advance who will be in Heaven and who won't.

5a. because our gospel came to you not simply with words but also with power, with the Holy Spirit and deep conviction.

Paul now summarizes the evidence that the Thessalonian Christians are among God's chosen. They could easily have believed a false religious message. Their world is full of competing religions and philosophies, and not all of them can be true. But Paul reminds the Thessalonians that by believing the *gospel*, they have received something else: the *power* that comes only from *the Holy Spirit*.

> **What Do You Think?**
> ▶ What are some guardrails we can erect to ensure that our accomplishments for Christ are "not by [human] might . . . but by [God's] Spirit" (Zechariah 4:6)?
> *Digging Deeper*
> How do the general principles in Matthew 7:15-23; Romans 8:5-11; 1 Corinthians 14:18-25; Galatians 5:22-26; and 1 John 4:1-3 help you answer this question with specifics?

There is no specific mention of miracles in the account of Paul's time in Thessalonica (Acts 17:1-9). But the account's brevity probably indicates that many things are left out. The references in the verse before us to power, the Holy Spirit, and *deep conviction* may be another way of referring to "signs and wonders, through the power of the Spirit of God" (Romans 15:19) done among the Thessalonians by Paul and his traveling companions. Though Luke (the author of Acts) provides no list of miracles taking place in Thessalonica, Paul's work recorded in Acts 14:8-10 and 16:18 hints that such work likely has included healings and exorcisms.

The signs of the Holy Spirit in Thessalonica provide assurance for those chosen. These signs assure not just the Greek believers but also Paul (see on 1 Thessalonians 1:4, above). Where there are believers, beloved and chosen by God, the Holy Spirit is present also.

Paul's presentation differs from that of traveling pagan teachers of his day. They often seek to impress audiences with lofty rhetoric and inspiring words (followed by gifts of money to the speakers). But Paul has no interest in flattering the Thessalonians to get money from them (1 Thessalonians 2:5; compare 2 Corinthians 10:10, 11). The veracity of his gospel, his message of the good news of salvation through Jesus Christ, comes from divine testimony, God's confirmation through miracles in their midst (see 2 Corinthians 12:12).

5b. You know how we lived among you for your sake.

Paul indicates that the Thessalonians can judge his character and that of his companions by their actions to this point. The result will be to know *how [they] lived among* the Thessalonians. None of them has sought to dominate the Thessalonians by authoritarian tactics (1 Thessalonians 2:6). Instead, the evangelists have cared for the Thessalonians as a mother and father care for their children (2:7, 11). Rather than requiring payment, Paul and his companions do other work for wages to support themselves (2:9; see Acts 18:3; compare 1 Corinthians 9:3-12).

B. Reputation for Joy (v. 6)

6a. You became imitators of us and of the Lord,

Paul's affectionate memories continue, recalling how the believers *became imitators* of him and his companions. He is not attempting to replace Jesus as their rightful Lord but indicating they joined Paul and his fellows as disciples of Christ (compare 1 Corinthians 11:1). Their lives are examples

HOW TO SAY IT

Achaia	Uh-*kay*-uh.
Corinthians	Ko-*rin*-thee-unz (*th* as in *thin*).
Macedonia	Mass-eh-*doe*-nee-uh.
Philippi	Fih-*lip*-pie or *Fil*-ih-pie.
Philippians	Fih-*lip*-ee-unz.
Silas	*Sigh*-luss.
synagogue	*sin*-uh-gog.
Thessalonians	*Thess*-uh-*lo*-nee-unz (*th* as in *thin*).
Thessalonica	*Thess*-uh-lo-*nye*-kuh (*th* as in *thin*).
Via Egnatia	*Vee*-uh Eg-*nah*-tee-uh.

of what it looks like to be Christ followers as well as pointers to the perfect example of Jesus himself.

Here Paul is especially stressing that the Thessalonian Christians have imitated him in accepting hardships that have come because of their faith. The core of the gospel is Jesus' willing death on the cross in submission to God. Jesus' followers will face hardships that call for similar faithfulness (John 15:20). If we understand the cross, we realize that following Jesus will mean accepting hardship, daily carrying our own crosses (Luke 9:23, 24).

What Do You Think?

What will you do to ensure that your spiritually healthy devotion to a church leader doesn't become unhealthy?

Digging Deeper

How does contrasting Paul's praise to the Thessalonians with his criticism of the Corinthians in 1 Corinthians 1:10-17 help form your response?

6b. for you welcomed the message in the midst of severe suffering with the joy given by the Holy Spirit.

This is not an easy time. Paul remembers *severe suffering*, not just for himself but also for the Thessalonian believers (see Lesson Context). He makes sure to note that their suffering has been answered by the comforting *joy given by the Holy Spirit*. Circumstances may seem to dictate that a morose and downtrodden spirit is justified. But the presence of the Spirit counteracts that in a powerful way (see Acts 13:50-52; Romans 14:17).

❧ THE TEST OF SPIRITUALITY ❧

In a church where I once ministered, we had a member whose focus in faith leaned heavily toward the charismatic. Any discussion of Christian faith with him quickly turned to talk of the Holy Spirit and the question of whether a person had a certain spiritual gift. This was the man's only real test of whether a person was Christian. He claimed to have the appropriate spiritual gift and claimed that his teenage son did too.

The son's behavior indicated otherwise. He seemed incorrigible, continually causing trouble in the youth group! Attempts to point out this inconsistency fell on deaf ears. Since this supposedly Spirit-led boy was not bringing joy to the church, one wonders if the father's assessment was accurate.

Paul refers to his own exemplary behavior in Thessalonica as evidence that the Spirit was at work in his life. How does the Spirit lead you to bring joy to others?   —C. R. B.

III. Examples
(I THESSALONIANS 1:7-10)
A. Announcing the Gospel (vv. 7, 8)
7. And so you became a model to all the believers in Macedonia and Achaia.

Macedonia is the region of northern Greece in which Thessalonica is located. *Achaia* is the region of Greece just to the south of Macedonia that includes both Athens and Corinth. The Thessalonian believers are models worthy of being copied by others far and wide.

> *What Do You Think?*
> What steps could we take to assess the reputation of our church in our community?
> *Digging Deeper*
> How can we improve that reputation without compromising beliefs?

8a. The Lord's message rang out from you not only in Macedonia and Achaia—your faith in God has become known everywhere.

The Thessalonians' steadfastness under affliction gives credence to their testimony to the message of the gospel. It enhances their opportunities to evangelize others. Their name *has become known* far beyond their city of Thessalonica.

Occurring only here in the New Testament, the Greek verb translated *rang out* can also imply a crashing sound. The "noise" of the Thessalonians' faith is not subtle but blaring out all around the Roman world.

8b. Therefore we do not need to say anything about it,

Praising the Thessalonians' faith in places where Paul travels is unnecessary because all who believe already know of it.

B. Embracing Christ (vv. 9, 10)
9. for they themselves report what kind of reception you gave us. They tell how you turned to God from idols to serve the living and true God,

Many of the Thessalonian believers are Gentiles (Acts 17:4), and therefor had been pagans who venerated false gods and worshipped *idols*. Temples for the gods and goddesses are found in even small Greek towns. A larger city like Thessalonica is thick with them (compare Paul's experience in Athens; 17:16). If worshipping one god is good, the thinking goes, then worshipping several is even better!

Temples and their idols are normal to Gentiles but abhorrent to Jews. Through general revelation, pagans know there is only one true God, but in rebellion they choose to suppress that truth (Romans 1:18-23). But now they have another chance to embrace the true God, who mercifully grants another chance through Jesus.

To abandon idolatry involves a complete change of life—a social, cultural, and religious upheaval. The Thessalonians embrace this radical change, having *turned* away from false gods and to *the living and true God*. The Thessalonians may feel insignificant, but they are at the very center of God's work in the world. Through the spread of the gospel, God is doing what he promised: making himself known to the nations (compare Isaiah 2:2-4; 42:6; Micah 4:1-3; Zechariah 8:20-23).

> *What Do You Think?*
> What steps can we take to identify and displace the idols in our lives?
> *Digging Deeper*
> At what point does something become an idol? Why?

10a. and to wait for his Son from heaven,

This is the first of three phrases by which Paul sums up his gospel message. He left the Thessalonians with hope, causing them *to wait* in anticipation for God's *Son* to return *from heaven*. Focusing on that return will allow the Thessalonians to endure any temporary affliction in the meantime. The doctrine of Christ's return is very important to the Thessalonians, and Paul addresses some of their misunderstandings about it in both letters to them (see 1 Thessalonians 5:1-11; 2 Thessalonians 1:7-10). Paul reminds these suffering Christians that they still look forward to God's final victory.

10b. whom he raised from the dead—Jesus,

Paul's second phrase is also a message of hope. He will later clarify a misunderstanding concerning the relationship between the coming of Christ and the resurrection (1 Thessalonians 4:13-18), but this is a start. Death is not the end; since Jesus was raised from the dead, so can we be. The chosen will be taken home to be with Jesus forever when he comes again (4:17).

10c. who rescues us from the coming wrath.

Paul's third phrase also conveys hope: the Thessalonian believers need not fear God's *wrath*. Many of them were not previously part of God's covenant people but now are through faith in Jesus' atoning death.

God's wrath is real, and Paul has much more to say about it elsewhere (Romans 1:18-31; 2:5, 8; etc.). Some may challenge the idea of a wrathful God whose punishment can be retribution rather than restorative. But that viewpoint misses the idea that the loving God is also the holy God.

Conclusion

A. Simple Gospel, Good Example

Is it possible to make the gospel too simple? Some preachers and churches seem to think so. They preach a highly refined version of the Christian message in which their followers must maintain correct views about many obscure doctrines, must adhere to certain social standards, and so forth. Could it really be so simple that Paul could express the essentials in a couple of verses?

Our gospel message must be centered on Jesus and his work. While there are many important aspects to the Christian life that call for study and practice, the core of the gospel need not be cluttered. Paul's message for the Thessalonians was that Jesus Christ came and died for their sins, that he was raised from the dead, and that he will come again. This simple yet powerful message was

Visual for Lesson 11. *Ask the class to contemplate this question in conjunction with the discussion of 1 Thessalonians 1:7.*

enough for hardened pagans in ancient Thessalonica to turn from their idols and embrace faith in Christ. Their hearts were filled with joy and with the Holy Spirit. Their transformation was so radical that their reputation spread over two Roman provinces.

Their testimony is worthy of our attention. Though this congregation experienced severe trials, the people refused to let their faith fade into the background. Instead, the Thessalonians stepped up their loving works so much that Paul touted them as already being an example to other congregations.

We sometimes distance faith from works in our teaching, not wanting to mislead Christians into thinking they can earn their salvation. However, the two are sometimes paired in the New Testament (see 2 Thessalonians 1:11; Revelation 2:19). What can be missing is the connecting factor: love. May we believe as the Thessalonians believed and then act on our faith as they did: full of the Holy Spirit and love.

B. Prayer

Father, turn our hearts from idols so we can serve you in faith and love. May we long for the return of your Son. We pray in his name. Amen.

C. Thought to Remember

The essentials of the gospel
are simple and life-changing.

INVOLVEMENT LEARNING

Enhance your lesson with NIV Bible Student *(from your curriculum supplier) and the reproducible activity page (at www.standardlesson.com or in the back of the* NIV Standard Lesson Commentary Deluxe Edition*).*

Into the Lesson

Number class members off in threes. Ask all the number 1s to gather in one part of your classroom as the 2s and 3s each gather in other areas. Distribute on handouts (you prepare) the following questions to be discussed. **1s Group:** What reputation does our church have in this community? **2s Group:** What reputation does our church have in our country? **3s Group:** What reputation does our church have in the world?

After two or three minutes, have class members take their seats for whole-class discussion of the three questions. Then say, "Today's Bible study shows us a first-century church whose positive reputation was known far and wide. Let's see what we can learn from its reputation."

Into the Word

Give a brief overview of Paul's history with the Thessalonian church. Then tell class members that today's text paints a positive picture of these ancient Christians whose faith can be an example for us today. As a volunteer reads 1 Thessalonians 1:2-10 aloud, have the class listen for phrases that spell out positive aspects of the Thessalonians' faith that we can pursue too.

After the reading, ask class members to name positive descriptions from the text; jot responses on the board. Ask class members to put verse references beside the items listed on the board (or do it yourself). Encourage volunteers to name any further items that should be on the list.

Divide the class into three groups. Ask each group to discuss and answer their assigned question: **Paul Group:** How did the influence of Paul deepen and develop the faith of the Thessalonians? **God Group:** How did the power of God deepen and develop the faith of the Thessalonians? **Thessalonian Group:** How did the faith of the Thessalonians encourage believers in other places? After a few minutes, allow each group to

share their responses with the whole class. Ask, "What was at the center of the transformation of the Thessalonians?" Point to verses 9 and 10 and emphasize that faith in the basic elements of the gospel was the heart of Thessalonian Christians' testimony and example.

Into Life

Before class, recruit two or three class members to prepare two-minute testimonials they will share with the whole class at this time. Their speeches should describe another Christian who demonstrated "endurance inspired by hope in our Lord Jesus Christ" (1 Thessalonians 1:3).

After each testimony, ask class members to tell what they found most convicting or helpful about it. Ask how each person's good reputation has made a positive impact for the cause of Christ. Ask how each person described "turned to . . . serve the living and true God" (1:9).

Ask class members to think of items, activities, or goals that can become idols. Point out that anything that takes the place of God in our hearts or thinking has become an idol. As they consider that definition, ask class members, one at a time, to come to the board and write an item that can become an idol for Christians. After a few minutes, ask the class whether any of the listed items surprise them.

Close by asking class members to offer one-sentence prayers out loud. Ask for each prayer to fit this pattern: "Lord, help us to make you Lord by banishing [insert one item listed on the board] as an idol from our lives."

Alternative. Distribute copies of the activity page, which you can download. Students can complete the "Counterfeit Gods" activity in pairs or groups. If you have time, ask class members to share their responses. Then point students to the "Composing a Prayer" activity at the bottom of the sheet as the closing activity.

FAITH THAT IS FOCUSED

DEVOTIONAL READING: 1 Peter 1:3-12
BACKGROUND SCRIPTURE: Galatians 5:22, 23; 1 Peter 1

1 PETER 1:13-25

¹³ Therefore, with minds that are alert and fully sober, set your hope on the grace to be brought to you when Jesus Christ is revealed at his coming. ¹⁴ As obedient children, do not conform to the evil desires you had when you lived in ignorance. ¹⁵ But just as he who called you is holy, so be holy in all you do; ¹⁶ for it is written: "Be holy, because I am holy."

¹⁷ Since you call on a Father who judges each person's work impartially, live out your time as foreigners here in reverent fear. ¹⁸ For you know that it was not with perishable things such as silver or gold that you were redeemed from the empty way of life handed down to you from your ancestors, ¹⁹ but with the precious blood of Christ, a lamb without blemish or defect. ²⁰ He was chosen before the creation of the world, but was revealed in these last times for your sake. ²¹ Through him you believe in God, who raised him from the dead and glorified him, and so your faith and hope are in God.

²² Now that you have purified yourselves by obeying the truth so that you have sincere love for each other, love one another deeply, from the heart. ²³ For you have been born again, not of perishable seed, but of imperishable, through the living and enduring word of God. ²⁴ For,

"All people are like grass,
  and all their glory is like the flowers of
    the field;
the grass withers and the flowers fall,
²⁵ but the word of the Lord endures
    forever."

And this is the word that was preached to you.

KEY VERSES

As obedient children, do not conform to the evil desires you had when you lived in ignorance. But just as he who called you is holy, so be holy in all you do. —1 Peter 1:14, 15

RESPONDING TO GOD'S GRACE

Unit 3: Faith Leads to Holy Living

LESSONS 10–13

LESSON AIMS

After participating in this lesson, each learner will be able to:

1. State the definition of holy.

2. Contrast holy conduct with unholy conduct.

3. Create a plan to identify and correct areas of sinfulness in his or her own life on an ongoing basis.

LESSON OUTLINE

Introduction
  A. Holiness Encounter
  B. Lesson Context
  I. Focusing Our Minds (1 PETER 1:13-16)
    A. With Sobriety (v. 13)
    B. With Holiness (vv. 14-16)
      Seek Ye First
  II. Focusing Our Faith (1 PETER 1:17-21)
    A. In Christ (vv. 17-19)
    B. In Resurrection (vv. 20, 21)
  III. Focusing Our Love (1 PETER 1:22-25)
    A. For Fellow Believers (vv. 22, 23)
      Holiday Humility
    B. For God's Word (vv. 24, 25)
Conclusion
  A. Holiness Gaps
  B. Prayer
  C. Thought to Remember

Introduction

A. Holiness Encounter

Have you ever had what seemed to be a surprising encounter with God's holiness? If so, how did you react? Some may claim to have holiness encounters in certain places (compare Genesis 28:16, 17). Others may claim to encounter God's holiness in certain people (compare 2 Kings 4:9). It seems more likely, however, that we will have encounters with unholiness in this fallen world (compare Genesis 6:5; 19:4, 5; Romans 3:10-18). And before we crave encounters with God's holiness, we may wish to examine biblical incidents of those first!

One example to consider is that of Moses in Exodus 3:1–4:17. At age 40, Moses fled from Egypt and lived in Midian for many years (Exodus 2:12, 15, 22; Acts 7:23). There he did the lonely job of shepherding, moving his flock from pasture to pasture. On one occasion, Moses found himself at the foot of Mount Horeb, later called Mount Sinai. There he encountered a marvelous sight: a fiery bush that didn't burn up. Curiosity resulted in his standing on "holy ground" (Exodus 3:1-5). Moses had encountered the holy God.

The voice in the bush told Moses he would return to this holy place with the people of Israel to worship the Lord (Exodus 3:12). When Moses did return, he encountered not a burning bush but a mountain on fire (19:18)—the holiness of God on a grand scale! Such encounters and others (Isaiah 6, etc.) have lessons to teach about holiness.

B. Lesson Context

Peter is a perplexing figure in the Gospel accounts. He tended to blurt out whatever was on his mind at the time, sometimes seeming to contradict himself in the process (examples: Matthew 16:22, 23; 26:35; Mark 9:5, 6; John 18:25-27). He was impulsive and recklessly bold, often acting before thinking (Matthew 14:22-33; John 18:10). In short, Peter was an apostle we can relate to.

A dramatic change came over Peter after Jesus' resurrection. He grew spiritually, constantly preaching, teaching, and healing in Jesus' name (Acts 2:14-39; 3:1-8, 12-26; 10:34-43, 47, 48; etc.).

This confident Peter is the same man who wrote the letters of 1 and 2 Peter. In his first letter, Peter addressed "exiles scattered throughout the provinces of Pontus, Galatia, Cappadocia, Asia and Bithynia" (1 Peter 1:1). These regions encompass a very large swath of land in northeastern Asia Minor, now Turkey. Such a large expanse of land suggests that a large number of people were also meant to be reached. The majority of Peter's audience were likely Gentile believers (consider 1:14; 2:9, 10; 4:3, 4).

A time of terror, of living day to day and being tempted to abandon the faith, forms the backdrop for Peter's two letters. His first letter mentions being in "Babylon" (1 Peter 5:13), a derogatory code term for the city of Rome (consider Revelation 14:8; 16:19; 17:5; 18:2). After a fire in Rome in AD 64, Emperor Nero blamed the Christian population of the city, putting many of them to death. Both Peter and Paul were in Rome in the mid–AD 60s while Nero persecuted anyone who put their faith in any lord but him. Reliable church tradition maintains that Peter was crucified in Rome in AD 67 or 68.

I. Focusing Our Minds
(1 PETER 1:13-16)
A. With Sobriety (v. 13)

13a. Therefore, with minds that are alert and fully sober,

Therefore indicates that this train of thought is a conclusion of previous statements regarding the work of prophets. Their work was not only for their contemporary audiences but also to minister to those who hear and believe the gospel later (see 1 Peter 1:12). To have *minds that are alert* suggests that one is prepared with focused attention.

HOW TO SAY IT

Bithynia	Bih-*thin*-ee-uh.
Cappadocia	Kap-uh-*doe*-shuh.
Galatia	Guh-*lay*-shuh.
Horeb	*Ho*-reb.
Nero	*Nee*-row.
Pontus	*Pon*-tuss.

A *fully sober* mind is an alert mind, undistracted and engaged in one's current situation with seriousness. The Greek word translated "sober" does not necessarily relate to alcohol consumption such as we use that word today. Rather, it is concerned with self-control in a broader sense.`

13b. set your hope on the grace to be brought to you when Jesus Christ is revealed at his coming.

Believers' focus should be on the return of Jesus. This gives *hope* because of the promise of *grace* associated with that event. Grace here refers to the good news of Christ's return—good news for believers, bad news for their persecutors. Hope gives strength to endure hard times, because present troubles pale in comparison to future glory (Romans 8:18-39). With his faith that Jesus can return at any moment, Peter reminds us of Jesus' own warning to be ready for his return (see Mark 13:32-37).

B. With Holiness (vv. 14-16)

14. As obedient children, do not conform to the evil desires you had when you lived in ignorance.

Focused minds must produce focused lives. Peter urges his readers to demonstrate their readiness for Jesus' return by the way they live. Believers must not be distracted by desires to return to sinful behaviors but instead be like *obedient children*.

This seems to be particularly directed to Gentile believers, who formerly engaged in drunkenness, sexual immorality, and idolatry—having considered such things normal (see 1 Peter 4:3; Lesson Context). To return to *evil desires* shows a reverting to *ignorance*, a willful obliviousness to the possible return of Jesus at any time. That would be to ignore the consequences of sinful behavior (Ephesians 4:18). Such ignorance reminds us of Jesus' illustration of the servants who were unprepared when the master returned home (Matthew 24:45-51).

15. But just as he who called you is holy, so be holy in all you do;

Being *holy* concerns two different but related concepts. First, holiness implies being separate or different. One foundational difference between

God and false gods (idols) is that God made people in his image (Genesis 1:27) and not the other way around (Exodus 20:4-6; Psalm 97:7). Like their God, the nation of Israel was to be unique: a different type of people, a kingdom of priests, a holy nation (Exodus 19:6).

Second, holiness demands moral purity. God's actions are pure and righteous (Ezra 9:15; Psalm 7:11), so his people's actions should also be pure and righteous. Israel was not to be like the other nations, which lived wickedly (2 Samuel 7:23; contrast Ezra 9:2). To approach a holy God, a person must have clean hands and a pure heart (Psalm 24:3, 4). This twofold cleanliness is expressed in right attitudes and actions.

> **What Do You Think?**
> What can our church do to help people have a better understanding of what holiness is and what it looks like in practice?
> *Digging Deeper*
> How do we do so without creating a judgmental, "holier than thou" impression that drives people away?

16. for it is written: "Be holy, because I am holy."

Peter's instructions are not new revelations for the church but those of the *written* precepts for the people of God. These instructions were first found in the Law of Moses. When the Lord called Israel out of Egypt and guided them to be his chosen nation, he demanded one central thing: holiness (Exodus 19:6; 22:31; Deuteronomy 7:6; 14:2; etc.). They were not to be like other nations with their ruthless kings, immoral practices, and injustice toward the poor. They were to *be holy because* God is holy (Leviticus 11:44, 45; 19:2; 20:7; etc.).

In times of suffering such as the church is experiencing when Peter writes, fulfillment of personal longings for material things, health, happiness, and even security seems elusive. But suffering or persecution cannot be allowed to diminish holiness and dedication to God and his ways. If persecution causes Peter's audience to turn away from

holiness, they will no longer be lights pointing to God (Matthew 5:14-16). When we choose holiness, we are choosing to be faithful.

> **What Do You Think?**
> How should we deal with the "gray areas" of what is holy and what is not?
> *Digging Deeper*
> In answering this question, use as a starting point the assumption that the New Testament is more concerned with *principles* in contrast with the Old Testament's concern for *rules*.

❧ *Seek Ye First* ❧

I was angry. My husband had lost his job, making cash flow a real concern. My oldest son was almost expelled from school, and my daughter was sneaking out at night.

I wasn't just angry; I was scared. Instead of consulting God's Word, I took matters into my own hands. I criticized my husband for any minute that was spent not looking for a job or working around the house. I snapped at my children. Consequentially, my children continued to misbehave. My husband lost interest in searching for another job and forgot to do little maintenance chores around the house. My unholy behavior triggered these.

We are to be holy as God is holy. When we are unholy, we aren't in communion with God. The moment I turned to the Lord for guidance, I no longer experienced separation from him. If you feel separated from God right now, could the problem be a lack of holiness?   — P. L. M.

II. Focusing Our Faith
(1 PETER 1:17-21)
A. In Christ (vv. 17-19)

17a. Since you call on a Father who judges each person's work impartially,

To refer to God as *Father* reflects Peter's internalization of Jesus' teachings. Jesus frequently referred to God as "my Father" (for example, Matthew 18:10; Luke 10:22; John 5:17) and encouraged his followers to see God as Father as well

(Matthew 6:9; John 20:17). This relationship implies that the children of the Father will relate to him in trust, obedience, and love.

Fathers must sometimes act as judges of their children's behavior and discipline them accordingly; so it is with God. Many people claim that one of their siblings is the parental favorite and therefore receives special treatment. Not so with God the Father. As Peter himself stressed years earlier, "God does not show favoritism" (Acts 10:34); no one gets preferential judgment. He expects the same holy thoughts, attitudes, and actions from all his obedient children.

17b. live out your time as foreigners here in reverent fear.

As children, we may have been able to hide some disobedience from our parents. That's not so with God, for he knows all. Therefore, we should have a sense of *reverent fear* that leads us to obedience (Leviticus 19:37; 25:17, 36, 43; Deuteronomy 5:29; 6:2; Isaiah 8:13; etc.).

Since Peter's message of salvation is a message of grace, that we are saved by faith (see 1 Peter 1:5; 5:10), then where does fear of God fit in? Doesn't 1 John 4:18 say "perfect love drives out fear"? Indeed it does. But Peter's idea here is that since the tests his audience faces can lead them to unfaithfulness, a proper fear for God is necessary to yield faithfulness instead (Psalm 86:22; 2 Chronicles 19:9; Hebrews 11:7).

18, 19. For you know that it was not with perishable things such as silver or gold that you were redeemed from the empty way of life handed down to you from your ancestors, but with the precious blood of Christ, a lamb without blemish or defect.

Peter's tack now is to establish the value of his readers' redemption by stressing its cost. Had their redemption been purchased *with perishable things such as silver or gold*, then its staying power would have been the same. It would have no eternal value.

In making this point, Peter is likely addressing Christians from a Gentile background since the phrase *the empty way of life handed down to you from your ancestors* would not refer to Judaism. That way of life was established by God. By con-

trast, Ephesians 4:17-19 speaks to the utter worthlessness of paganism.

The subphrase *from your ancestors* can remind us that many sinful and destructive behaviors are carried across generations. People too often find themselves in toxic lifestyles that parallel the life of a parent. But Jesus can rescue us from this cycle as he opens the path to new life available only in him (Romans 6:4; 2 Corinthians 5:17; Ephesians 4:24; etc.). This new life is possible only because Jesus was without sin, likened to a perfect *lamb* (compare Exodus 12:3-5; Hebrews 9:14).

Remembering this puts Christian ethics in perspective. If Jesus, the one without blame or sin, died willingly to offer salvation to all people, should we not strive for blamelessness ourselves (Philippians 2:14, 15)? This striving is the correct response to the holiness and love of Jesus' life, not an attempt to earn our salvation.

> ### What Do You Think?
> What visual aids can you use daily to remind you that the fact of 1 Peter 1:19 should result in holy living?
> ### Digging Deeper
> How might those visual aids differ from life context to life context (work, church, home, etc.)?

B. In Resurrection (vv. 20, 21)

20a. He was chosen before the creation of the world,

Peter wipes away all the patterns that influence evil behavior by going back to the earliest era: *before the creation of the world*. Even then—before forming the heavens and the earth, before creating men and women, and before the first sin—God had planned for our salvation through the spotless Lamb who is his Son. God's plans are deliberate and eternal.

20b. but was revealed in these last times for your sake.

The 2,000 years of Jewish history preceding Peter's ministry anticipated this coming Messiah. The revelation of this chosen one of God has come *in these last times* for Peter's first-century readers in Rome (compare Acts 2:14-21; 1 John

2:18; Revelation 22:7, 10, 12, 20). We are still in those last times. What follows this epoch is the end: Jesus' return to judge and save. As Peter's readers eagerly awaited Christ's return, so do we.

21. Through him you believe in God, who raised him from the dead and glorified him, and so your faith and hope are in God.

This verse forms a balance for the expectation of Christ's return. Christians hope for this return daily in our painful world. If he does not come in our lifetime, our hopes are not dashed. Our *hope* focuses on the Lord *God*, the one *who raised* Jesus from the grave to glory and will do so for us too.

III. Focusing Our Love
(1 Peter 1:22-25)
A. For Fellow Believers (vv. 22, 23)

22. Now that you have purified yourselves by obeying the truth so that you have sincere love for each other, love one another deeply, from the heart.

One word defines how Christians are meant to treat *each other* in the faith: *love*. This is more than an act of obedience. Our love for each other should be *sincere*, done with a pure heart, and felt *deeply*. We must do more than act like we love each other. We must truly care for each other as deeply as we care for ourselves (Matthew 22:37-40). Such love-motivated acts are the obedience to truth that Peter wants his readers to practice.

> **What Do You Think?**
> How can you try to improve your relationship with a person who seems suspicious of your motives and intentions?
> *Digging Deeper*
> Which passages about God's love most influence your response? What does the context surrounding Paul's note on unfeigned love in 2 Corinthians 6:6 contribute?

❧ HOLIDAY HUMILITY ❧

Thanksgiving was just around the corner when my sister blew apart my holiday spirit: she had invited her best friend. This was someone with whom I had been feuding for decades, fueled by harsh words and emotional wounds. I felt incredibly disrespected that this woman was invited.

I cried out to the Lord to help me face this ordeal. When I finished voicing my frustration and pain, I felt oddly renewed, as if I had sloughed off something dead. I still dreaded the upcoming holiday, but I knew what God wanted me to do: I needed to love her with a pure heart.

We said our first hellos with wary politeness, but two days later as she was leaving for the airport, we hugged and wished each other well. When we see people in the way God sees them, it allows us to love them with an otherwise impossible love. Who is God calling you to love impossibly?   — P. L. M.

23a. For you have been born again, not of perishable seed, but of imperishable,

Peter likely learned from Jesus to speak of salvation as being *born again* (John 3:3, 7). Peter's speech after healing a man uses a similar idea that he called "times of refreshing" from the Lord (Acts 3:19; compare Romans 12:2). The Christian life is a radically changed life, going from lost to saved, from sinner to saint, from living for oneself to living for Jesus. We commonly refer to this as "conversion," the starting point for a new, *imperishable* life (compare John 3:3-5).

23b. through the living and enduring word of God.

Becoming a believer is more than emotions, although it can be an emotional experience. We believe because we have learned from *the living and enduring word of God* the truth about Jesus. People cannot believe unless they hear or read about Jesus and his saving work (Romans 10:14). The gospel is still powerful today, 2,000 years after Jesus first preached it. It does not grow old or lose its potency.

B. For God's Word (vv. 24, 25)

24. For, "All people are like grass, and all their glory is like the flowers of the field; the grass withers and the flowers fall,

Peter quotes an abbreviated form of Isaiah 40:6-8, which uses the illustration of seasonal *grass* and *flowers*. They sprout, grow, bloom, then die. *People* and animals are like that too. Our life spans are limited, and death overtakes us all.

25a. "but the word of the Lord endures forever."

Not all things die (see Isaiah 40:8). Peter's claim of the everlasting power of *the word of the Lord* is bolstered by his use of a prophecy from Isaiah that was already ancient as Peter writes: the Word of God will never die.

> *What Do You Think?*
> How much time should we spend studying the Old Testament when we combine (1) the fact that God's Word endures permanently with (2) the factual change noted in Colossians 2:14?
>
> *Digging Deeper*
> How do Romans 15:4 and 1 Corinthians 10:11 help shape your response?

25b. And this is the word that was preached to you.

Peter ties the words of the prophet Isaiah to his own ministry. The ancient and eternal Word lives again in the preaching of the gospel, *the word* of God's grace and mercy. For those experiencing uncertainty and fear in persecution, the promise that the gospel is eternal invites them to experience peace and hope.

Conclusion

A. Holiness Gaps

Not long ago, a friend told me he thought "Be holy, because I am holy" to be the most neglected command in the church. The great apostle Peter did not think holiness should be neglected or dismissed. He held it as a core element of the gospel he preached. Our failures to be holy ultimately misrepresent our belief in the holiness of God. Since God is holy, then we should care about our own holiness. When we behave, think, or speak in unholy ways, we diminish our relationship with God.

Are there holiness gaps in your life, pockets of sinful attitudes and actions you harbor and pro-

Visual for Lesson 12. *Start a discussion by pointing to this visual as you ask how focused faith helps with the "gray areas" of holiness.*

tect? Are there areas where a holy God is not welcome, where your privacy rights are paramount? Sometimes the holiness gaps are not private at all. Others can see uncontrolled anger, lack of integrity, shameful treatment of a spouse, etc. But no matter how private your hold is on your sinfulness, God is a witness (1 Peter 1:17).

This lesson helps us understand why and how to live in stressful times and maintain our faith. We may not face imminent arrest and death for being Christians, but we have trials all the same. Many things call us to acknowledge them to be "lord" in place of Jesus. Peter's guidance helps us to focus on what is important, to live without fear, to strive for holiness, and to always remain faithful to our calling as followers of Jesus. His words encourage us to remain confident in Jesus, no matter what problems might threaten. Peter would do the same.

B. Prayer

Lord God, free us from sinful behaviors that weigh us down and cause us to stumble. Through your Holy Spirit, we ask that you empower us to strive for holiness so that we may be more like you. We pray in the name of Jesus, the spotless and holy Lamb of God. Amen.

C. Thought to Remember

God's holiness motivates
our desire for holiness.

INVOLVEMENT LEARNING

Enhance your lesson with NIV Bible Student *(from your curriculum supplier) and the reproducible activity page (at www.standardlesson.com or in the back of the* NIV Standard Lesson Commentary Deluxe Edition*).*

Into the Lesson

Ask students, in pairs or triads, to consider these quotations:

> Things that are holy are revealed only to men who are holy. —Hippocrates

> Anybody can observe the Sabbath, but making it holy surely takes the rest of the week. —Alice Walker

> However many holy words you read, however many you speak, what good will they do you if you do not act upon them? —Gautama Buddha

> We ought to fly away from earth to heaven as quickly as we can; and to fly away is to become like God, as far as this is possible; and to become like Him is to become holy, just and wise. —Plato

> He who has learned to pray has learned the greatest secret of a holy and happy life. —William Law

> No man should desire to be happy who is not at the same time holy. He should spend his efforts in seeking to know and do the will of God, leaving to Christ the matter of how happy he should be. —A. W. Tozer

Options. Either (1) duplicate all quotes on handouts or (2) give groups only one quote each to consider. Either way, ask students to decide why they agree or disagree with the quote(s). Ask how the quotation under consideration fits their understanding of the biblical concept of holiness.

After students have discussed the quotes in groups or pairs, allow them to share their conclusions with the whole class. Ask, "Which quote seems most valid for a Christian to heed today?"

Alternative. Place in chairs copies of the "What Does It Mean to Be Holy?" exercise from the activity page, which you can download, for learners to begin working on as they arrive. Tell them to feel free to work with a partner to find the answers.

After learners solve the puzzle, Ask, "Why should these words describe the Christian?"

After either activity, say, "Today's Scripture challenges every Christian to be holy and also tells us why and how."

Into the Word

Tell students they will use today's Scripture to complete a chart with these column headings: *What Holiness Does / What Holiness Avoids / Why Be Holy?* Write the three headings on the board, and ask students to listen for phrases that belong in each column as you read the Scripture aloud once or twice. Have a scribe jot students' answers on the board.

Options. Ask students in groups to complete the chart before discussing it as a whole class. Or give each heading to a different third of the class, and ask students to make a list under their headings for ensuing whole-class discussion.

Alternative. Distribute copies of the "My Life Is Yours, Lord" exercise from the activity page. This activity challenges students to compare the lyrics of the hymn "Take My Life and Let It Be" with the admonitions of today's Scripture.

Into Life

Ask students to evaluate their lists in the first two columns of the chart above. Ask, "Which of the attributes of holiness in today's Scripture do you find most lacking in the world today? in the church today? Which of them do you think are the most difficult to attain? How does this passage help us believe it is possible to be holy?"

Use the lyrics from "Take My Life and Let It Be" (found on the activity page) as a closing activity. Ask different members of the class to read stanzas while the rest of the class assumes an attitude of prayer. Or lead the class in singing the hymn. You may also find video or audio of the hymn to play as the closing prayer.

FAITH THAT
ESCAPES CORRUPTION

DEVOTIONAL READING: Psalm 90
BACKGROUND SCRIPTURE: 2 Peter 1

2 PETER 1:1-15

¹ Simon Peter, a servant and apostle of Jesus Christ,

To those who through the righteousness of our God and Savior Jesus Christ have received a faith as precious as ours:

² Grace and peace be yours in abundance through the knowledge of God and of Jesus our Lord.

³ His divine power has given us everything we need for a godly life through our knowledge of him who called us by his own glory and goodness. ⁴ Through these he has given us his very great and precious promises, so that through them you may participate in the divine nature, having escaped the corruption in the world caused by evil desires.

⁵ For this very reason, make every effort to add to your faith goodness; and to goodness, knowledge; ⁶ and to knowledge, self-control; and to self-control, perseverance; and to perseverance, godliness; ⁷ and to godliness, mutual affection; and to mutual affection, love. ⁸ For if you possess these qualities in increasing measure, they will keep you from being ineffective and unproductive in your knowledge of our Lord Jesus Christ. ⁹ But whoever does not have them is nearsighted and blind, forgetting that they have been cleansed from their past sins.

¹⁰ Therefore, my brothers and sisters, make every effort to confirm your calling and election. For if you do these things, you will never stumble, ¹¹ and you will receive a rich welcome into the eternal kingdom of our Lord and Savior Jesus Christ.

¹² So I will always remind you of these things, even though you know them and are firmly established in the truth you now have. ¹³ I think it is right to refresh your memory as long as I live in the tent of this body, ¹⁴ because I know that I will soon put it aside, as our Lord Jesus Christ has made clear to me. ¹⁵ And I will make every effort to see that after my departure you will always be able to remember these things.

KEY VERSE

He has given us his very great and precious promises, so that through them you may participate in the divine nature, having escaped the corruption in the world caused by evil desires. —**2 Peter 1:4**

RESPONDING TO
GOD'S GRACE

Unit 3: Faith Leads to Holy Living
LESSONS 10–13

LESSON AIMS

After participating in this lesson, each learner will be able to:

1. State from memory several elements of Peter's list of godly traits.

2. Explain the connection between faith, knowledge, and behavior.

3. Recruit an accountability partner to help identify and eliminate threats to his or her calling and election.

LESSON OUTLINE

Introduction
A. Making Every Effort

Students can be divided into four categories according to ability and effort. First are the highly capable students who work hard and excel beyond the course requirements. They get great benefit from the class. Second are less capable students who work hard even to meet the minimum requirements. They too get huge benefit from the class. Third, there are highly gifted students who do not work hard. They may pass the course (or not) but gain little benefit from it. Fourth, there are students with low academic ability who do not expend much effort. They tend to fail the course and receive little or no benefit.

Which type of student is the greatest joy to a teacher? Many instructors prefer the second category, the student who works hard to overcome academic deficiencies. The least favorite student is the third type, the student with great potential who squanders learning opportunities through laziness or neglect. During today's lesson, perhaps you will see a need to change your student-type!

B. Lesson Context

Peter's second letter consists of only three chapters (61 total verses), yet it presents several intriguing connections to other books of the New Testament. Many have noted the overlap of material between 2 Peter and Jude. Both letters express concern that false teachers would try to lead Christians astray (compare 2 Peter 1:20; 2:2-4, 10, 12-15, 18-22; 3:3-5, 17 with Jude 3-16). Such teachers claimed authority and insight from God that they did not have. The warning from the apostle Peter is stated in terms of "destructive heresies" (2 Peter 2:1).

Another cross-connection is found in 2 Peter 1:16-18, which refers to the transfiguration of Jesus recorded in the Gospels (compare Matthew 17:1-5). That pivotal and spectacular event revealed the true nature of Jesus and his glory to his inner circle of disciples of Peter, James, and John. Peter continued to tell of this event for some 30 years, bringing credibility to his preaching and teaching (Acts 2:14-36; 8:25; 1 Peter 2:23-25; etc.).

An obvious connection between 1 and 2 Peter is not so clear however. The style of writing in 2 Peter is much rougher than the elegant Greek of 1 Peter. This difference may be explained in 1 Peter 5:12, which indicates that Peter had the help of Silas in writing the first letter. There is no record that Silas, perhaps a more educated man, helped write 2 Peter. Without a writing partner, it makes sense that Peter's solo work on 2 Peter resulted in a different style than that of 1 Peter.

Peter wrote his second letter in the context of the persecution of Christians in the city of Rome. He wrote under duress, believing his own death to be near (see commentary on 2 Peter 1:13-15, below). The grim reality of persecution in Rome under Emperor Nero (reigned AD 54–68) served to focus Peter's thoughts in the direction we see in today's lesson text.

I. Greeting
(2 PETER 1:1, 2)

A. Through God's Righteousness (v. 1)

1a. Simon Peter, a servant and apostle of Jesus Christ,

Simon Peter identifies himself with both his Hebrew and Greek names. His given Hebrew name can also be spelled "Simeon" (see Genesis 29:33; 49:5). If names in two languages were not enough, Jesus called Simon "Cephas," the Aramaic version of Greek "Peter" (John 1:42); both names mean "rock" (Matthew 16:18).

Peter further identifies himself in terms of two roles. The word *servant* (absent from 1 Peter 1:1) implies that one has a master (compare 2 Peter 2:19). Such a master is the servant's "lord." In calling himself a servant *of Jesus Christ*, Peter identifies his Lord.

HOW TO SAY IT

Aramaic	Air-uh-**may**-ik.
Cephas	See-fus.
heresies	hair-uh-seez.
Nero	Nee-row.
Plato	Play-tow.
Silas	Sigh-luss.

Peter's use of the designation *apostle* reminds his readers that he has been given authority by Christ himself (see Matthew 10:2; 28:16-20; Galatians 2:8; 1 Peter 1:1). This title reveals that the person who is so designated is sent by or on behalf of someone else. To accept a role as Jesus' apostle means Peter believes that his mission and authority come from his Lord Jesus, not from Peter's own aspirations.

Simon Peter referred to himself only as Peter in his first letter (see 1 Peter 1:1). The lengthening of his name may suggest that he is asserting his authority more strenuously than before. This impulse is probably linked to the false teachers that have him concerned for his audience (see the Lesson Context). Peter is fighting for and exercising his apostolic voice.

1b. To those who through the righteousness of our God and Savior Jesus Christ have received a faith as precious as ours:

Those to whom Peter writes possess *a faith as precious as* his own. By use of the plural *ours*, he is including other firsthand witnesses of Jesus' ministry, especially the other apostles (compare 2 Peter 3:2). Such faith comes as a gift because of *the righteousness of our God*, which has made a way for all people to come to saving faith in Jesus.

Peter presents a high view of the deity of Christ, the apostle's remembered and living Lord (compare John 14:7-11). Most scholars believe that by the phrase *God and Savior Jesus Christ*, Peter refers not to Father and Son, but to the Son only. In so doing, Peter emphasizes Jesus' deity instead of his humanity.

B. Through Knowledge of God (v. 2)

2. Grace and peace be yours in abundance through the knowledge of God and of Jesus our Lord.

Peter's desire that *grace* (a Greek greeting) and *peace* (a Hebrew greeting) *be yours in abundance* in the lives of his readers echoes his salutation in 1 Peter 1:2 (see Lesson Context of lesson 12). This speaks to having peace with God, not mere earthly peace. Although Peter was primarily an apostle to the Jews (Galatians 2:9), he was the one chosen to reveal God's will for including Gentiles in salvation (Acts 10:1–11:18). Because of God's grace, everyone can experience peace with him.

The fact that such peace comes *through the knowledge of God and of Jesus* (also 2 Peter 2:20; 3:18) involves much more than "head knowledge." Peter will make this abundantly clear as this letter unfolds. What should be clear at this point is that by equating knowledge of Jesus with knowledge of God, Peter again affirms that Jesus is God (see 2 Peter 1:1b, above).

Referring to Jesus as *our Lord* groups Peter's audience with the apostles once again. Not only do they share the faith (again, see 2 Peter 1:1b); they also share in their roles as servants of the Lord. No one can follow the Lord without being subject to the Lord (contrast 2:1-3).

II. Godliness
(2 PETER 1:3-11)
A. Glory (vv. 3, 4)

3. His divine power has given us everything we need for a godly life through our knowledge of him who called us by his own glory and goodness.

God interacts with believers through *his divine power*, and the results are gifts we need. Specifically, God's working in our lives provides life defined by godliness. His *glory and goodness* call us when we recognize that only Jesus can lead us to true life.

All of this depends on *our knowledge of him*, which is not so much a propositional or "book knowledge" as it is a personal relationship (see commentary on 2 Peter 1:2, 8). As we know God better, we live the *godly life* more completely. We will never match God's perfect standards, but we still progress toward excellence in our lifestyle. This kind of excellence is characterized by *goodness*. Behind this translation is a Greek word that older versions of the Bible render as "virtue."

The concept of virtue is well known to the Greek philosophers. Those great thinkers argue about what should be the primary characteristics of moral and ethical behavior. Before Peter's day, Plato proposed the cardinal virtues of discernment, courage, moderation, and justice. To the philosophers, virtue yields the best life. But the Greeks do not look to their gods as examples of virtuous goodness; those (fictitious) deities are often seen to be petty, dishonest, and capricious.

Peter will discuss specific virtues later, based not on philosophical musings and human wisdom but on the character of God and revelation of Jesus (see commentary on 2 Peter 1:5-8). Christian virtues and moral characteristics are defined by God and known as godliness.

4a. Through these he has given us his very great and precious promises, so that through them you may participate in the divine nature,

Related to God's working with divine power are certain *promises* for believers that result in being granted the privilege of participating *in the divine nature*. This is a striking way of talking about the gift and presence of the Holy Spirit in our lives. Sharing in godly behavior shows the hand of God in our transformed lives.

4b. having escaped the corruption in the world caused by evil desires.

To be granted the privilege just discussed is based on the fact that we see here. Worldly *desires* are destructive, driving us away from God and his people. Peter speaks of *corruption* not as the breakdown of the body but as the depravity of the soul. Our self-inflicted moral wounds begin to heal as we experience the Holy Spirit in our hearts and yield to the Spirit's influence in our lives.

B. Morality (vv. 5-9)

5a. For this very reason, make every effort to add to your faith goodness;

Godly habits do not happen without real effort. Peter warns against a lazy attitude in pursuit of godly traits, knowing that making *every effort* toward godliness is crucial to one's relationship with God. We don't know God in any identifiable way if our lives do not reflect our commitment to him.

All godly habits flow from *faith*, based on our committed relationship to God. Peter presents seven characteristics to look for in terms of a connected chain. He starts with *goodness,* which we noted can be translated "virtue," reflecting moral excellence. This is the opposite of sinfulness. Christians should be morally excellent; everyone we meet should be able to recognize virtue and goodness in our lives.

❧ THE SOUND OF MUSIC ❧

On my way to work one morning, I flipped on a popular music station. The upbeat music made the hour-long drive pass by effortlessly. Throughout the day, I found myself singing those same songs.

This particular morning, I heard one of my favorite songs. Turning it up, the song's meaning suddenly became quite apparent. I cringed; I had sung that song a hundred times but had never considered its vulgar message. The lyrics had been there all along, but somehow I was hearing them for the first time. I quickly shut the radio off.

We are told to make every effort to supplement our faith with goodness. I needed to surround myself with things that would help me look upward, toward God, not keep me focused on worldly desires. While the Spirit guides that change, we must nurture it with godly, virtuous things. What tune are you singing all day long?

— P. L. M.

5b. and to goodness, knowledge;

Second, virtuous *goodness* should lead to *knowledge*, clear understanding of the parameters of the Christian life. Knowing God and knowing about God will result in knowing how to behave in a godly manner (compare Proverbs 2:1-10). This is self-knowledge based on God-knowledge.

6a. and to knowledge, self-control;

Third, our *knowledge* of God and his expectations for us should produce *self-control*. Such self-control should be applied to all facets of life.

6b. and to self-control, perseverance;

Fourth, *self-control* leads to *perseverance*, which is steady endurance. For Peter's audience in an environment of persecution, perseverance is necessary. God fulfills promises in his timing, not ours. Sometimes we can only wait patiently on him (Isaiah 40:31).

6c. and to perseverance, godliness;

Fifth, we should be refining our *godliness*, our patterns of devotion and respect for the Lord. This cannot be done passively, just as none of the other

Visual for Lesson 13. *Start a discussion by pointing to this visual as you pose the question that is associated with 2 Peter 1:8, below.*

Christian traits discussed so far can be obtained through inaction. Human hearts are inclined to evil (Genesis 6:5; Psalm 14:1-3; Jeremiah 17:9; Romans 7:18-20); without the Holy Spirit's work and our own persistence, we will cultivate evil instead of godliness.

7. and to godliness, mutual affection; and to mutual affection, love.

We group the sixth and seventh characteristics together because *mutual affection* is so closely related to *love*. Love that results in action with and for fellow Christians is to be a hallmark of believers (John 13:34, 35; Romans 13:8; 1 John 4:19-21; etc.). This primary characteristic of the church defines how we are to relate to one another (Romans 12:10). This should flow naturally from patient endurance and godliness. Loving others often requires great patience and requires many other godly traits to be exercised in a holy way. Unselfish love is motivated by a concern for others that has greater weight than concern for oneself. What Peter began with faith (see 2 Peter 1:5), he ends with love (compare 1 Corinthians 13:13).

> **What Do You Think?**
> Of the characteristics listed, which one will pose the greatest challenge to Christians in general in the year ahead? Why?
> **Digging Deeper**
> How will you in particular meet the challenge?

8. For if you possess these qualities in increasing measure, they will keep you from being ineffective and unproductive in your knowledge of our Lord Jesus Christ.

Diligent attention to these faith-based characteristics will result in spiritual fruit (compare Galatians 5:22-25). Growing in Christ is based on our *knowledge* of him (see commentary on 2 Peter 1:3, 5b). As we know him more fully, it is reflected in our lives. As we develop these characteristics of godliness, we know him better.

What Do You Think?
How will you assess your personal progress in the areas Peter mentions?
Digging Deeper
Under what circumstances would having an accountability partner be better than performing a self-assessment? Why?

9. But whoever does not have them is nearsighted and blind, forgetting that they have been cleansed from their past sins.

Does the neglect of the godly characteristics that flow from faith *result from* or *result in* a blindness to what God has done for a person? Perhaps it's both, in a mutually reinforcing and vicious cycle (compare Matthew 15:14; 2 Corinthians 4:3, 4; 1 John 2:9-11). This cycle must be broken or, better, not allowed to start in the first place. The beginning point is always to keep in mind that we have been *cleansed from* our *past sins*, and they no longer condemn us.

❧ *Blind Spot* ❧

My phone dinged. *Who is texting me so late?* It was a male coworker with a joke. I laughed and replied quickly. I was brushing my teeth when a second text came through. My husband walked into the bathroom with a puzzled look on his face. "Who's texting you 'good night, sleep tight'?" With a flushed face, I spat out the toothpaste and practically spat at him, "It was just a friend." My husband backed off.

Six months later, the texting had almost ended my marriage. I should have recognized the danger the moment I felt the urge to hide my phone.

I told myself it was innocent even though my face would flush with excitement at the thought of the next text.

When we are saved, we receive a new nature, one that opens our eyes to temptation. We are to want what God wants and hate what God hates. How can you discover your own blind spots and learn to see clearly? — P. L. M.

C. Calling (vv. 10, 11)

10. Therefore, my brothers and sisters, make every effort to confirm your calling and election. For if you do these things, you will never stumble,

To be called is to be invited; to be elected is to be chosen. These are not separate concepts but different aspects of the same thing. God both chooses and calls us to be part of his people. (On the relationship between these terms and the concepts of human freewill and God's foreknowledge, see commentary on 1 Thessalonians 1:4 in lesson 11.) We *confirm* our status by making the practice of godly habits a priority. We are not earning our salvation but living it as God expects. The practice of godliness becomes a beloved lifestyle, not a burden.

What Do You Think?
What steps can we take to ensure that a strength doesn't lapse back into a weakness?
Digging Deeper
What common preconditions to spiritual lapses have you seen?

11. and you will receive a rich welcome into the eternal kingdom of our Lord and Savior Jesus Christ.

The risen Christ promised the church in Smyrna that the one who is faithful until death will be given a crown of life (Revelation 2:10). Peter offers a similar promise to the ones who strive for godliness. This reminds us of Jesus' teaching about the *kingdom* of God, which Peter heard often (Matthew 6:33; 19:16-30; Mark 4:10-20; Luke 8:1; etc.).

Jesus warned the unbelieving Jews of his day that they would be barred from the kingdom of

God because of their failure to produce fruit that God desired (Matthew 21:43). They were blind to his will and would suffer the consequences (Mark 4:11, 12; see commentary on 2 Peter 1:9).

III. Remembering
(2 PETER 1:12-15)
A. To Establish Truth (v. 12)

12. So I will always remind you of these things, even though you know them and are firmly established in the truth you now have.

Peter commits himself to helping his audience remember and practice these important components of Christian living (compare Psalm 119:52-56; Ezekiel 20:43; 1 Corinthians 11:23-29). This is not a new endeavor for the apostle. His readers already *know* how they should live to be *firmly established in the truth*. Peter's concern is that they not grow tired in the midst of persecution or fall for compromises offered by false teachers who would demolish the foundation Peter has built with them (2 Peter 2:1-3).

> *What Do You Think?*
> What good aids have you discovered for remembering your status in Christ?
> *Digging Deeper*
> Which would you recommend that all Christians use? Why?

B. Because Time Is Short (vv. 13-15)

13, 14. I think it is right to refresh your memory as long as I live in the tent of this body, because I know that I will soon put it aside, as our Lord Jesus Christ has made clear to me.

Peter is feeling his mortality. Choosing to refer to his life as a *tent* recalls the temporary structure that housed God's presence in the desert wanderings (Exodus 29:43, 44; 33:9, 10; 1 Kings 8:10-12, 27-30; 1 Corinthians 6:19). Christians look forward to the new, resurrection bodies that we will be given after our temporary, earthly bodies die.

The brevity of Peter's remaining time has been revealed to him by *Jesus* himself, although Peter does not explain how (compare John 21:18, 19).

He believes his last days are best served by refreshing believers' memories concerning the important lifestyle matters just presented. In this way, they will be prepared for the return of Jesus or their own deaths, perhaps as a result of the murderous Roman persecution.

15. And I will make every effort to see that after my departure you will always be able to remember these things.

The Christian life is not about seeking new commands or innovative doctrine. Quite the opposite: the Christian life is about remembering and practicing the old, that which has already been given (see 1 John 2:7, 8; 2 John 5, 6). Nothing pleases Peter more than for his readers to do so.

> *What Do You Think?*
> How can our church help older believers leave a positive legacy of faithfulness to younger generations?
> *Digging Deeper*
> Is it better to approach this ministry with whole-church programs or on a person-to-person basis? Why?

Conclusion
A. Christian Efforts

Christians cultivate godly characteristics and habits as modeled by Christ. This is essential in following Jesus as Lord. Our values and attitudes flow from faith in Christ. This is the Christian life as Peter presents it to his readers.

We do not live without guidance in how to do this. We have Jesus' example and the Holy Spirit to guide us. God has shown us what he values. Are you making every effort to confirm your calling, to live your faith virtuously?

B. Prayer

Lord, guide us as we seek to live out our faith. May we not be useless, unfruitful, or blind. We pray in the name of Jesus our Lord. Amen.

C. Thought to Remember

The condition of our faith
defines our lives.

INVOLVEMENT LEARNING

Enhance your lesson with NIV Bible Student *(from your curriculum supplier) and the reproducible activity page (at www.standardlesson.com or in the back of the* NIV Standard Lesson Commentary Deluxe Edition*).*

Into the Lesson

As class members arrive, write "Last Words" on the board. Begin today's lesson by asking students if they can remember the last words someone spoke to them just before dying. Let several share. Or, before class, look up "Last words of famous people" on the internet and bring a list of these to share with the class.

Option. Distribute slips of paper to the class and ask students to write down what they hope will be remembered about them after they die. Tell them not to sign their names. Collect the slips and read some of them to the class.

Lead into Bible study by telling the class, "Today's Scripture text includes some of the final words the apostle Peter wrote as he was anticipating his death. They demand our attention perhaps more than any other 'last words' we've heard today."

Into the Word

Distribute handouts (you prepare) that list the following words in random order (not the order indicated here) in one column: *faith, goodness, knowledge, self-control, perseverance, godliness, mutual affection, love.* (*Alternative.* Write them on the board instead.)

Tell students that Peter challenged his readers to pursue each of these virtues, with one paving the way for the next. Challenge learners to put the virtues in the correct order without looking at today's text. Do this as an all-class activity, or allow pairs or triads to try putting the words in order. Then turn to 2 Peter 1:5-7 to get the order correct.

Next, show students the following list of definitions (or these could be listed, again in random order, in a new column on your handout): belief in God expressed in a committed relationship with him / moral excellence / intimate familiarity with God / self-restraint / steady endurance / patterns of devotion and respect for the Lord / love motivated by affection / love motivated by concern for others.

Challenge students to match these definitions to the list of virtues. Again, do this as an all-class discussion or ask students to complete the assignment in the pairs or triads formed earlier.

Completed lists should look as follows: Faith: belief in God expressed in a committed relationship with him / Goodness: moral excellence / Knowledge: intimate familiarity with God / Self-control: self-restraint / Perseverance: steady endurance / Godliness: patterns of devotion and respect for the Lord / Mutual affection: love motivated by affection / Love: love motivated by concern for others.

Ask students, "How can we hope to demonstrate such a challenging list of virtues?" Ask a class member to read verses 3 and 4 from today's lesson text. Then ask, "Why should we pursue these virtues?" Ask a class member to read verses 8-11. Ask, "Why was Peter so eager for his readers to live by these virtues?" Read verses 12-15. Encourage free discussion.

Into Life

Give class members one minute to rearrange the list of virtues according to how difficult they are to demonstrate in their personal lives. Ask, by a show of hands, how many rated each item on the list as most challenging. Write the virtues in order on the board and record the numbers beside each item.

Point to the item with the most votes and ask class members to suggest steps for developing and demonstrating that virtue in their own lives. Give class members one minute to write down one step they can take to increase the presence of one virtue from the list in their own lives this week.

Alternative. Distribute the exercises titled "What Do They Need?" and "What Do You Need?" from the activity page. After the first, review class members' answers and discuss questions. After the second, ask volunteers to share which quality they've chosen as a goal for this week.

HONORING GOD

Special Features

Lessons

Unit 1: David Honors God

Unit 2: Dedicating the Temple of God

Unit 3: Jesus Teaches About True Worship

QUARTERLY QUIZ

Use these questions as a pretest or as a review. The answers are on page iv of This Quarter in the Word.

Lesson 1
1. Only the _____ could carry the ark of God. *1 Chronicles 15:2*
2. Who saw David dancing? (Saul, Michal, Jonathan?) *1 Chronicles 15:29*

Lesson 2
1. We are to _____ the Lord in the splendor of holiness. *1 Chronicles 16:29*
2. According to David, the trees sing at the presence of the Lord. T/F. *1 Chronicles 16:33*

Lesson 3
1. David spoke to Nathan about the location of the _____. *1 Chronicles 17:1*
2. David sought to build an altar on Nathan's threshing floor. T/F. *1 Chronicles 21:24*

Lesson 4
1. Mary called Elizabeth "blessed." T/F. *Luke 1:41, 42*
2. How long did Mary stay with Elizabeth? (three days, three weeks, three months?) *Luke 1:56*

Lesson 5
1. God made the people of _____ his forever. *1 Chronicles 17:22*
2. What did David's heart move him to do? (sing, kneel, pray?) *1 Chronicles 17:25*

Lesson 6
1. Along with the ark of the Lord, Solomon brought up the _____ and all the sacred furnishings. *1 Kings 8:4*
2. The ark was filled with scrolls, incense, and other items from Israel's history. T/F. *1 Kings 8:9*

Lesson 7
1. It was in the heart of _____ to build a house for the name of the Lord. *1 Kings 8:17*
2. What object was said to contain the covenant that the Lord made with the Israelites? (the tabernacle, the ark, the temple?) *1 Kings 8:21*

Lesson 8
1. Solomon prayed that David's descendants would inherit the throne of Israel. T/F. *1 Kings 8:25*
2. Solomon wanted God to hear the people's prayers and (bless, heal, forgive?) them. *1 Kings 8:30*

Lesson 9
1. Solomon told the assembly that God was faithful to the promise given through _____. *1 Kings 8:56*
2. Solomon wanted all earth's people to know that the Lord alone was God. T/F. *1 Kings 8:60*

Lesson 10
1. How many days did Jesus fast before he was tempted? (4, 14, 40?) *Matthew 4:2*
2. How many times did Satan tempt Jesus in the wilderness? (once, thrice, five times?) *Matthew 4:3-8*

Lesson 11
1. Jesus said to give openly to set a good example for others. T/F. *Matthew 6:3, 4*
2. When we pray in secret, the Father will openly _____ us. *Matthew 6:6*

Lesson 12
1. The Lord's prayer begins, "Our Father in heaven, _____ be your name." *Matthew 6:9*
2. What daily provision did Jesus say to pray for? (bread, wages, rent money?). *Matthew 6:13*

Lesson 13
1. What three words of Jesus create the acronym ASK? _____ *Luke 11:9*
2. Jesus used "how much more" logic when comparing what earthly fathers give with what the heavenly Father gives. T/F. *Luke 11:13*

QUARTER AT A GLANCE

by Jim Eichenberger

IN A COURTROOM, the judge is referred to as "Your *Honor.*" Chivalrous men vow to protect their ladies' *honor.* High-achieving students work to make the *honor* roll. At a small bed-and-breakfast, guests might find a basket of snacks and be trusted with paying on the *honor* system.

This English word is very old, with its first usage being traced to the thirteenth century. *Honor* means "fame earned," recognition based on merit. An appointed or elected jurist, a chaste person, an exceptional student, and trusted clientele gain a reputation by past behavior.

More than any human being, God has earned his fame. This quarter is designed to explore how the Bible teaches us to express honor to God. To do so, these lessons will focus on three studies from Scripture.

David and Mary Express Honor

In Shakespeare's *Julius Caesar,* Brutus defends the assassination of Caesar as a noble deed. Antony undercuts Brutus's credibility, sarcastically repeating, "For Brutus is an honorable man." Antony insists that the claim that Brutus was acting honorably when killing the ruler of Rome must be measured by Brutus's inner character.

People often honor God with their lips without their hearts being in it (Isaiah 29:13). Four lessons from 1 Chronicles 15–17 reveal that David's praise of God was not superficial or self-serving, but truly came from his heart. King Saul was *not* an honorable man and placed his own ambition before honoring God. One way this was shown was in how he all but ignored the ark of the covenant. In contrast, David made arrangements for moving the ark to Jerusalem and even expressed a desire to build it a permanent home.

In a song that rivals David's own for beauty, Mary celebrated being given the honor of becoming the Messiah's mother (Luke 1:47-55). True honor will always be an expression of inner character.

Solomon Creates a Place of Honor

Sometimes a specific place helps focus our expressions of honor. People of faith know that the essence of a departed loved one does not lie in a grave, yet we lay flowers at the grave site to honor that person's memory. Believers agree with Paul that our God "does not live in temples built by human hands" (Acts 17:24), yet we find a physical meeting place helpful for corporate worship.

The second unit in this quarter moves from focus on inner attitude to a physical structure. David was bothered that the symbolic presence of God was housed in a tent while David lived in luxury (1 Chronicles 17:1). Solomon fulfilled David's dream of building a temple. Solomon's words and actions at its dedication are explored in four lessons from 1 Kings 8. For years, the temple served as a focal point where God's people honored him.

Jesus Teaches Practices of Honor

On Flag Day, June 14, 1923, representatives of over 60 organizations met to write the United States' National Flag Code. The code standardized practices for treating the flag to honor the nation it represents. Honor can be expressed personally, in an arranged location, but also by specific observances that can be held anytime and anywhere.

> *True honor will always be an expression of inner character.*

The third unit in this quarter examines patterns Jesus established for honoring God. He showed us how to resist the temptation to give to others the honor that belongs to God alone, to reject superficial piety, and to pray with purpose and persistence.

This quarter's lessons encourage us to think more deeply about our relationship to God. We are *honor*-bound to do the *honor* of inviting him to be the guest of *honor* in our lives.

GET THE SETTING

by Christopher Cotten

PIETY. What comes to mind when you think of this word? In some contexts, it can refer to sincere religious devotion. But quite often in our increasingly secular culture, piety has a negative connotation: "She's so pious" likely implies that the person being spoken of is stuck-up, self-righteous, or even hypocritical.

Our focus for this quarter is on ways of honoring God through worship. In a variety of Old and New Testament texts, we will see manifestations of Israelite and early Christian piety. These lessons reveal a full exposition of the biblical notion of piety—by David's desire to build a temple, in the ceremonies presided over by Solomon when the temple was dedicated, through Mary's song celebrating God's great works, and within the teachings of Jesus about what constitutes acceptable worship. Yet this was not a concept that developed in a vacuum. Ancient understandings of piety help illuminate our understanding of the biblical teaching on this subject.

Greek and Roman Understandings

The pagan conception of piety consisted of duty to the gods. This definition was generally accepted but was also subject to questioning. In Plato's *Euthyphro*, Socrates (470–399 BC) seeks a definition of piety that is applicable to all of humanity. His dialogue partner, a man named Euthyphro, at one point suggests that piety is whatever is approved by the gods. Even so, repeated attempts to reach a precise definition failed, resulting in frustration.

For the Romans, the matter was clearer. Piety to them generally referred to performing all of one's religious obligations with care. Roman statesman Cicero (106–43 BC) defined piety as "justice toward the gods," noting also that "piety warns us to keep our obligations to our country or parents or other kin."

Perhaps there is no better example of ancient piety than Aeneas, the Trojan warrior who settled in the area that later became the city of Rome. Aeneas is remembered as being "pious" because of his devotion to his family and his people in seeking out a new homeland for them.

Piety in the Old Testament

The basis of piety in ancient Israel was the covenant between God and his people, mediated through the prophet Moses at Mount Sinai. There God created a people for himself (see Exodus 19:5, 6). The Law of Moses outlined for God's people a life of personal and communal holiness and purity. This was manifested through a range of sacrifices and worship practices. What piety meant for the Israelites was this: to keep covenant by obeying God's commandments. This quarter we will see some of the high points of Israel's piety and devotion to God.

Israel's relationship with God quite often strayed far from these high points of devotion. The prophets indicate that the people thought that simply performing the sacrifices and observing the annual festivals—apart from a life of holiness and devotion—was enough to keep them in God's favor.

Piety According to Jesus

By the time of Jesus, this same emphasis on performance of ritual had become associated with the sect of the Pharisees. But the motives were different. The rules and regulations advocated by the Pharisees were an attempt to put a hedge around the law. The piety that this mindset encouraged missed the mark and was heavily criticized by Jesus (Matthew 23). The Pharisees often paid attention to the external act of tithing without giving heed to the condition of the heart behind the tithe. Jesus calls for the two—the external act and the internal condition of the heart—to be one. In that unity we find the basis for the specific teachings of Jesus on prayer, giving, and fasting.

THIS QUARTER IN THE WORD

Answers to the Quarterly Quiz on page 114

Lesson 1—1. Levites. 2. Michal. Lesson 2—1. worship. 2. true.
Lesson 3—1. ark. 2. false. Lesson 4—1. false. 2. three months.
Lesson 5—1. Israel. 2. pray. Lesson 6—1. tent of meeting.
2. false. Lesson 7—1. David. 2. the ark. Lesson 8—1. true.
2. forgive. Lesson 9—1. Moses. 2. true. Lesson 10—1. 40.
2. thrice. Lesson 11—1. false. 2. reward. Lesson 12—1. hallowed. 2. bread. Lesson 13—1. ask/seek/knock. 2. true

FROM TEMPLE TO DYNASTY TO TEMPLE

PROMISED TO DAVID	FULFILLED IN CHRIST	ESTABLISHED IN YOU?
1000 BC	AD 30	AD 2020
1 CHRONICLES 17:9-14 ACTS 7:44-47	LUKE 1:69 ACTS 2:22-36	2 CORINTHIANS 6:16 1 PETER 2:4,5

Photos © iStockphoto by Getty Images

THE CROWN OF CREATION

Teacher Tips by Jim Eichenberger

THIS SERIES addresses an issue that you may have noticed in your congregation. While members may generally agree about religious practice, they are miles apart when it comes to godly thinking. How can a Bible study leader help a group develop a Christian worldview?

A Christian worldview is supported by certain pillars. One of those examines the nature of God, who created the universe out of nothing (*ex nihilo*). God is separate from all creation, the entity who loves his creatures.

A second pillar is that of our having been created in God's image (*imago dei*). Not only did God create everything out of nothing, he also chose to make one species of his creatures in his own image. We reflect the very nature of the Creator. This premise affects the way Christians think about all people.

Human Value Is Intrinsic, Not Extrinsic

Our fallen nature encourages us to associate with the "right people." We value other human beings based on how useful they can be to us. Extrinsic characteristics—strength, beauty, wealth, intelligence, and a host of skills—become the basis for human worth. But human value is "baked in" by God. People are precious because of the intrinsic characteristics present due to our being created in his image. Extrinsic differences of ethnicity, physical abilities or limitations, or social standing do not alter our inherent worth. Simply by being human, all people are the "right people"!

Humans Are Diamonds, Not Apples

The value of ripe fruit plummets as it begins to rot. Gemstones, in contrast, neither ripen nor spoil. The age of a diamond does not change its worth. Likewise, *imago dei* establishes that whether in the cradle or in a nursing home, a human being has great value. The luster of God's crown jewels is intended never to fade with age.

Humans Are Royalty, Not Slaves

We may keep a dog on a leash or a chicken in a coop. But doing the same with another person is abhorrent! From ancient times, conquering armies have justified enslaving the captured enemy. Nevertheless, this is not the natural state of humankind. All people are born to a state greater than servitude. Because we share the image of the king of the universe, we are born to rule (Genesis 1:26, 28), not to be repressed.

You can teach the principle of *imago dei* in nearly every Bible study. When studying the interaction between David and God in lessons 3 and 5, point out that David and his descendants were not chosen because of their physical size or military skills. David's deposed predecessor looked the part based on extrinsic values, but David was chosen for his intrinsic *imago dei* value (1 Samuel 9:2; 16:1-13).

Though common wisdom debates when a fetus "ripens" to become a person, the Bible does not. When Mary, pregnant with Jesus, visited Elizabeth, pregnant with John, the fruit of their wombs were *not* spoken of as "potential human life." Both mothers and their unborn sons are spoken of as fully human (lesson 4).

Throughout the Old Testament, God is introduced as the one who frees from slavery (example: Exodus 20:2). David's song of praise (lesson 2) readily recognized that God saves and delivers from potential conquerors. When Jesus taught his disciples to pray (lessons 11 and 12), he taught us to affirm that we are born of a royal Father in Heaven, who prepares us as part of his kingdom.

As a Bible teacher, you have no need to feel apprehensive speaking about social justice, affirming the sanctity of human life, and rejecting the evils of racism. These positions flow seamlessly from the second pillar of a biblical worldview. Such views should unify and never divide the people of God.

DAVID'S WORSHIP

DEVOTIONAL READING: 1 Chronicles 16:7-13, 28-33
BACKGROUND SCRIPTURE: 2 Samuel 6:12-16; 1 Chronicles 15

1 CHRONICLES 15:1-3, 14-16, 25-29A

[1] After David had constructed buildings for himself in the City of David, he prepared a place for the ark of God and pitched a tent for it. [2] Then David said, "No one but the Levites may carry the ark of God, because the LORD chose them to carry the ark of the LORD and to minister before him forever."

[3] David assembled all Israel in Jerusalem to bring up the ark of the LORD to the place he had prepared for it.

. . . .

[14] So the priests and Levites consecrated themselves in order to bring up the ark of the LORD, the God of Israel. [15] And the Levites carried the ark of God with the poles on their shoulders, as Moses had commanded in accordance with the word of the LORD.

[16] David told the leaders of the Levites to appoint their fellow Levites as musicians to make a joyful sound with musical instruments: lyres, harps and cymbals.

. . . .

[25] So David and the elders of Israel and the commanders of units of a thousand went to bring up the ark of the covenant of the LORD from the house of Obed-Edom, with rejoicing. [26] Because God had helped the Levites who were carrying the ark of the covenant of the LORD, seven bulls and seven rams were sacrificed. [27] Now David was clothed in a robe of fine linen, as were all the Levites who were carrying the ark, and as were the musicians, and Kenaniah, who was in charge of the singing of the choirs. David also wore a linen ephod. [28] So all Israel brought up the ark of the covenant of the LORD with shouts, with the sounding of rams' horns and trumpets, and of cymbals, and the playing of lyres and harps.

[29a] As the ark of the covenant of the LORD was entering the City of David, Michal daughter of Saul watched from a window. And . . . she saw King David dancing.

KEY VERSE

All Israel brought up the ark of the covenant of the LORD with shouts, with the sounding of rams' horns and trumpets, and of cymbals, and the playing of lyres and harps. —**1 Chronicles 15:28**

HONORING
GOD

Unit 1: David Honors God

LESSONS 1–5

LESSON AIMS

After participating in this lesson, each learner will be able to:

1. Describe the steps taken by David to bring the ark of the covenant to Jerusalem.

2. Tell how taking the time to prepare for this time of worship enhanced Israel's experience of the occasion.

3. List one specific way that he or she can better prepare for worship and make a plan to do so.

LESSON OUTLINE

Introduction
  A. "In Tents" Worship
  B. Lesson Context
I. Preparations (1 CHRONICLES 15:1-3, 14-16)
  A. Creating a Place (v. 1)
  B. Carrying the Ark (vv. 2, 3, 14, 15)
    Warning!
  C. Conducting Worship (v. 16)
II. Ceremony (1 CHRONICLES 15:25-29a)
  A. A Time of Joy (v. 25)
  B. A Time to Sacrifice (v. 26)
  C. A Time to Worship (vv. 27-29a)
    Riding High
Conclusion
  A. Intent on Worship
  B. Prayer
  C. Thought to Remember

Introduction

A. "In Tents" Worship

Several years ago, the college where I was teaching broke ground in preparation for a new building that would house, among other things, an auditorium to be used for weekly chapel services. During the time the building was under construction, the services were held outdoors under tents that had been set up in a parking area across from the main campus. On one occasion, the school's president commented that the worship on campus had become much more "in tents" (pun intended!).

B. Lesson Context

Four of the five lessons in this unit address David's worship life as recorded in 1 Chronicles. The books of 1 and 2 Chronicles (treated as one book in Hebrew texts) appear to be among the final Old Testament books written, most likely in the latter half of the fifth century BC.

Though authorship is uncertain, themes and writing style suggest that the author could be Ezra. This noted scribe and teacher of God's law ministered to the exiles who returned to Jerusalem from captivity in Babylon (Ezra 7:6, 10). However, events that took place after Ezra's death are included in the text, making clear that even if Ezra began the work, he did not write its final words. For this reason, scholars most often refer to the writer simply as the Chronicler.

Most of the first volume covers the reign of King David over Israel from 1010 to 970 BC (1 Chronicles 10:14–29:30). Much of this is material found within other books of the Old Testament, especially 1 and 2 Samuel. So why were 1 and 2 Chronicles written? In short, because the people's situation had changed along with their needs; they desired new histories that emphasized God's care following the exile, a theme that was unnecessary for historians writing earlier.

Interestingly, the title of Chronicles in the old Greek version (the Septuagint) is translated "things omitted" or "things passed over." This fact may speak to an ancient viewpoint regarding why the books were written.

By the time the books were completed, some 100 years had passed since the return of God's people from captivity in 538 BC. The temple in Jerusalem had been rebuilt (Ezra 1:7-11; 6:13-18), and the wall around the city had been completed under Nehemiah's leadership (Nehemiah 6:15, 16).

However, many prophecies of Jerusalem's greatness and of God's special blessing had not been fulfilled. These included the establishment of a new covenant (Jeremiah 31:31-34) and the rise of a king reminiscent of David (Jeremiah 33:15; Ezekiel 37:24). In fact, God's people remained under the control of Persia. Many Jews likely expressed doubt and frustration at the uncertainty of their status as a nation.

The Chronicler reassured members of the postexilic community that they had not been abandoned and that they were very much a part of God's sovereign plan. God required and rewarded their obedience (2 Chronicles 17:1-6; 29:1, 2; 31:20, 21; 34:1, 2, 33; contrast 1 Chronicles 21:7; 2 Chronicles 20:35-37; 32:31; 35:21-24).

The Chronicler emphasizes David's obedience (1 Chronicles 14:2, 10, 16; 18:14; 21:19; etc.). That king's passion for finding a proper place for the ark of the covenant, the sacred symbol of God's presence with his covenant people, showed David's dedication to God and his people.

The record of David's reign focuses on the strengthening of his kingdom (1 Chronicles 11–12; 14; 18–20) and encouraging worship

HOW TO SAY IT

Abinadab	Uh-*bin*-uh-dab.
Abiathar	Ah-*bye*-uh-thar.
Asaph	*Ay*-saff.
Kenaniah	Ken-uh-*nee*-nah.
Heman	*Hay*-man.
Kiriath Jearim	*Kir*-ih-ath *Jee*-uh-rim.
Levites	*Lee*-vites.
Obed-Edom	O-bed-*Ee*-dum.
Philistines	Fuh-*liss*-teenz or *Fill*-us-teenz.
Septuagint	Sep-*too*-ih-jent.
Uzzah	*Uz*-zuh.
Zadok	*Zay*-dok.

within it (13:1-14; 15–17; 21–29). Of special importance to this lesson, David had already attempted to bring the ark of the covenant to Jerusalem. The ark had been placed on a cart and carried from the house of Abinadab in Kiriath Jearim (a little more than 10 miles west of Jerusalem), the place where it had been kept since the time of Samuel (1 Samuel 7:1, 2).

During the joyous procession, the oxen hitched to the cart stumbled. Concerned that the ark might be damaged, a man named Uzzah reached out and touched the ark to steady it. Immediately he fell dead. David's initial reaction to the death was one of great dismay and fear (1 Chronicles 13). How, he wondered, would he ever move the ark to Jerusalem?

I. Preparations
(1 Chronicles 15:1-3, 14-16)
A. Creating a Place (v. 1)

1. After David had constructed buildings for himself in the City of David, he prepared a place for the ark of God and pitched a tent for it.

The City of David is Jerusalem, which David conquered not long after becoming king (1 Chronicles 11:4-9; 14:1). Joab, leader of the army, assisted with building activity (11:6, 8). Rebuilding a captured city is standard procedure in David's time, especially when the newly acquired city is to become the king's new capital.

> *What Do You Think?*
> What are some ways to show respect for a church building without seeing it as God's temple?
> *Digging Deeper*
> How do Exodus 25–27 and 1 Corinthians 3:16, 17; 6:19 help you identify principles of tabernacle maintenance that are appropriate to apply to us as temples of the Holy Spirit?

David intends to do more than make Jerusalem a political capital or a city for his own personal enjoyment. He desires for Jerusalem to become the residence for the *ark of God* in the *tent* that he will provide for it. The ark of the covenant was fashioned under Moses' supervision as part of the construction of the tabernacle (Exodus 25:10-22). It represents God's dwelling place on earth and symbolically his presence with his covenant people, Israel (Exodus 25:16-22; Leviticus 16:2; Numbers 10:35, 36; 1 Chronicles 28:2; etc.). The tent in Jerusalem is not to be confused with the tabernacle of Moses, which remained at Gibeon during David's reign (see 1 Chronicles 16:39; 21:29).

B. Carrying the Ark (vv. 2, 3, 14, 15)

2. Then David said, "No one but the Levites may carry the ark of God, because the LORD chose them to carry the ark of the LORD and to minister before him forever."

When David had first attempted to bring *the ark* of the covenant to Jerusalem, the results were disastrous (see Lesson Context). Before a second attempt, David realized that the ark had not been carried in the manner prescribed by the Law of Moses: using poles inserted in the rings attached to the ark at the corners of its base (Exodus 25:10-16).

No text specifies that Uzzah was a Levite, which likely means the ark was transported by unauthorized individuals. Only *the Levites*, and specifically those descended from Levi's son Kohath, were chosen to be "responsible for the care of the sanctuary" (Numbers 3:32; see 3:17, 27-31; 4:1-6, 15; 7:9).

Forever in this case conveys the idea of "for all time to come until its purpose has been served." For as long as the ark of the covenant was present and needed to be moved, only the Levites were to do so. Today, this injunction is no longer needed because of the establishment of the better, new covenant (Hebrews 7:11-28; 9:1-15; 10:11-18; contrast Revelation 11:19).

❧ WARNING! ❧

Many product manufacturers place warning labels on merchandise to caution users not to use them improperly. This seems to be a logical precaution. But some warnings can be downright silly!

A steam iron once included the caution, "Never iron clothes on the body." The makers of a popular brand of sunglasses thought it prudent to warn, "It is not suitable for driving under conditions of poor light." To the true do-it-yourselfer, makers of a certain rotary tool advised, "This product is not intended for use as a dental drill." And would you be surprised to be warned that pepper spray "may irritate eyes"?

A warning label on the ark of the covenant could have been, "Can be moved only in the manner prescribed by the Law of Moses." This should have been as obvious to David as instructions to open a package before eating the peanuts within it! Are you ignoring any "warning labels" from God?   —J. E.

3. David assembled all Israel in Jerusalem to bring up the ark of the Lord to the place he had prepared for it.

David repeats the steps he had taken earlier *to bring up the ark* to Jerusalem (1 Chronicles 13:5, 6). This time, however, the Levites alone are permitted to carry the ark. The entire nation is invited to witness this momentous event, and citizens from all 12 tribes undoubtedly are present.

First Chronicles 15:4-13 records the names of six leaders among the Levites and the number of fellow Levites under their direction who serve on this occasion. David addresses these leaders along with two priests, Zadok and Abiathar (1 Chronicles 15:11, not in today's text). He charges them to consecrate themselves so they can carry out their God-appointed responsibility to transport the ark (15:12).

14. So the priests and Levites consecrated themselves in order to bring up the ark of the LORD, the God of Israel.

The priests and Levites comply with David's directions (compare 1 Chronicles 15:12, not in today's text). To be *consecrated* means to set apart someone or some object for a sacred purpose. The priests probably follow the guidelines for purification given to Moses (Exodus 19:10, 15; 29:1-37; Numbers 8:5-19). Such careful steps had not been taken the first time the ark was transported (compare 1 Chronicles 13); in fact, the focus there had been on what seemed right to the people (1 Chronicles 13:2-4).

15. And the Levites carried the ark of God with the poles on their shoulders, as Moses had commanded in accordance with the word of the LORD.

This verse highlights that authorized *Levites* are carrying the *ark* (see commentary on 1 Chronicles 15:2). The ark is conveyed on the Levites' *shoulders*, using *poles* as *the Lord* had said (compare Numbers 7:9). These poles are inserted into the rings at the corners of the ark so that it can be lifted and carried without touching it (Exodus 25:13-15). Those responsible for the ark fulfill their sacred duty according to what *Moses had commanded*. Everything is done *in accordance with the word of the Lord* to Moses concerning how the ark is to be moved.

C. Conducting Worship (v. 16)

16. David told the leaders of the Levites to appoint their fellow Levites as musicians to make a joyful sound with musical instruments: lyres, harps and cymbals.

David probably speaks to the six Levites named earlier (1 Chronicles 15:11, not in today's text). These men are to *appoint their fellow Levites* to lead in the worship that accompanies the ark's journey and arrival in Jerusalem. Some will be responsible for singing songs of joy; others will accompany them using the *instruments* noted. Clearly, David intends this to be a festive occasion!

The verses that follow record the names of those individuals appointed for the worship duties (1 Chronicles 15:17-24, not in today's text). Some names appear elsewhere in Scripture, most notably in connection with their authorship of certain psalms (Asaph of Psalms 50; 73–83 and Heman of Psalm 88).

II. Ceremony
(1 CHRONICLES 15:25-29a)
A. A Time of Joy (v. 25)

25. So David and the elders of Israel and the commanders of units of a thousand went to bring up the ark of the covenant of the LORD from the house of Obed-Edom, with rejoicing.

The ark had been taken to *the house of Obed-Edom* after the death of Uzzah and remained there for three months (1 Chronicles 13:13, 14). This second, successful endeavor to move the ark includes not only the aforementioned Levites but also *the elders of Israel* and the military leaders of the nation. They too are to share in the joy of this special day.

B. A Time to Sacrifice (v. 26)

26. Because God had helped the Levites who were carrying the ark of the covenant of the LORD, seven bulls and seven rams were sacrificed.

A consistent and prominent theme throughout both 1 and 2 Chronicles is that *God blesses obedience and punishes disobedience* (see Lesson Context). The Lord's directions are followed in this second endeavor (see commentary

Visual for Lesson 1. *Point to this visual as you ask how a shout or other verbal expression reveals the joy that worship can spark in our hearts.*

on 1 Chronicles 15:2, 14, 15). Because *the Levites* have obeyed God, he helps them. This point provides a stark contrast of the present effort with the failed first attempt.

Once the ark has been placed in the tent provided for it in Jerusalem, "burnt offerings and fellowships offerings" are to be offered there (1 Chronicles 16:1; compare 2 Samuel 6:13). The sacrifices likely are meant to express the Levites' gratitude for the Lord's help and for allowing them to be part of this sacred procession.

> **What Do You Think?**
> What one or two procedures can your church implement to convey that the offering time is itself a significant act of corporate worship?
>
> **Digging Deeper**
> What's the single most important thing your church can do to honor both monetary and nonmonetary sacrifices appropriately?

C. A Time to Worship (vv. 27-29a)

27. Now David was clothed in a robe of fine linen, as were all the Levites who were carrying the ark, and as were the musicians, and Kenaniah, who was in charge of the singing of the choirs. David also wore a linen ephod.

David has no intention of being a mere spectator for this event. He desires to express his own joy on this occasion. He dresses not in royal garments but instead in clothes like the *Levites* and *musicians*. The Levite *Kenaniah* leads the singing because of his great skill (compare 1 Chronicles 15:22).

David wears *a robe of fine linen* and *a linen ephod*, which are both associated with the priesthood (Exodus 39:27-29; 1 Samuel 2:18; 22:18). This ephod is a vest or apron-like garment worn over the chest. The high priest wears a special kind of ephod (Exodus 28:15-30), though a more generic ephod is not forbidden to the general population.

David's choice of clothing suggests that he views himself as fulfilling a priestly rather than political or military role. Some see King David's being dressed in priestly attire as foreshadowing the greater Son of David, who will combine the roles of priest and king (compare Genesis 14:18 and Hebrews 5:6).

❧ RIDING HIGH ❧

We often speak of degrees of power in terms of elevation: *upper* management, *higher* authority, the *top* dog, etc. Throughout history, these figurative designations became very literal when transporting an important ruler. A litter was basically a seat attached to poles. The poles rested on the shoulders of servants.

In ancient India, this type of vehicle was called a palanquin. The palanquins of rulers were rectangular wooden boxes. Their windows and doors were screened by curtains or shutters, and their interiors were lavishly furnished and ornamented. In Korea, similar litters were called *gamas*. This type of royal transport was enthusiastically adopted by European rulers and is often known as a sedan chair.

In Egypt, the people of Israel may have seen the pharaohs carried in such an elevated fashion. They would have recognized the imagery of the Levites bearing the ark of the covenant on their shoulders. They transported the very throne of the true king of Israel, Yahweh himself. How do you lift God up as your true king?   —J. E.

28. So all Israel brought up the ark of the covenant of the LORD with shouts, with the

sounding of rams' horns and trumpets, and of cymbals, and the playing of lyres and harps.

A similar description accompanied the first attempt to transport *the ark of the covenant* (1 Chronicles 13:8). Unlike that trip, this occasion does not dissolve into fear but continues in a vein of praise and thanksgiving to *the Lord. All Israel* joins with the leaders already listed in a show of unified worship to the Lord.

29a. As the ark of the covenant of the LORD was entering the City of David, Michal daughter of Saul watched from a window. And . . . she saw King David dancing.

There is, however, one exception to the rejoicing that fills the day's activities. *Michal daughter of Saul* has opted not to attend the festivities; her choice is to be a bystander, watching all the proceedings from her *window.*

Michal is David's wife (1 Samuel 18:27), but she is not referred to that way here. The designation as daughter of Saul associates her more closely with her father's faithlessness than with her husband's faithfulness (compare 1 Samuel 15:10, 11; 19:11-16). King Saul, David's predecessor, had shown little interest in *the ark of the covenant.* Only once did Saul pay any attention to it, and in that case he treated it merely as an object to consult during a time of war (1 Samuel 14:16-23; compare chapter 4). Saul seemed oblivious to its spiritual significance.

Saul clearly did not have the passion for spiritual matters that David possesses (1 Chronicles 10:13, 14). David commented on Saul's neglect during the first effort to carry the ark to Jerusalem (13:3). It appears that the same level of apathy is shared by his daughter. Her attitude is a clear contrast to David's enthusiastic *dancing* as an expression of his worship.

Conclusion
A. Intent on Worship

King David fulfilled his "in-tent" to establish a place for the ark of the covenant in Jerusalem. The ceremony during which the ark was carried to its new home was an occasion of great celebration and worship in which David himself participated with enthusiasm. The experience was indeed *intense!*

A significant amount of preparation went into finally bringing the ark of the covenant to Jerusalem. This task was not handled in a shoddy, careless manner. David's concern for conveying the ark properly brings to mind Paul's admonition to the Corinthians that their worship "be done in a fitting and orderly way" (1 Corinthians 14:40). David made sure the Levites carried the ark in the manner prescribed by the Law of Moses. The king also appointed individuals to supervise the various expressions of worship that would accompany bringing the ark into the city. Such a sacred object, and more importantly the God whose presence it represented, deserved the utmost care.

We do not have an ark or other sacred object to carry to a designated place. However, the New Testament indicates that Christians are sacred objects because God's Spirit dwells among us (1 Corinthians 3:16). So, what can we do to prepare our temples for worship (6:19, 20)? How can we prepare to bring our best to God when we gather for worship? What can we do to foster a frame of mind that contributes to worship instead of distracting from it? The old adage, "You get out of something what you put into it" applies to worship. How much do we really "put into" worship?

B. Prayer

Father, as temples of your Holy Spirit, may we worship and draw others to worship you through even the most mundane tasks that we carry out. May every day thus become a day of worship. We pray in Jesus' name. Amen.

C. Thought to Remember

Our weekly worship should not be entered into weakly.

VISUALS FOR THESE LESSONS

The visual pictured in each lesson (example: page 126) is a small reproduction of a large, full-color poster included in the *Adult Resources* packet for the Winter Quarter. That packet also contains the very useful *Presentation Tools* CD for teacher use. Order No. 2629120 from your supplier.

INVOLVEMENT LEARNING

Enhance your lesson with NIV Bible Student (from your curriculum supplier) and the reproducible activity page (at www.standardlesson.com or in the back of the NIV Standard Lesson Commentary Deluxe Edition*).*

Into the Lesson

Ask participants to imagine that a new classroom is being constructed for your group. Your class is to move items from your existing classroom to this new room. Jot ideas on the board as the class brainstorms things to do to complete this undertaking. Expect possible responses of collecting boxes for packing, finding carts or dollies to move furniture, deciding how to arrange the new room, etc. Follow up by asking learners to consider how long this process will take and what the sequence should be.

Alternative. Distribute copies of the "Making a Move" exercise from the activity page, which you can download. Have students work in pairs to complete this very difficult matching quiz.

After either activity say, "Whether we are moving the contents of one room into another or moving a household across the country, we need to prepare for the task to do it properly. We may be surprised to know that King David has something to teach us in this regard."

Into the Word

Divide the class in half, designating them the **Initial-Move Group** and the **Final-Move Group**. Task each group to prepare a skit in which David is interviewed after a movement of the ark per 1 Chronicles 13 (Initial-Move Group) and 1 Chronicle 15 (Final-Move Group). Distribute handouts (you prepare) with the following questions to be asked of each group's "David": 1–Why did you think that moving the ark of the covenant was important? 2–What plans did you make to move the ark? 3–How did the move go overall?

Stress that this is just the skeletal framework of the skits. Learners should be free to ad lib with follow-up questions.

For the **Initial-Move Group,** expect interview responses along these lines: 1–Since the ark was not given the respect it deserved during the reign of Saul, it needed to be moved to Jerusalem (13:3). 2–I, David, consulted the people and they agreed that it was a good idea to move the ark (13:4). We found a new oxcart and loaded the ark on it (13:7). 3–The move ended in loss of life! The Lord struck Uzzah dead after that man touched the ark to steady it when the oxen stumbled. I was afraid to move it again (13:10-13).

For the **Final-Move Group,** expect interview responses along these lines: 1–With other buildings finished and a tent constructed for the ark, it was time to move it to Jerusalem (15:1). 2–I, David, was impulsive on my first attempt to move the ark. This time, I ensured that the ark was moved by Levites (1 Chronicles 15:2). 3–What a tremendous success! The accompanying worship, characterized by music and sacrifices, could not have gone better (15:26-28).

Alternative. Distribute copies of the "David's Moving Plans" exercise from the activity page. Use the five lines with the scrambled words as outline points for further discussion.

Into Life

Write the following on the board as a possible outline of a personal worship plan:

I. **Before worship**
    A. *Plan for a "moving" experience.*
    B. *Have a clear "in-tent."*
II. **During worship**
    A. *Lift him high!*
    B. *Celebrate and sacrifice.*

Point to this outline as you pose one or more of the following questions for discussion: 1–What can we do to make our worship experience more powerful? 2–What are some needed preparations before worship? 3–How can we ensure that worship is truly uplifting for all as it exalts God? 4–What can we do to keep worship joyful yet reverent? (Note: allow discussion on one question before posing the next.) Close in prayer, asking for God's help in efforts to honor him in worship.

DAVID'S
GRATITUDE

DEVOTIONAL READING: Deuteronomy 26:1-11
BACKGROUND SCRIPTURE: 1 Chronicles 16:7-36

1 CHRONICLES 16:8-12, 28-36

8 Give praise to the LORD, proclaim his
   name;
   make known among the nations what
     he has done.
9 Sing to him, sing praise to him;
   tell of all his wonderful acts.
10 Glory in his holy name;
   let the hearts of those who seek the
     LORD rejoice.
11 Look to the LORD and his strength;
   seek his face always.
12 Remember the wonders he has done,
   his miracles, and the judgments he
     pronounced,

· ·

28 Ascribe to the LORD, all you families of
   nations,
   ascribe to the LORD glory and strength.
29 Ascribe to the LORD the glory due his
   name;
   bring an offering and come before him.
Worship the LORD in the splendor of his
   holiness.

30 Tremble before him, all the earth!
   The world is firmly established; it can-
     not be moved.
31 Let the heavens rejoice, let the earth be
   glad;
   let them say among the nations, "The
     LORD reigns!"
32 Let the sea resound, and all that is in it;
   let the fields be jubilant, and everything
     in them!
33 Let the trees of the forest sing,
   let them sing for joy before the LORD,
   for he comes to judge the earth.
34 Give thanks to the LORD, for he is good;
   his love endures forever.
35 Cry out, "Save us, God our Savior;
   gather us and deliver us from the
     nations
   that we may give thanks to your holy name,
   and glory in your praise."
36 Praise be to the LORD, the God of Israel,
   from everlasting to everlasting.
  Then all the people said "Amen" and "Praise
the LORD."

KEY VERSE

Give praise to the LORD, proclaim his name; make known among the nations what he has done.
—1 Chronicles 16:8

· 129

HONORING
GOD

Unit 1: David Honors God

LESSONS 1–5

LESSON AIMS

After participating in this lesson, each learner will be able to:

1. Tell why much of the text is in the nature of a psalm.

2. Explain how David's gratitude is reflected in the imperatives give, sing, remember, etc.

3. Identify one of those imperatives most lacking in his or her worship and make a plan for improvement.

LESSON OUTLINE

Introduction
   A. "The King of . . ."
   B. Lesson Context
   I. Call to Worship (1 CHRONICLES 16:8-12)
   A. Praise the Lord (vv. 8-10a)
   B. Seek the Lord (vv. 10b, 11)
      Facial Recognition
   C. Remember His Works (v. 12)
   II. Call Extended (1 CHRONICLES 16:28-33)
   A. To the Nations (vv. 28, 29)
   B. To All Nature (vv. 30-33)
      All Nature Sings
   III. Call Concluded (1 CHRONICLES 16:34-36)
   A. Repeated Praise (v. 34)
   B. Request for Deliverance (v. 35)
   C. Response of Praise (v. 36)
Conclusion
   A. Eyes of Gratitude
   B. Prayer
   C. Thought to Remember

Introduction

A. "The King of . . ."

Even though we may not live under a monarchy, the word *king* is still an important part of our vocabulary. We often use it to signify that someone or something is the best in its category. In baseball the pitcher who leads the major league in strikeouts is termed the Strikeout King, and the leader in home runs is called the Home Run King. NASCAR driver Richard Petty became known as simply the King because of his accomplishments in the sport.

In music, Elvis Presley is generally given the title of King of Rock and Roll, while Michael Jackson receives the accolade of King of Pop. Fans of the genre would likely disagree over who the King of Country is, depending on their preference for older or more contemporary versions.

If one were to create a title such as "King of Psalms," there is no question who would be the recipient of that honor; it would have to be given to King David. It is he who became known as the "sweet psalmist of Israel" (2 Samuel 23:1, King James Version). If David were to be offered such an honor, he most likely would refuse to accept it because his music was devoted to the praises of a far greater king: the Lord God of Israel. Whatever talent David possessed, he recognized it as being a gift from that same God.

B. Lesson Context

Today's lesson text closely follows the passage covered last week. There David brought the ark of the covenant to Jerusalem amidst great celebration and joy (see 1 Chronicles 15; lesson 1). After the ark was placed inside the tent that David had provided for it, burnt offerings and fellowship offerings were sacrificed (16:1). These expressions of worship were needed following the first attempt to transport the ark (see chapter 13). Likely they were partly given in repentance for the previous flippant attitude toward transporting the ark; partly they were offered undoubtedly to thank God for restoring and repairing their relationship with him.

A burnt offering was completely consumed

on the altar, signifying the worshipper's complete devotion to the Lord. Fellowship offerings were given with a desire to establish fellowship or communion between the worshipper and the Lord. They included a shared meal among the worshippers. On this occasion, David blessed the worshippers, then provided each one with food for their meal (1 Chronicles 16:2, 3).

David then appointed some of the Levites "to minister before the ark of the Lord" (1 Chronicles 16:4). That ministry was to focus primarily on leading the people in worship, specifically in the area of music. David desired to show utmost reverence toward the sacred space associated with the ark of the covenant. He assigned specific individuals to play certain instruments and even appointed two priests, Benaiah and Jahaziel, to sound trumpets regularly before the ark (16:4-6).

Chief among the men appointed by David for these sacred tasks was Asaph, who had already assisted in bringing the ark to Jerusalem (1 Chronicles 15:17). Asaph's authorship of certain psalms was noted in last week's study (see lesson 1 commentary on 1 Chronicles 15:16). David commissioned a special psalm of thanksgiving for Asaph for use on this important day and then for use in any future occasions of celebration and praise (16:7). David did not want Asaph to sing a solo or lead a professional chorus. Instead, this appears to have been an opportunity to teach the people a new worship song.

The resulting psalm contains sections that are similar to three psalms found in the book of Psalms (compare 1 Chronicles 16:8-22 to Psalm 105:1-15; 1 Chronicles 16:23-33 to Psalm 96; and 1 Chronicles 16:34-36 to Psalm 106:1, 47, 48). None of these three psalms are credited to David, nor is the psalm in 1 Chronicles 16 specifically attributed to him. He could have commissioned another writer to provide a psalm for Asaph (1 Chronicles 16:7). David, whose heavy involvement in this ceremony has already been noted, also could easily have composed a psalm for this occasion. The new song called attention to the Lord's goodness to his people throughout their history. It also challenged his people to give God the glory due his great name.

I. Call to Worship
(1 CHRONICLES 16:8-12)
A. Praise the Lord (vv. 8-10a)

8. Give praise to the LORD, proclaim his name; make known among the nations what he has done.

Not only does David desire that all of God's people engage in giving *praise to the Lord,* he also intends for *the nations* to hear about what the Lord *has done* (see 1 Chronicles 16:19-27).

9. Sing to him, sing praise to him; tell of all his wonderful acts.

The exhortation continues with the command to *sing praise* to the Lord. As in the previous verse, the worship of the Lord is not always meant to be private. The worshipper is to *tell* of the Lord's *wonderful acts.*

The world could use more talk about the Lord. Such conversations include telling *all* of what God has done in creation and the history of his people. We should also share personal testimonies about his work in our lives as David models elsewhere (Psalms 19, 30, 34, 63, 142, etc.). Christians have a greater story to share than David knew: we tell of Jesus' mighty work for all the nations (Matthew 28:18-20; Ephesians 2:11-22; Hebrews 11:32-40; Revelation 15:3, 4; etc.).

> *What Do You Think?*
> What are some of God's wonderful works we can and should proclaim in worship services?
> *Digging Deeper*
> In what ways have you found memory and proclamation of God's work to be connected to your own moral behavior?

10a. Glory in his holy name;

The Hebrew word *hallelujah* is translated here as *glory.* The *holy name* of the Lord is ample reason to glorify him. In a biblical context, one's name is associated with the person's character or reputation (Exodus 20:7; Proverbs 22:1). The name of the Lord is truly above all names, for his character and reputation are far superior to any possible rival (Exodus 3:14, 15; Psalms 8:1, 9; 20:1, 5, 7; etc.; compare Philippians 2:9-11).

B. Seek the Lord (vv. 10b, 11)

10b. let the hearts of those who seek the LORD rejoice.

Today, the heart is connected primarily to romantic affections. Throughout the Old Testament, the word *heart* often indicates the inner person that is home to one's deepest desires (Genesis 6:5; Exodus 4:21; 35:21; etc.). For one's heart to *rejoice* shows that the heart is pursuing or has found what it most wants.

The discipline of seeking the Lord is found throughout the Old Testament (Deuteronomy 4:29; 1 Chronicles 22:19; 2 Chronicles 14:2-4; Isaiah 55:6; Jeremiah 29:13). The Psalms regularly admonish worshippers to *seek the Lord* (Psalms 9:10; 24:6; 27:8; etc.). The people do not seek someone who intends to stay hidden. God has revealed himself in many ways throughout history (Hebrews 1:1, 2). This seeking is an unending though fruitful quest on earth (1 Corinthians 13:9-12). Our search will be completed when we are with the Lord for eternity (Revelation 21:3).

11. Look to the LORD and his strength; seek his face always.

The Israelites may be tempted to *look* for strength by the worship of foreign gods (Exodus 32:1; Numbers 25:1-3; 1 Kings 18:18-40) or by forming treaties with other nations (Exodus 34:12, 15; Joshua 9:3-15; 2 Chronicles 35:20-24). Instead of trusting God, the Israelites may be tempted to put their trust in a mighty military (Judges 7:1-8; 1 Samuel 8:10-12; 1 Kings 22:1-39) or by using oppressive economic practices to make them secure in wealth (Isaiah 10:1, 2; Amos 2:6, 7; 8:4-6). Instead of relying on these worldly sources of power, David exhorts the people to seek God's *strength* (compare 1 Samuel 2:10; Isaiah 45:24).

HOW TO SAY IT

Asaph	*Ay*-saff.
Benaiah	Be-*nay*-juh.
Jahaziel	Juh-*hay*-zuh-el.
Levites	*Lee*-vites.
Uzza(h)	*Uz*-zuh.

To *seek* the Lord's *face always* suggests that a person should strive to know him well. Moses is described as someone "whom the Lord knew face to face" (Deuteronomy 34:10). Yet, not even Moses was permitted to see the face of the Lord in the sense of viewing his glory directly (Exodus 33:18-20). Jesus later tells his disciples that seeing him is seeing God (John 12:44; 14:7, 9; compare Colossians 1:15-20). The climax of seeking the Lord's face will be seeing him face-to-face in the New Jerusalem (Revelation 22:4).

❧ FACIAL RECOGNITION ❧

Specialized computer applications identify a person by examining his or her face. In the mid-1960s, programmers Woody Bledsoe, Helen Chan, and Charles Bisson used computers to select from a database a small group of faces that most nearly resembled the face in a photo. As one might expect, results changed when photos varied by lighting, camera angle, and even facial expression of the subject.

Nevertheless, the technology continued to improve. Today, an algorithm analyzes the position, size, and shape of the subject's eyes, nose, cheekbones, and jaw. By looking at specific characteristics, the program can seek the face of a person with increasing accuracy.

A common command in Scripture is to use "facial recognition" of a sort to know God! How are you growing in your recognition of God's face?

—J. E.

C. Remember His Works (v. 12)

12. Remember the wonders he has done, his miracles, and the judgments he pronounced.

The exhortation to *remember* the Lord is common in the Old Testament (examples: Deuteronomy 8:2, 18; Ecclesiastes 12:1). His people tend to forget him without constant reminders (Deuteronomy 32:7-9, 18; Judges 3:7; 1 Samuel 12:9-15; compare 1 Corinthians 11:20-29). If we remember *the wonders he has done* and *his miracles,* we will be less apt to act unfaithfully.

The judgments of the Lord refer to more than judicial decisions and can be translated "justice" (Deuteronomy 16:19; 2 Samuel 15:6; etc.). The

Hebrew word can refer to the principles and commandments he has given his covenant people to live by (Exodus 21:1; Deuteronomy 4:14; etc.). For the people to have received such judgments from the Lord is just as much a sacred privilege as having witnessed his wonders (Psalm 147:20).

First Chronicles 16:13-27 (not included in today's text) highlights the Lord's works on behalf of his covenant people—works they should remember. Also included are exhortations to sing to the Lord and to speak of his great works to other peoples (1 Chronicles 16:23, 24).

II. Call Extended
(1 Chronicles 16:28-33)
A. To the Nations (vv. 28, 29)

28. Ascribe to the Lord, all you families of nations, ascribe to the Lord glory and strength.

God has always had a plan to provide salvation for the *families of nations*. Within the Old Testament, in which the nation of Israel is God's "treasured possession" (Exodus 19:5), there are hints of his intention to bless all the nations in the entire world (Genesis 3:15; 22:18; Isaiah 2:2; 11:9; Micah 4:1; etc.). Jesus fulfills that plan (2 Corinthians 5:17-19; Colossians 1:21-23). It will come to full fruition in Heaven, where the righteous "from every nation, tribe, people and language" will find their home (Revelation 7:9).

29. Ascribe to the Lord the glory due his name; bring an offering and come before him. Worship the Lord in the splendor of his holiness.

True worship is expressed in more than words. It must include action, specifically *an offering* (Leviticus 7:29; 9:7; 22:29; contrast Psalm 51:17; Micah 6:6-8). Such an offering could be an animal, raw grains or other produce, fruits and grains already prepared as food and drink, or other valuable goods (Exodus 25:21-29; Leviticus 2; 22:21; 23:13, 18, 37; etc.). The most important feature of an offering is the excellence of the gift—so good as to be perfect (example: Leviticus 3:6).

One should keep in mind the historical backdrop of this psalm: proper transportation of the ark of the covenant following an improper attempt (1 Chronicles 13, 15)—an attempt that was unholy in manner. The quality of *holiness* is central to God's character (Joshua 24:19; 1 Samuel 2:2; etc.). To worship in *the splendor of his holiness* means not only being aware of God's holiness but also approaching him as his holy people (1 Peter 1:15, 16). This can happen only as we obey him. God desires that his covenant people live holy lives. Christians must understand that this is the primary reason God has given us his Holy Spirit (1 Thessalonians 4:7, 8; compare Hebrews 12:14).

> *What Do You Think?*
> What are some ways to ensure that your worship is characterized by a holiness that honors God's holiness?
> *Digging Deeper*
> How should holiness in worship reflect the fact that God's people are set apart for his special purposes in the world? How do Psalm 29:1, 2 and 1 Peter 1:15, 16 inform your response?

B. To All Nature (vv. 30-33)

30. Tremble before him, all the earth! The world is firmly established; it cannot be moved.

The command to *tremble* reflects a concern that proper reverence be shown to the Lord, particularly in light of what happened during the first attempt to carry the ark (see 1 Chronicles 13). The phrase *all the earth* is emphasized by appearing three times within this psalm (see 16:14, 23). The Lord's control over the entire *world* stabilizes and sustains it. Nothing throws it out of its orbit; the planet remains in the place assigned by its Creator. When God desires to remove it from its place in order to establish the new heaven and earth, that will indeed happen (2 Peter 3:10-13).

31. Let the heavens rejoice, let the earth be glad; let them say among the nations, "The Lord reigns!"

The entire *heavens* and *the earth,* which the Lord has created (Genesis 1:1), are now called on to *rejoice* in their Maker. People—who are not only created by God but made in his image (1:27)—should witness *among the nations,* in the chorus with all creation, that *the Lord reigns!* None other is worthy of this declaration.

32a. Let the sea resound, and all that is in it;

The members of this choir continue to grow in number as the waters and the land and all their inhabitants add their voices. *The sea,* far from being a tranquil retreat, often represents chaos (Psalm 46:2, 3; Proverbs 8:29; Habakkuk 1:14). Its worship of the Lord reveals that even the seemingly untamable depths, with all its creatures, falls under God's power and yearns to see his greatness (Job 41; Psalm 74:13; Jonah 1:17; 2:10).

32b. let the fields be jubilant, and everything in them!

The fields represent a contrast to the sea. Far from being chaotic, they can be depended on to provide for the people as long as God blesses the fields to yield their bounty. Their rejoicing looks like bountiful food for people and their animals, a riot of thriving vegetation.

33. Let the trees of the forest sing, let them sing for joy before the LORD, for he comes to judge the earth.

Elsewhere *trees* "clap their hands" in praise to the Lord (Isaiah 55:12). This image helps round out the growing picture of all creation worshipping the Lord. It does so because the Lord's judging will include the release of all creation from the curse of sin. Paul pictures the creation as groaning even now for that deliverance from the "bondage to decay" (Romans 8:19-23) that will one day take place.

> *What Do You Think?*
> What can you do to become more aware of
>   God's presence in the everyday world?
> *Digging Deeper*
> Which psalms do you find especially suited to
>   teaching how to see God's world in a way that
>   is worshipful to him?

❧ ALL NATURE SINGS ❧

Throughout history, natural sounds and patterns have shaped the works of classical composers. Antonio Vivaldi's *The Four Seasons* is an example of this. This work consists of four concertos, each incorpo-rating the sounds of each of the four seasons. Ludwig van Beethoven's sixth symphony, also known as the *Pastoral Symphony,* takes the listener on a leisurely stroll in the Vienna countryside. Claude Debussy clearly identifies his inspiration for *La Mer (The Sea)* as he takes us on an ocean voyage. Chirping birds greet the dawn in Edvard Grieg's *Peer Gynt,* and a frantic piccolo takes us on Nikolai Rimsky-Korsakov's *Flight of the Bumblebee!*

Long before any of these composers lived, another songwriter sang of the music of nature. David heard these sounds as worship. The roar of the oceans, the rustling of the trees, and the gentle whisper of the winds over a field all sing of the sovereignty of God. Are we listening?   —J. E.

III. Call Concluded
(1 CHRONICLES 16:34-36)
A. Repeated Praise (v. 34)

34. Give thanks to the LORD, for he is good; his love endures forever.

The final two phrases of this verse are repeated with slight variations several times within the Old Testament, often accompanied by a command to *give thanks* (2 Chronicles 5:13; 7:3; Ezra 3:11; Psalms 107:1; 136; Jeremiah 33:11). Such repetition suggests the refrain's importance. No one can overstate the fact that *the Lord . . . is good.*

Being repeatedly reminded of God's goodness and *love* prompts his people to thank him for all that he does. That thankfulness in turn should direct the people to walk in the Lord's ways (Romans 2:4).

> *What Do You Think?*
> How would you explain God's goodness to
>   someone who wonders why there is so much
>   evil in the world?
> *Digging Deeper*
> Under what circumstances would you use or not
>   use the Bible in your explanation ?

B. Request for Deliverance (v. 35)

35. Cry out, "Save us, God our Savior; gather us and deliver us from the nations, that we may

give thanks to your holy name, and glory in your praise."

Thus far this psalm has featured a series of exhortations to *praise, give thanks to,* and worship the Lord. For the first time, words of request appear. The people's praying to be delivered *from the nations* reveals that salvation in this context concerns physical well-being, not primarily spiritual realities.

The nations are called to know that the Lord is king (1 Chronicles 16:31), but the song recognizes that they often pose a threat to God's covenant people. The plea for deliverance springs not from selfish or vengeful motives but from a desire that the Lord's *name* (his character and reputation) be exalted (Psalm 115). When *God* acts on behalf of his people, he gives them fresh material for which to *give thanks.*

Visual for Lesson 2. *While discussing the questions associated with verse 33, have learners consider this poster and its implications for their responses.*

> **What Do You Think?**
> What techniques can we use to ensure that we continue worshipping God actively during difficult times?
> *Digging Deeper*
> What do the successes and failures in this regard reveal about human nature? Give biblical examples.

C. Response of Praise (v. 36)

36a. Praise be to the LORD, the God of Israel, from everlasting to everlasting. Then all the people said "Amen" and "Praise the Lord."

The psalm concludes with a final tribute of praise that foreshadows the very picture of Heaven (Revelation 7:11, 12; 21:22-27). God by his nature is to be praised, and the saved will spend eternity praising him.

One can only imagine the rousing response of *Amen* that climaxes this unforgettable day. *The people* react as the songwriter and leaders intend.

Conclusion
A. Eyes of Gratitude

I'll never forget the first time I put glasses on, back in the seventh grade. My teacher had noticed my squinting to see the blackboard. I went through the tests with an eye doctor and didn't think too much about it. Then came the day when I first put on my glasses. Just before doing so, the lady said to me, "Look across the street." I did. Then she had me put on the glasses, and she said again, "Look across the street." I couldn't believe how clear everything was; it was amazing! I had no idea how poor my vision was until I could see clearly.

We are accustomed to praying with our eyes closed. That way, we can shut out distractions and approach prayer with the right frame of mind. But it doesn't hurt to pray with our eyes open—to see the many reasons around us for which to be thankful. This is something we can do as we drive (we don't want to close our eyes then, anyway!) or when we walk through the neighborhood or look out the window—or across the street. Such a practice can enhance our spiritual vision and deepen our sense of God's presence in everyday life.

B. Prayer

Father, we thank you for the mercy you demonstrated to all of humanity in the sending of Jesus, our Creator and Savior. May our worship of him be offered each day in word and deed from grateful hearts. We pray in Jesus' name. Amen.

C. Thought to Remember
Make each and every day
a day of thanksgiving.

INVOLVEMENT LEARNING

Enhance your lesson with NIV Bible Student *(from your curriculum supplier) and the reproducible activity page (at www.standardlesson.com or in the back of the* NIV Standard Lesson Commentary Deluxe Edition*).*

Into the Lesson

Option. For your early arrivers, place in chairs copies of the "Reasons to Celebrate" exercise from the activity page, which you can download.

When the time to start class arrives, have playing in the background a song that speaks of "celebration" in some way. Ask what memories this kind of song (but not necessarily this particular song) evokes. Follow up by discussing various reasons such songs give for celebrating.

Say, "We like parties—and there are so many reasons for celebration. But do we ever celebrate for reasons similar to those of Bible characters? Let's take a look at one and find out!"

Into the Word

Divide students into three groups with the following designations and focus texts: the **Remember Group** (1 Chronicles 16:8-12), the **Give Group** (1 Chronicles 16:28-30), and the **Sing Group** (1 Chronicles 16:31-36). Ask groups to express the content of their respective texts in a four-line poem. Move among the groups as they work, helping them understand and summarize their texts. For groups having trouble getting started, give these examples:

The Remember Group
We look for God and he is easily found—
  Signs of his presence are always around.
We cannot keep silent when we recall
  All he has done; we shout praises to all.

The Give Group
What can we give to our glorious king?
  The one who has given us everything!
We bring praise without condition,
  And surrender ourselves in full submission.

The Sing Group
All is at peace with God on his throne.
  For ages unnumbered he calls us his own.
He shows us mercy and is our salvation.
  So we echo the songs sung by all creation.

After no more than 15 minutes, allow groups to share their poetry. Comment as necessary to make sure all points are made clearly and completely.

Move into the final section of the lesson by saying, "David instructed the Israelites how to show their gratitude to Almighty God, recognizing his presence in Jerusalem. How are we doing with these same instructions? Let's evaluate our worship in terms of how we remember, give, and sing."

Into Life

Before class, gather enough of the following items so each student will have one of each: thin ribbons cut to 5"lengths, gift tags, and jingle bells. (These are available readily and inexpensively at craft stores this time of year.)

Say, "By means of the psalm found in the text, David showed his gratitude when bringing the ark of the covenant to Jerusalem. He gave Israel a clear formula for evaluating their praise. These items will help us evaluate our worship."

Distribute the ribbons as you ask, "In what ways can you use this ribbon to remind yourself of everything God has done in your life?" One response to expect is to use it in a way similar to the old idea of tying a string around a finger to remember something.

Distribute the gift tags as you ask, "What is the best gift we can offer God?" If no one says "ourselves," lead to that with a hint: "What does he want more than anything?"

Distribute the bells as you ask, "As you hear these bells as they are being passed around, would you say that their sound is in their primary nature, or is it secondary?" After the obvious answer, say, "May it be so with us as we sing God's praises."

Option. Distribute copies of the "Party Animals" exercise from the activity page as a take-home for personal self-evaluation. Promise to discuss results during next week's class.

DAVID'S HOUSE

DEVOTIONAL READING: Psalm 138

BACKGROUND SCRIPTURE: 2 Samuel 7:1-17; 24:18-25;
1 Chronicles 17:1-15; 21:18-31

1 CHRONICLES 17:1, 3, 4, 11-14

¹ After David was settled in his palace, he said to Nathan the prophet, "Here I am, living in a house of cedar, while the ark of the covenant of the LORD is under a tent."

. . . .

³ But that night the word of God came to Nathan, saying:

⁴ "Go and tell my servant David, 'This is what the LORD says: You are not the one to build me a house to dwell in.'"

. . . .

¹¹ "'When your days are over and you go to be with your ancestors, I will raise up your offspring to succeed you, one of your own sons, and I will establish his kingdom. ¹² He is the one who will build a house for me, and I will establish his throne forever. ¹³ I will be his father, and he will be my son. I will never take my love away from him, as I took it away from your predecessor. ¹⁴ I will set him over my house and my kingdom forever; his throne will be established forever.'"

1 CHRONICLES 21:18, 21-27

¹⁸ Then the angel of the LORD ordered Gad to tell David to go up and build an altar to the LORD on the threshing floor of Araunah the Jebusite.

. . . .

²¹ Then David approached, and when Araunah looked and saw him, he left the threshing floor and bowed down before David with his face to the ground.

²² David said to him, "Let me have the site of your threshing floor so I can build an altar to the LORD, that the plague on the people may be stopped. Sell it to me at the full price."

²³ Araunah said to David, "Take it! Let my lord the king do whatever pleases him. Look, I will give the oxen for the burnt offerings, the threshing sledges for the wood, and the wheat for the grain offering. I will give all this."

²⁴ But King David replied to Araunah, "No, I insist on paying the full price. I will not take for the LORD what is yours, or sacrifice a burnt offering that costs me nothing."

²⁵ So David paid Araunah six hundred shekels of gold for the site. ²⁶ David built an altar to the LORD there and sacrificed burnt offerings and fellowship offerings. He called on the LORD, and the LORD answered him with fire from heaven on the altar of burnt offering.

²⁷ Then the LORD spoke to the angel, and he put his sword back into its sheath.

KEY VERSES

When your days are over and you go to be with your ancestors, I will raise up your offspring to succeed you, one of your own sons, and I will establish his kingdom. He is the one who will build a house for me, and I will establish his throne forever. —1 Chronicles 17:11, 12

HONORING
GOD

Unit 1: David Honors God

LESSONS 1–5

LESSON AIMS

After participating in this lesson, each learner will be able to:

1. Summarize David's intention, God's response, and David's reaction regarding construction of a house (temple) for God.

2. Explain why David refused to offer sacrifices that cost him nothing.

3. Prepare a testimony of a time when he or she expected to serve God in a certain way, but found the plans redirected by him.

LESSON OUTLINE

Introduction

A. Doors, Windows, and Houses

Most of us have heard the saying, "When God closes a door, he opens a window," or some variation of that. The specific origin of that popular proverb is unknown. Many know it from the movie *The Sound of Music.* The would-be nun Maria speaks the words to herself as she unexpectedly leaves the abbey to serve as a governess.

The statement describes how, when one opportunity disappears, in time another opportunity will present itself. People of faith view these situations as much more than coincidence or luck. They see the sovereign hand of God at work to provide in his special and often surprising ways.

B. Lesson Context

Last week's lesson examined a psalm that David commissioned for use in celebrating the arrival of the ark of the covenant in Jerusalem (1 Chronicles 16:8-36). The text does not indicate how much time passed between bringing the ark to the city and the events studied in today's text. David became troubled by a glaring discrepancy, which is the point at which today's text begins.

The accounts in this lesson have parallel records in 2 Samuel 7 and 24. The first parallel, concerning David's impulse to build a house, shows little variation between 2 Samuel and 1 Chronicles 17. The second parallel, which follows David's taking a census in Israel (2 Samuel 24:1-17; 1 Chronicles 21:1-17), is more detailed in 1 Chronicles than in 2 Samuel. The details differ significantly. Those differences pertinent to the printed text will be considered in the commentary below.

I. Building a House

(1 CHRONICLES 17:1, 3, 4, 11-14)

David captured the city of Jerusalem following his being anointed as king of Israel (1 Chronicles 11:3-5). He took up residence "in the fortress" (11:7). This is either a preexisting structure in Jerusalem or, more likely, the home that King Hiram of Tyre had built for David out of cedar (2 Samuel 5:11).

A. A Realization (v. 1)

1. After David was settled in his palace, he said to Nathan the prophet, "Here I am, living in a house of cedar, while the ark of the covenant of the LORD is under a tent."

David becomes disturbed by the contrast between his own permanent *house* and the place in which *the ark of the covenant* now sits. It is still *under a tent* that David had erected in Jerusalem (2 Samuel 6:17). While Israel was walking through the desert, a portable home for the Lord was required. So the design of the tabernacle was given by God at Mount Sinai (Exodus 24:15–25:9; 26). Now that the Israelites are settled in the land, a permanent structure makes sense, at least to King David. *Cedar* is a strong, durable wood, frequently used in the Ancient Near East for building and decorating temples and palaces.

The Lord has not mentioned wanting a new residence (compare 2 Samuel 7:6, 7; 1 Chronicles 17:5, 6). However, David believes that the portable tabernacle has become obsolete. A permanent home should be erected for God in the land he has given to his people. Why should David, a mere human king, have a more elaborate residence than the king of the universe?

David voices his concern to *Nathan the prophet*. Apparently, Nathan has served as a counselor to David for spiritual matters (2 Samuel 7:1-4, 17; 12:1-14, 25; 1 Kings 1). Though many prophets experience tumultuous relationships with kings (1 Kings 18:1–19:9; 2 Kings 6:24-33; Jeremiah 38:1-13; etc.), David respects God and his messengers (1 Samuel 22:5; 2 Samuel 7:17-29; 12:1-14; 24:10-17; 1 Kings 1). First Chronicles 17:2, not in today's text, records Nathan's initial response to David's observation: he encourages David to pursue the matter, assuming with the king that this is what the Lord would have David do. David and Nathan make their plan without consulting God first.

B. A Word (vv. 3, 4)

3a. But that night the word of God came to Nathan,

The Lord wastes no time in reacting to Nathan's counsel to David. The phrase *the word of God came* indicates that what follows will not reflect a human's understanding. Though *Nathan* has presumed God's approval in responding to David, God now makes known what he really wants.

3b, 4. saying, "Go and tell my servant David, 'This is what the LORD says: You are not the one to build me a house to dwell in.'"

The Lord makes his will for *David* quite clear to Nathan. But God's denying David his desire is not the Lord's final word. In the following verses (1 Chronicles 17:5-9, not in today's text), the Lord clarifies that he has not asked for a temple. He reminds David through Nathan of God's abundant blessings for David. But the Lord has even more planned for his faithful servant.

What Do You Think?
What habits can you cultivate to help you remain faithful when your prayers result in answers that are not what you hope for?
Digging Deeper
In what ways can or should 2 Corinthians 12:8, 9 help frame your response?

C. The Plan (vv. 11-14)

11. "'When your days are over and you go to be with your ancestors, I will raise up your offspring to succeed you, one of your own sons, and I will establish his kingdom.

The Lord declares that he will build "a house for [David]," not the other way around (1 Chronicles 17:10, not in today's text). God makes clear that his intention is not to replace the physical house of cedar David already has. Instead, after David has gone *to be with* his *ancestors*—an expression describing death (compare 2 Samuel 7:12)—one of his sons will succeed him as king over Israel.

At this point, it is not obvious to David which son this will be; he has several sons, by several wives, who could seek the throne (1 Kings 1:5-14; 1 Chronicles 3:1-9). For God to *establish his kingdom* suggests that he will bless the line of the next king with longevity on the throne (compare 1 Kings 11:9-13; 2 Kings 8:19; 2 Chronicles 21:7).

12a. "He is the one who will build a house for me,

God addresses David's concern for the Lord's house. His word for David is not that building a temple is an absurd idea. Instead, God reveals that the man to *build* the *house* will be the son that God raises up after David (2 Chronicles 2:1–5:1).

❧ UNFULFILLED DREAM ❧

Chief Henry Standing Bear had a dream. He wrote to the Department of the Interior and offered to trade 900 acres of his farmland for Thunderhead Mountain, located about 17 miles from Mount Rushmore. The National Forest Service agreed. Standing Bear commissioned Korczak Ziolkowski to carry out his dream: to carve the image of Sioux warrior, Crazy Horse, into the mountain.

The memorial has been under construction since 1948 and is far from finished. Standing Bear died in 1953 and saw little of the progress made on fulfilling his dream. Forty-five years later, the face of Crazy Horse was completed and dedicated. When completed, the monument will be the world's largest sculpture, measuring 641 feet wide and 563 feet high.

King David dreamed of building a temple to honor the God of Israel. Like Standing Bear, David died before his dream was fulfilled. Both men planned for a future they would not see. What dreams can you only see by faith?   —J. E.

12b. "and I will establish his throne forever.

After assuring David that the temple will be built, God reveals his greater plan. This plan will encourage David to think in far more sweeping terms about his legacy. The promise that the *throne* of David's successor will last *forever* will cause confusion for the exiles, especially during the events surrounding the Babylonian exile (Jeremiah 25:1-14). Ultimately, this promise is fulfilled in Christ in a much greater way than David could imagine (Isaiah 11:1-9; Matthew 22:41-45; Romans 1:2-4).

13. "I will be his father, and he will be my son. I will never take my love away from him, as I took it away from your predecessor.

God had indeed removed his *love* from Saul who was king before David. The same Hebrew word translated love is also translated "kindness" (Genesis 24:27) or "mercy" (Hosea 6:6). God did not stop loving Saul, but he did remove the kind blessings that the first king in Israel had enjoyed for a time.

As a result, Saul was tormented (1 Samuel 16:14, 15, 23; 19:9, 10), and his line did not continue on Israel's throne (16:1; 23:16-18; 24:16-20). In contrast, a strong bond will be established between the Lord as *father* and the *son* who will build the Lord's house. Solomon will fall far short of being the greatest fulfillment of the promises within this verse (1 Kings 11:1-13). Once again, the promise is fulfilled in Christ (Luke 1:31-33; 24:44-49).

14. "I will set him over my house and my kingdom forever; his throne will be established forever."'

Twice in this verse the Lord emphasizes the eternal nature of the *house*, *kingdom*, and *throne* that he will establish. It becomes clear that God's promises look beyond the circumstances of David and his son, even beyond the construction of the Lord's house in Jerusalem. His intentions for David's family are very grand indeed.

When Gabriel will speak to Mary about becoming the mother of Jesus, he will echo God's promise here. Mary's son will inherit a throne, house, and kingdom forever (Luke 1:32, 33). Jesus is a far greater son of David than Solomon (Matthew

HOW TO SAY IT

Araunah	A-*raw*-nuh.
Gad	*Gad* (*a* as in *bad*).
Jebusites	*Jeb*-yuh-sites.
Joab	*Jo*-ab.

12:42; John 18:36; Acts 2:29-31). The eternal realm of Heaven is the consummation of the throne, house, and kingdom (Revelation 7:9-17; 11:15).

II. Providing a Site

(1 Chronicles 21:18, 21-27)

Following several military victories (1 Chronicles 18–20), David commanded Joab (the king's chief military commander) to conduct a census in Israel (21:1-17). Taking the census either reflected pride on the king's part or revealed a lack of faith in the Lord's protection. Joab objected to the order but yielded to the king's demand.

As Joab anticipated, the Lord was displeased with David's action. The Lord sent a seer, Gad, to give David a choice of three punishments. David chose a plague from the Lord that would last for a period of three days. As a result, 70,000 men perished in Israel (1 Chronicles 21:14).

A. A Command (v. 18)

21:18. Then the angel of the LORD ordered Gad to tell David to go up and build an altar to the LORD on the threshing floor of Araunah the Jebusite.

The angel of the Lord has been sent to destroy Jerusalem, but now the Lord's mercy prevails to spare the city. The angel is stopped at *the threshing floor of a Jebusite* (1 Chronicles 21:15).

The Jebusites have long lived in the promised land (Genesis 15:18-21; Exodus 3:8, 17); they inhabited Jerusalem before David conquered the city (Joshua 15:8). The Jebusites continued to live in the land until David's taking Jerusalem (15:63; Judges 1:21; 2 Samuel 5:6, 7), at which point they rapidly fade from history. This account concerning *Araunah* and his threshing floor constitutes one of the final references to Jebusites in the Bible.

The angel of the Lord who has been inflicting the plague now speaks to the prophet *Gad*. That man has not been mentioned in 1 Chronicles until now. He was with David during the attempt to escape from the hand of jealous King Saul (1 Samuel 22:5). The instruction to *build an altar* marks the end of God's punishment of Israel for David's sin (1 Chronicles 21:17). Altars built by the patri-

FROM TEMPLE TO DYNASTY TO TEMPLE

PROMISED TO DAVID — FULFILLED IN CHRIST — ESTABLISHED IN YOU?

1000 BC — AD 30 — AD 2020

1 CHRONICLES 17:9-14 / ACTS 7:44-47 — LUKE 1:69 / ACTS 2:22-36 — 2 CORINTHIANS 6:16 / 1 PETER 2:4, 5

Visual for Lessons 3 & 4. *Point to this timeline as you ask the class how it helps Christians understand their role as God's temple today.*

archs and the nation of Israel often mark locations where God had done something incredible (Genesis 12:7, 8; 22:9, 13; 26:24, 25; 35:1-7; Exodus 17:15; Judges 6:23-32; etc.). This particular altar on Araunah's threshing floor will remind the nation not only of the plague they have suffered but, more importantly, God's mercy in cutting it short (1 Chronicles 21:15).

> **What Do You Think?**
> What procedure can we adopt to discern that a person's counsel to us represents God's will?
> *Digging Deeper*
> What would make you suspect that a person's well-intentioned counsel is not truly from God? How does 2 Samuel 7:3-5 help frame your response?

B. A Negotiation (vv. 21-25)

21. Then David approached, and when Araunah looked and saw him, he left the threshing floor and bowed down before David with his face to the ground.

While threshing wheat, *Araunah* first sees the angel (1 Chronicles 21:20, not in today's text), then *David*. The man appropriately bows in homage as he recognizes the king.

22a. David said to him, "Let me have the site of your threshing floor so I can build an altar to the LORD,

A typical *threshing floor* is a level and hard piece of ground. It is usually located in the open air where the task of threshing (dividing the chaff from the usable grain in kernels of wheat) can be carried out. Building *an altar* implies that David plans to offer sacrifices.

22b. "that the plague on the people may be stopped. Sell it to me at the full price."

As king of Israel, David can simply seize Araunah's land for whatever reason desired. The Jebusites are a conquered people whose land had been promised to Israel (Exodus 3:8; 34:11; Deuteronomy 7:1). They were meant to be destroyed in the original conquest of the land (Deuteronomy 20:17). But instead of seizing what he requires, David insists on paying Araunah *the full price* for his property.

The angel of the Lord has stopped at the threshing floor (1 Chronicles 21:15, 16) because the next move is David's. Because *the plague* came on *the people* as a result of David's sin, he is responsible for the sin offering to show repentance (Leviticus 4:1–5:13). When the Lord forgives David, as the king believes God will do, the punishment on David and his people will come to an end.

What Do You Think?

▶ How visible should be our refusals to use power or privilege to personal advantage, considering the tension between Matthew 5:14-16 and 6:1-4?

Digging Deeper

Consider the relevance, or lack thereof, of John 7:4, 10; 13:15; and Titus 2:7, 8.

23. Araunah said to David, "Take it! Let my lord the king do whatever pleases him. Look, I will give the oxen for the burnt offerings, the threshing sledges for the wood, and the wheat for the grain offering. I will give all this."

Araunah holds nothing back. He is willing to give *David* everything the king needs in order to build the altar and offer sacrifices on it. No reason is noted for the generous offer. Given that he sees the angel of the Lord nearby (1 Chronicles 21:20), Araunah may recognize that the Lord has deter-

mined for David to receive this land and therefore doesn't desire to impede God's intentions.

24. But King David replied to Araunah, "No, I insist on paying the full price. I will not take for the LORD what is yours, or sacrifice a burnt offering that costs me nothing."

In refusing Araunah's counteroffer, *David* states an important principle: he will not take something for the Lord's use *that costs* him *nothing*. This is especially significant regarding animals that are used for burnt offerings. Such an offering ordinarily is to be taken from one's personal livestock and must always be "a male without defect" (Leviticus 1:1-3). Sacrifices are therefore costly in quality and quantity; to offer a sacrifice that is flawed or cheap suggests terrible things about one's reverence for the Lord (compare Malachi 1:8) and trust in his provision.

David knows that sin carries "wages" (a concept that Paul will later make clear in Romans 6:23). He has admitted that he and his family should have been plagued (1 Chronicles 21:17), not the 70,000 who have died thus far. For these reasons, nothing *Araunah* says can convince the king to take the property for free.

What Do You Think?

▶ How will you know when your personal giving moves from costing you little or nothing to being truly sacrificial?

Digging Deeper

Of Mark 12:41-44; 1 Corinthians 16:2; 2 Corinthians 8:1-15; 9:6-9, which most speaks to your heart in this regard? Why?

25. So David paid Araunah six hundred shekels of gold for the site.

The payment noted here is far more than the "fifty shekels of silver" noted in the parallel account 2 Samuel 24:24—perhaps 180 times as much when considering silver vs. gold. The difference may be explained by noting that 2 Samuel 24:24 mentions only the threshing floor and the oxen being purchased. The verse before us, however, appears to include the entire site, a much larger area (compare 1 Chronicles 21:28–22:1).

Today, the public might simply refer to the Teapot Dome incident as just another example of "pay-to-play" policy making. At the time, however, the scandal was considered sensational, tarnishing the administration of U.S. President Warren G. Harding.

To ensure that the navy had sufficient oil available, several oil fields, including Teapot Dome, were designated as Naval Oil Reserves. The Department of the Interior came to supervise the land in 1921. Harding's Secretary of the Interior, Albert B. Fall, had the authority to issue leases without competitive bidding. What he was *not* permitted to do was to accept money to influence his decisions. Following Congressional hearings, Fall was convicted of accepting bribes from two oil companies, bribes amounting to over $400,000.

Some leaders still view "pay-to-play" politics as a perk of governance. King David firmly rejected that view in the case of Araunah's threshing floor. David insisted that this site should cost him something. What do the value of your gifts to God say about your view of him?   —J. E.

C. An Altar (vv. 26, 27)

26a. David built an altar to the LORD there and sacrificed burnt offerings and fellowship offerings. He called on the LORD,

The scene is reminiscent of what occurred at the ceremony during which the ark of the covenant was brought to Jerusalem (1 Chronicles 16:1, 2). In both instances, David addressed acts of disobedience to the Lord (13:7-14).

26b. and the LORD answered him with fire from heaven on the altar of burnt offering.

The response of *fire* falling *from heaven on the altar* is similar to other occasions in the Old Testament, including Solomon's (future) dedication of the temple on this site (2 Chronicles 7:1) and the Lord's answer to Elijah's prayer on Mount Carmel (1 Kings 18:36-38). In these instances, God chooses to demonstrate dramatically his pleasure with the offerings.

Such scenes anticipate Pentecost, when tongues of fire will fall on the disciples. The coming of the Holy Spirit at that time will demonstrate God's

choosing and empowering them to carry out their mission (Acts 2:1-4).

27. Then the LORD spoke to the angel, and he put his sword back into its sheath.

David's offering provides the "aroma" that is "pleasing to the Lord" (Leviticus 1:9). The plague thereby ends, although one can imagine that this incident stays in David's memory long after it occurs.

Conclusion

A. Looking Ahead

God's saying *no* to something we propose to do can be devastating. Initially, David probably felt very good about his intended construction project. He had already brought the ark to Jerusalem. What better way to complete the task than to provide a dwelling place in honor of Israel's true king?

But God had other plans. He denied the king's plan, but then proclaimed his choice of David to participate in the building of the temple in a very important way. What had begun as a terrible punishment for sin resulted in David's offering sacrifices and purchasing the place for his son to build the Lord's house (1 Chronicles 22:1).

What was true with David applies to us as well: the Lord may reject what we have in mind, but that doesn't mean he rejects *us*. With the denial of David's desire came one of the most significant promises in all of the Old Testament: the Lord's promise to build a house for David.

The advice of Proverbs 3:5, 6 remains sound: "Trust in the Lord with all your heart and lean not on your own understanding; in all your ways submit to him, and he will make your paths straight." May we, like David, trust God in both his *yes* and *no* to use our lives to his glory.

B. Prayer

Father in Heaven, be our guide through times of discouragement. Open our eyes to see when your plans should replace ours. We pray in Jesus' name. Amen.

C. Thought to Remember

Trust God during times of both his *yes* and *no*.

INVOLVEMENT LEARNING

Enhance your lesson with NIV Bible Student *(from your curriculum supplier) and the reproducible activity page (at www.standardlesson.com or in the back of the* NIV Standard Lesson Commentary Deluxe Edition*).*

Into the Lesson

Tell this story:

In 1632, Emperor Shah Jahan commissioned the building of the Taj Mahal. This marble mausoleum on the banks of the Yamuna River in Agra, India, was constructed to house the remains of Jahan's favorite wife, Mumtaz Mahal. Construction of the complete 42-acre complex took 21 years to finish and employed 20,000 builders and craftsmen. The Taj Mahal attracts millions of visitors yearly and has been designated as one of the seven wonders of the modern world. The beautiful structure was named a UNESCO World Heritage Site in 1983 and is considered the best example of Muslim art in India."

Lead into Bible study by saying, "One thing all famous buildings have in common is *planning*. The need for that never changes. Another thing they all have in common is *unexpected roadblocks*. Today's text has something to teach us about how those may interrelate in service to God."

Into the Word

Divide the class into groups of three to five. Designate each group to be either a **God's Response Group** or an **Araunah's Offer Group**. If your class is large enough for three or more groups, merely bestow duplicate designations. Distribute handouts (you create) as follows.

God's Response Group(s). Read 1 Chronicles 17:1, 3, 4, 11-14 prior to considering these questions: 1–What interplay do you see between the literal and figurative uses of the word *house*? 2–How do 1 Chronicles 22:8 and 28:3 enhance your understanding of God's denial to David?

Araunah's Offer Group(s). Read 1 Chronicles 21:18, 21-27 prior to considering these questions: 1–In what ways does the alternate wording in 2 Samuel 24:18-25 enhance your understanding of this episode, if at all? 2–How is this purchase of property similar to and different from that described in Genesis 23?

Allow groups up to 10 minutes to discuss before sharing in whole-class discussion. If no one draws the conclusions that you (the teacher) have come to, be prepared to offer those yourself.

Expect those of the **God's Response Group(s)** to note that of the four occurrences of the word *house*, the three in verses 1, 4, and 12 refer to a literal, physical structure while the one in verse 14 is figurative. Point out that in all of 1 Chronicles 17 the total is 12—5 literal and 7 figurative uses. Expect learners to point out that the figurative is more important than the literal. Regarding the second question, push learners beyond merely parroting the texts' factual statements that David "shed much blood." Ask why God would consider that fact to be a disqualifier.

Expect those of the **Araunah's Offer Group(s)** to give personal responses to the first question. Regarding the second, expect learners to point out that while Abraham was in a position of weakness, David was not; as king, David may have been able to take the property without cost. (*Option*. Compare and contrast with 1 Kings 21:1-16.)

Option. Distribute copies of the "Fair or Unfair?" exercise from the activity page, which you can download, as a posttest.

Into Life

Discuss how human ideas, no matter how well-intentioned or logical, can fall short of better ideas God has. Ask participants to share a time when they expected to serve God in a certain way, but found the plans redirected by him.

Option. Distribute copies of the "Who Is in Charge?" exercise from the activity page for learners to complete in one minute or less. Give a token prize to the one who completes it the fastest. Discuss what the quote signifies.

Close with prayer asking God to help your learners trust that his plans are always superior to even the best of human intentions.

MARY'S PRAISE

DEVOTIONAL READING: 1 Samuel 2:1-10
BACKGROUND SCRIPTURE: Luke 1:39-56

LUKE 1:39-56

39 At that time Mary got ready and hurried to a town in the hill country of Judea, **40** where she entered Zechariah's home and greeted Elizabeth. **41** When Elizabeth heard Mary's greeting, the baby leaped in her womb, and Elizabeth was filled with the Holy Spirit. **42** In a loud voice she exclaimed: "Blessed are you among women, and blessed is the child you will bear! **43** But why am I so favored, that the mother of my Lord should come to me? **44** As soon as the sound of your greeting reached my ears, the baby in my womb leaped for joy. **45** Blessed is she who has believed that the Lord would fulfill his promises to her!"

46 And Mary said:
"My soul glorifies the Lord
47 and my spirit rejoices in God my Savior,
48 for he has been mindful
    of the humble state of his servant.
    From now on all generations will call me
        blessed,

49 for the Mighty One has done great things
        for me—
    holy is his name.
50 His mercy extends to those who fear him,
    from generation to generation.
51 He has performed mighty deeds with
        his arm;
    he has scattered those who are
        proud in their inmost thoughts.
52 He has brought down rulers
        from their thrones
    but has lifted up the humble.
53 He has filled the hungry with
        good things
    but has sent the rich away empty.
54 He has helped his servant Israel,
    remembering to be merciful
55 to Abraham and his descendants
        forever,
    just as he promised our ancestors."
56 Mary stayed with Elizabeth for about three months and then returned home.

KEY VERSES

Mary said: "My soul glorifies the Lord and my spirit rejoices in God my Savior." —**Luke 1:46, 47**

Honoring
God

LESSON AIMS

After participating in this lesson, each learner will be able to:

1. Retell the story of Mary's visit to Elizabeth and the song of praise that resulted.

2. Explain the significance of Mary's song with regard to its vision of the kingdom of God.

3. Write a prayer (or song) of thanksgiving that celebrates the ways in which God has blessed his or her life.

LESSON OUTLINE

Introduction
  A. A New Arrival
  B. Lesson Context
I. Family Visit (LUKE 1:39-45)
  A. Traveling (vv. 39, 40)
  B. Jumping for Joy (v. 41)
  C. Praising (vv. 42-45)
    Say Something Nice
II. Expectant Mother's Song (LUKE 1:46-56)
  A. Blessings for Mary (vv. 46-48)
  B. The Mighty One (vv. 49-51)
    All Generations
  C. A Great Reversal (vv. 52, 53)
  D. Blessings for Israel (vv. 54-56)
Conclusion
  A. A Song of Praise for All
  B. Prayer
  C. Thought to Remember

Introduction

A. A New Arrival

How do you react when you find out someone you love is expecting a child? For many people, the birth of a child is a time of great joy—and rightly so. A new baby signifies many things: the love between a husband and wife, the enlargement of a family, the arrival of a new generation, the extension of a family line, and so forth.

Yet sometimes other feelings surround the arrival of a child—feelings such as worry and anxiety for the future, fear or uncertainty about the reactions of others, and mistrust between the parents. The Scriptures reveal such instances. Consider the mixed feelings that must have attended the birth of Seth in the aftermath of the murder of Abel (Genesis 4:25). Or think of the fear that Moses' mother experienced that led her to hide her new baby boy in the reeds (Exodus 2:1-3).

Today's lesson concerns a birth announcement that was simultaneously incredible and terrifying to the young woman who received it. How would she respond to the announcement?

B. Lesson Context

Last week's lesson articulated God's great promise to David that the Lord would establish a kingdom from the line of David that would last forever. After many centuries have elapsed, today's lesson brings us to the fulfillment of that promise.

Luke's Gospel opens with the announcement of two very important births. The angel Gabriel appeared to the priest Zechariah to announce that his aging (and barren) wife, Elizabeth, was to bear a son to prepare Israel for the coming of the Messiah (Luke 1:17). In due course, Elizabeth's son was named John—eventually known to us as John the Baptist. The fact that Zechariah was rendered mute was a sign of the power of God and the certainty of his promise, as well as a rebuke to Zechariah's skepticism.

Some six months later, Gabriel appeared to the young virgin Mary in the town of Nazareth. Gabriel told her that she would give birth to a son to be named Jesus (Luke 1:31). The promises made about this child were of the highest order. He would be called the Son of God and was to sit on the throne of David forever (1:32, 33). Mary was overwhelmed by the magnitude of the news but nevertheless pledged her obedience (1:38). Today's lesson opens as she sets out to visit Elizabeth, a member of her extended family (1:36).

I. Family Visit
(LUKE 1:39-45)
A. Traveling (vv. 39, 40)

39, 40. At that time Mary got ready and hurried to a town in the hill country of Judea, where she entered Zechariah's home and greeted Elizabeth.

While the phrase *at that time* is not exceptionally precise, we should assume that the events of today's text occurred very shortly after Gabriel appeared to *Mary* (see Lesson Context).

The hill country refers to the region around Jerusalem (compare Luke 1:65). It is difficult to be more specific about the destination. Some commentators suggest that *a town* in *Judea* is a reference to the city of Hebron. The book of Joshua recounts that "Kiriath Arba (that is, Hebron), with its surrounding pasture land, in the hill country of Judah" was given to the priests (Joshua 21:10, 11). All of this matches up well with what we know about Zechariah and *Elizabeth* both being from priestly families (see Joshua 21:13; Luke 1:5).

If Mary travels from Nazareth to Hebron, her journey is at least 70 miles. The fact that Mary sets out on this journey is amazing. According to the customs of the day, she should be accompanied on a journey of such length. Luke's lack of details shows that he is more concerned with moving the narrative forward than on the minutiae of the journey.

Mary greets Elizabeth when she arrives in Elizabeth's home. This is important to Luke, given that he mentions it three times (see Luke 1:40, 41, 44). This initial greeting accords with the social norms of the day. Elizabeth is the superior of the two: she's considerably older than Mary (see 1:7), the wife of a priest, and thus a descendant of Aaron. Given these facts, it is proper for Mary to initiate the greetings.

B. Jumping for Joy (v. 41)

41. When Elizabeth heard Mary's greeting, the baby leaped in her womb, and Elizabeth was filled with the Holy Spirit.

We do not know the content of Mary's greeting, but we do know something of its results. Luke has already noted that John would be filled with the Holy Spirit in anticipation of the coming of Jesus (see Luke 1:15-17). When John leaps in his mother's *womb,* he begins to fulfill this role as the one who will go before the Lord to proclaim his coming.

But *Elizabeth* too is *filled with the Holy Spirit.* This is a clear indication that whatever she is about to say or do will be prophetic in nature (compare Acts 2:4-41).

C. Praising (vv. 42-45)

42. In a loud voice she exclaimed: "Blessed are you among women, and blessed is the child you will bear!

Elizabeth greets Mary with a surprising fullness and richness of language. She places herself in a subordinate role to Mary, who is *blessed . . . among women,* and whose child is likewise *blessed.* The form and content of Elizabeth's proclamation is definite in its prophetic quality. The *loud* volume of her *voice* in this context indicates conviction (compare 2 Chronicles 15:14; Ezra 10:12; Nehemiah 9:3-5). Similar language is used elsewhere of Elizabeth's own son, John. John's preaching will be, in the words of Isaiah the prophet, as "a voice of one calling in the wilderness" (Mark 1:3; see Isaiah 40:3).

43. "But why am I so favored, that the mother of my Lord should come to me?

HOW TO SAY IT

Gabriel	*Gay*-bree-ul.
Hebron	*Hee*-brun or *Heb*-run.
Magnificat	Mag-*nif*-ih-cot.
Manoah	Muh-*no*-uh.
messianic	mess-ee-*an*-ick.
Zechariah	Zek-uh-*rye*-uh.
Zephaniah	Zef-uh-*nye*-uh.

In greeting Mary as *the mother of my Lord,* Elizabeth indicates her submission to Mary's unborn baby. Her use of the term *my Lord* is extremely significant, echoing earlier messianic prophecies (Psalm 110:1; compare Matthew 22:44; Mark 12:36). It anticipates Jesus' designation as Lord at his exaltation to the right hand of God (see Acts 2:33-36). Elizabeth expresses amazement that she is privileged to be a part of the work of God in and through Mary.

44. "As soon as the sound of your greeting reached my ears, the baby in my womb leaped for joy.

The Holy Spirit empowers Elizabeth to recognize the meaning of John's leaping and to articulate its significance in the moment. Luke connects *joy* with the coming of salvation and redemption (see Luke 1:14, 47). Leaping can be associated explicitly or implicitly with joy and salvation in Luke's writings (see 6:23; a different but related word is used in Acts 3:8; 14:10).

45. "Blessed is she who has believed that the Lord would fulfill his promises to her!"

Mary is additionally called blessed because she has believed what the angel revealed to her. Mary's acceptance obviously contrasts with Zechariah's reaction (Luke 1:20).

Elizabeth's first blessing was spoken in the second person (Luke 1:42: "Blessed are you"), while this one is pronounced in the third person (*blessed is she*). This more general address opens the blessing to all who believe what God reveals about his Son and respond in obedience (John 6:37-40; 17:20-26; 20:29).

❧ SAY SOMETHING NICE ❧

Most funerals feature a eulogy. This compound Greek word could be translated "good words." It can be tricky to create a eulogy for certain people! Take President Richard Nixon for example. His legacy is always associated with Watergate. What "good words" could be spoken at his funeral?

President Bill Clinton delivered a memorable tribute to President Nixon in 1994. Clinton acknowledged Nixon's mistakes but declared that he should not be remembered solely for them. "May the day of judging President Nixon on any-

thing less than his entire life and career come to a close," Clinton implored. He instead focused on President Nixon's accomplishments.

While eulogies are associated with funerals, the eulogy of Jesus was given before he was born! Through the Holy Spirit, Elizabeth spoke good words that announced the good news about Jesus, even while he was still in the womb. How much more should we bless his name!   —J. E.

> **What Do You Think?**
> What one habit do you most need to develop to prepare you for times when God prompts you to speech or action?
> *Digging Deeper*
> What one habit do you most need to develop to know when to keep silent (Mark 9:5-7; etc.)?

II. Expectant Mother's Song
(LUKE 1:46-56)
A. Blessings for Mary (vv. 46-48)

46. And Mary said: "My soul glorifies the Lord

Mary responds to Elizabeth's greeting with the song that forms the bulk of today's text. Like the Psalms and other poetry of the Old Testament, Mary's Song (often referred to as the Magnificat) derives its poetic qualities not from meter or rhyme, but from the expression of ideas in parallels. Two, three, or more statements follow one another to express similar concepts. This creates a lyrical effect that conveys both thought and emotion.

The themes of Mary's song are familiar to readers of the Old Testament. Mary adapts traditional expressions of hope in God's promises as she reacts to God's announcement that he is about to fulfill those promises. Mary's song most closely resembles Hannah's prayer of praise after the birth of Samuel (see 1 Samuel 2:1-10).

For the Old Testament poets and prophets, the days when God would fulfill his promises lay in the uncertain future (Hebrews 11:1, 2, 39, 40). Those poets and prophets could not say when or how God would fulfill his pledge to bless his people (Romans 15:8; 2 Corinthians 1:20), restore them to himself (Isaiah 49:8; Hosea 14:4), and make all nations his (Psalms 46:10; 102:21, 22; Zephaniah 3:9). They could only affirm God's faithfulness: if he has made a promise, then he will fulfill it—period (Deuteronomy 32:4). In times of distress, hope is to be found in God's rock-solid faithfulness.

In contrast with the Old Testament poets and prophets, Mary stands at the very threshold of fulfillment. She is pregnant with the child through whom God will act to do what he has promised. But the fulfillment of God's promise comes at a cost: she is burdened with a pregnancy that will appear to everyone around her to be the result of sexual immorality (Luke 4:22), not divine intervention. And beyond the birth of her child, she too cannot say how God will go about fulfilling his pledge (2:34, 35, 41-51). Even so, she can, like the prophets before her, celebrate God's faithfulness.

47. "and my spirit rejoices in God my Savior,

The focus of Luke 1:46-50 is on God's blessings for Mary personally. An example of the parallelism characteristic of Hebrew poetry is Mary's use of soul and *spirit* in these first two verses to refer to the depths of her being (compare Isaiah 26:9).

The main idea of the verse before us is echoed in Habakkuk 3:18: "Yet I will rejoice in the Lord, I will be joyful in God my Savior." The term *Savior* highlights God's ability to rescue people from difficult circumstances (Isaiah 63:8, 9). In the immediate context, this may include Mary's amazement that God has healed the pain of Elizabeth's infertility. The theme of God's salvation and his ability to do what seems impossible underlies all of Luke 1, especially Mary's song.

48. "for he has been mindful of the humble state of his servant. From now on all generations will call me blessed,

As Mary's song progresses, she outlines the reasons for her praise. First, the fact that God regards *the humble state of his servant* reveals his character. The psalmist saw God's care for the lowly as central for understanding his work in the world (example: Psalm 138:6). The word translated *humble state* is also rendered "humil-

iation" (Acts 8:33; James 1:10; compare Philippians 3:21). Mary seems to be referring to the oppression of poverty that she—and Israel as a whole—are suffering under (see commentary on Luke 1:52, 53).

We should take special note of Mary's humility. To be God's *servant* echoes the similar expression in Hannah's song (see 1 Samuel 1:16, 18). The Greek word could be less poetically but more pointedly translated *female slave*. Mary's use of the term recalls her earlier response to the angel Gabriel after being told that she was to conceive miraculously (Luke 1:38). This is a response of total submission by one who recognizes her unworthiness to be *blessed* in such a manner.

> *What Do You Think?*
> Without giving advice, how might you counsel someone whose circumstances lead him or her to doubt God's goodness and mercy?
> *Digging Deeper*
> How would your counsel to a believer differ from counsel to an unbeliever? Why?

B. The Mighty One (vv. 49-51)

49. "for the Mighty One has done great things for me—holy is his name.

Mary gives a second reason for praise: she has some inkling of the nature of the *great things* God is doing through her. Two key attributes of God are emphasized as the cause of his work.

The title *the Mighty One* calls to mind the imagery of God as a warrior on behalf of his people that is found throughout the Old Testament (see Deuteronomy 10:17, 18; Isaiah 10:20-27; 49:25, 26). God's might cannot be separated from his holiness (Habakkuk 1:12). Isaiah frequently refers to God as "the Holy One" (Isaiah 1:4; 5:19, 24; 10:20; 12:6; etc.). The creatures that gather around the throne of God constantly say, "'Holy, holy, holy is the Lord God Almighty,' who was, and is, and is to come" (Revelation 4:8).

50. "His mercy extends to those who fear him, from generation to generation.

This verse shifts from focusing on God's might and holiness to his *mercy*. Indeed, his might and his mercy are joined together in a seamless whole in this song. The God who is a warrior also lifts up the lowly, shows mercy to *those who fear him,* fills the hungry, and so forth. The phrase *those who fear him* recalls the language of proverbs. The fear of God is associated with wisdom and with blessing (Proverbs 1:7; 3:7, 8; 9:10-12; etc.).

From generation to generation calls to mind the fact that God's promises endure; they do not fail (Exodus 20:4-6; Psalm 33:11; Isaiah 34:17).

❧ ALL GENERATIONS ❧

Generational differences are real! But what *are* these generations? Sociologists and others recognize several, though the dates can differ slightly.

Often referred to as the Greatest Generation (born 1901–1924), its members survived the Great Depression and World War II, leading the country to rebuild after both. The Silent Generation (born 1925–1942) followed and maintained their accomplishments.

Baby Boomers (born 1943–1964) came next. They have been referred to as idealists, not content with the world that was left to them. Generation X (born 1965–1979) has been called the latchkey generation; they cared for themselves, often with limited parental attention. Today, much focus is given to the Millennials (born 1980–2000) whose influence in shaping the world now predominates.

Mary recognized that the work God had done and would do through Jesus would affect *every* generation—those of her day and of all the days to come. What characteristics do you share with the Jesus Generation? —J. E.

51a. "He has performed mighty deeds with his arm;

With this verse, the lens begins to pan out to take in more of the surroundings. We move from a focus on Mary to a broader consideration of God's dealings with humanity. This is not the first time God *has performed mighty deeds with his arm* (see Deuteronomy 26:8; Psalms 89:10, 13; 136:12; Jeremiah 32:21); now he stands ready to do it again through the coming of his Son to redeem humanity.

51b. "he has scattered those who are proud in their inmost thoughts.

The Greek word behind *thoughts* refers to the understanding or the musings of a person (Ephesians 4:18; 1 John 5:20). God has *scattered* those who are arrogant in their understanding or their attitudes.

Though Mary exults in God's ability to know and judge the thoughts of the proud, we should assume these prideful attitudes are making themselves known in conduct as well. Pride contrasts with humility; only one of these attitudes finds a reward in God's presence (Proverbs 29:23).

> *What Do You Think?*
> How would you respond to those who point out situations where God seems to be absent because wicked people are prospering?
> *Digging Deeper*
> What teachings of Jesus' support your response? How would you use Judges 6:12, 13; Jeremiah 12:1; and/or Habakkuk 1:2-4?

C. A Great Reversal (vv. 52, 53)

52, 53. "He has brought down rulers from their thrones but has lifted up the humble. He has filled the hungry with good things but has sent the rich away empty.

The theme of reversal becomes explicit here. The *rulers* and *the rich*—those who exult in their own strength and power in opposition to God— are very often honored in this world. But in God's purposes, those who are *humble* and *the hungry* are the recipients of his gracious action (compare Matthew 5:45). Mary recognizes that her situation is only one example of a time when God has *lifted up* the lowly.

Jesus will reiterate the point made here in Luke 1:53 when he preaches his Sermon on the Plain. At that time, he will pronounce blessings on the hungry and the poor (Luke 6:20, 21)—blessings paired with woes on the rich and well fed (6:24, 25).

The rich, by contrast, are *sent . . . away empty.* They receive no consolation because they have placed all their earthly efforts into accumulating power and possessions for themselves. They have not cared about the suffering people who are around them (16:19-31). It is not to be so in the kingdom that God's Son comes to establish (Matthew 25:31-46).

D. Blessings for Israel (vv. 54-56)

54. "He has helped his servant Israel, remembering to be merciful

Mary's song now focuses on *Israel*. God is about to do something new through Mary, but that new thing is part of a long history of God's work through his covenant people. Mary sings that God *has helped . . . Israel.* God does this by *remembering to be merciful,* an idea found in the Old Testament (examples: Genesis 8:1; Psalms 25:6, 7; 98:3).

The people of Israel have languished under foreign domination for many centuries, most recently by the Romans. God has Israel in mind and is on the move to help them. But the help he is bringing is not what people anticipate.

55. "to Abraham and his descendants forever, just as he promised our ancestors."

The reasons for Mary's praise are embedded deeply in the original promise that God made to *our ancestors,* as well as *to Abraham and his descendants forever* (see Genesis 12:1-3; Galatians 3:16).

FROM TEMPLE TO DYNASTY TO TEMPLE

PROMISED TO DAVID — FULFILLED IN CHRIST — ESTABLISHED IN YOU?

1000 BC — AD 30 — AD 2020

1 CHRONICLES 17:9-14 ACTS 7:44-47 — LUKE 1:69 ACTS 2:22-36 — 2 CORINTHIANS 6:16 1 PETER 2:4, 5

Visual for Lessons 3 & 4. *While discussing the questions with verse 48, ask how Christians' being the temple of the Lord informs their answers.*

The coming of the Son is not a radical break with that promise but a fulfillment of it.

56. Mary stayed with Elizabeth for about three months and then returned home.

Since the six months of Luke 1:36 and the *three* of the verse at hand equals nine, we wonder if Mary stays long enough for John's birth. The text doesn't say.

Conclusion

A. A Song of Praise

God was working out his purpose for and through Mary. What he began in his humble servant has spread through the world as the good news of Christ is told in all nations to all people. Her song still resonates today as Christians seek to care for the lowly and disadvantaged, spreading hope that God sees every trial and has a plan to make salvation available to everyone. In this season, spread hope in God's Son!

B. Prayer

Father, we are thankful for your work through Mary. Teach us to see the ways in which you work through those the world considers "lowly." We pray in Jesus' name. Amen.

C. Thought to Remember

God works through even the lowliest to achieve his highest purposes.

INVOLVEMENT LEARNING

Enhance your lesson with NIV Bible Student *(from your curriculum supplier) and the reproducible activity page (at www.standardlesson.com or in the back of the* NIV Standard Lesson Commentary Deluxe Edition*).*

Into the Lesson

Divide the class in half. Members of one half will name a single blessing that most of them enjoy in common. Then the other half is to respond similarly, but the blessing they name must begin with the last letter of the first group's response. The first group then is to respond by naming a shared blessing that begins with the last letter of the second group's response. Encourage creative responses.

Play continues until one group is unable to answer. (Give groups enough time to confer when it's their turn, but don't let the game drag out.) Play as many rounds as time and interest allow.

Alternative. Distribute copies of the "Bless You!" exercise from the activity page, which you can download. Have students work individually to complete the activity as indicated in no more than one minute.

After either activity say, "To be blessed is to recognize and enjoy some kind of prosperity. In describing the visit of Mary to Elizabeth, Luke repeatedly wrote of blessing and being blessed. Let's see what this has to do with us."

Into the Word

Put students into three groups and give each a handout (you prepare) as follows: **"To Jesus and John the Baptist" Group:** Luke 1:39-44; see also Mark 1:1-4. **"To Mary" Group:** Luke 1:45-49; see also Luke 2:33-35. **"To All Generations" Group:** Luke 1:50-56; see also Matthew 19:28-30.

Include on each handout the following instructions: "Messages sent via Twitter (known as tweets) were limited to 140 characters originally. This was to ensure that users communicated succinctly. Do the same here, addressing your tweets to the namesake(s) of your groups. Use the passages on your handout as a source of content."

Give the groups 10 minutes to work on their tweets. Move among the groups to offer encouragement as needed. Use the commentary and these sample tweets to help groups that seem to be stuck.

"To Jesus and John the Baptist" Group: "You are relatives whose destinies were intertwined before birth. The older will introduce the younger to the world as the Lamb of God!" [134 characters including spaces, not including quotation marks]

"To Mary" Group: "Your faith and courage will allow the great things promised to you to be fulfilled. Joyful news now turns later into heart-piercing sorrow." [139 characters]

"To All Generations" Group: "Your world will be turned upside down! The Messiah will take the power from the arrogant. The downtrodden will be exalted." [122 characters]

Have groups explain their tweets. Point out that today's text sets the stage for the entire gospel.

Into Life

Say, "The word *blessed* occurs four times in today's text. In two of those cases, the word being translated is the source of our English word *eulogy*. We think of eulogies in terms of funerals, but in Luke 1:42b the word is used in anticipation of Jesus' earthly ministry. In what ways have you been blessed by him?" Depending on class size, this can be for discussions in small groups or as a whole class. Expect "eternal life" to be the first and top answer; if it's not, explore why.

Announce a time of singing about being blessed by God as you distribute hymnals or public-domain lyrics from the internet. Possible hymns are "Come, Thou Fount of Every Blessing," "Count Your Blessings," and "There Shall Be Showers of Blessings." Close with prayer, allowing participants to verbalize thanks to God for his blessings.

Option. As learners depart, distribute copies of the "Praying from the Psalms" exercise from the activity page as a take-home. To encourage completion, promise to discuss the results at the beginning of the next class.

DAVID'S PRAYER

DEVOTIONAL READING: Psalm 89:19-37
BACKGROUND SCRIPTURE: 2 Samuel 7:17-25; 1 Chronicles 17:16-27

1 CHRONICLES 17:16-27

[16] Then King David went in and sat before the LORD, and he said:

"Who am I, LORD God, and what is my family, that you have brought me this far? [17] And as if this were not enough in your sight, my God, you have spoken about the future of the house of your servant. You, LORD God, have looked on me as though I were the most exalted of men.

[18] "What more can David say to you for honoring your servant? For you know your servant, [19] LORD. For the sake of your servant and according to your will, you have done this great thing and made known all these great promises.

[20] "There is no one like you, LORD, and there is no God but you, as we have heard with our own ears. [21] And who is like your people Israel—the one nation on earth whose God went out to redeem a people for himself, and to make a name for yourself, and to perform great and awesome wonders by driving out nations from before your people, whom you redeemed from Egypt? [22] You made your people Israel your very own forever, and you, LORD, have become their God.

[23] "And now, LORD, let the promise you have made concerning your servant and his house be established forever. Do as you promised, [24] so that it will be established and that your name will be great forever. Then people will say, 'The LORD Almighty, the God over Israel, is Israel's God!' And the house of your servant David will be established before you.

[25] "You, my God, have revealed to your servant that you will build a house for him. So your servant has found courage to pray to you. [26] You, LORD, are God! You have promised these good things to your servant. [27] Now you have been pleased to bless the house of your servant, that it may continue forever in your sight; for you, LORD, have blessed it, and it will be blessed forever."

KEY VERSE

There is no one like you, LORD, and there is no God but you, as we have heard with our own ears.
—1 Chronicles 17:20

HONORING GOD

Unit 1: David Honors God
LESSONS 1–5

LESSON AIMS

After participating in this lesson, each learner will be able to:

1. Summarize the content of David's prayer.

2. Explain the importance of David's prayer in its historical context.

3. Recall prayers he or she prayed silently in class and offer them anew to the Lord daily throughout the week.

LESSON OUTLINE

Introduction
 A. Time-Out
 B. Lesson Context
I. Past Blessings (1 CHRONICLES 17:16-22)
 A. David's Smallness (vv. 16-18)
 B. God's Greatness (vv. 19, 20)
 C. Israel's Uniqueness (vv. 21, 22)
   No Place Like It
II. Future Blessings (1 CHRONICLES 17:23-27)
 A. For His Glory (vv. 23, 24)
   Antiestablishment?
 B. For His Servant (vv. 25-27)
Conclusion
 A. Upward and Inward
 B. Prayer
 C. Thought to Remember

Introduction

A. Time-Out

Many parents use the time-out method of discipline when their children misbehave. If a child has crossed the line in some way, he or she must go to a designated place for time-out. In some cases, the child must go to his or her room, and certain privileges are withheld. Some parents have the child sit in the corner of a room for a period of time, with no interaction with anyone. In either situation, the child is to think about what he or she has done and (perhaps) resolve it to avoid any future time-outs.

Time-outs can also be opportunities for children to calm down, whether or not misbehavior was a factor in their behavior. Walking away from an overly stimulating situation can allow children to return to interactions calmly. The time away may help them to deal with the situation more appropriately. A similar principle applies to any coach who takes a time-out to refocus the team at a critical juncture during a game.

In today's lesson, King David took a time-out from an overwhelming situation to sit before the Lord and talk about things. David's focus in this prayer is not repentance or a plea for help. Instead he praises God for the many good things the Lord has provided for him.

B. Lesson Context

Lesson 3 examined the special promise that God made to David in response to David's desire to build a house for God, one suitable for the ark of the covenant (1 Chronicles 17:11-14). Instead, the Lord announced his intention to build an eternal house, kingdom, and throne for David. That promise is fulfilled in the kingdom of Jesus, the son of David.

The prophet Nathan reported to David all the Lord's words concerning who would build a house for whom (1 Chronicles 17:15). That must have amazed David! We do not know how much time passed between Nathan's message and the prayer that David offered in response to the magnificent promise—today's text. Most likely it was not very long. The gratitude in David's heart for God's generosity had to be expressed; he could not keep it to himself. A second record of this prayer is found in 2 Samuel 7:18-29. The similarities are striking; differences of note will be discussed in the commentary below.

> **What Do You Think?**
> How will you realign your priorities to be able to reserve time and space for rest and spiritual reflection?
>
> **Digging Deeper**
> What cultural trend or expectation will most work against your doing so? Why?

I. Past Blessings
(1 Chronicles 17:16-22)
A. David's Smallness (vv. 16-18)

16. Then King David went in and sat before the LORD, and he said: "Who am I, LORD God, and what is my family, that you have brought me this far?

David sits awestruck at the message he has heard from Nathan. His seated posture may strike us today as casual. In his day, however, it is a posture of high respect for someone of greater honor. Likely David is sitting back on his heels, not on a plush throne or comfortable couch. King David knows that there is a much greater king to whom he must give allegiance (Psalm 5:2, 7, 8).

The prayer begins in great humility with words similar to David's reflections in Psalm 8:4. David's question here is very personal because of the promise he has been given. He views himself as unworthy of such treatment. David's humble *Who am I* contrasts with the arrogance of the Pharaoh in Egypt, who asked of Moses in derision, "Who is the Lord, that I should obey him and let Israel go?" (Exodus 5:2). Pharaoh's mind-set could be that of any ruler who believes he or she is an authority above God and need not be concerned about what God expects of earthly rulers. Such arrogance leads only to destruction (12:29-33; 14:5-28).

David alludes to how far the Lord has *brought* him. He is the youngest son of a rural family (1 Samuel 16:11-13). The Lord had previously mentioned David's humble beginnings as a shepherd (1 Chronicles 17:7). David went from literally tending the sheep to becoming the shepherd of God's covenant people (Psalm 78:70-72).

17. "And as if this were not enough in your sight, my God, you have spoken about the future of the house of your servant. You, LORD God, have looked on me as though I were the most exalted of men.

David knows that what *God* has done for him to this point is already significant—and yet there is more to come. He now reflects on what the *Lord* has planned. The Lord has told David of his intentions *for the future*, which include a kingdom and a throne with no end (2 Samuel 7:12, 13). Such treatment befits someone *exalted*—someone worthier, more honorable and impressive than a lowly former shepherd such as David.

David refers to himself as God's *servant* 10 times throughout this prayer. This repetition emphasizes his humility, especially when considering the amazing promise God has made. Referring to God as Lord at the same time positions David as a person who works on God's orders, not by his own authority. The repetition also contrasts David's status, high by human standards, with God's status, compared to whom no human has high status. David may be king of Israel, but he embraces his status as a mere servant of Israel's ultimate king.

> **What Do You Think?**
> What steps can Christians take to ensure that prayers are offered in a spirit of humility and patience?
>
> **Digging Deeper**
> Which of the following passages will help you most in this regard: 1 Samuel 2:1-10; 1 Kings 8:22-30; Psalm 51; Acts 4:23-30? Why?

18. "What more can David say to you for honoring your servant? For you know your servant,

At this point, *David* appears to be out of words to express his gratitude to the Lord. He acknowledges that the Lord knows him, a truth on which David elaborates in song, writing, "Such knowledge is too wonderful for me, too lofty for me to attain" (Psalm 139:6).

B. God's Greatness (vv. 19, 20)

19. "LORD. For the sake of your servant and according to your will, you have done this great thing and made known all these great promises.

David confesses the dual reasons for the Lord's generous dealings with him. Because of his love for David, God has chosen to bless David in this extraordinary, far-reaching manner (2 Samuel 7:16, 25; Isaiah 9:7; 37:35; 55:3). God has also demonstrated his greatness to David in keeping with God's own *will*. God takes great pleasure in doing *great* things and in making *great promises* to his faithful servants—to those who, like David, desire to honor him with their daily lives and their future plans (2 Chronicles 16:9).

What Do You Think?
  What guardrails can we erect to ensure we remain humble when God blesses us?
Digging Deeper
  In that regard, which of the following texts do you find most beneficial personally: Daniel 4:28-33; Acts 12:21-23; Philippians 2:1-11; James 4:13-17?

---

20. "There is no one like you, LORD, and there is no God but you, as we have heard with our own ears.

David acknowledges that the *Lord* is unique (compare Isaiah 44:6; 46:9). Indeed, not only is there no other god like Yahweh, he is the only *God*. This is a clear statement of the singular nature of God, one of the central tenets of biblical theology (Deuteronomy 4:35; 1 Samuel 2:2; Psalm 18:31; Isaiah 44:6; Mark 12:29b).

David's many conquests to this point have brought him and Israel into contact with other people groups and nations who worship and serve fictitious gods (1 Chronicles 11:4-25; 14:8-17). These peoples, who have seen the Lord work on behalf of David and Israel, have had to acknowledge that their own gods are weak and powerless compared to Israel's God (compare Moses' experi-

ences in Exodus 8:10; 9:14; 15:11). God's working on behalf of Israel has led their *ears* to ring with testimonies about how special the Lord really is.

This verse reflects on a fundamental understanding of who God is. Today we live in a world saturated with pluralism—the idea that one belief system is as good as any other. No religion has the right to claim to possess the truth or claim that its god is the only god. David disagrees. The Lord God who has revealed himself in the Bible as the one who creates (Genesis 1:1), sustains (Acts 17:28), redeems (Isaiah 47:4), and shepherds (Psalm 23) is indeed the only God.

It is good for us to include such an acknowledgment whenever we pray. Then we are better able to reject the barrage of pluralistic thinking that confronts us daily.

C. Israel's Uniqueness (vv. 21, 22)

21. "And who is like your people Israel—the one nation on earth whose God went out to redeem a people for himself, and to make a name for yourself, and to perform great and awesome wonders by driving out nations from before your people, whom you redeemed from Egypt?

God has chosen to express his power and uniqueness through his covenant with the *nation* of Israel. Just as there is no God like the Lord, there is no nation like his *people Israel*.

Much of what makes God unique is his holiness. Because of the nation's relationship with God, Israel could also rightly be called holy in the sense of being special and set apart from the *nations*. God blessed the Israelites by redeeming them from bondage in *Egypt* (Exodus 6:6) and then *by driving out* the nations that were residing in the promised land (Joshua 1:11). In so doing, God magnified his own *name*. Just as the Lord was able to take David from being a humble

HOW TO SAY IT

Molossia	Moe-*lahs*-ee-yah.
Pharaoh	*Fair*-o or *Fay*-roe.
Sinai	*Sigh*-nye or *Sigh*-nay-eye.
Yahweh *(Hebrew)*	*Yah*-weh.

shepherd to being king of Israel, so he was able to take Israel from being of inferior status among the nations to make it a nation of his covenant people (Deuteronomy 7:7, 8; 9:1).

That the Lord's name is *great and awesome* is recognized by the *nations* that God defeated on behalf of Israel (Psalm 102:12-17). It was his reputation (which is what *name* refers to) that caused the residents of Jericho to fear Israel (Joshua 2:9-11).

> **What Do You Think?**
> What can you do to strengthen your witness in terms of recalling God's past actions?
> **Digging Deeper**
> When witnessing to unbelievers, in what ways can we use such appeals without reference to the Bible (compare Acts 17:22-31)?

❧ *No Place Like It* ❧

The Republic of Molossia began as a joke. Ruled by self-proclaimed benevolent dictator Kevin Baugh, Molossia (population: 6) is located primarily on Baugh's front yard and backyard in Nevada. The currency of Molossia is the valora; its value is tied to the cost of a tube of chocolate chip cookie dough. Molossia remains at war with East Germany (which no longer exists) and enforces bans on guns, walruses, catfish, onions, and anything from Texas except pop star Kelly Clarkson. Truly, there is no nation like the Republic of Molossia!

King David announced with all certainty that no nation was like Israel. Israel was ruled by God, not by a self-proclaimed dictator. Israel was not at war with a nonexistent country but had been freed from a world power (Egypt). Israel was a land of milk and honey, not cookie dough! Baugh may pretend to be a sovereign ruler, but God's people need not pretend. We are ruled by the almighty God. There is no one like him!   —J. E.

22. "You made your people Israel your very own forever, and you, LORD, have become their God."

No other nation has received "most favored nation" status as *Israel* has. *God* bestowed that honor (accompanied by responsibilities) when

he established his covenant with the nation at Mount Sinai and designated them as his "treasured possession" from "out of all nations" (Exodus 19:5).

II. Future Blessings
(1 CHRONICLES 17:23-27)
A. For His Glory (vv. 23, 24)

23. "And now, LORD, let the promise you have made concerning your servant and his house be established forever. Do as you promised,

Having recounted the Lord's faithfulness to both him and to the nation of Israel, David now asks the *Lord* to establish that same faithfulness to him by bringing to pass all that the Lord has *promised* to David and *his house* (compare 1 Kings 8:22-26).

24. "so that it will be established and that your name will be great forever. Then people will say, 'The LORD Almighty, the God over Israel, is Israel's God!' And the house of your servant David will be established before you.

David desires that God keep his word. This hope is not solely so that David may benefit and receive all the good things God has promised. David also wants the Lord's reputation as a faithful, covenant-keeping God to receive additional acclaim. This concern for God's *name* to *be great forever* offers great insight into what makes David a man after God's own heart (Acts 13:22).

David also desires that *Israel* be recognized as the people whom God has singularly blessed. The continuation of his house, especially on the throne in Jerusalem, depends on Israel continuing as a nation. Of course, in Jesus we know that Israel did not have to continue to exist as a political entity for God to keep his promises. Christians today form the spiritual Israel over which Jesus reigns eternally (Romans 9:6-29; 1 Peter 2:9, 10, 25).

❧ *Antiestablishment?* ❧

Antiestablishment became a buzzword of the 1960s. Young people saw many wrongs perpetuated by society and began to question "The Establishment," the adults of the day. Ironically, the antiestablishment merely created an establishment of its own. T-shirts and jeans became the new establishment's uniform in opposition to the suits and ties of their parents. The evening martini was replaced by a joint, and ballroom dancing was rejected in favor of freestyle frolicking. And for all the passionate jargon, world problems remained unsolved. The generation promising to *fix* world problems is now being blamed by the younger generation for *causing* them!

David recognized that the solution to Israel's problems was not to make a new establishment but to submit to what God established. The throne of David was established by God to last forever. That true establishment still exists, ruled by the eternal son of David—Jesus. What is your role in spreading the establishment of God's kingdom?

—J. E.

B. For His Servant (vv. 25-27)

25. "You, my God, have revealed to your servant that you will build a house for him. So your servant has found courage to pray to you.

David's prayer has been grounded in the solemn promise the Lord made to *build a house for him*. Based on that sure word of the Lord, David has been stirred in his inner being to come to the Lord in prayer. It may be that, like David, our most fervent words spoken to God in prayer will come when they are based on the words he has spoken to us.

> **What Do You Think?**
> What are some appropriate ways to respond to fellow believers who claim that God told them to take or not take certain actions?
>
> *Digging Deeper*
> How would you further respond if the other believer quoted 1 Corinthians 2:14 to rebuff your reply?

Many outstanding books on prayer have been written over the years, but the Bible remains the best guide to prayer that one can use, in part thanks to David himself. One need only search the psalms to find David's prayers, available for the edification of God's people throughout gen-erations. God has promised to give us the confidence to come to him in prayer boldly (Hebrews 4:16). Daniel's awareness of the approaching end of the 70-year captivity of God's people (as foretold by the prophet Jeremiah) gave him the courage to pray and plead for God's mercy on his exiled people (Daniel 9:1-3).

26. "You, LORD, are God! You have promised these good things to your servant.

The root of the Hebrew word *promised* can also be translated "word" (1 Chronicles 10:13; 15;15; etc.). The Lord has always "worded" his *good things* to us in an abundance of promises. The strongest evidence of his goodness came when the Word became flesh and we could "read," not just the promise but the promise maker, on a deeply personal level (John 1:1, 14).

Grace was just as amazing to David in the Old Testament as it is for us under the new covenant. Any Christian might voice a similar prayer when he or she considers how abundant the Lord's goodness has been. We too have been given royal treatment, though our lives are riddled with sin and rebellion. God has lavished his mercy on us and made us his children. The apostle John says it well: "See what great love the Father has lavished on us, that we should be called children of God!" (1 John 3:1).

27. "Now you have been pleased to bless the house of your servant, that it may continue forever in your sight; for you, LORD, have blessed it, and it will be blessed forever."

Once more we see David expressing his desire that the *Lord* experience pleasure by blessing David's *house*. The prayer has been devoted to glorifying God, not David. David's two main motivations are the nature of God's blessings (abundant and sure) and David's deep comprehension of his own status as a mere *servant* whom the Lord has looked on with favor.

Although David's heir Solomon will turn from the Lord later in his life, the Lord will tear the kingdom away from Solomon's son, not Solomon himself. The reason? "For the sake of David your father" (1 Kings 11:12). God will also promise not to remove the entire kingdom but will leave one tribe for Solomon's son "for the sake of David my servant" (11:13; see 11:32, 36). Even after the nation divides, the Lord continues to honor David's legacy of faithful service. God will delay his judgment of the kingdom and of Jerusalem "for the sake of his servant David" (2 Kings 8:19; see also 19:34; 20:6).

David likely could not have anticipated the *forever* nature of the fulfillment of God's promises to him even as he trusted that they would be eternal (Psalms 16:11; 21:6). Lesson 3 noted that this fulfillment would come about through the great son of David, Jesus. He would establish the house, kingdom, and throne that God said would last forever (1 Chronicles 17:14). David's position may be likened to that of the Old Testament prophets who yearned to know more of how their prophecies would be fulfilled but which did not happen within their lifetimes (1 Peter 1:10-12; compare Hebrews 11).

David's prayer ends at this point. It is not hard to imagine that this devoted servant of the Lord remained seated for some time, simply reflecting on the mercies of God toward him and delighting in all that the Lord had promised.

Conclusion

A. Upward and Inward

All of us would do well to incorporate time-outs into our daily routine as David did. These times will help us develop the sense of gratitude that fills David's prayer. David began his prayer astonished at what God has just promised to provide for him. That God had promised to bless not only David but also his future house was an awe-inspiring thought. We can be assured, as David was, that God is sovereign in the present as proven by his past actions. He can take our lives and do great things with them, far beyond what we can imagine.

The other ingredient of prayer to be gleaned from our study deals with the matter of who we are. Today, many people revel in self-improvement, self-gratification, and self-fulfillment. The test of whether we are functioning at our highest levels is usually whether we are able to be independent. We expect to handle all sorts of problems—

O LORD, *there is none like thee, neither is there any God beside thee, according to all that we have heard with our ears.*
~1 Chronicles 17:20

Visual for Lesson 5. *Have the students pray this verse silently to themselves for one minute before closing the class with prayer.*

at home, at work, at church—on our own. When we begin to break down and think we might need help, we buy self-help books and resources. Such so-called solutions really mask the genuine root cause of humanity's problems. Any solution that leaves God the Creator out of the equation is doomed to failure. In the spiritual realm, the measure of our maturity is not our independence but our dependence on the Lord. If any of us asks the question, "Who am I?", the answer should be clear: "I am a servant of the Lord."

David found it difficult to come up with words to express his wonder at all that the Lord had promised to do for him. At times, we as followers of Jesus must also confess to being unable to express our gratitude for all we have been given because of his grace. What more can we say? Let our lives each day reflect our conviction that the God to whom David prayed and whom he served is our God. May such sacred times of prayer be part of our walk with the Lord as well.

B. Prayer

Father, stir us to give prayer the priority it must have in these perilous times. May we pray and live as people who know the truth that there is no other God but you. We pray in Jesus' name. Amen.

C. Thought to Remember

The most important time of any day
is spent with God.

INVOLVEMENT LEARNING

Enhance your lesson with NIV Bible Student *(from your curriculum supplier) and the reproducible activity page (at www.standardlesson.com or in the back of the* NIV Standard Lesson Commentary Deluxe Edition*).*

Into the Lesson

Before class, write familiar "best" or "of the year" honors on several index cards, one per card (examples: best dentist, grandparent of the year, top salesperson, spelling bee champion). Begin class by asking volunteers to draw cards and give an off-the-cuff acceptance speech for that award.

Alternative. Distribute copies of the "Exceptional Acceptance" exercise from the activity page, which you can download. Have class members work in pairs to discuss as indicated.

After either activity, discuss what makes a good acceptance speech. Lead into Bible study by saying, "When a person receives an honor, he or she may respond with gracious words. We can learn from David in this regard."

Into the Word

Divide the class into three groups. Give each group one of the following assignments on handouts (you prepare).

Humility Group: Read 1 Chronicles 17:16-19. 1—What was David's background (see also 1 Samuel 16:1-13)? 2—What merit did God see in David (see also Acts 13:22)?

Gratitude Group: Read 1 Chronicles 17:20-22. 1—Why was David grateful for being part of Israel (see also Deuteronomy 4:33, 34)? 2—What was God's intention for the nation of Israel from the beginning (see also Genesis 18:18, 19)?

Hope Group: Read 1 Chronicles 17:23-27. 1—What was the nature of the promise to David's descendants (see also Jeremiah 22:2-5)? 2—How was that promise fulfilled (compare Luke 1:29-33; Acts 13:32-35)?

After discussion winds down, have learners share their findings. Their results should be similar to these: **Humility Group**—David was not from Saul's royal line, but was the youngest son of a family of shepherds. God favored David, not because of his size or skill, but because David

shared God's heart. **Gratitude Group**—Israel was unique. God chose and protected a people to be the nation through which to reveal himself and his plan. Israel's origins are traced back to Abraham. The nation was to usher in the promised Messiah. **Hope Group**—Not every king in David's line obeyed God, and the nation suffered as a result. But the promise was never nullified. Jesus reigns eternally as David's descendant today.

Alternative. Distribute copies of the "How to Give an Acceptance Speech" exercise from the activity page. Have learners work in small groups to complete it. After either activity, lead into the final section of the lesson by saying, "David's prayer in this text provides us a good model for our own prayer lives. Let's see how we can apply what it teaches us."

Into Life

Close class by leading participants in a guided-prayer activity. Speak the words in italics, pausing as indicated for class members to respond with their own silent prayers.

Our God and Father of our Lord Jesus, we come to you in humility. We now confess reasons to you why we are unworthy of all you give us.

[Allow time for silent prayers in that regard.]

Nevertheless, you have promised that we are a royal priesthood and a holy nation according to 1 Peter 2:9. We ask that you help us be worthy of that calling this week as we seek to represent you in the following places.

[Allow time for silent prayers in that regard.]

We also come to you in gratitude for the people who minister to us in your name.

[Allow time for silent prayers in that regard.]

Finally, we come to you in hope, asking you to help us establish your throne in the hearts of those who do not yet know you.

[Allow time for silent prayers in that regard.]

We pray this in Jesus' name. Amen.

SOLOMON SUMMONS
THE ARK

DEVOTIONAL READING: Deuteronomy 31:7-13
BACKGROUND SCRIPTURE: 1 Kings 8:1-13; 2 Chronicles 5:1-14

1 KINGS 8:1-13

¹ Then King Solomon summoned into his presence at Jerusalem the elders of Israel, all the heads of the tribes and the chiefs of the Israelite families, to bring up the ark of the LORD's covenant from Zion, the City of David. ² All the Israelites came together to King Solomon at the time of the festival in the month of Ethanim, the seventh month.

³ When all the elders of Israel had arrived, the priests took up the ark, ⁴ and they brought up the ark of the LORD and the tent of meeting and all the sacred furnishings in it. The priests and Levites carried them up, ⁵ and King Solomon and the entire assembly of Israel that had gathered about him were before the ark, sacrificing so many sheep and cattle that they could not be recorded or counted.

⁶ The priests then brought the ark of the LORD's covenant to its place in the inner sanctuary of the temple, the Most Holy Place, and put it beneath the wings of the cherubim. ⁷ The cherubim spread their wings over the place of the ark and overshadowed the ark and its carrying poles. ⁸ These poles were so long that their ends could be seen from the Holy Place in front of the inner sanctuary, but not from outside the Holy Place; and they are still there today. ⁹ There was nothing in the ark except the two stone tablets that Moses had placed in it at Horeb, where the LORD made a covenant with the Israelites after they came out of Egypt. ¹⁰ When the priests withdrew from the Holy Place, the cloud filled the temple of the LORD. ¹¹ And the priests could not perform their service because of the cloud, for the glory of the LORD filled his temple.

¹² Then Solomon said, "The LORD has said that he would dwell in a dark cloud; ¹³ I have indeed built a magnificent temple for you, a place for you to dwell forever."

KEY VERSE

I have indeed built a magnificent temple for you, a place for you to dwell forever. —1 Kings 8:13

HONORING
GOD

LESSON AIMS

After participating in this lesson, each learner will be able to:

1. Retell the story of moving the ark of the covenant to the new temple in Jerusalem.

2. Explain the significance of that placement in historical context.

3. Propose a way to realize better God's presence in the church's corporate worship or in his or her life personally.

LESSON OUTLINE

Introduction

A. Dedication Ceremony

Crowds numbering more than 150,000 assembled on the National Mall in Washington, DC, on May 29, 2004. They had gathered for the dedication of the National World War II Memorial. The service was a time to remember the courage and sacrifice of 16 million men and women who served in the U.S. armed forces during World War II, especially that of the 400,000 who died. The millions who supported the war effort from home were also recognized. The service further celebrated the completion of 11 years of work on the memorial, which had begun in 1993 and involved thousands of individuals and many corporations throughout the country.

Celebrating the completion of massive projects is nothing new. First Kings 8 is an example of that fact as it narrates the dedication of the temple, which Solomon completed in about 959 BC. It was a time to celebrate! More importantly, it was a time to recall the truths and commitments that initiated the project in the first place.

B. Lesson Context

After King David's death, the Lord established Solomon on the throne in Israel (1 Kings 2:12). The new king attended to the mission his father, David, had given him: building a temple. David had streamlined the process by stockpiling materials Solomon's builders used for the awe-inspiring structure (1 Chronicles 22:2-6).

In addition, David had purchased the land for the temple, which had been Araunah's threshing floor (2 Samuel 24:18-25; 1 Chronicles 21:22–22:1; see lesson 3). This plot of land was north of the king's palace, in the ridge of hills known as Mount Moriah (2 Chronicles 3:1). This was the place where Abraham, in obedience to God's command, would have sacrificed Isaac as a burnt offering had the Lord not intervened (Genesis 22:2, 10-14).

The magnificent temple was completed in the eighth month of the eleventh year of King Solomon's reign. Skilled builders and artisans had labored on it for seven years (1 Kings 6:38). What David had proposed to do many years earlier had been accomplished by his son Solomon just as God instructed.

Today's lesson text picks up after the completion of the temple. Second Chronicles 5:2–6:2 contains a parallel account. The key difference between these two texts is found in 2 Chronicles 5:11-13, which adds details about the priests and musicians who were present.

I. The Ark on the Road
(1 KINGS 8:1-5)
A. The Assembly (vv. 1, 2)

1a. Then King Solomon summoned into his presence at Jerusalem the elders of Israel, all the heads of the tribes and the chiefs of the Israelite families,

The phrase *elders of Israel* is a broad term, referring to the informal heads of the various *Israelite families* (compare Numbers 7:2). The other two phrases refer to positions of authority of a more official nature within the clans and *tribes*.

> **What Do You Think?**
> What could be your part in improving the visibility of leadership unity in your church?
> *Digging Deeper*
> In what ways should that unity be evident in distinction from, say, that of a political party?

1b. to bring up the ark of the LORD's covenant from Zion, the City of David.

Solomon summons these influential leaders to celebrate the ark's journeying to the newly finished temple. *The ark of the . . . covenant* is a gold-covered wooden box with an ornamented lid known as the atonement cover. Two golden cherubim are mounted on the lid (Exodus 25:17-22). The box is two and a half cubits (three and three-quarter feet) long and one and a half cubits (two and a quarter feet) high and deep. The ark signifies the throne of God or his footstool on earth (1 Samuel 4:4; 1 Chronicles 28:2; Psalms 99:1, 5; 132:7, 8). Though the ark is now lost to history, John saw it in his vision of Heaven, once again housed in the temple (Revelation 11:19).

David had previously brought the ark to the city of Jerusalem but not the tabernacle, which housed it; instead, David had erected a tent for the ark within the old Jebusite fortress of *Zion* (2 Samuel 5–7; 2 Chronicles 1:3, 4). The designation Zion is often used in poetry to refer to Jerusalem (examples: Isaiah 1:8; 3:16; Lamentations 2:10; 4:2).

The leaders' gathering to *bring up the ark* from Zion indicates that the temple has been built outside the original confines of David's Jerusalem. The term Zion will come to designate the temple area as a whole (Isaiah 8:18; Amos 1:2) and then the entire city of Jerusalem (Isaiah 10:24; Amos 6:1). To refer to Zion as *the City of David* highlights God's choice of both.

2. All the Israelites came together to King Solomon at the time of the festival in the month of Ethanim, the seventh month.

The festival that occurs in *the seventh month* is the Festival of Tabernacles (Leviticus 23:34). It commemorates God's provision during the Israelites' wilderness wanderings as well as his giving them rest in Canaan (23:42, 43).

The fact that 1 Kings 6:38 says the temple is finished in "the month of Bul, the eighth month" creates an uncertainty when compared with the timing of the dedication in the seventh month. Many scholars propose the solution that the verse before us refers to the Ethanim of the year that follows. Eleven months thus pass between the end of construction and the dedication.

Others propose that the extended, 14-day celebration (1 Kings 8:65) begins in the seventh month and ends at the beginning of the eighth month. But this interpretation requires the feast to start later than the prescribed "fifteenth day" of that

HOW TO SAY IT

Araunah	A-raw-nuh.
Bul	Bool.
Ethanim	*Eth*-uh-nim.
Horeb	*Ho*-reb.
Kiriath Jearim	*Kir*-ih-ath *Jee*-uh-rim or Jee-*a*-rim.
Kohathite	*Ko*-hath-ite.
Obed-Edom	O-bed-*Ee*-dum.
tabernacle	*tah*-burr-*nah*-kul.

month (see Leviticus 23:34; Numbers 29:12). An extended application of the exception in Numbers 9:9-13 regarding Passover might allow this, however (compare 2 Chronicles 30).

We must not lose sight of the fact that the feast emphasizes the Lord's faithfulness to Israel. He has kept his promises to Abraham (Genesis 17:4-8). Now, the temple testifies to God's faithfulness to David as well (1 Chronicles 17:11, 12; see lesson 3). After the exiles return from Babylon, the feast will be celebrated again with great joy (Nehemiah 8:17).

B. The Procession (vv. 3, 4)

3. When all the elders of Israel had arrived, the priests took up the ark,

Although *the elders of Israel* represent the nation in the procession, *the priests* actually transport *the ark*. The Kohathites, a branch of the priestly tribe of Levi, have the exclusive responsibility of transporting the holy articles pertaining to the tabernacle, including the ark of the covenant (Numbers 4:1-5). They carry the ark on their shoulders, using two staves running through the four rings on the corners of the ark (Exodus 25:12-14; contrast 2 Chronicles 35:3).

David had reminded the levitical priests of the critical need to abide by this regulation (1 Chronicles 15:11-15). Unfortunately, David only reminded the priests of their duty after Uzzah, a non-priest, died during the first attempt to transport the ark from Kiriath Jearim to Jerusalem (13:5-10).

4. and they brought up the ark of the LORD and the tent of meeting and all the sacred furnishings in it. The priests and Levites carried them up,

Although the Kohathites bear *the ark,* other Levites apparently carry *the tent of meeting* and its furnishings. The division of labor and means of transporting the ark are both important for showing proper respect to God and avoiding his anger (1 Chronicles 15:13).

Solomon has constructed new furnishings for the temple (1 Kings 7:48-51). Among the tabernacle's original furnishings, only the ark remains in use because of its importance as a symbol of God's throne and reign.

C. The Gathering (v. 5)

5. and King Solomon and the entire assembly of Israel that had gathered about him were before the ark, sacrificing so many sheep and cattle that they could not be recorded or counted.

Having arrived at the temple grounds, the people gather around the king. Their position *before the ark* signifies the status of both *Israel* and *Solomon* as the Lord's subjects (see commentary on 1 Kings 8:1). God is their real king; Solomon is but his representative (see 1 Samuel 8:6-9).

The offering of a large number of sacrifices echoes at least two earlier events in Israel's history. Sacrifices were offered at the dedication of the tabernacle (Exodus 40:29), and David had sacrificed a bull and a calf after every six steps the priests took as they bore the ark from the house of Obed-Edom to Jerusalem (2 Samuel 6:9-15). Moreover, the fact that *so many* sacrifices are made *that they* cannot *be recorded or counted* echoes Solomon's description of Israel's population (1 Kings 3:8).

> *What Do You Think?*
> How can Christians determine the appropriate size of a personal lifestyle sacrifice or monetary offering in differing worship and service contexts?
>
> *Digging Deeper*
> How can churches as a whole do the same thing?

❧ PRAY IN, PRAY OUT ❧

The Ranch is a mission to young people whose lives have been twisted by addictions, sex, and a dysfunctional family life. These are youth who have been set up for hard adult lives.

When new students come to the Ranch, they are "prayed in." God's blessing is invoked on their season in the ministry. As the students come to the end of their time at the Ranch, they are "prayed out." The service dedicates the students to a new relationship with God and others. It also dedicates the young people to a new life of hope and accomplishment as well as asking for God's blessings.

Israel's dysfunctional past made it hard for them to live as the people of God. So the dedication of the temple was more than a ceremony for a new building. It was also a dedication of the nation to God's service. How does the dedication of your "temple" to God overcome your past?

—C. R. B.

II. The Ark at Home
(1 Kings 8:6-13)

A. In the Most Holy Place (vv. 6-8)

6. The priests then brought the ark of the Lord's covenant to its place in the inner sanctuary of the temple, the Most Holy Place, and put it beneath the wings of the cherubim.

The priests place *the ark* in *the inner sanctuary* of the temple as it had been in the tabernacle (Exodus 26:33; 2 Samuel 6:17). Because the ark is the symbol of God's presence, the temple could not be considered God's dwelling place until the ark was situated in *the Most Holy Place. The cherubim* are made of gold and figuratively guard the ark (Exodus 25:18, 19).

The word translated *temple* in this chapter is also appropriately translated "house" (examples: 2 Samuel 7:2, 16, 29). This marks the first of 21 times the underlying Hebrew word is used in this chapter. Its repetition highlights the Lord's promised presence. It also evokes memories of God's twofold promise that he would build David a "house" (dynasty) and that David's son would build the house for God (2 Samuel 7:11-13). Referring to the temple as a house implies that God has chosen to dwell in Israel.

7. The cherubim spread their wings over the place of the ark and overshadowed the ark and its carrying poles.

Within the Most Holy Place, *the ark* is placed under two large *cherubim* whose *wings* span the width of the chamber (1 Kings 6:23-30). In Ancient Near Eastern thought and art, cherubim are celestial beings who guard sacred spaces (compare Genesis 3:24). They commonly are depicted with the body of a lion, the wings of a bird, and the face of a human (Exodus 25:20; 37:7-9; contrast Ezekiel 1:6-11; 10:20-22). Whereas the cherubim on the atone-ment cover face each other (Exodus 25:17-20), these cherubim look out from the "innermost room of the temple" to face the places where the priests most frequently minister (1 Kings 6:27).

The ark's presence in this chamber makes it the most sacred space in Israel. Because the ark signifies the throne of God or his footstool (see commentary on 1 Kings 8:1), it also transforms this space into an earthly representation of God's heavenly throne room (Psalm 11:4). Only the great high priest can enter the Most Holy Place, once a year on the Day of Atonement (Leviticus 16; compare Hebrews 9:1-10).

8. These poles were so long that their ends could be seen from the Holy Place in front of the inner sanctuary, but not from outside the Holy Place; and they are still there today.

Even though the ark is now in its permanent location, *the poles* remain in place (Exodus 25:13-15). These poles can be seen by priests when the veil into *the Holy Place* is open, but not from outside. The statement that the poles *are still there today* implies that this section of 1 Kings was written before the temple was destroyed in 586 BC (2 Kings 25:8-15).

B. With Glorious Memories (vv. 9-12)

9. There was nothing in the ark except the two stone tablets that Moses had placed in it at Horeb, where the Lord made a covenant with the Israelites after they came out of Egypt.

At one time, the ark contained Aaron's budding staff (Numbers 17:10) and a jar of manna (Exodus 16:33, 34) as well as *the two stone tablets* that bear witness to the covenant God had made with Israel (24:12; 1 Kings 8:9; Hebrews 9:4). By this time, the pot of manna and Aaron's staff have gone missing. The Philistines may have removed them when they captured the ark during the days of Samuel (1 Samuel 4:1-11). The ark now contains only the two stone tablets of the law that God gave to *Moses* (Exodus 25:16).

Nevertheless, the presence of the two stone tablets represents the *covenant* relationship God initiated with Israel and the obligations Israel has as his covenant people. The Lord made this covenant with Israel *at Horeb*, also commonly called Mount

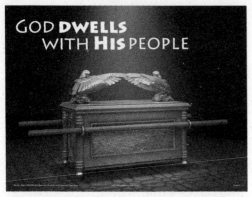

GOD DWELLS WITH HIS PEOPLE

Visual for Lesson 6. *As you discuss how to show God's presence, ask the class if your congregation is more like the ark (hidden) or temple (visible).*

Sinai (compare Exodus 19:20–20:21; Deuteronomy 5). The ark's moving to the temple represents God's continued, faithful presence with Israel.

What Do You Think?

How can our church help the members better understand the significance of Scripture to its identity and practices?

Digging Deeper

Consider ways that the congregation can do this both collectively and as individual members.

10. When the priests withdrew from the Holy Place, the cloud filled the temple of the LORD.

Allusions to the exodus and the dedication of the tabernacle at Horeb abound at the temple dedication. The first direct link between the two events is a physical sign. While the nation walked in the wilderness, Israel had been guided by a pillar of *cloud* filled with God's glory (Exodus 13:21, 22; 33:9, 10). When Moses ascended the mountain to receive the law, the cloud of God's glory looked like "consuming fire" (24:17). A cloud also filled the tabernacle during its dedication and stayed over it by day throughout Israel's wilderness sojourn (Leviticus 16:2; Numbers 9:15-23).

Later biblical texts will also employ images of the cloud of God's glory and presence. Unfortunately, the prophet Ezekiel will have a vision of the glory of God leaving the temple in response to Judah's sin (Ezekiel 10:3-5, 18, 19; 11:22, 23). This clearly represents God's removing his presence from the temple (contrast 43:1-5). On the Mount of Transfiguration, Peter, James, and John will be covered by a cloud from which the Father speaks (Matthew 17:1-7).These signs of God's presence reassure his people that he is not far away. He chooses to be near his people, so near that he will choose to take on flesh (Hebrews 2:17).

11. And the priests could not perform their service because of the cloud, for the glory of the LORD filled his temple.

The experience of *the priests* in the Lord's *temple* further alludes to the days of Moses. Not even that great prophet could enter the tent because *the glory of the Lord* descended on it and filled it (Exodus 40:34, 35). It took only the afterimage of God's glory to overwhelm the Israelites when they saw Moses' face after he received the law (34:29-35).

In a similar fashion, John's future vision will reveal servants of the Lord being prevented by the smoke of the glory of the Lord from ministering in God's heavenly temple (Revelation 15:8). From the days of Moses and Solomon until eternity, God's glorious presence overwhelms his servants.

❧ PRESENCE AND ABSENCE ❧

A married couple occasionally attended a church where I ministered. They earned their living teaching Dale Carnegie's principles from *How to Win Friends and Influence People.* Carnegie's principles were based to some extent on biblical teachings about caring for one's neighbors.

However, this couple found it easier to proclaim Carnegie's principles than to practice them. Their difficulties seemed to stem from using the principles to manipulate people; personal graces that come from the heart were absent.

Solomon's temple is said to have been the most magnificent building in the ancient world. However, it was nothing but an architectural marvel until God's presence—symbolized by the ark of the covenant and the cloud of glory—came to inhabit the place. In a similar way, we may build our lives to have a desirable outward appearance, but if our behavior fails to reflect the presence of God in our lives, what value is there? —C. R. B.

12. Then Solomon said, "The LORD has said that he would dwell in a dark cloud;

Solomon's statement serves to link again the temple he has built with memories of Israel's formation and the subsequent construction of the tabernacle (compare 2 Samuel 22:10). The statement in this verse is similar to the description of God's presence when Moses approached him to receive the law (Exodus 20:21).

While *a dark cloud* represents God's presence with Israel, it also stresses his holy hiddenness or otherness. A thick darkness engulfed Mount Sinai as God gave Israel the Ten Commandments (Deuteronomy 4:11; 5:22) and was one of the many phenomena that evoked great fear among Moses and the Israelites (Exodus 20:18; Hebrews 12:18-21). This display of God's power and majesty reminds the Israelites that the loving God who is near to them is also holy and transcendent above them. They must not treat him lightly. Remembering God's holiness will help Israel guard against sin, knowing that God's presence is both a comfort and a terror (Exodus 20:20).

> **What Do You Think?**
> In what ways can our church ensure that God's presence is not hidden to the surrounding community?
> **Digging Deeper**
> How do Matthew 5:14-16; 28:19, 20; 1 Timothy 6:12; and Revelation 2:13 inform your answer?

C. In a Permanent House (v. 13)

13. "I have indeed built a magnificent temple for you, a place for you to dwell forever."

Long before this dedication celebration, Moses had celebrated that God would establish himself among the people in the promised land (Exodus 15:17). Solomon's words connect the temple's completion to David's desire to build a *temple* for the Lord and God's promise that David's son would build it (2 Samuel 7:1-3, 12, 13). Solomon has been faithful to provide Israel a place for worshipping God. The Lord has been faithful to honor David's desire and the king's effort. Later

generations will continue to celebrate God's presence at Zion (Psalms 132:13; 135:21; etc.).

First Kings 8:27, 28 makes clear that Solomon does not believe that God can be contained in and confined to the temple or that God even needs the temple (compare Acts 17:24). Rather, the temple with the ark situated within reassures Israel of God's presence among them as their king. Centuries later, Jesus will make a similar point when he declares that anyone who swears by the temple really swears by God (Matthew 23:21). The temple in and of itself has no significance; the presence of the Lord in the temple means everything.

Conclusion

A. God Dwells Among His People

The procession of the ark into the temple of Solomon marked a central truth in Israel: the God of the universe was also the faithful God who had called the Israelites into covenant. He dwelled among them as king. The God whose presence was with Israel dwelled among us in the person of Jesus Christ (John 1:14). He now indwells us through his Spirit (Acts 1:8; 2:1-4; etc.). May we also celebrate that our God keeps his promises and stays close to his people!

> **What Do You Think?**
> What one area of spiritual growth will you pursue in order better to conduct yourself as a new-covenant temple of the Holy Spirit?
> **Digging Deeper**
> How do Ephesians 2:19-22; 1 Corinthians 3:6; 6:19; and 2 Corinthians 6:16 inform your answer?

B. Prayer

Lord, we praise you as our king who keeps his promises. We thank you that you dwelled among us in Jesus and dwell with us today in the Holy Spirit. We thank you as we pray in Jesus' name. Amen.

C. Thought to Remember

God still chooses to live among his people.

INVOLVEMENT LEARNING

Enhance your lesson with NIV Bible Student *(from your curriculum supplier) and the reproducible activity page (at www.standardlesson.com or in the back of the* NIV Standard Lesson Commentary Deluxe Edition*).*

Into the Lesson

Ask class members to recall the most spectacular celebration they've ever seen. If responses are slow in coming, mention categories such as patriotic and sports-related. (*Option.* Larger classes can keep this from dragging out by conducting this activity in small groups.)

Lead into Bible study by saying, "No matter how grandiose the celebrations of secular culture may be, they pale in comparison with dramatic events in the history of God's people. Let's consider what one of those has to teach us."

Into the Word

Have the lesson text of 1 Kings 8:1-13 read aloud. After the reading, advise participants to keep that text open before them. Then give each participant a copy of the following matching quiz, which you have duplicated in advance.

❧ PRECURSORS TO 1 KINGS 8:1-13 ❧

___ 1. Temple's Planning   A. Exodus 20:21
___ 2. City's Possession   B. Exodus 24:16, 17
___ 3. Dwelling's Placement   C. Deuteronomy 12:10, 11
___ 4. Cherubims' Positioning   D. 2 Samuel 5:6, 7
___ 5. Glory's Presence   E. 1 Chronicles 22:6-11
___ 6. Darkness Pervades   F. Psalm 99:1

Announce the quiz to be a speed drill with a one-minute time limit. After that minute, call time and announce the answers: 1–E, 2–D, 3–C, 4–F, 5–B, 6–A.

Say, "The background of the bringing of the ark to the temple is important. It was in the works for centuries before it actually happened—in the mind of God if not in the mind of humans." Then give each participant a copy of the following matching quiz, which you have duplicated in advance.

For completion of this quiz, put participants into study pairs or groups of three. Advise that this is not a speed drill since the expected responses are not as clear-cut as those of the first quiz. Recommend that if participants get stuck, they should

move on to the next; answers may ultimately be discerned through a process of elimination.

❧ PRESENTATION IN 1 KINGS 8:1-13 ❧

___ 1. Ark Ascends   A. 1 Kings 8:1
___ 2. Baggage Accompanies   B. 1 Kings 8:2, 3
___ 3. Carriers Assemble   C. 1 Kings 8:4
___ 4. Death Aplenty   D. 1 Kings 8:5
___ 5. Evening Appearance   E. 1 Kings 8:11
___ 6. Frozen Activity   F. 1 Kings 8:12

Expected responses: 1–A ("bring up"), 2–C (baggage = "sacred furnishings"), 3–B, 4–D, 5–F (taking the fading light of evening as darkness), 6–E.

Discuss results as whole class. Supplement responses with information from the commentary.

Option. Distribute copies of the "Glory, Glory, Glory!" exercise from the activity page, which you can download. Time allowing, have learners complete it in groups of three. It can be a take-home if time is short.

Into Life

Challenge class members to consider what they can learn about worship as they read the story of God's people bringing the ark to the temple. Make the following statements about today's text, and ask students to respond in ways they can do similar things in our worship today.

1–God's people remembered His work among them in the past.

2–God's people sought to honor Him with their worship.

3–God's people chose physical elements to represent spiritual truths.

4–God's people saw His presence among them as they worshipped.

Option. Distribute copies of the "God's Glory in Us" exercise from the activity page. Challenge class members to jot down a response to at least one of the questions before class adjourns. Call for volunteers to share what they've written, but don't put anyone on the spot.

SOLOMON SPEAKS TO THE PEOPLE

DEVOTIONAL READING: Psalm 132:1-5, 11-18
BACKGROUND SCRIPTURE: 1 Kings 8:14-21; 2 Chronicles 6

1 KINGS 8:14-21

14 While the whole assembly of Israel was standing there, the king turned around and blessed them. 15 Then he said:

"Praise be to the LORD, the God of Israel, who with his own hand has fulfilled what he promised with his own mouth to my father David. For he said, 16 'Since the day I brought my people Israel out of Egypt, I have not chosen a city in any tribe of Israel to have a temple built so that my Name might be there, but I have chosen David to rule my people Israel.'

17 "My father David had it in his heart to build a temple for the Name of the LORD, the God of Israel. 18 But the LORD said to my father David, 'You did well to have it in your heart to build a temple for my Name. 19 Nevertheless, you are not the one to build the temple, but your son, your own flesh and blood—he is the one who will build the temple for my Name.'

20 "The LORD has kept the promise he made: I have succeeded David my father and now I sit on the throne of Israel, just as the LORD promised, and I have built the temple for the Name of the LORD, the God of Israel. 21 I have provided a place there for the ark, in which is the covenant of the LORD that he made with our ancestors when he brought them out of Egypt."

KEY VERSE

Praise be to the LORD, the God of Israel, who with his own hand has fulfilled what he promised with his own mouth to my father David. —**1 Kings 8:15**

HONORING GOD

Unit 2: Dedicating the Temple of God

LESSONS 6–9

LESSON AIMS

After participating in this lesson, each learner will be able to:

1. Recall promises within the Lord's covenant to David.

2. Explain the purpose of remembering God's mighty works.

3. Create a plan to exhibit more faithfulness in one area of life in light of God's prior faithfulness to him or her.

LESSON OUTLINE

Introduction

A. Because He Said He Would

When asked to give the eulogy at his father's funeral, a young man named Alex Sheen decided to honor his dad by commemorating him as one who always kept his word. Sheen distributed "promise cards" with the words "because I said I would" written in the corner. He asked people to write promises on the cards and then to hand the cards to those to whom they made the promises. The persons making the promises would get the card back once they had fulfilled their word. Sheen then offered to send free cards to anyone who asked, no matter where they lived.

Word got out. Within 18 months, Sheen had kept *his* promise and sent out more than 250,000 cards. This response led to his establishment of the nonprofit organization "because I said I would." Since 2013, the organization has provided over eight million promise cards.

This week's text focuses on words Solomon spoke at the dedication of the temple. Those words highlighted promises made and kept. Because God said he would, he did.

B. Lesson Context

The faithful God of Israel had established David's son Solomon on the throne of Israel (1 Kings 2:12). God then enabled Solomon to complete the project his father had given him to build a house of worship for the Lord (1 Chronicles 22:6-13). First Kings 8:1-13 (last week's lesson) recounted the opening scenes of the dedication ceremony for the grand temple Solomon had built in Jerusalem for the God of Israel (see lesson 6). Today's account continues to examine that ceremony. A parallel account can be found in 2 Chronicles 6:3-11.

I. Blessings
(1 KINGS 8:14, 15)
A. For the People (v. 14)

14. While the whole assembly of Israel was standing there, the king turned around and blessed them.

Details in this account again recall events from the Israelites' time in the exodus (see lesson 6 regarding previous parallels). For example, when the glory of the Lord filled the tabernacle at Mount Horeb, the people stood in reverence (Exodus 33:10). Similarly here, the glory has filled the temple (1 Kings 8:11, last week's lesson) with the people standing before it. In the instance at hand, *the whole assembly* stands respectfully to hear *the king*, knowing that God is present (8:10-12).

Their standing in this context is a position of prayer. Though today we may think of kneeling as the most devout position, standing is often the preferred posture in ancient Israel (compare Leviticus 9:5; 1 Kings 8:22-61).

The king has been facing the sanctuary on a special bronze platform while the priests were at the altar (2 Chronicles 5:12; 6:13). Unlike the people, it appears that Solomon is kneeling as he speaks (6:13). Kneeling is not necessarily a posture of worship; this posture can be assumed in situations to express one's lowly position before a more powerful or important person. In the context at hand, kneeling conveys respect for the Lord and humility in his presence (1 Kings 8:54; Ezra 9:5; Isaiah 45:23).

In the world of the Bible, the act of blessing expresses one's desire that God's approval and goodwill will rest on a person or group. The content of Solomon's blessing is not recorded here. Later verses offer clues of what Solomon may pray as a blessing for the people (1 Kings 8:29-53, not in today's lesson text). Likely, the blessing the king seeks is for God to hear the people and forgive them when they repent of sins.

> **What Do You Think?**
> What will be your personal part in helping your congregation bless the people in its neighborhood?
> **Digging Deeper**
> What does Matthew 5:43-48 suggest regarding the form and content for your plan?

Solomon's blessing echoes Moses' blessing of the people following the completion of the tabernacle (Exodus 39:32, 43). The king's bless-

ing of *the whole assembly of Israel* highlights his role as a spiritual leader among the people as well as his identity as the nation's civic leader (compare Deuteronomy 17:14-20). Solomon's words of blessing nudge Israel toward greater faithfulness (1 Kings 8:65, 66).

B. For the Lord (v. 15)

15a. Then he said: "Praise be to the LORD, the God of Israel.

Having brought the ark of the covenant into the temple (1 Kings 8:6; see lesson 6), Solomon reminds Israel of the greatness of God (compare David's words in 1 Chronicles 16:36). The Hebrew word translated *praise* is the same as the word previously translated "blessed" (see 1 Kings 8:14). The NIV frequently translates the word as "praise" when referring to human action toward God (Genesis 24:27; Exodus 18:10; 1 Samuel 25:32, 39; 2 Samuel 18:28; 22:47; 1 Kings 1:48; etc.). Such passages emphasize that the Lord is worthy of reverence and worship.

Solomon begins the praise by addressing God with the extended title *the Lord, the God of Israel* (see 1 Kings 8:17, 20). The component parts of this address suggest much about God. In English translations, the small capital letters in LORD indicate that the name Yahweh is being used. This is the name that God revealed to Moses, translated "I Am Who I Am" (Exodus 3:14). At least two important attributes are suggested in this name: that God is eternal (compare 1 Timothy 1:17), and that he is unchanging (compare James 1:17).

In contrast with this special name, the Hebrew word translated *God* is much more generic. Many cultures in the Ancient Near East use a form of the same word to refer to the greatest of their gods.

HOW TO SAY IT

Ammonites	*Am*-un-ites.
Edomites	*Ee*-dum-ites.
Hiram	*High*-rum.
Moabites	*Mo*-ub-ites.
Philistines	Fuh-*liss*-teenz or *Fill*-us-teenz.
Syrians	*Sear*-ee-unz.
Tyre	Tire.

Except the LORD build the house, they labour in vain that build it. —Psalm 127:1

Visual for Lesson 7. *Point to this visual as you discuss the process of discerning one's role in God's work, whether in support or as a primary actor.*

In Israel, of course, the term refers to the true God only and ascribes all honor and power and glory and might to him.

The words *Lord* and *God* are frequently used together in the Bible, notably in Genesis 2. In combination, *Lord God* suggests that the most powerful god—the only God—is also a God who chooses to be close to his people, to reveal himself to them so that they can know him.

The phrase *of Israel* further emphasizes God's nearness—not just to his creation generally but to his chosen people specifically. The Lord God has chosen to create a covenant with Israel. Before revealing his name to Moses, the Lord indicated himself to be the God of Abraham, Isaac, and Jacob (Exodus 3:6). God connects his name to his people. Jesus will use this very name later to show that God is the God of the living, not the dead (Mark 12:24-27). The Lord God is the powerful, transcendent deity who is near to the Israelites and has made covenant with them.

15b. "who with his own hand has fulfilled what he promised with his own mouth to my father David. For he said,"

That Yahweh had spoken the promises to *David* with *his own mouth* points both to God's intimate involvement in the promise and to its reliability (compare Psalm 105:8; Hebrews 6:13-20). Working out those blessings *with his own hand* paints an image of sovereign power (Deuteronomy 3:24; 2 Chronicles 30:12; Ezekiel 20:33;

etc.). What the Lord had promised, he has now performed.

❧ UNFULFILLED DESIRES ❧

On May 25, 1961, President John F. Kennedy spoke to a joint session of Congress. He urged Congress to join with him in accomplishing an amazing and seemingly unreachable goal: "I believe that this nation should commit itself to achieving the goal, before this decade is out, of landing a man on the moon and returning him safely to the Earth."

Congress agreed, and work began in earnest. Tragically, Kennedy was assassinated less than six years before astronauts Neil Armstrong and Buzz Aldrin landed on the moon on July 20, 1969.

Neither President Kennedy nor King David lived to see their dreams fulfilled. However, their dreams inspired others who followed them. What dreams do you have that can challenge others to greatness in the cause of Christ and his kingdom?

—C. R. B.

II. Promises
(1 KINGS 8:16-21)
A. For David (vv. 16-18)

16a. "'Since the day I brought my people Israel out of Egypt,

Solomon joins Moses, Joshua, and Samuel as leaders of a given generation of Israelites who review significant events of their nation's past (Deuteronomy 1–4; Joshua 24; 1 Samuel 12:6-15). We see in the Bible that remembering correctly is often the first step to acting rightly (Numbers 15:39; Deuteronomy 5:15; 1 Corinthians 11:23-34). Even God is said to remember his promises before taking action (Genesis 8:1; 9:15, 16; Exodus 2:24). Rehearsing national memories of what God has done helps orient a new generation toward God in preparation for a new era of his dealing with the nation (Exodus 13:3-16).

God's covenant with *Israel* and his actions in rescuing that people from *Egypt* had formed the basis for God's covenant with David (Exodus 19–24; 2 Samuel 7). The temple, obviously blessed by God with the presence of his glory (1 Kings

8:10, 11), now stands as a reminder of his continuing presence. It also serves as a portent of his future involvement in the nation (1 Kings 8:27-30; 2 Chronicles 6:10, 11). Should future generations dismiss God's presence among them, judgment will follow (Jeremiah 7:4-15; Ezekiel 10:18, 19). They will, and it does.

16b. "'I have not chosen a city in any tribe of Israel to have a temple built

Before *Israel* entered the promised land, Moses told the Israelites that the Lord would choose a place for their worship (Deuteronomy 12:4-7). For over four centuries, the portable tabernacle served as that sanctuary (Joshua 4:18, 19; 8:30-35; 1 Samuel 4:4; 1 Chronicles 17:5, 6).

During that time, Israel was meant to conquer the land (Joshua 1:3-6; Judges 1:19-21, 27-36). Israel's hold on the land, however, began to solidify once David came to the throne. David's victories over the Ammonites, Edomites, Philistines, Moabites, and Syrians (2 Samuel 5:17-25; 8) resulted in Israel's finally possessing the land the Lord had promised through Abraham and Moses (Genesis 15:18; Exodus 23:31; Deuteronomy 11:24). David's conquest of Jerusalem became the focal point of Israel's victories (2 Samuel 5:6-12).

16c. "'so that my Name might be there,

The *Name* of the Lord is invoked repeatedly in the dedication of the temple (1 Kings 8:16-20, 29, 33, 35, 41-44, 48). God's glory and his name are frequently invoked in similar ways. Both are used to speak of God's awe-inspiring, transcendent nature.

When Moses desired to see the Lord's glory, God allowed him instead to hear a proclamation of God's name and to see his goodness (Exodus 33:18, 19). The Lord later proclaimed his name again to Moses, telling what his interactions with Israel have revealed about God's character (34:6, 7). The glory of the Lord subsequently made Moses' face shine (34:29-35).

While God's glory suggests that he is unapproachable (compare 1 Timothy 6:16), his name speaks of Israel's ability to know and experience his goodness and mercy. Solomon goes on to speak of Israel praising the Lord's name (1 Kings 8:33-36). Similarly, the psalmists frequently write of calling on or trusting in God's name (Psalms 9:10; 80:18; 99:6; 105:1; 116:13, 17).

Attaching one's name to something like a building or someone such as a spouse or family lineage conveys association. The Lord does not belong to the temple, but he does allow the temple to be associated with his name. He does not dwell in the temple in the sense that it contains him. The Lord remains transcendent, free, and sovereign even though the temple is a place where worshippers can connect with God.

16d. "'but I have chosen David to rule my people Israel.'

Solomon's words suggest that the events in which the community is participating are part of the next major stage in the Lord's ongoing relationship with Israel. Instead of choosing a city in which to place his name, the Lord had chosen *David*. God promised that David would have an everlasting dynasty and that a son would build a temple for the Lord (2 Samuel 7:11-16).

Now the city David conquered has become the place the Lord allows to be the home of the temple that reflects his name (2 Chronicles 6:6). The temple becomes the authorized location for Israelites to worship (Deuteronomy 12:5).

17. "My father David had it in his heart to build a temple for the Name of the LORD, the God of Israel.

The events Solomon recalls here and in subsequent verses are narrated in more detail in 2 Samuel 7 and 1 Chronicles 17 (see commentary on 1 Kings 8:18, 19, below). Having conquered Jerusalem, *David* found an ally in Hiram, king of Tyre. Hiram aided in David's building projects by sending cedars from Lebanon as well as skilled workers to Jerusalem. These builders helped David construct a palace (2 Samuel 5:11). After its completion, David became concerned that he was living in a cedar palace while Israel worshipped the Lord in a tent (1 Samuel 7:1, 2). He then committed himself to build *a temple* for the Lord (1 Chronicles 22:7; Acts 7:46).

One inherently connects a person's name to that person's reputation. Therefore, David's desire to build a temple for God's *Name* expresses his desire to exalt *the Lord, the God of Israel* above the gods of the nations. This requires building the Lord an impressive house of worship that speaks of his glory and honor (Psalms 26:8; 132:5). Solomon will later connect the temple to the reputation of the Lord among the nations (1 Kings 8:41-43).

18. "But the LORD said to my father David, 'You did well to have it in your heart to build a temple for my Name.

Solomon's assertion here does not appear to be quoted from any recorded material of anything the Lord said to Nathan or David (see 2 Samuel 7:5-16; 1 Chronicles 17:3-14). Instead, Solomon's words make explicit that God had been pleased with David's intent but not his timing.

> *What Do You Think?*
> Even though the church building is not equivalent to the temple of the old covenant, in what ways should it and/or its furnishings be treated as holy, if any?
> *Digging Deeper*
> What role, if any, should local sensitivities be allowed to have in answering that question?

B. By the Lord (v. 19)

19. "'Nevertheless, you are not the one to build the temple, but your son, your own flesh and blood—he is the one who will build the temple for my Name.'

This verse highlights an important contrast: after God builds David's house, David's son will *build the temple* for God. Despite David's good intention, God did not desire that man to be the one who would build the temple (2 Samuel 7:5;

compare 1 Kings 5:1-4). God's pleasure with David's impulse to build the Lord's temple can be seen in the fact that God allows his son Solomon to build it (2 Samuel 7:12, 13; 1 Kings 6).

Though David and Solomon may not have realized it at the time, the Lord's promise to David will bring about fulfillments of promises made to the patriarchs as well. The Lord told Abraham that all people groups would be blessed through that man's descendants (Genesis 12:3; 22:15-18). This promise is kept with God's honoring Jacob's blessing of Judah (49:8-12) when Jesus Christ is born of the line of David in the tribe of Judah (Luke 1:46-55, 68-75; 3:23, 33, 34).

> *What Do You Think?*
> How can we discern whether God is calling us to do something or is calling us to support someone else doing it?
> *Digging Deeper*
> How do passages such as Acts 15:37, 38; 17:7; Romans 16:21; 2 Timothy 4:16; and Philemon 1, 24 speak to your heart about the vital need to be a support person at times?

C. In Solomon (vv. 20, 21)

20. "The LORD has kept the promise he made: I have succeeded David my father and now I sit on the throne of Israel, just as the LORD promised, and I have built the temple for the Name of the LORD, the God of Israel.

Kings in the Ancient Near East often build or refurbish a temple to their patron god in order to establish the legitimacy of their reign. Politically, it makes sense to have a designated place of worship for an entire nation. This can create a more cohesive culture and nurture greater unity than if each village worships at its own altars and temples. Solomon affirms that he has not built the temple in order to establish himself—God has *already* done that (1 Chronicles 28:6, 7). God's placing of Solomon *on the throne* fulfills the Lord's *promise* to *David* (2 Samuel 7:12).

Peoples of the Ancient Near East consider their temples to be the houses or palaces of the deity. In fact, the Hebrew noun often translated *tem-*

ple can also refer to a palace (example: 1 Kings 21:1). Which use is intended must be determined by context. Because the Lord is both God and king, speaking of the temple can sound to Solomon's audience like speaking of God's palace. This reminds the audience of God's royal status as Israel's true king, residing in his palace in Jerusalem.

21. "I have provided a place there for the ark, in which is the covenant of the LORD that he made with our ancestors when he brought them out of Egypt."

The ark represents God's presence, throne, and reign (1 Samuel 4:4; 1 Chronicles 28:2; Psalms 99:1, 5; 132:7, 8; see lesson 6). The ark also testifies to *the covenant* relationship between the Lord and Israel (Numbers 10:33-36). Without the presence of the Lord that the ark represents, the temple is merely a majestic building. Without covenant faithfulness, neither the ark nor the temple mean anything (compare Jeremiah 7:1-15).

The ark contains the stone tablets of the covenant that the Lord had made in the desert with Israel. Solomon's reference to the ark thus underlines the tie between Israel's exodus experience and the Lord's covenant with David, emphasized earlier. God was utterly faithful to Israel's *ancestors* who made the journey through the wilderness.

> **What Do You Think?**
> What guardrails can we put in place to ensure that God receives appropriate credit for accomplishments?
> **Digging Deeper**
> Does this mean that we should never have recognition programs to acknowledge the work of fellow Christians? Why, or why not?

In some respects, the temple is analogous to the nation of Israel. The Lord will dwell in the temple just as he dwells within Israel. Just as the ark of the covenant is in the heart of the temple, so also the covenant is to be within the Israelites' hearts and actions. In a similar way, we speak today of believers as being the temples of the Holy Spirit (1 Corinthians 6:19). We must therefore be faithful to our covenant with the Lord (6:20).

❧ *KEEPING A PROMISE* ❧

"John did something terrible, but it was told to me in confidence. Promise to keep it a secret?" Some people find that the more scandalous the story, the harder it is to keep a promise not to spread the tale. Thus some people make promises they fully expect to break.

On the other hand, there are promises that we *do* intend to keep. The contract we sign when purchasing a house is one such promise, one with penalties if we break it. The promise we make to love and cherish a spouse "till death do us part" is a promise most people intend to keep. Then there are the promises of God, such as the ones Solomon recalled for Israel. God is the ultimate keeper of promises. We who are his children are called on to be as faithful as he is in keeping our word, whether to God or others. Do we?   —C. R. B.

Conclusion
A. God Is Faithful

Solomon's declarations highlight the power of God's promises. What God had promised to David, God fulfilled through Solomon. Just as the Lord God of Israel had kept his promises to the patriarchs, to Moses, and to Israel in general, so also he kept his promises to David. God's covenant to establish an everlasting dynasty for David finds its ultimate fulfillment in Jesus, the son of David (Matthew 1:1).

In response to God's promises, we are to be a covenant-keeping people. How we use our "temples" reflects our commitment to the Lord. Will others see God fulfilling his promises in us?

B. Prayer

Our Father, we thank you that you are the God of promises made and kept. We thank you for your presence with us through your Spirit. We pray in Jesus' name. Amen.

C. Thought to Remember

If God has promised it, he will do it!

INVOLVEMENT LEARNING

Enhance your lesson with NIV Bible Student (from your curriculum supplier) and the reproducible activity page (at www.standardlesson.com or in the back of the NIV Standard Lesson Commentary Deluxe Edition).

Into the Lesson

Before class members arrive, write *The Power of a Promise* on the board. Begin by pointing to the phrase as you ask, "What is the most powerful promise anyone ever made to you?" Allow several to answer.

Alternative. Tell class members the story behind the movement described in the lesson's Introduction. Ask some or all of the members to find the website and/or Facebook page on their smartphones. Allow two or three volunteers to share from these pages a few stories illustrating the power of a promise.

Lead into Bible study by saying, "As you know, our God is a promise-keeping God! Today, as we continue our study of the ceremonies surrounding the creation of the temple in Jerusalem, we will see why that fact is important."

Into the Word

Prepare in advance three strips of paper that have these phrases, one per strip: *God keeps his promises / God works in his own time / God sometimes says no.* Tell learners that the phrases you are about to read aloud state truths of today's text of 1 Kings 8:14-21 specifically and of life in general.

Read each statement twice. Then invite three shows of hands to indicate which statements your learners find most interesting. Form three groups according to the preferences indicated; give each of the three groups the appropriate strip of paper.

Ask class members to listen carefully as you read the lesson's Scripture text to see which part or parts illustrate their group's statement. You may decide to read the text aloud two or three times.

After the reading, give groups at least five minutes to agree on how the Scripture illustrates the groups' respective principles. Then call the groups together for whole-class discussion. Expect your groups to have seen at least these connections:

God keeps his promises . . . . verse 20
God works in his own time . . . . . verses 16, 21
God sometimes says no . . . . .verse 19

Groups may propose other connections of a more indirect nature. If so, ask for explanations.

Option. Distribute copies of the "Twelve of Many" exercise from the activity page, which you can download. Have learners work in study pairs to complete as indicated.

Into Life

Re-form the same three groups and ask them to brainstorm a list of situations in which people would be helped by believing the principle their group discussed. Allow just two or three minutes for groups to make lists as long as possible. (*Alternative.* Do this with the whole class, taking one principle at a time and writing responses on the board.)

Then lead a whole-class discussion, allowing participants to add more examples under the statements, which you have written as headers on the board. Probe deeper by asking when learners have experienced one or more of the truths personally. Allow several minutes for members to share their testimonies.

Option 1. Use the "One Favorite Promise" exercise from the activity page to expand the discussion. Students can pair off to discuss as indicated.

Option 2. Using the list of Scriptures containing promises on the activity page, recruit volunteers to look them up and read them aloud. Ask learners to adopt an attitude of worship as this sampling of God's promises is read.

Ask one person from each of the three groups to offer a prayer of thanks to God for keeping his promises and a prayer of petition for class members to keep promises to him.

Close by leading singing of the hymn "Great Is Thy Faithfulness" or another familiar composition that is similar in content.

SOLOMON SEEKS GOD'S BLESSING

DEVOTIONAL READING: 1 Timothy 2:1-6
BACKGROUND SCRIPTURE: 1 Kings 8:22-53; 2 Chronicles 6:12-42

1 KINGS 8:22-30, 52, 53

22 Then Solomon stood before the altar of the LORD in front of the whole assembly of Israel, spread out his hands toward heaven 23 and said:

"LORD, the God of Israel, there is no God like you in heaven above or on earth below—you who keep your covenant of love with your servants who continue wholeheartedly in your way. 24 You have kept your promise to your servant David my father; with your mouth you have promised and with your hand you have fulfilled it—as it is today.

25 "Now LORD, the God of Israel, keep for your servant David my father the promises you made to him when you said, 'You shall never fail to have a successor to sit before me on the throne of Israel, if only your descendants are careful in all they do to walk before me faithfully as you have done.' 26 And now, God of Israel, let your word that you promised your servant David my father come true.

27 "But will God really dwell on earth? The heavens, even the highest heaven, cannot contain you. How much less this temple I have built! 28 Yet give attention to your servant's prayer and his plea for mercy, LORD my God. Hear the cry and the prayer that your servant is praying in your presence this day. 29 May your eyes be open toward this temple night and day, this place of which you said, 'My Name shall be there,' so that you will hear the prayer your servant prays toward this place. 30 Hear the supplication of your servant and of your people Israel when they pray toward this place. Hear from heaven, your dwelling place, and when you hear, forgive.

. . . .

52 "May your eyes be open to your servant's plea and to the plea of your people Israel, and may you listen to them whenever they cry out to you. 53 For you singled them out from all the nations of the world to be your own inheritance, just as you declared through your servant Moses when you, Sovereign LORD, brought our ancestors out of Egypt."

KEY VERSE

Hear the supplication of your servant and of your people Israel when they pray toward this place. Hear from heaven, your dwelling place, and when you hear, forgive. —**1 Kings 8:30**

HONORING GOD

Unit 2: Dedicating the Temple of God

LESSONS 6–9

LESSON AIMS

After participating in this lesson, each learner will be able to:

1. Identify two fulfilled promises of the Lord.

2. Relate the key verse to leading ideas in the lesson text.

3. Suggest ways in which Solomon's prayer provides models for the Christian's prayers.

LESSON OUTLINE

Introduction
  A. Gateway to the West
  B. Lesson Context
I. God in Israel (1 KINGS 8:22-26)
  A. Past Faithfulness (vv. 22-24)
    Faithful Year After Year
  B. Future Faithfulness (vv. 25, 26)
II. God in Heaven (1 KINGS 8:27-30)
  A. Praise of Sovereignty (v. 27)
  B. Prayer for Attention (vv. 28-30)
    God Answers Prayer
III. God in All the Earth (1 KINGS 8:52, 53)
  A. Summary of Requests (v. 52)
  B. Reason for Requests (v. 53)
Conclusion
  A. Access in Christ's Name
  B. Prayer
  C. Thought to Remember

Introduction

A. Gateway to the West

Where is the Gateway to the West in the United States? While the young country was still struggling to spread westward, the Cumberland Gap was one of the easiest land crossings through the Appalachian Mountains into the wild frontier of Tennessee. On the other hand, Pittsburgh's location at the meeting of three rivers made it a great place to begin a westward journey down the mighty Ohio River. Fort Wayne, Indiana along with St. Louis and Kansas City have also been acclaimed as the Gateway to the West. None of these today is the nationally recognized Gateway to the West.

In a similar way, Israel lacked one place that was *the* gateway to God. Where could they go to connect with him?

B. Lesson Context

First Kings 8:1-21 narrates the initial stages of the dedication ceremony Solomon orchestrated for the temple he had built in Jerusalem for the God of Israel (see commentary lessons 6, 7). The priests carried the ark of the covenant to the temple and placed it within the temple's innermost chamber, the Most Holy Place. The Lord's glory then filled the temple, signaling God's approval of Solomon and the temple.

Solomon related to the congregation of Israel the story of the Lord's covenant faithfulness to David. The evidence for this was Solomon's coming to the throne in the place of his father and in the completion of the temple.

I. God in Israel

(1 KINGS 8:22-26)

A. Past Faithfulness (vv. 22-24)

22. Then Solomon stood before the altar of the LORD in front of the whole assembly of Israel, spread out his hands toward heaven

The *altar* that *Solomon* stands in front of is most likely the bronze altar of burnt offering in the temple courts (1 Kings 8:64). If it were a different altar, he would be standing in the temple, out of sight from *the whole assembly.*

Solomon's posture is one of prayer. Whereas we traditionally pray with folded hands and closed eyes, the ancient Israelites typically look up *toward heaven* or toward the temple, God's house on earth (1 Kings 8:29, 30). Their lifted, empty *hands* express petition and supplication (Exodus 9:29, 33; Psalm 143:6). This stance demonstrates both their need and their confidence that they will receive from God (1 Kings 8:38, 54; Psalms 63:4; 88:9; 143:6). Though the temple was built as God's home on earth, Solomon recognizes that the Lord's true home is in Heaven rather than in any one location on the earth (see on 1 Kings 8:27, below).

> **What Do You Think?**
> What level of attention should Christians in general give to the issue of physical posture(s), if any, in prayer? Why?
>
> *Digging Deeper*
> How do Deuteronomy 9:18, 25; Psalm 123:1; Luke 18:13; John 17:1; Acts 20:36; 21:5; and 1 Timothy 2:8 influence your conclusion?

23a. and said: "LORD, the God of Israel, there is no God like you in heaven above or on earth below—

Solomon continues to address God as the *Lord . . . God of Israel* (1 Kings 8:15, 17, 20, 25; see commentary lesson 7). He calls on the powerful, transcendent deity who is also near to Israel and keeps covenant with the nation. Solomon's affirmation of the Lord's uniqueness *in heaven* and *on earth* echoes Moses' words: "The Lord is God in heaven above and on the earth below. There is no other" (Deuteronomy 4:39; compare Exodus 15:11; Deuteronomy 7:9, 12; Nehemiah 1:5).

> **What Do You Think?**
> What are some ways to demonstrate more respect to God when praying?
>
> *Digging Deeper*
> Consider not only your prayers' contents (what you say) and contexts (when, where, and with whom you say them) but also how content and context interrelate.

23b. "you who keep your covenant of love with your servants who continue wholeheartedly in your way.

The Hebrew word translated *love* further highlights God's fidelity as it denotes loyalty and faithfulness to covenant obligations. The same word is translated "kindness" (Joshua 2:12; 2 Chronicles 24:22; etc.) and even "unfailing kindness" (Jeremiah 31:3). The Lord is loyal to his servants who demonstrate fidelity to him by walking before him *wholeheartedly* (Daniel 9:4). To *continue in* God's *way* suggests walking the correct path, a frequent biblical metaphor that designates one's conduct or process of living (Deuteronomy 8:6; Micah 6:8; etc.). The heart speaks to what is in the core of one's being; it designates one's intellect, emotion, or will (1 Samuel 2:1; 1 Chronicles 16:10; Psalm 9:1). Solomon calls the people to be wholly devoted to the Lord.

The command to love the Lord with all one's heart is part of the ancient prayer called the *Shema* (Hebrew for "hear") passage of Deuteronomy 6:4, 5. It constitutes Israel's central obligation to the Lord within the covenant (Deuteronomy 10:12; 26:16; Joshua 22:5; 1 Samuel 7:3). Solomon had been specifically charged by his father, David, to love the Lord with all his heart so that David would never fail to have a successor on the throne of Israel (1 Kings 2:1-4). Jesus later will declare the *Shema* to be the greatest commandment. Together with Leviticus 19:18, these two summarize the Law and Prophets (Matthew 22:34-40).

❧ FAITHFUL YEAR AFTER YEAR ❧

Tabloid headlines scream the latest gossip about which celebrity is having an affair this week or whose marriage is crumbling due to unfaithfulness. While sad examples like these abound, we occasionally read wonderful stories of couples whose marriages have lasted. For five years, Herbert and Zelmyra Fisher held the Guinness World Record for the longest marriage of a living couple: 86 years! When she was 103 years old, Zelmyra was asked the secret for their long marriage. She replied that only God could have kept them together.

What a wonderful example of human faithfulness! But it pales in significance to the eternal faithfulness of God. As Solomon noted, God remains true to his people, generation after generation. What a blessing and an example to us!

—C. R. B.

24. "You have kept your promise to your servant David my father; with your mouth you have promised and with your hand you have fulfilled it as it is today.

Three references to *your servant David my father* punctuate 1 Kings 8:24-26. Referring to King David as a *servant* contrasts David's role in Israel with the Lord's. Though David was the earthly leader of Israel, he was always subordinate to God. Earlier, the Lord had used the phrase "my servant" to refer to Moses (Numbers 12:7, 8; Joshua 1:2, 7) and Caleb (Numbers 14:24) while Joshua was designated as the Lord's servant (Joshua 24:29). Solomon also will speak of himself as the Lord's servant (1 Kings 8:28, 29, 52). This further ties Solomon to his father not just by blood but by acceptance of his role under God.

Solomon celebrates the Lord's covenant faithfulness to David. Solomon's place on the throne and the temple's completion represent the fulfillment of the Lord's promise to David found in 2 Samuel 7:13. The king had earlier praised God for establishing with his *hand* what he had promised (1 Kings 8:15). Hand is an image of God's power and authority (Exodus 13:3; 2 Chronicles 30:12; Isaiah 41:10; etc.). That God had spoken the promise to David by means of his own *mouth* testified to God's intimate involvement in the promise and to its reliability. Solomon praises the Lord as the one who had committed himself to

David and who had been able to perform what he had promised in establishing Solomon on David's throne. God has empowered Solomon to complete the temple.

B. Future Faithfulness (vv. 25, 26)

25. "Now LORD, the God of Israel, keep for your servant David my father the promises you made to him when you said, 'You shall never fail to have a successor to sit before me on the throne of Israel, if only your descendants are careful in all they do to walk before me faithfully as you have done.'

The word *now* signals a transition in Solomon's prayer: he seeks God's present and future faithfulness (compare 1 Chronicles 17:10-14, 23; 2 Chronicles 1:9). The Lord had promised David that he would establish David's dynasty and throne forever (2 Samuel 7:15, 16). Solomon echoes the words David used as recorded in 1 Kings 2:1-4 to recount to his son that covenant promise. In that recollection, David had highlighted a conditional element within the Lord's covenant. In order to enjoy its benefits, David's descendants must walk in God's ways (1 Kings 2:3). If David's descendants follow the Lord fully, then David will never fail to have a successor on the throne of Israel (2:4).

The phrase *if only* indicates the conditions under which Solomon can expect the Lord to continue to honor the promises he made. When David's descendants *are careful in all they do,* they will be established on his throne. When they are not, they will face God's judgments.

> **What Do You Think?**
> What is one of God's fulfilled promises that you can help your church celebrate to better effect? How will you do so?
>
> **Digging Deeper**
> Where should that better effect be focused: on worship, evangelism, discipleship, or something else? Why?

26. "And now, God of Israel, let your word that you promised your servant David my father come true.

HOW TO SAY IT

Deuteronomy	Due-ter-*ahn*-uh-me.
Egypt	*Ee*-jipt.
exilic	eg-*zil*-ik.
Leviticus	Leh-*vit*-ih-kus.
Moses	*Mo*-zes or *Mo*-zez.
Shema (Hebrew)	*She*-muh.
Solomon	*Sol*-o-mun.

Solomon anticipates God's future faithfulness to the *word* he had spoken to *David* (2 Samuel 7:25). The ultimate fulfillment of the Lord's gracious promise will come in the person and work of Jesus Christ, who will be born from the house of David (Luke 1:27, 69; Acts 2:29, 30) and be given "the throne of his father David" (Luke 1:32).

II. God in Heaven
(1 KINGS 8:27-30)
A. Praise of Sovereignty (v. 27)

27. "But will God really dwell on earth? The heavens, even the highest heaven, cannot contain you. How much less this temple I have built!

Having restated highlights from God's covenant with David, Solomon proclaims the wonder of the *God* who has established that covenant. Solomon contrasts the limits of the *temple* he built with the limitless God for whom it has been built (compare Psalm 139:7-16; Jeremiah 23:24). There is no God like the Lord in *the heavens* above or on the *earth* beneath (1 Kings 8:23), and both Heaven and earth belong to him (Deuteronomy 10:14). Not even the *highest heaven* can contain the Lord.

In Israelite thought, there exist three layers of heavens above the earth (compare 2 Corinthians 12:2). Beneath the earth can be found the abode of the dead. All of these tiers belong to the Lord, and not even the most magnificent of them can be said to contain God. Consequently, the newly constructed temple certainly cannot confine him (2 Chronicles 2:6; Isaiah 66:1; Acts 17:24).

The Israelites will err if they think they can confine God within a temple and use it to manipulate him the way neighboring nations seek to manipulate their gods (compare 1 Kings 18:26-29). Indeed, Stephen will quote both Solomon and Isaiah when he condemns the Jewish leaders for their reliance on the law and the rebuilt temple in their rejection of Jesus (Acts 7:47-53). This building represents the dwelling of the Lord among his people, but it will be a blessing for them only if they humbly obey the God who dwells among them (compare Jeremiah 7:1-15).

B. Prayer for Attention (vv. 28-30)

28. "Yet give attention to your servant's prayer and his plea for mercy, LORD my God. Hear the cry and the prayer that your servant is praying in your presence this day.

Solomon now begins to apply the title *servant* to himself as he links himself to God's promise and faithfulness (see commentary on 1 Kings 8:24, above). The king realizes that he has no claim on the *God* of Heaven. Solomon cannot force the almighty *Lord* to do anything. Yet God had made promises to David and to Israel, and Solomon could depend on the Lord's own word.

The nouns *prayer, plea,* and *cry* overlap greatly in meaning, each one offering a different emphasis. The first is the most generic, referring to any kind of praying to God. This word occurs over 70 times in the Hebrew Old Testament. *Plea* refers to prayers for God's intervention and assistance; it occurs only 25 times in the Hebrew Old Testament. *Cry* can refer to a ringing, emotional calling out to God either in joy or in pain, occurring 33 times in the Hebrew Old Testament.

What Do You Think?
 Without giving advice, how would you counsel
  discouraged people who believe their sins are
  so serious that God will not forgive?
Digging Deeper
What if a person points to passages such as
  Exodus 23:21; 2 Kings 24:4; Matthew 12:31,
  32; and/or 1 John 5:16b to maintain that he or
  she cannot be forgiven?

---

29. "May your eyes be open toward this temple night and day, this place of which you said, 'My Name shall be there,' so that you will hear the prayer your servant prays toward this place.

Solomon has clarified that the transcendent God cannot be confined within the temple. The king nevertheless prays that God will honor the newly constructed *house* as a place where the Lord can be approached.

The sensory metaphors of the Lord's seeing and hearing emphasize the receptivity that Solomon hopes and expects God will have toward his prayers (compare 2 Kings 19:16; Nehemiah 1:6;

Psalms 34:15; 101:6). Solomon does not just want God to see and hear; rather, Solomon wants God to act on behalf of his praying people on the basis of seeing and hearing (102:17). God promises that he will do so (2 Chronicles 7:15).

Solomon asks for God's constant attention *night and day* to the appeals of his people (compare Psalm 138:2; Daniel 6:10). God does not sleep; he is able to *hear* prayers always (Psalms 34:17, 18; 121:3-8). Furthermore, the Lord has provided his *Name* to Israel so that the people can know him (Exodus 3:13-15). They are to call on his name in praise, prayer, and trust (1 Kings 8:33, 35; 1 Chronicles 16:8; Psalm 9:10; etc.). God's name being associated with the temple conveys the idea of his possession of that space. Israel belongs to God as the nation called by God's name (Deuteronomy 28:10; 2 Chronicles 7:14; Isaiah 43:1; see lesson 7).

❧ GOD ANSWERS PRAYER ❧

When Mary was a month old, she had her first checkup. Everything seemed fine until the next day, when she appeared to be getting a cold. Pat and I took turns tending to our baby to keep her comfortable. About midnight, I turned Mary's care over to my wife. I tossed in the bed before praying, "God, if Mary will be all right, let me go to sleep so I will be alert for church." About 2:00 a.m., I heard my wife scream. I reached her in time to hear Mary take her last breath.

God didn't answer prayer for Mary's recovery the way we wanted. Instead, he gave us a gift of ministry. Many times, Pat and I had the privilege of sharing our story and God's comfort with other parents in similar circumstances.

In the years following Solomon's prayer, Israel walked far away from God. God's answer to Solomon's prayer was not always what the king would have expected. But God's answer was always intended to bless Israel, calling the people back to their mission. 　　　　　—C. R. B.

30. "Hear the supplication of your servant and of your people Israel when they pray toward this place. Hear from heaven, your dwelling place, and when you hear, forgive."

Solomon's requests recognize God's openness and receptivity to prayers. Solomon previously had asked the Lord to hear his own prayer; now Solomon explicitly includes the *people* of *Israel* among those to whom the Lord should listen. Israel will pray toward the temple, but God will hear from Heaven (1 Kings 8:32, 34, 36, 39, 43, 45, 49).

Solomon's specific requests that follow imply that Israel will pray in repentance (1 Kings 8:39, 47; compare Exodus 34:9; Leviticus 26:40-42). Solomon pleads that the Lord not only will hear Israel, but that he also will *forgive* Israel (1 Kings 8:34, 36, 39, 50). Elsewhere, God promises that he hears the prayers of his repentant people (Exodus 34:7; Jeremiah 29:12).

It is significant that Solomon links forgiveness to the Israelites' prayers rather than to their sacrifices—acts normally associated with temples. The temple is certainly the place for sacrifices (Deuteronomy 12:1-18), but sacrifices are offered in the context of prayer (Psalm 141:2; Isaiah 56:7). This distinction will be important for the future exilic and post-exilic communities that will experience disruptions in their ability to offer sacrifices after the temple is destroyed. While the nation might worry that God will not hear their prayers without sacrifice, Solomon's words serve as reassurance that the prayers behind the sacrifice are pleasing to God.

> *What Do You Think?*
>   What causes you to think that at times the Lord does not hear your prayers? Why?
> *Digging Deeper*
>   What are some ways Christians make sure not to confuse the issue of *hearing* prayers with that of *heeding* prayers?

III. God in All the Earth
(1 Kings 8:52, 53)

A. Summary of Requests (v. 52)

52. "May your eyes be open to your servant's plea and to the plea of your people Israel, and may you listen to them whenever they cry out to you.

In 1 Kings 8:31-51 (not in today's text), Solomon offers seven petitions to God concerning various circumstances his people may experience. These specific petitions will be very reassuring to the generations that will live during and after the Babylonian exile. Despite the judgments to come, Solomon expectantly prays that God will continue to care for his people.

First Kings 8:52 picks up key elements from previous portions of Solomon's prayer. Just as Solomon has prayed that God's *eyes* will be open toward the temple (8:27, 28), the king now prays that God's *eyes* will be *open* to his *plea* and to that of *Israel*, and that God will hear them (8:28, 29).

B. Reason for Requests (v. 53)

53. "For you singled them out from all the nations of the world to be your own inheritance, just as you declared through your servant Moses when you, Sovereign Lord, brought our ancestors out of Egypt."

Solomon is confident that the Lord will be attentive because the Israelites are his people whom he has rescued from Egyptian slavery (8:51; compare Psalm 3:4; contrast Job 30:20; Psalm 22:2). God has proven himself to Israel time after time.

Solomon began his prayer in 1 Kings 8:23 by addressing the *Lord,* the God of Israel. He now ends by appealing to the *Sovereign Lord* who had brought Israel *out of Egypt*. As he has done in the first part of his prayer (1 Kings 8:15, 16), Solomon connects the fulfillment of God's promises to David with the story of *Moses* and the exodus. Calling Moses a *servant* connects both David and Solomon to the earlier leader of Israel (8:28, 29, 30, 52; see commentary on 8:24).

God had chosen Israel *from all the nations of the world* to be his inheritance and special possession (Exodus 19:5, 6; 34:9; Deuteronomy 4:20; 7:7, 8; Psalm 33:12). He had delivered Israel in order for that nation to be a blessing in and to the world (Genesis 12:2; 22:17, 18; Exodus 19:5, 6). God has been faithful to his people, and he will fulfill his purposes for them. Those purposes are ultimately fulfilled in his Son, Jesus, and in the ministry and message of reconciliation he commits to Christ's church (2 Corinthians 5:14-19).

God made the world and everything in it—He does not dwell in temples made by hands.
—from Acts 17:24

Visual for Lesson 8. *Point to this visual to start a discussion about why it is good news that God does not dwell in temples.*

Conclusion

A. Access in Christ's Name

Solomon's temple-dedication prayer highlights the Lord's faithfulness to his covenant with David. The establishment of Solomon as king and the completion of the temple bore witness to God's faithfulness to David and to Israel. That past faithfulness formed the basis for Solomon's expectation of and his petition for the Lord's continued covenant loyalty. He prayed that the Lord would hear his people when they prayed toward the temple Solomon had built for the Lord's name (1 Kings 8:29). God agreed to use the temple as a gateway to him.

Jesus, the ultimate fulfillment of the covenant promises to David, spoke of himself as a temple (John 2:19, 21). Believers have access to God through Christ (Ephesians 2:18), and in his name we are able to approach God boldly and to pray in confidence that God will hear (John 14:13, 14; 15:16; Ephesians 3:12; Hebrews 4:16).

B. Prayer

Our Father, we praise you for your faithfulness to your people throughout all generations and to us in our time. We pray in Jesus' name. Amen.

C. Thought to Remember

God is faithful to hear us when we pray.

INVOLVEMENT LEARNING

Enhance your lesson with NIV Bible Student *(from your curriculum supplier) and the reproducible activity page (at www.standardlesson.com or in the back of the* NIV Standard Lesson Commentary Deluxe Edition*).*

Into the Lesson

Begin a brainstorming as you ask learners to name special events that usually call for a special prayer. Allow 90 seconds; have a scribe jot responses on the board as they are shouted.

After time is up, work back through the list, asking for shows of hands whether learners have heard or offered a prayer in each situation. Keep a tally on the board.

Lead in to Bible study by telling students that today's lesson will consider the prayer Solomon offered as the new temple was dedicated. Tell them to watch for how meaningful this prayer was to those who heard it originally.

Into the Word

Briefly recap the previous two lessons. Then ask a volunteer to read aloud today's lesson text of 1 Kings 8:22-30, 52, 53. Challenge class members to listen for what Solomon's prayer illustrates about God and how we might pray.

After the reading, ask students if they know what promises Solomon is referring to in verses 24 and 25. If 2 Samuel 7:13 and 1 Kings 2:4 aren't mentioned, do so yourself.

Then have students imagine a conversation they might have with Solomon after the dedication of the temple. Have half the class (in groups of no more than four) decide what the prayer teaches us about God. The other half (also in groups of no more than four) should determine what is appropriate to ask of God. After about five minutes, ask group members to share their conclusions.

Option 1. Provide students with copies of the three-column chart below. Suggest that learners use this as a note taker. Note that not every verse contains something to list under both of the other two headings. Inform learners also that some of the entries will be listed more than once.

Option 2. Provide copies of the same chart for students to complete in study pairs.

Verse(s)	Learned About God	Asked of God
22		
23		
24, 25		
26		
27		
28-30		
52		
53		

Option 3. Distribute copies of the "Seven Prayers, Seven Principles" exercise from the activity page, which you can download. Have learners complete as indicated, considering 1 Kings 8:31-51 as background. If distributed as a take-home, promise to discuss results next week.

Into Life

Put learners into four groups and give each group one of the following statements on a handout (you prepare):

1–God, there is no one like you.

2–God, because you're a promise keeper, we're asking you to keep your promises to us.

3–God, we can't contain you in this room, but we want you to be here with us.

4–God, help your people with the challenges we're facing in this world.

Include the following instructions on each handout: Identify the section(s) of today's text reflected in the supplication you've been given. Write a few sentences of a prayer that expresses the idea in your sentence.

In the ensuing whole-class discussion, allow volunteers to share what they've written. Probe further by asking which sentences remind them of prayers they regularly pray. Follow by asking which challenge them to pray in a new way and why.

Option. Distribute copies of the "Prayer Emphasis" exercise from the activity page as a take-home. To encourage completion, state that you will call for volunteers to share results next week.

SOLOMON
ANTICIPATES PRAISE

DEVOTIONAL READING: Psalm 136:1-16, 23-25
BACKGROUND SCRIPTURE: 1 Kings 8:54-66; 2 Chronicles 7:4-9

1 KINGS 8:54-61

54 When Solomon had finished all these prayers and supplications to the LORD, he rose from before the altar of the LORD, where he had been kneeling with his hands spread out toward heaven. 55 He stood and blessed the whole assembly of Israel in a loud voice, saying:

56 "Praise be to the LORD, who has given rest to his people Israel just as he promised. Not one word has failed of all the good promises he gave through his servant Moses. 57 May the LORD our God be with us as he was with our ancestors; may he never leave us nor forsake us. 58 May he turn our hearts to him, to walk in obedience to him and keep the commands, decrees and laws he gave our ancestors. 59 And may these words of mine, which I have prayed before the LORD, be near to the LORD our God day and night, that he may uphold the cause of his servant and the cause of his people Israel according to each day's need, 60 so that all the peoples of the earth may know that the LORD is God and that there is no other. 61 And may your hearts be fully committed to the LORD our God, to live by his decrees and obey his commands, as at this time."

KEY VERSES

May the LORD our God be with us as he was with our ancestors; may he never leave us nor forsake us. May he turn our hearts to him, to walk in obedience to him and keep the commands, decrees and laws he gave our ancestors. —1 Kings 8:57, 58

HONORING
GOD

LESSON AIMS

After participating in this lesson, each learner will be able to:

1. Summarize the content of Solomon's final words at the temple dedication.

2. Explain the relationship between the Israelites' living faithfully and remembering God's fulfilled promises.

3. Write a prayer that recalls God's faithfulness and that anticipates his future work.

LESSON OUTLINE

Introduction
  A. Remembering for the Future
  B. Lesson Context
I. Solomon's Blessing (1 KINGS 8:54-56)
  A. For Israel (vv. 54, 55)
  B. Of the Lord (v. 56)
    Blessed
II. Solomon's Desire (1 KINGS 8:57-61)
  A. For the Lord's Presence (vv. 57, 58)
  B. For the Lord's Help (vv. 59, 60)
    Faith of the Generations
  C. For the People's Hearts (v. 61)
Conclusion
  A. Faithful to the Faithful One
  B. Prayer
  C. Thought to Remember

Introduction

A. Remembering for the Future

In his 1990 remarks on the dedication of the Washington National Cathedral, President George H. W. Bush alluded to the initial laying of its cornerstone as well as to the future use of the building. He stated, "Eighty-three years ago on this spot, President Teddy Roosevelt said: 'God speed the work begun this noon.' And today I say: God speed the work completed this noon and the new work yet to begin."

President Bush looked to the past and offered hope for the future. Solomon, in his dedication address for the temple in Jerusalem, likewise called Israel to look to the past while hoping for the future.

B. Lesson Context

The narrative of 1 Kings 8 is devoted to the greatest moment of Solomon's reign: the dedication of the temple (about 960 BC). By that time Solomon was about 10 years into his 40-year reign. His fame had spread far and wide during that time (1 Kings 4:29-34). But the focus of the 10-year period was the construction of the temple. The required materials and manpower stagger the imagination (see 1 Kings 5:13-18; 2 Chronicles 2:1, 2, 17, 18).

The lesson text for this week comprises the final words of King Solomon's dedicatory address. A parallel account is found in 2 Chronicles 5–7. The dedication ceremony closed with a 14-day celebration, an expansion of the great annual harvest feast known as the Festival of Tabernacles (Leviticus 23:34; 1 Kings 8:2, 65).

Solomon's opening and closing remarks demonstrate similarities that make them fitting bookends for his prayer. The narration of the transporting of the ark of the covenant to the temple (1 Kings 8:1-11, lesson 6) prefaced Solomon's first oration (8:12-21) as the narration of the offering of dedicatory sacrifices (8:62-64) followed his final words. Solomon's final blessing (8:55-61) focused broadly on Israel in a fashion similar to his opening blessing, which focused on David and Solomon himself (8:15-21, lesson 7).

I. Solomon's Blessing
(1 KINGS 8:54-56)
A. For Israel (vv. 54, 55)

54. When Solomon had finished all these prayers and supplications to the LORD, he rose from before the altar of the LORD, where he had been kneeling with his hands spread out toward heaven.

Because the congregation of Israel is gathered within the temple courts, *the altar of the Lord* refers to the bronze altar of burnt offering located there (1 Kings 8:64; see commentary in lesson 8). Solomon has been kneeling on a special platform that is three cubits (four and a half feet) high (2 Chronicles 6:12, 13). *Kneeling* and offering *prayers* no doubt signify the king's respect and humble submission to the Lord (contrast 1 Kings 19:18; 2 Kings 1:13; Isaiah 45:14). The Israelites will also bow down in worship to God during this dedication ceremony (2 Chronicles 7:3; compare Psalm 95:6).

The king's stretching out *his hands . . . toward heaven* further expresses an attitude of petition and supplication (compare Exodus 9:29, 33; 1 Kings 8:22; Psalms 63:4; 88:9; 143:6). This demonstrates not only a sense of need but also confidence that God can and will respond to his requests (compare Exodus 9:29, 33).

What Do You Think?
Considering the prayer template **A**doration, **C**onfession, **T**hanksgiving, and **S**upplication (ACTS), how can you make sure the elements are in proper balance?
Digging Deeper
Would it be a good experiment to focus on just one element for a time? Why, or why not?

---

55. He stood and blessed the whole assembly of Israel in a loud voice, saying:

Arising from his position of kneeling, Solomon blesses *the whole assembly* as he did earlier (1 Kings 8:14). To bless a person or group is to express a desire that God's approval and goodwill would rest on them. It invites God to invest them with success, fruitfulness, or long life (examples: Genesis 24:60; 27:1-41; 48:9–49:28).

Usually a priest blesses the people (Numbers 6:22-27), but exceptions certainly exist. Solomon's blessing echoes that of Moses when the Israelites finished work on the tabernacle (Exodus 39:43). Solomon also mirrors King David's act of blessing the people after he brought the ark of the covenant into Jerusalem (2 Samuel 6:17-19).

Solomon's blessing of Israel not only recalls his father's blessing but builds on it now that the ark has been brought to rest in its new home (1 Kings 8:6, 7, 21). The congregation will reciprocate the king's action by blessing Solomon before departing (8:66).

B. Of the Lord (v. 56)

56a. "Praise be to the LORD, who has given rest to his people Israel just as he promised.

Solomon's blessing on Israel actually begins with a pronouncement praising *the Lord,* the God of Israel. The Hebrew word translated *praise* here is the same word that is used to speak of people being blessed throughout 1 Kings 8. Whereas blessing a person expresses one's desire that God would esteem and benefit them, one praises the Lord by giving honor to him (Genesis 24:27; Exodus 18:10; 1 Samuel 25:32, 39; etc.). The fact that Solomon begins his blessing of Israel by praising God demonstrates the king's understanding that any blessings Israel experiences come from the Lord, the source of all blessings.

Solomon has previously spoken of how God fulfilled his promise that David's son would build a temple for the Lord (1 Kings 8:15-21, lesson 7). Here, he speaks of God's fidelity to the Israelites in providing them *rest* in the land of Canaan (Exodus 33:14). Through Moses, the Lord had *promised* to give Israel rest in Canaan from their enemies (Deuteronomy 12:9, 10). Joshua had subsequently referred to the conquest of Canaan as the Lord's act of giving Israel that promised rest on every side (Joshua 1:13). The result was to be able to flourish as the people dwelled in security.

Solomon undoubtedly sees the completion of the temple as the fulfillment of the Lord's promise of that rest. The nation has become secure under the 40-year rule by his father, David, and by events at the beginning of Solomon's reign (2 Samuel 7:1; 1 Kings 5:4).

> **What Do You Think?**
> How can you personally do better at balancing rest with work?
> *Digging Deeper*
> Which one or two of the following texts convict you most in this regard: Genesis 2:2, 3; Exodus 34:21; Matthew 11:28; Mark 6:31; Hebrews 4:1-11? How is Matthew 26:45 cautionary to you?

56b. "Not one word has failed of all the good promises he gave through his servant Moses."

Because the nation is experiencing the promised rest, Solomon can allude to Joshua's affirmation made centuries earlier: no good thing the Lord has promised *has failed* (Joshua 21:45; 23:14). Not only has the Lord been faithful to his promises to the house of David, he has kept promises he spoke to Moses regarding Israel. Indeed, the promises to David and that man's forefathers are integral to God's plan and purpose for Israel. Nevertheless, the rest Israel enjoys at this time is temporary. Israel's later sin will lead to two exiles after the nation divides (2 Kings 17:1-23; 25:1-21; 2 Chronicles 36:15-21).

The Lord always desires rest for his people (compare Jeremiah 29:10-14; 30:1-3, 8-10; etc.). The writer of Hebrews affirms that the ultimate rest will be experienced at the return of Christ (Hebrews 4:1-13).

❧ *BLESSED* ❧

As a sophomore in college, I acted on God's call to ministry. More than 60 years later, I retired from vocational ministry. God had led me to city and country churches, a mission field in Africa, teaching and administration in Christian colleges, hospice chaplaincy, and a ministry to at-risk young people.

When I retired at age 81, I had the time to reflect on those six decades. Not many people have had the opportunity to experience the joys, rewards, and satisfaction in service that I have, not to mention the challenges for personal growth. I now see, more than ever, that God has blessed me far more than I deserve. I can say with Solomon, "Not one word has failed of all the good promises" God gave me.

My prayer for you is that you can reflect on your life and see God's hand blessing you, even as Solomon reminded Israel of what God had done.
—C. R. B.

II. Solomon's Desire
(1 Kings 8:57-61)
A. For the Lord's Presence (vv. 57, 58)

57. "May the LORD our God be with us as he was with our ancestors; may he never leave us nor forsake us.

Having praised God for his past faithfulness to Israel, Solomon now voices desires for the future. The structure of 1 Kings 8:57, 58 pairs a stated desire with a purpose statement; the pattern repeats in the two verses that follow.

Solomon's desire is that the Lord's presence with Israel will continue. The king recognizes that Israel's special place as God's covenant people depends on God's continued willingness (Genesis 26:3; Deuteronomy 4:31; Joshua 1:5). It does not depend on any inherent entitlement the Israelites' may imagine.

The phrase *our ancestors* refers to the patriarchs as well as to the Israelites' leaders during the days of Moses and Joshua (Exodus 3:15; 1 Samuel 12:6). In the New Testament, the patriarch designation is applied specifically to Abraham, the sons of Jacob, and David (see Acts 2:29; 7:8, 9; Hebrews 7:4). We further think of Isaac and Jacob as members of this group. The Lord has surely kept his promises to them (see Genesis 26:3, 24; 28:15; 31:3; 46:1-4; etc.). God also kept the promise of his presence to Moses (Exodus 3:12; 33:14) as well as to Moses' successor, Joshua (Deuteronomy 31:6, 8; Joshua 1:9; 3:7).

As Solomon repeats this ancient promise, there can be little doubt that he recalls the words of his father, David. King David had promised Solomon that the Lord would not forsake him while Solomon worked on the temple's construction (1 Chronicles 28:20)—a promise obviously kept!

Later in the Old Testament, the prophet Isaiah will reiterate the promise of God's attentive and loving presence with his people (Isaiah 41:10, 17; 42:16; 44:21; 49:14-16). The Lord also encourages Jeremiah with the assurance of his presence (Jeremiah 1:8, 19; 20:11).

Our Lord has given this same pledge to new-covenant believers. Centuries after Solomon's day, Jesus promises his disciples that he will not leave them as orphans (John 14:18). Before ascending to the Father, Jesus vows his constant presence (Matthew 28:19, 20). The author of Hebrews assures us that God will never leave or forsake us (Hebrews 13:5; compare Deuteronomy 31:6).

> What Do You Think?
> In what ways can Christians demonstrate better that God is "with us"?
> Digging Deeper
> How do we keep that effort from crossing into "holier than thou" territory?

58. "May he turn our hearts to him, to walk in obedience to him and keep the commands, decrees and laws he gave our ancestors.

Moses had taught that a proper relationship with the Lord begins in the heart and then manifests itself *in obedience* (Deuteronomy 5:31–6:9; 11:18; 32:46). In that regard, Solomon desires that the Lord empower his people to obey him. If the holy God is to be present among the Israelites as Solomon desires (1 Kings 8:57, above), then they must conduct themselves in holiness (Leviticus 11:44, 45; 19:2).

The image of walking *in obedience* to the Lord highlights Israel's obligation. This image appears many times in the Old Testament (see Leviticus 18:3, 4; Deuteronomy 5:33; 8:6; 10:12; Psalm 119:105; etc.). Solomon equates such walking with keeping the Lord's *commands, decrees and laws* as Moses had also prescribed (Deuteronomy 26:17; 30:16). Specifying these three related categories emphasizes the need for total and unwavering obedience to God.

Even so, Solomon's previous acknowledgment that everyone sins and is in need of forgiveness (1 Kings 8:46) highlights Israel's inability to follow God's ways without his help. Scripture elsewhere testifies to the roles of both God and his people in faithfully keeping the covenant (compare Psalm 119:36 [where the word *statutes* refers to laws or decrees] and Joshua 24:23, respectively).

> What Do You Think?
> What are some ways you can help God help you obey him?
> Digging Deeper
> Rank the examples of biblical heroes in Hebrews 11 in terms of whom you most identify with and why.

We see this similarly in the New Testament. For example, Paul's declaration "It is by grace you have been saved, through faith" (Ephesians 2:8) affirms that God's initiative in grace is the necessary precondition for our faithful response to him. Moses had used the image of the circumcision of the heart (Deuteronomy 30:6) to speak of this inclining of the will (see also Ezekiel 11:19; 36:26). Such a circumcision is made available in the new covenant brought by Jesus (Jeremiah 31:31-34; Luke 22:19, 20; Colossians 2:11, 12) through the work of the Holy Spirit (Romans 2:29; 8:1-11).

B. For the Lord's Help (vv. 59, 60)

59. "And may these words of mine, which I have prayed before the LORD, be near to the LORD our God day and night, that he may uphold the cause of his servant and the cause of his people Israel according to each day's need,

Moving to expressing his second desire, Solomon prays that God will hear his prayers and champion *the cause of his people Israel*. Solomon had earlier stressed the faithfulness of the Lord in keeping his word (1 Kings 8:20, 56). God's faithfulness in the past inspires faith and trust in Solomon for the present and the future.

The needs of Solomon and of God's people have been expressed, in one way or another, in all of Solomon's *words* to this point. His summary of his prayer invites Israel to remember what Solomon has requested of the Lord: the king previously had prayed that God's eyes would be open toward the temple "night and day" and that he would listen to his servant's prayer made toward that place (1 Kings 8:29). Solomon prays now that God will hear his prayer on behalf of the people and will not forget.

The final phrase reminds God's people that in each day and in every way, we can depend on his faithfulness (compare Exodus 16:4; Matthew 6:11).

❧ FAITH OF THE GENERATIONS ❧

My grandfather was a troublemaker when he was young. But the Lord used his marriage to my grandmother to change him.

When Grandpa turned his life over to Christ, this often-angry drunk became a kind, peaceful man of faith. The couple's two older sons became ministers. Their younger son was a lifelong leader in the local church. One daughter married a minister, and another married an evangelist. The generations that followed have seen even more Christian leaders walking in the way of "their fathers" as ministers, teachers, and missionaries.

Other families could tell similar stories, demonstrating the value of the faithful generations that came before them. The faithful examples of our fathers and mothers can be honored only in continued faithfulness. When we make faith our own, God continues to honor his promises. Israel had to learn this lesson. We would be wise to learn it too.

—C. R. B.

60a. "so that all the peoples of the earth may know that the LORD is God

Solomon's dedicatory prayer now reflects God's ultimate desire. Reaching the goal of *all the peoples of the earth* knowing *that the Lord is God* must include the Lord's attentiveness to the prayers of the Israelites and their obedience to him. That's how Israel will be an instrument of God's blessing in the world (Genesis 12:1-3; 22:18; etc.).

God's plan and purpose in choosing Israel as his people has always been that the nations would come to know him (examples: 1 Chronicles 16:23,

24; Psalms 72:19; 96:1-10). When Israel is properly obedient, non-Israelites will be attracted to the one true God (see 1 Kings 8:41-43; compare 2 Chronicles 6:32, 33).

60b. "and that there is no other.

The words *there is no other* stand in stark contrast to the many-gods outlook of the ancient world. Each people-group has its gods and worships them in vain attempts to address various needs. The Israelites acknowledge powers at work in the world other than God (Exodus 12:12; 15:11; 18:11; Psalm 82:1; etc.). But at their best, the Israelites worship no so-called god; they worship the Lord only. Solomon's affirmation echoes the assertions of Moses in Deuteronomy 4:35-39. It also anticipates similar statements by the Lord through the prophet Isaiah (Isaiah 45:5, 6, 22).

C. For the People's Hearts (v. 61)

61. "And may your hearts be fully committed to the LORD our God, to live by his decrees and obey his commands, as at this time."

Whereas 1 Kings 8:58 spoke of God's initiative to empower Israel's holiness and obedience, this verse emphasizes Israel's side of the relationship that is made possible by God's initiative. Because there is only one God, Israel's devotion to him is to be total and undivided (Deuteronomy 4:35, 39; 6:5). Joshua had emphasized some 400 years earlier Israel's need to follow the Lord's commands so that blessings would continue in the land where God had granted the nation rest (Joshua 23:14-16; 24:14, 15, 20).

In biblical thought, the heart is the center of a person's character. It can refer to one's mind or will as the source of thoughts, words, actions, and feelings. Israel's obedience is to be complete and

HOW TO SAY IT

Canaan	*Kay*-nun.
Deuteronomy	Due-ter-*ahn*-uh-me.
Leviticus	Leh-*vit*-ih-kus.
Moses	*Mo*-zes or *Mo*-zez.
patriarchs	*Pay*-tree-arks.
Solomon	*Sol*-o-mun.
tabernacle	*tah*-burr-*nah*-kul.

entire (Psalm 119:80), as is Solomon's (1 Kings 9:4; 1 Chronicles 28:9; 29:19).

Solomon himself eventually proves to be unable to stay wholly committed to the Lord. Although he had prayed for Israel's hearts to be turned toward God, Solomon's many wives eventually turn his heart after other gods (1 Kings 11:4). This faithlessness will lead to the fracturing of the nation of Israel (11:9-13).

Kings that follow him won't do much better. Though some kings will be wholly devoted to the Lord (examples: 1 Kings 15:14; 22:43; 2 Kings 20:3; 2 Chronicles 17:6; 25:2), many more will reign with divided loyalties or in outright rebellion (examples: 1 Kings 13:33, 34; 15:3; 16:18-20, 25, 26, 30-33; 2 Kings 1:1, 16, 17). The Israelites, like their kings, will fail to live up to their obligation; as a result, they lose their rest in the land (2 Kings 17:7-23; 24:14-16; 25:8-12).

The parallel account in 2 Chronicles 5–7 indicates that fire comes down from Heaven when Solomon concludes his words. The fire consumes the burnt offerings and sacrifices that had been prepared (2 Chronicles 7:1). The glory of the Lord fills the temple (2 Chronicles 7:1-3) as it had earlier in the celebration (1 Kings 8:10, 11; 2 Chronicles 5:13, 14; compare Exodus 40:34-38). This signals the Lord's approval of the building and the king.

> ### What Do You Think?
> What specific steps can you take to ensure that your heart becomes better aligned with God's desires?
> ### Digging Deeper
> Which stands most in the way of your personal growth in obedience: (1) things you should do and think but don't or (2) things you should not do or think but do?

Conclusion

A. Faithful to the Faithful One

The dedication of the temple was a time to remember the past, to celebrate the present, and to anticipate the future work of God for and with his people. The Lord had done great things for

Visual for Lesson 9. *As you discuss verse 58, point to this visual as you ask "Why is the difference between hearing and heeding important?"*

Israel, and he could be trusted to bless the nation in the future. These blessings would turn out for good—not only for Israel but also for those who came to know the Lord as the only true God. Given God's past faithfulness and given the anticipation of his future faithfulness, Israel was reasonably called to have unswerving devotion to God.

The words of Solomon during the dedication of the temple highlight the loyalty God had demonstrated to his covenant people. Prayerful consideration of what God has already done for us in Christ, is doing for us in the present, and will do for us in the future likewise is to motivate us to lead holy, godly lives.

B. Prayer

Our Father, we praise you as the one who has never failed one word of all your good promises. We cherish your promise never to leave or forsake us. We praise you as the one who is faithful when we are not. Renew us by your Spirit so that we may have the desire and the power to walk in your ways. We pray this so that the world may know you and your Son. We pray in Jesus' name. Amen.

C. Thought to Remember

Each day and in every way,
God is faithful.
Am I?

INVOLVEMENT LEARNING

Enhance your lesson with NIV Bible Student *(from your curriculum supplier) and the reproducible activity page (at www.standardlesson.com or in the back of the* NIV Standard Lesson Commentary Deluxe Edition*).*

Into the Lesson

Before class, gather the wording inscribed on cornerstones of buildings in your town, including your church building. Share the inscriptions with the class. (*Option.* If you have several inscriptions, create a fun quiz for learners to match inscriptions to buildings.) Have participants evaluate how closely the inscriptions reflect the buildings' current uses.

Lead into Bible study by quoting 2 Kings 10:27 as an example that a structure intended for one purpose may end up serving quite the opposite! Say, "Today's text can serve as a prelude to such cautionary tales. Let's see how."

Into the Word

Have a volunteer read the entirety of 1 Kings 8:54-61. Begin by noting Solomon's posture of prayer: kneeling. Ask, "How might the Israelites have reacted to the fact that their king was kneeling?" Discuss implications. (You may wish to keep the time spent here short if you plan to use the option in the Into Life section.) Moving through verses 54-56a, take time to explain the words *supplication, blessed,* and *rest.*

As you continue from verse 56b, divide the class into thirds. For smaller classes, each third will be its own group; for larger classes, divide the thirds into smaller groups. Have slips of paper ready on which you have written these questions, one per slip:

What does Solomon say about the *past*?
What does Solomon say about the *present*?
What does Solomon say about the *future*?

Give each group one of the slips of paper as an assignment. Allow about five minutes for groups to work, during which time you can write the same three questions on the board. After calling groups back together for whole-class discussion, invite responses by asking learners to help you make a complete list of answers under each question. (*Expected categorizations*: v. 56, past; vv. 57-60, present; v. 61, future. Some learners might make a good case that certain verses overlap time categories; ask for explanations.)

Ask class members to draw on their knowledge of Israel's later history to summarize how things turned out. Use responses as a transition to the Into Life segment.

Into Life

Give students two minutes to call out answers to this question: "Which phrase from Solomon's address is the biggest challenge to how Christians live today?" Jot responses on the board for whole-class discussion after time expires. As you move down the list, ask for shows of hands regarding which entry the class thinks to be the single, biggest challenge for Christians. (*Option.* Ask how and why the biggest struggle might change from culture to culture.)

Re-form the class into their thirds from earlier. Inform groups that you want them to think about God's work in and through your own church. The first third is to make a list of God's blessings in the past. The second third is to list his present blessings. The final third is to list what has to happen for God's blessings to continue; ask this group to make their list similar in form to the future-looking statements in Solomon's address.

Reconvene for whole-class discussion after about five minutes. Encourage additional entries to all lists. End with prayers of thanks for God's faithfulness and prayers of commitment to honor his desires in the years ahead.

Option. Distribute copies of the "Standing (?) in Need of Prayer" exercise from the activity page, which you can download. Have learners work in groups of three or four to discuss as indicated. As group discussion winds down, ask learners if any postures have been left out. Discuss those and group conclusions as appropriate.

SINGLE-MINDED
OBEDIENCE

DEVOTIONAL READING: Psalm 91
BACKGROUND SCRIPTURE: Matthew 4:1-11

MATTHEW 4:1-11

¹ Then Jesus was led by the Spirit into the wilderness to be tempted by the devil. ² After fasting forty days and forty nights, he was hungry. ³ The tempter came to him and said, "If you are the Son of God, tell these stones to become bread."

⁴ Jesus answered, "It is written: 'Man shall not live on bread alone, but on every word that comes from the mouth of God.'"

⁵ Then the devil took him to the holy city and had him stand on the highest point of the temple. ⁶ "If you are the Son of God," he said, "throw yourself down. For it is written:

"'He will command his angels concerning you,
and they will lift you up in their hands,
so that you will not strike your foot against a stone.'"

⁷ Jesus answered him, "It is also written: 'Do not put the Lord your God to the test.'"

⁸ Again, the devil took him to a very high mountain and showed him all the kingdoms of the world and their splendor. ⁹ "All this I will give you," he said, "if you will bow down and worship me."

¹⁰ Jesus said to him, "Away from me, Satan! For it is written: 'Worship the Lord your God, and serve him only.'"

¹¹ Then the devil left him, and angels came and attended him.

KEY VERSE

Jesus said to him, "Away from me, Satan! For it is written: 'Worship the Lord your God, and serve him only.'" —**Matthew 4:10**

HONORING
GOD

LESSON AIMS

After participating in this lesson, each learner will be able to:

1. Define *temptation*.

2. Identify the core issue(s) behind each of Jesus' temptations.

3. Make a plan to overcome a specific area of temptation in his or her life.

LESSON OUTLINE

Introduction
    A. Conquering Our Appetites
    B. Lesson Context
  I. In the Wilderness (MATTHEW 4:1-4)
    A. Tempted by Bread (vv. 1-3)
    B. More than Bread (v. 4)
  II. At the Temple (MATTHEW 4:5-7)
    A. Tempted to Prove Love (vv. 5, 6)
      "It Can't Happen to Me"
    B. Trusting the Lord (v. 7)
  III. On a Mountain (MATTHEW 4:8-11)
    A. Tempted by Power (vv. 8, 9)
      Seeing Is Possessing
    B. The End Requires the Means (vv. 10, 11)
Conclusion
    A. Triumph over Temptation
    B. Prayer
    C. Thought to Remember

Introduction

A. Conquering Our Appetites

Churches with a liturgical heritage have long observed the "fast of Lent." Beginning on Ash Wednesday, Lent is a 40-day period of self-denial loosely patterned on Jesus' 40-day fast before his temptation. Traditionally, Lent has involved denying oneself certain foods.

However, many churches now promote fasting as a self-discipline during that 40-day period since many people are given to consuming large quantities of food. Other disciplines encouraged are those of Bible study and prayer as replacements for unhealthy practices involving body and/or spirit. The hope, of course, is that the 40 days will shape the rest of one's year.

Proverbs 25:28 likens the lack of self-control to a city whose walls are broken down and therefore defenseless. How Jesus maintained his self-discipline when his defenses seemed at their lowest is still a model for us some 20 centuries later.

B. Lesson Context

The time of preparation for Jesus' ministry was almost over but not quite. By the point where today's lesson begins, Matthew has told us of the work of John the Baptist, the forerunner of the Messiah (Matthew 3:1-12). John's ministry intersected with that of the Messiah himself at the baptism of Jesus. Done "to fulfill all righteousness" (3:15), Jesus' baptism was a kind of anointing. It showed that he had accepted the task given to him and that he had the approval of both the Holy Spirit and the Father (3:16, 17).

The account of Jesus' temptation as recorded in Matthew 4 gives far more detail than the summary in Mark 1:12, 13. The parallel account in Luke 4:1-13 offers additional insights. The most obvious difference between the accounts in Matthew and Luke is the order in which the temptations are recorded. Luke reverses the second and third from Matthew's order, which is usually understood to be the original. Luke's reason for this change is not immediately apparent. Otherwise, the three accounts agree regarding the historical fact of Jesus' temptations.

Use of the term "the holy city" to refer to Jerusalem in today's text reveals that Matthew was rooted in the Jewish faith (compare Matthew 4:5; 27:53 with Nehemiah 11:1; Isaiah 52:1). By contrast, Luke, of Gentile background (implied in Colossians 4:11, 14), never uses that term (contrast Matthew 4:5 with Luke 4:9).

I. In the Wilderness
(MATTHEW 4:1-4)
A. Tempted by Bread (vv. 1-3)

1. Then Jesus was led by the Spirit into the wilderness to be tempted by the devil.

Matthew presents the temptations of *Jesus* as part of God's plan, a leading of *the Spirit* (compare Mark 1:12, 13; Luke 4:1, 2). The word translated *tempted* can refer to a kind of test (compare the word's translations as "test" or "tested" in John 6:6; Hebrews 11:17; Revelation 2:2, 10; and "examine" in 2 Corinthians 13:5). To come through a test successfully means that one has proven oneself (compare Hebrews 4:15).

Similarities are found between Jesus' temptations and the trials Israel faced in *the wilderness* (compare Exodus 16; 32; Numbers 13:17-33). Though the events are not exactly parallel, the similarities set a challenge for Jesus. Israel was tempted repeatedly in the wilderness and failed the tests. Can the Messiah succeed as God's Son where the Israelites as God's children failed?

> *What Do You Think?*
> Should Christians intentionally seek out a "wilderness experience" for personal growth in Christ? Why, or why not?
> *Digging Deeper*
> How do passages such as 1 Kings 19:1-18; Luke 3:4; John 1:23; and/or Galatians 1:17, 18a inform your conclusion?

The devil, the agent of this temptation (compare Matthew 4:5, 8, 11), is also known as "Satan" (4:10). We are familiar with these designations as referring to the adversary of humankind. He is the one who seeks our downfall. The word *devil* means "accuser"; the word *Satan* means "adver-

sary" (compare Satan's role in Job 1:6-12; 2:1-7). Matthew also calls him "the tempter" (Matthew 4:3), a title that reminds us of the temptations of Eve and Adam in the garden (Genesis 3:1-7).

2. After fasting forty days and forty nights, he was hungry.

The wilderness experiences of Jesus and the nation of Israel find a point of similarity here. The Israelites spent 40 years in the wilderness to be prepared to enter the promised land (Joshua 5:6), and Jesus spends *forty days and forty nights* in the wilderness in preparation for his ministry.

Comparisons also can be drawn between Jesus' 40 days and Moses' time on Mount Sinai (Exodus 34:28) and Elijah's time traveling to Mount Horeb (1 Kings 19:8). Like Moses, Jesus has been fasting. Like Elijah, Jesus' ministry will be marked by faithfulness to the Lord, even though much of Israel will reject Jesus as the Messiah and even kill him (1 Kings 19:10, 14; Luke 4:24-30; 23:33). Jesus' connection with those two historical figures is presented powerfully at his transfiguration (see Matthew 17:1-3).

3. The tempter came to him and said, "If you are the Son of God, tell these stones to become bread."

At Jesus' point of greatest weakness, *the tempter* makes his appearance (compare 1 Thessalonians 3:5). His attack is intended to exploit Jesus' extraordinary hunger. A 40-day fast necessarily results in weakness, sometimes even disorientation.

The temptation here is not that of interrupting the fast, for it has run its course. Rather, the

HOW TO SAY IT

Deuteronomy	Due-ter-*ahn*-uh-me.
Elijah	Ee-*lye*-juh.
Horeb	*Ho*-reb.
Gethsemane	Geth-*sem*-uh-nee (*G* as in *get*).
Isaiah	Eye-*zay*-uh.
Kidron	*Kid*-ron.
Massah	*Mass*-uh.
Messiah	Meh-*sigh*-uh.
Nehemiah	Nee-huh-**my**-uh.
Sinai	*Sigh*-nye or *Sigh*-nay-eye.

temptation is that of using divine power inappropriately to exchange the less important for the more important.

We should note in passing that the statement *If you are the Son of God* does not reflect doubt on Satan's part regarding Jesus' identity; demonic forces recognize Jesus for who he really is throughout the Gospels (Matthew 8:28-34; Luke 4:31-35, 40, 41). No ordinary person can turn *stones* to *bread*. The Son of God, however, is no ordinary person, as the next verse reveals.

B. More than Bread (v. 4)

4. Jesus answered, "It is written: 'Man shall not live on bread alone, but on every word that comes from the mouth of God.'"

Jesus is not insecure. He knows he has the power to feed himself and alleviate his great hunger. We will see Jesus make bread and affirm in doing so that there is nothing inherently sinful in that action (see Matthew 14:13-21). Jesus' feeding miracles will reveal not only his divine status but also his compassion.

But yielding to the current temptation would mark Jesus as someone who is willing to recreate his God-given role as physical needs dictate. Jesus' response to Satan's suggestion comes directly from Deuteronomy 8:3, words spoken first by Moses. That verse reveals a lesson that Israel should have learned in the wilderness: the manna provided by the Lord wasn't just to feed them physically. More importantly, it was to feed them spiritually by pointing them to God as their provider (Exodus 16:15, 16).

Bread in and of itself cannot feed one's spirit. It sustains only one's body—and that only for a limited length of time. Sadly, the wrong attitude in this regard will make a return appearance after one of Jesus' feeding miracles (see John 6:25-27; compare 6:63).

Jesus' answer reveals how Scripture can be recalled in times of temptation. A deep knowledge of Scripture prepares us to recognize both the Spirit's leading and Satan's distractions. When we are in tune with God's Spirit and serious in our Bible study, it is amazing what godly truths will come to mind when needed.

II. At the Temple
(MATTHEW 4:5-7)

A. Tempted to Prove Love (vv. 5, 6)

5. Then the devil took him to the holy city and had him stand on the highest point of the temple.

The holy city is Jerusalem (see Lesson Context), the site of the temple. This temptation comes not in the privacy of the wilderness but in the busiest, most populated place in Judea.

The location of *the highest point of the temple* is uncertain. But it likely refers to the highest elevation on the temple's walls. Many students suggest this to be the southeast corner of the wall, which overlooks the Kidron Valley below. A drop from this spot would certainly be lethal.

6. "If you are the Son of God," he said, "throw yourself down. For it is written: "'He will command his angels concerning you, and they will lift you up in their hands, so that you will not strike your foot against a stone.'"

The tempter now changes his tactics in two ways. First, he attempts his own use of Scripture as he quotes Psalm 91:11, 12 to frame the temptation. But his use of Scripture is immediately seen as insincere when we consider the historical context that Satan conveniently leaves out: that God's protection is linked to obedient faithfulness (91:9, 14).

The tempter's second tactical change is to appeal to Jesus' relationship with the Father. All Jesus has to do to validate that relationship is jump from the pinnacle. This should be an act of sure death, preventable only by a miraculous intervention of the Lord. Satan quotes Scripture to give the impression that God has promised to protect his Messiah from danger by guarding his life with powerful angels (compare Matthew 26:39-

42; 27:40). *Lift you up* even suggests rescue by means of a midair intervention.

We must not think that all who quote Scripture do so properly or with godly motives (compare 2 Corinthians 11:14). Sincere believers may misuse Scripture unintentionally at times. Liars and charlatans do so knowingly and deviously (1 Timothy 1:3-8, 11; 2 Peter 2:1-3). When someone uses selected phrases from the Bible to justify sketchy actions, we have the responsibility to measure this by considering Scripture as a whole, not by cherry-picked proof texts divorced from context.

B. Trusting the Lord (v. 7)

7. Jesus answered him, "It is also written: 'Do not put the Lord your God to the test.'"

Jesus immediately sees that the temptation goes beyond pinnacle-jumping. It has to do with testing *the Lord your God* (see on Matthew 4:1, above). God invites tests in some circumstances (example: Malachi 3:10). But performing the kind of test we see here would reveal that Jesus doubts the Father. Satan intends to plant that seed of doubt in Jesus: *Does the Father love me enough to save me from my folly?* Of course, not being saved from foolishness does not indicate lack of love on God's part. We often face the consequences of our actions.

Jesus does not need such a test. He knows his relationship with the Father is secure without any doubt; it was affirmed several weeks earlier at Jesus' baptism (Matthew 3:13-17). In resisting Satan, Jesus quotes Deuteronomy 6:16. When Moses spoke these words originally, he was warning the Israelites not to tempt God as they had when they asked for water at Massah (Exodus 17:2-7; compare Psalm 95:9).

❧ "IT CAN'T HAPPEN TO ME" ❧

Many feats of derring-do end with great pain. People participating in extreme sports must feel, to some extent, an "it can't happen to me" attitude regarding the possibility of injury or even death.

Some of the most stunning examples of death-defying stunts are seen in videos of wing-suit fliers. The suit allows a parachute jumper to descend at a slower rate of fall while allowing a (somewhat) controllable gliding at up to 200 mph! Viewers can experience the rush of the stunt without experiencing the potentially life-ending consequences via cameras mounted to jumpers' helmets.

When the devil dared Jesus to jump off the pinnacle of the temple, he was asserting that the death-defying stunt would not kill Jesus. Satan was inviting Jesus to adopt an "It can't happen to me" attitude. Jesus' refusal to take the dare was not cowardly; he knew that legions of angels were at his disposal (Matthew 26:53). Rather, Jesus saw the dare in spiritual terms: he would have been challenging God to save him from a foolish act. Do we ever do the same?   —C. R. B.

> *What Do You Think?*
> ► How do you draw a reasonable line between stepping out in faith and testing God?
> *Digging Deeper*
> Consider biblical examples in Exodus 17:2, 7; Judges 6:36-40; 1 Samuel 17; Daniel 6:10-12; and Acts 21:10-12. Also consider the directives and advisories in Malachi 3:10; Luke 14:31-33; Acts 15:10; Romans 12:2; and 1 Corinthians 10:9.

III. On a Mountain
(MATTHEW 4:8-11)
A. Tempted by Power (vv. 8, 9)

8. Again, the devil took him to a very high mountain and showed him all the kingdoms of the world and their splendor.

We are not told where the *very high mountain* is. No mountain in the world can make visible *all the kingdoms,* anyway. What is suggested, rather, is a visionary experience (compare 2 Corinthians 12:2). Whether a physical location or spiritual experience, it is very real for Jesus. Being shown the *splendor* of all the kingdoms means he sees their power and wealth (compare Revelation 21:24, 26).

9a. "All this I will give you," he said,

Satan is a liar (John 8:44), and he has misused Scripture already. Does he really presume to have the authority to give Jesus *all this*?

There is a sense in which Satan does indeed rule this world (see John 12:31; 2 Corinthians 4:4;

Ephesians 2:2). But his influence is temporary and limited (Revelation 12:9; 20:2, 7-10). Ultimately, Satan has no authority and will be destroyed. He offers a promise that he cannot keep, even if he wanted to do so.

9b. "if you will bow down and worship me."

To gain absolute power over the human realm, Jesus is to give allegiance to Satan. That allegiance is to take the form of *worship*. To *bow down* in that regard is to assume a prostrate position (compare Daniel 3).

Such an act would have at least two implications. First, Jesus would be turning his back on the glories of Heaven and its perfection for the pleasures of and power over the corrupt earth. It wouldn't be *both/and*; it is *either/or*.

Second, this reward would come at an unimaginable price: placing Jesus' authority under that of the devil rather than God. Yielding to this temptation would mean rejecting God's timing concerning when the Messiah is to receive authority (Matthew 28:18). The shortcut to prestige Satan offers may be appealing by sidestepping the pain and humiliation of death on a Roman cross. But the offer is a fiction and a mirage.

What Do You Think?
What techniques can we use to uncover a hidden agenda before we allow someone to "help" us?

Digging Deeper
How do passages such as Matthew 7:1, 15-20; 10:16; 24:4, 5; Mark 15:10; Luke 20:20-26; John 8:6; and/or 11:48 help you frame your response?

B. The End Requires the Means (vv. 10, 11)

10. Jesus said to him, "Away from me, Satan! For it is written: 'Worship the Lord your God, and serve him only.'"

When Peter later denies that Jesus will be killed, Jesus' rebuke is sharp: "Get behind me, Satan! You are a stumbling block to me" (Matthew 16:23). Thus the idea that the Messiah does not need to die is confronted more than once.

Jesus' response in the case at hand comes from Deuteronomy 6:13. That chapter is packed with short axioms that define Israel's relationship with the Lord (examples: Deuteronomy 6:4, 14). Only God is worthy of *worship*. For this reason, the ancient Israelites were constantly reminded to *serve* the Lord *only* (Exodus 20:3, 4; Joshua 24:14; Nehemiah 9:6; etc.). The same challenge confronts Christians (Revelation 22:8, 9; etc.). For Jesus to worship Satan would be not only a cardinal sin but also a repudiation of his nature as the Son of God—an impossibility.

What is the key for us to have victory over the temptations that come our way? Paul points out that one of the deficiencies in our lives is lack of self-control, which Satan exploits (Titus 2:12; compare Galatians 5:22-26). In the lesson's account of Jesus' temptations, we see superlative self-control. Jesus maintains a fast for 40 days. He resists three tantalizing temptations, each targeting a potential weakness in his self-control.

11a. Then the devil left him,

The fact that *the devil* leaves at Jesus' command shows who's really in charge here (compare Romans 16:20). The authority of Jesus prevails (compare Matthew 8:28-34; Mark 1:21-34; Luke 11:14-26).

11b. and angels came and attended him.

The angelic ministry that follows likely involves tending to both Jesus' physical and spiritual fatigue. This quick appearance of angels is also instructive for us. To experience temptation does not mean that God has forsaken us. Times of temptation can indeed test us to our limits. But the Bible promises that God will not allow us to be tried beyond our strength (1 Corinthians 10:13). God will always give us a way out. When we fortify our hearts with Scripture and earnestly seek the Lord, we will be prepared for the Holy Spirit to guide us through great tests without us betraying our faith in Jesus (2 Thessalonians 2:13-15).

The righteous way that Jesus chose led him all the way to the Garden of Gethsemane. In that garden, he again resisted temptation, yielding obediently to death to atone for the sins of the world (Mark 14:32-42). His strength can be ours.

The December 17, 2017, issue of *Time* magazine announced "The Silence Breakers" as the magazine's Person of the Year. This collective "person" represents numerous women who spoke out against sexual harassment and assault they had been subjected to by powerful males in their workplaces.

The hurt and anger these women experienced became part of the #MeToo movement. Women involved in the movement sought to hold men accountable for their *own* actions, not implicate all men unjustly for the misdeeds of some.

Vulnerable people throughout history have been considered mere parts of various "kingdoms" over which those in power have exercised authority. Many of the powerful give in to the desire to possess whatever they see. Uncontrolled sexual desire (contrast Genesis 38:15-18 with 39:1-10 with 2 Samuel 11) and lust for land (1 Kings 21) are just two examples. Even though Jesus didn't fall for it, that hasn't discouraged the devil from using this chance to sin on humans. Reason: it works.　　　　　　　　　　　　　—C. R. B.

Conclusion

A. Triumph over Temptation

Matthew's presentation of Jesus as the man who did not yield to temptation was confirmed during the three years Matthew lived closely with Jesus. Therefore, with full confidence that it was true, Matthew was able to write today's account of Jesus' successfully resisting temptations.

Jesus' wilderness experience involved genuine temptations, offering him the opportunity to sin. God was surely looking on this episode with a great desire and confidence that Jesus would not succumb. Even so, the Father probably still saw this as an important test of Jesus' character.

This is true for us as well. God knows we are tempted (Hebrews 4:15). Some situations may even function as needed tests of our faith (1 Corinthians 11:19; James 1:1-3). God may test us (Exodus 16:4; etc.), but he never tempts us to sin (James 1:13-15). Successfully overcoming temptation builds character (1:2-4) and results in eternal life (1:12). Winning interim battles against every-

Visual for Lesson 10. *Point to this visual as you ask learners what locations tend to get overlooked as potential places of temptation.*

day temptations prepares us for the great testing of faith that comes with life crises.

How do we gain such triumphant self-control? This lesson gives us a pathway in that regard. First, self-control builds confidence as it is exercised. Second, self-control must be guided by Scripture. Third, we are never to forget that God is with us in our times of trial. Self-control is more successful when we know others are watching and supporting us. May we cooperate with God in allowing him to strengthen our self-control!

> *What Do You Think?*
>   What guardrails can you erect to prevent tests
>   of character from turning into surrender to
>   sin?
> *Digging Deeper*
>   Consider how thoughts and actions interrelate.

B. Prayer

Heavenly Father, be merciful to us, for we often give in to temptation. May we draw on your strength when we are weak. May our willingness to grow spiritually in self-control reap a harvest of eternal life among those who follow our example. We pray in Jesus' name. Amen.

C. Thought to Remember

God gives us the resources to overcome temptation. Use them!

INVOLVEMENT LEARNING

Enhance your lesson with NIV Bible Student *(from your curriculum supplier) and the reproducible activity page (at www.standardlesson.com or in the back of the* NIV Standard Lesson Commentary Deluxe Edition*).*

Into the Lesson

Ask class members to think of at least one thing their parents forbade them to do but they did anyway. Prime the pump for discussion by sharing an example from your own life. If you have time, class members can share their answers with a partner before you ask for volunteers to share with everyone.

Lead into Bible study by saying, "The examples we've shared only begin to include all the temptations we've faced. Some of these may be similar to the temptations Jesus faced. Let's see."

Into the Word

Before class, write the following questions on three slips of paper, one each. Divide your class into three groups, and give a slip to each group. (Larger classes can create more than three groups with assignments duplicated.)

1–How may Jesus have wrestled with himself as he considered Satan's temptations?

2–How did Jesus affirm his faith in God during Satan's temptations?

3–How was Jesus prepared by his past to conquer these temptations?

Have groups read Matthew 4:1-11 as they consider their questions. After five minutes, ask each group to pass its slip to a different group so that each group discusses two of the three questions. After five more minutes, call the class to order and allow members to share their insights in whole-class discussion.

Consider the following points in response to the questions if groups miss them:

1–In the first testing, Jesus was tempted to take control of the situation for himself rather than trusting God to provide. In the third testing, the devil offered Jesus worldly fame and glory greater than ever known by any human.

2–In the first testing, Jesus needed to trust God, rather than himself, to meet his needs. In the second testing, Jesus needed to affirm his

knowledge that God was in control and committed to his best; Jesus didn't need to test God in order to prove that.

3–Jesus' knowledge of Scripture (more complete than any other human can achieve) prepared him to contrast the devil's misuse with the truth of God (compare Luke 2:46-52).

Option. As a posttest, have learners complete the "True or False?" exercise on the activity page, which you can download and reproduce.

Into Life

Write the following phrases on the board:

1. *Trust God to provide.*
2. *Worship God only.*
3. *Prepare for temptation.*

Ask class members to reassemble into their groups. Remind the class that these phrases summarize how and why Jesus won his victory over temptation. Ask class members to list specific temptations that threaten to keep Christians from following each of the three principles.

After five minutes, reassemble the class for whole-class discussion and ask for responses. Jot suggestions on the board.

Alternative. Distribute copies of the "Tempted Like Jesus" exercise on the activity page. Have learners complete it in study pairs before moving to the final commitment activity.

Remind class members that temptation is not sin; yielding to it is the sin. Ask them to choose one temptation the devil uses to try to separate them from God. Distribute blank slips of paper and ask students to write on it their completion to this sentence:

I can resist the temptation to _____
by remembering to _____.

If this is too personal for your group, it can be a take-home activity.

GOD-HONORING
PIETY

DEVOTIONAL READING: Luke 11:1-13
BACKGROUND SCRIPTURE: Ecclesiastes 5:1-6; Matthew 6:1-18

MATTHEW 6:1-8

[1] "Be careful not to practice your righteousness in front of others to be seen by them. If you do, you will have no reward from your Father in heaven.

[2] "So when you give to the needy, do not announce it with trumpets, as the hypocrites do in the synagogues and on the streets, to be honored by others. Truly I tell you, they have received their reward in full. [3] But when you give to the needy, do not let your left hand know what your right hand is doing, [4] so that your giving may be in secret. Then your Father, who sees what is done in secret, will reward you.

[5] "And when you pray, do not be like the hypocrites, for they love to pray standing in the synagogues and on the street corners to be seen by others. Truly I tell you, they have received their reward in full. [6] But when you pray, go into your room, close the door and pray to your Father, who is unseen. Then your Father, who sees what is done in secret, will reward you. [7] And when you pray, do not keep on babbling like pagans, for they think they will be heard because of their many words. [8] Do not be like them, for your Father knows what you need before you ask him."

KEY VERSE

Be careful not to practice your righteousness in front of others to be seen by them. If you do, you will have no reward from your Father in heaven. —**Matthew 6:1**

HONORING GOD

Unit 3: Jesus Teaches About True Worship

LESSON AIMS

After participating in this lesson, each learner will be able to:

1. Describe *hypocrisy*.
2. Contrast hypocritical and sincere attitudes.
3. Identify his or her motivations in giving and actively repent of ungodly motives.

LESSON OUTLINE

Introduction
  A. Christian Charity
  B. Lesson Context
I. On Giving (MATTHEW 6:1-4)
  A. As a Hypocrite (vv. 1, 2)
    The Best Giver
  B. As a True Worshipper (vv. 3, 4)
II. On Prayer (MATTHEW 6:5-8)
  A. Seen by Others (v. 5)
  B. Seen by God (v. 6)
    Better at Doing or Telling?
  C. Many Words or Few? (vv. 7, 8)
Conclusion
  A. Publicly or Privately?
  B. Prayer
  C. Thought to Remember

Introduction

A. Christian Charity

In a church I served for several years, we once had a "burn the mortgage" campaign. The leaders launched the campaign to raise the $100,000 needed to retire the congregation's only debt. Several members were capable of writing a check for the entire amount, so it seemed like the project should be quick and successful.

I was surprised, however, when raising the final $20,000 stalled for several weeks. Wondering why, I was told that two of the wealthier men of the church were each intending to give $10,000, but each one wanted to be recognized as the person who put the campaign "over the top." Both men desired to be seen by the congregation as timely and generous; both believed there was room for only one person in this honored position.

Eventually, the two men worked this out somehow, and neither was announced as the final giver. This was as it should have been. While this giving was not directly for relief of the poor (a context of this week's lesson), its intent to eliminate the congregation's debt would free up budget funds for international missions giving and support of the city's rescue mission.

The campaign was never intended to be a contest for recognition. Today's lesson tells us how that turn could have been prevented.

B. Lesson Context

The literary context of today's lesson is Jesus' Sermon on the Mount, which encompasses chapters 5–7 of Matthew's Gospel. This sermon is Jesus' exposition of what it means to live under the reign of God in the kingdom of Heaven, as Matthew calls it (Matthew 4:17; 11:11, 12; 16:19; 18:1; etc.; the other Gospels use the phrase "kingdom of God"). Early in the sermon, Jesus pronounced blessing on "those who hunger and thirst for righteousness" (5:6) and the "pure in heart" (5:8). A little later, Jesus warned that those who belong to God's kingdom must have righteousness greater than that of the teachers of the law and Pharisees (5:20). The middle section of Jesus' sermon explains those challenging ideas.

Jesus stressed that true righteousness means righteousness not just on the outside but on the inside as well. Obedience to God means not just avoiding murder but controlling anger (Matthew 5:21-24); not just avoiding adultery but controlling lustful thoughts (5:27-30). Genuine purity is that of the heart. Those who live under the rule of God are obedient not just where everyone can see but even in places God alone can see. This leads up to Jesus' condemnation of hypocrites and hypocrisy.

Today's text introduces the first of a series of Jesus' teachings regarding motives of the heart. His preferred method of teaching was to use parables (Matthew 13:34). But today's text is a picture of Jesus teaching by means of plain-spoken directives.

I. On Giving
(MATTHEW 6:1-4)
A. As a Hypocrite (vv. 1-2)

1. "Be careful not to practice your righteousness in front of others to be seen by them. If you do, you will have no reward from your Father in heaven.

Righteousness in this context refers to actions done in keeping with the expectations of a Jewish person who follows the Law of Moses. To show mercy to the poor is a central duty of the righteous who seek to obey the law (see Deuteronomy 15:11). God is not concerned with only the outward appearance of doing what is right. He also looks to the heart (1 Samuel 16:7; Matthew 9:4). He desires our good deeds to come from pure motives not from a desire for accolades.

> **What Do You Think?**
> What guardrails can Christians erect to ensure proper motives regarding any reward they expect as a result of giving?
> **Digging Deeper**
> How can Christians keep those guardrails from becoming legalistic (Mark 7:13)?

2. "So when you give to the needy, do not announce it with trumpets, as the hypocrites do in the synagogues and on the streets, to be honored by others. Truly I tell you, they have received their reward in full.

In the Galilee of Jesus' day, there are no funds coming from the Roman government to alleviate the grinding poverty that many experience. The Jewish community sees a duty in making sure its most vulnerable members (especially widows and orphans) do not starve or go without housing or clothing. Jesus' criticism does not target this worthy activity in and of itself, for the early church continues to care for the poor (see Matthew 19:21; 25:37-40; Luke 19:8; Acts 6:1-3; Galatians 2:10). Jesus has no problem with poverty relief; he assumes that his followers will practice giving to the poor.

Jesus' concern, rather, is that of hypocrisy. To confront this problem, he presents extreme examples of hypocritical behavior in this area. One can imagine a rich man staging a parade from his house to his synagogue. Accompanied by trumpeters and lavishly dressed attendants, the spectacle is intended to create maximum exposure of his generous gift. Such behavior is hardly for relief of the poor but for garnering public praise for a rich person—who himself may be complicit in the poverty of the oppressed (see Matthew 23:5-7; Luke 11:39-42; James 2:6, 7; 5:1-5). It is a created drama with the rich person playing the leading role: that of a praiseworthy benefactor. The short-lived *reward* for this hypocritical behavior is like the theater crowd's applause: when the hands quit clapping and the sound fades, nothing is left.

Hypocrites are the common target of today's lesson text. Various forms of this Greek term occur about two dozen times in the New Testament; the majority of those are in Matthew. A well-known background for the word *hypocrite* is the Greek drama tradition. A hypocrite in that context was an actor, one who played a role and pretended on stage to be a character created by a writer. Such actors traditionally used theatrical masks to define their characters. Such masks were known to the Greeks as "faces."

Therefore, the word *hypocrite* did not have the negative connotation that we understand today. The hypocrites who are targeted in this lesson are play-acting religious roles. These religious hypocrites perform for the audience of the adoring public. They wear masks of piousness to hide their hearts of evil (Matthew 23:27). Their pretense may fool the crowds but not Jesus. He knows their hearts (9:4). Jesus never uses the word *hypocrite* in a positive or even a neutral sense, although the larger culture of his day might do so. For Jesus, the hypocrite is a deceiver, a pretender who conceals true motives for actions.

Jesus often exposes his opponents' hypocrisies. Among these foes are the esteemed religious leaders of the Jews: the teachers of the law and Pharisees (see Matthew 23:13, 15, 16, 23, 25, 27, 29). Jesus identifies his opponents' false representations and lays bare their deviousness. He rips off the masks the hypocrites have been hiding behind, revealing their true faces.

> **What Do You Think?**
> In what ways, if any, does the kind of hypocrisy noted here call for different guardrails than those of the hypocrisies of Matthew 7:1-5 and 22:15-18? Why?
> **Digging Deeper**
> Which type poses the greatest danger to Christianity in general? Why?

❧ THE BEST GIVER ❧

Years ago, I was hired by a certain parachurch ministry. During my first board meeting, a glowing picture was painted of the organization's financial future, which was based on a program of receiving real-estate donations.

The program was promoted by a strong-willed board member whose term expired at that very meeting. Within a few months, we found the program was costing the ministry money. In the interests of good stewardship, we canceled it.

The former board member demanded to speak at the next board meeting as a result. He began, "I'm the largest single contributor to this ministry." His pride convinced him that he had the right to continue to exert influence over the ministry. But that man didn't contribute the most. My wife worked in the financial office—she knew.

Jesus warned that boasting about our righteousness brings into question the sincerity of our motives. How do you avoid temptation in this regard?
                                        —C. R. B.

B. As a True Worshipper (vv. 3, 4)

3. "But when you give to the needy, do not let your left hand know what your right hand is doing,

Jesus assumes that his followers will continue giving for relief of the poor, and he offers an unhypocritical way to do so. As with his extreme example of the rich man's parade, Jesus paints an equally extreme picture of privacy. For a person's *left hand* not to *know* what the *right hand is doing* is a near, if not outright, impossibility! But Jesus often paints extreme pictures to make an extreme point. In this case, giving should be done with as much secrecy as possible. This will ensure motives that are centered on concern for others not that of garnering attention for oneself.

At first glance, this teaching may seem to contradict what Jesus has already said in this sermon. How can good deeds be a light to others (Matthew 5:16) if they are to be a secret even from oneself (if that were even possible)? As always, the human heart is the very center of the matter. It seems that we are tempted to hide what we ought to show and to show what we ought to hide! Doing a good deed from the heart, whether in secret or in the open, pleases the Lord. Going through the motions—whether for attention or because we believe that outward actions can save us—never pleases God.

> **What Do You Think?**
> What are some practical ways you can honor Jesus' imagery of the left and right hands?
> **Digging Deeper**
> How do you personally temper Jesus' directive here with His remarks in Matthew 5:16 concerning your own giving?

When you give of your resources to help people, you are continuing a long tradition of the church, with even older roots in ancient Israel. Wealth, however, can always be transferred inappropriately. That happens when the gift is leveraged to be more for the advantage of the giver than the receiver. If the left hand doesn't know what the right hand is doing, it cannot expect a kickback. We are to give when we see a need and realize we can help not for recognition or praise.

4. "so that your giving may be in secret. Then your Father, who sees what is done in secret, will reward you.

Aiding the poor is a godly action, showing we love poor people as does our *Father* in Heaven (Deuteronomy 15:7-11; Luke 1:52, 53; James 1:27). By mentioning a *reward* from the Father, Jesus is not saying we can earn salvation by our good works. Rather, Jesus is stressing that God does indeed notice, for he sees all things, even those done *in secret* (compare Matthew 6:6, 18; James 2:18, 26).

God is the only audience that matters, and he will surely be pleased by properly motivated actions. Such actions will be rewarded eternally. That will happen very publicly at the appropriate time (Colossians 3:23, 24; Revelation 22:12).

II. On Prayer
(MATTHEW 6:5-8)
A. Seen by Others (v. 5)

5. "And when you pray, do not be like the hypocrites, for they love to pray standing in the synagogues and on the street corners to be seen by others. Truly I tell you, they have received their reward in full.

Jesus now turns to a second act of righteousness practiced by hypocritical Jews of the first century AD: prayer. Again, he presents an extreme example for effect. In Jesus' day, many prayer postures are acceptable (see Numbers 16:22; 1 Samuel 1:26; 2 Samuel 7:18; 2 Chronicles 6:13). The problem with *the hypocrites* is not their standing posture in and of itself during times of prayer. Rather, the problem is their attitude of desiring to *be seen by others*.

Prayer is regularly offered three times daily: "Evening, morning and noon I cry out" (Psalm 55:17; compare Daniel 6:10; Acts 3:1). Prayer within the confines of *the synagogues* would seem to be the ideal place for it, right? Not if the desire is to be seen and thought highly of.

The same is true even of (or especially of) prayer in the temple. And Jesus has a parable in that regard: that of the Pharisee and the tax collector (Luke 18:9-14). In this parable, the motives of the hypocrite are seen in the content of the Pharisee's prayer: "God, I thank you that I am not like other people. . . . I fast twice a week and give a tenth of all I get" (18:11, 12). This is hardly communication with God! It is merely self-serving praise and self-justification. It is the prayer a trained actor on stage might recite from a script. As with the applause of a theater crowd, the *reward* is only for the performance and quickly fades.

Shifting location from synagogue to *the street corners* changes nothing. Praise-seeking hypocrites are drawn to public places like a moth to a flame. But for Jesus, motives trump location in all cases and at all times.

B. Seen by God (v. 6)

6. "But when you pray, go into your room, close the door and pray to your Father, who is unseen. Then your Father, who sees what is done in secret, will reward you.

Jesus describes the sincere, unhypocritical prayer practice in extreme terms as well: prayer should happen in *your room*. The Greek word refers to a room not intended for social purposes (compare Matthew 24:26; Luke 12:3). To *close the door* prevents the possibility of even an accidental crowd.

The *Father* sees into the room, though, for nothing is *secret* from him. The only purpose of such a prayer is the true one: communication with God. The prayer does not have to be eloquent or perfect, only sincere (compare Romans 8:26). God *will reward* such praying by listening and caring.

We should note in passing that some Christians take this passage quite literally. They do so by designating a closet intended for storage as the only

HOW TO SAY IT

Baal	*Bay*-ul.
Deuteronomy	Due-ter-*ahn*-uh-me.
Galatians	Guh-*lay*-sunz.
Galilee	*Gal*-uh-lee.
Gethsemane	Geth-*sem*-uh-nee (*G* as in *get*).
Pharisees	*Fair*-ih-seez.
synagogue	*sin*-uh-gog.

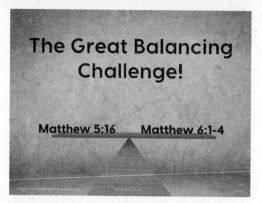

The Great Balancing Challenge!

Matthew 5:16   Matthew 6:1-4

Visual for Lesson 11. *Begin a discussion by pointing to this visual before you read aloud the two texts listed.*

proper place for their prayer. While there is nothing inherently wrong with this practice, there is nothing particularly virtuous about praying inside a broom closet per se. The issue is one of privacy.

Private prayer can be accomplished almost anywhere. It only requires a place where the one praying won't be distracted by surroundings or tempted to display one's self-thought righteousness to others. This requires planning and deliberate effort, because our world is full of distractions. Take time to turn off the television, silence your phone, and be alone.

Though some have thought this verse causes issues with public prayer in worship, elsewhere the first-century church is seen to engage in this very practice (see Acts 1:24; 3:1; 4:24-30). Today, congregational prayers have nearly disappeared in some churches. But this should not be the case. The one offering such a prayer should be prepared to do so while remembering that leading the congregation to the throne of God is not a performance.

⚜ *BETTER AT DOING OR TELLING?* ⚜

I entered seminary as a young man. At a retreat for incoming students, we had opportunity to get acquainted with our professors outside of the formal classroom setting. A featured speaker was a leader widely known in Christian circles for his devotional life. It seemed we were in for a treat.

The "treat" turned into a "treatment." The speaker described in great detail how he arose early every morning to pray for four hours—detailing everything he thought the Lord needed to know. Not once did he mention listening to what God might be trying to tell *him*.

I admit that my prayer life is less disciplined, and possibly even less effective, than that of our speaker. And yet something about the whole experience seemed to be a bit *off* in light of Jesus' admonishment about making a public display. Are you better at doing or telling?   —C. R. B.

> *What Do You Think?*
> What steps can you take to create time for "in secret" prayer in your daily schedule?
> *Digging Deeper*
> Under what circumstances should you, like Daniel in Daniel 6:10, 11, intentionally let others see you praying, if ever? How do the public prayers in Matthew 14:19; Acts 1:24; 3:1; 20:36; 21:5; etc., further inform your decision?

C. Many Words or Few? (vv. 7, 8)

7. "And when you pray, do not keep on babbling like pagans, for they think they will be heard because of their many words.

Jesus now expands his teaching on prayer beyond that of hypocritical practices. His next target are the Gentiles (that is, non-Jews) and their pagan practices. The fictitious gods they pray to are seen as having human weaknesses. They can be moved to action by long, wordy, repetitious prayers (of which we have written examples).

The idea behind their prayer blabber is that such repetition will grab the gods' attention and wear them down. Eventually the god gives in to grant the request. This is a little like the parent who says no to a child's request a hundred times, then finally yields with a yes simply to get the child to be quiet. Because the gods are seen as not inclined to listen or care, one needs to say a lot, over and over, in hopes of receiving a response.

Another aspect of praying to these fickle gods is their assumed short attention span and tendency to be easily distracted by other matters. Pagans praying to their gods may think such deities are too busy for them. We see this in Elijah's mocking of the prayers of the prophets of Baal. At the famous contest on Mount Carmel, those prophets leaped on their altar and shouted to their god from early morning until noon. Elijah encouraged these rival prophets to pray louder and more vigorously, because their god may have been busy, or sleeping, or on a journey (1 Kings 18:26, 27).

Then Elijah prayed a brief prayer to God. Then "the fire of the Lord fell" to consume his sacrifice (1 Kings 18:38). Elijah was in public, but his prayer was not a look-how-great-I-am show. His desire was for the Lord to show himself as the only God who listens and acts (18:36).

This is the kind of prayer Jesus teaches his followers to pray. His instructions contrast with pagan fears that their gods are not inclined to listen. God hears even a few words (Ecclesiastes 5:2).

We should point out that this verse doesn't mean that we can't or shouldn't be persistent in prayer (Luke 18:1-8). In the Garden of Gethsemane, Jesus will repeat his own prayer (Matthew 26:39, 42, 44). It's all the pointless *babbling* that we are to avoid.

What Do You Think?
How can you ensure that your repeated prayers do not result in the prayer style that Jesus condemns?

Digging Deeper
How does Jesus' instruction in Luke 18:1-8 inform your prayer style in this regard?

---

8. "Do not be like them, for your Father knows what you need before you ask him."

Unlike fictitious heathen gods, our *Father* does not need to be convinced of our needs. He already knows them (compare Matthew 6:31, 32). Some have therefore asked, "Why, then, ask God for anything since he already knows what we need?" This misses the point. Prayer is a way of developing a relationship with God. God himself is not psychologically needy, desiring for us to ask to satisfy something lacking in his personality. The point is that praying helps us learn to trust that he already knows what we need *before* we *ask him*.

We do still bring our petitions before the Lord (for example, Matthew 6:9-13, next week's lesson).

But what are proper things to ask God for, and what are improper? We dare not treat prayer as if we are on the lap of the department store Santa, giving him our Christmas list (compare James 4:3). Yet we should be bold to ask God for those things we need (see Hebrews 4:16). We ask God because we believe that he cares. We ask because it positions us properly within his will. It meets his desire that our relationship with him would grow and flourish. God wants us to share our hearts with him.

Conclusion

A. Publicly or Privately?

How public should our religious acts be? Should we expect public/published recognition when we give? Professional fund-raisers tell us that public recognition is important and motivating. But this seems to be contrary to Jesus' teaching.

Public acts of worship are not necessarily hypocritical. The issue is motive. Are we drawing attention to ourselves or pointing others to God? Is our giving intended to draw the praise of people or to encourage others to give? Are our public prayers designed to impress or to lead others to God's throne?

Jesus' teaching in this regard has not grown stale. It is still needed in the church and the lives of Christians. Jesus expects his disciples of any era to be different, rejecting the ways of the world. We should not try to impress either God or others.

We all struggle with hypocrisy at some level, whether we call it mixed motives or desire for respect. However, we can examine our hearts and motives as we live to please our Lord. May we seek to eliminate our hypocrisy by focusing on a true, sincere relationship with the Lord.

B. Prayer

Father, we often act the part of the righteous person to impress others, not to serve you. Give us new, pure, unhypocritical hearts, Lord. We pray in Jesus' name. Amen.

C. Thought to Remember

Hypocrisy cannot be overcome until it is identified and acknowledged.

INVOLVEMENT LEARNING

Enhance your lesson with NIV Bible Student *(from your curriculum supplier) and the reproducible activity page (at www.standardlesson.com or in the back of the* NIV Standard Lesson Commentary Deluxe Edition*).*

Into the Lesson

Play a game of "Raise Your Hand If" with your class as you pose each of the following:

You have received an anonymous gift.
You have given an anonymous gift.
You were embarrassed by a gift you received.
You've given a "needed" instead of "wanted" gift.
You've wanted something for more than a year.

Lead into Bible study by telling the class, "God's answers to our prayers are, in effect, gifts from him. Jesus has quite a bit to say about this, as do the inspired writers of Scripture. Today's study takes us down this vitally important road."

Into the Word

Announce a Bible-marking activity. Provide copies of Matthew 6:1-8 for those who do not want to write in their own Bibles. Provide handouts (you create) with these instructions:

1–*Underline* everything Jesus says not to do.
2–Put an *asterisk* beside everything Jesus wants His listeners to do.
3–Put a *question mark* beside any phrase or section that you want to understand better.
4–Put an *exclamation mark* beside any prohibition or command you find especially challenging.

Read the Scripture aloud (or ask volunteers to do so) slowly at least twice and as many as four times. As the Scripture is read, class members are to mark their copies in the ways noted.

After the final reading, launch a class discussion by working through each of the four instructions. After thoroughly considering Jesus' don'ts and dos, ask class members to share sections they'd like to understand better. Allow other learners to respond; use the commentary to fill in gaps.

Finally, ask for volunteers to share what they find especially challenging in the text.

Help students refine their views on all issues by leading them to compare the commands of Jesus in Matthew 6:1-8 with his words in Matthew 5:13-16. (The lesson for July 7, 2019, will help, if you have access to it.) Do so by forming groups of no more than three. Give each group one of the following two tasks on handouts (you prepare), assigning them among groups as evenly as possible: 1–What results of our faith should be seen in order to impact the world for the gospel? 2–What aspects of authentic faith are to be seen only by God?

Instruct that each group should refer to Matthew 5:13-20 and 6:1-8 to support conclusions.

After a few minutes call the class to order and let volunteers share their lists. Help class members reconcile what may seem like contradictory commands by focusing on the issue of motive.

Alternative. Distribute copies of the "Giving, Prayer, and Heart" exercise from the activity page, which you can download. Have learners complete it in study pairs or groups of three. (*Option.* You can change the seven questions into seven skits for learners to act out for discussion.)

Into Life

Distribute copies of the following self-rating activity regarding personal motives. Have learners complete it very quickly, marking first impressions on each of the three actions noted. Assure learners that you will not collect the results.

I (1) attend church, (2) serve the church, and (3) give to the church in order to be . . .

<—————————————————————————————>
seen by people   *known by God*

What needs to change for you to improve in each area?

Option. If you did not do so earlier, distribute copies of the "Giving, Prayer, and Heart" exercise from the activity page as a take-home. To encourage completion, promise to discuss results next week.

KINGDOM-SEEKING PRAYER

DEVOTIONAL READING: Psalm 40:1-10, 16, 17
BACKGROUND SCRIPTURE: Matthew 6:9-15

MATTHEW 6:9-15

⁹ "This, then, is how you should pray:
"'Our Father in heaven,
hallowed be your name,
¹⁰ your kingdom come,
your will be done,
    on earth as it is in heaven.
¹¹ Give us today our daily bread.
¹² And forgive us our debts,
    as we also have forgiven our debtors.
¹³ And lead us not into temptation,
    but deliver us from the evil one.'"

¹⁴ For if you forgive other people when they sin against you, your heavenly Father will also forgive you. ¹⁵ But if you do not forgive others their sins, your Father will not forgive your sins.

KEY VERSE

Your kingdom come, your will be done, on earth as it is in heaven. —**Matthew 6:10**

Honoring
God

LESSON AIMS

After participating in this lesson, each learner will be able to:

1. Recite the Lord's Prayer.
2. Explain the petitions of the Lord's Prayer.
3. Write a prayer that focuses on one aspect of the Lord's Prayer he or she tends to overlook.

LESSON OUTLINE

Introduction
 A. The Rightful King
 B. Lesson Context
I. The Prayer (MATTHEW 6:9-13)
 A. Holiness (v. 9)
  Our Father(s)
 B. The Kingdom (v. 10)
 C. Daily Needs (vv. 11-13)
II. On Forgiveness (MATTHEW 6:14, 15)
 A. For Others (v. 14)
  Forgive Every Debtor?
 B. For Ourselves (v. 15)
Conclusion
 A. Proclaiming the Kingdom
 B. Prayer
 C. Thought to Remember

Introduction

A. The Rightful King

Fairy tales and legends often feature stories about a just, good king to come. One famous example is that of Arthur Pendragon. When Arthur's father, King Uther Pendragon, died, there were many who wanted to be crowned king. There was a test, however: a sword embedded in a stone and engraved, "Whoso pulleth out this sword of this stone is the rightwise born king of all England."

Many tried to pull the sword, but could not. Yet young Arthur, almost by accident, effortlessly pulled the sword from the stone. He was immediately recognized by all the knights and nobles as the new king. Heralds were sent throughout England to proclaim the new sovereign: King Arthur.

Christians also anticipate the coming of a king. The prayer that Jesus taught his disciples gives us insight into what we can expect from the king whose kingdom is breaking into the world. Though many "kings" try to claim our allegiance, this king alone gives us everything we need and is worthy of our deepest loyalty.

B. Lesson Context

Last week's lesson on Matthew 6:1-8 revealed Jesus' teaching on the dangers and follies of hypocrisy in the areas of giving and prayer. As with that lesson, the historical setting of today's lesson text is Jesus' Sermon on the Mount (Matthew 5–7).

Today's text studies one of two versions of the Lord's Prayer, the other being found in Luke 11. Regarding distinctives, the prayer in today's text differs from its counterpart in Luke 11 in various ways. For one, Jesus' teaching on prayer that begins in Matthew 6:9 occurred as part of teaching that he was already engaged in. "When Jesus saw the crowds, he went up on a mountainside and sat down. His disciples came to him" (Matthew 5:1). Luke is more specific in noting that the version of the prayer he records happens after "one of his disciples said to him, 'Lord, teach us to pray, just as John taught his disciples'" (Luke 11:1).

Another major difference between Matthew and Luke is in the length of the prayer: Luke's version is much more concise than Matthew's. The content is very similar, but Luke has recorded a very minimal prayer. The differences suggest that Jesus taught about prayer more than once. Doing so allowed his disciples to learn through repetition what Jesus wanted them to know.

Just before our lesson's opening verse, Jesus had criticized hypocritical and pagan prayer, advising privacy and sincerity rather than public performance and verbosity. He followed those negative examples with a positive alternative.

I. The Prayer
(MATTHEW 6:9-13)
A. Holiness (v. 9)

9a. "This, then, is how you should pray:

The Lord's Prayer is not simply a masterpiece to be put behind glass in a museum. It is not to be kept unopened and pristine on a bookshelf. Jesus' prayer is intended to be a model prayer. As such, it teaches *how* his disciples *should pray*. For this reason, the prayer remains a wonderful resource for the church. It can be prayed as recorded in the text, and it can be studied as a pattern that teaches how to be concise and orderly in praying. The prayer consists of four couplets and an ending pronouncement, as follows.

9b. "'Our Father

The first couplet in the Lord's Prayer consists of the address, seen here, and the first petition, seen in verse 9d, below. While God surely discerns our hearts and intents in prayers, it is important for us to remember the one to whom we are praying.

The way we address God at the outset establishes the tone for the rest of the prayer. Will we address him flippantly and casually, expecting to receive whatever we ask? Will we approach him in terror, paradoxically afraid both of being heard and of being ignored? Or will we speak to him in a manner befitting the Creator of the universe and lover of our souls (Psalm 63:2, 3)?

Jesus teaches us to address God in two ways. First, he is *our Father*. First-century Jews have many ways to describe God, but this one is used relatively less frequently than others (compare Isaiah 63:16; 64:8). God is more often referred to as Creator, Lord, or King. But the fact that it is entirely appropriate to address God as Father is an understanding that runs throughout the recorded teachings of Jesus. This is so especially in the Sermon on the Mount (see Matthew 5:16, 45, 48; 6:1, 4, 6, 8, 18, 26, 32; 7:11).

Note that in the verse at hand, Jesus does not refer to God as Father simply because Jesus is the Son (John 1:14, 18, 49). He does not say *my* Father as he does in John 14:23. He says *our* Father, thereby including his disciples (compare Romans 1:7; Galatians 1:3; etc.). Christians have access to God the Father in prayer on an intimate level, the level of a son or a daughter talking with a loving parent. For some people, this is problematic. None of our fathers were perfect. Some people have no positive memories in that regard. Maybe he was abusive or absent. For this reason, many men (and women) live trying not to become their fathers; they struggle against that bad example for years.

Even so, we should discern carefully an implication of what Jesus teaches. We do not judge God by our earthly fathers.

One of the benefits of having the gift of the Holy Spirit (Acts 2:38) is that we can address God as Father (Mark 14:36; Romans 8:15). Christians have a restored relationship to God as His sons and daughters. He is truly the perfect Father who will never desert us or abuse us. Our Father will never fail us.

The second way Jesus teaches us to address God our Father comes next.

HOW TO SAY IT

Colossians	Kuh-*losh*-unz.
Corinthians	Ko-*rin*-thee-unz (*th* as in *thin*).
Deuteronomy	Due-ter-*ahn*-uh-me.
Ephesians	Ee-*fee*-zhunz.
Ezekiel	Ee-*zeek*-ee-ul or Ee-*zeek*-yul.
Galatians	Guh-*lay*-shunz.
Jeremiah	Jair-uh-*my*-uh.
Malachi	*Mal*-uh-kye.
Thessalonians	*Thess*-uh-**lo**-nee-unz (*th* as in *thin*).

My father died when I was 9 years old, and it has always troubled me that I don't have many memories of him. Although my older siblings have filled in gaps with positive impressions, my prominent emotional recollection is that my father was stern and intimidating.

When I became a father myself 36 years ago, I was determined to do my best to provide my son with an example that would influence his perception of his Father in Heaven in a positive way. I am blessed to observe that he seems to have a very healthy relationship with our Father.

How are negative memories of your earthly father (or mother) affecting your view of God? Ask our Father to help you relate to him as loving and holy as his Word clearly reveals him to be.

—A. S.

9c. "'in heaven,

To address God as "our Father" is to speak to only part of our relationship to him. The true God is the God *in heaven*. He is not part of the physical universe he created. He is separate from it (transcendent). Although we are created in his image and can have fellowship with him, the God of Heaven is not one of us. His heavenly abode is beyond any physical location that we can understand (compare 2 Corinthians 12:2-4).

This results in an important truth that is implied in Jesus' words: we are not God. As we begin to understand this, it makes the prayer even more marvelous. We, mere men and women who are not God, are nonetheless privileged to speak with the God of Heaven!

9d. "'hallowed be your name,

Following the address of God in Heaven is the first of the seven petitions, as distributed among four couplets, in this prayer. A petition in prayer is simply a request. Along with praise, thanksgiving, and confession, petitions are an expected, normal, healthy part of a believer's prayer life. Though God anticipates our needs (Matthew 6:8), he still desires for us to ask him for what we need. Doing so expresses and strengthens our knowledge of our reliance on God for every provision (John 1:3; Acts 17:24-28).

At the most basic level, petitioning for the *name* of the Lord to be *hallowed* is a commitment to honor the third commandment: "You shall not misuse the name of the Lord your God" (Exodus 20:7). When we pray for God's name to be hallowed, we pray for his name to be treated as holy. Such a prayer is a commitment to God to do so oneself. We are saying that we intend to reflect his holiness among men and women, using our influence to his glory, not to his shame or to our own ends. We are also asking to be empowered not to misuse his holy name.

In this first couplet of the Lord's Prayer, we run into a great paradox. On the one hand, we are taught to address God as Father. On the other hand, we do this while we acknowledge that God is completely other, completely without sin, completely worthy of honor, completely holy. Intimacy with the Father as his children is to be yoked with our respect for the Holy One. We are encouraged in the Lord's Prayer to be intimate with God as our Father, to share with him the deepest things of our hearts. Yet we are also warned to be respectful of God, not forgetting our position in the hierarchy of the universe. God is great, and we are small. God is holy, and we are sinners saved only through the blood of Jesus (Hebrews 7:27, 28).

> *What Do You Think?*
> What can our church do to help people gain a better understanding of the concept of holiness?
> *Digging Deeper*
> What would a failure to grasp the importance of this concept look like?

B. The Kingdom (v. 10)

10. "'your kingdom come, your will be done, on earth as it is in heaven.

The second couplet features petitions number two and three of the seven petitions of this prayer. Petition number two is for the *kingdom* of *heaven* to *come*. When we pray this, we are asking for the establishment of God's reign and sovereign rule. Petition number three asks for God's *will* to *be done.* When we pray this, we are asking that the will of God be carried out in all things at all times.

These twin petitions cannot be separated. To pray for the establishing of God's kingdom is to pray for the accomplishing of his will. To pray for the accomplishing of his will is to pray for the establishing of his kingdom.

The two petitions are connected by a joint qualifier: *on earth as it is in heaven.* This serves for both petitions. When we pray these petitions, we are praying that God's reign—the kingdom of Heaven—will be established in its ultimate fullness. To pray this is to pray that God's sovereign will, as realized in Heaven, will prevail in our world as well. We are praying that all opposition to God will cease, that all men and women will submit to his will (Revelation 21:22-27). We are praying that the last remnants of rebellion in our universe will be vanquished, and that we will experience his peace (21:1-6).

More than this, our praying for the establishment of God's kingdom and the working of his will on earth commits ourselves to help achieve those results (contrast Revelation 3:1-3). We are to desire God to reign in our hearts and in our world. We are to labor that God's will, his purpose, and his plans will come to fruition here and now. And we do our part of the work in this regard. We should not pray these petitions and then stand back and wait for God to do the work he intends us to do (compare James 1:23-25, 27).

> *What Do You Think?*
> ► What are some tangible ways you can help speed the inbreaking of God's kingdom?
> *Digging Deeper*
> How do 2 Peter 3:12; Revelation 11:17; and 22:20 help frame your decision?

C. Daily Needs (vv. 11-13)
11. "'Give us today our daily bread.

Matthew 6:11 and 12 form the third of the four couplets in this prayer. This couplet features the fourth and fifth of the prayer's seven petitions. The fourth petition, in the verse before us, calls us to go straight to the source for our most basic needs. *Bread* refers to food in general. In this case, it even seems to refer to all the essentials we need to live: food, water, clothing, shelter, etc. When we pray this petition, we recognize our dependence on God. We are affirming our belief that God will supply our every need (compare Luke 12:27-31). God is the ultimate source of our livelihood (Deuteronomy 8:18; James 1:17).

This does not mean we should expect to find manna on our breakfast table when we awake (compare Exodus 16). We commit to working to supply our needs as honest laborers in the world (compare 2 Thessalonians 3:12). But we also trust that God will care for us no matter what reversals and hardships come our way (compare Proverbs 30:8). We may be down to our last dollar and our last can of beans. But we trust that God has not forgotten us and will provide. When our resources are depleted, we may be surprised at how God supplies our daily bread!

But as we pray for bread, we should remember that "man shall not live on bread alone" (Matthew 4:4, lesson 10). We should also think about Jesus, who is the "bread of life" (John 6:48). He came down from Heaven to give us eternal life. Just as our bodies need physical food, our souls need spiritual food.

> *What Do You Think?*
> ► What are some steps you can take to ensure that your prayers for material needs matches the spirit of this verse?
> *Digging Deeper*
> What disciplines can you adopt to ensure that petitions for material needs do not eclipse the prayer elements of Matthew 6:9, 10?

12. "'And forgive us our debts, as we also have forgiven our debtors.

The fifth petition of the seven is unique for a couple of reasons. First, it is tied to the concept of daily provision. In this case, the provision sought is that of forgiveness of *our debts,* another term for sin (compare Matthew 18:23-35). This petition, like that for daily bread, invites repetition because of the problem of ongoing sin in our lives. Though the Holy Spirit is renewing us (Titus 3:5), we are not perfectly without sin. We still need to recognize the reality of sin (1 John 1:8-10).

We note that this petition is conditional: as we ask for God's forgiveness, we promise to be forgiving of others. We do not expect to receive from God what we do not extend to others (compare Luke 6:37). This is the only petition in the prayer that receives an immediate additional comment from Jesus (see on Matthew 6:14, 15, below).

13. "'And lead us not into temptation, but deliver us from the evil one.'"

The fourth and final couplet features the sixth and seventh petitions. These are two sides of the same coin. When we pray *lead us not into temptation,* we are recognizing both lurking sin (Genesis 4:7) and our inability to conquer it on our own. Thus we ask for God's mercy to help us in the times of trial, in the occasions of temptation. Of course, God does not tempt us (James 1:13), though he does test us (Hebrews 11:17).

When we pray *deliver us from the evil one,* we are again admitting our inability to deal with Satan's attacks in our own strength (compare 1 Corinthians 10:13). This petition acknowledges not just evil in the abstract but also the evil one himself: the devil, who tempts people to commit sin. Here we see part of the prayer's assurance. Powerful as he is, Satan is no match for Almighty God (John 17:15; 2 Thessalonians 3:3; 2 Timothy 4:18). One who is delivered from evil is to produce the fruit of the Spirit (Galatians 5:22-25). As we do, we constantly wear "the full armor of God" to "take [our] stand against the devil's schemes" (Ephesians 6:11).

In translations that use later New Testament manuscripts, this verse ends with a pronouncement: "For thine is the kingdom, and the power, and the glory, for ever. Amen." While this conclusion is beautiful and appropriate, older manuscripts do not include it. But with echoes of 1 Chronicles 29:11-13, it nevertheless expresses a biblical idea based on biblical language. It fits well as a restatement of the themes in the petitions: God's coming *kingdom,* his *power* to provide, and our glorious deliverance from temptation and evil.

II. On Forgiveness
(MATTHEW 6:14, 15)
A. For Others (v. 14)

14. "For if you forgive other people when they sin against you, your heavenly Father will also forgive you.

Having ended the model prayer, Jesus digs deeper to ensure that his listeners understand the implications of the fifth petition (see Matthew 6:12, above). The word translated *sin* here can also be translated "trespass" (example: Romans 5:15-18, 20) or "transgressions" (example: Ephesians 2:1, 5).

Receiving and extending forgiveness are inseparable. To experience the forgiveness of God, our hearts must be prepared to forgive others (Mark 11:25). Forgiveness of sin is essential to the church's identity, as implied in the words of Jesus at the last supper: "This is my blood of the covenant, which is poured out for many for the forgiveness of sins" (Matthew 26:28). The church should be a forgiving place, encouraging both the receiving and extending of this act of grace (Ephesians 4:32; Colossians 3:13).

When we come to the point of realizing how much God has forgiven us, our forgiveness of others will be natural and easier. We forgive as the Scripture requires us to, harboring no anger or grudges against others.

❧ *FORGIVE EVERY DEBTOR?* ❧

On June 17, 2015, 21-year-old Dylann Roof walked into the Emanuel African Methodist Episcopal Church in Charleston, South Carolina. For about an hour, he listened as the small Wednesday night group discussed the Scriptures. Then he stood up and pulled out a gun and began shooting. Nine church members died as a result.

Two days later Roof appeared in court, and several family members of those slain addressed him. One person, whose mother was one of the victims, stated, "You took something very precious from me. . . . But I forgive you." Another person in mourning added, "I am very angry. But [my sister] taught me that we are the family that love built. We have no room for hating, so we have to forgive."

Some may question the appropriateness of extending forgiveness in cases that do not involve repentance (Luke 17:3, 4). But a more basic issue here is the *willingness* to forgive.

Hard as they may be, Jesus' instructions regarding forgiveness aren't framed as optional. To have God's forgiveness, we must forgive others. Let these examples inspire and motivate self-examination: Whom do *you* need to forgive today?

—A. S.

B. For Ourselves (v. 15)

15. "But if you do not forgive others their sins, your Father will not forgive your sins."

Jesus ends with a warning. If you bypass step one of forgiving others, don't expect step two, the Father's forgiveness. Don't miss the point. This is not some sort of bargain we are making with God, as though he must forgive us if we forgive others. It is a request, a plea to God to help us have a spirit of forgiveness. Forgiveness, like love, is hard (compare Matthew 5:44; Luke 6:28; Acts 7:59, 60). We need God's help, and he's just the one to give it!

> *What Do You Think?*
> What would be your starting point for encouraging a person who struggles to extend forgiveness to one who has harmed him or her?
> *Digging Deeper*
> Would that starting point differ depending on the nature of the harm (emotional, physical, financial, etc.)? Why, or why not?

Are you asking for the right things?

Visual for Lesson 12. *Begin an interaction with this visual by asking learners what images they would replace on this poster with others.*

Conclusion

A. Proclaiming the Kingdom

Matthew's text of the model prayer has been prayed by Christians since the earliest days of the church. It's a simple prayer, with an introduction, seven petitions within four couplets, and a closing pronouncement. Each element teaches about God and how to relate to him in prayer.

Jesus' teaching shows us how we can assess our prayer lives. We need to acknowledge God as our Father, who loves us and gives us what we need. In that light, we need to be completely honest before him, concerned about his will and power not our own standing with others. Moment by moment we need to rely on him to provide what we need for life and for spiritual wholeness.

When we pray for the coming of the Father's kingdom, we pray for the coming of a king. When we proclaim the kingdom of Heaven, we proclaim that God *is* king. The Christian message is the good news that God is king, and the king has come to save us.

B. Prayer

Our Father in Heaven, may we be a praying people! As we are, may we respect you in the holiness you deserve. We pray in Jesus' name. Amen.

C. Thought to Remember

Our privilege is to approach the king in prayer.

INVOLVEMENT LEARNING

Enhance your lesson with NIV Bible Student *(from your curriculum supplier) and the reproducible activity page (at www.standardlesson.com or in the back of the* NIV Standard Lesson Commentary Deluxe Edition*).*

Into the Lesson

Write these unfinished statements on the board:

1. The hardest thing about requesting help is . . .
2. Help requests go unanswered when . . .
3. When I request help, what happens is . . .

Ask learners to take no more than one minute to write a conclusion to at least one of these sentences. Then have learners pair off to share what they wrote. After a few minutes, reconvene for whole-class discussion. Ask for shows of hands regarding how many completed each sentence. Allow volunteers to voice what they wrote, but don't put anyone on the spot to do so.

Use this discussion to remind students of last month's sessions regarding prayer. Lead into today's study by saying, "This week we have the opportunity to think about a prayer template offered not by King Solomon, but by Jesus himself."

Into the Word

Lead students in repeating the Lord's Prayer, Bibles closed. Ask, by shows of hands, how meaningful the prayer is to them on a scale from 1 (lowest) to 10 (highest). Record tallies on the board. Invite explanations for ratings given. (*Option.* For deeper discussion, call for separate self-usefulness ratings of *form* and *content* of the prayer.)

Say, "An analysis of the prayer might help it become more meaningful as a template for your own prayers." Distribute handouts (you prepare) that feature the following chart as a note taker.

Verse	Petition	How It Will Happen
9	_____	_____
10a	_____	_____
10b	_____	_____
11	_____	_____
12	_____	_____
13a	_____	_____
13b	_____	_____

In whole-class discussion, call for volunteers to name the seven easy-to-spot petitions included in this prayer, as the verse designations indicate. Expect everyone to fill in the middle column as a result.

Then have learners pair up with their original partners. After they do so, ask each pair to join another pair for resulting groups of four. Challenge these groups to complete the last column in the chart, thinking about this question: "If this prayer is answered, what will we see happen?"

After several minutes, discuss the chart as a class. Expect learners to fill in the blanks as you share insights from this week's lesson commentary. After considering verse 13, pause to see if anyone's blanks do not have an entry; review as necessary.

Then ask a volunteer to read aloud Matthew 6:14, 15. Ask, "Why did Jesus choose this one petition of the seven for further commentary?" Again, use the commentary to provide insight and fill in knowledge gaps.

Option. Distribute copies of the "Forgiveness Pointers" exercise from the activity page, which you can download. If you wish learners to work alone, allow one minute for selecting one quotation and reacting as indicated. If learners work in pairs, adjust your request as appropriate for your class. Limit the time for whole-class discussion so it won't drag out.

Into Life

Recalling the handout distributed earlier in Into the Word, ask students to put a star beside the petition that is the biggest challenge to their prayer lives, the petition they most often neglect when praying. Stress that this biggest challenge is also the biggest opportunity to improve their prayers!

Option. Distribute copies of the "Forgiveness Challenge" exercise on the activity page. Due to the highly personal nature of this exercise, it should be given as a take-home as learners depart.

Ever-Persevering Petitions

DEVOTIONAL READING: Psalm 13
BACKGROUND SCRIPTURE: Luke 11:1-13

LUKE 11:5-13

5 Then Jesus said to them, "Suppose you have a friend, and you go to him at midnight and say, 'Friend, lend me three loaves of bread; 6 a friend of mine on a journey has come to me, and I have no food to offer him.' 7 And suppose the one inside answers, 'Don't bother me. The door is already locked, and my children and I are in bed. I can't get up and give you anything.' 8 I tell you, even though he will not get up and give you the bread because of friendship, yet because of your shameless audacity he will surely get up and give you as much as you need.

9 "So I say to you: Ask and it will be given to you; seek and you will find; knock and the door will be opened to you. 10 For everyone who asks receives; the one who seeks finds; and to the one who knocks, the door will be opened.

11 "Which of you fathers, if your son asks for a fish, will give him a snake instead? 12 Or if he asks for an egg, will give him a scorpion? 13 If you then, though you are evil, know how to give good gifts to your children, how much more will your Father in heaven give the Holy Spirit to those who ask him!"

KEY VERSE

I say to you: Ask and it will be given to you; seek and you will find; knock and the door will be opened to you. —**Luke 11:9**

HONORING GOD

Unit 3: Jesus Teaches About True Worship

LESSONS 10–13

LESSON AIMS

After participating in this lesson, each learner will be able to:

1. State the main lesson of the parable.

2. Explain how prayer is asking, seeking, and knocking.

3. Identify one reason for lacking persistence in prayer and make a corrective plan.

LESSON OUTLINE

Introduction

A. Seeking a Blue Doorknob

A *shaggy-dog story* is a long-winded tale with an underwhelming punch line. The point of such a story is that the joke is on the listener, who has paid attention for far too long and has not been rewarded. One shaggy dog story tells of the search for a magical blue doorknob in the Empire State Building. The storyteller can stretch this joke to include as many of the building's 102 floors as desired (each with dozens of doors with knobs). The story can end with the questioning of a janitor on the top floor who says, "Oh, they took out all the colored knobs years ago."

Have you ever experienced frustrating and fruitless searches, quests that are like the punch line in what turns out to be a shaggy-dog story? Have you ever made repeated requests of someone and not received any kind of response? Have you ever knocked on a door when you knew someone was behind it but did not hear a word?

The fruitless search makes us think, *Give it up!* The ignored requests say, *Don't bother me!* The unopened door says, *Leave me alone!*

Perhaps your prayer life has felt that way at times. Your prayers seem to float to the ceiling and no farther. Earnest petitions yield silence day after day. Lamentations 3:44 seems all too real: "You have covered yourself with a cloud so that no prayer can get through." What are we to make of these times when God seems slow to answer?

B. Lesson Context

Luke's two books, Luke and Acts, have repeated mentions of people praying and frequent teachings on prayer. We cannot read these two books without noticing that Jesus was a man of prayer (see Luke 5:16; 6:12; 9:18, 28; 11:1; 22:40, 41, 44, 46; etc.) and that the first-century church was a community of prayer (see Acts 1:14; 13:3; 21:5; etc.). The Jerusalem church made prayer a priority (2:42). Cornelius, a Gentile, was a God-fearing man before his conversion, partly because he devoted himself to prayer (10:2).

The church inherited this reverence for prayer from its Jewish roots. Ancient Jewish synagogues and the temple itself were ideally houses of prayer (see Isaiah 56:7; Matthew 21:13; Mark 11:17; Luke 19:46), dedicated spaces where people could pray alone or in community.

Prayer by Jesus and first-century Jews was rooted in the Scriptures (Genesis 21:16-18; Exodus 32:11-13; Jeremiah 10:23-25; etc.). The Old Testament shows prayer as addressing the Lord as the God who hears, cares, and is powerful to act (Exodus 2:23-25; Psalm 65:2; Daniel 9:19).

The previous lesson looked at the Lord's Prayer as found in the Sermon on the Mount (Matthew 6:9-15; see lesson 12); Luke's parallel for that teaching opportunity (although not his version of the Lord's Prayer itself) is the Sermon on the Plain (Luke 6:17-49). Between that event and today's lesson occurs a miraculous healing and a resurrection (7:1-17); interactions with various people (7:18-50); more teaching (8:1-21; 10:38-42); calming a storm (8:22-25); an exorcism, resurrection, and healing (8:26-56); sending of the 12 (9:1-9); a miraculous feeding (9:10-17); private conversations and the transfiguration (9:18-36); another exorcism (9:37-43a); conversations and opposition (9:43b-62); and the sending of the 72 (10:1-24). Only then do we arrive at Luke's version of the Lord's Prayer (also known as the model prayer) and today's text that follows it.

As Luke 11 opens, Jesus was praying. When he had finished, a disciple asked him to teach them how to pray. Jesus' response was to offer the prayer of Luke 11:2-4. The text for today's lesson offers further insights on prayer.

I. Persistent Request
(LUKE 11:5-8)

A. Inconvenience (vv. 5-7)

5, 6. Then Jesus said to them, "Suppose you have a friend, and you go to him at midnight

HOW TO SAY IT

Cornelius	Cor-*neel*-yus.
Gentiles	*Jen*-tiles.
Judea	Joo-*dee*-uh.
synagogues	*sin*-uh-gogs.

and say, 'Friend, lend me three loaves of bread; a friend of mine on a journey has come to me, and I have no food to offer him.'

The setting of this parable is that of the relationship of two friends who are also neighbors. These are people who are likely to have engaged in sharing and borrowing things from each other over many years. Such a relationship is to be assumed as normal and healthy by Jesus' audience.

Midnight in Judea is truly the middle of the night. Because providing light after dark uses expensive oil for lamps, people rise shortly before sunrise and are in bed an hour or two after sundown. A normal day near the equator might begin about 5:00 a.m., and a household might be in bed by 7:00 or 8:00 p.m. By midnight, families are sound asleep, having been so for four or more hours.

An unexpected visitor turns one *friend* into a host in this parable. Ancient customs of hospitality differ from ours. A person on a journey might drop in unannounced, leaving a host scrambling to provide food at unusual hours. A host's failure to provide a meal for his visitor is a social error of inhospitality, even without prior notice of arrival (compare Genesis 19:1-3). Yet, we should not accuse the host of poor planning. His family may have eaten every piece of bread at the evening meal, assuming their supply would be replenished the next day. The unanticipated guest has created a crisis, and the rules of hospitality must be honored.

The host needs bread, *three loaves*. His claim to have *no food* may be a way of saying that his food stock is quite inadequate. Bread is baked frequently, even daily. It does not keep long and tastes best when fresh. Friend A is hoping that sleepy Friend B has some bread left over from the previous day.

7. "And suppose the one inside answers, 'Don't bother me. The door is already locked, and my children and I are in bed. I can't get up and give you anything.'

Jesus' disciples are undoubtedly surprised at the reaction of Friend B. They understand the inconvenience, but they also know that the expectation of village hospitality makes it imperative that the sleeping friend help, even at midnight. He says he can't get up, but the truth is that he lacks the willingness to get up and help. The parable thereby contrasts an ungracious attitude to God's graciousness as revealed in the model prayer (see Luke 11:3).

B. Yielding (v. 8)

8. "I tell you, even though he will not get up and give you the bread because of friendship, yet because of your shameless audacity he will surely get up and give you as much as you need.

Friendship alone is not a strong enough motivation for the man to help. Not even social customs of the day move him to action. What finally motivates him to action is his neighbor's *shameless audacity*.

The Greek word being translated, used only here in the New Testament, normally carries the sense of shamelessness. That sense can fit the context here if "shameless" is in the sense of "boldness." The idea is that of desperation that overrides shame. The friend pushes past courteous politeness (that might easily take no for an answer) to ask again and again until the request is granted.

The point as it applies to prayer must not be missed: persistence is important. Prayer is a laying bare of the heart before God. If a request is not worth repeating as a daily petition, it may be deemed as whimsical or unimportant. Prayer that is persistent and personal is powerful in God's eyes. Needs are daily; therefore our practice of prayer must be ongoing, never taking for granted the gracious provision of God.

We should take care here, though. Persistence in prayer is not effective because we somehow wear God down (see last week's lesson). That's not how it works with God. Persistence in prayer is a test for us, not for him.

> **What Do You Think?**
> What are some ways to increase your bold persistence in prayer?
> *Digging Deeper*
> Considering passages such as Job 38:1, 2; Jonah 4; and Malachi 2:17, what guardrails should you put in place to ensure that your boldly persistent prayers do not cross lines that they shouldn't?

For two years, my oldest boy struggled. A small legal problem became a two-year string of escalating trouble. His trouble stemmed from continuing to seek out the wrong crowd and flouting every rule the county set forth. My family prayed constantly, but the situation just kept deteriorating. He lied and stole. He became violent. He had to be placed in a shelter; he was admitted to the hospital for an overdose.

I cried out to the Lord, for what seemed like the millionth time, to deliver my son and my family from the constant chaos. Like the neighbor in need, I persisted. I prayed. I asked for strength when my despair threatened to overcome me. I didn't stop knocking until, in all his great mystery and love, God answered my prayer with a yes. My son began to improve and remains healthy to this day.

As Jesus tells us, we must never stop knocking. And unlike that frustrated friend who grudgingly got up to answer the door, Jesus is never reluctant to answer our prayers. His timing is perfect, and we err when we interpret a delayed answer with reluctance.   —P. M.

II. Tenacious Prayer
(Luke 11:9, 10)
A. Asking, Seeking, Knocking (v. 9)

9. "So I say to you: Ask and it will be given to you; seek and you will find; knock and the door will be opened to you.

The parable of the two friends gives context to the famous verse before us. It is the application of the parable (compare Matthew 7:7). The host has asked for bread, sought bread, and knocked on his neighbor's door until it was opened for him. All of these are presented by Jesus as commands of what we are to do: *ask, seek, knock*. All three have a sense of continuation: keep asking, keep seeking, keep knocking.

In this chapter, it is unmistakable that the asking, seeking, and knocking are referring to prayer. This persistence is unlike the prayer practices of pagan Gentiles of Jesus' day. Greek and Roman religions often view prayer as a device to manipulate or cajole a god or goddess to shower fortune on the person praying. For this reason, Jesus previously warned his disciples not to follow these empty practices (Matthew 6:7). Fundamentally, the Gentiles are unsure their gods hear them or will want to help even if they are listening. Jesus' disciples need have no such fears; unlike the inhospitable neighbor, our God loves to give us what we need when we ask (6:8, 11).

> **What Do You Think?**
> What are some steps to strengthen the process of asking, seeking, and knocking?
> **Digging Deeper**
> Will it be important in answering that question to distinguish asking from seeking from knocking? Why, or why not?

B. Receiving, Finding, Opening (v. 10)

10. "For everyone who asks receives; the one who seeks finds; and to the one who knocks, the door will be opened.

The potential for misunderstanding here is great. So it bears repeating that we must not see these verses as teaching that we can wear down God by endless, repeated requests until he gives in. Prayer in that case is not a conversation with our Father. Rather, it becomes a tirade that will not cease until demands are met. This danger of misapplication is also a caution for the similar parable of the unjust judge (Luke 18:1-8). The thrust of this parable is that we "should always pray and not give up" (18:1).

The thing to remember is that in both of these parables the persons who grant the requests are not sterling role models for us. Jesus' listeners do not want to be the inhospitable and insensitive sleeping friend of the two-friends parable. They also abhor the judge who does not care about justice. Does this, then, teach us anything about God? Is God, who hears and grants our requests in prayer, anything like these two men?

The answer is obviously no; God is not like this (Jonah 3:6-10; 4:2). The parables, at one level, set forth a lesser-to-greater comparison: if the lesser one grants the request, how much more is the

greater one (God) willing to do so! At another level, these parables teach us about the nature of prayer and how we should practice it. We must be persistent. A prayer life that makes a request once then abandons it is not much of a prayer life.

God is always faithful to respond appropriately to our needs. But let's be honest: Are we sometimes too proud to ask God (or anyone else) for help? Do we think we always should try to meet our own needs without God's help? Though asking for what we need goes against cultural expectations of rugged individualism, God expects us to ask him for what we need each day. We do not have access to the decision-making process of God when it comes to our prayer requests. But in all cases, we can remain confident that God is hearing us every time we pray and giving us the answer that best suits his purposes and our needs.

An important point in this and the previous verse is that a specific kind of person is in view here. Today's lesson text occurs within a long teaching section that deals with how Jesus' disciples are to think and behave. Thus when Jesus refers to people who ask, seek, and knock, he is referring to the kind of person who has the sort of relationship with God that Jesus has been describing all along. In other words, these verses are directed to the kind of people who ask, seek, and knock while having godly motives and goals.

> **What Do You Think?**
> What are some ways to model persistence in prayer when you yourself have not yet received, found, or had doors opened?
> **Digging Deeper**
> At what point in a Christian's prayer persistence should he or she reexamine the nature of the unanswered prayer itself?

III. Faithful Response
(Luke 11:11-13)

A. Imperfect Givers (vv. 11, 12)

11, 12. "Which of you fathers, if your son asks for a fish, will give him a snake instead? Or if he asks for an egg, will give him a scorpion?

Jesus begins a second illustration about prayer to make a different point. Only a heartless father would ignore the pleas of a hungry child; only the cruelest of fathers would respond to cries of hunger with the substitutions of *a snake* for *a fish* or *a scorpion* for *an egg*. Beyond being not edible by a child, such things are outright dangerous: a snake would bite a child rather than the reverse; a scorpion would sting.

> **What Do You Think?**
> ▶ How can we encourage those who feel God has given them "a scorpion" for "an egg"?
> *Digging Deeper*
> As you encourage such a person, how will you know when the time is right or wrong to point out passages such as Psalm 13; Jeremiah 20:7-13; and/or Romans 8:28?

B. The Perfect Father (v. 13)

13. "If you then, though you are evil, know how to give good gifts to your children, how much more will your Father in heaven give the Holy Spirit to those who ask him!"

Jesus drives home his major point: even comparatively *evil* human fathers can and do *give good gifts to* their *children* (compare Matthew 7:11). This principle is also true of the sleepy friend of the parable just considered and of the unjust judge in Luke 18. Even the worst of humans sometimes do the right thing, the good thing. However grudgingly, they are able to give good gifts to others. This is a bit like saying that even a blind squirrel finds a nut occasionally. An endorsement, but not a glowing one!

Yet even the best of people are evil when compared to the Lord (Romans 3:5, 10-18, 23). Thus, Jesus employs a lesser-to-greater argument: if certain good things about us frail humans are true, then *how much more* will good actions come from our perfect *Father in heaven,* who has no human weaknesses?

Moreover, the Father's capacity to grant requests far exceeds giving pieces of fish or boiled eggs. Our Father in Heaven gives believers a gift far greater than the most wealthy and generous parent on earth can: his *Holy Spirit.* Our God can fulfill not only our physical needs, he can also satisfy our greater spiritual needs. The gift of the Holy Spirit is one of the greatest blessings of the Christian believer. Luke expands on this in Acts 1:8; 2:38; 5:32; 15:8; etc. Focusing on the gift of the Holy Spirit calls Christians to hope even when in material want.

A caution: Jesus' teaching is not that God is required to better our lives through material possessions. A popular perception of God says that if you want a better car or a bigger house, all you need to do is ask for it in faith. This theory carries the assumption that God promises us health and wealth; it is a "name it and claim it" view of the gospel. But there is no such promise in the New Testament. Jesus is teaching us how true disciples understand the nature of God; Jesus is not teaching that we can get from God all we want simply by virtue of persistence.

> **What Do You Think?**
> ▶ What are some things your church should be more persistent in asking of the Lord? Why?
> *Digging Deeper*
> How will you need to change your own prayer priorities so you can best help your church change its prayer priorities?

❧ GOOD, GOOD FATHER ❧

A few years back, work transferred my husband to Nebraska. The family soon followed. We felt God's hand in all of it, despite having to uproot our lives. We—two adults, two teenagers, a cat, and a dog—were staying in a hotel room with two double beds and a kitchenette while we searched for a permanent home. But we were struggling to get credit approval.

When an apartment we had been hoping for turned us down, a feeling of worthlessness filled me. As I prayed through those despondent emotions, I remembered who God was. I remembered his clear desire to move our family. Suddenly, I was no longer worried about where we would live. I knew who my Father was.

The next Sunday, the call came that we had

been approved for the only rental house available within our children's school district. Just like that, we had a home. I have a good, good Father in Heaven, one who knows how to give good gifts. Do you? — P. M.

Conclusion

A. How Should I Pray?

There are many misconceptions about prayer among Christians. These erroneous beliefs can become debilitating. Some say that if God knows all, including our needs, we don't need to ask for anything. What can we tell God if he already knows everything? "Nothing!" some say. Therefore, this logic says, prayer is pointless. We don't want to pray wrongly, and we don't want to suffer from prayer paralysis. We also don't want to oversimplify prayer, for it represents a relationship with our heavenly Father.

Jesus used two analogies, images we would not expect, to teach us about our prayers to God. First, he spoke of borrowing loaves of bread. Second, he referred to a father providing wholesome food for his child. Sandwiched between (pun intended!) is one of Jesus' most profound teachings on prayer in all the Bible: his admonition to ask, seek, and knock without giving up. Jesus ends with a reference to the Holy Spirit, presenting this as the ultimate answer to prayer and the gift of the Father.

Just as the unprepared host did not stop knocking or give up his search for bread, so we should not give up on asking God for the things we need. Prayer must be an ongoing conversation with the Lord. Jesus taught the disciples to ask for "daily bread" (Luke 11:3), leaving us to conclude that this request must be done every day. Prayer is a lifetime of activity, not an essay we write and file away forever.

Jesus teaches us that we are not abandoned by God. For this reason, we do not need to devise effective prayer strategies on our own. He has given us examples, and he has given us his Holy Spirit. Paul notes the value of this for us when he teaches that even though we are inadequate in our prayer lives, God's Spirit will intercede for us to make up for our weaknesses (Romans 8:26).

Visual for Lesson 13. *As you discuss verse 9, point to this visual and ask how the image relates to the discipline of asking, seeking, and knocking.*

God not only hears our prayers, he will help us if we let him.

Jesus' encouragement in Luke 11 is to never give up on prayer, no matter how unfruitful it may seem on any given day. The key is that we keep praying. We keep asking God, seeking his will, and knocking on the doors of Heaven with our requests (using James 4:3 as a caution: "Ye ask, and receive not, because ye ask amiss, that ye may consume it upon your lusts"). Few of us would count ourselves as giants in the world of prayer, so we can make this same request: "Lord, teach us to pray" (Luke 11:1)! Jesus was both a master teacher and the greatest pray-er of all time. His centuries-old words still guide us in this crucial spiritual matter today.

B. Prayer

Father God, we do have daily needs, things like food and drink that our bodies require. We have personal needs, to be loved by others and to have others to love. Most of all, we have spiritual needs that will only be satisfied by your Holy Spirit. We knock on your door to ask that you supply all our needs, all that we seek. We ask this in the name of Jesus, who graciously taught us to pray. Amen.

C. Thought to Remember

"The worst sin is prayerlessness."
—P. T. Forsythe (1848–1921)

INVOLVEMENT LEARNING

Enhance your lesson with NIV Bible Student *(from your curriculum supplier) and the reproducible activity page (at www.standardlesson.com or in the back of the* NIV Standard Lesson Commentary Deluxe Edition*).*

Into the Lesson

Pose this question: "What are some things you have asked a loved one to give you when you were a child?" Expect responses such as a toy, a bike, a pet, a favor, or permission to participate in an activity or special event. Jot responses on the board as they are voiced.

Follow up by asking, "What was something you asked for that was met with refusal, and why?" Jot responses on the board again; allow time for the class to discuss, but don't let this drag out.

Alternative. Distribute copies of the "Handling Personal Requests" exercise from the activity page, which you can download. Have students work in pairs to complete as indicated. (*Option.* Reduce the number of questions to be discussed as time constraints dictate.)

After either activity, lead into Bible study by saying, "Those who can grant our desires sometimes say yes, sometimes they say no, and sometimes change their no to yes because of our persistence. Let's see how Jesus used this common experience to teach about our relationship with the heavenly Father."

Into the Word

Divide the class into three small groups of three or four. Distribute handouts (you create) of the following group assignments.

Persistence Group: Read Luke 11:5-8 and answer these questions: 1–When was a time you were this persistent in making a request of a family member or friend? 2–What caused you to be so insistent? 3–What was the outcome of a time you were this persistent in prayer?

Ask, Seek, Knock Group: Read Luke 11:9, 10 and discuss these questions: 1–When was a time you can characterize your prayer as having *asked* and *sought* but not *knocked*? 2–What was the result of a time when you did all three? 3–What causes us either to skip a step or do all three?

Confidence Group: Read Luke 11:11-13 and discuss these questions: 1–How do these three verses relate to verses 5-10? 2–Why can we have so much more confidence in God to give us good gifts than we can in the people who love us? 3–What would happen if people were given everything they desire?

After group discussion, call for conclusions. Expect a wide variety of responses due to the personal nature of several questions. The **Persistence Group** may note that the more urgent the need, the more persistent the prayer. The **Ask, Seek, Knock Group** may respond similarly regarding their third question. Be prepared to distinguish between asking, seeking, and knocking. If the **Confidence Group** has trouble with its first question, use the commentary to fill in gaps.

Into Life

Make a transition by saying, "Some Christians seem to have many excuses for not praying consistently and persistently. What are some reasons you have heard in that regard?" Jot responses on the board. Expect responses such as too busy, not knowing how to pray, being easily distracted, uncertainty about God's will or love. (*Option.* Time allowing, you can interject for discussion the issue of wrong motives per James 4:3.)

As the discussion winds down, distribute blank index cards, one to each person. Say, "Write on your card one personal weakness when it comes to persistence in prayer and how you will correct that problem in the week ahead. I will not collect the cards; they are for your personal use only." Challenge learners each to post it in a place where they will see it daily.

Option. Distribute copies of the "A Pathway to Prayer" exercise from the activity page. This is best used as a take-home due to its personal nature. Stress that you will begin next week's class by asking for volunteers to share conclusions.

JUSTICE AND THE
PROPHETS

Special Features

Note: Special Features are minimized this quarter due to 14 lessons instead of the usual 13. Some lessons are shorter than normal for the same reason.

Lessons
Unit 1: God Requires Justice

Unit 2: God Promises a Just Kingdom

Unit 3: Called to God's Work of Justice

QUARTERLY QUIZ

Use these questions as a pretest or as a review. The answers are on page iv of This Quarter in the Word.

Lesson 1
1. The day of the Lord is light, not darkness. T/F. *Amos 5:18*
2. "But let _____ roll on like a river, _____ like a never-failing stream!" *Amos 5:24*

Lesson 2
1. What was Habakkuk's role? (prophet, king, priest?) *Habakkuk 1:1*
2. Men are referred to as fish that have no what? (ruler, sense, food?) *Habakkuk 1:14*

Lesson 3
1. One should build a town with blood and guts. T/F. *Habakkuk 2:12*
2. The earth will be filled with the knowledge of the Lord's _____. *Habakkuk 2:14*

Lesson 4
1. The author questions the leaders of Israel regarding their practice of _____. *Micah 3:1*
2. Actions that the Lord requires are to act justly, love mercy, and walk _____. *Micah 6:8*

Lesson 5
1. The role of priest included that of what? (judge, messenger, prophet?) *Malachi 2:7*
2. The priests had failed to keep the covenant of Levi. T/F. *Malachi 2:8*

Lesson 6
1. To whom will the servant bring forth judgment? (Jews, Canaanites, the nations?) *Isaiah 42:1*
2. God will not give his _____ to another. *Isaiah 42:8*

Lesson 7
1. What did Paul preach to the Corinthians? (the gospel, the law, tithing?) *1 Corinthians 15:1*
2. There were only a few witnesses to Christ's resurrection. T/F. *1 Corinthians 15:5-8*

Lesson 8
1. Who conspired against Esther and her people? (Xerxes, Mordecai, Haman?) *Esther 7:6*
2. The conspirator was impaled on the pole he had prepared for another. T/F. *Esther 7:10*

Lesson 9
1. The Lord loves justice and hates robbery. T/F. *Isaiah 61:8*
2. Who will provide a new name for God's people? (Gentiles, kings, the Lord?) *Isaiah 62:2*

Lesson 10
1. The author calls Daughter Jerusalem to do what? (sing, shout, rejoice?) T/F. *Zephaniah 3:14*
2. "I will give you honor and praise among all the _____ of the earth." *Zephaniah 3:20*

Lesson 11
1. Who expressed jealousy? (the Lord, Zion, Judah?) *Zechariah 8:2*
2. Sound judgment must be executed in _____. *Zechariah 8:16*

Lesson 12
1. Which empire was to destroy Jerusalem? (Assyria, Babylon, Persia?) *Jeremiah 21:10*
2. Punishment is determined according to one's deeds. T/F. *Jeremiah 21:14*

Lesson 13
1. Jeremiah condemned the hand of whom? (liar, oppressor, false prophet?) *Jeremiah 22:3*
2. If the people did not obey, the Lord would still restore their fortunes. T/F. *Jeremiah 22:5*

Lesson 14
1. God mourned for Israel as a parent for a _____. *Hosea 11:1*
2. God's roar like what creature was to call Israel home? (bear, lion, tiger?) *Hosea 11:10*

THIS QUARTER IN THE WORD

Answers to the Quarterly Quiz on page 226

Lesson 1—1. false. 2. justice, righteousness. **Lesson 2**—1. prophet. 2. ruler. **Lesson 3**—1. false. 2. glory. **Lesson 4**—1. justice. 2. humbly with God. **Lesson 5**—1. messenger. 2. true. **Lesson 6**—1. the nations. 2. glory. **Lesson 7**—1. the gospel. 2. false. **Lesson 8**—1. Haman. 2. true. **Lesson 9**—1. true. 2. the Lord. **Lesson 10**—1. rejoice. 2. peoples. **Lesson 11**—1. truth. 2. the Lord. **Lesson 12**—1. Babylon. 2. true. **Lesson 13**—1. oppressor. 2. false. **Lesson 14**—1. child. 2. lion.

A CALL TO
ACCOUNTABILITY

DEVOTIONAL READING: Psalm 97
BACKGROUND SCRIPTURE: Amos 5

AMOS 5:18-24

18 Woe to you who long
   for the day of the LORD!
Why do you long for the day of the LORD?
   That day will be darkness, not light.
19 It will be as though a man fled from a lion
   only to meet a bear,
as though he entered his house
   and rested his hand on the wall
   only to have a snake bite him.
20 Will not the day of the LORD be darkness,
      not light—
   pitch-dark, without a ray of brightness?
21 "I hate, I despise your religious festivals;
   your assemblies are a stench to me.
22 Even though you bring me burnt offerings
      and grain offerings,
   I will not accept them.
Though you bring choice fellowship
      offerings,
   I will have no regard for them.
23 Away with the noise of your songs!
   I will not listen to the music of your
      harps.
24 But let justice roll on like a river,
   righteousness like a never-failing
      stream!"

KEY VERSE

Let justice roll on like a river, righteousness like a never-failing stream. —**Amos 5:24**

JUSTICE AND THE PROPHETS

Unit 1: God Requires Justice
LESSONS 1-5

LESSON AIMS

After participating in this lesson, each learner will be able to:

1. Summarize the misconceptions concerning the day of the Lord.

2. Explain why the Lord detested the people's worship rituals.

3. Recruit an accountability partner to implement one lifestyle change to improve his or her obedience to the imperative of the key verse.

LESSON OUTLINE

Introduction
  A. A Red-Letter Day?
  B. Lesson Context
I. Dismal Day (AMOS 5:18-20)
  A. Of Delusion (v. 18)
    It Seemed Like a Good Idea
  B. Of Danger (v. 19)
  C. Of Darkness (v. 20)
II. Disappointed God (AMOS 5:21-24)
  A. Not Religious Ritual (vv. 21-23)
    Flood
  B. Meaningful Worship (v. 24)
Conclusion
  A. The Misuse of Worship
  B. Prayer
  C. Thought to Remember

Introduction

A. A Red-Letter Day?

A red-letter day is a day that is memorable in some way, usually because something positive occurred on that day. The term appears to be derived from the practice of marking holy days in red letters on church calendars. *The Book of Common Prayer,* issued in 1549, included a calendar with holy days marked in red ink. Some calendars mark Sundays in red.

In Old Testament times, many of God's people in Israel viewed the coming day of the Lord as a red-letter day. They did not know exactly when it would occur, but they assumed it would be a happy, special day that they would always remember fondly.

B. Lesson Context

Today's lesson begins a new quarter of studies on the topic "Justice and the Prophets." The lessons in the first unit are drawn from the writings of Amos, Micah, Habakkuk, and Malachi. These four books make up one-third of the 12 Old Testament books that we call the Minor Prophets. The word *minor* has nothing to do with their degree of importance. The term highlights the length of these 12 books; all are much shorter than the majority of books described as *major* (Isaiah, Jeremiah, Lamentations, Ezekiel, and Daniel). Lamentation's inclusion in the major writings reflects the fact that the book was written by the major prophet Jeremiah.

The prophet Amos is unique among the writing prophets in two ways. First, he is a prophet who had another occupation to which he returned after delivering his prophecies (see Amos 1:1; 7:14, 15). Second, Amos was from the southern kingdom of Judah but was commanded by the Lord to speak his message in the northern kingdom of Israel (1:1). We do not need to imagine the reception that this outsider got when he prophesied against Israel (2:6-16; 7:10-17). Though he prophesied against several nations (1:3–2:5), Amos had the most to say about the sins of Israel.

Amos began his ministry around 760 BC. By then, God's people had been divided for approximately 170 years. Amos 1:1 mentions the two kings who were in power at the time of his ministry: Uzziah of Judah (also called Azariah; 785–734 BC; 2 Kings 15:1-3; 2 Chronicles 26:1-5) and Jeroboam (II) of Israel (786–746 BC; 2 Kings 14:23, 24). In Israel, an apathy toward God's laws had set in among the majority of the people. Life was good for them; the nation was prospering, and nations that often posed a threat to them (such as Assyria and Egypt) were weak and ineffective. What could this prophet possibly have to say to them? Why had he traveled from Judah to disturb their life of ease?

In the verses immediately preceding the start of our lesson text, Amos clearly revealed the cause of his ministry. At seemingly every turn, Israel chose evil over good (Amos 5:7-15). The prophet accused them of mistreating the poor (5:11). He then highlighted the people's numerous other sins (5:12-15): they punished those who sought justice, they accepted bribes, and they discriminated against the poor in lawsuits. With these admonitions still ringing in the air, Amos delivered the word of the Lord found in today's lesson text.

I. Dismal Day
(Amos 5:18-20)
A. Of Delusion (v. 18)

18a. Woe to you who long for the day of the Lord! Why do you long for the day of the Lord?

Woe is common in prophetic language. It introduces messages of warning and judgment (Jeremiah 22:13; Ezekiel 13:3, 18; Amos 6:1; etc.). Ideally, God's people should desire the day of the Lord, just as Christians desire the return of Jesus (2 Corinthians 1:14; 2 Peter 3:12).

However, Amos's audience longs for the day of the Lord for twisted, selfish reasons. Though they do not prioritize faithfulness to their covenant with the Lord, they believe that the day of the Lord will be a day of blessing for them. They have forgotten that covenant blessings are contingent on covenant faithfulness, and faithlessness will be met by judgment (Deuteronomy 28, 29).

The *day of the Lord* is a common theme in the Old Testament prophets (Isaiah 2:12-21; Ezekiel

30:3; Joel 1:15; 2:1, 2; Obadiah 15; Zephaniah 1:7-18; etc.). The verse at hand implies that in Amos's time the popular thinking surrounding the day of the Lord in Israel is gravely flawed. Israel believes that the Lord will arise on behalf of his people and defeat their enemies in a mighty display of his power on that day. Conveniently, God's people consider themselves exempt from judgment on that day because of their status as his chosen, covenant people (compare Judah's attitude in Jeremiah 7:2-11).

What prophets like Amos point out is that being the covenant people does not come without obligation. Elevated status before God also elevates the degree of accountability to him (Amos 3:2; compare Luke 12:47, 48). True, God's unique relationship with Israel provides them with special blessings and privileges, but it also comes with a solemn responsibility for faithful obedience to him. The people in Amos's day have come to expect the privileges, but they have abandoned the responsibility.

18b. That day will be darkness, not light.

Because of their false beliefs, the people will find themselves surprised that *the day* will be *darkness* for them, *not light* (compare Isaiah 5:30; Jeremiah 13:16). They would have cheered the judgment that Amos proclaimed on their enemies (Amos 1:3–2:5). The darkness and judgment that the other nations will experience will also fall on Israel, for Israel is no different from those nations (contrast Exodus 19:6).

> *What Do You Think?*
> Which three modern thoughts and/or behaviors of what we might call "interim darkness" do you think God will condemn most harshly on the day of ultimate darkness? Why?
> *Digging Deeper*
> Which one of those three is most challenging to Christians generally? Why?

❧ *It Seemed Like a Good Idea* ❧

Well-meaning lawmakers sometimes find that their decrees end up doing more harm than good. This phenomenon is called the "law of unintended consequences." When the U.S. Congress imposed a 10 percent luxury tax on yachts, some felt relief: the rich would finally pay their fair share of taxes!

But within eight months after the law took effect, the largest U.S. yacht manufacturer had laid off more than 80 percent of its employees and closed one of its two manufacturing plants.

In the first year, one-third of U.S. yacht-building companies stopped production. Ultimately, 25,000 workers in that industry lost their jobs, and 75,000 more jobs were lost in companies that supplied yacht parts and materials. Jobs shifted to companies in Europe and the Bahamas. The U.S. Treasury collected zero revenue from the sales driven overseas.

Amos warned that those who spoke of a victorious day of the Lord would face unintended consequences too. Counting on religious ritual to yield divine reward would result in God's wrath.

—J. E.

B. Of Danger (v. 19)

19. It will be as though a man fled from a lion only to meet a bear, as though he entered his house and rested his hand on the wall only to have a snake bite him.

Amos illustrates the plight of the people with two darkly humorous pictures. In both images, *a man* believes himself to be safe right before he meets his doom. He discovers that *a bear* is as deadly as *a lion* (compare Lamentations 3:10) and not even the man's *house* can keep him safe from *a snake* that has slithered inside (compare Deuteronomy 32:24; Ecclesiastes 10:8).

What Do You Think?
When you have one of those bad-to-worse kind of days, what encouragement from Scripture gets you back on track most quickly?
Digging Deeper
Under what circumstances would you not use that particular Scripture to help someone else through such a day? Why?

Two lessons should be drawn from these scenarios. First, like escaping a lion only to meet a bear, it is impossible to hide from judgment on the day of the Lord (compare Job 20:24; Isaiah 24:17, 18; Jeremiah 15:2, 3; 48:44). As the saying goes, "You can run, but you can't hide." In Amos's illustration, even one's own home, which might be considered a truly "safe place," will provide no refuge from what the day of the Lord will bring. The apostle John pictures individuals from all walks of life crying for the rocks to hide them from the Lamb on "the great day of their wrath," but such cries are futile (Revelation 6:15-17).

Second, the day of the Lord and its accompanying judgment arrive without warning. A person believes him- or herself to be safe from harm, when unanticipated danger strikes. Both Jesus and Paul use the illustration of the thief in the night to describe the sudden and unexpected nature of the day when Jesus returns (Matthew 24:42-44; 1 Thessalonians 5:1, 2). Paul adds that people will be claiming "peace and safety" when inescapable sudden "destruction" comes (5:3).

C. Of Darkness (v. 20)

20. Will not the day of the LORD be darkness, not light—pitch-dark, without a ray of brightness?

Amos reiterates his earlier point that the *day of the Lord* will be a time of *darkness, not light*. The Hebrew word translated *pitch-dark* comes from the same root word that describes the "total darkness" that fell upon the land of Egypt for three days during the ninth of the 10 plagues (Exodus 10:22). The judgment delivered shortly after that day resulted in the Israelites' being delivered from their enemy, from slavery to freedom. The day of the Lord, however, promises to be a reversal of both what Israel had experienced and what they expect to happen once more (see Ezekiel 7:7; Zephaniah 1:15).

What Do You Think?
What common but wrong assumptions do Christians have about Christ's return that may end up leading to the darkness of Amos 5:20 rather than the light of Titus 2:13?
Digging Deeper
What guardrails will you erect to protect yourself against these wrong assumptions?

II. Disappointed God
(AMOS 5:21-24)
A. Not Religious Ritual (vv. 21-23)

21. "I hate, I despise your religious festivals; your assemblies are a stench to me.

Though Amos has been speaking for God up until now, the Lord himself steps in to express his extreme displeasure with Israel's *religious festivals* (see Exodus 23:14-18; 34:22-25). These would include annual feasts like Passover and the Feast of Tabernacles (Leviticus 23). Though the Lord had ordained these feasts for his people, he now refers to them as *your* (the people's) religious festivals. The Lord does not want to be associated with them in any way. God rejects mere observance of days.

The Lord voices his disdain especially for the people's *assemblies* (Leviticus 23:36; Numbers 29:35; Deuteronomy 16:8). The Lord hates how the people have twisted religion to their own ends instead of honoring the assemblies as he intends (compare Leviticus 26:30, 31; Hosea 2:11).

Israel scorns anyone who tries to correct the people's wicked behavior and promote what is upright and good (Jeremiah 44:4, 5). Amos challenged the people to hate what is evil and love what is good (Amos 5:15, 20, 21; compare Isaiah 5:20).

The language of being offended by the smell reflects the Old Testament sacrificial system. The Lord had stated that he took pleasure in the aroma of offerings presented to him (examples: Genesis 8:21; Exodus 29:18; Numbers 29:2). In Amos's day, however, the pleasing aroma has become a *stench* in the Lord's nostrils. This is the first of three sensory reactions the Lord has to the worship of the unholy, faithless people.

22. "Even though you bring me burnt offerings and grain offerings, I will not accept them.

HOW TO SAY IT

Amos	*Ay*-mus.
Habakkuk	Huh-*back*-kuk.
Jeroboam	Jair-uh-*boe*-um.
Uzziah	Uh-*zye*-uh.

Though you bring choice fellowship offerings, I will have no regard for them.

The three offerings noted here are required by the Lord as part of the Old Testament sacrificial system. *Burnt offerings* are foundational. These are completely consumed by the sacrificial fire, except for the skin (Leviticus 1:6-9; 7:8). A burnt offering is to be offered every morning and evening for all Israel (Exodus 29:38-42).

Grain offerings are offerings of flour and oil. The best part of the grain is to be given to the Lord through this offering (6:14, 15). This offering celebrates that the Lord is the provider of what the land produces.

Fellowship offerings are shared by the priest, the one who brought the sacrifice, and others (Leviticus 7:15, 16, 28-36). Thus the offering becomes part of a communal, or fellowship, meal. The word *choice* refers to the best of the herd or flock that was used for the fellowship offering.

For God to refuse to *accept* these offerings that he has commanded indicates that something is terribly amiss with the people who are bringing them (Isaiah 1:11-15; Jeremiah 14:11, 12). It is especially ironic that the Lord has *no regard* for the fellowship offerings that are intended to establish a sense of closeness between God and his people. The Hebrew suggests that God refuses to even see these offerings—the second of the three sensory reactions first mentioned in Amos 5:21.

23. "Away with the noise of your songs! I will not listen to the music of your harps.

The Lord's strong disapproval also applies to the music presented by the people at their worship assemblies (compare Amos 6:1, 5). Whether the music is vocal, expressed through their *songs*, or instrumental, played by the *harps*, God wants no part of it. Just as the offerings are a stench in his nostrils, the *music* makes him want to cover his ears.

What is the reason for such harsh words directed against actions that the Lord has specifically commanded in his law given through Moses? The problem is that worship practices such as the sacrifices and the music have become an end in themselves. The people of God are merely going through the motions and words of worship,

Join the river of righteousness

Visual for Lesson 1. *When discussing verse 24, ask the class what obstacles they face when joining the river of righteousness.*

divorcing that worship from any real impact on their daily conduct. The words of Isaiah, which Jesus will apply to the Pharisees of his day, could be spoken by Amos to his audience: they are people who "come near to me with their mouth and honor me with their lips, but their hearts are far from me" (Isaiah 29:13; compare Matthew 15:7-9).

> **What Do You Think?**
> How would we recognize whether the Lord has grown to "hate" a particular practice of our church?
>
> **Digging Deeper**
> Would a good way to avoid the problem be to automatically cancel all programs every year so that discussion is required to reinstate them? Why, or why not?

❧ FLOOD ❧

It is not surprising that hurricanes cause the greatest amount of water damage to American homes. But the second-greatest culprit in that regard starts out small and often goes unnoticed until it is too late.

According to government sources, approximately 10,000 gallons of water a year slowly enter U.S. homes as small trickles. A crack in a pipe rarely stays small. A burst water pipe can turn a minor drip into a house-soaking flood. Plumbing leaks are more than a nuisance; left unchecked, they can lead to tremendous cost for the homeowner. For this reason, experts suggest that homeowners not let small leaks go unresolved.

The people of Israel became complacent. They overlooked seemingly minor "leaks" in their nation's obedience to God. What seemed to be minor cracks in their obedience would result in a flood of God's judgment. What spiritual leaks do you need to fix this week?　　　　—J. E.

B. Meaningful Worship (v. 24)

24. "But let justice roll like a river, righteousness like a never-failing stream!"

While the people have become quite content with shallow gestures of worship, the Lord expects and deserves much more. Amos specifically highlights the issues of *justice* and *righteousness*. Justice concerns the fair, lawful practices of a society that honors the Lord. Practicing justice requires a person to be actively concerned about not only knowing what is just but also choosing to do it. An individual who really cares about justice becomes passionate about making sure that it is carried out in his or her surroundings and in the lives of others (see Jeremiah 22:3; Micah 6:8).

That the northern kingdom does not uphold justice is clear from the indictments that Amos brings against the people (see Lesson Context). Such conduct makes their so-called acts of worship nothing but a sham. No wonder the northern kingdom is ripe for divine judgment! This is why the day of the Lord that the people so fervently desire will be a time of darkness rather than light (Amos 5:18, 20).

Righteousness is closely tied to justice. To live righteously is to make certain that God's standards of what is right guide one's daily decisions. When justice and righteousness are pursued habitually day after day, they flow like waters in a *never-failing stream* (compare Isaiah 45:8). But how can this happen when the people have clogged the flow through their stubborn and rebellious hearts and their contempt for God's righteous standards?

The call to exercise justice and righteousness

has echoed through the centuries to God's people of every era. The laws set forth by Moses laid out what those qualities should look like in the promised land (for example, Deuteronomy 15:1-18; 24:14, 15, 17-22). Joshua affirmed these laws (Joshua 1:7-9; 24:14, 15). Isaiah will be bold in decrying the empty worship of his audience (Isaiah 1:10-17). Jeremiah will describe those who make the Lord's temple in Jerusalem a "den of robbers" (Jeremiah 7:8-11), mouthing the words "the temple of the Lord" like a mantra that can save them (7:4), while treating the people in need around them with the utmost scorn. God's desire for justice and righteousness is not a fad; his people do well to take him seriously.

Conclusion

A. The Misuse of Worship

Diet Eman was a young Christian girl growing up in Holland when Adolf Hitler invaded the country and began his horrible persecution of the Jews there. Eman, along with some fellow Christians, determined to do something about this injustice and became part of an underground movement to rescue the Jews in Holland.

But Eman also tells the story of a rail line that was used by the Nazis during World War II to transport boxcars jammed with Jews and others whom the Nazis considered "undesirables." Many times the trains were sidetracked for hours while the people inside begged for food, water, and mercy. There were no bathroom facilities for the journey, which could last four days or longer. Along the train's route was a small church located close enough to the rail line to hear the cries coming from within the boxcars. The church people attending services were deeply disturbed by these "distractions," so they began singing more loudly so they would not have to hear them.

We are likely not in a setting where a train filled with suffering people is traveling by the place where we worship. However, our place of worship may well be in a community where many people are hurting and in need. It is certainly located in a community that needs righteousness to be practiced daily. We cannot allow ourselves to think that we have somehow fulfilled our Christian duty by simply attending worship services and then returning to our routines while ignoring the needs of those around us. Feast days and burnt offerings are not part of our worship observances, but do we offend the Lord today with our closed eyes and deaf ears to the hurts of those around us?

> ### What Do You Think?
> Where is the most pressing need for justice in the community in which your church is located? Why do you say that?
> ### Digging Deeper
> What guardrails can your church erect to ensure that its work for earthly justice does not eclipse the primary task of evangelism for eternal life? Or is that even a danger?

Christians should consider Jesus' call to be salt and light (Matthew 5:13-16) as a call to practice the kind of lifestyle encouraged by the prophets. Righteousness cannot be practiced in isolation from other people; it requires contact with the world, a world that is often characterized by injustice and unrighteousness. To be salt and light is to have a noticeable impact on our surroundings, and that is what followers of Jesus have always been called to do. Without these practices, we too may see the day of the Lord not as a day of celebration but as a day of judgment to our great shame.

B. Prayer

Father, may *justice* and *righteousness* be more than mere words to us; may they be part of our daily conduct. We pray in Jesus' name. Amen.

C. Thought to Remember

We worship God through the offerings of our daily lives.

VISUALS FOR THESE LESSONS

The visual pictured in each lesson (example: page 234) is a small reproduction of a large, full-color poster included in the *Adult Resources* packet for the Spring Quarter. That packet also contains the very useful *Presentation Tools* CD for teacher use. Order No. 3629120 from your supplier.

INVOLVEMENT LEARNING

Enhance your lesson with NIV Bible Student *(from your curriculum supplier) and the reproducible activity page (at www.standardlesson.com or in the back of the* NIV Standard Lesson Commentary Deluxe Edition*).*

Into the Lesson

Have this quip displayed as class begins:

If life were fair, we would all get speeding tickets.

Ask class members to explain this saying and how it does or does not challenge typical ideas of fairness.

Alternative. Distribute copies of the "Fair Enough" exercise from the activity page, which you can download. Have students work in small groups to discuss the fairness of the situations described. Note that there are no clear right or wrong responses. Limit discussion time to no more than five minutes.

After either activity, pose one or more of the following questions for a whole-class discussion: 1–What frequently causes people to complain about being treated unfairly? 2–Why is self-interest the worst criterion by which to evaluate fairness? 3–What better criteria exist?

Make a transition by saying, "People want fairness and expect justice—it's human nature. But is justice a matter of personal, subjective expectation? Let's see what God had to say about this through the prophet Amos."

Into the Word

Divide the class into groups of three to five. Ask them to imagine a letter from God in response to one of the following letters, which you distribute as handouts you prepare. God's response should be derived from the cited portion of the text.

Day of the Lord Group (Amos 5:18-20)—Dear God, life is good for me. But I guess it will be even better when you bring judgment during your promised day of the Lord. Tell me what good things I can expect!

Good-Religion Group (Amos 5:21-24)—Dear God, I know you expect your people to worship you. I think we have done a pretty good job of that, but we would like to hear you tell us so.

Allow groups adequate time to prepare their letters, but no more than 20 minutes. Then allow groups to share their letters. Expect responses similar to these:

Day of the Lord Group—Do you really expect my day of judgment to make life even better for you? I tried to warn you—it is not going to be a brighter day for you, but a much darker one. My judgment will devour you because you are unjustly devouring others.

Good-Religion Group—Are you kidding? Frankly, your worship stinks! Your songs hurt my ears! You should put hands and feet to your worship by showing compassion to others. As it is, your so-called worship is just a show!

Use the lesson commentary as necessary to correct learners' misconceptions.

Option. If your class needs a refresher on the four categories of justice, be prepared to discuss the differences between *distributive justice* (economic fairness), *procedural justice* (due process), *restorative justice* (making restitution), and *retributive justice* (punishment).

Into Life

Before class, prepare plastic bags with a few candy kisses in each. Tie each bag with a ribbon attached to a tag saying, "Righteousness and peace have kissed each other" (Psalm 85:10).

After you distribute the bags, pose this question for whole-class discussion: Can justice occur where peace and righteousness do not "kiss"? After a few minutes, move the ensuing discussion from the abstract to the personal by noting the value of having an accountability partner to encourage practicing the imperative of the key verse, Amos 5:24.

Alternative. Distribute copies of the "Seven Days of Justice and Righteousness" exercise from the activity page as a take-home. As an incentive to complete it, promise that you will begin next week's class by discussing results.

A PRAYER FOR JUSTICE

DEVOTIONAL READING: Psalm 73:1-3, 21-28
BACKGROUND SCRIPTURE: Habakkuk 1

HABAKKUK 1:1-4, 12-14

¹ The prophecy that Habakkuk the prophet received.

² How long, LORD, must I call for help,
    but you do not listen?
Or cry out to you, "Violence!"
    but you do not save?
³ Why do you make me look at injustice?
    Why do you tolerate wrongdoing?
Destruction and violence are before me;
    there is strife, and conflict abounds.
⁴ Therefore the law is paralyzed,
    and justice never prevails.
The wicked hem in the righteous,
    so that justice is perverted.

· ·

¹² LORD, are you not from everlasting?
    My God, my Holy One, you will never
        die.
You, LORD, have appointed them to exe-
        cute judgment;
    you, my Rock, have ordained them to
        punish.
¹³ Your eyes are too pure to look on evil;
    you cannot tolerate wrongdoing.

Why then do you tolerate the treacherous?
    Why are you silent while the wicked
        swallow up those more righteous than
        themselves?
¹⁴ You have made people like the fish in the
        sea,
    like the sea creatures that have no ruler.

KEY VERSE

Why then do you tolerate the treacherous? Why are you silent while the wicked swallow up those more righteous than themselves? —**Habakkuk 1:13b**

Justice and the Prophets

Unit 1: God Requires Justice

Lesson Aims

After participating in this lesson, each learner will be able to:

1. Summarize Habakkuk's two complaints.

2. Explain the specific issue of justice with which Habakkuk was wrestling.

3. Watch and pray to see how God is working in difficult situations this week.

Lesson Outline

Introduction
  A. What a (Sometimes) Wonderful World
  B. Lesson Context
I. Dilemma (Habakkuk 1:1-4)
  A. God's Inaction (vv. 1, 2)
  B. The World's Iniquity (vv. 3, 4)
II. Deliberations (Habakkuk 1:12-14)
  A. Unmatched Sovereignty (vv. 12, 13a)
    Turning a Blind Eye
  B. Unexplained Silence (vv. 13b, 14)
    Power in Numbers?
Conclusion
  A. The Prophetic Job
  B. Prayer
  C. Thought to Remember

Introduction

A. What a (Sometimes) Wonderful World

Years ago the great jazz musician Louis Armstrong popularized a song entitled "What a Wonderful World." With his trademark raspy voice, Armstrong sang of the beauty of creation. Most would agree with Mr. Armstrong's sentiments—there is much about this world that makes it wonderful indeed: the people we love and the sights and sounds that add so much to our lives on a daily basis.

At the same time, there is much in this world that causes us great sorrow and pain. Some things are not wonderful in the least. As followers of God and readers of his Word, we understand that this heartache is the result of the curse brought about by humanity's sin. That does not ease the hurt we feel. It can even cause us to question God and his purpose for the difficult circumstances that we or those we love endure. Our faith can be shaken to the very core.

B. Lesson Context

Habakkuk is another of the 12 books at the end of our Old Testament, which we call the Minor Prophets (see Lesson Context in lesson 1). Unlike the prophet Amos (see lesson 1), Habakkuk mentions no kings of either Israel or Judah in his book. One benefit of this decision is to make the book more universal. Instead of being very obviously tied to a situation concerning this or that king, the book can be applied more generally to any similar situation.

Habakkuk is a challenging book to date. A key to placing this prophet historically is found in Habakkuk 1:6. There we read of God's promise to raise up Babylon to inflict judgment on the wayward nation of Judah (the southern kingdom). The Babylonians are described as a cruel and vicious people who let nothing stand in their way as they swallow up peoples and territories (Habakkuk 1:6-11, not in today's text). Since the northern kingdom of Israel had been conquered by Assyria in 722 BC, Habakkuk's complaints and God's responses must concern the southern kingdom of Judah.

The Babylonians had replaced the Assyrians on the center stage of world history by first gaining independence from the Assyrians in 626 BC and then eventually dismantling Assyria's remaining control in a series of battles from 615 to 612 BC. Thus Habakkuk's prophecy should likely be dated within the latter years of the seventh century BC as the Babylonians' growing dominance over the ancient Near East became clear. This puts his ministry in the same time frame as Jeremiah's (see lessons 12 and 13). Both prophets interpreted the Babylonians' rising to power as ordained by God, to be used to judge Judah for its wickedness (compare Jeremiah 22:25).

I. Dilemma

(HABAKKUK 1:1-4)

These verses introduce Habakkuk and his complaint to the Lord. In his rather heated exchange with the Lord, Habakkuk's manner of speaking resembles Job's words when he expressed his own frustration with the Lord. Yet the reasons for these men's questions toward God are grounded in different circumstances. Job's anguish was rooted in the tragedy of his personal suffering (Job 1, 2). Habakkuk's concern, however, is much broader in scope.

A. God's Inaction (vv. 1, 2)

1. The prophecy that Habakkuk the prophet received.

Prophecy translates a Hebrew word that can refer to loads carried by animals (2 Kings 5:17; 8:9; etc.) or people (Numbers 11:11, 17; etc.). The same Hebrew word is used frequently to introduce prophetic messages that are threatening or ominous in nature; the NIV translates it with the more benign "prophecy" or "word" regularly (examples: Isaiah 13:1; Nahum 1:1; Zecha-

HOW TO SAY IT

Asaph	*Ay*-saff.
Assyrians	Uh-*sear*-e-unz.
Babylonians	Bab-ih-*low*-nee-unz.
Habakkuk	Huh-*back*-kuk.
Nineveh	*Nin*-uh-vuh.

riah 9:1; Malachi 1:1). Such messages may be seen as burdensome—weighing heavily on the prophet's mind. He must speak them in order to relieve himself of the burden that he feels.

The Hebrew word behind the translation *received*, also translated "saw," is frequently used to describe the prophetic experience (Isaiah 1:1; Amos 1:1; etc.). The word can indicate that visions are seen or simply that a message is received from the Lord. It marks the prophet as a man of unique spiritual vision or insight; he sees with vision that is empowered by the direction of the Holy Spirit (compare 2 Peter 1:20, 21).

2a. How long, LORD, must I call for help, but you do not listen?

Habakkuk wastes no time in getting to the heart of his concern. This is a prophet who is deeply troubled and believes that the *Lord* has ignored his concerns (compare Jeremiah 14:9). The phrase *how long . . . must I call for help* indicates that Habakkuk has voiced these concerns to the Lord repeatedly (compare Psalms 6:3; 13:1, 2). The prophet fears that the only explanation for God's apparent lack of concern is that he is choosing *not* to *listen* to Habakkuk (compare 22:1, 2).

> **What Do You Think?**
> On a scale of 1 (low) to 10 (high), what is your tolerance for waiting in line at a store compared with waiting for answers to prayer? What does this say about you?
> **Digging Deeper**
> What has to happen to get your tolerance for waiting on God's answer up to a 10?

2b. Or cry out to you, "Violence!" but you do not save?

Habakkuk rightly assumes that the just and righteous God cares deeply when *violence* goes unchecked (see Genesis 6:11-13; compare Job 19:7). Furthermore, the Lord is known as a God who will *save* his people when they call on him (2 Chronicles 20:9; Psalm 107:13, 19; etc.).

B. The World's Iniquity (vv. 3, 4)

3a. Why do you make me look at injustice? Why do you tolerate wrongdoing?

This half verse introduces us to two of six words Habakkuk uses to describe the chaos he sees everywhere he turns (see verse 3b). Chaos stands in opposition to the order that God created in the world (see Genesis 1, 2; John 1:1-5; Acts 17:24-28). For this reason, the existence of chaos, especially in the land God promised to his people, is deeply problematic for Habakkuk (compare Job 9:23).

Habakkuk, like Job before him, asks questions of the Lord that presuppose God's character (Job 3:11, 12, 20, 23; compare Habakkuk 1:13, below). Habakkuk's questions are not primarily about why he sees *injustice* and his reasons to be grieved, though it may seem that is his focus. The answer to that question is quite simple: people are sinful, and so Habakkuk sees sin around him. The subtext of this question, rather, is why the Lord has not put an end to these things.

Thus the questions are based in the assumption that God is holy and good. Given this fact, it makes no sense to Habakkuk that God is not acting to right the horrible wrongs that the prophet witnesses.

> **What Do You Think?**
> In what circumstances should you ask the same kind of "why" question that the prophet asks? What should be the motive for asking?
> *Digging Deeper*
> How can we keep our questions from crossing a line that results in God's rebuke, as in Job 38?

3b. Destruction and violence are before me; there is strife, and conflict abounds.

Destruction might be associated specifically in the original context with warfare and the taking of plunder from others (example: Isaiah 16:4). When paired with *violence*, it emphasizes the horrible results often associated with war (examples: Jeremiah 6:7; 20:8; Ezekiel 45:9; Habakkuk 2:17).

Strife and *conflict* add explicitly chaotic overtones to Habakkuk's description (compare Jeremiah 15:10). Taken together, Habakkuk longs for the order that the Creator has graced the world with.

4a. Therefore the law is paralyzed,

In an environment such as Habakkuk describes,

there is clearly no respect whatsoever for authority or *law* (compare Isaiah 1:23; 29:21; Ezekiel 9:9). The Hebrew word translated *paralyzed* elsewhere refers to being made feeble (Psalm 38:8), and that is the sense here. The law is inactive and essentially lifeless. By pointing this out, Habakkuk hopes to see God move to action (compare 119:126).

4b. and justice never prevails.

In parallel to the weakened law, *justice* is also powerless. The situation is similar to the time of Amos, who expressed God's desire that justice and righteousness flow like a never-failing stream (Amos 5:24; see lesson 1). Those qualities are as absent in Habakkuk's surroundings as they were in Amos's.

> **What Do You Think?**
> What problems may a person avoid by not using an absolute word like "never" in a prayer?
> *Digging Deeper*
> How will you guard against such problems?

4c. The wicked hem in the righteous,

It is not hard to imagine that in the conditions described, *the wicked* appear to be in complete control. They *hem in the righteous*—surrounding them to suppress any effort the righteous put forth to express their concerns (compare Psalms 17:9; 22:16). Again, the situation is reminiscent of how Amos described his environment: "The prudent keep quiet in such times, for the times are evil" (Amos 5:13). David also pondered the prevalence of wickedness (Psalm 11:1-3; compare Job 21:7-13). The reader might be reminded of the sad moral climate that prevailed during the time of the judges in Israel, when everyone did whatever they thought best (Judges 17:6; 21:25).

4d. so that justice is perverted.

Perverted justice becomes the norm under such conditions. This is a violation of what God intends for his covenant people to maintain in their courts (Deuteronomy 16:18-20; compare Isaiah 5:20).

II. Deliberations
(HABAKKUK 1:12-14)

In Habakkuk 1:5-11 (not in our printed text), the Lord responds to Habakkuk's concerns. God intends to do things that Habakkuk could not believe even if the Lord revealed his plans to the prophet (1:5). The Lord tells the troubled prophet that he will raise up the violent Babylonians to administer the Lord's disciplinary measures to his wayward people (1:6, 9; see commentary on 1:12b). Thus God will respond to the violence in Judah by bringing the violence of the Babylonians against it.

A. Unmatched Sovereignty (vv. 12, 13a)

12a. LORD, are you not from everlasting? My God, my Holy One, you will never die.

Habakkuk speaks again, reacting to the Lord's planned discipline of his people. The prophet ponders what he knows to be true of the Lord. The phrase *my Holy One* is unique in the Old Testament, occurring only here. Similar phrases emphasize God's relationship with all Israel, not with one individual (Isaiah 31:1; 37:23). Habakkuk appears to be alone in referring to the *Lord* as his personal holy *God*. This confidence in his relationship with God probably explains Habakkuk's frank speech.

Ancient scribal tradition holds that Ezra changed this verse to read *you will never die*. Originally, it is argued, the text read, "we shall not die." If the latter reading is taken as original, then there is more at stake than simply acknowledging that God lives forever. God's eternal nature seems to be the basis of Habakkuk's assertion that God's people *will never die*. Because God is *everlasting* and has made everlasting promises, the prophet feels confident that God cannot really intend to destroy his people utterly (compare Psalm 118:17). Yet the situation around Habakkuk suggests that his confidence might be misplaced (contrast Isaiah 10:5-7).

12b. You, LORD, have appointed them to execute judgment; you, my Rock, have ordained them to punish.

Habakkuk acknowledges the decision of the *Lord* in order to set up the prophet's question in Habakkuk 1:13b, below. *Them* refers to Babylon. The facts as Habakkuk sees them are that the people are marked for *judgment* and punishment, even though they would be the instrument to bring correction to Judah.

Calling the Lord *my Rock* conveys the security of resting in his changeless character (Genesis 49:24; Deuteronomy 32:4; 1 Samuel 2:2). God's history of interactions with his people has proven that he really is faithful and consistent. His decision to correct them seems to contradict his character to some degree.

One should note that Habakkuk has no reservations whatsoever about God's people deserving to be punished for their many transgressions. The way they have trashed the Lord's covenant with them and trampled on his law in the manner already described is unacceptable and cannot be tolerated (Habakkuk 1:2-4). But using the wicked Babylonians to carry out the punishment certainly does not seem a fair or just punishment to Habakkuk.

13a. Your eyes are too pure to look on evil; you cannot tolerate wrongdoing.

Habakkuk's words reflect once again his understanding of the holy, righteous character of God. God's purity in regard to sin does not even allow him *to look on evil*, meaning not that God does not see but that he does not see without action (see Psalm 18:26; Lamentations 3:34-36). How can the Lord who cannot tolerate the presence of any kind of *wrongdoing* allow the obviously despicable Babylonians to overpower the people of Judah (contrast Psalm 25:1-3)?

❧ TURNING A BLIND EYE ❧

The idiom "turning a blind eye" has an interesting origin. Admiral Horatio Nelson (1758–1805) was a hero of the British Royal Navy. Nelson was known as a bold and unconventional leader. His tactics led to some decisive British naval victories, most famously at the Battle of Trafalgar in 1805, where he was killed in action. Before that he had been wounded several times in combat, one wound resulting in blindness in one eye.

Nelson turned this disability into an asset at the Battle of Copenhagen in 1801. During the battle, Nelson's commanding officer, who was on a different ship, signaled him to disengage the enemy. When Nelson's crew pointed him to the signal, he lifted his telescope up to his blind eye. He told the men he did not see the signal and continued to fight. The result was a British victory. When Nelson's superior was recalled, Nelson was promoted. And "turning a blind eye" has come to mean "intentionally ignoring undesirable information."

When the Lord revealed that he was going to allow the ruthless Babylonians to execute judgment on his people, Habakkuk was incensed! How could the righteous God turn a blind eye to the sins of a nation that was more wicked than faithless Judah? Yet God had already taken that fact into account (see Habakkuk 2:4-17).

God has no blind eye. He sees all. Any seeming defect in how he should act is our own blindness, not his.   —J. E.

B. Unexplained Silence (vv. 13b, 14)

13b. Why then do you tolerate the treacherous? Why are you silent while the wicked swallow up those more righteous than themselves?

Habakkuk is incredulous as he considers the people whom God has chosen to chastise Judah. The Babylonians are described with exceptionally derogatory language by the Lord himself (see Habakkuk 1:6-11). How can they be the ones whom God will use as the rod of discipline? To Habakkuk, to do so seems to compromise qualities that the Lord is known for.

True, the people of Judah deserve the Lord's judgment, but so do the Babylonians. Habakkuk, knowing his own people's evil as he does, contends that Judah is *more righteous than* the Babylonians. At least those in Judah are part of God's covenant people; the Babylonians are wicked idolaters. Habakkuk has not hesitated to voice his dismay over the Lord's inaction toward Judah's wickedness and his proposed course of action using Babylon to deal with that wickedness. Yet the Lord seems to remain *silent* and unmoved by what the prophet sees as obvious injustice (compare Job 21:7-13).

> **What Do You Think?**
> What methods can we use to keep from misinterpreting God's silence?
> **Digging Deeper**
> When God seems to be silent, how do you know whether He wants you to do something rather than wait on Him—or vice versa?

Habakkuk and Jonah are an interesting prophetic pair: Habakkuk questioned God for using a pagan nation to punish his people, while Jonah questioned God for forgiving a pagan nation on the verge of facing his judgment. Jonah's objections were the product of seeing the Assyrian people in Nineveh accept his message, repent of their sins, and thus escape the Lord's wrath. He resented the Lord's compassion toward the Assyrians, insisting that God ought to punish them instead of showing them mercy (Jonah 4:1, 2).

14. You have made people like the fish in the sea, like the sea creatures that have no ruler.

When God created the first man and woman, he gave them dominion over all other created beings, including *the fish* and all *sea creatures* (Genesis 1:26). Habakkuk, in his bewilderment over God's dealings with his people, wonders whether the Lord is treating human beings as no more than fish and other creatures that are allowed to be captured and killed at random. Apparently there is *no ruler* to hold the Babylonians accountable, or at least it appears that way to Habakkuk.

In the remaining verses of chapter 1 (not in this lesson), Habakkuk continues his marine metaphor by comparing the wicked Babylonians to a fisherman who gathers fish in nets and takes great pleasure in doing so. The Babylonians are portrayed as worshipping their net; that is, they are congratulating themselves and their ability to overpower whomever they please. They are as suited to violence as the fisherman is to fishing.

❧ POWER IN NUMBERS? ❧

Fish benefit from being a part of a school. Together they are able to detect nearby predatory animals, find food, or locate potential mates. But as every fisherman knows, schools of fish are easy targets for human predators. Productive fishing happens in places where fish are found in a group. Fishermen can lure and hook one after another! Those fishing with nets can lower them into a school, capturing dozens of fish at once. Lacking an alpha leader, fish swim around without leadership, almost begging to be caught!

Habakkuk used such imagery to compare Babylon to a fisherman and describe the nations they conquered as helpless fish. Just like fish that have no ruler are easily hooked or captured in a net, weak nations are easy prey for the strong and ruthless. So too a "school" of people suffer without the leadership of a knowledgeable teacher. How does your community stay connected to our great teacher and leader Jesus?　　　　　—J. E.

Conclusion

A. The Prophetic Job

Habakkuk's nation, Judah, was in a spiritual free fall, ripe for the judgment of almighty God. God's method for providing that judgment was not at all wonderful in Habakkuk's eyes. The prophet did not view it as an acceptable solution to the problem. Habakkuk struggled to reconcile his understanding of God with the uncertain world around him.

Habakkuk's concern has been voiced repeatedly through the years. For example, Asaph, the author of Psalm 73, was deeply troubled over what he saw as God's unfair treatment of the wicked. They appear to prosper and live carefree lives while completely oblivious to God and his ways. Psalm 10 begins by expressing similar disappointment in God's seemingly uncaring attitude about injustices in the world. The wicked do just as they please and benefit from their evil while their victims suffer. Doesn't God see? And if he does, doesn't he *care*?

> *What Do You Think?*
> How do we know when it's appropriate to cry out to the Lord (Psalm 22:2) vs. when we should keep silent (Habakkuk 2:20)?
> *Digging Deeper*
> Are you more likely to cry out when you should keep silent, or the opposite? What's the cure?

This is a struggle with which nearly all of us can readily identify. When we find ourselves questioning God or his purpose for the circumstances we are confronting, we are in good company. Prophets like Habakkuk and righteous people like Job

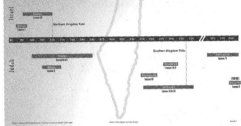

GOD SPEAKS
THROUGH THE PROPHETS

Visual for Lesson 2. *While introducing the lesson, use this time line to orient the class to Habakkuk's ministry in reference to others' from this quarter.*

were some of the most outspoken in their questions and accusations directed toward the one who called them to his service (compare Numbers 11:10-15; 1 Kings 19:4; Psalm 13:1-4; Jeremiah 20:7, 8; Matthew 11:1-3).

God is not caught off guard with such language. Indeed, sometimes he even chooses to engage our questions, though the answers may not be what we hope to hear. With Habakkuk, our knowledge of the Lord can lead us to conclusions that seem correct but in the end require correction from God (compare Job 38:1–40:2).

In all of life's circumstances, but especially in times of discipline, let us rest in the knowledge that God does not change (James 1:17). He is working in our world to accomplish his purposes for us and through us.

B. Prayer

Father, our times often resemble those of the prophet Habakkuk. Many solutions are offered to address such problems, but most ignore your wisdom and fail to see situations through your eyes. Empower your church by your Holy Spirit to speak forth with courage and clarity the love of Christ and the power of the gospel. We pray in Jesus' name. Amen.

C. Thought to Remember

Even when God seems far away,
he is always working in our circumstances.

INVOLVEMENT LEARNING

Enhance your lesson with NIV Bible Student *(from your curriculum supplier) and the reproducible activity page (at www.standardlesson.com or in the back of the* NIV Standard Lesson Commentary Deluxe Edition*).*

Into the Lesson

Before class, write the names of six fictional villains on 3" × 12" strips of paper, one name per strip. Possibilities include Professor Moriarty, Simon Legree, Norman Bates, the Joker, Captain Hook, the Wicked Witch of the West, Grendel, Lord Voldemort, Darth Vader, Hannibal Lecter, and Freddy Krueger.

Use the strips in a pyramid game. Call for two volunteers. Seat one volunteer with his or her back to a blank wall. On the wall behind that volunteer, attach three strips of paper to form a pyramid (triangle). Position the second volunteer facing the first volunteer and having a clear view of the pyramid. Starting at its peak, the second volunteer should quickly give clues to the identities of the villains to the first volunteer. Time how long it takes for the first volunteer to guess correctly all three. Then have another pair of volunteers do the same for the second set of three names.

Alternative. Distribute copies of the "Tyrants in Power" exercise from the activity page, which you can download. Have students work individually for no more than a minute (or in small groups for a few minutes) to complete as indicated.

After either activity say, "We recognize that this world has bad guys in it—not just fictional but terribly real. If God is good and all powerful, why doesn't he stop them? This is not a new question, as today's text reveals."

Into the Word

Divide students into two groups (or multiple groups if the class is large). Allow both groups access to Bibles. Give each group one of the two following handouts (you prepare):

Questioning Group—*God will not tolerate his people's questioning what he does or how he does it.* Modify this statement after reading Genesis 18:16-33; Jeremiah 20:7-18; Habakkuk 1:1-4; 2:20. Compare and contrast with Job 38–41.

Judgment Group—*God will only use those who follow him to execute judgment on others.* Refute this statement after reading Genesis 50:15-21; Jeremiah 43:10-13; Habakkuk 1:12-14.

After 15 minutes, allow groups to present their findings. The Questioning Group should point out that Habakkuk did indeed question God's apparent lack of action when the Babylonians prepared to attack Judah. But this was nothing new. Abraham questioned God about his plan to destroy Sodom, and Jeremiah complained that God allowed him to be ridiculed for speaking God's words. Even so, Habakkuk 2:20 and Job 38–41 reveal God's limits to humans' questioning his justice.

The Judgment Group will have found that God destined the wicked Babylonians to execute judgment on Judah. Joseph's brothers, in trying to kill their brother, were being used by God to save many people.

Alternative. Distribute copies of the "It Doesn't Add Up!" exercise from the activity page. Have students work in small groups to complete as indicated.

After either activity, point out that because God is sovereign, he can and does use even the actions people intend for evil to accomplish his will.

Into Life

Brainstorm a list of situations in which one might wonder if God is inactive. Consider especially violence and injustice. Then have the class choose one situation and discuss it as you pose these questions: 1–What might God be accomplishing in this situation? 2–Who are the instruments he may be using to do so? 3–How can we help achieve God's purposes in this situation? (Teaching tip: Do not pose all three questions at once. Instead, let the discussion run its course on one question before posing the next.)

If time allows, do the same with a second and third situation.

CONSEQUENCES FOR INJUSTICE

DEVOTIONAL READING: Psalm 130
BACKGROUND SCRIPTURE: Habakkuk 2

HABAKKUK 2:6-14

⁶ "Will not all of them taunt him with ridicule and scorn, saying,

'Woe to him who piles up stolen goods
and makes himself wealthy by
extortion!
How long must this go on?'

⁷ Will not your creditors suddenly arise?
Will they not wake up and make you
tremble?
Then you will become their prey.

⁸ Because you have plundered many
nations,
the peoples who are left will plunder
you.
For you have shed human blood;
you have destroyed lands and cities and
everyone in them.

⁹ Woe to him who builds his house by
unjust gain,
setting his nest on high
to escape the clutches of ruin!

¹⁰ You have plotted the ruin of many
peoples,
shaming your own house and forfeiting
your life.

¹¹ The stones of the wall will cry out,
and the beams of the woodwork will
echo it.

¹² Woe to him who builds a city with
bloodshed
and establishes a town by injustice!

¹³ Has not the LORD Almighty determined
that the people's labor is only fuel for
the fire,
that the nations exhaust themselves for
nothing?

¹⁴ For the earth will be filled with the
knowledge of the glory of the LORD
as the waters cover the sea."

KEY VERSE

Woe to him who builds a city with bloodshed and establishes a town by injustice! —**Habakkuk 2:12**

JUSTICE AND THE PROPHETS

Unit 1: God Requires Justice
LESSONS 1–5

LESSON AIMS

After participating in this lesson, each learner will be able to:

1. List some characteristics and consequences of injustice.

2. Contrast "the knowledge of the glory of the Lord" with human knowledge and its consequences.

3. Make a plan to exchange unholy human thought for "the knowledge of the glory of the Lord" in one regard in the week ahead.

LESSON OUTLINE

Introduction

A. Gone with the Fire

One of the most riveting scenes in the classic movie *Gone with the Wind* is the burning of Atlanta. The scene is incredible to watch—the intensity of the flames, the collapse of all the buildings. As the city burns, Rhett Butler says to Scarlett O'Hara, "There goes the last of the Old South." Everything they had amassed was gone with the fire.

The destruction of all that Judah had amassed took several years to accomplish. However, when God had finished with his discipline of the people, the old Judah was just as surely gone.

B. Lesson Context

Today's lesson is taken once again from the writings of the prophet Habakkuk (see lesson 2). The Lesson Context from last week's study therefore applies, and so that material need not be repeated here. Even so, more can be said. Habakkuk 2 begins with Habakkuk's description of himself standing watch on a tower to wait for the Lord's response to his objections (Habakkuk 2:1). The Lord tells Habakkuk to record on tablets the "revelation" he is about to receive so that a messenger can deliver it (2:2). Though the prophecy could be read and understood easily, it was ambiguous regarding its timing. But when the time came, events unfolded quickly (2:3).

The Lord also described the lawless, arrogant attitude and lifestyle of the typical Babylonian leader (Habakkuk 2:4, 5). In this way, God emphasized that he was not unaware of their faults; nevertheless, he had work for them to do.

I. First Woe
(HABAKKUK 2:6-8)
A. Unbridled Greed (v. 6)

6a. "Will not all of them taunt him with ridicule and scorn, saying,

Him refers to the Babylonian Empire, personified as a single representative person. The word *them* refers to nations and people who are the victims of the Babylonians' aggression and brutality

(Habakkuk 2:5). The Babylonians will experience an unpleasant role reversal: the people they victimize will be in a position to *ridicule* them (see also Isaiah 23:13).

The Hebrew word translated *taunt* can also be rendered "proverb" (examples: 1 Kings 4:32; Proverbs 1:1; Ezekiel 12:22). In certain contexts like this one, the word can take on negative overtones, such as "byword" (example: Psalm 44:14). In context, Habakkuk describes a mocking kind of speech, perhaps similar to what is referred to today as trash talk. It is only fitting that such language be directed toward the Babylonians, a people who have become renowned for ravaging other peoples and their lands and possessions.

6b. "Woe to him who piles up stolen goods

Woe introduces judgment (Amos 5:18; see lesson 1). This particular woe is the first of five within Habakkuk 2 (see also Habakkuk 2:9, 12, 15, and 19). The judgment introduced is directed against the one who takes what is not his, a clear violation of Israel's eighth commandment (Exodus 20:15).

> *What Do You Think?*
> Which problem should take priority in being addressed: greed that leads to injustice, or the injustice itself?
> *Digging Deeper*
> Does the answer change depending on local context? Why, or why not?

We do well to note that the Babylonians never pledged faithfulness to a covenant with God. Though they have their own laws that prohibit stealing and other offenses, they are not bound by the Ten Commandments in the same way that the Israelites are. Even so, the Babylonians still violate what they know to be right (compare Romans 2:14, 15). The Babylonians simply do not care about theft when conquered people are concerned. The wealth of weaker nations is theirs for the taking.

6c. "'and makes himself wealthy by extortion! How long must this go on?'

The phrase *makes himself wealthy by extortion* probably is an idiom that implies involvement in threats of violence. Such a person is part of a group whose members are as "thick as thieves." Like any thief or extortionist, the Babylonians' trade practices burden their trade partners and take no concern for the needs of others. Habakkuk points out that even the Babylonians' normal legal practices are unethical and immoral.

The prophet himself has already asked the question *how long?* (Habakkuk 1:2; see lesson 2). Here the question is a part of the taunt that the people of the earth direct against the seemingly invincible Babylonians.

B. Unexpected Punishment (vv. 7, 8)

7a. "Will not your creditors suddenly arise? Will they not wake up and make you tremble?

The word *creditors* refers to those in the previous verse whose possessions have been unjustly seized by the Babylonians. The vagueness of this word could refer to many different groups of people since Babylon oppresses many different nations. This prophecy therefore expresses God's concern not only for Judah but for all who suffer because of Babylon. Eventually, however, the Babylonians will be on the receiving end of hostile treatment.

Although this verse is addressed to *you*—the Babylonians—this text may never be read by any of them. Even if they do read it, they are not the intended audience. Judah remains Habakkuk's focus. The prophecy's intent is to reassure Judah that the people's oppressors will not always have the upper hand.

The role reversal pictured will be sudden and unexpected. This agrees with the Lord's earlier word that when the fulfillment of the prophet's "revelation" occurs, it will come without delay

HOW TO SAY IT

Babylonians	Bab-ih-*low*-nee-unz.
Jehoiachin	Jeh-*hoy*-uh-kin.
Edom	*Ee*-dum.
Habakkuk	Huh-*back*-kuk.
Obadiah	O-buh-*dye*-uh.
seraphim	*sair*-uh-fim.
Zechariah	Zek-uh-*rye*-uh.

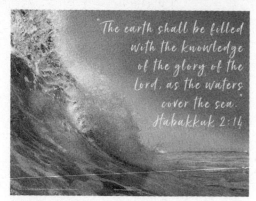

The earth shall be filled with the knowledge of the glory of the Lord, as the waters cover the sea.
Habakkuk 2:14

Visual for Lesson 3. *Ask the class to focus on verse 14, imagining what the earth will be like when it is filled with this knowledge, before closing in prayer.*

(Habakkuk 2:3). God says that the problem will not continue indefinitely. The Babylonians will receive their just deserts. The tables will be turned when the abuser becomes the abused.

The language anticipates the description of the suddenness of Jesus' return. People will be feeling quite comfortable and at ease when sudden destruction comes—destruction they cannot escape (1 Thessalonians 5:1-3).

> **What Do You Think?**
> What are some practical ways to exercise a faith that says "God is still in charge" during periods of societal unrest?
> *Digging Deeper*
> How would you explain to someone that such faith isn't a blind faith, but is faith based on the evidence of history?

7b. "Then you will become their prey.

This idea builds on the previous one. The word translated *prey* refers to the spoils of victory (compare the translation of the same word in Isaiah 42:24). The Babylonians take an abundance of spoils from those they conquer. But soon it will be their turn to experience the trauma of powerlessness in the face of a stronger foe (compare Proverbs 29:1; Ezekiel 39:10; Zechariah 2:8, 9). Indeed, Babylon will fall to the Persians in 539 BC (see 2 Chronicles 36:20).

8. "Because you have plundered many

nations, the people who are left will plunder you. For you have shed human blood; you have destroyed lands and cities and everyone in them.**

This verse again emphasizes the reversal of fortunes that the Babylonians will suffer. Those who have suffered because of the Babylonians' cruelty will no doubt take pleasure in gaining the upper hand on their tormenter. Obadiah's rebuke of Edom also applies to Babylon: "As you have done, it will be done to you" (Obadiah 15; compare Isaiah 33:1; Habakkuk 2:17; Galatians 6:7).

Condemning the Babylonians for destroying both *lands and cities* is a way of holding them accountable for the mistreatment that happens throughout every nation where they hold power (compare Jeremiah 50:17, 18). The note of violence against *everyone in them* further emphasizes the totality of Babylonian guilt. They have not harmed just one city or one group of people; everyone who deals with Babylon suffers.

❧ To Rob a Thief ❧

A popular genre of movies is the heist flick, in which characters assemble to commit a bold robbery. The victim of the theft is usually a person who gained wealth by dishonest means. Such a movie has an appeal across cultures, as the existence of such movies originally produced in many of the world's languages demonstrates.

In the comedic Spanish-language heist movie *To Rob a Thief,* two former thieves plot to rob the biggest thief they know: a TV infomercial producer. That shyster had made a fortune by selling worthless products to poor Latino immigrants. The two would-be thieves assemble a team of ordinary refugees to pull off a bold crime of revenge. The plot involves gaining entry into a well-guarded mansion, accessing a vault, and then getting the money off the property.

To Rob a Thief has joined the ranks of many other Hollywood "caper" movies. But the basic plot is centuries old. Though the Babylonians had long stolen from others, they would be stolen from by the very people they had wronged. There's more than a ring of truth to the axiom "What goes around, comes around." How do we keep from getting caught in that vicious loop?

—J. E.

II. Second Woe
(HABAKKUK 2:9-11)
A. Built to Escape Evil (vv. 9, 10)

9. "Woe to him who builds his house by unjust gain, setting his nest on high to escape the clutches of ruin!

This is the second of the woes uttered by Habakkuk in our lesson text. It calls attention to the Babylonians' breaking of the tenth commandment by their *unjust gain* brought on by covetous desire (compare Exodus 20:17; see on Habakkuk 2:6b, above). Such a person *builds his house* with self-centered pride (compare Jeremiah 22:13). Habakkuk compares him to a bird that sets its *nest on high* in order to escape potential threats. The higher the structure, the more secure is the resident from *ruin* or harm—or so he thinks (contrast Isaiah 10:12-14). This person seeks to remove himself or herself from the problems of society by residing above it all. This person wants to live in the fortress of an enclave of wealth, which is untouched by the poor and needy.

> *What Do You Think?*
> How can you recognize when your desire for something crosses the line into greed or covetousness?
> *Digging Deeper*
> What blind spots do you see in others in this regard? How will you keep those blind spots from becoming your own?

The prophet's language echoes again what the prophet Obadiah says of the arrogance of the people of Edom. They have built their dwellings in "the clefts of the rocks," and they feel safe from any danger (Obadiah 3). But the Lord says, "Though you soar like the eagle and make your nest among the stars, from there I will bring you down" (v. 4).

❧ *LIVING HIGH* ❧

Since the eighteenth century, the phrase *high life* has been an English expression describing a lifestyle of luxury. In the 1920s, however, the term developed a very literal application.

The economic growth of the roaring twenties brought a construction boom to New York City. The wealthiest business people in the city sought to live above it all—literally. The idea of a penthouse apartment was born. Those who could afford them built luxury apartments on the top floors of buildings, apartments with views of the city above the crowds.

Habakkuk's description of the proud Babylonians sounds eerily like the financial high rollers of the 1920s. But just as the financial boom raised them up high, the stock market crash of 1929 brought them down. What "penthouses" might God be preparing to bring low in our lives?

—J. E.

10. "You have plotted the ruin of many peoples, shaming your own house and forfeiting your life.

The Lord highlights the violence wrought by the Babylonians against *many peoples*. The Babylonians view what they do as a legitimate expression of their power and dominance. The plotting of the *ruin* of these people described here may refer to the way in which the Babylonians abuse helpless people and take their goods in the process of constructing their own lavish homes.

> *What Do You Think?*
> In what contexts of modern injustice will declarations of shame be either effective or ineffective? Why?
> *Digging Deeper*
> In what ways do 1 Corinthians 4:14; 6:5; and 15:34 influence your response?

According to the Babylonians' worldview, "might makes right." But God sees their actions for what they really are: a sin against him and against themselves (compare Jeremiah 26:19; Habakkuk 2:16, not in our text). From the safety of a fortress-home, the greedy person continues to oppress the poor. The sin is so serious that God says this person has shamed his *own house*, referring to the inner person. Therefore, that person's *life* is now forfeit; the God of justice will respond with wrath.

B. Buildings Protest Evil (v. 11)

11. "The stones of the wall will cry out, and the beams of the woodwork will echo it.

We sometimes say, "If these walls could talk." Oh, the stories an old house could tell! The aforementioned house has been constructed with suspect motives and methods. Habakkuk pictures the *stones* and wooden *beams* crying out against their selfish builders (compare Joshua 24:27; Luke 19:40). The house may be solid structurally and made of the highest quality materials, but it will not be able to withstand the Lord's judgment.

Sadly, the Babylonians are not alone in their repulsive building practices. The prophet Jeremiah, a contemporary of Habakkuk, speaks of how King Jehoiachin of Judah has constructed his house unrighteously. He has done so by withholding fair wages from those who did the work (Jeremiah 22:13). A king who rules the Lord's covenant people should possess an understanding of what he requires (Deuteronomy 17:18-20). But this king has acted no better than the Babylonians.

For this reason, Jehoiachin and his people will find themselves in Babylonian captivity (Jeremiah 22:25-27). This will happen even though the Babylonians overall are arguably more wicked than the people of Judah.

III. Third Woe
(HABAKKUK 2:12-14)

A. Fiendish Cities (v. 12)

12. "Woe to him who builds a city with bloodshed and establishes a town by injustice!

Habakkuk now presents his third *woe* against the Babylonians. This woe builds on the previous two. The prophet pronounces judgment on the Babylonians for the heartless way in which they have built entire towns and cities. Accusing them of building *a city with bloodshed* does not mean that blood is literally a building material. Instead, the accusation focuses on the means by which the people came to build. In this case, violence and *injustice* account for the prosperity that built the cities (compare Ezekiel 22:2). Spilled blood will cry out like the stones and beams in Habakkuk 2:11 (above), and it will cry out for the Lord's vengeance, even as Abel's blood cried out from the ground to indict his brother Cain (Genesis 4:10).

Once more the Babylonians are not alone in their guilt for such deplorable actions. The leaders in Jerusalem, the site of Solomon's great temple, built that city using the same resources highlighted by Habakkuk: *bloodshed* and *injustice* (Micah 3:9, 10; see lesson 4).

B. Futile Human Efforts (v. 13)

13. "Has not the LORD Almighty determined that the people's labor is only fuel for the fire, that the nations exhaust themselves for nothing?

Thus far in this series of charges directed against the Babylonians, the Lord's name has not been mentioned. Now it becomes explicit that he is the one who will hold these people accountable for their actions. His intention is that all that the Babylonians have constructed—the houses and towns of which they are so excessively proud—will be cast into the *fire* (compare Isaiah 50:11). The builders are willing to *exhaust themselves* as they pour themselves into their work, since they are certain that what they do will last far into the future. But God says that their work will come to *nothing*.

Jeremiah uses language very similar to Habakkuk's as part of an extensive message of judgment on Babylon (see Jeremiah 50, 51). The walls and gates of Babylon will be destroyed by fire (51:58). Centuries later, the apostle Peter will write of a similar conflagration to occur on the day of the Lord, the day when Jesus returns (2 Peter 3:10).

C. Future Divine Plan (v. 14)

14. "For the earth will be filled with the knowledge of the glory of the LORD as the waters cover the sea."

Like many passages from the prophets, the predictions of doom and gloom are not the last word. Habakkuk ends this section with a word of hope, looking forward to a time when there will be universal acknowledgment of the Lord God.

The prophet Isaiah, whose ministry began well before Habakkuk's, also spoke of a global *knowledge of the glory of the Lord,* even using the same water comparison that Habakkuk does (Isaiah 11:9). All people will be engulfed by this spiritual deluge. There will be no holdouts who continue to deny the greatness and majesty of the Lord.

> **What Do You Think?**
> What are some ways to use Habakkuk 2:14 as a faith anchor in the face of injustice?
> *Digging Deeper*
> How can we ensure that we won't use the promise of this verse as an excuse not to act against injustice?

People such as the Babylonians, who view themselves as invincible, will find themselves brought to their knees before almighty God. They will learn what real glory is (compare Exodus 16:6, 7). It is not found in the accomplishments of empires such as Babylon, which are destined for the fire as Habakkuk has just declared. Rather, it is found in the worldwide recognition that the Lord reigns supreme as "all in all" (1 Corinthians 15:28).

It is true, as the seraphim proclaimed to Isaiah during his prophetic call, that even now "the whole earth is full of [God's] glory" (Isaiah 6:3; see also Numbers 14:21). But the knowledge or recognition of that glory is something that proud, defiant individuals and nations refuse to acknowledge. Individuals see evidence of that glory every day, but will not humble themselves in worship to the source, the creator God.

But a day is coming when "every knee should bow . . . and every tongue acknowledge that Jesus Christ is Lord, to the glory of God the Father" (Philippians 2:10, 11; compare Isaiah 45:23). Habakkuk sees that day of global glory coming. The administration of final judgment at the end of time when Jesus returns may well be part of what Habakkuk meant when he declared that the whole earth will fully know the glory of the Lord. True justice carried out by an all-wise God will be something glorious indeed!

In the last chapter of his book, Habakkuk looks forward to a time when God's glory will cover the heavens and the earth will be filled with his praise (Habakkuk 3:3). This promise comforted the suffering saints of Habakkuk's day and gives hope to Christians today. Centuries after Habakkuk, the apostle Peter offered similar hope when he wrote that we "participate in the sufferings of Christ, so that you may be overjoyed when his glory is revealed" (1 Peter 4:13).

Conclusion
A. Justice for All

What *Gone with the Wind* so dramatically portrayed about the 1864 burning of Atlanta is what Habakkuk said awaited the Babylonians. All their possessions would be fuel for the fire (Habakkuk 2:13). This is in fact the future that awaits the entire world (again, 2 Peter 3:10). Today's lesson reminds us that the Lord will make certain that justice is carried out against evildoers.

"Justice for all" is very easy to say and desire. But putting hands and feet to this desire is quite another matter. Cries for justice echo throughout every society. Acts of violence against individuals or groups are followed by demands that justice be served and those responsible for the violence be punished. Systems that methodically keep people in positions to be mistreated are protested because they perpetuate injustice—sometimes on a massive scale. The whole world longs for justice.

Today's study from Habakkuk, along with the testimony of Scripture as a whole, assures us that God will right all wrongs committed by human beings. Sinners may escape the punishment required by human law, but they cannot dodge Heaven's law so cleverly.

B. Prayer

Father, may the works of our hands anticipate the day when the earth will know your glory. We pray in Jesus' name. Amen.

C. Thought to Remember

The Lord, the righteous judge, makes certain that justice prevails.

INVOLVEMENT LEARNING

Enhance your lesson with NIV Bible Student (from your curriculum supplier) and the reproducible activity page (at www.standardlesson.com or in the back of the NIV Standard Lesson Commentary Deluxe Edition).

Into the Lesson

Before class, write these situations on the board:

A 10-year-old leaves dirty clothes on the floor.
A 15-year-old wants to set his own bedtime.
A young teen refuses to shower regularly.
A 9-year-old keeps leaving toys outside.
A 7-year-old cheats at board games.

Have the class speculate as to what the natural consequence of each bad decision may be. Jot responses on the board.

Alternative. Distribute copies of the "Consequotation" exercise on the activity page, which you can download. Have students work in pairs to complete the puzzle as directed.

After either activity say, "The fact is, actions have consequences. Let's see what the ancient prophet Habakkuk learned from God in that regard."

Into the Word

Divide the class into three groups. Give each group one of these Scripture segments:

Powerful Plunderers Group: Habakkuk 2:6-8
High Houses Group: Habakkuk 2:9-11
Bloody Builders Group: Habakkuk 2:12-14

Have groups summarize their texts with four-line poems. Give them about 15 minutes to work. For groups slow to start, use one or more of the following as samples:

Powerful Plunderers Group (Habakkuk 2:6-8):
A nation that lies, cheats, and steals
* May enjoy luxury and sumptuous meals.*
But the tables will turn one day,
* And they will be the ones who pay!*

High Houses Group (Habakkuk 2:9-11):
They build their castles in the sky
* And look down on the one who passes by.*
But when their houses are filled with strife,
* They'll lose their home and lose their life!*

Bloody Builders Group (Habakkuk 2:12-14):
They have it all and still want more,
* So they build a kingdom by blood and war.*
But the world is not conquered by any who sin.
* At the end of it all, only God wins!*

Next, make and distribute copies of the following matching activity for learners to complete individually. Inform learners that this is a Bible speed drill; you will call time in 60 seconds.

HUMAN THOUGHT VS. GOD'S WISDOM

___1. Get rich by charging high interest rates
___2. Enjoy life by eating and drinking in quantity
___3. Build luxurious houses while others are in need
___4. Sacrifice the good of family to build wealth
___5. Seek stability through bribes and bloodshed
___6. Work oneself to death to get rich

a. Proverbs 11:29   b. Proverbs 15:25
c. Proverbs 23:20, 21   d. Proverbs 23:4
e. Proverbs 28:8   f. Proverbs 29:4

Directions: Match the example of wrong thinking against the wisdom of God found in Proverbs.
[Do not put these expected matches on the handout: 1–e; 2–c; 3–b; 4–a; 5–f; 6–d]

Option. Distribute copies of the "From the Dustbin of History" exercise from the activity page. After learners complete it in pairs, discuss why people don't seem to learn the lessons that the examples of failed despots have to teach.

Into Life

From the matching exercise above, challenge learners to choose the proverb that speaks to them most strongly. Ask for volunteers to state which and why, but don't put anyone on the spot. Propose that they pray over it daily in the week ahead, having the goal of exchanging an unholy human thought for "the knowledge of the glory of the Lord." State your intention to ask at the beginning of next week's class how things went.

An Argument Against Corruption

DEVOTIONAL READING: Zechariah 7:8-10; Deuteronomy 24:17-22
BACKGROUND SCRIPTURE: Micah 3–6

MICAH 3:1-3, 9-12

¹ Then I said,
"Listen, you leaders of Jacob,
    you rulers of Israel.
Should you not embrace justice,
²   you who hate good and love evil;
who tear the skin from my people
    and the flesh from their bones;
³ who eat my people's flesh,
    strip off their skin
    and break their bones in pieces;
who chop them up like meat for the pan,
    like flesh for the pot?"

· ·

⁹ Hear this, you leaders of Jacob,
    you rulers of Israel,
who despise justice
    and distort all that is right;
¹⁰ who build Zion with bloodshed,
    and Jerusalem with wickedness.
¹¹ Her leaders judge for a bribe,
    her priests teach for a price,
    and her prophets tell fortunes for
        money.
Yet they look for the LORD's support and
    say,

"Is not the LORD among us?
    No disaster will come upon us."
¹² Therefore because of you,
    Zion will be plowed like a field,
Jerusalem will become a heap of rubble,
    the temple hill a mound overgrown
        with thickets.

MICAH 6:6-8

⁶ With what shall I come before the LORD
    and bow down before the exalted God?
Shall I come before him with burnt
        offerings,
    with calves a year old?
⁷ Will the LORD be pleased with thousands
        of rams,
    with ten thousand rivers of olive oil?
Shall I offer my firstborn for my
        transgression,
    the fruit of my body for the sin of my
        soul?
⁸ He has shown you, O mortal, what is
        good.
    And what does the LORD require of you?
To act justly and to love mercy
    and to walk humbly with your God.

KEY VERSE

He has shown you, O mortal, what is good. And what does the LORD require of you? To act justly and to love mercy and to walk humbly with your God. —**Micah 6:8**

JUSTICE AND THE PROPHETS

Unit 1: God Requires Justice
LESSONS 1–5

LESSON AIMS

After participating in this lesson, each learner will be able to:

1. Summarize the condition of Judean leadership of the late eighth century BC.

2. Explain why the requirements of Micah 6:8 were especially necessary for leaders of the day.

3. Write one prayer per day in the week ahead for different church leaders—that the standards of Micah 6:8 would be theirs as well.

LESSON OUTLINE

Introduction
  A. Warped
  B. Lesson Context
  I. Hateful Leadership (MICAH 3:1-3)
  A. Despising Principles (vv. 1, 2a)
  B. Consuming People (vv. 2b, 3)
    Cannibalism
  II. Hypocritical Leadership (MICAH 3:9-12)
  A. Guilty Leaders (v. 9)
  B. Greedy Leaders (vv. 10, 11a)
  C. Declaring God's Presence (v. 11b)
  D. Deserving God's Judgment (v. 12)
    Indulgences
  III. Heavenly Living (MICAH 6:6-8)
  A. People's Ideas (vv. 6, 7)
  B. God's Ideal (v. 8)
Conclusion
  A. Humbly in Justice and Mercy
  B. Prayer
  C. Thought to Remember

Introduction
A. Warped

A certain funeral home sets up a nativity scene on its front lawn each Christmas season. One year, someone vandalized the nativity set. The perpetrator stole the Christ-child figure and replaced it with a stuffed monkey. The vandal also broke off the fingers of other figures and let the live sheep, goats, and donkeys out of the fenced area.

A few days later, the vandal confessed and returned the stolen figure of the baby Jesus. Even so, one can empathize with the funeral director's frustration when he said, "Why people would come here and show such disrespect, I don't know. You have to have a warped mind to do something like this."

The prophet Micah indicted the leaders of his day for their own brand of vandalism. But Micah described how real people were being abused and mistreated by those responsible for their care. They too were guilty of having warped minds. And such minds tend to excel at hiding behind warped self-justification.

B. Lesson Context

The book of Micah is another of the 12 Minor Prophets. Micah's ministry took place in the second half of the eighth century BC. His times were full of turmoil and uncertainty for both Israel (the northern kingdom) and Judah (the southern kingdom). The Assyrians were a formidable threat to both kingdoms. They were the instrument in God's hands to carry out his judgment against Israel when the capital city of Samaria fell in 722 BC.

Micah's ministry may have overlapped with that of Amos (see lesson 1). While the ministry of the latter is dated during the reign of Uzziah king of Judah (about 785–734 BC; Amos 1:1), Micah 1:1 describes Micah's ministry as occurring during the reigns of Jotham (Uzziah's son), Jotham's son Ahaz, and Jotham's grandson Hezekiah. Jotham's reign, however, overlapped Uzziah's. While Uzziah was confined during the latter years of his reign, Jotham ruled in his stead (2 Chronicles 26:16-23).

Micah and Isaiah were contemporaries (compare the lists of kings in Isaiah 1:1 and Micah 1:1). Both ministered in Jerusalem. Micah's message included words of judgment against both Israel and Judah. His book begins with a reference to Samaria and Jerusalem, representing Israel and Judah respectively (1:1). Both are indicted for rebellion against the Lord (1:5-9).

I. Hateful Leadership
(MICAH 3:1-3)

In Micah 3, the source of today's study, we see language reminiscent of that found in the previous study from Habakkuk 2 (see lesson 3). Habakkuk, however, was describing the conduct of the foreign Babylonians. Sadly, Micah is describing the behavior of those who are part of God's covenant people and should know better.

A. Despising Principles (vv. 1, 2a)
1. Then I said, "Listen you leaders of Jacob, you rulers of Israel. Should you not embrace justice,

The Hebrew word translated *listen* often introduces prophecy in the book of Micah (examples: Micah 1:2; 3:1, 9; 6:1, 2; contrast "obeyed" in 5:15). The same word introduces Deuteronomy 6:4, 5, which Jesus will call "the first and greatest commandment" (Matthew 22:38). The implication of its use is not just that ears will hear but that hearts will comprehend the words and lives will change as a result (contrast Isaiah 6:9, 10).

The designations *Jacob* and *Israel* refer historically to one man who had his name changed (Genesis 32:28; 46:2). As here, the names are often paired in Hebrew poetry as parallel expressions that refer to the same thing: God's covenant people (examples: Psalm 14:7; Isaiah 9:8). Similarly, *leaders* and *rulers* both refer to the same group of people (see Numbers 1:16; Joshua 22:30).

Micah begins his address to the leaders with a rhetorical question about their knowledge of *justice*. The question implies that leaders ought to know what true justice is and how to exercise it faithfully and consistently (see commentary on Micah 3:9; Amos 5:24 in lesson 1).

Justice requires God's people to behave according to His righteous standards (contrast Jeremiah 5:5; Matthew 23:23). Exercising justice reflects a person's awareness of God's standards of right and wrong (example: Leviticus 19:15).

2a. "you who hate good and love evil;

The leaders' hatred for *good* and *love* for *evil* makes it impossible for them to administer proper justice. Their moral compass points in the wrong direction. Both Isaiah (in Judah) and Amos (in Israel) address this perversion of values at about the same time (Isaiah 5:20; Amos 5:14, 15). Both northern and southern kingdoms are guilty of rejecting the Lord's standards.

> *What Do You Think?*
> How would you explain to someone the difference between good and evil?
> *Digging Deeper*
> Considering 1 Corinthians 9:19-23, how would your explanation to Christians differ from an explanation to unbelievers, if at all? Why?

B. Consuming People (vv. 2b, 3)
2b. "who tear the skin from my people and the flesh from their bones;

Micah uses graphic language in portraying how offensive and destructive the leaders' behavior is (compare Psalm 53:4; Ezekiel 22:27). But this is only the beginning of his shocking description.

One should understand that these gruesome actions are not happening in a literal, physical sense. There are references to and predictions of literal cannibalism in the Bible (example: 2 Kings 6:26-29), but this is not one of them. Rather, Micah uses figurative, symbolic language to illustrate the extreme degree to which these leaders hate the good and love the evil (compare Psalm 14:4; Proverbs 30:14; Zephaniah 3:3). They are so indifferent to the people they are meant to serve that they can be compared to butchers.

3. "who eat my people's flesh, strip off their skin and break their bones in pieces; who chop them up like meat for the pan, like flesh for the pot?"

Micah continues building on the cannibalistic

overtone of the previous verse. For the leaders to *strip off* the people's *skin* implies excessively cruel treatment. The leaders are meant to administer justice and uphold righteousness. Doing so would allow the people to flourish, both physically and spiritually. Instead, the leaders do the opposite by perverting justice and thwarting righteousness. Ezekiel, whose ministry will take place more than a century later among the captives in Babylon, uses similar language (Ezekiel 11:2-7; 24:3-6).

Centuries later, Jesus will describe the leaders' greediness when he speaks of how the teachers of the law "devour widows' houses" (Luke 20:46, 47). Paul in turn warns Christians against our own type of cannibalism in Galatians 5:15.

❧ CANNIBALISM ❧

The practice of humans eating the flesh of other human beings is well documented. Chinese emperors ate human flesh as a delicacy. Christopher Columbus reported on cannibalism in the Caribbean, at least partly so that he could conquer the islands by whatever means he desired. Throughout the sixteenth and seventeenth centuries, some Europeans ingested human body parts for medicinal purposes. As recently as the 1960s, the Fore people of Papua, New Guinea, traditionally ate parts of the bodies of recently deceased relatives.

Micah used images of cannibalism as a shocking illustration of the unjust practices in his day. He condemned Israel's leaders for treating people as sources of nourishment instead of as creatures made in God's image. Christians today must still beware of the tendency to use people to get what they need instead of valuing them simply as God's beloved creatures. How do you resist "cannibalizing" others?　　　—J. E.

> **What Do You Think?**
> What modern imagery would you use to describe corrupt leaders today? Why?
> **Digging Deeper**
> How do you harmonize your response with Acts 23:5; Romans 13:1, 2, 7; 1 Timothy 2:1, 2; 1 Peter 2:17; and Jude 8, 9?

II. Hypocritical Leadership
(MICAH 3:9-12)

In Micah 3:4-8 (not in today's lesson), the prophet declares the Lord's judgment on the leaders (compare Deuteronomy 1:45). Then Micah exposes false prophets (Micah 3:5-7; compare Isaiah 29:10). Micah contrasts their selfish motives with the divine authority that undergirds his own prophetic ministry (Micah 3:8). This sets the stage for further condemnation, next.

A. Guilty Leaders (v. 9)

9. Hear this, you leaders of Jacob, you rulers of Israel, who despise justice and distort all that is right;

Micah again calls on the *leaders* and *rulers* of God's people to *hear* his message. But whereas in Micah 3:1 the prophet posed a rhetorical question to challenge the leaders in the matter of justice, here he bluntly accuses them of unjust behavior. They actually *despise justice* and twist the meaning of it to suit their own selfish purposes (compare Psalm 58:1, 2; Isaiah 1:23).

B. Greedy Leaders (vv. 10, 11a)

10. who build Zion with bloodshed, and Jerusalem with wickedness.

The final three verses of Micah 3 clearly focus on the southern kingdom of Judah and its capital city, *Jerusalem*. Though *Zion* was originally a specific location within Jerusalem, it gradually came to refer to the entire city. The two terms are therefore used together in parallel accusations against the city. Habakkuk indicted the Babylonians for building *with bloodshed, and . . . wickedness* (Habakkuk 2:12; see lesson 3). Here it is not the pagans but the leaders of God's covenant people who are charged with cruelty (compare Isaiah 59:7).

The implication, like that of the butchering image before, is that the leaders are taking advantage of the people for their own gain (compare Jeremiah 22:13, 17; Micah 7:2).

11a. Her leaders judge for a bribe, her priests teach for a price, and her prophets tell fortunes for money.

Three crucial leadership functions are listed here along with transgressions. When the Lord established the function of *judge*, he made it clear that those exercising this responsibility must never accept bribes or exhibit favoritism in their decisions (see Leviticus 19:15; Deuteronomy 16:18-20). The *leaders* in Micah's time blatantly ignore these standards (compare Malachi 2:9, next week's lesson). All they are interested in is what reward, in the form of *a bribe*, they can obtain for their services.

The *priests* and *prophets*, whose offices are especially sacred, are no better. They too are guided by financial rather than spiritual priorities. They are willing to lie in order to earn their fee (see Jeremiah 6:13; Ezekiel 13:19; 34:2). The prophets are described as those who *tell fortunes for money*. The practice of divination was strictly forbidden for God's people (Deuteronomy 18:10, 14). Its practice is listed as a reason why God's judgment fell on the northern kingdom of Israel (2 Kings 17:17, 18).

Paul will later teach that "those who preach the gospel should receive their living from the gospel" and be compensated for their work (1 Corinthians 9:14). His method and motive are very different from those condemned by Micah, however. The leaders of Micah's day are motivated by greed, and they use a forbidden method to satisfy that greed. Neither greed nor a forbidden method applies to Paul.

> ### What Do You Think?
> In what contexts and in what positions do (or would) you favor the idea of paying church leaders? Why?
> #### Digging Deeper
> How do the texts of Acts 18:3; 1 Corinthians 9:3-18; 2 Corinthians 2:17; 1 Thessalonians 2:5; 1 Timothy 5:17, 18; and/or 2 Peter 2:3 inform your response?

C. Declaring God's Presence (v. 11b)

11b. Yet they look for the LORD's support and say, "Is not the LORD among us? No disaster will come upon us."

As if these disgraceful practices are not enough,

these fraudulent leaders have the audacity to claim God's presence as a cover for their detestable conduct (see also Jeremiah 7:4). The Lord had promised to place his name in Jerusalem when Solomon built his temple there. But that promise remains contingent on the people's obedience (2 Chronicles 7:12-22). The leaders in Micah's day are prime examples of disobedience.

D. Deserving God's Judgment (v. 12)

12. Therefore because of you, Zion will be plowed like a field, Jerusalem will become a heap of rubble, the temple hill a mound overgrown with thickets.

Such arrogant, brazen behavior by the leaders of God's people cannot be tolerated. The "disaster" that the leaders confidently claim will never come (Micah 3:11b) will indeed come—and its arrival will be unforgettably severe. *Jerusalem,* the great city of David, will be reduced to *a heap of rubble* (compare Leviticus 26:31; Isaiah 6:11; Jeremiah 22:6). No longer will anyone travel to Jerusalem to worship (contrast Psalm 122:3, 4). Instead, they will go to marvel at the extensive destruction that has taken place (1 Kings 9:6-9; compare Ezekiel 5:14, 15). *Zion* will be treated as nothing more than a *field* for plowing (Lamentations 5:18). The *temple hill,* which refers to the location of the house of the Lord, will be reduced to a forested area.

Approximately 100 years after Micah's time, his prophecy of Jerusalem's demise will be quoted by some of the elders in Jerusalem as a warning not to ignore Jeremiah's message (Jeremiah 26:17, 18). They note that King Hezekiah heeded Micah's warning. Rejecting this example and ignoring Jeremiah will imperil the whole city (26:19).

HOW TO SAY IT

Ahaz	*Ay*-haz.
Babylonians	Bab-ih-*low*-nee-unz.
Hezekiah	Hez-ih-*kye*-uh.
Jotham	*Jo*-thum.
Micah	*My*-kuh.
Samaria	Suh-*mare*-ee-uh.
Uzziah	Uh-*zye*-uh.

Johann Tetzel (1465–1519) may have had as important a part in launching the Protestant Reformation as any of the great reformers had. Tetzel's notoriety, however, derives from his negative example.

Tetzel was a German Dominican friar of prominence in the Roman Catholic Church. He was known to grant indulgences on behalf of the church in exchange for money. An indulgence was claimed to allow a remission of punishment in purgatory, thereby allowing a deceased person quicker admission into Heaven. Martin Luther's strong condemnation of Tetzel's actions helped spark the Reformation.

Tetzel's lack of scruples, sanctioned by others in the hierarchy of the medieval church, led to the undermining of Roman Catholicism's power in Europe. Had that hierarchy paid closer attention to Micah 3, the outcome could have been different. Indulging in wickedness instead of righteousness invites God's disapproval and judgment. How can you keep from being a negative example in that regard?
—J. E.

III. Heavenly Living
(MICAH 6:6-8)

Micah 6 opens with the prophet's final appeal to the people to hear what the Lord has to say (see commentary on Micah 3:1). Whereas the previous call was aimed primarily at Judah's leadership, this one is directed at the people (6:3). The Lord portrays them as defendants on a witness stand, facing a series of questions from him. He proceeds to give the people a history lesson, recounting his gracious acts on their ancestors' behalf (6:4, 5).

A. People's Ideas (vv. 6, 7)

6. With what shall I come before the LORD and bow down before the exalted God? Shall I come before him with burnt offerings, with calves a year old?

Micah appears to put himself in the position of the defendants who are on trial before the Lord (see Micah 6:2, 3). The questions he poses may reflect the people's genuine puzzlement (compare

6:7). More likely, they are meant to expose the people's willful ignorance (contrast Psalms 40:6-8; 51:16, 17).

Burnt offerings are foundational in the Old Testament sacrificial system (Leviticus 1). The daily requirement is two unblemished year-old lambs (Numbers 28:3). *Calves a year old* are even more costly than the two lambs. The question here suggests that God asks too much of his people! At least, this is how the people seem to justify themselves for their iniquities.

7a. Will the LORD be pleased with thousands of rams, with ten thousand rivers of olive oil?

Micah continues his questions by increasing the quantity of what might be brought before the Lord. Do numbers impress God? Is he looking for *thousands of rams* or *rivers of olive oil*? Again, the implication is that the people cannot give enough to please the Lord. In a way, this is true: without the heart behind the sacrifice, nothing will please God (compare Isaiah 1:11; Amos 5:22).

7b. Shall I offer my firstborn for my transgression, the fruit of my body for the sin of my soul?

Micah raises the stakes even higher by suggesting the sacrifice of a *firstborn* child. The firstborn is of special significance to the Lord (Exodus 13:2). Child sacrifice is always forbidden (Leviticus 18:21; 20:2-5; Deuteronomy 18:10), but the argument here is not about child sacrifice. Rather, the people feel that not even giving the most extravagant sacrifice they can think of will please God.

B. God's Ideal (v. 8)

8a. He has shown you, O mortal, what is good.

God has not kept his desires secret; what he requires is not a mystery. God has revealed what he considers *good* and what he wants (see Deuteronomy 10:12, 13; Mark 12:33). It is not their gifts or offerings that God really desires. What he wants are the people themselves, given to the Lord in lives that reflect his priorities and passions (see 1 Samuel 15:22).

8b. And what does the LORD require of you? To act justly and to love mercy and to walk humbly with your God.

Acting *justly* should not be thought of strictly in terms of judgment. Treating people justly may be thought of as treating people just as God would treat them (examples: Isaiah 1:17; Jeremiah 22:3; Zechariah 7:9, 10). This includes extending *mercy*, which can be expressed as forgiveness in many ways.

The key to understanding both justice and mercy lies in a relationship with God, which is where the challenge to *walk humbly* applies (see 2 Kings 22:19; Isaiah 57:15). Apart from such a walk, justice and mercy are unattainable.

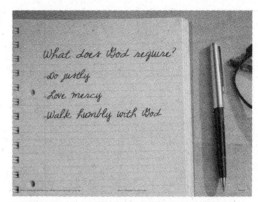

Visual for Lesson 4. *Ask the class how adding these three items to their to-do list changes their priorities for the upcoming week.*

> **What Do You Think?**
> What plan can you make to identify and improve the requirement in Micah 6:8 that is most lacking in your life?
> **Digging Deeper**
> How would you expect attention to the other two requirements to influence the one most lacking?

These requirements given by Micah for coming before the Lord should not be used to justify salvation by works. Micah is not addressing the question, "What must I do to be saved?" The issue is that God's covenant people must conduct themselves in ways pleasing to him. Micah's audience is wrong to think that their offerings and rituals alone will please God. Christians today who think the same about their "Sunday only" acts of worship are equally misguided.

Conclusion

A. Humbly in Justice and Mercy

Micah courageously confronted the tragic lack of godly leadership for the people of God. While Micah's words in the concluding portion of our printed text apply to all God's people, they most certainly need to be exemplified in the lives of their leaders. One thinks of how Jesus looked at the masses in his day and saw them as "sheep without a shepherd" (Matthew 9:36). The same terminology could have been used to describe the people in Micah's day, given how corrupt the leadership had become. What a difference it would have made if those leaders had taken the words in Micah 6:8 to heart!

Church leaders today would do well to make those words their standard of conduct. But whether Christian leaders are aligned with God's will or not, the priesthood of all believers must still bring their lives to God as sacrifices (Romans 12:1; 1 Peter 2:5). Jesus has paid the price (Hebrews 7:27, 28). We do not worry about offering rivers of oil or thousands of animal sacrifices. Let us therefore search our hearts for strongholds that resist practicing justice and mercy. In humility, may we seek to please the Lord with our whole lives.

> **What Do You Think?**
> Which prophetic words of this lesson and the previous three challenge you most to act? Why?
> **Digging Deeper**
> What is your plan for action?

B. Prayer

Father, thank you for godly leaders! May the power of your Holy Spirit help us all to seek and do your will, even when—and especially when—our leaders stray from your paths. We pray in Jesus' name. Amen.

C. Thought to Remember

God has revealed how to please him.

INVOLVEMENT LEARNING

Enhance your lesson with NIV Bible Student *(from your curriculum supplier) and the reproducible activity page (at www.standardlesson.com or in the back of the* NIV Standard Lesson Commentary Deluxe Edition*).*

Into the Lesson

Begin by reading this true story:

When discussing corruption of the nineteenth century, one name surfaces often: that of the infamous William "Boss" Tweed (1823–78). In the mid-1800s, he and his cronies delighted in finding creative ways to use the New York City treasury to enrich themselves. Tweed once bought 300 benches for $5 each, then sold them to the city for $600 each. Quite a profit! When New York City Hall was under construction, Tweed charged the city $7,500 for every thermometer, $41,190 for each broom, and nearly $5.7 million for furniture and carpets. Tweed's graft today would be in the $200 million range! There was no happy ending for Boss Tweed though. He was arrested and died in prison in 1878.

Alternative. Distribute copies of the "Scandalous History" exercise on the activity page, which you can download. Have students work in pairs to complete it as indicated.

After either activity, ask, "Is abuse of power really anything new? The ancient prophet Micah has the answer."

Into the Word

Divide the class into three groups: **How Corrupt Leaders View People** (Micah 3:1-3) / **How Corrupt Leaders See Themselves** (Micah 3:9-12) / **How Corrupt Leaders Approach God** (Micah 6:6, 7). Give each group markers and a poster board. Have groups write the title and Scripture reference at the top of their posters. Then have them use stick figures, line drawings, and short phrases to illustrate the images in their Scripture passage. Stress that the artwork need not be detailed. But it should communicate the content of Micah's words. Allow about 15 minutes.

Expect that the **View People** group will have very violent images, since Micah's descriptions in these verses are quite graphic! The poster may feature people with sharp teeth, armed with hatchets, and filling cooking pots.

The **See Themselves** group may show pious-acting people with dollar signs in thought balloons. Phrases such as "priest for hire" and "all is well" may be scattered around the poster.

The **Approach God** group may have stick figures performing rituals and making extravagant offerings. Phrases or images reflecting "rivers of olive oil" and "thousands of rams" may be expected on the poster.

Have groups explain their posters. Offer insights from the commentary as appropriate.

Then turn to Micah 6:8. Help learners evaluate the corrupt leaders of Micah's day by the standards of this verse. Pose the following questions: 1–How did they fall short of acting justly? 2–Why did their actions not demonstrate mercy? 3–What evidence do you see that they did not approach God with humility?

Into Life

Make and distribute copies of the following prayer calendar:

Monday–leader and duty: _____

Tuesday–leader and duty: _____

Wednesday–leader and duty: _____

Thursday–leader and duty: _____

Friday–leader and duty: _____

Saturday–leader and duty: _____

Sunday–leader and duty: _____

Challenge learners to use it as a reminder to write one prayer per day in the week ahead for different church leaders—praying that the standards of Micah 6:8 would be theirs as well.

Option. Distribute copies of the "Micah 3 & 6 Interview Questions" exercise from the activity page to groups of three to five. During whole-class discussion after groups complete as indicated, work through the lesson text carefully to see if learners have missed anything.

NEED FOR JUST LEADERS

DEVOTIONAL READING: Psalm 50:1-15
BACKGROUND SCRIPTURE: Malachi 2, 3

MALACHI 2:1-9

¹ "And now, you priests, this warning is for you. ² If you do not listen, and if you do not resolve to honor my name," says the LORD Almighty, "I will send a curse on you, and I will curse your blessings. Yes, I have already cursed them, because you have not resolved to honor me.

³ "Because of you I will rebuke your descendants; I will smear on your faces the dung from your festival sacrifices, and you will be carried off with it. ⁴ And you will know that I have sent you this warning so that my covenant with Levi may continue," says the LORD Almighty. ⁵ "My covenant was with him, a covenant of life and peace, and I gave them to him; this called for reverence and he revered me and stood in awe of my name. ⁶ True instruction was in his mouth and nothing false was found on his lips. He walked with me in peace and uprightness, and turned many from sin.

⁷ "For the lips of a priest ought to preserve knowledge, because he is the messenger of the LORD Almighty and people seek instruction from his mouth. ⁸ But you have turned from the way and by your teaching have caused many to stumble; you have violated the covenant with Levi," says the LORD Almighty. ⁹ "So I have caused you to be despised and humiliated before all the people, because you have not followed my ways but have shown partiality in matters of the law."

MALACHI 3:5, 6

⁵ "So I will come to put you on trial. I will be quick to testify against sorcerers, adulterers and perjurers, against those who defraud laborers of their wages, who oppress the widows and the fatherless, and deprive the foreigners among you of justice, but do not fear me," says the LORD Almighty.

⁶ "I the LORD do not change. So you, the descendants of Jacob, are not destroyed."

KEY VERSE

"If you do not listen, and if you do not resolve to honor my name," says the LORD Almighty, "I will send a curse on you, and I will curse your blessings. Yes, I have already cursed them, because you have not resolved to honor me." —**Malachi 2:2**

JUSTICE AND THE PROPHETS

Unit 1: God Requires Justice

LESSONS 1–5

LESSON AIMS

After participating in this lesson, each learner will be able to:

1. Describe the conduct of the Judean priesthood of the late fifth century BC.

2. Explain why God held the priesthood to a high standard.

3. Create a plan to improve one aspect of his or her own priestly ministry (1 Peter 2:5).

LESSON OUTLINE

Introduction
A. A Model for Leadership
B. Lesson Context

I. Failing the Call (MALACHI 2:1-9)
A. Hear the Lord (vv. 1-4)
   Take That!
B. Fear the Lord (vv. 5-7)
   Reliable Delivery
C. Follow the Lord (vv. 8, 9)

II. Renewing the Call (MALACHI 3:5, 6)
A. Trying Offenders (v. 5)
B. Unchanging God (v. 6)

Conclusion
A. "Familiarity Breeds Contempt"
B. Prayer
C. Thought to Remember

Introduction

A. A Model for Leadership

In the late 1940s, Billy Graham's ministry was becoming well known. Graham realized that he needed to hold himself and his ministry to an extremely high standard of conduct for the sake of the gospel message he proclaimed. In 1948, Graham and his staff created what they called the "Modesto Manifesto." They pledged themselves to follow the highest standards of conduct in every area of their lives.

When the evangelist died in 2018, tributes to Graham poured in. Many of them cited his uncompromising integrity. Even those who did not accept Graham's message had to acknowledge that he was a man who practiced what he preached. During a time when many public figures were caught up in scandalous behavior, Graham remained a consistent model of faithfulness to Christ.

In the days of the prophet Malachi, the leaders of God's people took the polar opposite approach. What we might call "Malachi's Manifesto" exposed the corruption of these leaders and called attention to what God has always desired.

B. Lesson Context

Malachi mentions no kings at the beginning of his book. This makes establishing an approximate date for the prophet's ministry challenging. Even so, the book's contents offer some clues.

The issues addressed by Malachi are similar to those facing God's people in the time of Nehemiah in the fifth century BC. With permission from King Artaxerxes of Persia, Nehemiah had traveled from Persia to Judah around 445 BC to rebuild Jerusalem's walls.

Some issues addressed by both Nehemiah and Malachi include mixed marriages (Nehemiah 13:23-27; Malachi 2:11), the failure to tithe (Nehemiah 13:10-14; Malachi 3:8-10), and corrupt priests (Nehemiah 13:4-9; Malachi 1:6–2:9). These similarities point to a date for Malachi that is post-exilic. That means the setting is an era after the exile in Babylon ends in 538 BC (see Ezra 1:1-4).

Bolstering the conclusion that Malachi is post-exilic is the use of the title "governor" (Malachi 1:8). This was Nehemiah's official title (see Nehemiah 5:14; compare Haggai 1:1; 2:21); before the exile, Judah had kings, not governors. Based on these and other facts, scholars conclude that Malachi is chronologically the last of the prophets, of about 430 BC.

The Babylonian captivity occurred between the ministries of Micah (see lesson 4) and Malachi. The delinquent leadership against which Micah spoke so passionately had resurfaced in Malachi's day. And it was just as displeasing to the Lord in Malachi's time as it had been in Micah's.

I. Failing the Call
(MALACHI 2:1-9)

Up to the point where our lesson text begins, Malachi has written in dialogue format. This involves first stating a proposition from the Lord or presenting a scenario, then anticipating a response. That response is followed by the Lord's rejoinder. Variations of this technique are found throughout the book. This is Malachi's method of challenging his audience to rethink their practices and alter their way of living.

A. Hear the Lord (vv. 1-4)

1. "And now, you priests, this warning is for you.

At the point where our lesson begins, Malachi has already said much about the poor quality of leadership demonstrated by the *priests*. When the prophet first mentions the priests, he describes them as despising the Lord's name (Malachi 1:6). The priests are abusing their sacred office by offering defective, unacceptable sacrifices (1:7, 8).

God has made it clear in the Law of Moses that only the best is to be brought to him in worship. In the case of animals, only those unblemished are to be brought (examples: Leviticus 1:3, 10; 3:1). But instead of finding delight in the privilege of preparing such offerings, these priests look on their work as a "burden" (Malachi 1:13). The *warning* about to be voiced is an invitation to

hear God anew and repent. The verse before us therefore begins the transition from problem to solution—or consequences for allowing the problem to continue.

2. "If you do not listen, and if you do not resolve to honor my name," says the LORD Almighty, "I will send a curse on you, and I will curse your blessings. Yes, I have already cursed them, because you have not resolved to honor me.

The Lord issues a solemn warning to the delinquent priests. Their ministry is intended to bring *honor* to the Lord's *name* (compare Matthew 15:7-9; 1 Timothy 6:16; Revelation 5:12, 13). He is the one they serve. The work they do is to be viewed as a privilege.

But if the priests are unwilling to *resolve* to take seriously what the Lord says, then the Lord will *send a curse on* them and even *curse* their *blessings* (compare Deuteronomy 11:26; 28:20; Jeremiah 13:17). This may refer to the blessing that the priests are to pronounce on the Israelites (Numbers 6:22-27). If so, then God will make that declaration null and void. The unfortunate truth is that unholy priests cause suffering for all the people.

Another possible interpretation is that God will curse the harvest so that the crops will not produce as they should. This happened in the time of Haggai nearly a century earlier (Haggai 1:5-11). Since the Law of Moses commands that a tithe of the harvest be given to the Levites (Numbers 18:21), a poor crop means a reduced provision for them. (We remind ourselves that all priests were Levites but not all Levites were priests.)

> **What Do You Think?**
> What are some ways to discern a pending problem of cursed blessings today?
> **Digging Deeper**
> When difficult times do come, how will you determine if the problem is one of cursed blessings rather than random occurrence?

Referring to God as *the Lord Almighty, which literally means "Lord of hosts,"* emphasizes his power, especially as a warrior in prophetic books (examples: Isaiah 10:24-26; Jeremiah 11:20; Nahum 2:13). So serious is the heart condition of these priests and the shameful conduct that is the outcome, God says he has *already cursed* their blessings.

3. "Because of you I will rebuke your descendants; I will smear on your faces the dung from your festival sacrifices, and you will be carried off with it.

Sinful behavior of a person or group often has consequences for their *descendants* (example: 1 Kings 14:9, 10). God declared this to be so in his instructions that accompanied the second commandment (Exodus 20:4, 5).

The Lord's *rebuke* is depicted in a most shocking manner. Normally the *dung* of animals that are sacrificed, along with the contents of their intestines, is to be taken outside the camp of the Israelites and burned (Exodus 29:14; Leviticus 4:11, 12). To have dung on one's face is to be massively dishonored. The language is probably not to be viewed in literal, physical terms. Rather, it is a way of vividly describing how repulsed the Lord is by the priests' conduct.

> *What Do You Think?*
> How can churches do a better job in the area of holding their leaders accountable?
> *Digging Deeper*
> Which of these texts best support your response: Matthew 18:15-17; Romans 16:17, 18; 1 Corinthians 5:11-13; 2 Thessalonians 3:14, 15; 1 Timothy 6:3-5; Titus 1:10-16; 3:10? Why?

❧ TAKE THAT! ❧

In the early twentieth century, the pie-in-the-face sight gag was introduced as a staple of slapstick comedy. Later, it became an act of political protest. Though pieing was originally intended primarily to be funny, as a political act it is intended to make an opponent look foolish.

Thomas King Forcade was probably the first to employ this method of political protest. In 1970, he pied Otto N. Larsen, chairman of the Commission on Obscenity. Aron Kay witnessed the event and went on to have a storied pieing career himself, hitting the likes of William Buckley Jr., E. Howard Hunt, G. Gordon Liddy, and Andy Warhol. Noel Godin, another noted pie thrower, hit Bill Gates and several others.

Malachi spoke of God's threatening to smear the faces of his delinquent priests with something far less palatable than a whipped cream–topped pie! Such a humiliation would be accompanied with very real consequences.

In what way does your conduct most invite humiliation—or worse—from the Lord? —J. E.

4. "And you will know that I have sent you this warning so that my covenant with Levi may continue," says the LORD Almighty.

The delinquent priests have forgotten, either through passive carelessness or by active intent, the roots of their sacred office and heritage. The priestly *covenant* goes back to Jacob's son *Levi*, some of whose descendants are assigned the priesthood (Numbers 3:5-13). Anytime a role is inherited instead of earned by merit, the danger is greater that a person will simply go through the motions. Those of the Levitical priesthood are not immune to this pitfall.

B. Fear the Lord (vv. 5-7)

5. "My covenant was with him, a covenant of life and peace, and I gave them to him; this called for reverence and he revered me and stood in awe of my name.

The special blessings promised to Levi were *life and peace*, spiritual blessings associated with the Levites' special place in God's service. Levi's descendants in turn were to respond to these favors with *reverence*, expressed as grave respect for

HOW TO SAY IT

Artaxerxes	Are-tuh-*zerk*-seez.
Levites	*Lee*-vites.
Levitical	Leh-*vit*-ih-kul.
Malachi	*Mal*-uh-kye.
Nehemiah	Nee-huh-**my**-uh.
Persia	*Per*-zhuh.
Shechem	*Shee*-kem or *Shek*-em.

the godly tasks they were given (compare Hebrews 12:28, 29).

When one looks at the life of Levi himself, he does not appear to exemplify a great deal of fear toward the Lord. He and his brother Simeon misused the covenant sign of circumcision to avenge the cruel treatment of their sister, Dinah, by Shechem (Genesis 34; 49:5). The Lord's words here perhaps describe what was true of Levi's descendants when Moses pronounced his final blessing on that tribe (Deuteronomy 33:8-11). Later, the Levites did prove themselves to be a God-fearing tribe (see Exodus 32:25-29; Numbers 25:6-13).

6a. "True instruction was in his mouth and nothing false was found on his lips.

Three important responsibilities for priests are highlighted in this verse. First, they are to give *true instruction* faithfully (Deuteronomy 33:10). That involves communicating the Lord's requirements to his people (17:9-13). *Nothing false* is to be *found* in a priest's speech, a characteristic highly commended by James for the new covenant era (James 3:2).

6b. "He walked with me in peace and uprightness,

Second, the priest's daily walk is to be consistent with his faith profession (compare Genesis 5:22). To be a person of *peace* goes hand in hand with loving God's law (Psalm 119:165). The Hebrew word underneath the translation *uprightness* can also be translated "level" or "smooth" as opposed to "rough" (see Isaiah 40:4; 42:16), and that is the sense here. It indicates that the person is virtuous and lacks any deceit (compare John 1:47). The faithful priest exhibits high moral character (compare Psalm 25:21).

6c. "and turned many from sin.

Third, the faithful priest is dedicated to helping others (compare James 5:19, 20). The priest is to set the kind of example that draws others to follow and imitate his righteous lifestyle.

7. "For the lips of the priest ought to preserve knowledge, because he is the messenger of the LORD Almighty and people seek instruction from his mouth.

The priests in Malachi's day neglect and even abuse the divinely given role they are called to fulfill: every priest is the Lord's *messenger*. Priests are, in a very real sense, the Lord's representatives to the people as those priests bring God's message (examples: Ezra 7:11; Nehemiah 8). Priests are to look to him for the *knowledge* and *instruction* found only in his law (compare Leviticus 10:11).

> **What Do You Think?**
> In what ways is the admonishment to the priests applicable to Christians today, given the reality of our own priesthood (1 Peter 2:9)?
> *Digging Deeper*
> If no one seeks God's Word from you as a messenger of the Lord, what problem and solution do you see?

❧ RELIABLE DELIVERY ❧

In most parts of the United States, packages can be delivered efficiently by car or truck. But in the central business districts of crowded metropolitan areas, motor vehicles can be hindered. In such areas, businesses often count on bicycle messengers for reliable delivery.

In 1945, one of the earliest recorded American bicycle courier companies was founded. Carl Sparks began Sparkies, an all-bicycle delivery service in San Francisco. By the late 1970s, bicycle messenger and delivery services existed in many of this country's major cities.

Though the end of bicycle couriers has been predicted, technological innovation has not yet significantly reduced the demand for their services. Many items can be sent most efficiently by bike: corporate gifts, original artwork, clothes for photo shoots, and original signed documents are but a few. Some companies would rather send sensitive information by courier to avoid the risk of having their email hacked.

God established a type of delivery service when he founded the nation of Israel. Priests were to transmit God's law from generation to generation. Theirs was precious cargo that the people needed. But there's an even bigger picture to consider: the nation as a whole was to communicate

Visual for Lesson 5. *As the class discusses Malachi 2:2, ask them what situations they currently need to listen to the Lord about; pray for these in closing.*

the future arrival of the Messiah to the waiting world.

The task of communicating the reality of that arrival now belongs to Christians. What will be your part in doing so?　　　　　　—J. E.

C. Follow the Lord (vv. 8, 9)

8. "But you have turned from the way and by your teaching have caused many to stumble; you have violated the covenant with Levi," says the LORD Almighty.

The task of keeping *the covenant with Levi* means nothing to the delinquent priests (compare Jeremiah 2:8). Whether the problem is one of mere negligence or of active rebellion, the result is the same: *many* people *stumble* (compare 18:15; Hosea 4:6; Mark 9:42).

> *What Do You Think?*
> What are some good ways your church can acknowledge its leaders who are doing the opposite of Malachi 2:8?
> *Digging Deeper*
> What will be your part in this initiative?

9. "So have I caused you to be despised and humiliated before all the people, because you have not followed my ways but have shown partiality in matters of the law."

This verse makes the case that the problem is not just one of negligence; if it were, the verse

could stop with the phrase *you have not followed my ways.* The phrase *but have shown partiality in matters of the law* points to conscious, intentional disregard of God's ways (compare, from the era of the judges, 1 Samuel 2:27-33). To be partial in applying the law is abhorrent to the Lord; frequent warnings against doing so are found within the Law of Moses (examples: Leviticus 19:15; Deuteronomy 16:19).

II. Renewing the Call
(MALACHI 3:5, 6)

The Lord does not merely state a problem and stop there. He goes on to state the solution, which begins in Malachi 3:1 (not in today's text): his "messenger" will "prepare the way" before him. John the Baptist is the one who will fulfill Malachi's prophecy (Matthew 11:10).

Malachi goes on to speak about a second messenger's coming, actions, and results. The refining and purifying mentioned fit Jesus' work in raising up in his church those who will faithfully serve him (Malachi 3:3, 4). Though judgment will be brought against all individuals who have violated the covenant, the Levites are still called out specifically (3:3); as teachers, theirs is the greater accountability.

A. Trying Offenders (v. 5)

3:5a. "So I will come to put you on trial. I will be quick to testify against sorcerers, adulterers and perjurers,

This half-verse and the next elaborate on the judgment and *trial* to be carried out by the second messenger (see Malachi 3:2, not in today's text). Sorcery and related practices are strictly forbidden in the Law of Moses (example: Deuteronomy 18:9-14). This prohibition in part prevents Israel from seeking to manipulate the Lord with "secret arts" and "spells" (examples: Exodus 7:11; Isaiah 47:9). Adultery violates the seventh commandment (Exodus 20:14; compare James 2:11; 2 Peter 2:12-14); to swear falsely breaks the ninth (Exodus 20:16; compare Leviticus 19:11, 12; Jeremiah 7:9).

5b. "against those who defraud laborers of their wages, who oppress the widows and the

fatherless, and deprive the foreigners among you of justice, but do not fear me," says the LORD Almighty.

The Lord also calls to account all who take advantage of the most vulnerable in Israelite society. The Law of Moses included specific directives to care for each of these groups (examples: Leviticus 19:13; Deuteronomy 24:14-22).

Although *the laborers* and *the widows and the fatherless* are likely fellow Israelites, *the foreigners* refers specifically to those who do not belong to the covenant people by lineage. God shows a special concern for the foreigners who live in Israel. He calls his people to remember their own time of oppression while they lived as foreigners in Egypt and to treat foreigners in their own land quite differently (Exodus 22:21).

Ultimately such disregard for these peoples in need and for the principles found in the Law of Moses can be traced to a lack of reverence for the lawgiver, the Lord himself (compare Deuteronomy 31:12, 13; Isaiah 1:2). The *fear* of the Lord has always been "the beginning of knowledge" (Proverbs 1:7); lack of such fear leads to certain ruin (example: James 5:1-6).

> ### What Do You Think?
> In what ways can you use Malachi 3:5 as a source of comfort or encouragement in the face of today's negative headlines?
>
> ### Digging Deeper
> In what ways can you be an empathizer in passing that encouragement along to the oppressed as named in this text?

B. Unchanging God (v. 6)

6a. "I the LORD do not change.

God can change his mind (example: Jonah 3:10), but he does not change his character (see James 1:17). His standards of right and wrong always hold true. He will be consistent in carrying out judgment on those who violate these standards, as he has made abundantly clear throughout Scripture.

6b. "So you, the descendants of Jacob, are not destroyed."

The *descendants of Jacob,* referring to the Israelites, have not been *destroyed* by God's wrath—yet (compare Hosea 11:8, 9). The Lord is merciful because of his promises—and his unchanging character means he will keep those promises.

Conclusion

A. "Familiarity Breeds Contempt"

Malachi's words should serve as sobering warnings to leaders in the church. Dangers abound when we become casual about doing God's work. It's a small step from an attitude of indifference to one of antibiblical rationalizing by those who serve the Lord in leadership positions. The late Dallas Willard once observed, "The greatest threat to devotion to Christ is service for Christ."

Those who earn wages by serving the church or a parachurch ministry can come to see what they do merely as a source of income. They forget that theirs is a ministry done in service to the Lord and for his glory. Certain words and actions become part of the routine, of what is expected according to their job description. It's a slippery slope.

One source of help may be for the leader to arrange to meet with a group of fellow leaders (either within or outside of the congregation) for mutual prayer and encouragement. Many have found such accountability groups greatly beneficial in keeping them spiritually sharp and providing valuable counsel when temptations or other challenges occur (compare Malachi 3:16).

Speaking honestly to one another can be of immeasurable value in avoiding the spiritual barrenness that brought God's harsh criticism of the priests in Malachi's day. Inviting candid feedback from a fellow servant of Christ is always preferable to being on the receiving end of God's correction!

B. Prayer

Father, keep us from handling sacred duties in such a way that we lose sight of you. Empower our church to remember our covenant with you. In Jesus' name we pray. Amen.

C. Thought to Remember

Working for God requires faithfulness.

INVOLVEMENT LEARNING

Enhance your lesson with NIV Bible Student (from your curriculum supplier) and the reproducible activity page (at www.standardlesson.com or in the back of the NIV Standard Lesson Commentary Deluxe Edition).

Into the Lesson

Before class, recruit a class member to assist you secretly. Instruct this representative to purposely disobey the instructions his or her partner will give. Begin class with a game of tic-tac-toe. Select three volunteers (the third of whom will be your prepared accomplice) to play the game on the board.

Play your variation of the game as follows: Player One makes any move he or she wishes to make. Player Two cannot speak aloud, but can only make a move by whispering his or her move to an assistant, your prepared accomplice. The assistant, according to your earlier instruction, will disregard Player Two's wishes and purposely make bad moves!

Play two or three games, allowing Player Two's confusion to grow. Then reveal the reason the assistant made the bad moves.

Option. Before class begins, place in chairs copies of the "Fair Representation" puzzle from the activity page, which you can download. Your early arrivers can begin work on this before class begins. If time allows, discuss at conclusion of the class.

Make a transition by asking, "When a leader of God's people falls short of what the responsibility requires, is it usually through simple negligence or intentional misconduct?" After brief whole-class discussion, say, "Let's see what today's lesson from Malachi has to say about the distinction and about God's standards, as the prophet describes the conduct of the Judean priesthood of the late fifth century BC."

Into the Word

Write this text at the top of the board:

I will come to put you on trial.
—Malachi 3:5a

Read aloud today's lesson text; follow that with an explanation of the context. Inform the class that the group activity will be to act out Malachi's prophecy as a trial.

Divide the class into the following groups, asking each group to prepare a portion of the trial as the group designation suggests:

Priests' Duty Group (Malachi 2:4-7)
Priests' Failure Group (Malachi 2:1, 2, 8)
God's Judgment Group (Malachi 2:3, 9; 3:5, 6).

Allow about 10 minutes for groups to prepare their respective portions of the trial; then let the trial begin. Exercise reasonable creativity for assigning group discoveries to those from each group playing the parts of prosecutor, defendant, and judge.

In general, expect these conclusions:

• **Priests' Duty Group** stresses that Levitical priests were to revere God as they taught his standards.

• **Priests' Failure Group** lists ways the priests failed in their duty.

• **God's Judgment Group** lists consequences promised and delayed for priests' failures with regard to God's covenant promise(s).

Conclude the trial by having the judge declare either a verdict of (1) not guilty, (2) guilty of simple negligence, or (3) guilty of intentional malfeasance. Follow with whole-class agree/disagree discussion.

Into Life

Read 1 Peter 2:4-12 aloud to launch a discussion regarding what it means for every Christian to be a priest. Write this question on the board: *What is the nature of the spiritual sacrifices (v. 5) that we are to offer?* Jot responses underneath the question. After the discussion winds down, pose this question for 15 seconds of silent, personal reflection: *What commitment can I make to improve?*

Option. Distribute copies of the "My Priesthood" exercise from the activity page as a take-home for further self-evaluation.

A JUST SERVANT

DEVOTIONAL READING: Psalm 98
BACKGROUND SCRIPTURE: Isaiah 42

ISAIAH 42:1-9

¹ "Here is my servant, whom I uphold,
   my chosen one in whom I delight;
I will put my Spirit on him,
   and he will bring justice to the nations.
² He will not shout or cry out,
   or raise his voice in the streets.
³ A bruised reed he will not break,
   and a smoldering wick he will not snuff
     out.
In faithfulness he will bring forth justice;
⁴   he will not falter or be discouraged
till he establishes justice on earth.
   In his teaching the islands will put their
     hope."
⁵ This is what God the LORD says—
   the Creator of the heavens, who stretches
     them out,
   who spreads out the earth with all that
     springs from it,
   who gives breath to its people,
   and life to those who walk on it:
⁶ "I, the LORD, have called you in
   righteousness;
   I will take hold of your hand.

I will keep you and will make you to be a
   covenant for the people
   and a light for the Gentiles,
⁷ to open eyes that are blind,
   to free captives from prison
   and to release from the dungeon those
     who sit in darkness.
⁸ "I am the LORD; that is my name!
   I will not yield my glory to another
   or my praise to idols.
⁹ See, the former things have taken place,
   and new things I declare;
before they spring into being
   I announce them to you."

KEY VERSE

Here is my servant, whom I uphold, my chosen one in whom I delight; I will put my Spirit on him, and he will bring justice to the nations. —**Isaiah 42:1**

JUSTICE AND THE PROPHETS

Unit 2: God Promises a Just Kingdom

LESSONS 6–9

LESSON AIMS

After participating in this lesson, each learner will be able to:

1. Identify the Lord's servant and the servant's task.

2. Explain the fulfillment of the lesson text found in Matthew 12:15-21.

3. Sing a hymn or song that is based on Isaiah 42.

LESSON OUTLINE

Introduction

A. Champions of Justice

A few years ago, the Consumer Attorneys of California created the "Champions of Justice Award" to honor extraordinary service among the association's members. Sandra Ribera Speed received the award in 2015. This honor was awarded to her in part for her involvement in a case involving a runaway delivery truck that crashed into a family vehicle.

Sandra's law firm at the time wanted nothing to do with fighting this case against a powerful company and its army of attorneys. But Sandra believed the case had merit and refused to give up. She used all her savings and incurred credit card debt in order to work on the case by herself for six months. She was so well prepared that the seven lawyers from the prestigious firm representing the delivery company settled the case on the first day of trial. In addition to serving her clients well, Sandra's portion of the settlement allowed her to establish her own law firm.

About 2,700 years ago, the prophet Isaiah foretold the coming of the ultimate champion of justice. He would fight for, defend, and serve not just one person but all those who would accept his help.

B. Lesson Context

This lesson begins unit 2, which emphasizes God's promises of a just kingdom. The prophets foretold the coming of the Messiah as the champion of justice. Such prophecies, of course, have direct bearing on Palm Sunday. As appropriate, some of these connections will be explored in the commentary below.

The prophet Isaiah, for his part, had a lengthy ministry, from about 740 to 680 BC. The book featuring his name as its title is comprised of two parts. Isaiah 1–39 has been described as the Book of Judgment; it focuses on the sins of the people of Judah. Isaiah 40–66, the Book of Comfort, looks forward about a century and a half to the time when Judah's exile in Babylon is about to end. We keep in mind that the exile did not even begin until 586 BC.

The end of exile is foreseen in the chapter preceding our lesson text: God called "one . . . in righteousness" (Isaiah 41:2) to bring the captivity to its end. That man was Cyrus, the king of Persia who conquered Babylon in 539 BC (see 44:28 and 45:1, where he is designated "shepherd" and "anointed," respectively). He issued a decree permitting the exiled Jews to return to Jerusalem beginning in 538 BC (Ezra 1:1-8).

The word *servant* occurs more than three dozen times in the book of Isaiah. In chapter 41, the Lord applies it to "Israel, my servant" (Isaiah 41:8, 9). This servant was fearful. For that reason, God reassured the people of his love. They didn't need to fear; their exile in Babylon was not evidence that God had cast them away forever. He promised Israel that they were still his covenant people. The Lord encouraged his helpless servant Israel by stating that the people need not fear, because God would help them (41:10, 13, 14).

The Lord then addressed, in a courtroom setting, the nations and their idols. He challenged the nations to provide evidence that idols had ever correctly predicted the future. After announcing judgment on the false gods, the Lord proclaimed that he had "stirred up one from the north" (Isaiah 41:25)—surely once again alluding to Cyrus. Although the Persian emperor hailed "from the east" (41:2), he conquered several kingdoms north of Babylon before eventually attacking Babylon from that direction. Against this backdrop of a pagan king as an instrument of God to rescue an exiled people, Isaiah introduced the intriguing servant of the Lord.

Isaiah 42:1-9 (today's text) is the first of Isaiah's five "servant songs," in which the servant is identified with the Messiah to come (see 49:1-6; 50:4-9; 52:13–53:12; 61:1-4). These messianic songs highlight what the servant is to accomplish on behalf of the world.

I. Presentation
(ISAIAH 42:1-4)
A. God's Servant (v. 1)

1a. "Here is my servant, whom I uphold, my chosen one in whom I delight;

The *servant* introduced here bears some similarities to the anointed shepherd Cyrus and servant Israel in having God's approval (see the Lesson Context). However, this servant is profoundly different from both; the quotation of Isaiah 42:1-4 in Matthew 12:18-21 establishes this to be Jesus. God both supports and delights in him (Matthew 3:16, 17). This suggests the servant will be obedient and godly in a way like no other.

1b. "I will put my Spirit on him,

Members of ancient Israel did not experience the indwelling of the Holy Spirit as Christians do today (see Joel 2:28-32; Acts 2:14-21, 38). Thus the servant is marked as special for a special purpose, and Jesus' baptism clearly points back to this verse. On that occasion the Spirit will descend on him after he rises from the water as the Father expresses his pleasure with his Son (Luke 3:21, 22; see also Isaiah 11:1-5).

1c. "and he will bring justice to the nations.

We cannot miss the servant's mission of bringing *justice* to the world, since it is mentioned three times in the first four verses of Isaiah 42. The concept of justice encompasses much more than judicial equity in a courtroom, a fair redistribution of goods in society, etc. The justice that the servant *will bring* also includes making available the salvation of God. Isaiah's prophecy includes *the nations* in this plan (compare Isaiah 42:6, below). Although Israel often found itself being enemies with surrounding nations, God's plan ultimately is to make one people of many (compare Genesis 49:10; Romans 5:18, 19; Galatians 3:26-29).

HOW TO SAY IT

Babylon	*Bab*-uh-lun.
Cyrus	*Sigh*-russ.
Davidic	Duh-*vid*-ick.
Isaiah	Eye-*zay*-uh.
Judah	*Joo*-duh.
Messiah	Meh-*sigh*-uh.
messianic	mess-ee-*an*-ick.
Nazareth	*Naz*-uh-reth.
Persia	*Per*-zhuh.

B. Gentle and Just (vv. 2-4)

2. "He will not shout or cry out, or raise his voice in the streets.

This servant of the Lord will be quite different from the typical king or conqueror who calls attention to himself through loud proclamations (example: Acts 25:23). No, he won't even *shout or cry out*, nor *raise his voice in the streets*. God's answer to the world's arrogance is not more arrogance.

> **What Do You Think?**
> What are some issues you believe the Lord doesn't want you to voice publicly "in the street" in imitation of this characteristic? Why?
> **Digging Deeper**
> How do Matthew 5:14-16; 6:5; and 22:9 inform your response?

The crowds at Jesus' triumphal entry will shout, "Blessed is the king who comes in the name of the Lord!" (Luke 19:38). Notice that while the crowd speaks "in loud voices" (19:37), Jesus never says a word. He will be silent just as this prophecy says. Jesus will not speak up even to defend himself against false accusations (Acts 8:32-35, quoting Isaiah 53:7, 8).

As in ancient times, many people are attracted to leaders who draw attention to themselves, boasting of their abilities and accomplishments (see Acts 8:9-11). Christians do well to remember that Jesus didn't boast. Paul also refused to boast about anything "except in the cross of our Lord Jesus Christ" (Galatians 6:14; compare 2 Corinthians 10:17, 18).

3a. "A bruised reed he will not break, and a smoldering wick he will not snuff out.

Instead of using his power to crush the mighty, the servant will be so gentle that he won't even *break* off *a bruised reed* that is bent over (compare Matthew 11:29). With gentleness, the servant will support the weak and mend the broken.

❧ A PIGGYBACK SERVANT ❧

On a trip to Israel, our church group had walked about 30 minutes to get to a site. A woman in the group slipped and fell. She was immediately in a great deal of pain, learning later that she had broken a bone in her foot.

The concerned group began discussing the dilemma of getting her back to the bus. Then Bill stepped forward and lowered himself to his hands and knees, indicating that he would carry her. When the woman was securely attached to Bill's back, he stood up. He carried her, piggyback style, to the bus. Telling the story at Bill's celebration, our preacher concluded, "Bill is one who comes alongside others and carries their burdens."

Isaiah 42 introduces us to the Lord's servant, one who would not break an already-damaged plant. How willing are you to follow the example of the Lord Jesus and "lower" yourself to support those who are weak or broken? —A. S.

> **What Do You Think?**
> Which characteristic of Jesus most stirs you to act and speak on His behalf: that of Matthew 12:20 (which quotes Isaiah 42:3) or of Matthew 21:12, 13? Why?
> **Digging Deeper**
> What examples can you list of situations calling for a Matthew 12:20 response rather than one of Matthew 21:12, 13—and vice versa?

3b. "In faithfulness he will bring forth justice;

We are told again that the servant's mission is tied to *justice*. This is most fitting for a king from David's line (see David's words in 1 Chronicles 16:14, repeated in Psalm 105:7; see further his son Solomon's words in 72:2). But now the qualifier *in faithfulness* is added. Where servant Israel has failed (see Isaiah 48:1; 59:12-15), servant Jesus will succeed. Indeed, Jesus will prove himself to be the very embodiment of faithfulness (2 Timothy 2:13).

4a. "he will not falter or be discouraged

We see here a hint of the suffering the servant will experience, since this prediction presupposes the presence of things that can result in failure or discouragement. This finds full expression in the fourth servant song (Isaiah 52:13–53:12). Although surrounded by many chances to depart from God's chosen path, the servant will faithfully and obediently remain true to God's mission.

4b. "till he establishes justice on earth.

Here we have the climax of Isaiah's statements regarding *justice* in Isaiah 42:1-4. The servant won't merely preach justice as a desirable goal; he will enact it (compare Isaiah 9:7; 16:5; 54:14). Although the servant will be exceedingly gentle, he will not be weak. Establishing justice—God's divine order—*on earth* is a huge task. It requires unimaginable power. It is not the power that is typically used when trying to establish governments (compare 2:4; 51:4).

Centuries later, the people in Malachi's day will ask, "Where is the God of justice?" (Malachi 2:17). Malachi's prophetic response is fulfilled in John the Baptist, who prepares the way for the Messiah (see 3:1; Matthew 11:10). The Messiah in turn inaugurates justice (example: Luke 1:46-55).

4c. "In his teaching the islands will put their hope."

Islands is likely Isaiah's way of referring to distant places on the earth. These far places are meant to indicate that the prophecy concerns the entire world (compare Genesis 49:10; Isaiah 11:11; Matthew 12:17-21). The whole world is to have an opportunity to *put their hope* in and depend on the servant's *teaching*.

⚜ HUMBLE RESEARCH ⚜

Does humility come with any benefits? Social scientists are inclined to say yes! Studies indicate that humble people tend to be secure in their identity. They have an accurate sense of their own strengths and weaknesses, which gives them stability in their character.

Humble people also are aware that they aren't the center of the universe. Far from this realization getting them down, it allows them to enjoy their strengths and seek to improve their weaknesses.

Isaiah 42 reveals that the Lord's servant is not like leaders who draw attention to themselves. Such people boast about their abilities and accomplishments, but Jesus calls us to follow his humble example. What steps do you need to take to reorient your beliefs and behavior to align with Christ's attitude toward humility? How will you do that both in how you perceive others and in how you present yourself?　　　　　　　　—A. S.

II. Commission
(ISAIAH 42:5-9)
A. Called by the Creator (v. 5)

5. This is what God the LORD says—the Creator of the heavens, who stretches them out, who spreads out the earth with all that springs from it, who gives breath to its people, and life to those who walk on it:

The Lord is not merely Israel's *God* but is *the Creator* of all things (Genesis 1:1, 9; Psalm 102:25; Isaiah 48:13; etc.). On this basis, God rightly claims authority not just over the land and people of Israel but over all nations (Psalm 82:8; etc.).

More significantly, he is the one who gives *breath* and *life* to *people* (Genesis 2:7; compare Acts 17:24, 25). How sadly ironic that those very people in turn create idols that have no breath themselves (Jeremiah 10:14; 51:17), let alone being able to impart breath to others!

> **What Do You Think?**
> In what ways might your life change, were you to be more consistent at reminding yourself of God's position and role of Creator?
> **Digging Deeper**
> How can your church encourage its members to do likewise?

B. Called to Covenant (vv. 6, 7)

6a. "I, the LORD, have called you in righteousness; I will take hold of your hand. I will keep you

Having presented the servant and his mission, now *the Lord* addresses and commissions his servant. God has *called* the servant according to his own nature—his *righteousness* (compare Jeremiah 23:6). The servant doesn't have to fulfill the mission by himself; God *will take hold of* him tightly by the *hand* and won't let go (see Isaiah 41:9, 10, 13). The servant will do the Lord's work in God's power according to God's will.

6b. "and will make you to be a covenant for the people and a light for the Gentiles.

At the heart of that work is the fact that the servant will initiate *a covenant*. We know from other

Scriptures that the Messiah is to fulfill the Davidic covenant and establish a new covenant through personal sacrificial death (compare 2 Samuel 7:12-16; Isaiah 55:3; Jeremiah 31:31-34; Hebrews 8:6-13; 9:15). This covenant is without end (Isaiah 54:10; 59:21; 61:8).

The people refers to those who have already received God's revelation—the Israelites (see Isaiah 49:8). Their role as a priestly nation is meant to draw other nations to the Lord (Exodus 19:6; compare 1 Peter 2:9). The scope of the servant's ministry reflects this concern as he also becomes *a light* on behalf of *the Gentiles* (compare Isaiah 49:6; Luke 2:29-32; Acts 26:18, 22, 23).

7. "to open eyes that are blind, to free captives from prison and to release from the dungeon those who sit in darkness.

Ancient prisons are extremely dark, both literally and figuratively. The light-imparting ministry of the servant will indeed be welcomed by *those who sit in darkness* (see Isaiah 49:9; 51:14). Light would come through freedom, not by the installation of lamps or windows. The *eyes* of the *blind,* whether physical or spiritual in nature, are to be opened by the servant as a sign of his identity and call (compare Psalm 146:8; Isaiah 32:3; Matthew 11:5).

As is often the case with the Old Testament prophets, this prophecy likely carries a double meaning. In the first sense, Isaiah is probably looking about 150 years ahead to his people's release from captivity in Babylon (Isaiah 48:20; 52:2; compare Zechariah 2:7). In the context of the calling of the servant, however, Judah's deliverance from exile can only serve as a foretaste of the release of people from the bondage of sin and ignorance. While Cyrus, an instrument of the

Lord, will provide deliverance from the oppression of Babylon, this servant will provide liberation from the bondage of sin (compare Acts 26:18; 2 Timothy 2:26; Hebrews 2:14, 15).

This fulfillment will come into sharp and dramatic focus when Jesus reads Isaiah 61:1, 2a in Nazareth (Luke 4:18, 19). God offers deliverance from the imprisonment of sin to everyone—whether Jew or Gentile—who accepts Jesus as the Messiah according to the biblical plan of salvation (John 3:16; etc.).

C. Called for God's Glory (vv. 8, 9)
8a. "I am the LORD; that is my name!

The Lord's declaring of his *name* recalls the scene of Moses at the burning bush. There God revealed his personal name to Moses at the event that commissioned that man for his task. That task was to go back to Egypt so that the Lord could establish his covenant with Israel at Sinai (Exodus 3:13-15; 6:3; 19:1-6; compare Psalm 81:10; Isaiah 43:3, 11).

8b. "I will not yield my glory to another or my praise to idols.

Isaiah's own calling has surely impressed on him the fact that the Lord is holy and "the whole earth is full of his glory" (Isaiah 6:3). God alone has all authority; *idols* cannot share his *glory* or *praise* (compare Exodus 8:10; 20:4). Both the servant and Isaiah's audience are reminded that the servant's mission will confirm that God is beyond comparison.

9. "See, the former things have taken place, and new things I declare; before they spring into being I announce them to you."

In Isaiah 41:22 (not in our lesson text), God challenges the idols to reveal *the former things*—

the things God has revealed in prophecy and brought to pass later. Of course they cannot. God can reveal not only those things but also the ultimate end result. Events predicted about both Cyrus and the servant *have taken place*. This confirms the Lord's sovereign authority.

The *new things* of the Old Testament era likely point to Israel's restoration following the end of the Babylonian exile (see Isaiah 43:19-21). Once again, though, historical hindsight tells us that God's plan for his people will remain largely unfulfilled until the coming of the servant Jesus and his perfect work. Because of this, there is hope for all the world.

Regarding the beginning of the New Testament (new covenant) era, the Jews of Jesus' day will hope for a militaristic Messiah to come and, like Cyrus, deliver them from the oppression of a foreign nation. To be rid of Roman rule would be the new start they want. During Jesus' triumphal entry into Jerusalem, the people will cry out "Hosanna" (Matthew 21:9), which means "save" (compare 2 Samuel 14:4; 2 Kings 6:26). This is both an appeal of prayer and an exclamation of praise.

Jesus is certainly worthy of loud and absolute praise (Revelation 5:12)! Yet the humble Messiah ends up being much different from what anyone expects. The past, present, and future king of the universe comes not as one to be served "but to serve, and to give his life as a ransom for many" (Mark 10:45).

Conclusion
A. In His Steps

The biblical concept of judgment represents God's righteous world order. At his first coming, Jesus treated people more than justly; when Jesus walked the earth, he overcame enemies with gentleness and love. When he returns, he will judge the world based on how each person treated "the least of these" (Matthew 25:45). At his first coming, the Lord's servant inaugurated God's just and right order from a position of apparent weakness when compared to worldly strength; in so doing, he is an example for us so that we can "follow in his steps" (1 Peter 2:21-23).

Visual for Lessons 6 & 7. *Ask what part of Isaiah's prophecy about the Servant was fulfilled in the most surprising way in Christ.*

We have a part to play in the servant's task of bringing light to the nations and to our neighbors who live in darkness. The Holy Spirit, working through Scripture and circumstances, motivates Christ's followers to take his gospel to the ends of the earth. For more than 2,000 years, Christians have borne witness to Jesus through evangelism (see Matthew 28:18-20) and ministries of mercy: establishing hospitals and schools, caring for prisoners and the poor, and participating in countless other charities (25:34-40).

Particularly challenging for most of us is following the manner and attitude of the servant's life and ministry. It's not easy to surrender the self-centeredness and assertiveness that has been with us since birth in the surrounding culture. But God's Word calls us to pattern our lives after his servant Jesus (Philippians 2:4-8). How will you follow the example of Jesus? How will you *serve*?

B. Prayer

We thank you, Father, for sending the promised servant to save us and inaugurate your justice on earth. May the Holy Spirit empower us with the courage to follow your servant's humble example as we serve him and those around us. In Jesus' name we pray. Amen.

C. Thought to Remember

Jesus is the champion of justice and the servant of all servants.

INVOLVEMENT LEARNING

Enhance your lesson with NIV Bible Student (from your curriculum supplier) and the reproducible activity page (at www.standardlesson.com or in the back of the NIV Standard Lesson Commentary Deluxe Edition).

Into the Lesson

Have these quotes displayed or on handouts (you prepare) as class begins, but without the names of the authors:

Human progress is neither automatic or inevitable. . . . Every step toward the goal of justice requires sacrifice, suffering, and struggle; the tireless exertions and passionate concern of dedicated individuals.
—Martin Luther King Jr.

Justice in the life and conduct of the State is possible only as first it resides in the hearts and souls of the citizens. —Plato

I want to be remembered as someone who used herself . . . to work for justice and freedom. . . . I want to be remembered as one who tried. —Dorothy Height

Have displayed separately the names of the three authors along with these five additional names (or others of your choosing): Gandhi, Rosa Parks, Nelson Mandela, Abraham Lincoln, and George Washington. (Avoid using names that run the risk of politicizing the discussion.)

If using handouts, allow a minute for matching the quotes to correct authors. If using the board, don't allow anyone to make a second guess before everyone has had a chance to make a first guess. Discuss results as appropriate.

Lead into the Bible study by saying, "We may wonder if the ideals of justice that were to be inaugurated by the servant in Isaiah's five 'servant songs' is identical or similar to the concerns for justice in these quotes. Today's lesson provides us some insight in that regard."

Into the Word

Begin by identifying Isaiah's five servant songs by using their description in the Lesson Context. Then divide your class into three groups, assigning each a section of the lesson text as follows:

Qualifications Group (Isaiah 42:1-4)
Task-Description Group (Isaiah 42:5-7)
Sponsor Group (Isaiah 42:8, 9)

Include on handouts (you prepare) that groups are to summarize their segment of today's lesson text in the form of a brief career post or bio. The post/bio will either describe the servant's qualifications, his task, or the sponsor that backs him, according to the title of the group.

Possible responses are as follows:

Qualifications Group—The servant is chosen by God as evidenced by God's Spirit on him; exhibits a unique combination of gentle firmness; able to work tirelessly, ignoring naysayers.

Task-Description Group: makes things happen as empowered by the ultimate authority of the universe; initiates the covenant for everyone—no exceptions.

Sponsor Group: no better or more powerful sponsor for the servant's task can or will be substituted; the sponsor's power is proven by sole-source ability to predict events and make them happen.

After whole-class discussion of groups' responses, note that the three categories are not airtight; each segment of text may contain elements of qualifications, task descriptions, and/or descriptions of the servant's sponsor.

Into Life

Have advance preparations in place for learners to sing one or more of the following hymns or songs that are based on, or allude to, Isaiah 42:1-9: "Jesus, Lover of My Soul," "Behold My Servant! See Him Rise!" "Mighty Yet Meek," "Hark! The Distant Isles Proclaim," "Take My Hand, Father," "Open the Eyes of My Heart," or another of your own research. After singing, match elements of the lyrics to today's text.

Option 1. After the above, distribute copies of "A Case Study" from the activity page, which you can download. Have learners work in groups to discuss as indicated. *Option 2.* Distribute copies of "The Ultimate Servant" puzzle from the activity page as a take-home.

A RESURRECTED SAVIOR

DEVOTIONAL READING: Isaiah 53:4-12
BACKGROUND SCRIPTURE: Mark 16; 1 Corinthians 15

1 CORINTHIANS 15:1-8, 12-14, 20-23, 42-45

1 Now, brothers and sisters, I want to remind you of the gospel I preached to you, which you received and on which you have taken your stand. 2 By this gospel you are saved, if you hold firmly to the word I preached to you. Otherwise, you have believed in vain.

3 For what I received I passed on to you as of first importance: that Christ died for our sins according to the Scriptures, 4 that he was buried, that he was raised on the third day according to the Scriptures, 5 and that he appeared to Cephas, and then to the Twelve. 6 After that, he appeared to more than five hundred of the brothers and sisters at the same time, most of whom are still living, though some have fallen asleep. 7 Then he appeared to James, then to all the apostles, 8 and last of all he appeared to me also, as to one abnormally born.

· ·

12 But if it is preached that Christ has been raised from the dead, how can some of you say that there is no resurrection of the dead? 13 If there is no resurrection of the dead, then not even Christ has been raised. 14 And if Christ has not been raised, our preaching is useless and so is your faith.

· ·

20 But Christ has indeed been raised from the dead, the firstfruits of those who have fallen asleep. 21 For since death came through a man, the resurrection of the dead comes also through a man. 22 For as in Adam all die, so in Christ all will be made alive. 23 But each in turn: Christ, the firstfruits; then, when he comes, those who belong to him.

· ·

42 So will it be with the resurrection of the dead. The body that is sown is perishable, it is raised imperishable; 43 it is sown in dishonor, it is raised in glory; it is sown in weakness, it is raised in power; 44 it is sown a natural body, it is raised a spiritual body.

If there is a natural body, there is also a spiritual body. 45 So it is written: "The first man Adam became a living being"; the last Adam, a lifegiving spirit.

KEY VERSES

If only for this life we have hope in Christ, we are of all people most to be pitied. But Christ has indeed been raised from the dead, the firstfruits of those who have fallen asleep. —1 Corinthians 15:19, 20

JUSTICE AND THE PROPHETS

Unit 2: God Promises a Just Kingdom

LESSONS 6–9

LESSON AIMS

After participating in this lesson, each learner will be able to:

1. List the key elements of the gospel as Paul sees them.

2. Explain why Christ's resurrection is the key to understanding everyone's future.

3. Describe changes in his or her dedication to Christ after reading the entirety of 1 Corinthians 15 each day in the week ahead.

LESSON OUTLINE

Introduction

A. Will We Live Again?

In the midst of his suffering, Job asked rhetorically, "If someone dies, will they live again?" (Job 14:14). He soon answered his own question when he declared, "After my skin has been destroyed, yet in my flesh I will see God" (19:26). Centuries later, God put a massive exclamation point on Job's conclusion when Jesus rose from the dead. Easter Sunday worship services today will likely feature songs, Scripture readings, and preaching to celebrate that fact—the cornerstone of the Christian faith. Many Christians even prefer to call this Resurrection Sunday.

For the first-century church, every Sunday was Resurrection Sunday. Every week was a celebration and recognition that they served a living Savior. But at least one church had problems with regard to the implications of Jesus' resurrection.

B. Lesson Context

The city of Corinth was located on the Isthmus of Corinth. That was a narrow strip of land, about five miles wide, that connected upper Greece with the Peloponnesian Peninsula to the south. This allowed Corinth to prosper as a trade center for goods coming from the eastern Roman Empire across the Aegean Sea to the Gulf of Corinth on their way to Italy and Rome (and vice versa). Corinth became a large, wealthy city made up of a business class, workers, and—sadly—slaves. The city attracted entrepreneurs from around the empire, giving the city a cosmopolitan culture and a mix of religions.

The apostle Paul's first visit to the city of Corinth turned into a stay of 18 months in the early AD 50s (Acts 18:11). That was some two decades after the death and resurrection of Christ. Paul ended up planting a church of considerable diversity in Corinth, including Gentiles from many different religious backgrounds and Jews (see 18:8). After Paul's departure, the Corinthian church endured many self-inflicted problems (examples: 1 Corinthians 3:3, 4; 5:1, 2; 7:1-16). He wrote his first letter to the church in Corinth in AD 56 to address these issues.

Perhaps the most serious of the Corinthians' problems was a misunderstanding of the nature and significance of the resurrection of Jesus. Paul understood that the resurrection could not be neglected; there could be no compromise about it. This issue is dealt with more completely in 1 Corinthians 15 than anywhere else in the Bible. For this reason, the chapter is often called the Resurrection Chapter.

I. Key to Preaching
(1 Corinthians 15:1-8)
A. Not in Vain (vv. 1, 2)

1. Now, brothers and sisters, I want to remind you of the gospel I preached to you, which you received and on which you have taken your stand.

Although Paul has been absent for several years, many in the Corinthian church remember his preaching. He reminds the Corinthians that what he taught them in the past is still valid. Since they had *received* his message as truth, Paul can say that the Corinthians *stand* on his preaching. They continue to believe *the gospel* (see on 1 Corinthians 15:3b-8, below; compare Galatians 1:8). They can still use his teaching as a guide for their faith and practice.

2. By this gospel you are saved, if you hold firmly to the word I preached to you. Otherwise, you have believed in vain.

It is the continuing acceptance of Paul's *gospel* that gives the Corinthians assurance that they *are saved* from eternal punishment for their sinful rebellion against God (see also Romans 1:16). Paul urges the Corinthians not to forget his gospel essentials (which he is about to review). Otherwise, all their earlier commitments will be *in vain*.

What Do You Think?

▶ What favorite memory-recall technique can you share with a fellow Christian to help him or her stay strong in the faith during trying times?

Digging Deeper

In what way does 1 Peter 3:15 help form your response? Explain.

B. According to the Scriptures (vv. 3, 4)

3a. For what I received I passed on to you as of first importance:

Paul presents himself as a conduit of his message; he is neither its originator nor its final recipient. He *received* it from the Lord himself (Galatians 1:12). Paul's plan for evangelism has always been to deliver the gospel to faithful people who will pass it on to others (see 2 Timothy 2:2).

The phrase *first importance* indicates that what Paul is about to say is of primary, bedrock, and central importance.

3b. that Christ died for our sins according to the Scriptures,

From his birth to his death, Jesus' life provides the ultimate example of God's love and the ideal human reaction to that love. No one, including Paul, seeks to trivialize Jesus' life and ministry. But for Paul, the very core preaching of the gospel requires three things: Jesus' death, burial, and resurrection.

Jesus' death was scandalous, the execution of an innocent man through treachery and injustice (compare Galatians 1:4). Though history bears witness to many unjust deaths, Jesus' death is unique because he *died for our sins* (John 1:29; 1 Peter 2:24), something no other human could do. In that regard, his death served as a propitiation, which means "something that turns away wrath" (see Romans 3:25; 1 John 2:2; 4:10).

All this took place *according to the Scriptures* (see Isaiah 53:5, 6; Psalm 16:8-11). God had planned the gospel events before they happened. And the Old Testament Scriptures, written centuries beforehand, bear witness to this preordained design (compare Matthew 26:24; Luke 24:27, 44; Acts 17:2).

4a. that he was buried,

Paul insists that proclamation of the gospel must include the fact that Jesus *was buried* (see Matthew 27:59, 60). Mary Magdalene and other women, not to mention Peter and other apostles, went to Jesus' tomb fully expecting to find a corpse (Luke 24:5; John 20:13). The angelic report that the tomb was empty and Jesus was alive was soon backed up by personal experience (Matthew 28:8-10; Luke 24:1-49; John 20:14-29).

The Resurrected Servant

Visual for Lessons 6 & 7. *While discussing all of the witnesses Paul lists, asks how Christians today witness Jesus' resurrection and are witnesses to it.*

During Paul's ministry, lies were circulating that Jesus' body had been stolen from his tomb (Matthew 28:12-15). Paul does not tolerate such nonsense. The security surrounding that burial is well attested (Matthew 27:57-66; etc.). And no one contests that the burial took place.

4b. that he was raised on the third day according to the Scriptures,

Jesus' lifeless body lay in the tomb all day Saturday. Then he *was raised* from the dead, brought back to life by the Father (1 Corinthians 6:14; 15:15), *on the third day.* That is the day of the week we call Sunday. On the phrase *according to the Scriptures,* see reference to Jonah 1:17 by Jesus in Matthew 12:40 (compare John 2:19-22.)

The resurrection serves as God's stamp of approval for all time on Jesus (compare Acts 2:29-32; Romans 1:4). He was not a madman when he claimed to be God's Son. God had designated him as the sacrificial Lamb who would take away the sin of the world (John 1:29). That happened when he paid sin's price by dying on the cross.

C. Testifying to the Resurrection (vv. 5-8)

5a. and that he appeared to Cephas,

The Gospels record that one of the first witnesses of the risen Christ was Mary Magdalene (John 20:16; compare Matthew 28:1; Luke 24:1, 10; Mark 16:1). Paul begins his list instead with *Cephas,* the apostle Simon Peter (compare Luke 24:34). Peter boldly proclaimed the resurrection

of Christ (Acts 2:24; 3:15; 10:40; 1 Peter 1:3). Peter might have visited the Corinthian church, giving him special influence there (see 1 Corinthians 9:5). Indeed, a factional party within this church identified itself as Peter's followers (1:12). For the believers in Corinth, Peter's witness holds great weight.

5b, 6. and then to the Twelve. After that, he appeared to more than five hundred of the brothers and sisters at the same time, most of whom are still living, though some have fallen asleep.

Paul then expands the list of witnesses to all 12 apostles; these are 11 of the original 12, now minus Judas but replaced by Matthias (Acts 1:12-26). As the number of witnesses expands from a few to a group of *more than five hundred,* we see rapid and exponential expansion. It leaves the impression there are many more post-resurrection witnesses that might be included.

We have no other information on the appearance of Christ to the crowd of more than 500. But Paul's statement that *some* of these *have fallen asleep* suggests that he knew some of these folks personally and had kept track of them.

We should also take care to note the importance of the words *brothers and sisters.* With one exception, there is no record of Jesus appearing to any of his enemies or to unbelievers after his resurrection, only to believers. That one exception is Paul, when he was known as Saul (see 1 Corinthians 15:8, below).

7. Then he appeared to James, then to all the apostles,

We take care to note that this *James* is neither of the apostles of that same name in Matthew 10:2-4. Since those two men are included in "the Twelve" of 1 Corinthians 15:5b, above, they are already accounted for. This James is one of Jesus' half brothers (Mark 6:3).

Jesus' brothers did not believe in him before his death (John 7:5), but they did afterward (Acts 1:14). The mention of James in the text before us coincides with the fact of his leadership in the first-century church (15:13-21; 21:18).

The mention of James helps us understand why Paul writes here *then to all the apostles* when "the Twelve [apostles]" have already been noted two verses prior. The solution is simple: more individuals in the New Testament have the designation "apostle" than just the 12. James, the Lord's half brother, is one of them (see Galatians 1:19; compare Acts 14:14; Romans 16:7).

8. and last of all he appeared to me also, as to one abnormally born.

Paul ends his list of witnesses to the resurrection with himself. He did not see the risen Jesus during the 40-day period between the resurrection and the ascension. Paul's personal encounter with the risen Lord came later, while he was a persecutor of Christians (Acts 9:1-6, 17; 22:6-9; 26:12-15). That encounter means that Paul is not merely repeating stories as secondhand hearsay (Galatians 1:1, 11, 12).

> **What Do You Think?**
> In what situations should your personal testimony be included in a gospel presentation and in what situations should it not? Why?
> **Digging Deeper**
> What biblical examples can you list for each of the two scenarios?

Paul's status is the same as that of Peter or James (see 1 Corinthians 9:1). Yet he acknowledges that he came to this position based solely on an untimely and unexpected event. For Paul to be visited by the risen Christ (*appeared to me also*) was not in keeping with any predictable pattern, but out of the mercy and plan of the Lord.

II. Key to Faith
(1 Corinthians 15:12-14)
A. False Teaching (v. 12)

12. But if it is preached that Christ has been raised from the dead, how can some of you say that there is no resurrection of the dead?

Paul has now emphasized both the centrality of Jesus' resurrection and the credible evidence for it. This is a review of things the Corinthians had heard him preach when he was among them.

Despite what Paul taught the Corinthians, there are some in the church who want to deny the possibility of *resurrection* while still maintaining that *Christ* had risen *from the dead*. So Paul proceeds to

rebut this illogical position. The rhetorical question of the verse before us begins that rebuttal.

B. Futile Belief (vv. 13, 14)

13, 14. If there is no resurrection of the dead, then not even Christ has been raised. And if Christ has not been raised, our preaching is useless and so is your faith.

Denying all *resurrection* logically denies Jesus' own resurrection. If we affirm his resurrection but deny the possibility of bodily resurrection for all people, then we are negating Jesus' humanity (contrast John 1:14). Such a denial nullifies the sacrificial power of Jesus' death that gives us new life (compare 11:23-26; 1 Thessalonians 4:14). That would mean that we are still liable to the penalty for our sins (1 Corinthians 15:18). Without the possibility of resurrection from the dead, the entire Christian message collapses; the Christian life becomes an exercise in futility (compare 2 Timothy 2:18).

> **What Do You Think?**
> Given culture's growing secularism, what are some ways you can remind yourself continually of the truth of verses 13, 14?
> **Digging Deeper**
> When/how have you seen secular culture cause the most damage in denying Christ's resurrection?

❧ OF LOGIC AND TRUTH ❧

Did you know that what is true and what is logical aren't necessarily the same thing? I took a college course in philosophical logic. In it I learned how to analyze three-sentence arguments called syllogisms. In a syllogism, the first two sentences are premises and the third one is the conclusion. My task was to determine whether a given syllogism was constructed with logical correctness.

Here is an example of a syllogism:

1. Major premise: All insects are blue.
2. Minor premise: All ants are insects.
3. Conclusion: Therefore, all ants are blue.

From experience we recognize that the first premise is patently false; so, therefore, the conclusion is false as well. Nevertheless, this syllogism is constructed in a logically correct way.

Paul used logic and also factual evidence to challenge error. When the Corinthians started with a false premise, no valid conclusion could result. What lie or false logic most challenges you today?　　　　　　　　　　　　　　—L. H-P.

III. Key to Hope
(1 CORINTHIANS 15:20-23, 42-45)
A. Firstfruits (v. 20)

20. But Christ has indeed been raised from the dead, the firstfruits of those who have fallen asleep.

Paul pivots from arguing about the centrality of resurrection for all believers to some specific implications of Christ's resurrection. The agricultural metaphor of *firstfruits* invokes the idea of the choice parts at the outset of a harvest (example: Exodus 34:26a). It is the opposite of leftovers. There is no harvest produce that comes earlier than the firstfruits. This is true of the resurrection of Christ. His is only the first resurrection of many to come (Acts 26:23; 1 Corinthians 15:23; 1 Peter 1:3).

B. New Adam (v. 21-23)

21, 22a. For since death came through a man, the resurrection of the dead comes also through a man. For as in Adam all die,

Genesis identifies *Adam* as the first human being. He disobeyed God and brought sin into the human realm. The inevitable result of this sin was *death* (Genesis 2:17; Romans 5:12, 14). Adam is thus the prototype of a sinner under the curse of death. Adam is humanity's father of sin and death.

22b. so in Christ all will be made alive.

The new prototype or template is *Christ* (Romans 5:14-19). Christ has overcome the power of death through his resurrection (Acts 2:24; Hebrews 2:14). This has two implications. First, there is an order to the resurrection of humankind. As the author of Hebrews puts it, Jesus is the "captain" of our salvation, implying his priority and leadership (Hebrews 2:10; compare 12:2).

23. But each in turn: Christ, the firstfruits; then, when he comes, those who belong to him.

Second, the resurrection of Christ is not the end of God's display of resurrecting power. We will follow in due time according to God's plan (1 Corinthians 6:14). Paul ties this fact to the second coming of Christ (15:52, not in our printed text).

> **What Do You Think?**
> In what area of study do you feel most deficient: on the significance of resurrection in general or the significance of Christ's resurrection in particular?
> *Digging Deeper*
> What plan will you form to correct this?

C. Resurrected Body (vv. 42-45)

42, 43. So will it be with the resurrection of the dead. The body that is sown is perishable, it is raised imperishable; it is sown in dishonor, it is raised in glory; it is sown in weakness, it is raised in power; it is sown a natural body, it is raised a spiritual body.

Paul later deals with questions concerning the nature of the resurrection body we will enjoy (1 Corinthians 15:35-41, not in our printed text). His premise is that all bodies have their own unique characteristics. Though we do not know what our resurrection bodies will be like, we can be sure that God has determined this.

Paul characterizes our current bodies as *perishable* (subject to deterioration), dishonorable (associated with shameful acts), and weak (limited in strength and endurance). By contrast, our new bodies will be *imperishable* (not subject to disease or decay), glorious (free from sin and shame; compare Philippians 3:21; Colossians 3:4), and powerful (completely adequate in all things to serve the Lord).

44. it is sown a natural body, it is raised a spiritual body. If there is a natural body, there is also a spiritual body.

Our current bodies are *natural* (subject to the physical laws of nature). But our new bodies will be *spiritual*. We understand this incompletely, but Paul is likely aware of the appearance of the resurrected Jesus to his disciples in a room with locked doors; that was something no natural body could do (John 20:19, 20). Jesus did not become some sort of spiritual blob or glowing mist (Luke 24:39, 40). He had a recognizable body, one that even carried the scars of crucifixion on his hands, feet, and side (Luke 24:39, 40). We will recognize each other after our resurrections too.

⚜ THE PROMISE OF RESURRECTION ⚜

As a child, I feared death. I dreaded funerals and absolutely protested viewing of bodies of the deceased. It was not until my grandmother died that my fear of death dissipated. I grieved her death, yet I was at peace with it. How could this be?

My grandmother was a devout Christian. She discipled me, teaching me how to study the Bible, pray, fast, and serve others. When she came to the end of her earthly journey, there was no need to fear for her: through Christ she had eternal life. Her body that had suffered would be resurrected and changed by Christ's power. Her physical death was the end of her life on earth, but her life was not over. She has eternal life through Christ.

Better grasping the promise of resurrection changed not only my view of death but also my view of life. This transformative promise prompts us to yield our lives in service to Christ. Have hope for his return and the resurrection!   —L. H-P.

45. So it is written: "The first man Adam became a living being; the last Adam, a life-giving spirit."

Paul uses the two-Adams analogy again, but in a different way than to contrast sin and death versus eternal life. He reminds us that Adam's body was lifeless until God breathed life into it (Genesis 2:7). Only then did Adam become *a living being.*

In the resurrection, our dead bodies will receive

life again, given by *the last Adam,* who is Christ. The risen Christ participates as *a life-giving spirit* in our bodies' return to life from death (compare John 5:21; 6:54). Christ is the one who has the power to recreate and restore life to our bodies. The new body in and of itself is not enough, even if it is imperishable, glorious, and powerful.

> *What Do You Think?*
> What additional steps can your church take in transforming people from being less like Adam and more like Christ?
> *Digging Deeper*
> What could be your part in this plan?

Conclusion
A. The Twinkling of an Eye

Before and during the first century AD, there were instances of the miraculous restoration to life of a dead person (examples: 2 Kings 4:32-35; 13:21; Luke 7:11-17). But those people eventually died again. Jesus' resurrection, however, was different. He rose from the dead never to die again. Because he lives, we can be confident that we will live with him in resurrected bodies, never again to face death (Romans 8:2).

Paul's Corinthian readers had produced fruit and would continue to do so as long as they remained faithful. However, their faith was endangered by the choices some had made to abandon the doctrine of the resurrection—and so the danger is with us. We should join Paul therefore in seeing resurrection as victory over humanity's greatest enemy: death. On the glorious day of Christ's return, we will be changed (1 Corinthians 15:52). As we celebrate the resurrection of Christ, let us anticipate the promise of our own resurrection.

B. Prayer

Father God, we look forward to the resurrection of the dead, made possible by your Son, Jesus Christ. We pray in Jesus' name. Amen.

C. Thought to Remember

Christ's resurrection gives us the certain hope for life after death.

HOW TO SAY IT

Aegean	A-*jee*-un.
Cephas	*See*-fus.
isthmus	*i*-smes.
Matthias	Muh-*thigh*-us (*th* as in *thin*).
Peloponnesian	*Pell*-uh-puh-*nee*-shen.
propitiation	pro-*pih*-she-*ay*-shun.
syllogism	*si*-le-ji-zem.

INVOLVEMENT LEARNING

Enhance your lesson with NIV Bible Student *(from your curriculum supplier) and the reproducible activity page (at www.standardlesson.com or in the back of the* NIV Standard Lesson Commentary Deluxe Edition*).*

Into the Lesson

Give each learner several index cards. Then challenge learners to use their cards to create a two-story structure (on a table) without working together or modifying the cards in any way. As learners finish and admire their handiwork, talk about the first floor of each structure. Discuss the necessity of ensuring its soundness for supporting the second story. Offer good-natured comments on the efforts of learners who had difficulty in that regard.

Make a transition by saying, "The resurrection is the foundation for our faith. Without that foundation, Christianity would—and should—collapse. Today's lesson explains why."

Into the Word

Begin a three-phase discussion by dividing the class into three groups. Give each group one of the following discussion assignments on handouts (you prepare).

Necessary-Death Group. 1–In what ways was/is the death of Jesus a necessary part of the Christian faith? 2–What would Christianity be like if Jesus had not died? 3–Which specific Scriptures of today's lesson text support your answers?

Necessary-Burial Group. 1–What role does the burial of Jesus play in establishing the foundation of Christianity? 2–How would the credibility of Christianity be different if Jesus had not been buried? 3–Which specific Scriptures of today's lesson text support your answers?

Necessary-Resurrection Group. 1–In what ways is the resurrection of Jesus necessary to the Christian faith? 2–What would Christianity be like if Jesus had not risen from the dead? 3–Which specific Scriptures of today's lesson text support your answers?

Groups should ideally be no larger that five learners each. For larger classes, form extra groups and give duplicate assignments.

As group discussion winds down, reconvene for whole-class discussion of each group's conclusions in turn. Use the commentary to correct factual mistakes and resolve misunderstandings.

Option 1. Following the above, write these three phrases on the board to probe further the importance of evidence:

> *Faith in spite of evidence to the contrary*
> *Blind faith*
> *Faith based on evidence*

Ask learners to give examples of each. Be prepared to defend the supreme importance of faith based on evidence. (For best preparation, consult the books *Cold-Case Christianity* and *Forensic Faith* by J. Warner Wallace and/or see his YouTube channel.)

Option 2. Distribute copies of the "My Resurrection Body" exercise from the activity page, which you can download. Have learners complete it in pairs.

Into Life

Distribute copies of the following seven-day chart that you have copied and enlarged:

Day	Thoughts on 1 Corinthians 15
Sun	
Mon	
Tue	
Wed	
Thu	
Fri	
Sat	

Challenge learners to read all of 1 Corinthians 15 daily in the week ahead and make notes of renewed commitment to Christ based on that text.

Alternative. Distribute copies of the "Proclaim the Resurrection" exercise from the activity page for learners to discuss and use as indicated.

AN EXECUTED SCOUNDREL

DEVOTIONAL READING: Luke 19:11-26
BACKGROUND SCRIPTURE: Esther 3, 5, 7

ESTHER 7:1-10

¹ So the king and Haman went to Queen Esther's banquet, ² and as they were drinking wine on the second day, the king again asked, "Queen Esther, what is your petition? It will be given you. What is your request? Even up to half the kingdom, it will be granted."

³ Then Queen Esther answered, "If I have found favor with you, Your Majesty, and if it pleases you, grant me my life—this is my petition. And spare my people—this is my request. ⁴ For I and my people have been sold to be destroyed, killed and annihilated. If we had merely been sold as male and female slaves, I would have kept quiet, because no such distress would justify disturbing the king."

⁵ King Xerxes asked Queen Esther, "Who is he? Where is he —the man who has dared to do such a thing?"

⁶ Esther said, "An adversary and enemy! This vile Haman!"

Then Haman was terrified before the king and queen. ⁷ The king got up in a rage, left his wine and went out into the palace garden. But Haman, realizing that the king had already decided his fate, stayed behind to beg Queen Esther for his life.

⁸ Just as the king returned from the palace garden to the banquet hall, Haman was falling on the couch where Esther was reclining.

The king exclaimed, "Will he even molest the queen while she is with me in the house?"

As soon as the word left the king's mouth, they covered Haman's face.

⁹ Then Harbona, one of the eunuchs attending the king, said, "A pole reaching to a height of fifty cubits stands by Haman's house. He had it set up for Mordecai, who spoke up to help the king."

The king said, "Impale him on it!" ¹⁰ So they impaled Haman on the pole he had set up for Mordecai. Then the king's fury subsided.

KEY VERSE

They impaled Haman on the pole he had set up for Mordecai. Then the king's fury subsided.

—Esther 7:10

JUSTICE AND THE PROPHETS

Unit 2: God Promises a Just Kingdom

LESSONS 6–9

LESSON AIMS

After participating in this lesson, each learner will be able to:

1. State how Haman's plan backfired.

2. Suggest elements of the account that are more likely to be providential than others.

3. Repent of a sin of omission concerning a time when he or she should have opposed injustice but did not do so.

LESSON OUTLINE

Introduction

A. An Outrageous Injustice

After serving nearly 25 years for the murder of his wife, 57-year-old Michael Morton walked out of a Texas prison on October 4, 2011. He was released and officially exonerated after DNA evidence proved his innocence and pointed to the crime's true perpetrator.

Investigation into the initial prosecution of the crime also revealed that the district attorney in the case had illegally concealed evidence that pointed to Mr. Morton's innocence. As a result, the district attorney spent time in jail himself and was stripped of his law license.

Miscarriages of justice and abuses of power stir our outrage all the more when they involve officials who have been entrusted with maintaining a just society. Today's lesson will identify a corrupt, prejudiced official whose abuse of power could have resulted in the destruction of God's covenant people. Little did this individual realize that certain Jews were in positions to foil this genocidal intent.

B. Lesson Context

The story of Esther is one of several in the Old Testament to portray the success of Israelites living in foreign surroundings. In a few noteworthy cases, these Israelites rose to influential positions (examples: Genesis 41:40-43; Nehemiah 1:11; Daniel 2:48, 49).

These accounts illustrate God's care for his covenant people. They also illustrate his resolve to use them as agents of influence even when (or especially when) they faced opposition, criticism, and ill-treatment.

The events in the book of Esther take place in the Persian citadel of Susa during the reign of Xerxes I, also known as Ahasuerus (485–465 BC; see Esther 1:1, 2). Key figures in the account are the close relatives Mordecai and Esther. They were part of a Jewish community that had remained in the area even after a decree in 538 BC allowed them to return home (Ezra 1:1-4; Esther 2:5-7).

Esther became queen after Vashti, the previous queen, was divorced by Xerxes (Esther 1:10-22).

Xerxes subsequently replaced Vashti by holding a beauty pageant, which Esther won (2:1-18).

Throughout the selection process, Mordecai forbade Esther from revealing her nationality, and she complied (Esther 2:10). There is no indication that the king himself would have held her Jewish identity against her. Perhaps Mordecai was aware of a general prejudice among the members of the royal court in the larger community.

Eventually, a scheme to destroy the Jews materialized. Xerxes' highest official, Haman, had developed a fierce animosity for Mordecai (Esther 3:1-5). This resulted in Haman's seeking an edict from Xerxes for the annihilation of all Jews throughout the Persian Empire (3:6). Haman secured this edict without revealing to Xerxes which people he had targeted for destruction. A date for their eradication was set, and the Jews found themselves in grave peril (3:7-15).

Mordecai convinced Esther to act, at the risk of her own life, to save her people (Esther 4). A key part of his appeal was to consider the possibility that divine providence was at work. This possibility can be seen in his question, "Who knows but that you are come to your royal position for such a time as this?" (4:14). Esther's subsequent resolve is seen in her reply, "I will go to the king, even though it is against the law. And if I perish, I perish" (4:16).

After three days of fasting, Esther went before Xerxes and received his mercy (Esther 4:16–5:2). She asked that he and Haman join her in a banquet, where she would answer the king (5:3, 4). When prompted at the meal to offer her petition, she requested only that they come to another feast the next day (5:5-8).

I. Scheme Explained
(ESTHER 7:1-4)
A. Second Banquet (vv. 1, 2a)
1. So the king and Haman went to Queen Esther's banquet,

Esther's invitation to *the king and Haman* results from Mordecai's telling her about Haman's plan to slaughter the Jews (see Esther 4:7, 8, 15, 16). The *banquet* hosted here is the second the two men attend at Esther's request (see the Lesson Context).

2a. And the king said again unto Esther on the second day at the banquet of wine.

Overindulgence of *wine* seems to have contributed mightily to Vashti's dismissal as queen (Esther 1:7-10). At Esther's *banquet*, however, *the king* seems much better behaved.

B. Second Request (v. 2b)
2b. and as they were drinking wine on the second day, the king again asked, "Queen Esther, what is your petition? It will be given you. What is your request? Even up to half the kingdom, it will be granted."

Xerxes once again expresses his willingness to hear Esther's *petition* (see the Lesson Context). Having been asked to wait during the banquet of the night before, he is no doubt intensely curious about what's on Esther's mind. Thus his exaggerated offer of up to *half the kingdom* (see also Esther 5:3; 9:12; compare Mark 6:23).

C. Second Response (vv. 3, 4)
3. Then Queen Esther answered, "If I have found favor with you, Your Majesty, and if it pleases you, grant me my life—this is my petition. And spare my people—this is my request.

In ordinary circumstances, *Esther* may have drawn out the process over more days with more banquets and wine. Xerxes himself may have expected the process to draw out further, given the custom of multi-day banquets (Esther 1:5). But for Esther and her people, time is running out. At least two months have elapsed since the king's extermination order was issued, leaving less than nine months before it is to be enacted (3:7; 8:9,

HOW TO SAY IT

Ahasuerus	Uh-haz-you-*ee*-rus.
eunuch	*you*-nick.
Haman	*Hay*-mun.
Harbona	Hahr-*boh*-nuh.
Mordecai	*Mor*-dih-kye.
Susa	*Soo*-suh.
Xerxes	*Zerk*-seez.

12). That may seem like plenty of time in a modern sense. But it's not, given the vast expanse of the Persian Empire and the limitations of ancient methods of communication.

Therefore Esther does not waste time on any multi-day etiquette of presenting a request, beyond the single-day delay so far. She has a history of modesty in her requests (Esther 2:15), so she probably knows that the king will assume that she won't ask for anything extravagant now. Esther has been queen for several years at this point (compare 2:16 with 3:7), so it's quite likely that she has developed a sense of when to push the king and when not to!

> What Do You Think?
> What does the timing of Esther's request with regard to the king's state of mind teach you about how to time your own initiatives?
> *Digging Deeper*
> Defend or refute this statement by Thomas Jefferson: "A good cause is often injured more by ill-timed efforts of its friends than by the arguments of its enemies."

4a. "For I and my people have been sold to be destroyed, killed and annihilated.

Esther begins to expose Haman's plot to destroy the Jews (Esther 3:9). Haman must be the one to connect the dots first: Esther is a Jew! Her statement *my people have been sold,* phrased in the passive voice, avoids implicating the king (see also 4:7). The heaping up of phrases—*to be destroyed, killed and annihilated*—emphasizes the dire consequences of her *people* being sold.

4b. "If we had merely been sold as male and female slaves, I would have kept quiet, because no such distress would justify disturbing the king."

The second part of Esther's statement is difficult to interpret. Esther could mean that she would have kept silent if her people were "only" *sold* into enslavement rather than to death. On the other hand, Esther might mean that she would keep silent if economic loss from their enslavement would not equal the loss from their deaths. Oppression in slavery would still hold out the

possibility for God to release his people (compare Psalm 81:10), but death would not. Either way, this is Esther's diplomatic way of stressing the extreme importance of the issue.

> *What Do You Think?*
> Where might God be calling you to speak up for justice on behalf of others?
> *Digging Deeper*
> How can you ensure that more harm than good won't result?

Esther conveys that she has seriously weighed the situation before speaking up. She may not realize that Haman has withheld the identity of the people he has targeted for destruction (Esther 3:8-11). One would think that the king himself would have asked that identity. The fact that he didn't indicates his absolute trust in Haman. And since the decree has now been sent all over the Persian Empire, one wonders if the king is still unaware of the identity of the group being targeted (compare 3:12-15 with 8:9). Such lack of awareness would indicate the extreme isolation of the king.

II. Culprit Exposed
(ESTHER 7:5-8)
A. King's Question (v. 5)

5. King Xerxes asked Queen Esther, "Who is he? Where is he—the man who has dared to do such a thing?"

Some wonder why the king can apparently be so clueless. But the questions are reasonable given the facts that (1) it's been several weeks since he was involved in this issue (comparing the time references of Esther 3:7, 12; 8:1, 9); (2) kings are busy people and therefore delegate tasks to subordinates (3:10, 11); and (3) the king is just now being made aware that *Esther* is part of the target group. In any case, the king is still trying to put together the bigger picture.

B. Queen's Answer (v. 6)

6a. Esther said, "An adversary and enemy! This vile Haman!"

If *Esther* has been concerned that Xerxes would become defensive, here she is probably relieved to be able to point the finger squarely and only at *Haman*. She does not identify him as her personal enemy but as *an adversary and enemy.*

Esther has stated her concern with humility and deference, following the expected protocol of the royal court. Tact is of utmost importance (compare Daniel 2:14), given that Esther is accusing the king's most trusted adviser of treachery that involves misuse of the king's own power. She is careful to level this accusation at Haman without implicating Xerxes himself.

Visual for Lesson 8. *Before ending class, discuss how Esther's providential story serves as encouragement for believers' seeking God's hand at work.*

> **What Do You Think?**
> Under what circumstances is it appropriate, if ever, for Christians to describe opponents with negative terms rather than sticking solely with the facts of what they did? Why?
>
> *Digging Deeper*
> How do texts such as Matthew 23:27; Acts 23:1-5; James 4:11; and Jude 9 help you make defensible decisions in this regard?

6b. Then Haman was terrified before the king and queen.

Haman's reaction is like that of many who are caught in wrongdoing: his once steely exterior becomes a "deer caught in the headlights" look. Interpreters often identify this moment as the climax of the entire story. *Haman* knows he is exposed; the only question is how *the king* will react. Esther has completed her speech and speaks no further in this chapter.

C. Culprit's Arrest (vv. 7, 8)

7a. The king got up in a rage, left his wine and went out into the palace garden.

With his blood boiling (compare Esther 1:12), *the king* storms out. He need hear no self-defense from Haman. The king has put the pieces together, and Haman's guilt is obvious. The king's highest official has abused royal authority, though the king does not know why. Haman has had his own best interests, not the king's, in mind.

7b. But Haman, realizing that the king had already decided his fate, stayed behind to beg Queen Esther for his life.

The king's intentions toward *Haman* are clear (compare Proverbs 20:2). Haman must do something, but he has no good option. He cannot follow *the king* outside, nor can he add to his guilt by fleeing. The warning from his wife and friends, thematic of the book as a whole, should have been heeded: "Since Mordecai, before whom your downfall has started, is of Jewish origin, you cannot stand against him—you will surely come to ruin!" (Esther 6:13). Their words are certainly coming true.

8a. Just as the king returned from the palace garden to the banquet hall, Haman was falling on the couch where Esther was reclining.

Persian royal banquets involved reclining on beds, like couches, instead of sitting at a table (compare Esther 1:6). Desperate for mercy, *Haman* approaches the queen who is reclined on her *couch* to plead for his life. Her silence may have increased his desperation, for he falls onto her couch. Ironically, Haman was enraged earlier when a Jew would not bow down to him (3:5), but now he will find himself at the feet of one of those same Jews.

8b. The king exclaimed, "Will he even molest the queen while she is with me in the house?" As soon as the word left the king's mouth, they covered Haman's face.

How *the king* might have handled Haman's treachery before seeing the man on his queen's couch no longer matters. Xerxes indicts Haman for violating harem protocol and, even worse, appearing to *molest the queen* (compare Genesis 34:7; 39:14). In the Persian system, the only men allowed near the queen or the king's other wives and concubines were eunuchs. Otherwise, an advance on any member of the harem was considered an affront to the king himself (example: 2 Samuel 16:21, 22).

The king's officials thus act on what they recognize as a capital offense. They cover *Haman's face* because he is no longer worthy to see the king.

> **What Do You Think?**
> Under what circumstances, if any, should you correct a misperception of an enemy's action? Why?
>
> **Digging Deeper**
> Does Romans 12:19-21 (quoting Proverbs 25:21, 22) inform your answer? Why, or why not?

❧ RULES OF THE HAREM ❧

Having multiple wives and concubines was common among the nobility of the ancient world (example: 2 Chronicles 11:21). These women were kept from contact with men other than their master. Centuries later, the Arabic word *harem* came into use to describe these women and their living spaces.

Harem etiquette was governed by royal edicts. Wives and concubines were not supposed to be seen in public. They were guarded by eunuchs and could only leave the harem when appropriately covered. The women of the harem lived in seclusion.

It is easy to understand the outrage of the king when he thought he saw Haman attempting to assault the queen. If the man's fate wasn't sealed before, it was then! And it all traced back to a personal vendetta against an honorable man: Haman's grudge against Mordecai. How do we stop such a vicious cycle before it starts?   —J. E.

III. Scoundrel Executed
(ESTHER 7:9, 10)
A. Just Idea (v. 9)

9a. Then Harbona, one of the eunuchs attending the king, said, "A pole reaching to a height of fifty cubits stands by Haman's house. He had it set up for Mordecai, who spoke up to help the king."

Esther has taken some of the king's *eunuchs* into her confidence during the passage of years (see Esther 2:8, 9, 15; 4:4, 5). One of them has knowledge of Esther's difficulty, probably from joining in her fast (4:16; compare 1:10).

The eunuch *Harbona* speaks up to inform *the king* that *Haman* has erected a high structure for a humiliating execution of *Mordecai*. Haman had left the first meal in high spirits. But after another confrontation with Mordecai on the way out, he once again became enraged. At the suggestion of his wife and friends, he had gallows set up with the intent of having Mordecai hanged on it (Esther 5:9-14). The height of *fifty cubits* (about 75 feet) reveals Haman's intent for Mordecai's demise to be a brazen public display.

9b. The king said, "Impale him on it!"

If *the king* had any remaining notions of sparing Haman's life, those thoughts now leave him permanently. Mordecai had saved the king's life previously (Esther 2:19-23; 6:1-11); the king now returns the favor.

B. Just Result (v. 10)

10. So they impaled Haman on the pole he had set up for Mordecai. Then the king's fury subsided.

The execution takes place immediately, given the time indicator in Esther 8:1. For *Haman* to meet his end in the manner *he had set up for Mordecai* is the supreme irony of the book (compare Proverbs 11:5, 6; 26:27); it is a prime example of poetic justice. Such an outcome points to God's work on behalf of his covenant people. God brings Haman's wickedness down on his own head in the same way the Bible often declares (examples: Psalm 9:16; Matthew 7:1, 2). Before that day's end, Xerxes will give to Mordecai the signet ring that he had entrusted to Haman, along with the position and authority that Haman had held (Esther 8:2; 10:2, 3). The Jews find deliverance by a second decree of the king (8:11, 12). The Feast of Purim (derived from the word *pur*; see 3:7; 9:24, 26) commemorates this deliverance each year. This celebration includes not only a meal but also hearing the book of Esther read aloud in a synagogue and giving food and other forms of charity.

> **What Do You Think?**
> How will you know when celebrating an enemy's defeat is appropriate (Esther 8:15-17; 9:16-28) and when it is not (Proverbs 24:17, 18)?
> **Digging Deeper**
> What other Scripture texts inform your answer?

❧ ISN'T IT IRONIC? ❧

Piracy of digital property is an ongoing problem in the age of the internet. Adobe, Apple, and Microsoft were losing profits when businesses illegally copied software. In early 2014, the help of the Business Software Alliance (BSA) was enlisted. The BSA ran online ads offering a reward to employees who informed them that a company was copying software illegally. This effort backfired in an ironic manner.

It was soon revealed that the image on one of these ads—a pot of gold—was published without the group's having acquired a license to do so. The ad meant to fight digital piracy contained a pirated picture! The very problem that they were trying to solve ended up indicting themselves.

Poetic justice involves ironic twists of fate. Jesus' warning in that regard still applies: "For in the same way you judge others, you will be judged, and with the measure you use, it will be measured to you" (Matthew 7:2).   —J. E.

Conclusion

A. Behind the Scenes

Like many people, I count the story of Esther among my favorites in the Bible. Though the book famously does not mention God by name any-

where, its many twists and turns strongly hint at God's providential hand with his covenant people. From Esther's selection as queen, to Haman's execution, to the Jews' deliverance—the eyes of faith clearly see these events as much more than luck or happenstance. Rather, God was at work behind the scenes.

We therefore should see God as the main character in the account. The actions of its human characters are of mixed quality. Xerxes consistently acted under the influence of alcohol and with a hot temper. Haman always acted in self-interest and pride. Esther and Mordecai seem not to have resisted Esther's participation in a contest that resulted in marriage to a pagan king (contrast Ezra 10). But God worked his will through all parties nonetheless.

Like Esther and her relative Mordecai, we are God's imperfect servants in rectifying the wrongs in the world. But God can and does work through us nonetheless. There are two extremes to avoid: (1) thinking that confronting evil is all up to us and (2) thinking that confronting evil is all up to God. The proper path to take in any given situation will depend on prayer, Bible study, and openness to the leading of the Holy Spirit. We must always consider the possibility that God has placed us in a circumstance "for such a time as this" (Esther 4:14).

There is no guarantee that every incident in the lives of God's people will have a tidy ending, as the book of Esther does. Evil sometimes enjoys temporary victories. The path to triumph over evil is often unclear, recognized only in twenty-twenty hindsight. But with Christ working in us and through us, we can live with the assurance that "in all things God works for the good of those who love him" (Romans 8:28).

B. Prayer

Father, open our eyes to the opportunities you have for us. Give us courage to act, even when we don't know your plans. We pray in Jesus' name. Amen.

C. Thought to Remember

Act justly in every situation.

INVOLVEMENT LEARNING

Enhance your lesson with NIV Bible Student *(from your curriculum supplier) and the reproducible activity page (at www.standardlesson.com or in the back of the* NIV Standard Lesson Commentary Deluxe Edition*).*

Into the Lesson

Tell the following story:

A Florida couple was arguing over possession of a pickup truck to which each claimed rightful ownership. The man came up with a plan to plant cocaine in the vehicle, hoping that his girlfriend would get caught with it and the vehicle would then be his. The plan went awry when police caught him in the act of planting the drugs. He was arrested.

Allow time for volunteers to share one or two stories of revenge gone wrong. Then say, "There's something very satisfying about proper vindication and retribution. That's exactly what our lesson is about today."

Option. Before class begins, place in chairs copies of the "Revenge Gone Wrong" exercise from the activity page, which you can download. Learners can begin working on this as they arrive.

Into the Word

Have learners take turns reading aloud the lesson text of Esther 7:1-10. Then place learners into groups of three or four; give each learner a handout (you prepare) on which you have reproduced a copy of the lesson text. Title the handouts "Normal or Providential?" and have these identical instructions on each:

1. Circle all the verbs and other action words in the text of Esther 7:1-10.

2. Put a *P* next to each word you circled that is much more likely to have happened as a result of God's providential intervention rather than normal human behavior or random chance.

3. Put an *N* next to each word you circled that is much more likely to have happened as a result of normal human behavior or random chance rather than God's providential intervention.

4. Put a *?* next to each word you think could go either way.

Introduce the activity by saying, "Even though God is not mentioned in the book of Esther, many of the events seem providential. As your group works through the actions of the text, mark your conclusions in that regard as indicated. While there are no definitive answers, be prepared to give reasons to support your conclusions."

After groups complete their work, reconvene for whole-class discussion to determine consensus or lack thereof. Wrap up this section by asking, "What other book of the Bible does not mention God by name?" (*answer: Song of Songs*). Follow by discussing what difference this makes in understanding these two books, if any.

Into Life

Write the following on the board. Pause for discussion of each scenario before writing the next.

Your supervisor uses unethical business practices that put you in compromising situations.

An acquaintance asks you to go to a rally to support a cause that violates your beliefs.

Someone you care about is being unfairly attacked on social media.

During whole-class discussion, encourage free response. Jot responses on the board. (*Option.* Arrange the class into study pairs to discuss one scenario per pair. Distribute handouts [you prepare] that list the scenario for a given pair to discuss.)

After discussing conclusions, give each learner a blank index card. Have learners write on their cards this lead-in phrase: "If only I had . . ." Instruct them to write a prayer of repentance about a time when they could have opposed an injustice but failed to do so. Assure learners that you will not ask to collect the cards. Encourage learners to take the card home as a reminder to thank God for his forgiveness.

Option. Distribute copies of the "Teamwork Under Fire" exercise from the activity page. Promise to discuss answers when the class next meets.

A Justice-Loving God

DEVOTIONAL READING: Isaiah 42:1-9
BACKGROUND SCRIPTURE: Isaiah 61:8–62:12

ISAIAH 61:8-11

8 "For I, the LORD, love justice;
  I hate robbery and wrongdoing.
In my faithfulness I will reward my people
  and make an everlasting covenant with
    them.
9 Their descendants will be known among
    the nations
  and their offspring among the peoples.
All who see them will acknowledge
  that they are a people the LORD has
    blessed."
10 I delight greatly in the LORD;
  my soul rejoices in my God.
For he has clothed me with garments of
    salvation
  and arrayed me in a robe of his
    righteousness,
as a bridegroom adorns his head like a
    priest,
  and as a bride adorns herself with her
    jewels.
11 For as the soil makes the sprout come up
  and a garden causes seeds to grow,

so the Sovereign LORD will make righteous-
    ness and praise
  spring up before all nations.

ISAIAH 62:2-4A

2 The nations will see your vindication,
  and all kings your glory;
you will be called by a new name
  that the mouth of the LORD will bestow.
3 You will be a crown of splendor in the
    LORD's hand,
  a royal diadem in the hand of your
    God.
4a No longer will they call you Deserted,
  or name your land Desolate.

KEY VERSE

I, the LORD, love justice; I hate robbery and wrongdoing. In my faithfulness I will reward my people and make an everlasting covenant with them. —**Isaiah 61:8**

Photo: Tanjulchik / iStock / Thinkstock

JUSTICE AND THE PROPHETS

Unit 2: God Promises a Just Kingdom

LESSONS 6–9

LESSON AIMS

After participating in this lesson, each learner will be able to:

1. Identify the everlasting covenant.

2. Explain why Old Testament parallelism promotes fuller understanding of the text.

3. Repent of a sin of commission concerning a time he or she promoted an injustice.

LESSON OUTLINE

Introduction

A. Contrasts

The father of one of my high school friends was a coach for a nearby college basketball team. A group of us went to one of the games. I had gone to many high school basketball games, but this was my first college game. I was immediately struck by how much faster and more highly skilled the players were. My appreciation for their abilities was due to the contrast of what I had observed at the college level compared to high school.

Another time, I overheard two high school boys conversing at a hamburger stand. Before leaving, one realized he had been given too much change. As he started to give it back, his friend said, "If you give that back, you're stupid!" The young man gave the money back anyway. His simple act was a contrast to the habits of his friend, who clearly had a different set of values.

Lifestyle contrasts can indeed reveal important truths. Today's lesson will leave no doubt about that fact!

B. Lesson Context

Isaiah (ministered about 740–680 BC) lived in the days when Israel, the northern kingdom, was struggling against Assyria and was finally exiled from the land. For a time, the northern kingdom sent tribute to Assyria; however, Israel's King Hoshea sought an alliance with Egypt in order to end Israel's vassal relationship to the Assyrian oppressors. The consequence of Israel's rebellion against Assyria was that they were carried away into captivity by the Assyrians in 722 BC (2 Kings 17), never to be restored.

The southern kingdom of Judah remained, but Isaiah predicted punishment for its disobedience as well (example: Isaiah 3). His predictions were fulfilled almost a century after his ministry. God used the Babylonians as his instrument to bring down the monarchy of Judah and destroy the temple in 586 BC (see 2 Chronicles 36:15-21; Habakkuk 1:6).

The Lord, in faithfulness to his covenant with David (2 Samuel 7:1-17), brought back the Jews from exile in 538 BC and reestablished them as a nation. He used the Persians as his instrument to accomplish that restoration (2 Chronicles 36:22, 23; Ezra 1:1-8).

The book of Isaiah is typically viewed in terms of two large sections: chapters 1–39 and chapters 40–66 (see Lesson Context of lesson 6). Most of Isaiah 40–66 is conveyed in a poetic style. These chapters can be read as an ancient play.

Imagine a large stage with all the characters present. On one side of the room, there is Heaven with the Lord and the heavenly host present; on the other side, the earth and its inhabitants. Different characters speak, are addressed, or are discussed. The characters are the nation of Israel and the nations.

Within Israel there are the righteous and the wicked, the leaders and the commoners, and the servant of the Lord. The Gentile nations are distant but interested observers. Usually they are talked about, whether for future judgment or for blessing. But sometimes they are addressed directly.

On two occasions, Cyrus, the future king of Persia, is specifically named (Isaiah 44:28; 45:1-7; again, see Lesson Context of lesson 6). Isaiah is at times an actor onstage with the other characters; sometimes he is an offstage narrator to the readers, who are the theater audience.

Isaiah 56–66 begins with the prediction of the salvation of the nations (56:1-8). The text then describes the punishment of the wicked of Israel, especially the leaders (56:9–57:21), for their ritual and ethical sins (chap. 58).

But the Lord is able and willing to deliver the repentant (Isaiah 59). As a result, Israel will become a light to the nations (chap. 60) and embrace its priestly role (chap. 61).

Then comes a lengthy description of Israel's glorious future with the arrival of their triumphant Lord (Isaiah 62–65). The grand conclusion describes the blessings and ministry of the contrite and the ultimate punishment of the wicked (chap. 66).

Isaiah 61:1-11 is a sequence of four speeches that follow up on the Lord's declaring Israel a light to the Gentiles in Isaiah 60. The identity of the speakers is not always clear. But paying attention to changes in pronouns helps the reader identify different parts:

Verses	I/We	Thou/Ye/You
1-4	Messenger	Zion
5-7	Isaiah	Zion
8, 9	The Lord	The Messenger and Zion
10, 11	Zion	The Lord and the Messenger

I. The Priestly Nation
(Isaiah 61:8-11)
A. Attitudes and Actions (v. 8)
8a. "For I, the Lord, love justice;

Isaiah 61:8 identifies the third speaker as *the Lord* (see Lesson Context). The conjunction *for* links verses 8, 9 to the previous verses and explains what it means for God's people to be a nation of priests (see Isaiah 61:6).

First, the priestly people have moral requirements that stem from the very character of God. One of these is to practice *justice* (compare Isaiah 5:16). The word *justice* as commonly used today implies judgment and condemnation. It can mean that in the Bible as well (example: 34:5). However, the meaning of justice here has more to do with God's character and what he expects from his people.

The Lord himself is just (Deuteronomy 32:4), and he requires the same of his people (compare Proverbs 21:3; Isaiah 56:1). This applies especially to their leaders (Proverbs 16:10; 29:4; etc.). Justice has to do with the setting right of wrongs (example: Isaiah 1:17). In many cases it refers to moral behavior: the Hebrew word being translated "justice" is used in Genesis 18:19 to describe the actions of God and in Proverbs 21:15 the actions of the righteous.

8b. "I hate robbery and wrongdoing.

Contrasted with the justice that the Lord loves is *robbery* that he hates, along with all types of *wrongdoing*.

The Hebrew of the Old Testament was originally written in consonants only. Vowels were not put in until centuries after Christ. This gives translators problems because words with identical consonants can change meaning with different vowels—just like in English. That is the case here with the word *wrongdoing*; with different vowels it can also be translated "burnt offering," as it is in the NIV translation of this verse. And there's always the possibility that the writer intends a double meaning—a play on words.

In his condemnation, Isaiah may be casting the spotlight on the practice of fulfilling requirements of sacrifices only ritually, without keeping the moral requirements of the law (example: Isaiah 1:10-17). God makes clear that acts of worship from those who do not follow him wholeheartedly are repulsive (example: Amos 5:21-24). The Lord intends to bring about dramatic changes in his people; his righteous standards do not vary.

> **What Do You Think?**
> Which kind of change do you need to work on most: learning to love what the Lord loves, or learning to hate what the Lord hates? Why?
> **Digging Deeper**
> How could enlisting the aid of an accountability partner help you do better in this regard?

8c. "In my faithfulness I will reward my people

In my faithfulness refers to God's character and the certainty of his direction or rewarding.

8d. "and make an everlasting covenant with them.

The Lord is giving his assurance that he will not forget his people in their exile. He will keep his promise to them. At the same time, however, those to return from exile likely prefigure the new-*covenant* people of God (see Jeremiah 31:31-34; Hebrews 8:6-13; 9:15; 10:14-22).

The Hebrew word translated *everlasting* can refer to an indefinite period of time that has no discernible end from the point of view of the original reader. The word is used frequently in that way with regard to Old Testament laws and ordinances that do not apply in the New Testament era (compare "lasting" in Exodus 12:24; Leviticus 3:17; etc.). In the verse before us, however, it refers to a truly eternal *covenant* (compare Hebrews 13:20).

Centuries later, the New Testament writers will confirm the fact of the Lord's preservation of Israel for the inauguration of a permanent new covenant through the Messiah (see Romans 9:3-5; 11:1-10; Hebrews 8:7-13; etc.). The salvation brought about by the one-time sacrifice of Jesus produces a covenant that is absolutely everlasting.

B. Results and Reactions (vv. 9-11)

9. "Their descendants will be known among the nations and their offspring among the peoples. All who see them will acknowledge that they are a people the Lord has blessed."

One of the most easily observable characteristics of Hebrew poetry is parallelism. This involves using, in adjacent lines, words having either similar or opposite meanings. These phrases can explain each other or offer a contrast. Repetition through the use of parallel terms emphasizes whatever truth the writer is trying to convey.

The verse at hand offers an excellent example of such parallelism in Hebrew poetry: *their descendants* parallels *their offspring*, and *the nations* parallels *the peoples*. The repetitions found in these parallel phrases highlight one aspect of the dramatic transformation to come regarding the ancient Israelites' reputation. In their future captivity, the Israelites will be derided by foreigners (Deuteronomy 28:36, 37); God's covenant people will become a "scorn and reproach" to the nations around them (example: Jeremiah 29:17-19).

The prophet Isaiah, however, predicts a time when that reputation is to change. The release from captivity and subsequent events will result in the descendants of Isaiah's current audience being known as *a people the Lord has blessed* (compare Genesis 12:2; Isaiah 43:5; 48:19).

> **What Do You Think?**
> What adjustments do Christians need to make in how they view the concepts of legacy and heritage? Why do you say that?
> **Digging Deeper**
> What secular stumbling blocks most need to be identified for improvements to happen?

10a. I delight greatly in the LORD; my soul rejoices in my God.

The speaker here is Zion (see the Lesson Context). The partial verse before us and the two that follow each feature a poetic pair in the mold of Hebrew parallelism, just discussed. The parallel here is easy to see:

I	delight greatly	in the Lord,
↓	↓	↓
my soul	rejoices	in my God.

We normally think of cause and effect in just that order. But here Isaiah starts with the effect, then moves to state the cause.

10b. For he has clothed me with garments of salvation and arrayed me in a robe of his righteousness,

The second poetic pairing states the cause of Zion's rejoicing. Note that we say "cause," not "causes." There is one cause mentioned here, not two. That's a key to interpreting Hebrew parallelism properly. The phrases *clothed me* and *arrayed me* point to one action by God, expressed twice with different words. Likewise, the *garments of salvation* equate to *a robe of his righteousness*. These are figurative descriptions of a vitally important reality: they describe a person fully clothed by God so as to be acceptable in his sight (see Revelation 3:4, 5; 19:8; contrast Isaiah 64:6).

The parallelism further shows that salvation and righteousness are closely related. Of course, no one earns salvation through personal righteousness (see Ephesians 2:8, 9; Titus 3:5). Instead, the Lord imputes, or credits, his own righteousness to the sinner to make salvation possible. We see the need when we realize that "all our righteous acts are like filthy rags" (Isaiah 64:6; see also Philippians 3:9; Romans 1:16, 17; 10:3). To have salvation is to have the imputed righteousness of God.

10c. as a bridegroom adorns his head like a

HOW TO SAY IT

Assyria	Uh-*sear*-ee-uh.
Cyrus	*Sigh*-russ.
Deuteronomy	Due-ter-*ahn*-uh-me.
Habakkuk	Huh-*back*-kuk.
Hoshea	Ho-*shay*-uh.
Isaiah	Eye-*zay*-uh.
Persia	*Per*-zhuh.

priest, and as a bride adorns herself with her jewels.

The third pair uses a comparison to describe the beauty of the clothing. The garments given by the Lord are as magnificent as the finest accessories worn by a *bride* and groom at their wedding (compare Isaiah 49:18). We may wonder what kind of adornments a *bridegroom* wears. The Hebrew word seems to refer to some type of headdress, as the word is used in Ezekiel 24:17, 23; 44:18. A bridegroom in biblical times usually wore a head-piece that resembled a turban.

> **What Do You Think?**
> Which of these additional clothing texts motivate you most to praise their "tailor": Luke 12:28; Romans 13:14; 2 Corinthians 5:2-5; Galatians 3:27; 1 Peter 5:5; Revelation 3:4, 5, 18?
> **Digging Deeper**
> With reference to 1 Timothy 2:9, 10, how can you use your credit-card statement to evaluate where your priorities need to change with regard to spiritual vs. physical clothing?

The analogy involving a bridegroom and a bride brings to mind the relationship between Jesus and his church (Ephesians 5:22-33). While recognizing that the language of the verse before us is spoken by Zion, we also note that the blessings described are blessings Jesus shares with his followers. Revelation 19:7-9 informs us of the special clothing that awaits those who are part of the "wife" of the Lamb; he prepares us to join him at his "marriage" (compare 21:2).

❧ ROYAL DRESS CODE ❧

How do royal families decide what to wear? In Britain, tradition old and new often dictates the answer.

Some rules about dress are driven by the current queen's preferences. For example, Queen Elizabeth II is not a fan of beards. Another of the queen's fashion no-nos is for women to wear shoes with wedge heels. And these ladies would not dare be seen wearing bright fingernail polish!

Other rules stem from long-practiced traditions. Even when there is a nip in the air, the boys

Not just long life —everlasting life!

Visual for Lesson 9. *While discussing the questions associated with verse 9, ask learners how their answers are affected by the promise of eternal life.*

of royalty wear shorts and high socks in public. Hats are fine, but women of royalty should not wear them indoors after 6:00 p.m. And please— no bare legs! Pantyhose are a must, ladies.

British royalty does not have a monopoly on royal dress codes. Long before, Isaiah spoke of the dress code God requires for those who would enter his presence. But once we have such clothing through Christ, are we careful to respect his dress code? —J. E.

11. For as the soil makes the sprout come up and a garden causes seeds to grow, so the Sovereign LORD will make righteousness and praise spring up before all nations.

This verse features two pairs. The first pair introduces the main thought by an analogy. *Righteousness and praise* will grow out of *all nations* just like plants grow in *the soil* and in *a garden*. God causes all things to grow—not just flowers or trees but also right living and worship (compare Isaiah 45:8).

The Lord God's grace shown to Israel will in turn cause *all nations* to bloom with the same *righteousness* and subsequent *praise*. The righteousness that Zion displays will have an effect on the nations as well. They too will know the Lord. The theme of people from among the nations coming to the Lord is highlighted throughout Isaiah (examples: Isaiah 2:2-4; 5:26; 49:6; 60:3; 66:18-20). Their praise is an intended consequence of God's faithfulness to Israel.

II. The Righteous Nation
(ISAIAH 62:2-4a)
A. New Name Predicted (v. 2)

2a. The nations will see your vindication, and all kings your glory;

In this pair, the second thought builds on the first. *The nations* in the first line corresponds to *all kings* in the second. Kings represent the other nations because of their leadership roles. The word *your* refers to Zion, also called Jerusalem (Isaiah 62:1).

The Hebrew word here translated *vindication* is frequently translated "righteousness" (see Job 29:14; Psalm 9:8; Isaiah 51:5; etc.). Righteousness most often refers to moral integrity in doing what God declares right (example: Psalm 7:8). And so it is here. Parallel to *vindication* in the first line is *glory* in the second. Beyond simple restatement, the glory seen by the kings describes the magnitude of the righteousness of Zion. The people of Zion will live lives so markedly distinct from sin that the nations will take notice (compare 67:2; Isaiah 40:5; 45:14).

2b. you will be called by a new name that the mouth of the LORD will bestow.

A general prediction is made before specifying that the Lord will be the one who acts. Renaming in the Bible communicates some new characteristic of the one renamed. The new name is prophetic, either in condemnation (example: Hosea 1:4-9) or commendation (example: Genesis 32:28).

Isaiah often uses prophetic name changes for the redeemed (examples: Isaiah 1:26; 44:5; 45:4). Christians look forward to the new names the Lord will grant after the resurrection of the dead (Revelation 2:17; compare 3:12).

B. Old Name Discarded (Isaiah 62:3, 4a)

3. You will be a crown of splendor in the LORD's hand, a royal diadem in the hand of your God.

The second statement once again builds on the first. *A crown* is often made of gold and worn by a king (example: 2 Samuel 12:30); *diadem* occurs parallel to the crown. They both signify the *splen-*

dor of the Lord and his royalty. Zion is the crown or diadem *in the Lord's hand* (contrast Isaiah 28:5; compare 1 Thessalonians 2:19). To be in the hand of the Lord is to be under his control (compare Psalm 75:8; Proverbs 21:1).

4a. No longer will they call you Deserted, or name your land Desolate.

The Hebrew word translated *Deserted* is used over 20 times by Isaiah and represents a theme in the book. Israel forsook the Lord (Isaiah 1:4, 28). Because of this, the land was to be deserted (32:14). From all appearances, the people will seem to be forsaken in the Babylonian captivity to come (49:14). Once they yield to become the righteous crown in God's hand, they will know they are not forsaken (42:16; 60:15).

The Hebrew word translated *Desolate* is used six times in Isaiah, and in every case it predicts the destruction of the land of Israel (Isaiah 1:7 [two times]; 6:11; 17:9; 64:10). Here alone is desolation set in a positive light, because it will be permanently ended.

> *What Do You Think?*
> Were God to allow you to choose your future "new name" right now, how would you use Revelation 2:17 as a basis for doing so?
>
> *Digging Deeper*
> With regard to your former self (per Romans 6:6, Ephesians 4:22-24, and Colossians 3:9, 10), in what one way can you live more victoriously now in light of your future "new name" (Revelation 3:12)?

❧ *FUN NAMES* ❧

A popular feature on some social media sites is games that give users new nicknames. Matching initials, birthdays, or other information allows users to generate novel names for themselves. For example, John, who was born March 3 might find that his superhero name is The Radioactive Hairy Mutant. His friend Linda, born November 27, is now The Daring Masked Cat!

Marketers use such features to draw people to their websites. A desire to discover a "new identity" as a superhero, a rock star, a unicorn, etc.,

can entice us to be open to a sales pitch we would never have considered otherwise.

The Lord promised a new name to those who would accept his righteousness as their own. Human desire to have a special identity and a fresh start is understood by God. How will we recognize sales pitches that offer us new names (reputations) that don't line up with God's intentions?   —J. E.

Conclusion

A. Blessed and Blessing

A few years ago I went on an outing to a retreat center. Among the many activities was horseback riding. One of the wranglers told me two things about horses. First, he said horses can live 50 years or more. Domesticated horses live longer and healthier lives than wild ones because of care. Second, horses thrive when they have work to do.

We are similar. As we place ourselves in the hand of God, under his care and control, we live better: we are blessed. Whether our years be many or few, they are of higher quality. In turn, living under the control and care of God comes with a mandate to take Christ to the world (see Matthew 28:19, 20).

> *What Do You Think?*
> In what ways have your views of justice been challenged because of our studies over the past several weeks?
>
> *Digging Deeper*
> What viewpoint do you continue to hold even though you sense God wants you to change?

B. Prayer

Heavenly Father, empower us by your Spirit to let our lights shine! May others see your Son in our good works and give glory to you. We pray in Jesus' name. Amen.

C. Thought to Remember

Obeying the righteous God of justice blesses ourselves and others.

INVOLVEMENT LEARNING

Enhance your lesson with NIV Bible Student *(from your curriculum supplier) and the reproducible activity page (at www.standardlesson.com or in the back of the* NIV Standard Lesson Commentary Deluxe Edition*).*

Into the Lesson

Begin by distributing handouts (you prepare) that list these four activities:

engaging in small talk   exercising

cooking   playing board games

Say, "There are things in life that people either love or hate. If you personally feel strongly about anything on the list, mark those with either an *L* or an *H*." After a few seconds, say, "Let's see how well you know your classmates." Then proceed to (1) write the four activities on the board, (2) take a poll regarding which of the four your class believes will get the most *L*s and which the most *H*s, and (3) collect the (anonymous) handouts and tally the actual results.

Invite reactions as you compare and contrast the predicted results with the actual results.

Alternative. Distribute copies of the "Would You Rather . . . ?" quiz from the activity page, which you can download. After learners complete as indicated, have them pair off and take turns trying to guess the other person's choices.

After either activity state, "Most of our preferences are morally neutral. They are neither right nor wrong, but are simply matters of taste. Today we'll explore whether the same is true of God."

Into the Word

Read Isaiah 61:8 (only), then lead a discussion of the significance of the word *everlasting*. Ask five volunteers to read these passages, one each: Genesis 9:15, 16; Genesis 17:8; Genesis 21:33; Galatians 6:8; Isaiah 61:8. Pause after each reading to discuss whether the idea is of something truly eternal (lasting throughout eternity) or is of something that lasts for an indefinite period of time, with no end in sight. Use the commentary on Isaiah 61:8d as needed. Then have the entire lesson text read.

After the reading, distribute identical handouts (you prepare) titled "Parallelism in Isaiah 61:9-11 and 62:2-4a." Have printed below that title the

following verse indicators down the far left side: 61:9 / 61:10a / 61:10b / 61:10c / 61:11 / 62:2 / 62:3 / 62:4a. Leave plenty of space between each of these. As you give a handout to each student, explain *parallelism* as a feature of Hebrew poetry, per the commentary on Isaiah 61:9, 10a. As an example, write out verse 61:9 (only) on the board in such a way as to reveal its parallel structure.

Then divide your class in half. Assign one of the halves verses 61:10a; 61:10b; 61:10c; and 61:11. Assign the other half of the class verses 62:2; 62:3; and 62:4a. Challenge each half to write out their assigned segments in such a way that the parallelisms are readily apparent. Walk around the room to monitor progress. At this stage, give as much help as needed but as little as possible.

When groups finish, reconvene for whole-class discussion to achieve consensus. Ask, "Why is it important to recognize parallelism where it exists?" *(Expected response: to avoid seeing two distinct things or ideas where only one thing or idea exists but is expressed in similar terms.)*

Into Life

Remind learners of the index cards they received at the conclusion of last week's lesson. They were challenged to write on those cards the lead-in phrase "If only I had . . ." regarding a sin of omission in the form of a prayer of repentance. Give each learner a blank index card on which they are to do the same thing again, but this time regarding a sin of *commission* concerning a time when they acted as an opponent of justice. As before, assure learners that you will not ask to collect the cards. Encourage learners to take their cards home as a reminder to thank God for his forgiveness.

Alternative. Distribute copies of the "Did You Ever . . . ?" exercise from the activity page to complete as indicated. Assure learners that you will not ask for these back or put anyone on the spot to reveal responses to the class.

PROPHESYING RESTORATION

DEVOTIONAL READING: Psalm 47
BACKGROUND SCRIPTURE: Zephaniah 3

ZEPHANIAH 3:14-20

¹⁴ Sing, Daughter Zion;
    shout aloud, Israel!
Be glad and rejoice with all your heart,
    Daughter Jerusalem!
¹⁵ The LORD has taken away your
      punishment,
    he has turned back your enemy.

The LORD, the King of Israel, is with you;
    never again will you fear any harm.
¹⁶ On that day they will say to Jerusalem,
    "Do not fear, Zion;
    do not let your hands hang limp.
¹⁷ The LORD your God is with you,
    the Mighty Warrior who saves.
He will take great delight in you;
    in his love he will no longer rebuke you,
    but will rejoice over you with singing.
¹⁸ I will remove from you
    all who mourn over the loss of your
      appointed festivals,
    which is a burden and reproach for you.
¹⁹ At that time I will deal
    with all who oppressed you.
I will rescue the lame;
    I will gather the exiles.
I will give them praise and honor
    in every land where they have suffered
      shame.
²⁰ At that time I will gather you;
    at that time I will bring you home.
I will give you honor and praise
    among all the peoples of the earth
when I restore your fortunes
    before your very eyes,"
            says the LORD.

KEY VERSE

At that time I will deal with all who oppressed you. I will rescue the lame; I will gather the exiles. I will give them praise and honor in every land where they have suffered shame. —**Zephaniah 3:19**

JUSTICE AND THE PROPHETS

Unit 3: Called to God's Work of Justice

LESSONS 10–14

LESSON AIMS

After participating in this lesson, each learner will be able to:

1. Identify themes of restoration.
2. Explain the significance of those themes.
3. Use daily for a week a favorite hymn or song that praises God for his promise and work of restored relationship with him.

LESSON OUTLINE

Introduction

A. An Amateur Restorer

In 2012, the *New York Times* reported on what it called "probably the worst art restoration project of all time." A small church in Spain had a famous painting of Jesus that was deteriorating due to age and moisture. Painted directly on the stone wall by nineteenth-century artist Elías García Martínez, the picture portrayed Jesus wearing a purple robe and a crown of thorns.

One day, church officials found the work of art changed beyond all recognition, and authorities suspected vandalism. The modified painting, which quickly became famous on the internet as "Monkey Jesus," had none of the grace or artistry of the original. While investigating the crime, authorities were shocked to discover that the perpetrator was no young vandal, but rather Cecilia Giménez, an 80-something-year-old member of the church. Cecilia, distressed at the deteriorating state of the painting, had taken it upon herself to restore it. Sadly, her skills were nowhere near up to the task

When a priceless work of art needs to be restored, it's foolish to trust the job to anyone but the best. Like the painting, Israel needed true restoration. Was anyone willing and able to take on the job?

B. Lesson Context

Zephaniah was a prophet in the southern kingdom of Judah in the seventh century BC. His lineage suggests that he may have been of royal blood (see Zephaniah 1:1). This family background would have given him deep insight into the state of the nation and impact his understanding of God as king of Israel. Zephaniah understood the importance of leadership and what its absence could do to a nation.

Zephaniah likely wrote in the late 620s BC before King Josiah's spiritual reforms. The prophet is primarily concerned with Judah's continued rebellion against God (see 2 Kings 22:1–23:28). The first two chapters of the book of Zephaniah describe a coming Day of the Lord, in which Judah is to face judgment for idolatry. This judgment is to come in the form of both the natural consequences of that nation's choices and as a tool of God for purifying his people.

God's process of purification would remove the rebellious in order to ensure the survival of those remaining faithful—"the remnant of Israel" (Zephaniah 3:12 [v. 13 in NIV 1984]; see also 2:7, 9; compare Isaiah 10:20-22). The prophet's warnings to Judah carried weight given the fact of the deportation of the northern kingdom (Israel) by Assyria in 722 BC. That reality and its associated horror underlined the fact that Zephaniah's warning was not an idle threat.

Zephaniah's prophecy of God's judgment came true in 586 BC. That was the year the Judeans were cast into Babylonian exile (2 Kings 25:1-21). The prophesied restoration would not begin until 538 BC, when Jewish captives were allowed to return to Judah (Ezra 1:1-4).

The ancient writers' fondness for using parallelism (structural doublets) is important to keep in mind when reading Old Testament passages composed as poetry. Previous discussions in lessons 4 and 9 regarding how to recognize this feature still apply, so that information need not be repeated here. We should, however, stress anew the significance of this technique: when the second phrase in lines of poetry echoes the first phrase, only one thing or action is in view, not two. One happy result of this fact is that when part of a verse is difficult to understand, its companion phrase may be used to interpret the more difficult portion.

Zephaniah's prophecy presents us with a sharp change of theme beginning in Zephaniah 3:9, as restoration of a remnant takes center stage. The Lord promises that the "meek and humble . . . . will trust in the name of the Lord" (3:12), untroubled by those who are proud and haughty. The remnant can freely celebrate captivity's end.

HOW TO SAY IT

Jerusalem	Juh-*roo*-suh-lem.
Judah	*Joo*-duh.
personification	per-*saw*-nih-fih-**kay**-shun.
Zephaniah	Zef-uh-*nye*-uh.
Zion	*Zi*-un.

I. Celebration
(Zephaniah 3:14, 15)
A. How to Praise (v. 14)

14. Sing, Daughter Zion; shout aloud, Israel! Be glad and rejoice with all your heart, Daughter Jerusalem!

Having been told why the remnant should celebrate (see the Lesson Context), the people are told how: they are encouraged to *sing, . . . be glad and rejoice* (compare Psalms 9:2; 95:1; contrast 137:1-4).

> *What Do You Think?*
> What are some techniques we can use to remind ourselves to express proper gratitude for God's promised care?
> *Digging Deeper*
> What is one specific way God's care for you in the past should cause you to sing a song of gratitude yet today?

The designation *Zion* originally referred to "the City of David" (2 Samuel 5:7); eventually Zion came to include the temple area just to the north (Micah 3:12). Zion often parallels (stands for) *Jerusalem* as a whole in poetry (example: Psalm 128:5), and that is the case here. Jerusalem is the capital of the southern kingdom of Judah (compare 2 Samuel 5:5).

The prophets frequently refer to Jerusalem and/or Zion in terms of a *Daughter* (examples: Isaiah 37:22; Lamentations 2:13). This is a literary technique known as personification, in which the writer assigns the qualities of a person to something that isn't human. And since Jerusalem is the location of the temple, this imagery emphasizes the value of God's covenant people. It also stresses God's unique claim to stand as their champion.

The word *Israel*, for its part, can designate different things depending on historical context. Sometimes it refers to the entirety of the 12 tribes (example: 1 Kings 4:7). At other times it refers only to the 10 tribes of the northern kingdom of the divided monarchy (example: 2 Kings 3:1). Here the word seems to refer to the faithful remnant; as do the two uses of *Daughter*.

Some students propose that use of the word

Visual for Lesson 10. *While discussing verse 20, ask how God's gathering people from "every land" changes our relationships to strangers now.*

Israel signifies the completeness of God's welcome home. That is quite possible as long as it is accompanied with the realization that the completeness Zephaniah prophesies refers to the completeness of a remnant, not the whole (see Lesson Context).

B. Whom to Praise (v. 15)

15a. The LORD has taken away your punishment, he has turned back your enemy.

After the prophesied Day of the Lord and the *punishment* that characterizes it (see Zephaniah 1:7-10, 14-16, 18; 2:2, 3), God will step into the situation in a new way. Although the nation of Judah as a whole has disobeyed and turned its back on him, God will not abandon the faithful among his covenant people. The Lord's anger regarding Judah's sin (see 1:4-6, 8-16; 2:1-3) will subside. After God uses Babylon as his agent to discipline his people, he will then defeat Babylon, thus ending the oppression Judah faced during that time. Judah will indeed have to face the consequences of its choices, but God will not allow those consequences to destroy completely. Instead, like a parent considering a punishment to be sufficient, he will end it (compare Isaiah 40:1, 2). God's affirmation of his faithful remnant is to be the cause for the joyful celebration just noted above.

The faithful remnant will suffer along with the unfaithful majority. But when the time comes for God to turn back the *enemy,* he will bring the fullness of his presence to bear in rescuing his rem-

nant. The nature of the forthcoming exile may suggest God's complete abandonment. But that is never true for those who remain faithful (compare 1 Kings 19:18).

15b. The LORD, the King of Israel, is with you;

In the ancient Near East, the presence of a k*ing* was essential to the well-being of his people. An absentee ruler cannot judge disputes. People begin to think, *While the cat's away, the mice can play* (compare Matthew 24:48, 49). A ruler who is present and active is expected to provide some degree of protection and justice. So when Zephaniah describes God as *the King* present with his people, the prophet is telling a powerful story of God's protective rule (compare Isaiah 54:14; Zechariah 9:8, 9).

This language of presence foreshadows significant New Testament themes. God's promise to dwell with his people was fulfilled in Jesus. As the incarnate Word, he physically lived among people (John 1:1-18). Before he ascended, Jesus promised that "where two or three gather in my name, there am I with them" (Matthew 18:20). The indwelling of the Holy Spirit for the Christian is a blessed reality (Romans 8:9-11; 1 Corinthians 6:19; 2 Timothy 1:14).

15c. never again will you fear any harm.

The promised restoration in general and this verse in particular in no way suggest that God will exempt his people from experiencing the natural consequences of their choices. The context, rather, is that of God's removal of those who instigate *harm* against the remnant. The promise of God's restoration, with the peace and protection he gives, offers hope to God's people in the midst of judgment against the rebellious. There is joy coming in the morning, even after the tears of the night before (Psalm 30:5).

The promise of restoration does not end with Zephaniah's prophecies to pre-exilic Judah that is to become the post-exilic remnant. In the Lord's Prayer, Jesus teaches his disciples to pray for restoration in terms of God's kingdom coming and God's will being done (Matthew 6:10)

As Jesus proclaims that coming kingdom during his time on earth, he does not consider the restoration to be accomplished fully during his earthly ministry. Just before his ascension, his disciples ask if the time has come for the restoration of Israel (Acts 1:6). Jesus' response, coming on the heels of three years of proclamation that "the kingdom of God has come near" (Mark 1:15), shows that the disciples' expectation of an immediate physical-political fulfillment misses the point. Instead, restoration and the establishing of the kingdom of God are inaugurated. Fulfillment is in some sense both "now" and "not yet."

Full restoration in terms of new life in Christ is consummated at his return (1 Corinthians 15:52-57; Revelation 22). In the meantime, we allow the Holy Spirit to transform us daily (Romans 12:2).

❧ THE HEALING POWER OF LOVE ❧

Long ago, I knew a couple who wanted a baby but were unable to conceive. Eventually, they adopted. When I first visited the new family of three, I saw a sickly child covered with evidence of abuse. The infant had been removed from his home because his biological parents didn't love him or care for him. But his new parents gushed, "Isn't he beautiful?"

From my perspective, he was *not* beautiful—physically, anyway. However, the new parents' love enabled them to see beyond the evidence of his past and to his possibilities for a bright future. Not many weeks later, I saw him again. Their loving care had restored him to health; he was, indeed, a beautiful baby!

The idolatry of many of God's covenant children ended up leaving the Judeans bruised and beaten. The remnant suffered alongside the rest. But God's love enabled him to promise their future healing. What sins does God want to heal in your life?

—C. R. B.

II. Promise
(ZEPHANIAH 3:16-20)
A. In That Day (vv. 16-18)

16a. On that day they will say to Jerusalem,

Zephaniah's phrasing makes clear that the promise of restoration is certain even though the exact timing is unrevealed. *That day* points to a real occasion while leaving the timing wide open. Although people may fervently desire to know exactly when restoration is to come, God's fervent desire is that people be confident that the promise of the restoration is certain (compare Hebrews 11:1). What is to happen on the day mentioned here is the opposite of what will happen on the "that day" of Zephaniah 1:15.

16b. "Do not fear, Zion; do not let your hands hang limp.

It is no coincidence that there is no occasion for *fear* in God's restored kingdom. When the king of creation is fully present, peace and justice hold sway in his realm.

The Bible's imagery of hands can express strength or symbolize power (example: Micah 5:9). Imagery of weak or incapable hands can indicate a feeling of helplessness or hopelessness in situations characterized by fear (example: Isaiah 35:3, 4). Thus if *hands hang limp* after this pronouncement, it indicates the presence of unwarranted fear. That, in turn, indicates lack of faith (compare Matthew 14:26-31).

17. "The LORD your God is with you, the Mighty Warrior who saves. He will take great delight in you; in his love he will no longer rebuke you, but will rejoice over you with singing."

Zephaniah again presents a state of the future, followed by attendant results. The reason the people are not to fear is because *the Mighty Warrior* is present with them. The image Zephaniah paints is of a victorious king. Having defeated his enemy, God's entire focus shifts to his utter *delight* over once again being with his people, providing and caring for them (compare Isaiah 62:4).

The statement *in his love he will no longer rebuke you* may seem curious at first. It should be understood as God's shifting from a mode of active wrath to one of steady love. In that mode, the Lord will no longer punish the people (compare Hosea 14:4).

The cycle of joy is thereby complete: as God's people celebrate their restored relationship with him, God celebrates being present with them.

What Do You Think?
After you recover from surprise to learn that God sings, how will that fact influence your songs of praise?

Digging Deeper
How do you anticipate that your witness in that regard might affect others in a godly way?

18a. "I will remove from you all who mourn over the loss of your appointed festivals,

This verse presents some translation difficulties. Taken as a whole, however, the verse suggests that the *appointed festivals* that were instituted as an expression of faith have become a matter of shame instead. Another possibility is that because God has called the people to rejoice, he will remove those who choose to continue to wallow in sorrow; they will not be allowed to prevent others from expressing their joy.

18b. "which is a burden and reproach for you.

The language of *reproach* brings another dimension to the promise of restoration. The same word is translated "shame" elsewhere (example: Isaiah 47:3), and that may be the sense here. Shame and honor are more than simply matters of hurt feelings in the ancient Near East. Rather, those concepts speak to how people identify and value themselves. To be cast into exile will result in the Judeans no longer understanding who they are as a people (compare Psalm 74)

This *burden* will be lifted when God reclaims his remnant. Restored relationship means restored identity. God brings the joy of identity with him in the place of the shame of his rejection.

B. At That Time (vv. 19, 20)

19. "At that time I will deal with all who oppressed you. I will rescue the lame; I will

gather the exiles. I will give them praise and honor in every land where they have suffered shame.

The phrase *at that time* links this promise to the previous verses. The people are to experience restoration identity and more: the consequences to be suffered will come to an end as God removes the agents of judgment (see the Lesson Context for lesson 6). Judah will no longer be known as the people who abandoned their God (compare Deuteronomy 29:24, 25; Isaiah 60:18)

In the ancient Near East, physical handicaps often are considered evidence of a deity's judgment (see John 9:2). Similarly, enslavement by a hostile nation is thought to prove the inability of both king and deity to protect a people (compare Isaiah 14:1-8). Restored relationship with God removes and heals these purported signs of abandonment (see also Ezekiel 34:16; Micah 4:6). Physical healing, freedom, and return home are concrete ways God's justice and love will be announced.

Crippling helplessness and insufficiency will disappear in the face of God's power at work. The language of *shame* emerges again to highlight the remnant's restored sense of identity as God's people. The remnant's inability to protect themselves is to be negated as God exercises his own power to restore and reclaim. The alienation caused by sin in general and idolatry in particular is reversed when God is once again present with his people. Those willing to affirm allegiance to God alone, rejecting idolatry—the opposite of which will be the main reason for the forthcoming exile (Ezekiel 23)—are promised God's care in his plan to restore his people to wholeness (compare Psalm 68:6).

What Do You Think?
In what ways do you sense that God wants you to be His hands and feet with regard to restoring the lost to Him?

Digging Deeper
What criteria will you use to distinguish between what God wants you to do, what He wants others to do, and what He reserves for himself to do?

Young people don't seem to have the love affair with automobiles that older generations have had. They don't visit auto museums like generations before. As a result, many such museums are closing and cars are being auctioned off.

People such as William Harrah would restore the lost interest if they could. He loved cars, collecting over 1,400 in his lifetime. After he died in 1978, the National Automobile Museum was created to house about 225 of Harrah's cars. Each car (from late-1800s motorized buggies to mid–twentieth century classics) has been meticulously restored. The ravages of time, hard use, and neglect have been reversed.

New generations of Judeans had grown up with no interest in God, even though their land was a "museum" of the evidence of God's actions among them. As a result, God sent the oppressive Babylonians against Judah as the instrument of his judgment. We should be extremely careful about drawing any similar cause-and-effect conclusions today when we see a people group suffering; that's not our task. When we see suffering and its alienating effects, our tasks are found in Matthew 28:19, 20; James 1:27; etc.   —C. R. B.

20. "At that time I will gather you; at that time I will bring you home. I will give you honor and praise among all the peoples of the earth when I restore your fortunes before your very eyes," says the Lord.

Zephaniah again refers to *that time,* reinforcing the link between these promises. God's restoration of familial relationship goes hand in hand with restoring a sense of identity as God's covenant people. God's care is demonstrated in this renewed relationship and rediscovered identity.

What Do You Think?
  In what ways is God challenging you to bring back to Christ someone who needs to return from the captivity of sin?
Digging Deeper
  What techniques, in your experience, will not work in such a ministry? Why?

The phrase *when I restore your fortunes* should reemphasize to us that the terrible judgments of the Day of the Lord are yet to occur from the perspective of the original reader. And as the decades pass until those occur, it will be easy to forget or outright dismiss the predictions of exile and return (compare 2 Peter 3; Revelation 2:4, 5). Could there be anything sadder than to fail to be restored to relationship to God Almighty himself?

Conclusion

A. The Restoration Expert

The final words of the book of Zephaniah remind us that restoration requires the power and willingness of God. He and he alone is the one who has the power to make restored relationship with him possible. That's why Zephaniah's promise of restoration for the Old Testament remnant is relevant to us yet today: it foreshadows our restored relationship to God through Christ.

Christians have been delivered from the captivity of sin; yet we still live in a world that is mired in that captivity. Therefore the fullness of our deliverance is yet to come. We trust God to keep his promise in that regard because he has, among other things, "set his seal of ownership on us, and put his Spirit in our hearts as a deposit" (2 Corinthians 1:22). Although God's kingdom is not yet here in its fullest sense, his continuing work of restoration is guaranteed by the presence of his Spirit.

Let us therefore celebrate these grand realities! As we do, we can affirm with Paul "that neither death nor life, neither angels nor demons, neither the present nor the future, nor any powers, neither height nor depth, nor anything else in all creation, will be able to separate us from the love of God that is in Christ Jesus our Lord" (Romans 8:38, 39).

B. Prayer

Lord, open our eyes to ways in which you are present and restoring your kingdom in and around us. In Jesus' name we pray. Amen.

C. Thought to Remember

Celebrate the present and future reality
of restored relationship to God.

INVOLVEMENT LEARNING

Enhance your lesson with NIV Bible Student (from your curriculum supplier) and the reproducible activity page (at www.standardlesson.com or in the back of the NIV Standard Lesson Commentary Deluxe Edition).

Into the Lesson

Have the word *Restoration* written on the board as learners arrive. Ask for one success story and one failure story about projects that were intended to restore something to its former beauty and/or functionality. Be prepared with your own story or stories if one or both are not forthcoming from volunteers. (But don't let this drag out with many long stories.)

After this activity, inform the class that today's lesson deals with the vital theme of restored relationship with God by his initiative.

Into the Word

Write on the board the title and passage location of three or four well-known Scripture texts regarding the topic of "restoration" (example: the parable of the prodigal son, Luke 15:11-32). After doing so, write today's lesson title and the text as the final entry.

Then take a survey by asking for a show of hands as to which entry learners think of first, second, third, etc., when they think of the biblical topic of "restoration." Offer appropriate comments regarding where today's text scores in that regard.

Call on a volunteer to present a three-minute summary of the Lesson Context of today's passage. Ask this volunteer several days in advance to prepare this presentation; a possible outline to provide for the volunteer is:

    I. Who Zephaniah Was
    II. Who Received Zephaniah's Message
    III. What Zephaniah Said

Distribute paper to class members and inform them you have instructions for what they should write as today's text of Zephaniah 3:14-20 is read aloud. As you or a volunteer reads the text the first time, class members are to jot down all the things it says that *God will do.* After the reading, have learners voice the entries on their lists as you write

those, along with verse references, on the board. Add insight from the lesson commentary as (or after) you complete the list.

Then read the text again. As you do, have learners make notes about how the original audience might have reacted when they heard or read these predictions. Caution learners to bear in mind that the prophecy came several decades before the captivity of 586–538 BC even began. After this reading, do the same as you did after the first.

Next, ask students to turn to one or two neighbors to discuss this question: *What does this passage teach us about God?* Invite conclusions to be voiced in the whole-class discussion that follows.

Option. Distribute copies of the "The Promise of God's Presence" exercise from the activity page, which you can download. Have study pairs complete it as indicated. Call for insights during ensuing whole-class discussion.

Into Life

Form small groups of three or four for the task of creating lists of hymns, songs, and/or praise choruses that praise God for the fact that he has restored our relationship to him through Jesus. (*Option.* Distribute hymnals, etc., as research helps; expect many students to use their smartphones for this.)

Possible titles to expect learners to mention in ensuing whole-class discussion include "Amazing Grace," "Because He Lives," and "Nothing but the Blood." Encourage learners to pick their favorite and use it as a daily basis for their devotional time in the week ahead.

Option. If you used the first exercise from the activity page earlier, distribute copies of the second one, titled "Practicing God's Presence," as a take-home. To greatly increase the likelihood that learners will complete it (and not just leave it stuck in their Bibles), say that you will call for their conclusions at the beginning of the next class.

PROMISING
PEACE

DEVOTIONAL READING: Zechariah 8:18-23
BACKGROUND SCRIPTURE: Zechariah 8

ZECHARIAH 8:1-8, 11-17

[1] The word of the LORD Almighty came to me.

[2] This is what the LORD Almighty says: "I am very jealous for Zion; I am burning with jealousy for her."

[3] This is what the LORD says: "I will return to Zion and dwell in Jerusalem. Then Jerusalem will be called the Faithful City, and the mountain of the LORD Almighty will be called the Holy Mountain."

[4] This is what the LORD Almighty says: "Once again men and women of ripe old age will sit in the streets of Jerusalem, each of them with cane in hand because of their age. [5] The city streets will be filled with boys and girls playing there."

[6] This is what the LORD Almighty says: "It may seem marvelous to the remnant of this people at that time, but will it seem marvelous to me?" declares the LORD Almighty.

[7] This is what the LORD Almighty says: "I will save my people from the countries of the east and the west. [8] I will bring them back to live in Jerusalem; they will be my people, and I will be faithful and righteous to them as their God."

. . . .

[11] "But now I will not deal with the remnant of this people as I did in the past," declares the LORD Almighty.

[12] "The seed will grow well, the vine will yield its fruit, the ground will produce its crops, and the heavens will drop their dew. I will give all these things as an inheritance to the remnant of this people. [13] Just as you, Judah and Israel, have been a curse among the nations, so I will save you, and you will be a blessing. Do not be afraid, but let your hands be strong."

[14] This is what the LORD Almighty says: "Just as I had determined to bring disaster on you and showed no pity when your ancestors angered me," says the LORD Almighty, [15] "so now I have determined to do good again to Jerusalem and Judah. Do not be afraid. [16] These are the things you are to do: Speak the truth to each other, and render true and sound judgment in your courts; [17] do not plot evil against each other, and do not love to swear falsely. I hate all this," declares the LORD.

KEY VERSE

I have determined to do good again to Jerusalem and Judah. Do not be afraid. —**Zechariah 8:15**

JUSTICE AND THE PROPHETS

Unit 3: Called to God's Work of Justice

Lessons 10–14

LESSON AIMS

After participating in this lesson, each learner will be able to:

1. Describe the expressions of the peace that God promises.

2. Explain why jealousy is not a sin or character defect when applied to God.

3. Write a couplet that dedicates his or her life to embracing God's "new normal."

LESSON OUTLINE

Introduction
  A. Don't Forget Me!
  B. Lesson Context
I. Stability (Zechariah 8:1-8)
  A. Return to Zion (vv. 1-3)
  B. Restoration of Jerusalem (vv. 4-8)
II. Prosperity (Zechariah 8:11-17)
  A. Reversal of Fortunes (vv. 11-15)
      Used to Be Poor
  B. Renewal of Responsibility (vv. 16, 17)
Conclusion
  A. God Dwells with Us
  B. Prayer
  C. Thought to Remember

Introduction

A. Don't Forget Me!

There's a little-known psychiatric condition called athazagoraphobia. It refers to an irrational fear of being forgotten. The associated anxiety can be debilitating. Sufferers may feel the need to check in with family constantly while traveling. Or they might excessively remind a coworker about an upcoming meeting. Changes in plans can bring on panic attacks. Sufferers' lives are filled with anxiety and fear.

A few passages of the Bible speak of a fear of being forgotten by God (example: Lamentations 5:20); many more speak of the reality of people forgetting him (example: Jeremiah 3:21). That fact speaks directly to an important role of prophets: pointing out the reality of God's memory and its implications for us (example: Zechariah 10:9).

B. Lesson Context

By one count, there are at least 30 men in the Bible by the name of Zechariah. The one who wrote the book of today's study was a prophet from a priestly family; his recorded ministry occurred after the Babylonian exile (Ezra 5:1, 2; 6:14; Nehemiah 12:12, 16). The datings in Zechariah 1:1, 7; 7:1 compute to a time between late 520 BC and late 518 BC.

The setting in post-exilic Jerusalem is essential to understanding Zechariah's prophecies. Twenty years after returning from exile, signs of God's continued favor seemed to have disappeared (Ezra 4:24; Haggai 1:1-11). Many of those who returned undoubtedly wondered if God had forgotten them.

I. Stability

(Zechariah 8:1-8)

A. Return to Zion (vv. 1-3)

1. The word of the Lord Almighty came to me.

The phrase *the word of the Lord . . . came to* occurs dozens of times in the Old Testament as a standard introduction to a prophecy. Much rarer is inclusion of the description *Almighty,* most occurring in this book (compare Isaiah 39:5; Zechariah

7:4; 8:18). It serves to stress God's power. God is therefore both fully present and fully capable to accomplish whatever he determines to do.

2a. This is what the LORD Almighty says:

As if to doubly stress the Lord's power, the prophet uses the phrase *the Lord Almighty* again. A more literal translation of "hosts" (2 Chronicles 33:5) or "army" (33:11) reveals the military connotations of this title. God is the warrior who fights for his people. This is a favorite phrase of Zechariah, occurring more than 50 times in his book.

2b. "I am very jealous for Zion; I am burning with jealousy for her."

There is no doubt in the prophet's mind that the Lord has the right to be *jealous for* his people; they are his exclusively (see Joel 2:18). God's jealousy is not like that of a boy who has a fit if he sees his girlfriend flirting with someone else. The biblical concept of jealousy when applied to God indicates a profound sense of caring and commitment.

This is even more apparent where a word in the original language is translated "jealousy" in one passage but "zeal" in another. For example, the Hebrew noun translated "jealous" here and "jealousy" in Ezekiel 8:3, 5 is rendered "zeal" in Isaiah 9:7; 37:32; 59:17; 63:15. The Greek noun translated "jealousy" in 2 Corinthians 11:2 is the same one translated "zeal" in Philippians 3:6.

Overlap in meaning is affirmed in English by a dictionary entry that offers one meaning of *jealousy* as "zealous vigilance." The common idea is one of fervency. God's jealousy implies his right to protect his people and to be angry at those who would hurt them (Zechariah 1:14, 15). God will show what it means to have him fully present in his infinite power, intent on keeping safe those who are his own.

3a. This is what the LORD says: "I will return to Zion and dwell in Jerusalem.

Zechariah's ministry includes encouraging the returned exiles to finish rebuilding the temple (see

Ezra 4:24–5:2). When God declares his intention to *dwell in Jerusalem,* he refers specifically to the temple (see also Zechariah 1:16). *Zion* can refer to the entire city of *Jerusalem* or to only the temple area. Both of these represent the entire nation. For the returned exiles, God's presence signifies the restoration of his favor (compare Isaiah 52:8; Zechariah 2:10; contrast Ezekiel 10).

3b. "Then Jerusalem will be called the Faithful City,

Though the Jews had suffered judgment, Zechariah reinforces God's intentions on their behalf. God's renaming of *Jerusalem* uses a term that evokes themes of loyalty and trustworthiness (compare Isaiah 1:26; Jeremiah 33:16). Post-exilic Jerusalem is to have a reputation of residents who keep faith with one another. That trustworthiness is to be without limit as the covenant between God and his people is fully honored.

In the New Testament, the "new Jerusalem" represents the final, complete fulfillment of God's intention (Revelation 3:12; 21:2, 10; compare Galatians 4:26). In this sense, the city reflects the mountain about which Zechariah prophesies next.

3c. "and the mountain of the LORD Almighty will be called the Holy Mountain."

The renaming continues. The *mountain* to which Zechariah refers is the hill upon which the temple will be rebuilt. A comparison of the date in Ezra 6:15 (which computes to March 12, 515 BC) with that in Zechariah 7:1 (which computes to December 7, 518 BC) indicates that this rebuilding project is not yet complete.

To designate *the mountain of the Lord Almighty* as *the Holy Mountain* serves to set it apart from normal human activity; it is to be reserved wholly for God's use. Such an image of God's holy mountain shows up several times in prophecy in this regard (examples: Isaiah 66:20; Ezekiel 20:40; Joel 3:17; contrast Isaiah 65:11).

The redesignations of both the city and the mountain project the idea of uncompromised loyalty to God—true faithfulness.

B. Restoration of Jerusalem (vv. 4-8)

4. This is what the LORD Almighty says: "Once again men and women of ripe old age

HOW TO SAY IT

athazagoraphobia	*ay*-thaz-uh-gor-uh-*foe*-bee-uh.
Haggai	*Hag*-eye or *Hag*-ay-eye.
Zechariah	*Zek*-uh-*rye*-uh.

Are you fireproof or fuel for the fire?

Visual for Lessons 11 & 12. *As you reach the end of the lesson, point to this visual and ask how the imagery applies to today's study.*

will sit in the streets of Jerusalem, each of them with cane in hand because of their age.

A noticeable effect of God's active presence will be the longevity of God's people. Only a country enjoying peace and stability sees its citizens reach *old age*. Disease, war, and injustice attack the hardest those least able to protect themselves, and this certainly includes those of advanced age. But in the future prophesied, no one is neglected.

5. "The city streets will be filled with boys and girls playing there."

Similarly, there will be no injustice in *the city* to threaten the safety of *boys and girls*. Referring to the oldest and youngest is a way of expressing the totality of the security and stability in God's kingdom (compare Jeremiah 30:20). All God's people are to be deeply invested in extending his security and care toward one another. From the last generation to the next, all are to be safe from harm (compare 31:13). This is a powerful promise for those who had experienced the violence of exile.

> **What Do You Think?**
> What's the single most important thing your church can do right now to make it a welcome haven for people of all ages?
> **Digging Deeper**
> Is it important to know the demographics of your area before taking that action? Why, or why not?

6. This is what the LORD Almighty says: "It may seem marvelous to the remnant of this people at that time, but will it seem marvelous to me?" declares the LORD Almighty.

The new normal God is instituting is so *marvelous* as to seem fantastical, even impossible, to the original readers. The original word being translated "marvelous" is also translated "wonders," referring to miracles, in Psalm 78:11. People will undoubtedly struggle to believe what God promises to do. Perhaps doubt is here expressed in the model of Gideon's question in Judges 6:13. But for God it is no problem; *the Lord Almighty* has the power to fulfill each promise he makes.

7. This is what the LORD Almighty says: "I will save my people from the countries of the east and the west.

Again we see the imagery of extremes. The phrasing *of the east and the west* indicates a complete whole (compare Psalm 107:3; Isaiah 43:5). For the returned exiles, this likely recalls their fellow Israelites' being taken into exile in Assyria, as well as other migrations that seem permanent (compare 11:11).

The word translated *save* is frequently used in contexts of liberation from foreign oppressors (examples: Exodus 14:30; Judges 6:14). This association causes problems in the first century AD for those who think of this connection rather than that of being saved from the oppression of sin (compare and contrast Luke 1:71; Acts 1:6; Colossians 1:13).

8. "I will bring them back to live in Jerusalem; they will be my people, and I will be faithful and righteous to them as their God."

The powerful themes presented thus far are repeated. To exist fully as God's *people* suggests their taking his characteristics of being *faithful* and *righteous* as their own. God's loyalty to his people is thus to come full circle in their loyalty to him. That has been God's intent since the first sin (compare John 12:32). In the New Testament, God's intent to include Gentiles is sharply clear. Even so, that inclusion is nothing new, as underlined by quotations from the Old Testament in the New (see Acts 13:47; Romans 15:12; etc.). Zechariah's prophecy finds its ultimate fulfillment in the church.

II. Prosperity
(ZECHARIAH 8:11-17)
A. Reversal of Fortunes (vv. 11-15)

11. "But now I will not deal with the remnant of this people as I did in the past," declares the LORD Almighty.

Here God moves the new normal a step further. This time of restoration will not follow any pattern expected by *the remnant*. God has a change in mind that vastly exceeds what their recent experience may predict. Thus far, they have faced the uphill battles of reclaiming their land, rebuilding their heritage, and maintaining priorities while doing so (see Ezra 4; Haggai 1:2-4). The result has been poor harvests and inadequate clothing (1:5-11).

12. "The seed will grow well, the vine will yield its fruit, the ground will produce its crops, and the heavens will drop their dew. I will give all these things as an inheritance to the remnant of this people.

This promise reads like a reversal of the curse God put on all the earth after Adam and Eve's sinning (Genesis 3:17-19). Similar prophecies draw even clearer parallels (see Ezekiel 34:25-29; Haggai 2:15-19). Lists of blessings elsewhere reflect similar promises (example: Leviticus 26:3-10).

The promise of good harvests goes hand in hand with the promise of stability in the land. That in turn implies no war, no raids, and no political unrest to destroy the fruitfulness of the land.

> *What Do You Think?*
> What can Christian teachers do to head off misunderstandings of the "remnant" concept?
> *Digging Deeper*
> What forms might such misunderstandings take? Why do you say that?

❧ USED TO BE POOR ❧

When I was a kid, my family was poor. But we didn't know it because all our friends were also poor. I was born in the midst of the Great Depression. My parents provided for us what they could and taught us to be grateful to God.

When the post–World War II recovery came, being not quite as poor as we used to be made us think we were rich. How much richer could a family be than to have a new Chevrolet in the driveway, a 10-inch (black and white) television set in the living room, and two pairs of shoes for every child in the family?

Zechariah's people knew what it was to be poor. They had been political exiles and had returned to a land that had been plundered by the enemy. So when the prophet told them of peaceful prosperity that was coming, they would appreciate it as God's gift when it became reality.

What "poor" experiences help you anticipate the spiritual riches God is yet to give you?

—C. R. B.

13. "Just as you, Judah and Israel, have been a curse among the nations, so I will save you, and you will be a blessing. Do not be afraid, but let your hands be strong."

Bringing the themes of blessing and curse full circle, God reminds his people of his original promise to bless the nations through Abraham (Genesis 12:2, 3). They had been a *curse* in that while claiming to belong to God, they were disloyal and followed every kind of wrong behavior.

No one could have looked at pre-exilic Judah and understood either who God is or what belonging to him really means. Instead of drawing the nations toward God, their behavior ridiculed him. But now God's people will prove his love and his power in this new normal of living in God's presence. Just as Abraham was a blessing to the world by demonstrating a life lived in loyalty to God, so will they be. Despite their history of disobedience, God promises restoration without fear of reprisal.

Hands is frequently a symbolic reference of strength and ability in the Old Testament (see lesson 10). To strengthen one's hands is to renew one's power and motivation to act. This results in a person being encouraged and empowered to act confidently in the service of God.

14. This is what the LORD Almighty says:

"Just as I had determined to bring disaster on you and showed no pity when your ancestors angered me," says the LORD Almighty,

God reiterates the old pattern of relationship that characterized Israel and Judah before their exiles (compare Zechariah 8:11, 13, above). The phrase *showed no pity emphasizes that God did not give* them "comfort," as the same Hebrew word is translated in Isaiah 52:9; 66:13; etc.

15. "so now I have determined to do good again to Jerusalem and Judah. Do not be afraid.

Passages such as Jeremiah 4:27, 28 reveal God's former resolute intention to punish the people of the covenant. In something of a parallel, the verse before us now reveals God's resolute intent to do the polar opposite. On *do not be afraid,* compare the discussion on fear in lesson 10.

> *What Do You Think?*
> What are some ways to respond to those who resist the gospel on the basis that God is inconsistent in bestowing blessings?
> *Digging Deeper*
> Which contexts of response will call for discussion of Scriptures (such as Matthew 20:1-16) and which contexts will not (example: Acts 17:16-33)? Explain.

B. Renewal of Responsibility (vv. 16, 17)

16, 17. "These are the things you are to do: Speak the truth to each other, and render true and sound judgment in your courts; do not plot evil against each other, and do not love to swear falsely. I hate all this," declares the LORD.

God's people must reflect his character in their relationships. This is why the themes of *judgment* and *truth* turn up again. These two concepts go hand in hand and should define the lives of God's people.

The word *courts* refers to a city's entrance where legal issues were settled (example: Ruth 4:1, 2, 11). To practice justice there is to set the proper example for everyone watching to do so as well. There will be no bribes, no partiality shown to anyone (see Exodus 23:8; Isaiah 33:15, 16; etc.).

For God to state what he hates establishes boundaries of human behavior. This is reminiscent of other blessing/curse and love/hate declarations (examples: Deuteronomy 12:31; 16:22; Proverbs 6:16-19).

Ancient covenants established between kings and citizens frequently listed the positive attributes and actions of the ruler before listing the expected reciprocal responsibilities of the citizens. Zechariah's prophecy is essentially a covenant in miniature: it institutes a new normal of peace in light of God's presence with his people.

> *What Do You Think?*
> Which kind of change should you work on most: learning to love what the Lord loves, or learning to hate what the Lord hates? Why?
> *Digging Deeper*
> With two weeks having passed since posing this same question in lesson 9, is your response now the same, or different? Why?

Conclusion
A. God Dwells with Us

When a relationship needs to go from bad to good, someone has to make the first move. The text for today tells of a time when God did just that. The bad relationship between God and his covenant people was wholly the fault of the people. Logically, therefore, they should have made the first move. But God in his compassion took the initiative, promising great things to his people. And so it still is: God promises great things for us when we actually deserve quite the opposite. He is determined to redeem all who are willing to acknowledge him as sovereign Lord. Do you?

B. Prayer

Father, may our allegiance be to you alone! Strengthen us to reflect that value and your character daily. We pray for this in Jesus' name. Amen.

C. Thought to Remember

Only God offers true restoration and peace.

INVOLVEMENT LEARNING

Enhance your lesson with NIV Bible Student *(from your curriculum supplier) and the reproducible activity page (at www.standardlesson.com or in the back of the* NIV Standard Lesson Commentary Deluxe Edition*).*

Into the Lesson

Give each of four learners a slip of paper on which you have written the following, one per slip:

> *I feel most at peace when . . .*
> *My greatest hope for peace is . . .*
> *Peace seems most out of reach when . . .*
> *The best way to get peace is . . .*

Begin class by calling on the four students to read their statements aloud; then ask class members how they would complete it.

Alternative. Inform the class that you saw a bumper sticker that you can't understand. You need their help in deciphering it. Say "Here's what it said" as you write *Envision Whirled Peas* on the board. Learners should quickly see that this is a sarcastic recasting of *Envision World Peace.*

After either activity, lead into Bible study by saying, "If you're interested in hearing what God has to say about the concept of peace, today's study is for you!"

Into the Word

Using the Lesson Context, deliver a quick summary of the who, where, and when regarding the prophet Zechariah. Follow that by having two learners take turns reading the lesson text aloud: one learner can do the even-numbered verses, the other can do the odd-numbered ones.

Then distribute identical handouts (you prepare) on which are printed the list of symbols and statements below. *Be sure to arrange the statements in a different order from what's here, but keep each symbol with its original statement.*[1]

@ God is jealous for what is (or should be) already His.

$ God's people won't worry about the scorn of nations.

• God will once again be present in Jerusalem.

‡ Jerusalem will be a place of peace for all generations.

---

[1]Note: The listing here is in the order the answers occur in the text, for the teacher's convenience in working through the answers later. The statements have symbols rather than numerals so learners won't have a sequence crutch to lean on.

& God's desire to restore shouldn't be a surprise.

◊ God will protect Jerusalem from potential enemies.

Δ Agricultural efforts will flourish once again.

% God will not continue to express anger as before.

√ Certain traits must characterize God's people.

Tell class members that each statement is an explanation or paraphrase of a different verse or two in today's text. Ask them to work in pairs for two minutes to answer as many as possible. After two minutes, call time and have each learner switch to a different partner to keep working. (Each learner should be filling out his or her own handout to take along when the switch occurs.) Continue to call "switch" every two minutes until most or all handouts are complete.

Reconvene the class for whole-class discussion of the answers: @–verse 2; $–verse 2; •–verse 3; ‡–verses 4, 5; &–verse 6; ◊–verses 7, 8; Δ–verse 12; %–verses 14, 15; √–verses 16, 17.

Alternative. Distribute copies of the "Turn Lies into Truth" exercise from the activity page, which you can download. Have learners work in triads to complete as indicated. Include in the ensuing whole-class discussion a consideration of how easy it is to allow nonbiblical folk wisdom to direct our talk and actions.

Into Life

Ask class members which of the text's principles brings them the greatest assurance and which offers the greatest challenge. After everyone has had a chance to respond, distribute handouts (you prepare) on which are printed these directions: "Having considered your greatest assurance and greatest challenge from the text, write a couplet that dedicates your life to embracing God's 'new normal.'"

Option. As learners depart, distribute copies of the puzzle "Jesus Gives What I Know I Really Need" as a take-home. (This should not be an in-class exercise.)

PRACTICE JUSTICE

DEVOTIONAL READING: Psalm 86:1-13
BACKGROUND SCRIPTURE: Jeremiah 21

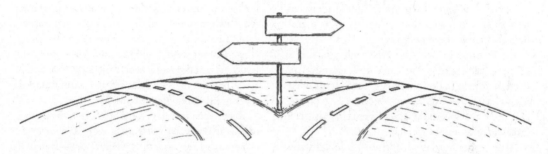

JEREMIAH 21:8-14

8 "Furthermore, tell the people, 'This is what the LORD says: See, I am setting before you the way of life and the way of death. 9 Whoever stays in this city will die by the sword, famine or plague. But whoever goes out and surrenders to the Babylonians who are besieging you will live; they will escape with their lives. 10 I have determined to do this city harm and not good, declares the LORD. It will be given into the hands of the king of Babylon, and he will destroy it with fire.'

11 "Moreover, say to the royal house of Judah, 'Hear the word of the LORD. 12 This is what the LORD says to you, house of David:

"'Administer justice every morning;
  rescue from the hand of the oppressor

the one who has been robbed,
  or my wrath will break out and burn like
    fire
  because of the evil you have done—
  burn with no one to quench it.
13 I am against you, Jerusalem,
  you who live above this valley
  on the rocky plateau, declares the
    LORD—
you who say, "Who can come against us?
  Who can enter our refuge?"
14 I will punish you as your deeds deserve,
  declares the LORD.
I will kindle a fire in your forests
  that will consume everything around
    you.'"

KEY VERSE

This is what the LORD says to you, house of David: "Administer justice every morning; rescue from the hand of the oppressor the one who has been robbed." —**Jeremiah 21:12a**

Photo: Zdenek Sasek / iStock / Thinkstock

JUSTICE AND THE PROPHETS

Unit 3: Called to God's Work of Justice

LESSONS 10–14

LESSON AIMS

After participating in this lesson, each learner will be able to:

1. Summarize Jeremiah's message to the people and the royal court.

2. Explain why God's covenant people sometimes suffered (or seemed to suffer) more severely under his judgmental wrath than did their pagan enemies.

3. Write a testimony of a time when negative consequences resulted in repentance and a long-term benefit.

LESSON OUTLINE

Introduction
   A. "Unexpected" Misfortune
   B. Lesson Context: Historical
   C. Lesson Context: Jeremiah 21
I. To the People (JEREMIAH 21:8-10)
   A. Choice to Make (v. 8)
   B. Consequence to Consider (vv. 9, 10)
      Groupthink
II. To the King's House (JEREMIAH 21:11-14)
   A. Judgment (vv. 11, 12)
   B. Punishment (vv. 13, 14)
Conclusion
   A. The End of the Line
   B. Prayer
   C. Thought to Remember

Introduction

A. "Unexpected" Misfortune

Some of the most disheartening, even frightening, times in life are those when we come face-to-face with the negative consequences of our poor decisions. Perhaps you can remember an instance in school when you didn't turn in an assignment on time and ended up severely damaging your grade in that class. Perhaps you even acted surprised when you received the penalty or tried to tell your teacher that it wasn't fair. In situations like this, the lessons we learn often turn out to be very valuable to us later on. And so it was—or should have been—with God's covenant people of the Old Testament era.

B. Lesson Context: Historical

The prophet Jeremiah ministered from about 626 to 575 BC. That ministry was to a people—the Judeans—who had disobeyed the Lord on a level far beyond the mundaneness of a late term paper. As a result, serious consequences loomed. God had sent prophet after prophet to warn both kings and commoners of pending destruction. But they didn't listen. They acted as though they had God's favor no matter what; they viewed Jerusalem's temple as a good-luck charm (Jeremiah 7:4).

The northern kingdom, Israel, had been taken into captivity by the Assyrians in 722 BC (2 Kings 17:6). A century later, the survival of the southern kingdom of Judah was by no means assured. The Assyrians were still the dominant military and political power in the ancient Near East.

King Ashurbanipal of Assyria died in 627 BC. Although he had been a strong ruler, his death laid bare serious internal weaknesses in Assyria. Disorder and revolt erupted in every part of that empire. Nineveh, the capital city, was destroyed in 612 BC (see the book of Nahum); the last vestiges of Assyrian might were wiped out at the Battle of Carchemish in 605 BC (Jeremiah 46:2).

The consequences of Assyria's decline were felt in Judah. After a reign of about 30 years, King Josiah was killed in battle in 609 BC. That happened as he attempted to halt the Egyptian army from aiding the remnants of the Assyrian army (2 Kings 23:29). The Babylonians stepped into the power vacuum left by the collapse of Assyria under the Babylonian king Nabopolassar and his son Nebuchadnezzar (reigned 626–605 and 605–562 BC, respectively). Babylon came to dominate much of Assyria's old territory. The last kings of Judah reigned in subservience to the Babylonians before the final exile of 586 BC (chap. 24, 25).

Jeremiah 1:2 places the beginning of Jeremiah's ministry at around 626 BC. The book of Jeremiah preserves a prophetic ministry that took place over the course of the next several decades—through the reigns of five Judean kings and a governor.

C. Lesson Context: Jeremiah 21

Jeremiah 21 is a coherent unit. The opening verses set the scene. Pashhur and Zephaniah were sent by Judah's final king, Zedekiah, to Jeremiah. Pashhur (not the same Pashhur as in Jeremiah 20) was a dogged opponent of Jeremiah, even trying to have him executed (see Jeremiah 38:1-4). Zephaniah, a priest (and not to be confused with the prophet of the same name), was not actively hostile to Jeremiah (see 21:1; 29:25-29).

The two emissaries intended to enlist Jeremiah's help in order to ensure God's aid against King Nebuchadnezzar of Babylon (Jeremiah 21:1, 2). King Zedekiah apparently thought that he would be aided by the Egyptians if he rebelled against the Babylonians (compare 2 Kings 18:21). The sit-

HOW TO SAY IT

Ashurbanipal	As-shure-*bah*-nee-pahl.
Carchemish	*Kar*-key-mish.
Jeremiah	Jair-uh-*my*-uh.
Josiah	Jo-*sigh*-uh.
Nabopolassar	Nab-uh-puh-*las*-uhr or Nab-oh-poh-*las*-er.
Nebuchadnezzar	*Neb*-yuh-kad-*nez*-er.
Nineveh	*Nin*-uh-vuh.
Pashhur	*Pash*-uhr.
Zedekiah	Zed-uh-*kye*-uh.
Zephaniah	Zef-uh-*nye*-uh.

uation quickly became desperate when Jerusalem was besieged (25:1, 2).

Zedekiah and his messengers had some confidence in God's willingness to help them, based on his past work on Judah's behalf. Since he had protected Jerusalem before (2 Kings 19:35, 36), couldn't he be counted on to do so again? As Jeremiah's response shows, the request demonstrated a fundamental misunderstanding of Judah's standing with God.

Jeremiah's response came in three parts. First came words against King Zedekiah himself (Jeremiah 21:3-7). The prophet was blunt: Jerusalem's weapons will become a liability as the Lord himself fights against the city. Today's text opens with the second section of Jeremiah's response.

> **What Do You Think?**
> How should we respond, if at all, to those whose prayers reflect their own desired outcomes more than openness to God's will?
> *Digging Deeper*
> How should our responses differ, if at all, when those prayers come from people having varying levels of spiritual maturity?

I. To the People
(JEREMIAH 21:8-10)
A. Choice to Make (v. 8)

8. "Furthermore, tell the people, 'This is what the LORD says: See, I am setting before you the way of life and the way of death.

Here in the second of Jeremiah's three-part response (see Lesson Context), the prophet turns his attention from the king (without excluding him) to *the people* in general. God sets before them a stark choice between *life* and *death*. Similar expressions are common throughout the Scriptures, but this one seems to especially recall the words of Moses: "See, I set before you today life and prosperity, death and destruction" (Deuteronomy 30:15).

Jeremiah's words of judgment and doom come in the context of God's covenant with the people. The Lord still requires obedience and loyalty.

The people's oft-repeated refusals to render to him their exclusive worship have brought them to this dire point.

The choice presented to God's people in the days of Jeremiah is also presented to us, collectively and individually, today. Jesus speaks of the choice between life and death as a choice between a wide gate and a narrow way (Matthew 7:13, 14). Each of us is called to choose the path we take. Though choosing life seems a no-brainer, many still choose death by trusting in their own wisdom (contrast Proverbs 3:5-7). Only following Jesus leads to life (John 14:6, 7).

B. Consequence to Consider (vv. 9, 10)

9. "'Whoever stays in this city will die by the sword, famine or plague. But whoever goes out and surrenders to the Babylonians who are besieging you will live; they will escape with their lives.

The choice that Jeremiah has just presented abstractly in the previous verse he now paints in real-life terms: to stay in Jerusalem and try to hold out against *the Babylonians* will mean certain death. The three vehicles of death—*by the sword, famine or plague*—are all typical of the results of a long siege (compare Ezekiel 5:12). Leaving the confines of the city and surrendering to the Babylonians is the only path to continued life (compare Jeremiah 14:12; 38:17; 40:9).

This is not the advice the people hope for in this situation. They want to stay *in this city* and be delivered by God. However, the ways of life and death that Jeremiah presents are the only options. God has decided to punish his people; there will be no deliverance from the Babylonians (compare Jeremiah 27:11, 12).

What Do You Think?
In what contexts could you use the counterintuitive nature of this choice facing the citizens of Jerusalem to illustrate the two eternal paths that exist for everyone to choose between?

Digging Deeper
In what contexts could such an approach be ineffective? Why?

The phrase *they will escape with their lives* in the original Hebrew is a military figure of speech, rendered in the KJV translation of this verse "his life shall be unto him for a prey" (examples: Jeremiah 38:2; 39:18; 45:5). A victorious army brings home booty like a predator brings home prey. A defeated army's best possible outcome is the life of its soldiers. In this situation, if they surrender to the Babylonians, the people will be rewarded with their lives and nothing more (compare 45:5).

10. "'I have determined to do this city harm and not good, declares the LORD. It will be given into the hands of the king of Babylon, and he will destroy it with fire.'

Jeremiah's address to the people closes with a sobering restatement of the truth as God has *determined* (compare Jeremiah 44:11; Luke 9:51). Translated literally, God has "set his face" against the people. He will *do this city harm and not good.*

Doubtless the idea that God will do *harm* against his own people is a shock (compare Jeremiah 44:26, 27; Amos 9:4). The concept of harm is closely related to cursing, especially in contrast to doing *good* as a blessing. God's harm is not intended only as retribution; it is intended also to correct his wayward children (compare Jeremiah 5:3; Hebrews 12:4-11).

Furthermore, we should understand that sometimes multiple layers are the nature of God's wrath. Sometimes it's purely retributive in nature. In those cases, God's wrath has no redemptive element at all; it's punishment simply because the one who receives the punishment deserves it (examples: Romans 2:5; 6:23; Colossians 3:5, 6).

The nation of Judah, represented by its capital *city* of Jerusalem, certainly deserves God's wrath in a retributive sense; if the pagan nations deserve punishment for their idolatry, how much more Judah! And the Judeans' preference to believe that God will punish only the enemies of the Jews—and thereby always deliver Judah—shows how badly they misunderstand what it means for God to be faithful. His wrathful judgment results from the actions of a people and their rulers who have received God's word as no other nation has. They are without excuse in their repeated rejections of him. What is happening to Judah now is the promised result of those actions (see Deuteronomy 4:25-28). Even so, God's wrath in this instance is also corrective in nature (see 4:29-31).

What Do You Think?
What filters can we use to evaluate claims that a given disaster today is from the Lord?
Digging Deeper
What can happen if we fail to do so?

All of this is a reminder of the absolute sovereignty of God. Zedekiah, in seeking to inquire of God (Jeremiah 21:2), seems to assume that the Lord is on call to perform miracles whenever the people desire. But God cannot be manipulated. The destruction of Jerusalem at *the hands of the king of Babylon* will happen because God has determined that it should (compare 20:4; 32:28). Nebuchadnezzar will indeed burn the city (2 Kings 25:8, 9).

❧ GROUPTHINK ❧

In 1979, I was called to be president of a Bible college in northern California. The campus was deteriorating and located in a declining area. A noisy, multilane highway had been built just a few yards away from our buildings.

My staff and I engaged in a years-long search for a perfect property. In hopeful consensus, we convinced ourselves that we should press ahead on one in particular. However, we soon began to

Visual for Lessons 11 & 12. *As you discuss verse 14, ask learners what parts of their lives the Lord desires to refine by fire, not just destroy.*

have nagging doubts. We eventually concluded that God was speaking to us through others who were raising critical questions. We backed out of the negotiations. A few years later, an earthquake made that property totally unusable. What folly if we had continued in perfect agreement with one another!

The bad kind of consensus-building we had engaged in has a name: groupthink. This kind of interaction results from listening only to those who agree with the group. Judah had a long history of groupthink, listening only to themselves rather than to the prophets' warnings. The result of their groupthink was the destruction of their nation. What kind of warning is there for us in all this?
—C. R. B.

II. To the King's House
(JEREMIAH 21:11-14)
A. Judgment (vv. 11, 12)

11. "Moreover, say to the royal house of Judah, 'Hear the word of the LORD.

The focus of Jeremiah's message shifts again as he begins the third of his three sections of address (see Lesson Context). In speaking *to the royal house of Judah,* the reference seems to be to all members of the royal court, those who live in the palace and assist in carrying out the affairs of state. They are not exempt from the indictment against king and commoner (compare Jeremiah 13:18).

12. "'This is what the LORD says to you, house of David: Administer justice every morning; rescue from the hand of the oppressor the one who has been robbed, or my wrath will break out and burn like fire because of the evil you have done—burn with no one to quench it.

In two words Jeremiah sets forth God's vision for kingship and for the responsibilities of the ruling elites toward the people. Those two words are *administer justice.* This is to be the foundational role of the ruling elites toward the people.

The justice spoken of here can be understood in a legal sense. That includes adhering to the Law of Moses with regard to how people are to be treated—especially those who are most vulnerable (Exodus 22:22; Leviticus 25:17; etc.).

The phrase *every morning* is a Hebrew idiom that implies "daily" or "regularly" (see Psalms 5:3; 59:16). It is customary for cases to be adjudicated at the city gates in the morning. Starting each day with right judgments will help ensure that the people act in ways pleasing to the Lord.

All this certainly includes the royals and officials of the *house of David* thwarting the evil schemes of *the oppressor.* Such people seek to take what is not theirs. If human judges refuse to end this injustice, God's *wrath* will be *like fire,* and will *burn* as a result. Fire is not typically literal in contexts such as this (see Psalms 79:5; 89:46), but sometimes it is (see 2 Kings 1:10; Job 1:16). The latter will be the case here when Nebuchadnezzar, as an instrument of God's wrath, burns Jerusalem.

B. Punishment (vv. 13, 14)

13. "'I am against you, Jerusalem, you who live above this valley on the rocky plateau, declares the LORD—you who say, "Who can come against us? Who can enter our refuge?"

The Lord addresses Jerusalem by way of its geographical characteristics. Both the *valley* and *the rocky plateau* make the inhabitants feel secure in the face of military advances. Jerusalem is bounded on three sides by deep valleys. Thus the city itself sits above its potential enemies on a defensive stronghold (compare Jeremiah 49:4).

The people of the city are overconfident in this situation (compare 2 Samuel 5:6, 7). The question *Who can come against us?* indicates just how little they understand about their vulnerability. This attitude is especially astounding given that it's not a foreign army that's the primary threat, but the Lord God himself. Can there be any worse words to hear from the Lord than *I am against you?*

14. "'I will punish you as your deeds deserve, declares the LORD. I will kindle a fire in your forests that will consume everything around you.'"

A reading of Joshua 5:13–6:27 should convince everyone that their walls offer no security against the Lord's wrath! When the Lord desires to pass judgment *as your deeds deserve,* he cannot be thwarted (Proverbs 1:31; Isaiah 3:10, 11).

What Do You Think?
How would you respond to someone who says that the Lord's promise to punish contradicts the claim that "God is love" in 1 John 4:8?
Digging Deeper
How would your response change, if at all, if talking with a sincere seeker rather than with a hardened skeptic who seems to have a list of "gotcha" questions?

Commentators disagree on what is being referred to as *your forests,* since there are no forests in the immediate vicinity of Jerusalem. One possibility is a figurative reference to the royal palace as being "the Palace of the Forest of Lebanon" in 1 Kings 7:2. It was referred to in this manner because of the quantities of cedar that went into its construction. Other homes were also constructed of wood, thus perhaps creating a kind of urban "forest" (compare 2 Kings 19:23).

Conclusion
A. The End of the Line

Today's lesson brings us to one of the most somber moments in the history of God's dealings with his covenant people. Jerusalem was beyond the point of repentance. The people's trust in their own wisdom meant death.

Whether or not we are immunized against such a mind-set depends on whether we are willing to learn from history. And we realize that the grace of God may come to us in the mere fact that we avoided the worst possible outcome of a bad decision or a bad pattern of living. "Consider therefore the kindness and sternness of God" (Romans 11:22). May we, unlike the people of Jeremiah's day, repent while there is time.

B. Prayer

Father, remind us daily that it's either the narrow way of life or the wide gate of destruction. We pray in Jesus' name. Amen.

C. Thought to Remember

Choose the way of life.

INVOLVEMENT LEARNING

Enhance your lesson with NIV Bible Student *(from your curriculum supplier) and the reproducible activity page (at www.standardlesson.com or in the back of the* NIV Standard Lesson Commentary Deluxe Edition*).*

Into the Lesson

Have the following statement on display as class begins: *People reap what they sow.* Ask learners to jot on scrap paper as many real-life examples as they can think of in one minute. After calling time, ask learners to call out their examples, using fewer than 10 words per example—no long stories!—as you write them on the board.

Inform the class that today's lesson illustrates this proverb in a "truer words were never spoken" kind of way.

Into the Word

Briefly summarize the Lesson Context or have a learner (whom you recruited in advance) do so. Have class members open their Bibles to today's lesson text. As a volunteer reads Jeremiah 21:8-10, write *Message to the People* on the left side of the board as a column heading. After the reading, write this question underneath that heading: *What difficult options did God present to the besieged people of Jerusalem?* After a learner voices the obvious answer and you record it under that question, write underneath it this follow-up question: *Why was there no third option of a more pleasant nature?* Write responses on the left side of the board.

Then as a volunteer reads Jeremiah 21:11-14 aloud, write *Message to the Royal Court* as a column header on the right side of the board. Write this question underneath it after the reading: *What primary fruit (v. 14) did Judean leadership lack?* Jot on the board the expected response of "administer justice" (v. 12) when someone vocalizes it.

Then form the class into groups of three to discuss these three questions, which you provide on handouts that you prepare: 1–In what ways were God's expectations of the common people similar or identical to what he expected from the nation's leadership? 2–In what ways, if any, did God's expectations differ regarding the two groups? 3–Why is such a compare/contrast important today?

As group discussion winds down, reconvene for whole-class discussion of conclusions.

Into Life

Distribute handouts (you prepare). As shown here, have this question at the top, with the bullet points following:

How does today's lesson text from Jeremiah 21:8-14 refute the thinking expressed in your assigned scenario?

• A person lives selfishly and sinfully for years, but when crisis comes to her life, she expects God to answer her prayer for help.

• A person's misbehavior causes him to lose his leadership role in the church, his family, and his reputation in the community. The best he can hope for is a low-paying job as he survives in a tiny apartment, away from what was once home.

• A woman leaves her family to pursue a pattern of adultery and drug addiction. She continues her willful ways despite the pleas of her husband and children. Eventually she discovers she has no relationship with any of them.

• A person has no obvious sins and leads a basically decent life. But going to church has never been important to her. She asks, "Does that make me a bad person?"

• One man admits, "Yes, I'm in a horrible situation. I stole funds donated to my charity. I'm going to jail. There's nothing I can do but serve my sentence."

Form the class into small groups and assign a different scenario to each. Allow five minutes for group consideration, then reconvene for whole-class discussion.

Finish with a brief time of reflection by asking learners to write a testimony of a time when negative consequences resulted in repentance and a long-term benefit. After learners finish, ask for volunteers to share their reflections, but don't put anyone on the spot.

Option. Distribute copies of both exercises on the activity page as take-home work. State that you will discuss results at the beginning of the next class.

REPENT OF INJUSTICE

DEVOTIONAL READING: Psalm 72:1-17
BACKGROUND SCRIPTURE: Jeremiah 22

JEREMIAH 22:1-10

¹ This is what the LORD says: "Go down to the palace of the king of Judah and proclaim this message there: ² 'Hear the word of the LORD to you, king of Judah, you who sit on David's throne—you, your officials and your people who come through these gates. ³ This is what the LORD says: Do what is just and right. Rescue from the hand of the oppressor the one who has been robbed. Do no wrong or violence to the foreigner, the fatherless or the widow, and do not shed innocent blood in this place. ⁴ For if you are careful to carry out these commands, then kings who sit on David's throne will come through the gates of this palace, riding in chariots and on horses, accompanied by their officials and their people. ⁵ But if you do not obey these commands, declares the LORD, I swear by myself that this palace will become a ruin.'"

⁶ For this is what the LORD says about the palace of the king of Judah:

"Though you are like Gilead to me,
    like the summit of Lebanon,
I will surely make you like a wasteland,
    like towns not inhabited.
⁷ I will send destroyers against you,
    each man with his weapons,
and they will cut up your fine cedar beams
    and throw them into the fire.

⁸ "People from many nations will pass by this city and will ask one another, 'Why has the LORD done such a thing to this great city?' ⁹ And the answer will be: 'Because they have forsaken the covenant of the LORD their God and have worshiped and served other gods.'"

¹⁰ Do not weep for the dead king or mourn
        his loss;
    rather, weep bitterly for him who is
        exiled,
because he will never return
    nor see his native land again.

KEY VERSE

This is what the LORD says: Do what is just and right. Rescue from the hand of the oppressor the one who has been robbed. Do no wrong or violence to the foreigner, the fatherless or the widow, and do not shed innocent blood in this place. —**Jeremiah 22:3**

JUSTICE AND THE PROPHETS

Unit 3: Called to God's Work of Justice

LESSONS 10–14

LESSON AIMS

After participating in this lesson, each learner will be able to:

1. State promised results of obedience to God and promised consequences for disobedience.

2. Compare and contrast God's statements regarding social justice and injustice with those in other lesson texts of this unit.

3. Evaluate his or her church's ministries to the most vulnerable and participate in a plan for improving those.

LESSON OUTLINE

Introduction

A. Natural Disasters?

On May 18, 1980, Mount St. Helens erupted in the state of Washington. It was the deadliest eruption ever in the United States. The estimated power of the blast was 1,600 times the size of the atomic bomb dropped on Hiroshima. Miles of forest were leveled by the direct blast, and the very earth was scorched by its power. Fifty-seven people and thousands of animals died as a result. What had previously been lush forest and vacation area looked like moonscape. The ash cloud turned the sky dark as far away as Montana. The blast was a violent reminder of nature's potential for destruction.

The utter devastation that was to follow the destruction of Jerusalem probably looked equally shocking. A once thriving city would be reduced to wilderness and wasteland. A primary thing to keep in mind, however, is that the devastation of Jerusalem was definitely supernatural in origin.

B. Lesson Context

The historical context of this lesson is the same as that of lesson 12, so that information need not be repeated here. Even so, we can say a bit more about the man Jeremiah himself.

God called Jeremiah as a young man to be his prophet to Judah; Jeremiah's own evaluation was that he was too young and not qualified to speak (Jeremiah 1:6). The forthcoming confrontations would seem, at times, to be just two against everyone else. But since one of those two was God (1:17-19), there could be no question regarding the outcome.

At times in Jeremiah's lengthy ministry, the stress was so great that it seemed as if he was at the psychological breaking point. Nothing Jeremiah did seemed to persuade people. One example of his extreme frustration is his series of complaints in Jeremiah 12:1-4 (also 20:7-18). God's response? If we could be permitted a very loose translation of Jeremiah 12:5, it would be something like, "Cowboy up and get with the program!" But Jeremiah's early years of prophetic ministry under King Josiah were easy compared to what was to come.

I. For Judah

(Jeremiah 22:1-5)

A. Audience Identified (vv. 1, 2)

1a. This is what the Lord says:

This is a common introductory phrase. It tells the reader that a new prophecy is beginning and to expect a change from the previous subject. Jeremiah is in Jerusalem as our text begins (compare Jeremiah 19:3).

1b. "Go down to the palace of the king of Judah and proclaim this message there:

Go down is probably a directional command in a literal sense. Jerusalem features elevation changes. So the directive suggests that Jeremiah receives it while at or near the temple mount and therefore will need to walk downward to get to *the palace of the king of Judah.*

Based on the timing of the prophecy, the king currently sitting on Judah's throne is probably Jehoiakim. However, God refers to the location of the king's palace instead of to the king himself. This implies that Jeremiah will not be speaking only to the king (contrast Jeremiah 13:18; 21:11 [lesson 12]; 34:2).

2a. "'Hear the word of the Lord to you,

This phrase is another introduction to prophecy (examples: Isaiah 28:14; Ezekiel 13:2). The expression demands not just listening but also comprehending and heeding the message (contrast Isaiah 6:9, quoted in Matthew 13:14). What Jeremiah is about to speak is an authoritative message. As such, it will be quite unlike the invented messages of Jerusalem's false prophets (Jeremiah 23:14; etc.).

2b. "'king of Judah, who sit on David's throne—you, your officials and your people who come through these gates.

HOW TO SAY IT

Babylonians	Bab-ih-*low*-nee-unz.
Gilead	*Gil*-ee-ud (*G* as in *get*).
Jehoahaz	Jeh-*ho*-uh-haz.
Jehoiakim	Jeh-*hoy*-uh-kim.
Josiah	Jo-*sigh*-uh.
Lebanon	*Leb*-uh-nun.
Shallum	*Shall*-um.

Referring to *David's throne* confirms the sense that this prophecy is directed toward all David's royal heirs and not necessarily to a single, specific *king of Judah* (compare Luke 1:32). Jeremiah explicitly extends this challenge to the king's court and all his *people* (all those in the palace household). The *gates* are the entrances to the palace (see also Jeremiah 22:4, below; contrast city gates in 17:25). Everyone should listen to and be responsible to respond to Jeremiah's words, but especially the leaders.

B. Message Delivered (v. 3)

3a. "'This is what the Lord says:

Again, Jeremiah emphasizes that *the Lord* is speaking. Jeremiah himself is only the messenger.

3b. "'Do what is just and right.

This is the point of leadership failure (compare Ezekiel 45:9; Amos 5:24). Doing *what is just* is to ensure fair treatment but is not limited to that. It also extends to developing and maintaining healthy, honest, and respectful relationships at all levels. To do . . . *right* is to create and maintain those kinds of relationships. Even so, we should not see too much of a distinction between being just and right, given their many uses as parallel terms in Hebrew poetry (examples: Isaiah 32:1; Amos 5:24; see discussions of parallelism in lessons 4, 9, and 10).

God's character sets the standard for what is just and right (compare Leviticus 25:17; Psalm 89:14; Isaiah 56:1; Micah 6:8). Both must be expressed toward everyone at all times. And it is the leaders who are to set the example.

3c. "'Rescue from the hand of the oppressor the one who has been robbed. Do no wrong

or violence to the foreigner, the fatherless or the widow, and do not shed innocent blood in this place.

Oppression flourishes where justice and righteousness are absent. In such circumstances, *the oppressor* can cheat and steal without consequence (see also Jeremiah 21:12, last week's lesson). The three kinds of victims mentioned are the most vulnerable in the ancient world. The three were mentioned together 16 times in the Hebrew Old Testament (compare 7:6). *The foreigner* (that is, a non-Israelite living among the covenant people) should have legal recourse for righting *violence* done to himself and his family. *The fatherless* and *the widow* are most susceptible to poverty, lacking a family breadwinner.

What Do You Think?
What stance(s) should Christians adopt regarding governmental policies and procedures that the Word of God says are wrong?
Digging Deeper
How do Acts 4:18-20; 5:27-29; and Romans 13:1-7 help shape your answer?

C. Consequences Specified (vv. 4, 5)

4. "'For if you are careful to carry out these commands, then kings who sit on David's throne will come through the gates of this palace, riding in chariots and on horses, accompanied by their officials and their people.

God frequently sets his commands in the context of consequences and blessings (example: Deuteronomy 11:26-28). Here, God promises again to extend David's legacy to David's royal descendants if they will *carry out these commands*—namely, practice justice and righteousness.

The bottom-line question is simple: Do those *who sit on David's throne* desire to keep their positions, or do they not?

5a. "'But if you do not obey these commands, declares the Lord,

A warning against refusing to *obey* and heed God's *commands* is in keeping with the blessing/curse pattern established early in the history of Israel (see Deuteronomy 28). Jeremiah does not use

that couplet specifically, but blessing-and-curse is indeed the sense here (compare Zechariah 8:13).

What Do You Think?
Which sins of injustice are most in need of correcting today: those of commission (doing wrong) or those of omission (failing to do right)? Why?
Digging Deeper
Which of those two areas are you best positioned to help correct? Why?

5b. "'I swear by myself that this palace will become a ruin.'"

To *swear* is a particularly weighty way of making a promise (compare Genesis 22:16). The more significant, permanent, or powerful the thing sworn on, the more definite and absolute the promise. There is nothing and no one more significant, permanent, or powerful than God (Hebrews 6:13). He will make sure he fulfills this promise if Judah refuses to respond obediently.

The consequences God describes are both symbolic and literal. The phrase *this palace* refers both to David's descendants and to the physical structure of their dwelling. If Judah's leaders disregard God, they will not only be dethroned; they also will be without a physical residence in Jerusalem (compare Jeremiah 39:4-8).

❧ HOUSE RULES ❧

When I was in high school, I met Sam. As we got acquainted, I began to hear from Sam about how unjust his father was. As Sam and I got closer, we would visit each other's homes. I began to see why Sam was frustrated. His father approached life with a critical, demanding spirit.

One day Sam said, "I wish my dad were more like your dad." Ironically, my dad had some of the same rules as Sam's dad. The difference was in approach. My father prioritized, helping me understand why the house rules were in place, as well as how they worked for my own good.

Jeremiah tried to help the leaders of Judah see that there were good reasons for God's rules. If God couldn't get the leaders' attention through prophecy, then he would get their attention through fulfillment of prophecy. What does it take for God to get your attention?   —C. R. B.

II. For the Nations
(Jeremiah 22:6-10)
A. Imagery of Destruction (vv. 6, 7)

6a. For this is what the Lord says about the palace of the king of Judah:

Again, Jeremiah restates that the words he speaks come from *the Lord* and are addressed to *the palace of the king*. There should be no mistake about either the source or the intended recipients!

6b. "Though you are like Gilead to me, like the summit of Lebanon, I will surely make you like a wasteland, like towns not inhabited.

God uses imagery to affirm how precious his people are to him. *Gilead* is an area just east of the Jordan River (Numbers 32:1-4, 19); *Lebanon* is located along the seacoast north of Israel. Those areas were known for their forests (Judges 9:15; etc.). Both David and Solomon used expensive wood from the areas in building projects (2 Samuel 7:2; 1 Kings 5:1-10; 7:2). Gilead was also known for its balm (Genesis 37:25; Jeremiah 8:22; 46:11).

Other than the text before us, mention of Gilead and Lebanon occur together in the same verse only in Zechariah 10:10. Just three verses later, that prophet speaks of fire destroying Lebanon's "cedars" and "oaks of Bashan"—an area lying north of and adjacent to Gilead (11:1, 2). The coming destruction will be heartbreaking. Though David's lineage is precious to the Lord, he will dispossess its kings if they don't change their unjust ways. But that is up to them.

7. "I will send destroyers against you, each man with his weapons, and they will cut up your fine cedar beams and throw them into the fire.

The *destroyers* to whom God refers are the Babylonians (2 Chronicles 36:17-19). Reference to *your fine cedar beams* may refer either to (1) trees of the forest or (2) the cedar used in construction for the wealthy, especially the king's palace. Considering the first possibility, the felling of trees is a natural thing for a besieging army to do for building

its siege ramps and towers (Jeremiah 6:6; compare 43:12; Isaiah 10:34).

Since an army would use the trees closest at hand, which probably wouldn't be cedar, the reference to cedar in the king's palace is more likely. Under either interpretation, the victorious besiegers will burn everything of significance before leaving for home (Jeremiah 52:13). Judah will be a deconstruction zone. The sense of the verse is of priceless things destroyed that need not have been.

B. Example of Disobedience (vv. 8, 9)

8. "People from many nations will pass by this city and will ask one another, 'Why has the Lord done such a thing to this great city?'

People of the ancient Near East generally linked the rise and fall of *nations* to the power of a nation's deities (see 1 Kings 20:23). Jerusalem's status as a *great city* has earned Judah a reputation for following a very powerful deity. This is what God intended (Genesis 12:1-3).

The injustice that infects Jerusalem and Judah does not draw the nations toward the just and holy God—the only God there is. Instead, the nations around Jerusalem see no difference between Judah's way of life and theirs, between their gods and Judah's God. And when those nations see the defeat and captivity of God's people, they will link it to God's activity. The scope of devastation Judah is to undergo will be so immense that everyone will conclude that it was a God-driven action. The extent of the destruction will accomplish what Jerusalem and her injustice had not: nations will acknowledge God in at least one sense.

9. "And the answer will be: 'Because they have forsaken the covenant of the Lord their God and worshiped and served other gods.'"

God's plan from the beginning has involved inviting others to experience and follow him. We see this in God's promise to Abraham, that Abraham will be a blessing to the nations (Genesis 12:1-3). We see this again in Zechariah 8:20-23, as God's restoration of Judah draws the nations to seek him. We see it again in the New Testament, when Peter challenges his readers to live lives that draw questions—all so that we may respond with Jesus as our answer (1 Peter 3:8-15).

Do no WRONG to the POWERLESS.

Visual for Lesson 13. *While discussing v. 3, have the class identify their responsibilities toward "the powerless" in the community.*

But in our text we see the opposite occurring. Jerusalem's injustice does not draw the nations to seek God, since they see no difference between Judah's actions and their own. So God plans to draw their attention to his ways of justice and righteousness by disciplining Judah for her failure to model God's character. That would invite others to see God for who he is (compare 2 Kings 22:17; Ezekiel 39:23). The forthcoming devastation will be seen as divine in origin. The predicted *answer* is nothing new (see Deuteronomy 29:25, 26; 1 Kings 9:8, 9; Jeremiah 16:10, 11).

C. Mourning for the Exiles (v. 10)

10a. Do not weep for the dead king or mourn his loss;

This lament is usually understood to refer to Josiah, Judah's last righteous king (2 Chronicles 35:25). Mourning *for the dead* is a significant ritual for cultures worldwide; the ancient Near East is no exception. Jeremiah's words suggest that there is a fate worse than death (compare Ecclesiastes 4:2).

10b. rather, weep bitterly for him who is exiled, because he will never return nor see his native land again.

The reference is to Shallum, also known as Jehoahaz (Jeremiah 22:11, 12, not in our printed text; 2 Kings 23:29-32). Shallum succeeded Josiah as king in about 609 BC. Reversing Josiah's initiatives, Shallum led Judah back into the evils of Josiah's predecessors; he was king for only three months,

then was exiled permanently to Egypt (23:33; the Shallum of 2 Kings 15 is a different person).

It seems odd to mourn the exile of an evil king yet not grieve the death of a godly king (compare Jeremiah 22:18, not in our printed text). The force of Jeremiah's prophecy has been God's warning of destruction and exile if Judah's leaders refuse to practice justice. Shallum is to serve as an example of the grief of all the exiles. Jeremiah holds him up as a warning of his hearers' own possible future.

> *What Do You Think?*
> In what ways does this verse help you in establishing priorities of focus?
> *Digging Deeper*
> What additional help do you find in 1 Corinthians 7:29-31 in this regard? How so?

Conclusion

A. Supernatural Restoration

The word from the Lord to the house of David features two promises: (1) If David's descendants would renounce injustice, then God would bless them, but (2) if not, they would suffer punishment. Judah would experience the full and recognizable consequences of disobeying God. God would therefore exhibit his character to the world and draw people to himself in one of those two ways.

God calls us to the same challenge he posed through Jeremiah. As we demonstrate God's righteous and just character in our actions, we also must expose the injustice inflicted on the powerless by oppressive people and systems. But we don't just draw people to God as an abstract. Rather, we draw people to the living Jesus. To reject this mission is to risk experiencing God in ways we will not like.

B. Prayer

Heavenly Father, help us see ways in which we have been unjust so that we may repent and model you as you would have us do. We pray in the name of the one who suffered great injustice, Jesus. Amen.

C. Thought to Remember

Does your example invite God's justice?

INVOLVEMENT LEARNING

Enhance your lesson with NIV Bible Student *(from your curriculum supplier) and the reproducible activity page (at www.standardlesson.com or in the back of the* NIV Standard Lesson Commentary Deluxe Edition*).*

Into the Lesson

Give to each of six class members a piece of poster board on which you have written one word of the following in very large letters:

Get while the getting is good.

Ask the six participants to come to the front and arrange themselves in the correct order. After they do so, merely say, "Hmmm . . . looks like we have some work to do." Then have half the class think of reasons why the sentence represents a correct worldview by which to live; the other half is to think of reasons it represents a defective worldview. Jot proposals on the board during ensuing whole-class discussion.

Announce that today's text will cast light on whether this axiom is biblically valid or defective.

Into the Word

Prepare handouts with the following headings and/or others as you see fit. Leave space between the headings for notes.

    I. What the leaders should do
    II. How God will respond
    III. What disobedience will bring
    IV. What the nations will conclude

Distribute the handout to groups of two to six to complete as the outline suggests. After five minutes, allow groups to share with the whole class.

Next, pose the following questions for whole-class discussion. (*Option.* To encourage balanced participation, say that no one gets to speak twice until everyone has had an opportunity to speak once.)

1–Why was God's exhortation aimed at the leaders rather than the population at large?
2–How is God's instruction here different from prophecies that focus on idol worship?
3–What makes God's promised punishment especially terrible?

4–Why would God predict the reaction of pagan nations?

Next, form the class into study pairs or triads to discuss these comprehension questions:

- How are God's statements regarding justice and injustice *similar to* his statements in the other lessons in this unit studied so far?

- How do God's statements regarding justice and injustice *differ from* his statements in the other lessons in this unit studied so far?

Point students again to the six-word sentence that began today's session. Ask, "How does today's text suggest an approach for God's people different from 'Get while the getting is good'?"

Into Life

Distribute handouts (you prepare) featuring the following categories:

___Victims of injustice   ___Foreigners
___Widows   ___Orphans

Ask learners to take 30 seconds to rank from 1 (best) to 4 (needs most improvement) how your church is doing in ministering to each category of people. Follow by creating an overall class tally on the board. Discuss reasons for different rankings. (*Option.* Precede this exercise by having study pairs complete the "Concern for the Vulnerable" exercise on the activity page, which you can download.) Remind students that each listed category is in Jeremiah 22:3.

Form small groups designated by the four categories above, one designation per group. Allow learners to be in the group of their choosing. Have groups propose how group members can help your church improve in that area of ministry.

Option. Conclude by distributing the "Prayer for Wisdom to Help" exercise at the bottom of the activity page as a take-home.

PURSUE LOVE AND JUSTICE

DEVOTIONAL READING: Deuteronomy 8:11-20
BACKGROUND SCRIPTURE: Hosea 11, 12

HOSEA 11:1, 2, 7-10

1 "When Israel was a child, I loved him,
   and out of Egypt I called my son.
2 But the more they were called,
   the more they went away from me.
They sacrificed to the Baals
   and they burned incense to images."

. . . .

7 "My people are determined to turn from me.
   Even though they call me God Most High,
   I will by no means exalt them.
8 "How can I give you up, Ephraim?
   How can I hand you over, Israel?
How can I treat you like Admah?
   How can I make you like Zeboyim?
My heart is changed within me;
   all my compassion is aroused.
9 I will not carry out my fierce anger,
   nor will I devastate Ephraim again.
For I am God, and not a man—
   the Holy One among you.
   I will not come against their cities.
10 They will follow the LORD;
   he will roar like a lion.
When he roars,
   his children will come trembling from the
      west."

HOSEA 12:1, 2, 6-14

1 Ephraim feeds on the wind;
   he pursues the east wind all day
   and multiplies lies and violence.
He makes a treaty with Assyria
   and sends olive oil to Egypt.
2 The LORD has a charge to bring against Judah;

he will punish Jacob according to his ways
   and repay him according to his deeds.

. . . .

6 But you must return to your God;
   maintain love and justice,
   and wait for your God always.
7 The merchant uses dishonest scales
   and loves to defraud.
8 Ephraim boasts,
   "I am very rich; I have become wealthy.
With all my wealth they will not find in me
   any iniquity or sin."
9 "I have been the LORD your God
   ever since you came out of Egypt;
I will make you live in tents again,
   as in the days of your appointed festivals.
10 I spoke to the prophets,
   gave them many visions
   and told parables through them."
11 Is Gilead wicked?
   Its people are worthless!
Do they sacrifice bulls in Gilgal?
   Their altars will be like piles of stones
   on a plowed field.
12 Jacob fled to the country of Aram;
   Israel served to get a wife,
   and to pay for her he tended sheep.
13 The LORD used a prophet to bring Israel up
      from Egypt,
   by a prophet he cared for him.
14 But Ephraim has aroused his bitter anger;
   his Lord will leave on him the guilt of his
      bloodshed
   and will repay him for his contempt.

KEY VERSE

You must return to your God; maintain love and justice, and wait for your God always. —**Hosea 12:6**

JUSTICE AND THE PROPHETS

Unit 3: Called to God's Work of Justice

LESSONS 10–14

LESSON AIMS

After participating in this lesson, each learner will be able to:

1. Identify Israel's problem.

2. Explain whether the predicted consequences of that problem better fit the concept of *restorative* justice or that of *retributive* justice.

3. Identify one or more modern parallels to elements of the text and develop responses.

LESSON OUTLINE

Introduction
  A. Rotten at the Core
  B. Lesson Context
I. Father's Faithfulness (HOSEA 11:1, 2, 7-10)
  A. God's Action (v. 1)
  B. Israel's Reaction (vv. 2, 7)
    Judgment Tempered by Love
  C. God's Decision (vv. 8, 9)
  D. Israel's Future (v. 10)
II. Lord's Resolution (HOSEA 12:1, 2, 6-14)
  A. Charges of Sin (vv. 1, 2)
  B. Direction for a Return (v. 6)
  C. Persistence in Wickedness (vv. 7, 8)
  D. Plan for Reconciliation (vv. 9, 10)
  E. Resistance to the Plan (vv. 11-14)
Conclusion
  A. Fruit for the Harvest
  B. Prayer
  C. Thought to Remember

Introduction

A. Rotten at the Core

One hot summer day, the cool green watermelon was as appealing as gourmet ice cream. A swift stroke of a knife later, though, and everyone gathered around the table winced in disgust. The watermelon had rotted from the inside out. The rind was perfect, but the dead white insides reeked of decay. Disappointment quickly gave way to revulsion as we tried to escape the nauseating stench. The beautiful fruit was rotten at the core.

The northern kingdom of Israel of the mid–eighth century BC looked beautiful on the surface as well, like the nation had it all together. But it too was rotten at the core. And God had had enough of Israel's revolting behavior.

B. Lesson Context

A general time line for Hosea's prophetic ministry is 755–725 BC. This is computed with reference to the reigns listed in Hosea 1:1, as well as the fact that the northern kingdom of Israel, Hosea's primary focus, ceased to exist in 722 BC.

Israel's King Jeroboam II, listed in Hosea 1:1, reigned from about 793 to 753 BC. He was a strong ruler politically. He expanded Israel's borders and made Israel the leading nation in Palestine and Syria (see 2 Kings 14:23-29). Israel was wealthy and proud of its success. Turning their backs on God, the people also found it all too easy to shift allegiance to the fictitious deity known as Baal (Hosea 2:8, 13); this went hand in hand with injustice (4:1, 2). In confronting this idolatry, God called Hosea to live out a unique and difficult parable of God's love for Israel (see chap. 1–3).

Hosea's style did not involve pronouncing what we might call highly directed prophecies—those beginning with the command "Hear," followed by named addressees—the way other prophets did (contrast Jeremiah 10:1; 22:2, last week's lesson; etc.). Two exceptions are found in Hosea 4:1 and 5:1. Following those pronouncements, Hosea simply continued his generalized prophetic pronouncements on wayward Israel. For this reason, the organization of the book can be difficult to determine.

I. Father's Faithfulness

(HOSEA 11:1, 2, 7-10)

A. God's Action (v. 1)

1. "When Israel was a child, I loved him, and out of Egypt I called my son.

Hosea tells the story of God's interactions with *Israel* beginning with the exodus *out of Egypt.* That event and the giving of the law at Sinai launched Israel as a nation. Calling Israel *a child* reinforces that this was a formative experience (compare Jeremiah 2:2). God is determined that the leadership and people of Israel understand the coming prophecy first and foremost in terms of his love.

Matthew uses this text to describe the return of young Jesus from Egypt (Matthew 2:15). That story too should be read in light of God's love. Jesus is the ultimate expression of that love.

B. Israel's Reaction (vv. 2, 7)

2. "But the more they were called, the more they went away from me. They sacrificed to the Baals and they burned incense to images."

The designation *Baal* refers to the fictitious god of other nations, particularly the Canaanites. This is a term that generally has the sense of "lord" or "master." But no matter how persistently God has *called* Israel to him, the people insist on doing the opposite and embracing idolatry (examples: 2 Kings 17:15, 16; Hosea 11:7, below; 13:1).

Though the people may still be offering sacrifices to the Lord and celebrating his festivals (Hosea 2:11), they also burn *incense* to idols (compare Jeremiah 1:16; 18:15; Hosea 2:13). The hearts of the people are untrue to the very God who gave birth to their nation by bringing them from Egypt and giving them a land of their own.

❧ *JUDGMENT TEMPERED BY LOVE* ❧

Andrew was a regular in a men's Bible study I led. But his participation could be problematic at times. Whenever our text dealt with judgment, Andrew questioned God's actions. He had trouble with Jesus' words about a final separation of saved and wicked. When the group discussed various ethical issues, Andrew was unfailingly lenient.

One day Andrew finally told us the reason for his difficulty. His father had been a judgmental, controlling person. The man was so mean-spirited that none of his three children went to his funeral! I watched the group as Andrew bared his soul to them. Where frustration had been, compassion began to blossom.

Andrew had turned away from a man who caused his family only pain. Israel had no such excuse: God was a loving Father whose judgment was tempered with love. What human failures continue to color your experience of your loving heavenly Father?
—C. R. B.

7a. "My people are determined to turn from me.

God's frustration with the Israelites is quite apparent. Their choice is not accidental due to ignorance. Quite the opposite—theirs is a committed intent to *turn* away from him. The northern kingdom of Israel mirrors the southern kingdom of Judah in this regard (example: Jeremiah 8:5).

7b. "Even though they call me God Most High, I will by no means exalt them.

The meaning of the Hebrew text is not entirely clear in this half verse. In the larger context of Hosea 11, it suggests that Israel is mixing practices and religious vocabulary. Likely the people are worshiping Canaanite deities even as they continue to say the right things about *God Most High.* Because of their utter refusal to abandon idolatry, God will not exalt them by delivering them.

C. God's Decision (vv. 8, 9)

8. "How can I give you up, Ephraim? How can I hand you over, Israel? How can I treat you like Admah? How can I make you like

HOW TO SAY IT

Admah	*Ad*-muh.
Baal	*Bay*-ul.
Ephraim	*Ee*-fray-im.
Gilead	*Gil*-ee-ud (*G* as in *get*).
Gilgal	*Gil*-gal (*G* as in *get*).
Zeboyim	Zeh-*bo*-im.

Zeboyim? My heart is changed within me; all my compassion is aroused.

The parallel structure of Hebrew poetry is evident here as the second question creatively rephrases the first. *Ephraim* is another way of referring to the northern kingdom of Israel (compare Hosea 5:3; 6:10; see also Genesis 41:50-52).

Likewise, the fourth question rephrases the third: *Admah* and *Zeboyim* were sister cities of the infamous Sodom and Gomorrah (Genesis 14:2, 8; Deuteronomy 29:23). The thought of punishing Israel as he did those cities breaks God's *heart*. He is one who takes "no pleasure in the death of the wicked, but rather that they turn from their ways and live" (Ezekiel 33:11).

Language of *changed* and *aroused* does not mean that God repented of his actions as though he has done or is planning to do wrong. Rather, the sense is that *compassion* tempers his anger; see the next verse.

9. "I will not carry out my fierce anger, nor will I devastate Ephraim again. For I am God, and not a man—the Holy One among you. I will not come against their cities.

This is not the first time that God's compassion tempers his anger (see 2 Samuel 24:15-25). Unlike people prone to overreact in their anger, God is always thoughtful and measured in his actions.

Visual for Lesson 14. *As you discuss verse 1, have the class reflect on situations that God's love has called them to leave behind.*

and love (compare 1 John 4:8, 16). Neither one is subordinate to the other. God's holiness calls forth retributive expressions of his wrath (examples: Genesis 6:5-7; Revelation 20:15), while God's love calls forth restorative expressions of his wrath (Deuteronomy 8:5; Hebrews 12:5-7).

Centuries after the time of Hosea, the self-sacrifice of Jesus on the cross will satisfy the requirements of both God's holiness and love. As sin is punished to satisfy the requirements of God's holiness, the path to eternal life is thereby opened in satisfying the requirements of God's love. Life in the presence of our holy God becomes possible as sin's price is paid (Romans 3:21-26).

D. Israel's Future (v. 10)

10. "They will follow the LORD; he will roar like a lion. When he roars, his children will come trembling from the west."

They will follow the Lord will be the result of God's restorative discipline. The figurative *roar like a lion* by God will be the sign for Israel to return home. The return from exile by the southern kingdom of Judah will be from the east, but this return with *trembling from the west* is clarified as "from Egypt, trembling like sparrows" in Hosea 11:11 (not in today's text; compare and contrast Isaiah 11:11). This brings us full circle to the "out of Egypt" of Hosea 11:1, above. But Israel should realize that God can just as well act as a lion in a destructive sense (see Hosea 5:14).

> **What Do You Think?**
> How can you use this text to encourage those who feel that their bad decisions cannot be forgiven?
> **Digging Deeper**
> What other texts have you found to be valuable in this regard?

For God to refer to himself as *the Holy One among you* reminds his covenant people that although he is present with them, he also is entirely different from them. His ways are not human ways (compare Numbers 23:19; Isaiah 55:8, 9).

This verse in its context is valuable for glimpsing God's two overarching characteristics of holiness (compare Isaiah 6:3; Revelation 4:8; etc.)

II. Lord's Resolution

(HOSEA 12:1, 2, 6-14)

A. Charges of Sin (vv. 1, 2)

1. Ephraim feeds on the wind; he pursues the east wind all day and multiplies lies and violence. He makes a treaty with Assyria and sends olive oil to Egypt.

For *Ephraim* (meaning Israel; see on Hosea 11:8, above) to feed *on the wind* and pursue *the east wind* can be another way of referring to *a treaty with Assyria* and an economic treaty with *Egypt* that involves *olive oil* (see 2 Kings 17:4; 18:21; Isaiah 30:7). Rather than seeking God as an ally, the king of Israel has turned to world powers for security (compare Hosea 5:13; 7:11).

> *What Do You Think?*
> How can we guard against allowing our trust in earthly covenants to supersede the new covenant we have in Christ?
> *Digging Deeper*
> What early warning signs have you noticed to be important in indicating that that is happening?

2. The LORD has a charge to bring against Judah; he will punish Jacob according to his ways and repay him according to his deeds.

This is the formal language of a lawsuit (compare Isaiah 3:13; Amos 3:13; Micah 6:2). Like any legal arrangement, there are consequences for breaking the contract. These consequences are agreed on before signing (example: Deuteronomy 11:16, 17, 28). As the name Ephraim in our text refers to the entire northern kingdom of Israel, so also *Jacob* here represents all of *Judah* (or even both kingdoms in totality). Judah would do well to see how God judges the north and repent while there is time.

B. Direction for a Return (v. 6)

6. But you must return to your God; maintain love and justice, and wait for your God always.

The language of *return to your God* is language of repentance from sin. But this turn of the heart must be evidenced by a turn in behavior. Any

turn of heart must be accompanied by exercising the *love and justice* that mirrors God's own character.

Further, to *wait for your God always* is not a suggestion of mere passive patience; rather, this imperative conveys the idea of an active and complete trust in God's plans and timing (examples: Psalm 130:5; Isaiah 8:17; Micah 7:7). This will demonstrate repentance from relying on earthly powers instead of the Lord.

> *What Do You Think?*
> What techniques can you pass on to others to help them wait for God?
> *Digging Deeper*
> Which mistake are Christians more likely to make: failing to wait for God, or waiting too long and therefore failing to keep up with Him? Why is that?

C. Persistence in Wickedness (vv. 7, 8)

7. The merchant uses dishonest scales and loves to defraud.

The nation is portrayed as a greedy shopkeeper who gleefully uses *dishonest scales* (false weights on a balance scale) to *defraud,* or cheat, customers (compare Leviticus 19:36; Amos 8:5; Micah 6:10-14).

8. Ephraim boasts, "I am very rich; I have become wealthy. With all my wealth they will not find in me any iniquity or sin."

Ill-gotten gain breeds arrogance (compare Ezekiel 28:5). Unchecked arrogance eventually results in a self-deluding sense of invincibility (*they will not find in me any iniquity or sin*). Revelation 3:17 warns against the same self-delusion in the first century AD. This danger seems even greater today.

D. Plan for Reconciliation (vv. 9, 10)

9. "I have been the LORD your God ever since you came out of Egypt; I will make you live in tents again, as in the days of your appointed festivals.

Mention of the exodus from *out of Egypt* again brings the prophecy back to Hosea 11:1. To *live in tents again* refers to the annual Festival of

Tabernacles. During this week-long observance, Israelites live in temporary huts, or booths (tabernacles), to remember their days of God's protection in the wilderness (Leviticus 23:33-36, 39-43). To bring the people back to him, God will send them through a wilderness experience again in the form of exile.

10. "I spoke to the prophets, gave them many visions and told parables through them."

By this time, God has spoken *to the prophets* plainly (examples: Leviticus 26:14-17; 1 Kings 18:21; 20:13-22). He has also communicated through *visions* (examples: Numbers 24:4, 16; 1 Samuel 3:15) and *parables* (Psalm 78:2; Proverbs 1:1-6).

E. Resistance to the Plan (vv. 11-14)

11. Is Gilead wicked? Its people are worthless! Do they sacrifice bulls in Gilgal? Their altars will be like piles of stones on a plowed field.

This is a good example of a prophetic parable in the form of a riddle God poses to Israel. Earlier in Hosea's prophecies, he had introduced *Gilgal* as the site of a major pagan shrine (Hosea 4:14, 15; compare Amos 4:4). Gilgal is west of the Jordan River and close to Jericho. The location of the city of *Gilead* is unknown, but it parallels Gilgal in wickedness (see Hosea 6:8). God speaks of the people's pride in both the shrine and their agricultural wealth. But Gilead's *altars* to other gods make it as unfruitful as if its fields were sown with rocks instead of fertile soil.

12. Jacob fled to the country of Aram; Israel served to get a wife, and to pay for her he tended sheep.

God continues the riddle by noting Jacob's experiences with Laban. Although *Jacob* initially *fled* to Laban for safety (Genesis 27:42-45), Jacob did not find the haven he hoped for. Jacob (later renamed *Israel*; 32:28) was deceived in marriage (29:14b-30) and ultimately sensed the need to flee (chap. 31). Similarly, Israel is looking to Egypt and Assyria for safety but will eventually find Egypt to be powerless and Assyria to be a deadly enemy.

13. The LORD used a prophet to bring Israel up from Egypt, by a prophet he cared for him.

God now speaks plainly again. Listening to Hosea is the same as listening to the *prophet* Moses of long ago. Both speak God's words. Just as God led *Israel up from* slavery under Moses, God can lead the Israelites away from a second captivity and exile if they listen to Hosea.

> *What Do You Think?*
> What do the text's frequent references to Egypt suggest to you about what to be on guard against in human nature, generally speaking?
> *Digging Deeper*
> What practices have you found useful in overcoming this human tendency? Be specific.

14. But Ephraim has aroused his bitter anger; his Lord will leave on him the guilt of his bloodshed and will repay him for his contempt.

God repeats his warning: *Ephraim* (Israel) will face the consequences of its actions (compare Ezekiel 18:13). God's protection will be withdrawn. Arrogant Israel's injustice and idolatry will result in national destruction.

Conclusion
A. Fruit for the Harvest

All too frequently we feel the sneaky satisfaction of having gotten away with something. And our choices often convey to others that we are the most important people in our lives. We feel secure because of what we own or who we know; when trouble comes, we try to solve our own problems by way of people and stuff. Suddenly Israel looks as familiar as our reflection in the mirror.

It's time to leave those things behind and trust in God. It's time to show through our actions that we follow God only.

B. Prayer

Dear Lord, help us put hands and feet to our claims to follow you—and convict us when we don't. In Jesus' name we pray. Amen.

C. Thought to Remember

Let love and justice characterize your life.

INVOLVEMENT LEARNING

Enhance your lesson with NIV Bible Student *(from your curriculum supplier) and the reproducible activity page (at www.standardlesson.com or in the back of the* NIV Standard Lesson Commentary Deluxe Edition*).*

Into the Lesson

Write the following on the board:

A parent shows love for his or her child by . . .

Invite responses, which you jot on the board. Then do the same with this sentence:

Children disappoint their parents when . . .

If you have learners who didn't respond to the first completion, give them priority in responding to this one.

Alternative. Distribute copies of the "Tell a Story" exercise on the activity page, which you can download. Have students work in pairs to complete as indicated. Call for ideas in the ensuing whole-class discussion.

Lead into Bible study by asking, "Do these sentences [or pictures, if you used the alternative] have anything to do with people's relationships with their heavenly Father? Let's find out!"

Into the Word

Write the following four themes on the board as a basis for the Bible study:

     I. The Mercy of God
     II. The Foolishness of the People
     III. The Rebellion of the People
     IV. The Demands of God

Choose one of the following two options as a way for students to discover which theme matches best to each verse of today's study.

Option 1. Assign each learner one theme at random. (Classes larger than four will naturally result in duplicate assignments.) Read aloud slowly the 17 verses of the text and the verse numbers. As you do, students can listen for verses that best fit their themes. Then read the text and verse numbers aloud a second time. Do not read it aloud a third time; instead direct learners to their Bibles if they need to process the text further.

After a few minutes, poll the class by show of hands for their conclusions for each of the 17 verses. After recording a complete tally for all four themes, focus on areas where the tally shows the least agreement. Use the commentary to correct misconceptions.

Option 2. Divide the class into small groups and assign all four themes to every group (you may wish to put the themes on handouts). After all groups finish matching verses to themes, proceed with the class as a whole to tally and discuss all results as above.

If you used the alternative "Tell the Story" exercise during Into the Lesson, have study pairs complete as indicated the "Find the Lesson" segment on that same downloadable page.

Into Life

Distribute handouts (you prepare) with the following statements:

A–Our country's best hope for security lies in a strong military and good foreign policy.
B–Sure, there are areas for creative interpretation in the contracts we give customers. If they don't read the fine print, that's their problem!
C–I go to church, take Communion, put money in the plate, and show up at fellowship dinners. With all those boxes checked off, I'm good with God.

Form small groups to develop responses to each statement, using concepts from today's text. Responses should include one or more phrases and/or verse references for each statement. Allow six to eight minutes before discussing conclusions with the class as a whole. *(Expected connections: A with 12:1; B with 12:7; C with 11:2 and/or 12:11. Learners may make a good case for others.)*

If you used the "Tell the Story" and "Find the Lesson" segments on the downloadable activity page, have learners complete as indicated the third segment, "Change Your Story," taking no more than one minute.

MANY FACES
OF WISDOM

Special Features

Lessons
Unit 1: Wisdom in Proverbs

Unit 2: Wisdom in the Gospels

Unit 3: Faith and Wisdom in James

QUARTERLY QUIZ

Use these questions as a pretest or as a review. The answers are on page iv of This Quarter in the Word.

Lesson 1

1. The fear of consequences is the beginning of knowledge. T/F. *Proverbs 1:7*

2. If _____ men entice you, do not go along with them. *Proverbs 1:10*

Lesson 2

1. To what two items is wisdom compared? (gold, silver, treasure, a lamp?) *Proverbs 2:4*

2. The Lord is the giver of wisdom, knowledge, and _____. *Proverbs 2:6*

Lesson 3

1. Wisdom is more valuable than rubies. T/F. *Proverbs 8:11*

2. Wisdom loves those who _____ her. *Proverbs 8:17*

Lesson 4

1. To go in the way of understanding, you must leave your _____ ways. *Proverbs 9:6*

2. If you give instruction to a wise man, he will become _____. *Proverbs 9:9*

Lesson 5

1. Who was the messenger sent ahead of Jesus? (Elisha, John the Baptist, Paul?) *Matthew 11:10, 11*

2. Jesus was criticized for being what? (dishonest, a friend of tax collectors and sinners, lustful?) *Matthew 11:19*

Lesson 6

1. Jesus' parents knew to look for Jesus in the temple. T/F. *Luke 2:46*

2. Jesus increased in _____ and stature. *Luke 2:52*

Lesson 7

1. A prophet is not without honor, except in his own _____. *Mark 6:4*

2. Jesus performed many miracles in his hometown. T/F. *Mark 6:5*

Lesson 8

1. Which of these things did Jesus reveal himself to be? (the way, the key, the answer?) *John 14:6*

2. Jesus said that those who have seen him have seen the Father. T/F. *John 14:9*

Lesson 9

1. If you lack wisdom and ask God for it, he will give it to you _____. *James 1:5*

2. James contrasts having faith with doubting. T/F. *James 1:6*

Lesson 10

1. James defines *self-deceit* as hearing God's Word but not obeying it. T/F. *James 1:22*

2. Which item is not included in James's definition of *pure religion*? (looking after widows and orphans, not being polluted by the world, being respected by the congregation?) *James 1:27*

Lesson 11

1. According to James, it doesn't matter if works accompany faith. T/F. *James 2:17*

2. James referred to Rahab as a positive example of works accompanying faith. T/F. *James 2:25*

Lesson 12

1. The tongue is like _____ that can set someone's life ablaze. *James 3:6*

2. A tongue used to bless God should not also _____ the people he made. *James 3:9, 10*

Lesson 13

1. What quality is evident in a person with wisdom? (confidence, humility, ability to convince?) *James 3:13*

2. Wisdom from above shows partiality toward rich people. T/F. *James 3:17, 18*

QUARTER AT A GLANCE

by Larry Shallenberger

WE ADMIRE WISDOM, but struggle to define the term. In 2016, a team of psychologists attempted to understand how people perceived the concept of wisdom. The team presented historical figures who were generally esteemed as being wise, then asked what specific qualities made them wise. Three templates emerged: practical wisdom, philosophical wisdom, and benevolent wisdom.

Scripture confirms that wisdom manifests itself in many ways. Bezalel was filled with wisdom for his work constructing the tabernacle (Exodus 31:2, 3). Joshua was filled with wisdom to lead Israel into the promised land (Deuteronomy 34:9). A wise woman persuaded her city to slay David's enemy and save themselves (2 Samuel 20:16-22). Even in biblical times, it was apparent that wisdom has diverse blossoms.

The Roots of Wisdom

True wisdom is rooted in a single source: God himself. We open unit 1 with a survey of wisdom in the book of Proverbs. King Solomon, the primary contributor to the anthology, taught young men that "the fear of the Lord is the beginning of knowledge" (Proverbs 1:7). The word *fear* is best interpreted as a worshipful awe and respect of God, not an unhealthy terror of the divine.

Solomon's belief that wisdom was accessible to anyone is evident through his anthropomorphizing (giving human characteristics to) wisdom as being a woman. She stands at the gates of the city and invites anyone who would come to partake in her lavish feast. But Solomon also recognized that wisdom wasn't the only voice calling out to his rising leaders.

The Embodiment of Wisdom

Wisdom became incarnate in Jesus, discussed in unit 2. The Gospel writers emphasized that Jesus was an unexpected and even unwelcome source of wisdom. As a boy, Jesus' understanding of Scripture flabbergasted the religious teachers of his day. His eccentric prophet, John the Baptist, preached in the badlands of Israel instead of from the comfort of the temple. The unprecedentedness of God's wisdom taking human form was highlighted when Jesus was rejected upon returning to his hometown.

Jesus captured the Hebrew concept of wisdom as a road to be followed when he declared, "I am the way and the truth and the life. No one comes to the Father except through me" (John 14:6). Wisdom could no longer be viewed merely as a collection of principles with which to organize one's life. In order to be wise, one must hear the words of Jesus, believe them, and then follow after him.

The Way of Wisdom

In unit 3, James examines the interplay between following Jesus and possessing faith. James reaffirms God's generosity in sharing his wisdom, which is especially needed in times of trouble. However, if a person's faith is not marked by acts of obedience to God's Word, then it is dead. Intellectual assent to God's ways isn't enough; wisdom is evidenced by a

> *Wisdom became incarnate in Jesus.*

transformed life. According to James, the quality of a person's speech and treatment of others is an accurate barometer for measuring one's pursuit of wisdom. James revisits Solomon's conviction that we are all presented with the choice of pursuing wisdom or folly. James details how possessing "wisdom that comes from heaven" (James 3:17) inevitably yields godly character.

May we trust God's generosity in sharing his wisdom with us as we study together this quarter.

GET THE SETTING

by Jeff Gerke

PART OF THE BEAUTY of the Bible is that it presents the whole range of human life, thought, and emotion. There is no situation, even in our confusing and high-tech lives, that Scripture doesn't touch on in some way.

Wisdom literature in the Bible is one place where writers step back and wrestle with the hard questions of life: What does it mean that the innocent suffer? Why do the unrighteous prosper? And what do we do with the fact that God doesn't answer prayers in ways we expect?

Wisdom Literature in the Near East

Other ancient cultures besides Israel took a lively interest in what wisdom is and how to obtain it. For instance, Egypt, Sumer, Syria, and Babylonia all had books of wisdom. Though all their works miss the mark of true wisdom, they do have some ideas similar to those found in the Bible.

The Egyptian tome *Instruction of Ptahhotep* talked about wisdom, *ma'at*, as a fixed principle that doesn't change: "Ma'at is good and its worth is lasting. . . . It lies as a path in front even of him who knows nothing." This sounds much like how Solomon discussed wisdom in Proverbs. Wisdom doesn't change based on a person's whims; it remains consistent and dependable.

The Sumerian book *The Instructions of Shuruppak* includes helpful proverbs like "Don't loiter about where there is a quarrel" and "A hateful heart destroys a family." In form and in content, this book is also similar to our own book of Proverbs. Still, it falls short of the mark by basing wisdom on human philosophy instead of on fear of the Lord.

These worldly sources of wisdom literature picture wisdom as hidden and secret. It was the kind of thing supposedly reveal only to kings and sorcerers. The elite could expect to find wisdom. But biblical wisdom rejects this claim.

Wisdom Literature in the Old Testament

Job, Psalms, Proverbs, Ecclesiastes, and the Song of Songs are considered wisdom literature. Proverbs points out that living in the fear of the Lord is the key to having a hope of living life to the fullest. But Job and Ecclesiastes point out that fearing God is not a guarantee of peace or happiness. You can be the picture of obedience to God and still struggle with various hardships. For this reason, it has been said that Proverbs presents the ideal and Ecclesiastes and Job present the struggle many of us face.

Psalms and the Song of Songs demonstrate wisdom in different ways. As the songbook of ancient Israel, Psalms gives words to the greatest hopes and fears of the people. The songs teach us how to speak to God in joy and in anger, in our communities and alone at home. The church has long read the Song of Songs as an allegory, which teaches us about the love of Christ for his bride (the church). Doing so emphasizes the wisdom of complete devotion to God, not allowing any earthly desires to come between us.

Wisdom Literature in the New Testament

Jesus' Sermon on the Mount, especially the Beatitudes (Matthew 5:3-12), would fit nicely into the book of Proverbs. Paul's lists of vices and virtues (Galatians 5:19-21; etc.) could almost form chapters of Ecclesiastes. So could his forays into ethical behavior and the deep meaning of the resurrection.

One example of wisdom literature in the New Testament is the book of James. James draws on his knowledge of the moral teachings of the Law and Jewish books of wisdom. The content of James's letter so echoes the Sermon on the Mount that it is almost a book of wisdom about that one sermon.

Wisdom—the art of successful living in light of God's ways—is a major topic of biblical writers from start to finish. That topic urges us to wrestle with the dilemmas of our own day.

THIS QUARTER IN THE WORD

Answers to the Quarterly Quiz on page 338

Lesson 1—1. false. 2. sinful. **Lesson 2**—1. silver, treasure. 2. understanding. **Lesson 3**—1. true. 2. love. **Lesson 4**—1. simple. 2. wiser. **Lesson 5**—1. John the Baptist. 2. a friend of tax collectors and sinners. **Lesson 6**—1. false. 2. wisdom. **Lesson 7**—1. town. 2. false. **Lesson 8**—1. the way. 2. true. **Lesson 9**—1. generously. 2. true. **Lesson 10**—1. true. 2. being respected by the congregation. **Lesson 11**—1. false. 2. true. **Lesson 12**—1. fire. 2. curse. **Lesson 13**—1. humility. 2. false.

Filled with...

Wickedness? (Leviticus 19:29)

The spirit of wisdom? (Deuteronomy 34:9)

Spiritual power? (Micah 3:8)

Violence? (Genesis 6:11)

Delight in God? (Proverbs 8:30)

Praise of God? (Psalm 71:8)

Envy and deceit? (Romans 1:29)

Drunkenness and sorrow? (Ezekiel 23:33)

The Spirit? (Ephesians 5:18)

The good things of God? (Psalm 65:4)

Filth? (Revelation 17:4)

Knowledge of the Glory of the Lord? (Habakkuk 2:14)

Joy? (2 Timothy 1:4)

Righteousness? (Psalm 48:10)

Shame? (Habakkuk 2:16)

Oppression? (Jeremiah 6:6)

Sheet 1—Summer 2020, Adult Resources, Standard Lesson Quarterly® Curriculum

Lesson 1

Photo © Getty Images

THE REST OF THE STORY

Teacher Tips by Jim Eichenberger

W<small>E ALL HAVE</small> acquaintances who *identify* themselves as Christians but do not *think* like Christians. One reason they don't is that the Western church has existed for decades in a culture where three beliefs have been taken for granted and therefore not considered needing much thought. Those three true and good beliefs are that (1) God is the Creator, (2) humans are fundamentally different from the rest of creation, and (3) there exists a universal natural law.

Since these have been assumed to be above question, Christian education primarily focused on a fourth pillar: the authority of the Bible as the written Word of God. As a result, some Christians have claimed to believe in the Bible (often a belief in no more than a few proof texts) without having a clear understanding of the nature of God, humanity, and the moral structure of the universe.

A sad result is that Christians are unable to push back the threat of false doctrine as Western culture becomes more pluralistic. We see that increasing pluralism as worldviews that deny the existence of God become mainstream. We see it all the more as self-identified Christians are unable to articulate why the Bible trumps all other books considered to be sacred. Such inability points to a worldview built but on a single wobbly pillar of a profession of faith in a book not often read.

This is a problem for Bible-study leaders. Their students who have not examined their Christian worldview may nod appreciatively in class, but walk away dismissing what they have heard as little more than an inspirational talk. In addressing this difficulty, those teaching the Word of God must show the Bible's connection with the other three pillars of a proper worldview.

The Bible Explains What We Sense

Strictly speaking, we do not need the Bible to prove the existence of the Creator God, that humans are fundamentally different from other creatures, or that a universal law of right and wrong exists. Creation itself is quite adequate in serving as evidence to all three (compare Psalm 19:1; Romans 1:19, 20; etc.). These foundational truths are so obvious that they have to be purposely suppressed if they are to be disbelieved (see Romans 1:21-25). What we *do* need the authoritative Word of God for is, among other things, to be able to explain the nature of God as that nature relates to his works of creating, ruling, and redeeming.

The Bible Confirms What We Know

The Bible speaks of real times and places in the past, thereby separating itself from mythology. In the pages of the Bible we see people of centuries ago behaving the same way as people today—for good and for ill. This separates the Bible from stories of idealized heroes. In Scripture we find a world of yesterday with real landmarks that exist today; even the most sympathetic heroes are presented with "warts and all" in plain view.

The Bible Promises What We Desire

To view the Bible narrowly as a list of actions that one must take to avoid the bad news of eternal damnation is to miss the point. The gospel speaks more to the human yearning for hope—inspiring good news. Humankind has always held out hope for victory over a world of violence and injustice. The Bible's message in this regard offers hope on the basis of grace (Romans 3:21-26)—a basis found nowhere else.

When reaching out to the current culture, Christianity's fourth pillar—the Word of God—is often best used as our closing argument rather than our opening (compare Acts 17:16-32). Beginning discussions with "The Bible says . . ." can lose us a hearing. Better is to start by searching for common ground among Christianity's other three pillars. But before your learners can do that with effectiveness, they must be able to defend them. Can they?

LISTEN TO GOD'S WISDOM

DEVOTIONAL READING: Psalm 34:11-18
BACKGROUND SCRIPTURE: Proverbs 1

PROVERBS 1:1-4, 7, 8, 10, 20-22, 32, 33

¹ The proverbs of Solomon son of David, king of Israel:
² for gaining wisdom and instruction;
    for understanding words of insight;
³ for receiving instruction in prudent behavior,
    doing what is right and just and fair;
⁴ for giving prudence to those who are simple,
    knowledge and discretion to the young.
. . . .
⁷ The fear of the LORD is the beginning of knowledge,
    but fools despise wisdom and instruction.
⁸ Listen, my son, to your father's instruction
    and do not forsake your mother's teaching.
. . . .
¹⁰ My son, if sinful men entice you,
    do not give in to them.
. . . .
²⁰ Out in the open wisdom calls aloud,
    she raises her voice in the public square;

²¹ on top of the wall she cries out,
    at the city gate she makes her speech:
²² "How long will you who are simple love your simple ways?
    How long will mockers delight in mockery
    and fools hate knowledge?"
. . . .
³² "For the waywardness of the simple will kill them,
    and the complacency of fools will destroy them;
³³ but whoever listens to me will live in safety
    and be at ease, without fear of harm."

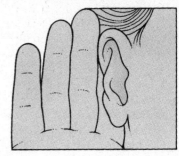

KEY VERSE

The fear of the LORD is the beginning of knowledge, but fools despise wisdom and instruction.
—**Proverbs 1:7**

Many Faces of
Wisdom

Unit 1: Wisdom in Proverbs
Lessons 1–4

Lesson Aims

After participating in this lesson, each learner will be able to:

1. Summarize the nature of biblical wisdom.
2. Contrast biblical and nonbiblical wisdom.
3. Propose one way for adults to model biblical wisdom at home and work.

Lesson Outline

Introduction
A. Commencement Season

June concludes the usual season for graduations from high school and college in the USA. Hearing a commencement speaker address the graduating body of students is a standard part of almost any graduation ceremony. Yet how much of what is said reflects genuine wisdom, and how much merely sounds good at the time?

Let's imagine for a moment a person getting up at any state university and presenting the graduation speech. The speaker begins, "I want you graduates to strive to be wise and prudent in your behavior. Do what is right and just and fair. Teach others the right way to live; pass along the knowledge that you have." Some polite applause would perhaps follow these statements. Then the speaker says, "And remember, graduates, the fear of the Lord is the beginning of wisdom."

In this secular setting, no doubt some in the audience would object to the use of religious language. Even more likely is that people would question the truth of the assertion that wisdom begins with the fear of the Lord. Yet a biblical understanding of wisdom must begin with the fear of the Lord. Like a college graduate starting the next chapter of life, we are invited in this lesson to choose what our lives will look like.

B. Lesson Context

The book of Proverbs is the third of the five books in the Old Testament that are often called "wisdom literature." (The group also includes Job, Psalms, Ecclesiastes, and Song of Songs.) When most people think of proverbs in general (not just the biblical ones), they probably call to mind pithy statements of truth that are good, general advice for navigating life. "Haste makes waste" and "He who hesitates is lost" are generally true statements, but one can see how these statements might contradict each other.

The wisdom of each saying is situational. Biblical proverbs are as well, though they are more than just good advice. They are godly advice, based on the crucial premise that "the fear of the Lord is the beginning of wisdom" (Proverbs 9:10).

Keeping that premise in mind helps the wise person discern when a certain course of conventional wisdom might not be best for obeying God's laws. Knowing God yields the wisdom to decide well.

The book of Proverbs divides itself into three major sections: (1) a long introduction to the collections of proverbs (chap. 1–9), (2) the collections of the proverbs themselves (10:1–31:9), and (3) an acrostic conclusion (31:10-31). There are six collections: (a) proverbs of Solomon (10:1–22:16), (b) words of the wise (22:17–24:22), (c) more words of the wise (24:23-34), (d) more proverbs of Solomon (25:1–29:27), (e) words of Agur (chap. 30), and (f) words of King Lemuel (31:1-9).

The four lessons in this unit are drawn from the nine opening chapters of Proverbs (1–9) that exhort the audience to choose to live by God's wisdom. In these chapters, we find more association between individual proverbs than the more randomized sayings that appear from chapter 10 forward. Most scholars see 10 fatherly appeals or lectures in chapters 1–9. These are 1:8-19; 2:1-22; 3:1-12; 3:21-35; 4:1-9; 4:10-19; 4:20-27; 5:1-23; 6:20-35; and 7:1-27. Our text today includes part of the first appeal.

I. Introducing a Book
(Proverbs 1:1-4)
A. Author (v. 1)
1. The proverbs of Solomon son of David, king of Israel:

King *Solomon* (reigned 970–930 BC) is mentioned by name at two other places in the book, establishing the origin of the book's contents (Proverbs 10:1; 25:1). According to the latter verse, "the men of Hezekiah king of Judah [compiled]" *the proverbs of Solomon* found in the succeeding chapters (25:2–29:27). Hezekiah (reigned about 729–700 BC) and his assistants may well have produced the final edition of the book of Proverbs, probably adding proverbs of Solomon that were not part of an earlier edition. Since Solomon produced 3,000 proverbs (1 Kings 4:30-32; see also Ecclesiastes 1:1), there was more than enough material to choose from.

Solomon's wisdom was a gift from God

(1 Kings 4:29-34). Like any spiritual gift, wisdom has to be accepted and practiced regularly. Though he was a wise man, the direction Solomon's life took shows how he himself ignored the very words with which he desired to guide others. Solomon married women from other nations who worshipped other gods; these women lured Solomon into worshipping those gods. As a result, the Lord told Solomon that the impressive kingdom that *David*, his father, had left for him to rule would be divided after Solomon's death (11:4-13). If anything, Solomon's failure to continue to practice wisdom underscores the accuracy and soundness of what is recorded in Proverbs (example: Proverbs 4:23).

B. Purpose (vv. 2-4)
2a. for gaining wisdom and instruction;

This verse and the next four (Proverbs 1:3-6) portray in broad strokes what this collection of proverbs intends to accomplish. *Gaining wisdom* is recognizing the best course of action for a given situation and following through on that action. The Hebrew word translated *instruction* carries the idea of admonishing or correcting someone. It implies disciplining (as a daily practice, not as punishment) a person in the correct way of living in the sight of God.

2b. for understanding words of insight;

Words of insight must become more than just theory or good advice. They must be personally embraced and applied in order to be of genuine value. Otherwise they are not really perceived.

> *What Do You Think?*
> What steps can we take to ensure that we not only hear but also apply God's wisdom?
> *Digging Deeper*
> How will those steps differ, if at all, when interacting with fellow believers vs. unbelievers?

3. for receiving instruction in prudent behavior, doing what is right and just and fair;

Instruction is repeated to emphasize its importance (see Proverbs 1:2). The word translated *prudent behavior* emphasizes discernment. In this verse, one sees the ways in which godly wisdom is to manifest itself. The Hebrew word translated *right* is translated elsewhere as "righteous" (examples: Deuteronomy 33:19; Psalm 4:1). Being *just* does not apply only to an ethical standard in a judicial setting. It also includes to the idea of applying good reasoning to situations that confront one daily, especially those involving others in need (example: Exodus 23:6, where it's translated "justice"). Fairness is closely tied to this and relates to our treatment of others.

> **What Do You Think?**
> In what ways should our church's concern for justice be apparent?
> *Digging Deeper*
> What would you like your neighbors to say about your commitment to justice?

Clearly, biblical wisdom is to be demonstrated in practical ways more than in one's academic prowess. Formal education has no bearing on whether a person can attain wisdom. Moreover, Solomon's call for his readers to learn the virtues of righteousness, justice, and fairness resonates in cultures around the world, regardless of religious belief or educational background.

4a. for giving prudence

The Hebrew word translated *prudence* can have a negative connotation (example: "schemes" in Exodus 21:14). In fact, one form of the Hebrew word is used of the serpent in Genesis 3:1; he was "more crafty" than any other creature the Lord had made. But the same root can also imply a more positive quality (examples: Proverbs 12:23; 13:16; 14:15). This positive nuance is what Solomon intends here.

4b. to those who are simple,

The victim of scheming and craftiness is someone who lacks life experience and knowledge (compare "the unwary" in Psalm 116:6; "anyone who sins . . . through ignorance" in Ezekiel 45:20). Such a person must be teachable , willing to listen to the instruction and discipline that wisdom has to offer.

4c. knowledge and discretion to the young.

The designation *the young* can refer to children or young adults. This suggests that the reason for ignorance is partially a matter of lack of time to have already learned. This usage complements the frequent references to "my son" in the first nine chapters of Proverbs (examples: Proverbs 1:8; 2:1).

This emphasis on the male child reflects the patriarchal society of that time and the importance placed on fathers to train their sons. Though the son is emphasized throughout Solomon's writings, the principles found throughout Proverbs are clearly valuable for both men and women.

The word translated *discretion*, like the Hebrew word for prudence, can have a positive or negative meaning (compare "schemes" in Job 21:27; "evil schemes" in Jeremiah 11:15); here again the positive meaning is clearly implied. Godly wisdom will help a young person navigate a sin-infested world by learning to choose what is right and acceptable in God's sight.

II. Introducing Wisdom
(Proverbs 1:7, 8, 10, 20-22, 32, 33)
A. Divine Origin (v. 7)

7a. The fear of the Lord is the beginning of knowledge,

Following additional descriptions of the wise person in Proverbs 1:5, 6 (not in our printed text), Solomon reveals that the key to obtaining *knowledge* is *the fear of the Lord* (see also Proverbs 9:10; 15:33). The word *fear* covers a broad range of mind-sets in the Old Testament, from simple respect to awe to sheer terror (examples: Genesis 20:11; Job 28:28; Psalm 55:5). In the context of this passage, it means primarily to acknowledge and submit to the Lord as the source of true knowledge and wisdom. If one is not grounded in that understanding of the Lord, knowledge and wisdom will remain foreign to that person.

HOW TO SAY IT

Agur	*Ay*-gur.
Ecclesiastes	Ik-*leez*-ee-*as*-teez.
Hezekiah	Hez-ih-*kye*-uh.
Lemuel	*Lem*-you-el.
patriarchal	pay-tree-*are*-kul.
Solomon	*Sol*-o-mun.

As long as an individual possesses the fear of the Lord, he or she is on the path to wisdom (compare 112:1; Isaiah 33:6; 50:10).

Though the world may agree that prudence, righteousness, justice, and fairness are worthy pursuits (Proverbs 1:3, above), many scoff at the assertion that knowledge of God's ways is necessary for human excellence in any field of inquiry. Wisdom comes from many places, it is thought, especially from the minds of people who have spent their lives thinking. Yet the rejection of the fear of the Lord as the basis for knowledge (and of the God who is the source of wisdom) is precisely the cause of the strife, turmoil, and disorder that mark current society (see 8:33-36).

> *What Do You Think?*
> What's one step you need to take to be more fully submitted to God?
> *Digging Deeper*
> What is your plan for putting that step into practice? What part will increased "fear of the Lord" have in your plan? Why?

❧ BEGIN HERE! ❧

The movie *Love Story* features a musical theme recorded by Henry Mancini. Realizing the popularity of the instrumental tune, the distributors of the movie's music decided that the tune needed lyrics to have greater commercial impact. So they contacted Carl Sigman, a man who later was inducted into the Songwriters Hall of Fame.

Imagine Sigman's surprise when the distributors promptly rejected his lyrics! Purportedly, Sigman was furious about being asked for a total rewrite. Still, he decided to try. He turned to his wife and asked, "Where do I begin?" That question became the first line of the rewrite, as well as the title for what would become a best-selling record! Crooner Andy Williams's recording of the song spent 13 weeks on the *Billboard* Hot 100 in 1971.

Every story—be it a love story, heroic tale, or book of wisdom—needs a place to start. In introducing the book of Proverbs, Solomon answered Sigman's lyrical query. Where does one begin in explaining the source of principles that can lead

to a successful life? If you are wondering where to begin (or begin *again*), start with fear of the Lord.

—J. E.

7b. but fools despise wisdom and instruction.

To ignore *wisdom* is to embark on the path of *fools*. Such individuals demonstrate their contempt for God and his *instruction* (see Proverbs 19:16). In general, foolish people can expect to experience unnecessary trials (13:18; 15:32).

B. Human Instruction (v. 8)

8. Listen, my son, to your father's instruction and do not forsake your mother's teaching.

Some have suggested that the term *son* in Proverbs should be interpreted as a disciple or student, as in the literal translation "sons of the prophets" (2 Kings 6:1, KJV). However, the context supports translating this word in familial terms instead of educational. Both father and mother are instrumental in teaching wisdom to their children (Proverbs 6:20). It is a team effort, very much in keeping with the counsel found in Deuteronomy 6:6, 7 (compare Proverbs 2:1-5; 3:1; 4:1; etc.). The consequences of not hearing, or of forsaking, the *instruction* and *teaching* of parents will be discipline and potential disaster (Deuteronomy 21:18-21).

> *What Do You Think?*
> What should a teacher of children do when realizing that a child's instruction received from a parent is unbiblical?
> *Digging Deeper*
> What are some examples of unbiblical "wisdom" you have heard from your own parents? How do you handle these in light of Exodus 20:12 and Ephesians 6:1-3?

C. Potential Opposition (v. 10)

10. My son, if sinful men entice you, do not give in to them.

Peer pressure has been around for all of human history (compare Genesis 3:6; 11:1-9; 1 Kings 12:1-14). The behavior of friends can influence one's behavior, often in a negative way (Psalm 1:1; Proverbs 16:29). The son's resisting invitations

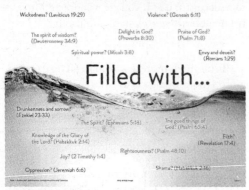

Filled with...

Wickedness? (Leviticus 19:29)   Violence? (Genesis 6:11)

The spirit of wisdom?   Delight in God?   Praise of God?
(Deuteronomy 34:9)   (Proverbs 8:30)   (Psalm 71:8)

Spiritual power? (Micah 3:8)   Envy and deceit?
(Romans 1:29)

Drunkenness and sorrow?
(Ezekiel 23:33)

The Spirit? (Ephesians 5:18)   The good things of
God? (Psalm 65:4)

Knowledge of the Glory of   Filth?
the Lord? (Habakkuk 2:14)   (Revelation 17:4)

Righteousness? (Psalm 48:10)

Joy? (2 Timothy 1:4)

Oppression? (Jeremiah 6:6)   Shame? (Habakkuk 2:16)

Visual for Lesson 1. *Use this visual as a discussion starter regarding what kind of wisdom fills your learners' lives.*

from *sinful men* will save the young man much trouble (compare Deuteronomy 13:6-10).

Proverbs 1:11-19, not in our printed text, includes more specific words of enticement from plotting, scheming sinners. They are not just out to participate in some good-natured fun. Rather, they clearly want to do harm to someone, to "lie in wait for innocent blood" (Proverbs 1:11; compare vv. 12-14). An extended plea from the father for his son to shun these wicked people follows (1:15-19). Danger awaits, not for the innocent victim of the sinners' plans, but for the perpetrators themselves. *They* are the ones who "lie in wait for their own blood; they ambush only themselves!" (1:18).

D. Powerful Outreach (vv. 20-22)

20a. Out in the open wisdom calls aloud, she raises her voice in the public square;

Whereas the father has been the one who issues warnings to his son to this point, now *wisdom* itself is pictured as appealing to anyone who will listen. Wisdom will be described (just below) with the pronoun *she*, perhaps in part because the Hebrew word for *wisdom* is a feminine noun. More importantly, wisdom's personification as a woman may also reflect the fact that the students are young men. By contrast, folly is portrayed as a loose woman who tempts men to their ruin (example: Proverbs 9:13-18; see lesson 4).

21. on top of the wall she cries out, at the city gate she makes her speech:

One must not overlook the places where the *voice* of Wisdom seeks an audience. Wisdom is not cloistered behind academia's ivy-covered walls. *She* is out *in the public square*, where life is lived each day, making her appeal. The square appears to describe any location that is busy, with lots of people moving about.

Portraying her *on top of the wall* emphasizes that she is calling as many people as possible to follow in her ways, rejecting foolish paths. *The city gates* are where business is often conducted and where key decisions or announcements occur (examples: Joshua 20:1-4; Ruth 4:1, 2, 11). Wisdom's words are desperately needed everywhere.

❧ SPEAKERS' CORNER ❧

Do you have something to say? Have you ever wanted to stand up in public and tell an audience exactly what you think? If so, consider visiting a speakers' corner.

The original Speakers' Corner is in the northeast corner of Hyde Park in London, England. The corner dates back to 1866. Riots occurred after large meetings of working-class protesters caused the government to lock the park. After heated political debate, the 1872 Parks Regulation Act established the right to free speech and association in Hyde Park. At Speakers' Corner, anyone can turn up unannounced and talk on almost any subject. Over the years, this spot was frequented by Karl Marx, George Orwell, Tony Benn, and many other notables.

The image of someone standing in public to proclaim a message boldly is nothing new. Solomon described Wisdom as doing that very thing (Proverbs 1:20, 21). What does wisdom call you to proclaim publicly?   —J. E.

22. "How long will you who are simple love your simple ways? How long will mockers delight in mockery and fools hate knowledge?"

Wisdom calls for people to rearrange their priorities, to reorient their entire value system. Instead of being *simple* and *mockers* who scorn Wisdom's invitation (Psalm 50:17; Proverbs 7:7), they are challenged to embrace *knowledge* (8:5; 9:1-4a; see lessons 3, 4).

Proverbs 1:23-31 (not in our printed text) includes a warning of the high price one will pay for continuing to scorn knowledge. The time will come when those who have done so will desire Wisdom's assistance. But by then they will have already reaped the consequences of their contempt.

E. Promising Offer (vv. 32, 33)

32. "For the waywardness of the simple will kill them, and the complacency of fools will destroy them;

The rejection of Wisdom's call is a decision that has a major impact on one's life. *The waywardness* of turning away from wisdom is fatal (Proverbs 5:22, 23; 15:10; Isaiah 66:4). The combination of *kill* and *destroy* conveys the great violence that awaits those who reject Wisdom's call. In context, *complacency* suggests being at ease or feeling secure because of one's situation, especially financially. There is a smugness that gives the foolish person a false sense of security.

33. "but whoever listens to me will live in safety and be at ease, without fear of harm."

This chapter closes with a statement of the blessings that follow from heeding Wisdom's invitation (compare Deuteronomy 33:28; Proverbs 3:23). Safety comes because the wise person has chosen to ignore foolish and sinful voices that offer invitations to pursue their path of wrongdoing.

The Hebrew word translated *harm* can be used in a moral sense, like "evil" (Proverbs 1:16). But in some cases it refers to the harm that is one of the consequences of living in a world under the curse of sin ("destruction" in Jonah 3:10; "disaster" in Micah 1:12). God, of course, does no moral evil. He does, however, judge justly and bring judgment. Unfortunately, judgment can be perceived as evil by those who experience it.

The wise do not need to *fear* the harm that often comes to those who live by the sinners' code. True, the wise or godly person may be the target of the ungodly and may suffer harm from them (or suffer other types of harm in this fallen world). But *fear* of such an outcome does not trouble or overwhelm the godly person. Instead, like any wise person, he or she is grounded in and guided by the fear of the Lord.

> *What Do You Think?*
> Without giving directive advice, how would you use this verse to support a fellow believer who is beset with anxiety?
> *Digging Deeper*
> How would you *not* use this verse? Why?

Conclusion

A. Heed Warnings

What happened to Solomon? Why didn't he follow his own advice? Thinking of Jesus' statement "Physician, heal yourself!" (Luke 4:23), we may wish we could advise Solomon by saying, "Wise man, heed your wisdom."

Can what happened to Solomon happen to us? Certainly! We will not be tempted, as Solomon was, by the beliefs and lifestyles of 700 spouses. But the need to guard our hearts and our ways is as urgent now as ever.

We should view Solomon with compassion, not criticism. Anyone's spiritual failures, whether we read about them in the Bible or see them reported in the media, should humble us. Paul's warning to the Corinthians contains its own words of wisdom: "If you think you are standing firm, be careful that you don't fall!" (1 Corinthians 10:12).

B. Prayer

Father, help us to heed your call to wisdom. As we do, may we lead others to heed your voice as well. In Jesus' name we pray. Amen.

C. Thought to Remember

Fear the Lord and learn wisdom.

VISUALS FOR THESE LESSONS

The visual pictured in each lesson (example: page 350) is a small reproduction of a large, full-color poster included in the *Adult Resources* packet for the Summer 2020 Quarter. That packet also contains the very useful *Presentation Tools* CD for teacher use. Order No. 4628120 from your supplier.

INVOLVEMENT LEARNING

Enhance your lesson with NIV Bible Student (from your curriculum supplier) and the reproducible activity page (at www.standardlesson.com or in the back of the NIV Standard Lesson Commentary Deluxe Edition).

Into the Lesson

Write this quote on the board:

I'm intolerant often, especially of incompetence, particularly my own.
—Liz Trotta

Ask volunteers to share times when they've felt incompetent. Discuss together reasonable ways to gain competence.

Alternative. Distribute copies of the "Decode It" exercise from the activity page, which you can download. Allow class members to work in pairs to complete the activity according to instructions. After completion, discuss conclusions by asking learners to identify the common theme of the decoded phrases, which relate to feelings of inadequacy or incompetence.

After either activity say, "We all have times when we feel unqualified, unprepared, or incompetent to address a task. How do we overcome these feelings? Let's find out."

Into the Word

Divide the class into groups of three to five. Give each group a copy of the lesson text, paper, and two or three nonfiction/how-to books with back-cover copy to use as an example. Give groups about 15 minutes to summarize the lesson text as back-cover copy promoting the entire book of Proverbs. Suggest this general format: 1–Choose a catchy title for the summary. 2–Tell what the reader will gain by reading the book of Proverbs (1:1-4). 3–Describe the basic point of the book of Proverbs (1:7, 8, 10). 4–Explain why the instructions in the book of Proverbs differ from advice from other sources (1:20-22, 32, 33).

As groups work, move among them to help them construct their summaries. Refer to the commentary to clarify the meanings of words or phrases in the text. Here is a sample of how such a summary might look:

Live Life Right!

This collection of wisdom from Solomon is a must-read for everyone seeking to live a successful life. This wise king offers to the young and inexperienced information everyone needs, including how to treat others fairly and helpful tips for making sound decisions.

Solomon teaches that there is a right way to live, and that way is found by listening to the right voices. Reverence for God and his words is credited as the starting point for everything worth knowing. Parental advice is praised, and peer pressure is discounted.

Other sources of advice entice a reader with cynicism or promises that one way is no better than any other. Proverbs is different. Solomon assures the reader that knowledge based in the fear of the Lord will lead to a godly life, while following the crowd is a path to failure.

Allow groups to read and explain their summaries. Make sure the contrast of earthly wisdom and godly wisdom is made clearly and accurately.

Into Life

Have a volunteer read Romans 2:18-24 aloud. Discuss what Paul says or implies about a believer who fails to practice biblical wisdom. (*Expected response:* those claiming to be Christians but who do not live accordingly give others an excuse to disbelieve.)

On the board write, "I know that a Christian should _____, but too often I am tempted to _____." Ask for volunteers to supply ways these blanks can be filled (example: "I know that a Christian should be honest, but too often I am tempted to slant the truth.") As you solicit responses, point out the importance of modeling biblical wisdom in various contexts of life.

Option. Distribute copies of the "On Trial" exercise from the activity page as a take-home to be completed as indicated. As a motive to complete it, state that you will begin the next class session by reviewing results.

VALUE WISDOM

DEVOTIONAL READING: Proverbs 2:12-22

BACKGROUND SCRIPTURE: Genesis 39; Proverbs 2

PROVERBS 2:1-11

¹ My son, if you accept my words
 and store up my commands within you,
² turning your ear to wisdom
 and applying your heart to
 understanding—
³ indeed, if you call out for insight
 and cry aloud for understanding,
⁴ and if you look for it as for silver
 and search for it as for hidden treasure,
⁵ then you will understand the fear of the
 LORD
 and find the knowledge of God.
⁶ For the LORD gives wisdom;
 from his mouth come knowledge and
 understanding.

⁷ He holds success in store for the upright,
 he is a shield to those whose walk is
 blameless,
⁸ for he guards the course of the just
 and protects the way of his faithful
 ones.
⁹ Then you will understand what is right
 and just
 and fair—every good path.
¹⁰ For wisdom will enter your heart,
 and knowledge will be pleasant to your
 soul.
¹¹ Discretion will protect you,
 and understanding will guard you.

KEY VERSE

For the LORD gives wisdom; from his mouth come knowledge and understanding. —**Proverbs 2:6**

Many Faces of Wisdom

Unit 1: Wisdom in Proverbs

Lessons 1–4

Lesson Aims

After participating in this lesson, each learner will be able to:

1. State promises and blessings associated with godly wisdom.

2. Compare and contrast uses of the words *wisdom, knowledge, understanding, treasure,* and *discretion.*

3. Begin keeping a journal of occasions when godly wisdom has "preserved" him or her.

Lesson Outline

Introduction

    A. More Valuable Than Gold

    B. Lesson Context

I. Earthly Father's Plea (Proverbs 2:1-5)

    A. Search for Wisdom (vv. 1-4)

    B. Find Wisdom (v. 5)

II. Heavenly Father's Word (Proverbs 2:6-11)

    A. Source of Wisdom (v. 6)

    B. Protection for the Wise (vv. 7, 8)

       Information That Protects

    C. Preservation in Wisdom (vv. 9-11)

       Well Preserved

Conclusion

    A. Seekers for Life

    B. Prayer

    C. Thought to Remember

Introduction

A. More Valuable Than Gold

Swimmer Michael Phelps electrified the sports world when he won a record eight gold medals at the 2008 Beijing Summer Olympics. But he had made a different kind of impact in the 2004 games in Athens, Greece. There Phelps, who had earned a spot in the 4x100-meter medley relay, decided to give up his spot to Ian Crocker. Crocker was swimming in what he thought was his final Olympics, and he had yet to earn gold thus far in Athens.

The American team won the relay, and Crocker received the gold medal that had eluded him. Phelps's gesture of withdrawing from a race for the sake of a teammate identified him as a gold medalist in more than swimming. It made him a champion of a different kind in the eyes of many.

Olympic athletes are known for their highly disciplined training in pursuit of world-class excellence and of winning the gold medal that distinguishes them as the best. In today's Scripture, Solomon encouraged his son (and all readers of his words) to pursue something far more valuable than any precious medal.

B. Lesson Context

Proverbs often uses a form of Hebrew poetry called *parallelism*. This is where two or more lines of text make the same point by using synonyms or near synonyms. For example, Solomon says of wisdom in Proverbs 3:17:

her ways are	pleasant ways
↓	↓
all her paths are	peace

In other words, all of wisdom's ways are the same as her paths, and they are both pleasant and peaceful. The effect of this literary technique is to emphasize the point being made. Parallelism occurs frequently in today's lesson.

Today's lesson continues the appeal from the father to the son (Proverbs 1:8, 10, 15; see lesson 1). Though the son could find many other enticing treasures to seek, the father impresses on the young man the superiority of finding wisdom.

I. Earthly Father's Plea

(PROVERBS 2:1-5)

A. Search for Wisdom (vv. 1-4)

1a. My son, if you accept my words

The father offers a conditional invitation. *If* the *son* will *accept* his father's *words*, then a certain reward will follow (see commentary on Proverbs 2:5 below). The second clause (in 2:1b below) clarifies what it means to *accept* these words. If the son will not listen to his father, he cannot expect to receive these blessings.

1b. and store up my commands within you,

Sometimes we *store up* objects to protect them from being used or harmed. *Storing* Scripture is for the purpose of having those items available to use whenever needed to provide the wisdom that only God's Word can supply (compare Psalm 119:11). Storing the father's *commands* will ensure that the son can refer to them at any time and so find his way in any situation.

2a. turning your ear to wisdom

The thought begun in Proverbs 2:1 continues. *Turning* one's *ear* creates an image of actively listening to whoever is speaking (Proverbs 4:20; 5:13). In other Scriptures, the same Hebrew word is used to ask the Lord to "hear" or "listen" to the praying person (examples: Psalms 17:1; 86:6; 142:6). Other passages tell how God's people failed to hear his teaching and for that reason came under his judgment (example: Zechariah 1:4). Here the son is encouraged to listen closely so that he will miss nothing that *wisdom* has to say.

Proverbs 9:10 teaches that wisdom begins with "the fear of the Lord." Does this mean that the wisest person is the one who cowers most in terror before God? Not exactly. It means that the

HOW TO SAY IT

Colossians	Kuh-*losh*-unz.
Corinthians	Ko-*rin*-thee-unz (*th* as in *thin*).
Hebrews	*Hee*-brews.
parallelism	*par*-al-lel-ism.
Phelps	*Fehlps.*
Solomon	*Sol*-o-mun.

wise person is the one who respects God to the point of obedience. We are on the path of wisdom when we hear and heed God's directions. This is the path that Solomon desperately wants his hearers to find and follow.

2b. and applying your heart to understanding—

Becoming wise involves more than just one's ears. The *heart* must be included as well. Biblically, the heart describes our ability to reason, think, and consider spiritual matters (example: the stubbornness of Pharaoh in Exodus 7:13; 8:15). Each person must "above all else, guard [his or her] heart" (Proverbs 4:23). Both wisdom and *understanding* have already been cited as part of the purpose for which the proverbs have been compiled (1:2; see lesson 1).

> *What Do You Think?*
> How do we go about being more receptive to wisdom?
> *Digging Deeper*
> How do texts such as Acts 17:18; 1 Corinthians 1:20; and Colossians 2:8 caution and challenge you in this regard?

3. indeed, if you call out for insight and cry aloud for understanding,

The son is now challenged to engage his *voice* in the pursuit of *insight* and *understanding*. His crying out will represent an intensifying search; the son is to be consumed with a desire for wisdom.

Again, Solomon uses a couple of vivid metaphors to describe the necessary quest *for understanding*. We are to bellow for it, raising our voices and clamoring for it. Previously, Wisdom was pictured as crying out in the public arenas (Proverbs 1:20-23). She longs to be heard, and she is looking for those who are desperate to follow after her (compare James 1:5). Now it is we who are to call out for her.

4. and if you look for it as for silver and search for it as for hidden treasure,

To illustrate how passionate the son's desire for wisdom must become, a comparison is introduced: he must become as earnest in his quest for wisdom as many are for the material wealth of *silver* and *hidden treasure* (compare Matthew 13:44-46).

Indeed, the drive for material wealth often drains the desire for wisdom. Jesus warns us to "be on [our] guard against all kinds of greed" (Luke 12:15) and tells a parable to illustrate how the obsession with material wealth and success can blind us to the things of God (12:16-21). People "put their hope in wealth" (1 Timothy 6:17) when their trust should be in God. He is the source of wealth that riches cannot provide: wisdom.

Job uses a similar comparison when he describes man's quest for wisdom (Job 28:1-11). The chapter concludes with a declaration that echoes Solomon's words: "The fear of the Lord—that is wisdom, and to shun evil is understanding" (28:28; compare Proverbs 9:10).

We also are to go on a treasure hunt for wisdom, seeking and searching. Wisdom is available but must be sought. We are not born wise. Wisdom is not intuitive; in fact, the wisdom of God is sometimes counter intuitive because it goes against our impulses of self-preservation, self-importance, and greediness.

> *What Do You Think?*
> Who could be your role model as one who lives out the implications of Proverbs 2:4?
> *Digging Deeper*
> To initiate a mentor-protégé relationship, what questions would you ask this person?

B. Find Wisdom (v. 5)

5a. then you will understand the fear of the Lord

This verse gives the conclusion (note the word *then*) to the previous four verses. There the interest in obtaining wisdom has been described in terms of increasing desire. If the son will dedicate himself fully to the search for wisdom, he will come to *understand the fear of the Lord*.

It bears noting that this is the third time the phrase "fear of the Lord/to fear the Lord" has been used in the first two chapters of Proverbs. It first appears in the opening verses of the book, introducing the reader to the "beginning of knowl-

edge" (Proverbs 1:7). The second time is when Wisdom herself cries out and urges passersby to heed her voice and not be among those who refuse to fear the Lord (1:20-29).

5b. and find the knowledge of God.

Having understood the fear of the Lord, the son will discover the key to *knowledge* (Proverbs 1:7). Wisdom and knowledge are not, biblically speaking, found through mastery of a body of facts or data. They are found in a relationship with the Lord that acknowledges him as their source. Neither wisdom nor knowledge is an end in itself; the Lord himself is the end of the quest.

> *What Do You Think?*
> How would you explain to a new believer the relationship between *fear* and *knowledge* as those terms are used in Proverbs 2:5?
> *Digging Deeper*
> How would your explanation differ for an unbeliever, if at all? Why?

In another sense, however, the quest has only begun. There are always new adventures and insights to receive as one learns to trust the Lord with all one's heart and acknowledge him in all one's ways (Proverbs 3:5, 6).

Such a discovery as this may seem foolish and hardly worth the effort in the eyes of the world. Secular culture fails to consider God at all when searching for the source of wisdom. But God's wisdom has always been scorned by the unbelieving world. This truth adds to the wonder of the gospel message, particularly as seen in the cross of Jesus (1 Corinthians 1:18-31).

II. Heavenly Father's Word
(Proverbs 2:6-11)
A. Source of Wisdom (v. 6)

6. For the Lord **gives wisdom: from his mouth come knowledge and understanding.**

God's *wisdom* results in fulfillment by leading people to develop the qualities emphasized as being necessary for a good life. *Knowledge and understanding* signify far more than intellectual prowess (see commentary on Proverbs 2:5 above);

apart from God, these are often used for violent, destructive purposes. Both knowledge and understanding have to do with learning God's character and recognizing what he desires.

The reference to the *mouth* of the Lord highlights his spoken and written Word as the source of wisdom. (Psalm 119:72 offers a similar comparison.) God's inspiring our Scriptures (2 Timothy 3:16, 17) gives them authority that mere humans writing on their own cannot achieve, no matter how wise. Jesus countered one of the devil's temptations with the words, "Man shall not live on bread alone, but on every word that comes from the mouth of God" (Matthew 4:4). Certainly, we need physical sustenance. But without knowledge from God, we are spiritually starving to death.

B. Protection for the Wise (vv. 7, 8)

7a. He holds success in store for the upright,

The idea of *holds . . . in store* may bring to mind Jesus' words in the Sermon on the Mount about storing up treasures in Heaven (Matthew 6:20). Whereas Jesus will call his disciples to store up for themselves, here the Lord himself is the one who holds in store *success* as a treasure *for the upright* (compare Psalm 84:11).

These are riches that one can draw from at any age and stage of life. One never outgrows the need for the Lord's wisdom. But a person must be willing to admit that need and express a humble dependence on what the Lord has provided in his Word.

7b. he is a shield to those whose walk is blameless,

A *shield* is usually buckled around the arm of the soldier to provide a means of defense against a sword, a spear, or an arrow. The soldier is then able to use his free hand to carry his own weapon into battle.

The Hebrew word translated *blameless* may also be rendered "integrity" (example: 1 Kings 9:4). Such a person is not half-hearted or superficial regarding devotion to wisdom. The individual has set foot on a path from which he or she does not intend to deviate (see Proverbs 4:25-27).

8. for he guards the course of the just and protects the way of his faithful ones.

To guard in this context means that the Lord watches over *the course of the just.* The Lord never abandons *the way of his faithful ones*; he guides and keeps them in his care in every circumstance. Numerous assurances provide strength and endurance to God's people who suffer because of the brokenness of the world (Psalm 91:1-4; Isaiah 40:31; Hebrews 13:5, 6).

The phrase *faithful ones* is often associated with holiness or being set apart in some way (1 Samuel 2:9; Psalm 97:10). Here it signifies those who are distinguished by their commitment to live by the wisdom that comes only from the Lord (compare Joshua 24:15; Acts 14:23; 1 Peter 4:19).

What Do You Think?
> What steps can we take to acknowledge more consistently the reality of God's constant protection?
Digging Deeper
What should others see in us when that happens?

❧ INFORMATION THAT PROTECTS ❧

Some information is essential for large groups of people to know. But how does one get them to listen? British actor and producer Richard Massingham offered one solution.

Massingham saw that many major problems in Great Britain could be avoided by an informed public's taking simple precautions. After much thought, Massingham left his first career in medicine and started his own company, Public Relationship Films, in 1938. In his films, Massingham played an absent-minded, ordinary man whose lapses in judgment allowed his audience to laugh at him and at themselves reflected in him.

This character suffered the consequences of his nonsensical decisions, thus demonstrating the importance of looking both ways before crossing the road, sneezing into a handkerchief to avoid spreading disease, and so on. In this way, the genre that became known as Public Information Films (PIF) in the United Kingdom was born.

Massingham's lighthearted but informational messages became a new standard for being heard by the public. Solomon knew that God-given wisdom would help his countrymen in their everyday affairs. Such wisdom would invite God to be their protection. What does God want wisdom to teach you?　　　　　　　　　　　　　　　—J. E.

C. Preservation in Wisdom (vv. 9-11)

9. Then you will understand what is right and just and fair—every good path.

As an individual follows the Lord's direction and receives his help in life, he or she gains experiential understanding of the qualities the Lord views as *good*: righteousness, justice, and fairness. All three recall the stated purpose for the book (Proverbs 1:3; see lesson 1).

Understanding these three virtues allows the people to pursue right and just relationships (example: Deuteronomy 1:16). Such a *path* is far different from the one that sinners entice people to travel, of which the son has already been warned (Proverbs 1:10-19).

10. For wisdom will enter your heart, and knowledge will be pleasant to your soul.

Heart and *soul* are difficult to distinguish in terms of what they specifically designate. In this poetic verse, they are intended to be parallel terms (see Lesson Context). The differences between the terms are less important than the similarities: both refer to the inner person, to his or her motivations.

Wisdom and *knowledge* must be internalized to the point that they impact the spiritual makeup of an individual. Accepting biblical wisdom is not solely a mental exercise, though the heart in Scripture is associated with the mind, as previously noted (see Proverbs 2:2 above).

11. Discretion will protect you, and understanding will guard you.

The promise of protecting and guarding the person who lives by godly wisdom uses the same verbs found in Proverbs 2:8: "for he guards the course of the just and protects the way of his faithful ones" (compare 1 Samuel 2:9. The father will find nothing more satisfying personally than to see his son walk in a way that marks him as one of those who is faithful to God (see also Psalms 31:23; 37:28).

What Do You Think?
> Should you set a goal to gain more discretion so that understanding may result, or should you set a goal to gain more understanding so that discretion may result?

Digging Deeper
How do the various uses of these same terms in Proverbs 1:4; 2:2, 3, 6; 3:13, 19; 5:2; 8:1; 10:23; 11:12; 14:29; 15:21; 17:27; 18:2; 19:8; 20:5; and 24:3 influence your response?

Proverbs 2:12-22 (not in our printed text) continues the father's description of the benefits of wisdom, especially in keeping the son from certain evildoers and one type of individual in particular. The first is "wicked men" whose "ways" and "paths" travel in the opposite direction from the way of wisdom (2:12-15). The other is the "adulterous woman" whose words are seductive and flattering but whose path leads to certain death (2:16-19).

The chapter concludes with another appeal to the son to "walk in the ways of the good and keep to the paths of the righteous" (2:20) and with a contrast between the upright and wicked (2:21, 22).

❧　WELL PRESERVED　❧

Across cultures, one fact remains: we all need to eat. But food begins to spoil as soon as it is harvested. For that reason, throughout history people have developed several methods of food preservation. Exactly what methods were adopted originally varied according to climate.

For instance, in cold climates, keeping food on ice was convenient. Freezing impedes the growth of bacteria that spoils a harvest. Cool temperatures above freezing slow decay, so cellars, caves, and cool streams also were used for preservation.

In tropical areas, drying was the preferred preservation method. The sun and wind would dry foods naturally. Evidence shows that Eastern cultures preserved fish, wild game, and other meats this way.

These and other preservation techniques are still used today. Fermentation, pickling, can-ning, and more allow food to be preserved for later consumption. Solomon spoke of wisdom as the ultimate method for guarding freshness and preserving usefulness of spiritual food. Solomon explained how God-given wisdom preserves us for his purposes. How do you experience God's preservation of the good in your life?　　　—J. E.

Conclusion

A. Seekers for Life

The challenge in today's text to find wisdom is expressed in terms of an intense search, not just a casual or passing interest. One must cry out for knowledge and lift up his or her voice for understanding, not whisper. One must be as passionate for wisdom as many are for material wealth. An individual must seek for the Almighty himself, not the almighty dollar.

For some, however, the seeking spirit—the passion for wisdom and for the God who is its source—diminishes with time. In the Western world especially, we settle into routines and expectations at church and in our faith. We become comfortable with where we are spiritually. We lose the hunger and thirst for righteousness (Matthew 5:6). We may not be guilty of any blatant wrongdoing against God or against others, but neither do we maintain our sense of seeking first the kingdom of God and his righteousness (6:33). Our cry for wisdom is reduced to a whimper.

Ultimately, addressing this matter requires that we undergo a serious self-examination. This is particularly so with regard to our relationship with God. Since "the fear of the Lord is the beginning of knowledge" (Proverbs 1:7), then maintaining a strong bond with the Lord and a reverence for him is pivotal to sustaining passion and growth. The spiritual disciplines of prayer, Bible study, and meaningful fellowship with other Christians dare not be neglected (Hebrews 10:24, 25; etc.).

Our lesson text also highlights the necessity for a human teacher to convey to students the value of wisdom and thus of the knowledge of the Lord. True, reading insightful works can be of great

Visual for Lesson 2. *Point to this visual as you ask how decisions become habits, whether wise ones or unwise ones.*

benefit; but nothing teaches wisdom better than a consistent personal example.

The best personal example is the one that a person sees daily in the home setting. Both mothers and fathers are to urge their children to receive their words and take to heart their commandments (Proverbs 1:8) so that wisdom and understanding can be theirs.

The responsibility then falls on the children to continue to cultivate their own desire for wisdom. They must cry out for it with raised voices. They must look for it as though seeking hidden treasure. Parents can model wisdom as they encourage their children to seek it, but each individual must do the seeking personally. The parents can put wisdom into a child's head. But the journey those few inches from head to heart is the task of the growing child.

B. Prayer

Heavenly Father, in a world where so many mock and scorn you and your Word, you are still the only wise God. May we keep our thoughts, words, and deeds in tune with your wisdom and not allow the many distractions around us to quell our seeking spirit. May we pant and thirst for you even as the psalmist did. In Jesus' name we pray. Amen.

C. Thought to Remember

God's wisdom never depreciates in value.

INVOLVEMENT LEARNING

Enhance your lesson with NIV Bible Student *(from your curriculum supplier) and the reproducible activity page (at www.standardlesson.com or in the back of the* NIV Standard Lesson Commentary Deluxe Edition*).*

Into the Lesson

Before class, hide 15–20 pieces of individually wrapped candy around your classroom. Make sure you remember where you concealed each piece.

After all class members have arrived, explain what you have done. Give the class about five minutes to find your hidden treasures. If some pieces are not found, reveal their locations and distribute those pieces as you see fit.

Alternative. Distribute copies of the "A Search for Information" exercise from the activity page, which you can download. Give class members five minutes to complete as indicated. Allow students to share what they have learned.

Discuss either activity with these questions: 1–What other types of treasure hunts have you enjoyed in the past? (*Possible responses:* scavenger hunts, Easter egg hunts, etc.) 2–Sometimes our searches are not games but rather are vital parts of life. What are some of those? (*Possible responses:* job search, researching a major purchase, etc.)

Lead into Bible study by saying, "Treasure hunts and similar games are fun, but we all participate in much more serious searches. Let's see what Solomon taught regarding the nature of the most important search."

Into the Word

Ask a volunteer to read the lesson text aloud. Point out that Solomon uses four different words to describe a hidden treasure we must seek. Help the group determine what these words in Proverbs 2:6-11 imply by saying, "While the four words are similar, they have slightly different meanings. Let's see what light dictionaries can shed." Distribute several of those for learners to use in the following small-group exercise.

Divide students into four groups: **Wisdom Group / Knowledge Group / Understanding Group / Discretion Group.** Ask each group to define the word for which its respective group is named. Also have them explain its importance in the context of the lesson text. Aid the groups with information from the lesson commentary as needed.

Allow the groups about 10 minutes for their research before asking them to share what they have found. Expect definitions along these lines:

- *Wisdom* is the ability to discern the right attitude, belief, or course of action.
- *Knowledge* refers to having a familiarity with facts and people that allows one to experience them intimately.
- *Understanding* is the faculty to process data reasonably to accomplish a task.
- *Discretion* speaks of the quality of having good judgment and making responsible decisions.

Option. Distribute copies of the "Fill It In" exercise from the activity page. Have students work in small groups to complete the puzzle.

Into Life

As you wrap up this session, display a life preserver. If one is not easily available, a picture of one or a similar type of flotation device will do. Then pose these questions: 1–How do devices like this preserve, or save, lives? (*Expected response:* they prevent us from being pulled under the water.) 2–How do we use phrases like "being a real lifesaver" in a figurative way? (*Expected response:* something or someone keeps us from experiencing negative consequences in a potentially dangerous situation.) 3–When has godly wisdom been a lifesaver to you? In other words, what are some times when applying Bible truth helped you avoid disaster? (*Option.* State that no one is allowed to respond twice before everyone has responded once.)

Encourage the class members to keep a journal of occasions when godly wisdom has "preserved" them. (*Option.* Supply the class with notebooks for this purpose.)

RECEIVE
WISDOM'S GIFTS

DEVOTIONAL READING: Job 28:12-28
BACKGROUND SCRIPTURE: Job 1; 42; Proverbs 8

PROVERBS 8:8-14, 17-21

8 All the words of my mouth are just;
    none of them is crooked or perverse.
9 To the discerning all of them are right;
    they are upright to those who have
      found knowledge.
10 Choose my instruction instead of silver,
    knowledge rather than choice gold,
11 for wisdom is more precious than rubies,
    and nothing you desire can compare
      with her.
12 "I, wisdom, dwell together with prudence;
    I possess knowledge and discretion.
13 To fear the LORD is to hate evil;
    I hate pride and arrogance,
    evil behavior and perverse speech.
14 Counsel and sound judgment are mine;
    I have insight, I have power."

17 "I love those who love me,
    and those who seek me find me.
18 With me are riches and honor,
    enduring wealth and prosperity.
19 My fruit is better than fine gold;
    what I yield surpasses choice silver.
20 I walk in the way of righteousness,
    along the paths of justice,
21 bestowing a rich inheritance on those who
      love me
    and making their treasuries full."

KEY VERSES

Choose my instruction instead of silver, knowledge rather than choice gold, for wisdom is more precious than rubies, and nothing you desire can compare with her. —**Proverbs 8:10, 11**

Many Faces of
Wisdom

Unit 1: Wisdom in Proverbs
Lessons 1–4

Lesson Aims

After participating in this lesson, each learner will be able to:

1. Describe the blessings of godly wisdom.
2. Explain why the benefits of godly wisdom far outweigh those associated with material wealth.
3. Write a prayer on behalf of someone that godly wisdom will guide his or her lifestyle.

Lesson Outline

Introduction

A. Dispersal of Wealth

My father passed away several years ago, my mother in December of 2015, and my older sister in the summer of 2017. My sister's passing left me to serve as executor of my parents' estate. My wife and I handled the sale of Dad and Mom's house, which closed title in May of 2018. About a month later, we closed the estate by distributing to the designated family members the money that remained in Mom's account.

While I appreciate what Dad and Mom were able to do to provide for their children financially, that is not the most valuable legacy that they left us. Both of them were faithful Christians who regularly took us to Sunday school and church. They taught us the wisdom that the book of Proverbs calls its readers to obtain and cherish; they were conscientious of the importance of laying up treasures in Heaven.

My parents stewarded both physical and spiritual wealth well. However, others are not so wise. Many are extraordinarily rich in the things that will not last and exceedingly poor in eternal wealth. How do we invest in the riches that come only through the pursuit of godly wisdom?

B. Lesson Context

Wisdom was highly valued in the ancient Near East. Most nations had wise men who held high rank in government because of their skill (examples: Exodus 7:11; 1 Kings 4:30, 31, 34; Jeremiah 18:18; Daniel 1:19, 20). The Old Testament mentions wise women as well (examples: 2 Samuel 14:2; 20:16). The people who filled these positions in government and society were considered exceptional in wisdom.

Wisdom such as that found within the book of Proverbs is not limited to a specialized class of people. It is intended for everyone to live by and practice, regardless of their social status. Proverbs describes four animals that are said to be "extremely wise" (Proverbs 30:24-28). These are not exceedingly brainy creatures, but they do have skills in practical areas of living that help them survive and thrive. The wisdom God has provided in Scripture helps us do the same. Thus, wisdom is far more than intellectual prowess. This practical knowledge guides as we navigate through life in this broken, sinful world—by instructing us how to act, speak, and respond in a wide variety of situations.

Today's lesson from Proverbs continues the appeal to follow the path of wisdom that is grounded in the fear of the Lord. The principles are found in the introductory nine chapters of the book (see Lesson Context in lesson 1). In these chapters, Wisdom is personified thrice as a woman and pictured as making her own appeal (see Proverbs 1:20-22 and commentary on lesson 1; 8:4-36, partially included in today's lesson text; 9:4-6 and commentary on lesson 4). Wisdom's foil is the seductive woman called Folly, whose tempting words lead to disaster.

Wisdom is described again as calling out and raising her voice (Proverbs 8:1; see 1:22-33). And as was the case in Proverbs 1:21, Wisdom is positioned at prominent, public locations so that her cry cannot be missed (8:2, 3).

I. Wisdom's Words
(PROVERBS 8:8-14)
A. Based on Truth (vv. 8, 9)

8. All the words of my mouth are just; none of them is crooked or perverse.

Wisdom has previously described her *words* as "trustworthy," "right," and "true" (Proverbs 8:6, 7). Furthermore, "[Wisdom's] lips detest wickedness" (8:7). A similar declaration occurs in the present verse. The claim is comprehensive; *all* of Wisdom's words are grounded in what is *just*. *Crooked* is a synonym for *perverse* (compare Job

HOW TO SAY IT

choleric	kah-*lay*-rihk.
Ecclesiastes	Ik-*leez*-ee-*as*-teez.
Hippocrates	Hih-*paw*-cruh-teez.
melancholic	mehl-ahn-*kah*-lik.
phlegmatic	flehg-*ma*-tik.
sanguine	*san*-gwin.
Solomon	*Sol*-o-mun.

5:13; 2 Samuel 22:27). The rightness of everything Wisdom says excludes any falseness, even from merely twisting the truth or omitting key details.

9. To the discerning all of them are right; they are upright to those who have found knowledge.

Though some assume that gaining wisdom is a complicated, high-level pursuit, Wisdom asserts that her ways are *right* to those who are *discerning*. Wisdom's counsel is also right in her straightforward goals. There is no hidden agenda or anything to be ashamed of when following Wisdom. There is no fine print to entrap someone later.

Words that are *upright* appeal to those who are guided by understanding and *knowledge*—the kind of knowledge that begins with the fear of the Lord (Proverbs 1:7). Such individuals see no need to debate the worth or value of these words; they make perfect sense. The only appropriate response to them is obedience.

B. Better Than Riches (vv. 10, 11)

10, 11a. Choose my instruction instead of silver, knowledge rather than choice gold, for wisdom is more precious than rubies,

Wisdom presents herself as the first of two choices facing a person. The second choice is the best material this world has to offer, represented by the precious metals *silver* and *choice gold* (implying gold of the finest quality; compare Psalm 19:9, 10) and the costly jewels *rubies* (compare Proverbs 3:13-15).

The offer of such abundant wealth would be hard to refuse. Yet wisdom possesses more lasting value and produces far more genuine pleasure and enjoyment than anything the world has to offer (see Job 28).

11b. and nothing you desire can compare with her.

This is perhaps the boldest statement in today's lesson text. Though the kind and amount of things people owned was different in biblical times, the desire for stuff, especially valuable stuff, still existed. All this and more amounts to nothing compared to the value of wisdom. This is true even if one were to obtain every desirable thing imaginable (compare Ecclesiastes 2:8-11).

Centuries later, Paul will have much to say to Timothy about the temptations associated with riches. The apostle will counter those who believe that "godliness is a means to financial gain" by declaring that godliness with contentment is itself the great gain (1 Timothy 6:5, 6). Those who set their hearts on obtaining riches are subject to many harmful desires that ultimately destroy them (6:9). In fact, the love of wealth is "a root of all kinds of evil" (6:10). If people desire to be rich, Paul will write, then they should seek to be "rich in good deeds" (6:18). The key questions are these: What do you love? Do you desire to be rich as God defines the term, or as the world does?

C. Bringing Discernment (vv. 12-14)

12. "I, wisdom, dwell together with prudence; I possess knowledge and discretion.

The father has encouraged his son to practice wisdom by keeping good company and avoiding those who would entice him into sinful practices (Proverbs 1:10; see lesson 1). Now we learn that Wisdom herself keeps good company. *Prudence* speaks of a person who is discerning in making choices, cautiously deciding what is right.

Wisdom also claims to be familiar with *discretion* (compare Proverbs 1:4; 3:21). In Proverbs 2:11, discretion is said to "protect" the person who possesses it. The present verse may then be highlighting Wisdom's ability to provide one with the necessary insight to spot harmful influences or people when they are encountered and take steps to avoid them.

The writer of Hebrews characterizes mature individuals as those who have practiced wisdom so that they can "distinguish good from evil" (Hebrews 5:14). This aligns with Wisdom's words here. Though the wise person will be innocent of evil, he or she must also recognize evil in order to avoid it (Matthew 10:16).

13. "To fear the LORD is to hate evil; I hate pride and arrogance, evil behavior and perverse speech.

The wisdom of demonstrating a healthy *fear of the Lord* is emphasized throughout the Old Testament (examples: Deuteronomy 6:2; Psalm 128:4; Jeremiah 26:19). The assumption is that a proper reverence and respect for God will result in obeying him (examples: Genesis 22:12; Exodus 20:20). One cannot keep his commands without learning *to hate evil* (compare Job 28:28; Jeremiah 44:4).

The attitudes cited in this verse are all sins that are part of *evil behavior*. They each detract from the life of blessing that is the fruit of prioritizing wisdom over material wealth. *Pride* and *arrogance* are used synonymously. This is the only place in the Old Testament where these two words occur together. Pride in particular is condemned because it stands in the way of the humble heart that the Lord both requires and honors (see Proverbs 6:16-19; 16:18). *Evil behavior* and *perverse speech* are built on pride and arrogance (compare 8:8). Speech that is perverse goes against what the Lord finds pleasing. It is counter to the kind of speech that Paul will state later that followers of Jesus are to demonstrate (Ephesians 4:29).

14. "Counsel and sound judgment are mine; I have insight, I have power."

Wisdom continues to make her case for earning both hearing and heeding from her listeners. The blessings that come with obtaining wisdom contrast sharply with what the Lord and Wisdom both hate (see Proverbs 8:13). The *insight* and *power* of wisdom elsewhere are said to overthrow entire cities (21:22; compare 16:32; Ecclesiastes 7:19).

> **What Do You Think?**
> If you suddenly had double the amount of godly wisdom you have now, what would neighbors notice differently about the way you live?
> *Digging Deeper*
> What would you be willing to give up in order to make time to devote to "wisdom doubling"?

❧ *TEMPERAMENTAL* ❧

Four centuries before Christ, Greek physician Hippocrates tried to explain why people have differing temperaments. He hypothesized that personality variations are related to internal secretions of one's body. The four temperaments he identified were caused by an imbalance of blood (a "sanguine" temperament), yellow bile (a "choleric" temperament), black bile (a "melancholic" temperament), or phlegm (a "phlegmatic" temperament).

Using these ancient terms, a sanguine person is optimistic, active, and social. Choleric individuals are independent, decisive, and goal-oriented. Melancholics tend to be deep, very traditional, and orderly. Finally, a phlegmatic individual tends to be relaxed and easygoing. Hippocrates suggested that these characteristics were balanced in an ideal personality type, with no one characteristic dominating.

Centuries before Hippocrates, Solomon described godly wisdom as a balance of personality characteristics. "Wisdom" and "prudence" coexist; "knowledge" and "discretion" work together, as do "insight" and "power" (Proverbs 8:12-14). Have you found balance in wisdom?
—J. E.

II. Wisdom's Wealth
(PROVERBS 8:17-21)
A. Promised to Seekers (v. 17)

17. "I love those who love me, and those who seek me find me.

Wisdom never spurns anyone who truly loves her (compare 1 Samuel 2:30; John 14:21-24). This verse also commends those who *seek* Wisdom, a challenge that was included in the previous study (Proverbs 2:4, 5 in lesson 2; compare 1 Chronicles 16:11; Matthew 7:7-11). Preferably, the seeking begins *early* in one's life so that an individual can gain the maximum benefit from wisdom (compare Ecclesiastes 12:1).

The quest for wisdom is not an impossible, idealistic dream walk. It is very much within our grasp if we turn to God. Our search is governed by our respect for God and his ways. Our goal is to know God and his ways more fully so that we may better follow them. This is a happy, joyous journey, the lifelong pursuit of godliness.

B. Providing Real Treasure (vv. 18-21)

18a. "With me are riches and honor,

Wisdom promises that *riches and honor* result from obeying her invitation. One is reminded of Solomon's request for wisdom. God not only granted the king's request but also gave him much that he had not asked for, including "both wealth and honor" (1 Kings 3:5, 10-14; compare Deuteronomy 8:18).

Some look at the promises of riches and honor that are associated with wisdom as an assurance that material wealth and prosperity will come to anyone who chooses to obey the Lord and live by his wisdom as found in Scripture. Other verses appear to offer such a guarantee (Proverbs 3:9, 10, 16; 10:22; 22:4).

Like all proverbs, however, caution must be exercised in interpreting these as guaranteed rewards for faithfulness. The proverbs in Scripture express principles that find fullest reward in eternity and do not always result in an easy life. One must not overlook the role that human free will and sin have in impacting how certain proverbs actually play out. For instance, Proverbs 22:6

Wisdom—
God gives generously

Visual for Lessons 3 & 9. *While discussing verse 18, point to the visual and ask class members to describe how God has given them greater wisdom.*

speaks of a child being well taught and still living in wisdom in old age. Yet we all know of cases where children went astray in spite of their parents' wise teachings. Or a statement such as "A gentle answer turns away wrath" (Proverbs 15:1) does not describe what happened to Jesus at his trial prior to his crucifixion. He gave such an answer to his opponents, and they still crucified him (see Luke 23:3-32).

These exceptions do not negate the truth found within a given proverb; they simply illustrate that we have to be cautious in expecting an ironclad guarantee in every case. For this reason, we must not be surprised that not everyone who lives a wise and godly life will experience material prosperity or even a perfectly peaceful life. One example of this is Jeremiah. Though he clearly lived his life in fear of the Lord and therefore wisely, the prophet suffered much in his ministry (examples: Jeremiah 26:8, 9; 38:4-6; 40:1). In contrast, the wicked often live prosperous and seemingly carefree lives (compare Ecclesiastes 7:15; 8:14).

18b. "enduring wealth and prosperity.

If we are ever troubled by circumstances, rest assured that we are not alone. The psalmist wrestled with the same issue and came to understand that material prosperity is only temporary; it ends when the Lord carries out his righteous judgment (Psalm 73:16-20). Real wealth, found in wisdom, is *enduring*. Like the treasures in Heaven, wisdom's *wealth* cannot decay or be stolen (Matthew 6:19, 20).

19. "My fruit is better than fine gold; what I yield surpasses choice silver.

The comparison with *fruit* goes well with wisdom's earlier portrayal as being a "tree of life" (Proverbs 3:18). Wisdom bears worthwhile fruit throughout one's life and provides invaluable insights for any age, stage, or circumstance of life. Once again, its reward is compared favorably to precious metals (compare Job 28:12-19; Proverbs 3:13, 14).

It is important when considering the promises of riches and wealth in Proverbs to examine another book that has much to say about wisdom: Job. The man himself is described at the outset as being of exemplary and upright character (Job 1:1). Yet we know the tragedies that befell him in the course of a single day. Though he was wise and praised God through all his trials, he still went through those trials. Wisdom did not save him from the sorrows that Satan visited on him (1:12–2:10). Job experienced an abundance of sorrow, in spite of conventional wisdom that said he would be blessed for his faithfulness (example: 4:7, 8).

Job's account assists us in maintaining a proper balance when we read promises such as those cited earlier from Proverbs or found elsewhere in Scripture. Jesus spoke of seeking the kingdom of God first; then "all these things" (the material goods that "non-kingdom" people are so preoccupied with) will be provided (Matthew 6:33). But Jesus was also honest about the persecution that his followers would suffer (5:10, 11) and the cost that accompanies choosing to follow him (Luke 9:23; 14:33). At such times, the true value of the gifts of enduring wealth that godly wisdom offers will manifest itself.

20. "I walk in the way of righteousness, along the paths of justice,

Wisdom's ties with what is right have already been established (see Proverbs 8:9), as have her links to what is just (see 2:8, 9). Whether *justice* is understood as judging right from wrong or as practicing fair judgment in one's daily contacts and circumstances, Wisdom feels right at home in the midst of such God-honoring decisions and actions.

21. "bestowing a rich inheritance on those who love me and making their treasuries full."

The word *inheritance* highlights the "enduring" nature of Wisdom's wealth (Proverbs 8:18). It is an inheritance that Wisdom bequeaths to those who sincerely, passionately seek her (8:17). Once again, *treasuries* can signify the material benefits that accompany living by the counsels of Wisdom (see 15:6; 24:4, where the word is translated "treasure[s]"). But these are not the primary riches for which Wisdom is to be known and followed. The inheritance Wisdom provides is one that can be passed on to one's children with the understanding that, if pursued diligently, Wisdom's treasures will become just as precious and valuable to them.

> **What Do You Think?**
> What opportunities do you have to teach children to distinguish worldly wisdom from godly wisdom?
> *Digging Deeper*
> How will you pray for the opportunity to do so?

❧ *A Different Inheritance* ❧

What happens to our wealth after we die? The usual answer is that it goes to our children. Some of the world's wealthiest individuals have different plans, however.

Rock star Gene Simmons made his fortune with hard work. He wants his children to learn the value of work too. Martial artist and movie star Jackie Chan plans to give most of his wealth to charity and not to his son. His logic is clear: "If he is capable, he can make his own money. If he is not, then he will just be wasting my money." Warren Buffett has promised not only to give away 99 percent of his wealth, he's also partnered with Bill Gates to persuade other super-wealthy individuals to do the same! Most of Buffett's fortune will go to charities, not to his children.

These and other incredibly rich people have expressed a Solomon-like wisdom when it comes to inherited wealth. Solomon recognized that the best gift we can leave our children is wisdom, not cash. When we live a life of righteousness, we ensure that our children will have a "rich inheritance" (Proverbs 8:21), not a life of ease and irresponsibility.

—J. E.

Conclusion

A. ... *And* Wise?

Some may ask, "Isn't it possible to be wealthy *and* wise?" True, the biblical record includes individuals who were both (examples: Genesis 41:41-44; 1 Kings 3:10-14; Job 1:1-5; 42:12-17). But the Bible clearly warns us about the spiritual dangers that material wealth and possessions can pose. The primary issue is the impact that this has on one's heart and thus on one's relationship with God (compare Psalm 52:5-7; Mark 10:17-23).

In his parable of the sower, Jesus warns of the "deceitfulness of wealth" that results in an individual's becoming unfruitful after receiving the gospel (Matthew 13:22). Similarly, Jesus asked, "What good will it be for someone to gain the whole world, yet forfeit their soul?" (16:26). Of course, the implied answer is, "Nothing." To gain all the world has to offer at the loss of wisdom results in tragedy. That is true despite all the abundance that the whole world can offer.

All these teachings are consistent with Wisdom's plea to choose her above any form of material wealth. No matter how many priceless artifacts we amass—or how useful the new gadgets, inventions, and technological devices are—all the things that we may desire cannot compare with the value of wisdom.

B. Prayer

Father, thank you for the abundance of gifts that you provide to those who choose to heed the call of Wisdom. Thank you for examples of that wisdom who have shaped us over the years. Help us to be such examples to those in our spheres of influence. In Jesus' name we pray. Amen.

C. Thought to Remember

Before wisdom's gifts can be opened and treasured, they must be sought.

INVOLVEMENT LEARNING

Enhance your lesson with NIV Bible Student (from your curriculum supplier) and the reproducible activity page (at www.standardlesson.com or in the back of the NIV Standard Lesson Commentary Deluxe Edition).

Into the Lesson

Ask class members to find merchants' reward cards that they have in their wallets/purses or on their key chains. Ask for volunteers to state the advantages they receive from using their cards.

Lead into Bible study by saying, "We like the discounts, bonus points, rebates, and other perks that reward cards provide. But Solomon speaks of wisdom as offering even greater rewards. Wisdom's value is our topic today."

Into the Word

Divide the class into three groups, designating them **Religious Group, Educational Group,** and **Domestic Group.** Explain that each group will be considering a case study of a challenge that a teenager named Sophia faces. Distribute three sets of handouts (you create), one for each group, with the following information.

Religious Group (Proverbs 8:8-11): Sophia exchanges text messages on a regular basis with friends in the youth group. Everyone gets along well, but Sophia is worried that some of their jokes involving Carlos may be crossing the line from good-natured teasing into bullying.

Educational Group (Proverbs 8:12-14): Sophia's school friends follow influential celebrities on social media. Some celebrities have good things to say; others, not so much. One particularly popular celebrity posts questionable content on a regular basis. But he's also really funny, and "following" him (in the sense that social media uses that term) could give Sophia something in common with most of her classmates.

Domestic Group (Proverbs 8:17-21): Sophia doesn't get along with her dad. They don't have many similar interests. His rules are stricter than those of her friends' parents. And he works a lot, so she doesn't see him often. She loves her dad, and she knows he loves her too, but the relationship needs some improvement.

Include on all handouts the following questions: 1–How did group members react in similar situations in their youth? 2–What options are available to Sophia? 3–What pluses and minuses does each option offer? 4–What does the assigned text offer in the way of wise counsel for Sophia?

After groups discuss their respective scenarios, have them summarize their answers to questions 2, 3, and 4 in whole-class discussion.

Alternative. Before class, recruit a volunteer (preferably female) to play the part of Wisdom in an interview. Pose the following questions, which you have given to your volunteer in advance, during the interview: 1–Why should people take you seriously? *(Proverbs 8:8-11)* 2–With whom do you associate and avoid association? *(8:12-14)* 3–What do people stand to gain from heeding your counsel? *(8:17-21)*. The parenthetical passage references need not be voiced during the interview, but should be the basis for the whole-class discussion that follows.

Option. Distribute to study pairs copies of the "Wisdom Wanted!" exercise from the activity page, which you can download. After pairs complete as indicated, start a discussion by asking which is truer: *we apprehend wisdom* or *wisdom apprehends us*.

Into Life

Have learners pair off to discuss one or two rewards of wisdom that members of the pair desire to experience. After several minutes, ask that each learner write a prayer for his or her study partner in light of the other person's expressed desire for wisdom. Close with your own prayer that encourages class members to pray their prayers for the others each day in the week ahead.

Option. To expand the previous activity, distribute copies of the "Wisdom Needed!" exercise from the activity page. Allow one minute for class members to complete as indicated.

FEAST WITH WISDOM

DEVOTIONAL READING: Psalm 119:97-104
BACKGROUND SCRIPTURE: Proverbs 9

PROVERBS 9:1-6, 8-10, 13-18

¹ Wisdom has built her house;
    she has set up its seven pillars.
² She has prepared her meat and mixed her
    wine;
    she has also set her table.
³ She has sent out her servants, and she
    calls
    from the highest point of the city,
⁴ "Let all who are simple come to my
    house!"
    To those who have no sense she says,
⁵ "Come, eat my food
    and drink the wine I have mixed.
⁶ Leave your simple ways and you will live;
    walk in the way of insight."

⁸ Do not rebuke mockers or they will hate
    you;
    rebuke the wise and they will love you.
⁹ Instruct the wise and they will be wiser
    still;

teach the righteous and they will add to
    their learning.
¹⁰ The fear of the LORD is the beginning of
    wisdom,
    and knowledge of the Holy One is
    understanding.

¹³ Folly is an unruly woman;
    she is simple and knows nothing.
¹⁴ She sits at the door of her house,
    on a seat at the highest point of the city,
¹⁵ calling out to those who pass by,
    who go straight on their way,
¹⁶ "Let all who are simple come to my
    house!"
    To those who have no sense she says,
¹⁷ "Stolen water is sweet;
    food eaten in secret is delicious!"
¹⁸ But little do they know that the dead are
    there,
    that her guests are deep in the realm of
    the dead.

KEY VERSE

Leave your simple ways and you will live; walk in the way of insight. **—Proverbs 9:6**

MANY FACES OF
WISDOM

Unit 1: Wisdom in Proverbs
LESSONS 1–4

LESSON AIMS

After participating in this lesson, each learner will be able to:

1. Summarize the two lifestyles personified by the two women.

2. Compare and contrast the appeals personified in the two women.

3. Role-play planning a dinner party both to seek and honor wisdom.

LESSON PLAN

Introduction
A. Life-Changing Meals

Has a dinner ever changed your life? Examples of meals that changed a person's life abound. For instance, without a dinner party during a ferocious storm in Switzerland in 1816, Mary Shelley's *Frankenstein* would never have been written. The name Henri Rousseau might mean nothing to the art world if not for the dinner thrown by Pablo Picasso in 1908. Without a meal at Dooky Chase's Restaurant in 1960, we may never have seen the brave example of the men and women who participated in the sit-ins that furthered the cause of the Civil Rights Movement in the USA. Most of all, without the Passover there would have been no precedent for the Lord's Supper, which continues to be the most important meal for Christians.

In today's Scripture text, Wisdom invites us into her house; her meal is prepared, and she is ready to give a party to change your life. Folly is also ready. The choice is yours to make: Who will be your hostess and change your life?

B. Lesson Context

Today's lesson concludes our studies from the book of Proverbs. It is drawn from the final chapter in the opening section of Proverbs (chapters 1–9), in which Wisdom (personified as a woman; see Lesson Context in lesson 3) presents her case for being embraced—and followed as a way of life—by the hearer or reader (see Proverbs 9). From Proverbs 10 on, the book consists primarily of brief sayings and statements of advice covering a wide range of topics, often contrasting the life of wisdom with the life of folly.

I. Wisdom's Home
(PROVERBS 9:1-6)
A. Preparations (vv. 1, 2)

1. Wisdom has built her house; she has set up its seven pillars.

The imagery of a house to represent wisdom is alluded to, from the close of the previous chapter (see Proverbs 8:34). Here *Wisdom* is described as having completed *her house*.

Pillars suggest stability and a degree of magnificence or stateliness. That Wisdom herself has worked to carve them out shows her to be associated with hard work. *Seven* is a number representing completeness or perfection throughout the Bible (examples: Genesis 2:3; Leviticus 25:8; Revelation 5:6), and it may be viewed so here. Wisdom's house has no flaws or defects; it is the ideal dwelling place.

2. She has prepared her meat and mixed her wine; she has also set her table.

Wisdom has prepared a sumptuous meal for her guests (compare Isaiah 25:6). *Wine* is something to be enjoyed (Genesis 27:28; Isaiah 55:1), though the Scriptures also warn of its abuse (Proverbs 23:29-35; 31:4, 5). Here it is part of what Wisdom has prepared to show that she has put forth her best efforts to prepare *her table*. All that is missing now are the guests (compare Luke 14:16-23).

B. Invitation (vv. 3-6)

3. She has sent out her servants, and she calls from the highest point of the city,

Wisdom publicizes her invitation using two means. First, she sends *out her servants*. Second, Wisdom herself goes out to invite people to come to her feast, which may represent the second and more urgent invitation since it comes directly from her. She utters her cry at prominent points where she can be both seen and heard (Proverbs 8:1-3). The setting is similar to that in chapter 1, where Wisdom cries out to passersby in public places to get their attention (1:20, 21).

What Do You Think?

What is one specific lifestyle change you can make to reduce the "noise" that interferes with your hearing Wisdom's call?

Digging Deeper

What accountability procedure can you adopt to keep you on track in that regard?

---

4. "Let all who are simple come to my house!" To those who have no sense she says,

Wisdom's appeal is aimed at the *simple,* a group mentioned at the outset of Proverbs as those who can benefit from the book's contents (Proverbs 1:4, 22). *Those who have no sense* parallel the simple. The wording describes people who may be viewed as "neutral" in terms of wisdom vs. foolishness. These individuals could be considered naïve or immature, people who clearly can benefit from what Wisdom has to offer but haven't yet chosen to do so.

5. "Come, eat my food and drink the wine I have mixed.

The invitation from Wisdom begins by asking those invited to take part in the meal that she has prepared. Sharing *food* in the biblical world is considered the epitome of intimate fellowship with another person (compare Psalms 42:2; 63:1; 143:6; Isaiah 44:3; John 7:37, 38).

The implied fellowship is why, for example, the Jewish Christians were initially so upset with Peter for having eaten with uncircumcised Gentiles (Acts 11:2, 3). Jesus uses the language of intimate fellowship in appealing to the church at Laodicea to give him the opportunity to eat with them (Revelation 3:20). His desire is for such warm fellowship to end the "lukewarm" condition of the church (3:16). Wisdom desires a similar intimacy with those who respond to her call.

6. "Leave your simple ways and you will live; walk in the way of insight."

For a person to accept Wisdom's invitation, the individual must abandon his or her *simple ways*. In so doing, that person will also turn from foolish actions that would hinder one's ability to follow wisdom consistently. A person cannot walk on both a wise and a foolish path any more than a person can serve both "God and money" (Luke 16:13). What Wisdom offers, though, is life (Proverbs 3:1, 2, 18; 8:35).

HOW TO SAY IT

Apollos	Uh-*pahl*-us.
Aquila	*Ack*-wih-luh.
Carnegie	Car-*nay*-ghee.
De Wallen (*Dutch*)	Deh *Wall*-ehn.
Laodicea	Lay-*odd*-uh-*see*-uh.
Priscilla	Prih-*sil*-uh.
Rembrandt	*Rehm*-brandt.
van Gogh	van *Gof* or van *Go*.

II. Becoming Wise

(PROVERBS 9:8-10)

A. Accepting Instruction (vv. 8, 9)

8. Do not rebuke mockers or they will hate you; rebuke the wise and they will love you.

One way in which *mockers* and *the wise* demonstrate how different they are is in how each group accepts criticism. Scornful or contemptuous people reject any attempt to correct their behavior or to show the error of their ways (see Proverbs 15:12; Matthew 7:6). Pride usually lies at the root of such people's conduct. On the other hand, the wise person will appreciate any correction and express that to the person who conveys it.

Just because a person is wise does not mean that he or she knows everything; indeed, genuine wisdom is characterized by humility and a teachable spirit. David, the man after God's own heart, was not too pious to say, "Let a righteous man strike me—that is a kindness; let him rebuke me—that is oil on my head. My head will not refuse it" (Psalm 141:5).

9. Instruct the wise and they will be wiser still; teach the righteous and they will add to their learning.

This expands on the second part of the previous verse. A truly *wise* individual admits that there is always more to learn (see Proverbs 1:5). He or she is not insulted by the person who offers *instruction*; the individual is grateful for whatever new insight or information is received (compare 12:15; 15:31; 19:25).

Apollos exhibited such an attitude when he was willing to receive the corrective teaching of Aquila and Priscilla. And Aquila and Priscilla demonstrated wisdom in the way they took Apollos aside in private in order to instruct him (Acts 18:24-26).

❧ WINNING THEM OVER ❧

We all want others to see things our way. But how is that done? Since 1936, many have found answers in a best-selling book that promises to tell *How to Win Friends and Influence People.*

Dale Carnegie (1888–1955), American writer and developer of self-improvement courses, was the author of this manual for building interpersonal skills. Carnegie believed that it is possible to change other people's behavior by changing one's behavior toward them.

Carnegie encouraged leaders to become good listeners and to take a genuine interest in others. By taking a real interest in another person's well-being, it becomes easier to suggest changes that the receiver can consider and accept as being his or her own conclusions. By building nurturing relationships, a successful leader can grow personally while helping others do likewise.

Solomon also advised how to influence others. Trading insults with a scorner will only feed antagonism. Helping someone who wants to be just will allow the relationship to flourish and improvement to continue. What kind of relationships are you nurturing?   —J. E.

B. Fearing the Lord (v. 10)

10. The fear of the LORD is the beginning of wisdom, and knowledge of the Holy One is understanding.

The truth expressed in the first part of this verse has been encountered already in the book (Proverbs 1:7). *The knowledge of the Holy One* refers to knowing the Lord (compare 2 Kings 19:22; Psalm 78:41; Isaiah 1:4; 43:3).

To many, the word *holy* implies a life that is removed from the practical concerns of this world and is thus unable to properly relate to it and live within it. But holiness implies a separation in a spiritual sense: being set apart for God. Though secular living (as the opposite of holy living) may seem fun, it detracts from a meaningful or enriching life. The best way to journey through life in a broken, sin-filled world is to follow the Creator's guidelines.

Lady Wisdom concludes her invitation (Proverbs 9:11, 12, not in our text) with the promise of rewards (not to be enjoyed by the scorner). These include a longer life (which is a general principle, not an ironclad guarantee).

III. Folly's Home
(Proverbs 9:13-18)
A. The Woman (v. 13)

13. Folly is an unruly woman; she is simple and knows nothing.

This verse introduces *Folly* to contrast with the woman known as Wisdom. She is described as *unruly*: noisy, loud, obnoxious (compare Proverbs 7:11). Whereas Wisdom sends her appeal to the simple (9:4), Folly herself *is simple* (that is, unfocused or wandering: compare 5:6). Though one gets the impression that she likes to sound knowledgeable, in reality she needs wisdom for she *knows nothing*.

B. The House (v. 14)

14. She sits at the door of her house, on a seat at the highest point of the city,

While Wisdom has built her house (Proverbs 9:1), nothing is said about Folly's efforts to build her own. Nor does the text indicate that she has prepared any meal as has Wisdom (9:2). Folly simply *sits* idly *at the door of her house* (contrast 9:4).

Folly, like Wisdom, locates herself at a prominent point *at the highest point of the city*. Some suggest that because of the way in which high places are often associated with pagan worship in the Old Testament, it may be that Folly is inviting passersby to join her in such worship (com-

pare Ezekiel 16:24, 25). If so, that adds to the suspect nature of her appeal. But since Wisdom also resides on a high place (Proverbs 9:3), Folly's character more than her location is what makes her suspicious as a good hostess.

> *What Do You Think?*
> How can we work to turn down the volume on foolishness in our surroundings without denying the right to free speech?
> *Digging Deeper*
> Comparing Proverbs 9:3 with 9:14, what are the "high places" from which wisdom and foolishness proceed most noticeably near you?

Folly is contrasted with Wisdom in a manner that calls to mind the parables of Jesus. The house imagery anticipates how Jesus will conclude his Sermon on the Mount, with an illustration of two houses built on two different foundations: rock and sand. Both houses are subject to the same circumstances (rain, floods, and wind). The house built on sand collapses, while the house built on a foundation of solid rock remains intact.

The two houses, as Jesus will explain centuries later, stand for two different ways of living. The one built on rock represents the life lived in obedience to his teachings; the one built on sand represents the person who hears his teachings but refuses to obey them (Matthew 7:24-27; Luke 6:48, 49).

C. Temptation (vv. 15-17)

15. calling out to those who pass by, who go straight on their way,

Folly provides a distraction from Wisdom's call; she is trying to lure people away from the course they are on (contrast Proverbs 1:20-23). Her intentions are questionable, to say the least.

16. "Let all who are simple come to my house!" To those who have no sense she says,

Folly words her invitation in a manner similar to Wisdom's (Proverbs 9:4, 5). In that regard, Folly's invitation is to the same naïve population to which Wisdom calls. In this case, *have no sense* means that a person lacks discernment.

17a. "Stolen water is sweet;

Here, however, we see the difference between the two invitations. And the two potential hostesses cannot be more distinct! Folly has nothing of her own to offer as she brazenly refers to her provision of *water* as *stolen* (contrast Proverbs 9:5). She further has the audacity to boast of how *sweet* such fare is to taste (compare 20:17).

There is no sense of shame or remorse in how Folly has acquired what she is offering. Quite the opposite—there is an unmistakable sense of perverse pride!

17b. "food eaten in secret is delicious!"

One can assume that the *food* to be *eaten in secret* is also stolen. That is why it is devoured where no one can discover the theft of the ones who enjoy it.

D. Departing Gift (v. 18)

18a. But little do they know that the dead are there,

Hebrews 11:25 describes the pleasures of sin as "fleeting"—they do not endure. This is illustrated by the *but* statement of the verse before us as it follows the seductive appeal of the previous verse. What Folly has made to sound so enjoyable and so satisfying leads to a *dead* end (compare Proverbs 2:18; 7:26, 27). Instead of being a lifestyle of pleasure, her path produces a "death-style."

One is reminded of the lie posed by the serpent in the Garden of Eden. The serpent promised much to the woman (and to the man through her) but could only deliver death, as God had warned (Genesis 2:17). Satan continues to be the master of deception. Jesus refers to the devil as the father of lies (John 8:44). One of his disguises by which he deceives is to appear as "an angel of light" (2 Corinthians 11:14). There is nothing sweet or pleasant in following his counsel. Only Wisdom offers the tree of life (Proverbs 3:18).

18b. that her guests are deep in the realm of the dead.

The Hebrew word translated *realm of the dead* can also be translated "the grave" (examples: Genesis 37:35; 1 Kings 2:6). It refers to the depths below the earth (Job 11:8; Psalm 139:8), not nec-

essarily to a place of punishment. The concept of Heaven and Hell as we understand today wasn't fully revealed by God when Solomon wrote. To grasp that entirety, one must consider the teaching of the entire New Testament. Only there is to be found the ultimate clarity on the subject of the afterlife (examples: Matthew 10:28; Mark 10:21; 12:25; 2 Peter 2:4; Revelation 21; 22).

The focus of the warning in the verse before us is that heeding Folly's invitation is a sure path to ruin. The clear contrast is found in Wisdom's appeal, which promises long life (Proverbs 3:16; 9:11). A life lived with wisdom, even one tragically cut short, is a good life. Since true wisdom begins with the fear of God, any such life, whether long or short, is the path to everlasting life with the Lord. In that way, a person can be said to have found the Old Testament's understanding of abundant life (compare John 10:10). And what has been avoided is the way of trespasses and sins, which leads to death (compare Ephesians 2:1).

> **What Do You Think?**
> Which Scriptures do you find most helpful in strengthening your resolve to make wisely measured decisions?
> **Digging Deeper**
> Which one of those Scriptures is most "shareable"? Why do you say that?

❧ TOURIST TRAP ❧

Amsterdam is a city with a rich history. For instance, the city claims that the Amsterdam Stock Exchange is the oldest in the world. Similarly, the Natura Artis Magistra is one of the oldest zoos in Europe and includes a planetarium and an aquarium. Museums display the works of renowned Dutch artists such as Rembrandt and van Gogh.

While these cultural sites attract their share of sightseers, one of the largest draws in Amsterdam is the neighborhood known as De Wallen, home of the famous red-light district. Prostitutes offer their services from behind the siren songs of windows illuminated with red lights. Beyond prostitution, the area also lures visitors with drug-related activities.

Wisdom offers a rich feast in all cities, even Amsterdam. But the call of unrestrained sensuality is strong. Although Wisdom is built on a solid foundation of truth, Folly appeals to people's basest instincts. Whose call do you follow?   —J. E.

Conclusion

A. Only Two Choices

When I was growing up in the 1950s and 1960s, the choice of breakfast cereals was limited. Today many grocery store aisles are filled with nothing but cereals. In fact, almost anything we buy today involves selecting from a huge (and often confusing) array of choices. Truly we live in a world with an abundance of choices in a variety of areas.

However, as today's lesson from Proverbs has pointed out, the essentials of life and eternity come down to a single choice. The first psalm concludes with a contrast of this choice: "The Lord watches over the way of the righteous, but the way of the wicked leads to destruction" (Psalm 1:6). The prophet Ezekiel urged the people of his day to turn from the way leading to death and thereby live (Ezekiel 18:23, 32). All this is reinforced by the teaching of Jesus concerning the good way leading to life versus the evil way (Matthew 7:13, 14), the two builders (7:24-27), and the two groups at the final judgment (25:31-46).

Throughout the book of Proverbs, the choices are presented as wisdom and folly (or foolishness) dozens of times. Following wisdom leads to life (Proverbs 9:6), folly to death (9:18). Today's Scripture text from Proverbs 9 uses the illustration of two houses and two hostesses to present the choice that we all face. This is consistent with the choice that Moses gave the Israelites:

> This day I call the heavens and the earth as witnesses against you that I have set before you life and death, blessings and curses. Now choose life, so that you and your children may live (Deuteronomy 30:19).

The same options are reflected in the choice that Joshua later gave to the Israelites as to whom

Visual for Lesson 4. *Start a discussion by pointing to this visual as you ask what habits learners can develop to help them to feast with Wisdom daily.*

they would serve: other gods or the true God (Joshua 24:15). Then as today, it's either/or, not both/and.

Despite the many who advocate that there are many paths to life from many different (and even contradictory) religions, the Scriptures still offer the only possibility. Jesus is the only way to life (John 14:6); every other path leads to death. This is why responding to the gospel with acceptance remains so crucial. It is a matter of great urgency because it makes all the difference between life and death.

Two houses stand, but one will fall. Two meals are offered, but one is poisoned. Two hostesses extend invitations, but one is deceptive. It is up to each individual to decide which house to enter, which meal to eat, and which invitation to accept. Choose wisely!

B. Prayer

Father in Heaven, thank you for Jesus, who reveals his treasures of wisdom and knowledge to those who seek him. Thank you for the holy Scriptures, which are able to make us wise concerning salvation. Grant us grace and strength to follow the way of wisdom, knowing that it is the way to life. We pray in Jesus' name. Amen.

C. Thought to Remember

The path of folly is not a lifestyle;
it's a death-style.

INVOLVEMENT LEARNING

Enhance your lesson with NIV Bible Student *(from your curriculum supplier) and the reproducible activity page (at www.standardlesson.com or in the back of the* NIV Standard Lesson Commentary Deluxe Edition*).*

Into the Lesson

Call for two volunteers to answer the following series of opinion questions (or others of your own devising):

What national park, monument, or historic site should everyone visit?

What is the best worship song or hymn?

What is the best fast-food restaurant?

What is the best movie ever made?

What is the tastiest snack food?

Alternate between the volunteers as to who answers first. After the last question, open the floor for the rest of the class to express their opinions as you repeat the questions.

Alternative. Distribute copies of the "Choices" exercise from the activity page, which you can download, for each learner to complete silently as indicated. Call time after no more than one minute. Tally responses on the board.

After either activity say, "Life is full of choices. Some are merely matters of personal taste, while others influence the very course of life. Let's see what Solomon had to say about the latter."

Into the Word

Divide the class in half, designating one of the halves as the **Wisdom Group** and the other as the **Folly Group**. Explain that the groups will debate this proposal: *Wisdom is better than folly.*

Each group is to prepare to debate either for or against the proposal as the group designations indicate. Stress that use of today's text of Proverbs 9:1-6, 8-10, 13-18 is to be first and foremost in their preparation. After several minutes, allow a representative of the **Wisdom Group** to go first in the giving of opening statements.

After both groups' opening statements, use a back-and-forth format appropriate for your class for groups to support and deny the proposal; an

internet search in advance will help you decide on the best format to use.

After an appropriate amount of time, move to closing statements, with the **Folly Group** going first. The **Wisdom Group** has the privilege of going last because it has the burden of proof regarding the proposal. In fairness, however, the **Wisdom Group** is not allowed to present new arguments or new Scripture support since the **Folly Group** will have no chance of rebuttal. Mention this at the outset of debate preparation.

Following the debate, ask the class how choosing between wisdom and folly is like and/or unlike the debate just witnessed. Jot responses on the board; correct misconceptions as they arise.

Into Life

Inform learners that next they will plan a dinner party intended to reflect appreciation for the guest of honor: Wisdom herself. In whole-class brainstorming, have learners suggest a guest list (people they know who reflect wisdom), the location of the banquet (a place wisdom is likely to be found), the menu (how wisdom results in spiritual nourishment), etc.

Returning to the guest list, ask learners to suggest the types of people (without using names) who would expect to be invited and who would be surprised when they weren't. Pause for a minute of silent reflection for learners to make private notes to themselves regarding what they need to do in the coming week to not be in that group.

Option. Distribute copies of the "Two Appeals" exercise from the activity page as a closing self-test. As you do, assure learners that you will not collect the results. Allow no more than one minute; have learners check their own answers.

Close with a prayer that thanks God for his rebukes and teachings in wisdom, asking that he will continue to teach wisdom to each member of the class.

VINDICATING WISDOM

DEVOTIONAL READING: Matthew 10:1-14
BACKGROUND SCRIPTURE: Matthew 11:1-19

MATTHEW 11:7-19

7 As John's disciples were leaving, Jesus began to speak to the crowd about John: "What did you go out into the wilderness to see? A reed swayed by the wind? 8 If not, what did you go out to see? A man dressed in fine clothes? No, those who wear fine clothes are in kings' palaces. 9 Then what did you go out to see? A prophet? Yes, I tell you, and more than a prophet. 10 This is the one about whom it is written:

"'I will send my messenger ahead of you,
who will prepare your way before
you.'

11 Truly I tell you, among those born of women there has not risen anyone greater than John the Baptist; yet whoever is least in the kingdom of heaven is greater than he. 12 From the days of John the Baptist until now, the kingdom of heaven has been subjected to violence, and violent people have been raiding it. 13 For all the Prophets and the Law prophesied until John. 14 And if you are willing to accept it, he is the Elijah who was to come. 15 Whoever has ears, let them hear.

16 "To what can I compare this generation? They are like children sitting in the marketplaces and calling out to others:

17 "'We played the pipe for you,
and you did not dance;
we sang a dirge,
and you did not mourn.'

18 For John came neither eating nor drinking, and they say, 'He has a demon.' 19 The Son of Man came eating and drinking, and they say, 'Here is a glutton and a drunkard, a friend of tax collectors and sinners.' But wisdom is proved right by her deeds."

KEY VERSE

The Son of Man came eating and drinking, and they say, "Here is a glutton and a drunkard, a friend of tax collectors and sinners." But wisdom is proved right by her deeds. —**Matthew 11:19**

MANY FACES OF
WISDOM

Unit 2: Wisdom in the Gospels

LESSON AIMS

After participating in this lesson, each learner will be able to:

1. Summarize Jesus' description of John the Baptist.

2. Explain why the generation that Jesus criticized displayed a lack of wisdom in its evaluation of both him and John the Baptist.

3. Make a plan for change in the area where he or she most needs to improve in the exercise of godly wisdom.

LESSON OUTLINE

Introduction

A. Love It or Hate It

Beauty is in the eye of the beholder . . . or the tongue of the taster or ear of the listener. We all make distinctions between what is good and what is bad, and sometimes these opinions are no more than personal taste. In the end, they don't really matter. How you decorate your home (or choose not to) is a matter of preference, one that can lead to conflict with others in the house who disagree. But there is no real right or wrong.

When preparing dinner, you may not have strong feelings about carrots, but you probably do about brussels sprouts and beets—if you even eat them! Some music blends into the background, while other songs you turn up and sing along to— or maybe turn off to stop the assault on your ears. The same may be true of movies or TV shows: most are average, neither great nor horrible. But others divide us between fans and critics.

Today's text explores the seemingly vast gulf between John the Baptist and Jesus Christ— and the variety of opinions surrounding them. Many loved them; many hated them. Yet loving or hating these two is very different from loving or hating carpeting or cushions, music or movies. Choosing to hate these two, even in their differences, is choosing to hate God's wisdom.

B. Lesson Context

The Gospel of Matthew is one of four books in the New Testament that tell the story of Jesus' life, death, and resurrection. Through Jesus, God was restoring his rule over his world, setting right what human rebellion had made wrong. Matthew put special focus on the surprising way in which God fulfilled his promises to Israel in Jesus.

For instance, we might expect God's true king to be warmly received. But in fact, Jesus met with hostility from his infancy (examples: Matthew 2:13; 21:45, 46; 27:20). Jesus warned his followers that they would meet with similar opposition (10:14-25, 34-36).

The same hostility is seen in the arrest and death of John the Baptist (Matthew 14:1-12), which foreshadowed Jesus' own crucifixion (26:1-

5, 14-16; 27:32-44). Yet this very climax of the hostility against God's wisdom was the means by which God fulfilled his wisdom, for Jesus died not merely as an innocent victim but as the willing and worthy sacrifice for the sins of humanity (20:28; 26:28).

God's victory came through rejection, death, and resurrection. Nothing could have been more contrary to expectations. In an episode preceding our text, the (to human thinking) upside-down wisdom of God proved confusing even to John the Baptist, the prophet who announced the nearness of God's reign and the coming of his true king (Matthew 3:1-3, 11, 12).

John had clearly identified Jesus as that promised king and had witnessed God's affirmation of Jesus as beloved Son (Matthew 3:13-17). John had been imprisoned for his declaration that Herod Antipas, ruler of Galilee, was wrong to have taken his brother's wife as his own (11:2a; 14:3, 4). John became distressed and sent messengers to ask Jesus whether he was indeed the promised king, as John had previously proclaimed (11:2b, 3). John's question expressed either doubt or impatience as he languished in prison.

Jesus' response affirmed that he was indeed the promised coming one (Matthew 11:4, 5). But what did that imply about John? Had his impatience or doubt demonstrated him to be a failure as God's prophet?

I. John the Baptist
(MATTHEW 11:7-15)
A. A Reed, a Royal (vv. 7, 8)

7. As John's disciples were leaving, Jesus began to speak to the crowd about John: "What did you go out into the wilderness to see? A reed swayed by the wind?

Concurrent with the departure of John the Baptist's *disciples* (see Lesson Context), Jesus speaks to *the crowd* regarding their attitude toward *John*. This large group likely includes those who already consider themselves students of Jesus, others who are merely curious about his power and teachings, and still others who are skeptical or even hostile.

Jesus' rhetorical questioning expects his audi-

ence to scoff at the idea that John has been timid. Certainly he is no easily shaken *reed,* bowing over in whatever *wind* came along. John boldly told the prominent and self-satisfied that they have no standing with God unless they repent (Matthew 3:7-10).

8. "If not, what did you go out to see? A man dressed in fine clothes? No those who wear fine clothes are in kings' palaces.

Being made entirely by hand, *clothes* in the ancient world were expensive. Ordinary people owned few garments, and those few were made of scratchy, uncomfortable fibers. Softer fabrics were too expensive for any but the wealthiest.

John's characteristic garb is made of camel's hair and is bound with a leather belt (Matthew 3:4). This perhaps imitates Elijah, the prophet who boldly confronted Israel's wicked King Ahab (2 Kings 1:1-8).

John's clothes are anything but *fine*! The contrast in clothing with that of people who live *in kings' palaces* points to a difference in lifestyle. John is a bold spokesman for God; are people able to look past his attire and see that? Individuals with a worldly agenda may try to get what they want by flattery (example: Acts 12:19b-22), but that won't work with John the Baptist! His attire suggests that he has nothing and wants nothing of earthly value.

> **What Do You Think?**
> ▶ What distinctive thing could you do this week to demonstrate a faithfulness to God when it would conflict with cultural expectations?
> **Digging Deeper**
> Contrasting Matthew 15:12-14 with 17:27, how do you gauge when the offense caused by going against cultural expectations will do more harm than good?

❧ *JUDGING APPEARANCES* ❧

Have you ever found yourself in front of a fruit stand, searching for the shiniest apple or the largest orange with the brightest color? You finally choose one, the best you can find, only to get home and discover it is no good on the inside.

It is either not quite ripe, or it has decayed inside and is no longer fit for consumption. Another, less beautiful fruit might have been the better choice after all.

Jesus asks in Matthew 11:7, 8, "What did you go . . . to see?" He tells us that men in fine clothing are to be found in kings' palaces, not in wilderness areas. Only earnest seekers would be able to look past John the Baptist's rough clothing to the truth he taught. His garments weren't sewn with gold stitching and his grooming was not up to par, but his message was!

When you hear the gospel preached, what matters more: the outward appearance of the messenger or the quality of the message itself?　—P. M.

B. A Prophet, a Messenger (vv. 9-15)

9a. "Then what did you go out to see? A prophet?

Having exposed as absurd the fictitious reasons for seeking out John, Jesus begins to offer the real one. People went to the wilderness to hear John the Baptist because they believed him to be God's *prophet* (Matthew 14:5; 21:26; Luke 1:67, 76), someone empowered to speak for God.

Often we associate the work of prophets with predicting the future. Certainly the biblical prophets did speak about the future (example: Isaiah 9:1-7). But their primary work was not prediction but proclamation (example: 1:10-15). The prophets were God's spokesmen in their own day and time, declaring to their own generations what God was doing or was about to do (example: 2 Kings 19:5-7).

Prophecies of all kinds were concerned with various aspects of God's promises. Having been taken captive by hostile nations, the Israelites heard the prophets promise that God would free them from captivity and return them to their homeland (examples: Isaiah 44:26; Jeremiah 16:15; Zechariah 10:6). This deliverance was to be so exceptional that it would demonstrate to the nations that Israel's God was and is the only true God (example: Isaiah 2:1-5).

Because this promised act of God so closely resembled his deliverance of Israel from slavery in Egypt, the prophets could speak of it in similar terms (example: Isaiah 4:2-6). God had visited his people in their distress in Egypt, defeating the rulers of Egypt and bringing his people into the promised land (Exodus 15; Joshua 1); he would do so again (Deuteronomy 30:1-10).

9b, 10. "Yes, I tell you, and more than a prophet. This is the one about whom it is written: 'I will send my messenger ahead of you, who will prepare your way before you.'

Jesus can affirm that John is *more than a prophet* because his appearance on the scene fulfills the promise of Malachi 3:1. God himself is the one who sends his *messenger ahead of* Jesus. Jesus has declared that he is the one about whom John spoke (Matthew 3:11). If John's role is to prepare the way for the Lord, and if John has indeed prepared the way for Jesus, then logically it follows that Jesus is the Lord, living among his people.

John's announcement of the nearness of God's kingdom and the coming of God's true king is the announcement that the Messiah's reign is about to begin (Matthew 3:1, 2; John 3:27-30). Other prophets had articulated this promise (example: Zechariah 9:9, 10). To John the Baptist has fallen the duty to proclaim that it was about to be fulfilled (Mark 1:2-4).

> *What Do You Think?*
> ▶ What's the most important thing you can do this week to prepare for the gospel message to be received favorably in your circle of influence?
> *Digging Deeper*
> Considering 1 Corinthians 12:12-31, in what way(s) might your response differ from that of other Christians?

11. "Truly I tell you, among those born of women there has not risen anyone greater than John the Baptist; yet whoever is least in the kingdom of heaven is greater than he.

In using the word *truly,* Jesus introduces this proclamation with an expression that affirms his trustworthiness (Matthew 5:18; 6:2, 5, 16; 8:10). But the declaration itself is very difficult for his audience to understand because it seems self-contradictory: first, Jesus says that *John the Baptist* is "more than a prophet" (see 11:9b, above), which places him among the greatest people in history. How then can someone who *is least in the kingdom of heaven* be *greater than he*?

Jesus is challenging his audience to rethink their understanding of the kingdom of Heaven (compare Matthew 5:3, 10, 19, 20; etc.). Jesus' contemporaries believe that the kingdom God will establish is to be a political continuation of David's throne (example: Acts 1:6). This interpretation means that Judah and Israel are to be restored as a united kingdom in political power, not subject to Rome or anyone else.

But God's intentions are much broader than that: his kingdom is his promised reign over the world (Philippians 2:10, 11), his restoration of wholeness to the world that currently suffers under the curse and brokenness of sin. It is the full realization of God's promises to all people.

Jesus spoke of God's kingdom in terms of three time frames: near, here, and yet to come. Like John the Baptist, Jesus speaks of God's reign as "near" (Luke 21:31). But as Jesus heals and drives out demons, he is more likely to be speaking of God's kingdom as already present (example: Matthew 12:26-28). And as he speaks of what his followers come to understand as his return, he speaks of the kingdom as a future reality (7:21-23).

From the perspective of the kingdom as either near or future, Jesus can speak of John as less than the least in God's kingdom. John is the herald of God's kingdom, first announcing its nearness. But he is not yet a subject of that kingdom in terms of its future reality, for it has not yet arrived in that sense. God has done great things through John, but God will do greater things through and for the subjects of God's kingdom by way of Jesus' death and resurrection (John 14:12).

12. "From the days of John the Baptist until now, the kingdom of heaven has been subjected to violence, and violent people have been raiding it.

Jesus follows one challenging saying with another that is even more challenging. The idea that God's *kingdom* can suffer *violence* seems absurd. How could the rule of the Almighty be challenged by anyone? Jesus seems to refer to the world's treatment of citizens of God's kingdom. One example is how Herod Antipas has imprisoned John the Baptist for speaking out against Herod's sin (Matthew 11:2; 14:3, 4). Herod later will have John killed (14:9, 10). Jesus himself will eventually be arrested and crucified (26:50-56; 27:32-50). Looking further into the future, Jesus has already spoken of the opposition that his followers will face (10:16-31).

God's kingdom is great, but until it comes in its fullness, God's people experience great hardships. God's kingdom enters the world in Jesus, but the fullness of God's reign, including the complete defeat of evil, awaits Jesus' return. Until then, Jesus' followers experience the blessing and power of God's reign in the midst of a world that opposes them and the king they serve. It is not an "all at once" kingdom. It is an "already but not yet" kingdom.

13. "For all the Prophets and the Law prophesied until John.

The Prophets and the Law is an expression referring to Israel's Scriptures that Christians call the Old Testament. Jesus says that John's work was the climax of the message of those books. Jesus speaks of the Old Testament in its entirety—the stories of the patriarchs and the nation of Israel, the laws, the teachings of the prophets—as coming together as a message of promise. They announced this promise *until John*, who was directed by God to announce the soon-to-be fulfillment of the promise.

14. "And if you are willing to accept it, he is the Elijah who was to come.

Underlining this point, Jesus identifies John as *Elijah*. That prophet had confronted the evil leaders of his day with the reality of God's powerful authority (example: 1 Kings 18:16-40). Generations later, the prophet Malachi promised that one

HOW TO SAY IT

Ahaziah	Ay-huh-*zye*-uh.
Herod Antipas	*Hair*-ud *An*-tih-pus.
Messiah	Meh-*sigh*-uh.
Malachi	*Mal*-uh-kye.
Nazirite	*Naz*-ih-rite.

like Elijah would appear as the forerunner of God's promised rule (Malachi 4:5, 6). John is this promised prophet like Elijah, the one who announces the fulfillment of God's long-awaited promises.

15. "Whoever has ears, let them hear."

Jesus sometimes ends a discourse with this word of warning and encouragement (Matthew 13:9, 43; Mark 4:9, 23; 7:16; Luke 8:8; 14:35). The saying encourages hearers to think carefully about what they have heard and to respond appropriately to the challenge it poses (contrast Mark 4:12).

> *What Do You Think?*
> What can you do to ensure that you do not become hard of hearing in a spiritual sense?
> *Digging Deeper*
> What would you say are the number 1, 2, and 3 causes of spiritual deafness?

II. This Generation
(MATTHEW 11:16-19)
A. Like Children (vv. 16, 17)

16. "To what can I compare this generation? They are like children sitting in the marketplaces and calling out to others:

The phrase *this generation* and expressions like it appear often in Jesus' teaching. He uses the phrase to focus on those who reject his message despite their having witnessed his mighty acts of power (Matthew 12:39-45; 17:17).

Though Jesus' contemporaries may not realize it, their refusal to trust God parallels the same attitude of their ancestors during the exodus. That refusal resulted in wandering in the wilderness until the generation died off (Numbers 26:62-65; 32:13).

17. "'We played the pipe for you, and you did not dance; we sang a dirge, and you did not mourn.'

Certain children in the marketplace call out to each other to express frustration that the other children will not respond to their playful activities. They have played a dance tune on their flutes, but the other children *did not dance*. So the children began to wail as at a funeral, but the other

children still did not join in. Regardless of the situation, the other children never offer the expected response. The idea seems to be that the generation Jesus is criticizing wants him to dance to their tune. But that doesn't happen.

> *What Do You Think?*
> What will motivate you to conquer stubbornness with trust?
> *Digging Deeper*
> In what situations have you seen people refusing to trust because of stubbornness? What do you learn from this?

❧ PLAY BALL! ❧

When I was young, summer days were full of outdoor sports. Sometimes we played until the streetlights came on, and then a few minutes more, testing the very limits of our parents' patience. But sometimes those games ended quickly. A kid on the losing team would yell, "I'll take my ball and go home!" When the sore loser was the only one with a ball—game over.

I've seen that same behavior manifested in adults, including Christians. People fight to have their way, stomping their feet; they storm out whenever the minister doesn't give them what they want. Instead of acting appropriately, they ignore everything but their own desires.

Children want their way and pout when it doesn't happen. Adults who act like this do not have ears to hear God. We become as children who can't see beyond their own wants. As adults, which describes us: those who look to God's desires or those who expect him to meet ours?   —P. M.

B. Like Fools (vv. 18, 19)

18. "For John came neither eating nor drinking, and they say, 'He has a demon.'

The two actions of the children in the marketplace suggest the contrast that Jesus now makes. John the Baptist lived under the vow of the Nazirite, refusing wine (Numbers 6:4; Luke 1:15) and adopting a diet symbolic of a great crisis (Matthew 3:4), refusing ordinary food. Jesus describes those who reject John's message as justifying their refusal by claiming that his strange actions indicate that he is possessed by *a demon*. Like the children just noted, John refuses to dance to their tune.

19. "The Son of Man came eating and drinking, and they say, 'Here is a glutton and a drunkard, a friend of tax collectors and sinners.' But wisdom is proved right by her deeds."

Jesus, by contrast, is known to attend banquets given by those on the margins of society (example: Matthew 9:9, 10). *Tax collectors* work for Rome and are regarded by fellow Jews as having forfeited their standing in God's people. *Sinners* are notorious in their communities for violating God's law. In contrast to John, Jesus is called *a glutton* and *a drunkard* for his association with such people at meals. Jesus, of course, has an explanation: he has come to save just such people (9:12, 13).

Visual for Lesson 5. *When considering verses 18 and 19, point to this visual and ask how its caption applies to different ministry approaches.*

What Do You Think?
How can you better equip yourself to refute the error in logic that Jesus is pointing out?
Digging Deeper
In what circumstances, if any, should you react as Paul did in Acts 18:6 when the message you bring is rejected? Why?

For those unwilling to heed God's wisdom, no messenger is good enough. Note the wrongheaded criticisms: John is too strict with himself and thus has a demon; Jesus is too indulgent. But God is at work in both, bringing his promises to fulfillment. The people of *wisdom*, those who responded to John and Jesus in faith, will prove the truth of what those two proclaim.

Conclusion

A. Paradox of God's Kingdom

If we think that the wisdom of God is bound to meet with universal acceptance, the New Testament tells us otherwise. The gospel has always been sharply divisive. Jesus inspired joyous faith from many but received powerful, even violent, opposition from others. God's wisdom appeals to some people as it addresses their deepest needs. But it repels others as it challenges their self-rule.

For those expecting a kingdom to come with

military and political power, Jesus seemed the opposite of God's true king. For those who expected God to bring an immediate end to injustice and suffering, Jesus' idea of God's kingdom seemed absurd. But for those with ears to hear and eyes to see, Jesus brings the fulfillment of every divine promise and the answer to every human need. That he was rejected comes as no surprise to us, for God's messengers have always been rejected by many.

How do you deal with the tension of God's kingdom, which is both "now" and "yet to be"? Circumstances can prove discouraging at times, but trusting that Christ reigns now and will reign fully in the future can provide strength and encouragement to meet even the biggest challenges. Those included even the challenge of Herod's prison for John and the challenge of the cross for Jesus. In the strength we have in Christ, we witness the vindication of God's wisdom.

B. Prayer

Father, as we rely on your power in good times and bad, teach us to trust your wisdom. May we not be so self-centered that we fail to hear your wisdom—wisdom that corrects wrong ideas and expectations. We pray in Jesus' name. Amen.

C. Thought to Remember

What seems like foolishness to humans is sometimes the wisdom of God.

INVOLVEMENT LEARNING

Enhance your lesson with NIV Bible Student (from your curriculum supplier) and the reproducible activity page (at www.standardlesson.com or in the back of the NIV Standard Lesson Commentary Deluxe Edition).

Into the Lesson

Have the following displayed on the board, and ask for responses as learners arrive:

What non-politician is the media currently reporting as creating controversy?

Jot responses on the board. Then select one entry and ask, "Why does this person create such different reactions among various groups?" Keep the discussion short.

Make a transition by saying, "Controversial figures have emerged throughout history. Today we'll explore differing opinions about the person and ministry of John the Baptist."

Option. Before learners arrive, place in chairs copies of the "Puzzling" exercise from the activity page, which you can download. Conduct an agree/disagree discussion as appropriate.

Into the Word

Distribute handouts (you prepare) that feature two blank columns and two blank rows. Have the left column headed *John the Baptist* and the right column headed *Jesus*. Title the first row *How they differed in lifestyle*. Title the second row *The logic people used to reject them*. Reproduce the same chart on the board. Encourage learners to use their handouts as note takers as they work through the text. Have a volunteer read Matthew 11:1-5 as a lead-in to the lesson text. Use the Lesson Context to ensure that students grasp the circumstances.

Invite a student to read Matthew 11:7, 8. Ask learners to define the term *rhetorical question*. Jot responses on the board. (This is a question that is asked without expectation of receiving an answer.)

Then form learners into small groups to engage in a *What's So/So What?* exercise. For the *What's So* part, groups are to decide whether Jesus' questions were or were not rhetorical in nature. For the *So What?* part, groups are to decide what difference it makes whether the questions were rhetorical in

nature. (Create handouts of these instructions if you think your class needs to have them in written format.)

After whole-class discussion of results, read Matthew 11:9-14 aloud. Then announce a small-group speed drill of this question: "What are the facts about John the Baptist as recorded in Scripture passages other than this one?" Have learners rejoin their groups to come up with group-based answers. Announce scoring of one point per fact and one point per Scripture reference that establishes that fact (time limit: four minutes). After calling time, poll the groups to determine the winner. Check results against your own research done during your preparation to teach the lesson.

At an appropriate point, sketch a bridge on the board with the words of Matthew 11:15 written beneath it. Ask how that verse can be seen as a bridge that connects the verses prior to it with those that follow. Allow up to a minute of dead silence to allow students time to think. If there are no responses, offer a hint *only* after a minute of silence. Then discuss Jesus' comparisons in verses 16-19 and how they are connected to his descriptions in verses 7-14.

Option. As a post-test, distribute copies of the "Correcting Falsehood" quiz from the activity page. Allow learners to score their own results after one minute.

Into Life

Distribute handouts (you create) on which are printed these words and phrases:

saving money / choosing friends / spending money / monetary giving / priorities in time expenditures / parenting / marriage / diet / exercise / [other]

Have learners circle the one area in which they most lack godly wisdom and jot down a "what's next" action to begin an improvement plan. Allow sharing from those who desire to do so.

THE BOY
JESUS

DEVOTIONAL READING: Leviticus 12:1-8; Numbers 3:11-13
BACKGROUND SCRIPTURE: Ecclesiastes 3:1-15; Luke 2:39-52

ECCLESIASTES 3:1, 7B

[1] There is a time for everything,
and a season for every activity under
the heavens.

. . . .

[7b] A time to keep silence, and a time to
speak.

LUKE 2:39-52

[39] When Joseph and Mary had done everything required by the Law of the Lord, they
returned to Galilee to their own town of
Nazareth.

[40] And the child grew and became strong; he
was filled with wisdom, and the grace of God
was on him.

[41] Every year Jesus' parents went to Jerusalem for the Festival of the Passover. [42] When he
was twelve years old, they went up to the festival, according to the custom. [43] After the festival was over, while his parents were returning
home, the boy Jesus stayed behind in Jerusalem, but they were unaware of it. [44] Thinking

he was in their company, they traveled on for a
day. Then they began looking for him among
their relatives and friends. [45] When they did
not find him, they went back to Jerusalem to
look for him. [46] After three days they found
him in the temple courts, sitting among the
teachers, listening to them and asking them
questions. [47] Everyone who heard him was
amazed at his understanding and his answers.
[48] When his parents saw him, they were astonished. His mother said to him, "Son, why have
you treated us like this? Your father and I have
been anxiously searching for you."

[49] "Why were you searching for me?" he
asked. "Didn't you know I had to be in my
Father's house?" [50] But they did not understand
what he was saying to them.

[51] Then he went down to Nazareth with them
and was obedient to them. But his mother treasured all these things in her heart. [52] And Jesus
grew in wisdom and stature, and in favor with
God and man.

KEY VERSE

The child grew and became strong; he was filled with wisdom, and the grace of God was on him.
—Luke 2:40

• 385

MANY FACES OF WISDOM

Unit 2: Wisdom in the Gospels

LESSONS 5–8

LESSON AIMS

After participating in this lesson, each learner will be able to:

1. Recall key elements of the story of the boy Jesus in the temple.

2. Explain how Jesus' defying of expectations was grounded in his unique nature and calling.

3. Write a prayer of commitment to choose godly wisdom over secular wisdom at all times.

LESSON OUTLINE

Introduction
  A. Raising a Child Star
  B. Lesson Context: Ecclesiastes
  C. Lesson Context: Luke
I. Wisdom in Seasons (ECCLESIASTES 3:1, 7b)
  A. In All Things (v. 1)
    There's a Reason for a Season
  B. In Speech (v. 7b)
II. Wisdom in Exceptions (LUKE 2:39-52)
  A. Ordinary Holiday (vv. 39-42)
  B. Disrupted Travel (vv. 43-48)
    Book Smart
  C. Precocious Saying (vv. 49, 50)
  D. Return to Ordinary (vv. 51, 52)
Conclusion
  A. Defying Expectations
  B. Prayer
  C. Thought to Remember

Introduction

A. Raising a Child Star

Ever since Shirley Temple (1928–2014) appeared in movies as a child, preteen actors have been a feature of popular entertainment. Children with exceptional talent consistently attract large audiences eager to be amazed at youngsters who can outperform adults.

Imagine being the adult who nurtures and guards such a child. It might seem that all the usual principles of parenting have to be ignored so that the child's full potential can be realized. Friends? School? Play? Discipline? There is no time for such matters when practice and performances beckon. How can caring parents ensure that the child's life is as "normal" as possible in the pressures of the limelight? The sad stories of many child stars suggest that their path to adulthood is not easy. Today's text narrates a never-to-be-repeated first-century version of this dilemma.

B. Lesson Context: Ecclesiastes

As one of the Old Testament books known as wisdom literature, Ecclesiastes explores the accumulated wisdom of its time and place. In so doing, it asks whether life has meaning. Its writer, "the Teacher" (Ecclesiastes 1:1), has long been identified as King Solomon. He alternates between principles of wise living and his own discouraged impression that "all of it is meaningless" (2:17). But in the end he concludes that the purpose of human life is to remember the Creator before our lives slip away from us (12:1). Therefore one must read the entirety of the book to glean the ultimate truth of it.

C. Lesson Context: Luke

Of the four Gospels, only Matthew and Luke give stories of Jesus' birth, and only Luke includes a story from Jesus' childhood. It comes just after the accounts of the announcement and birth of both John the Baptist and Jesus.

Luke portrays both births as vital parts of God's plan, closely linked to one another as the two men's ministries later would be linked. Even so, Jesus' uniqueness is evident from the beginning (Luke 1:32, 35; 2:11). As his story unfolds, we see that Jesus is greater than all others because he has the nature and authority of God himself (Matthew 28:18; Philippians 2:6). In Jesus, God entered the world to rescue his people (John 1:1, 9-14).

How we understand something so unusual, something that is fundamentally different from every other thing, is answered by today's text.

I. Wisdom in Seasons
(ECCLESIASTES 3:1, 7b)
A. In All Things (v. 1)

1. There is a time for everything, and a season for every activity under the heavens.

This verse introduces a meditation on the regularity of life (see all of Ecclesiastes 3:1-8). This introduction takes a form characteristic of Hebrew poetry: parallelism (see lesson 2). *Everything* and *every activity* are parallel, as are *time* and *season*. The writer considers how life begins, develops, and ends in largely consistent cycles. The wise person will understand those cycles and live in harmony with them. Since God created the emotions that attend these rhythms of life, those emotions should not be suppressed. Wise people accept even the burdensome or painful realities that we cannot change.

⁂ *THERE'S A REASON FOR A SEASON* ⁂

My husband and I were excited to have a second child. The time seemed right in every way. I was confident when I took a pregnancy test, already feeling a change in my body. Positive! I quickly called my husband. We soon told everybody in our family and at work.

I was pregnant for two months before having emergency surgery. Suddenly I had to explain to my 3-year-old daughter that her little brother or sister was not going to be with us. I had to tell my family and coworkers.

It's been 19 years since we lost our little one, and in that time my husband and I gained two beautiful children. But we still don't know why God allowed us such sorrow. Maybe it's not the season to know. Maybe we'll never know. Regard-less, we can rest peacefully in the knowledge that the Lord, the only one who needs to know, knows.
—P. M.

B. In Speech (v. 7b)

7b. A time to be silent and a time to speak.

The human capacity for communication is one of many things subject to regular patterns. We have many occasions *to speak* to one another, but no less important are occasions when speech is unnecessary, unwanted, or even harmful. In sickness or sadness, being *silent* may be more meaningful than speaking. In loving companionship, time spent in silence can be reassuring (compare Job 2:13; 13:5; 16:2, 3; etc.). And when standing before those who are older and wiser, we do well to listen silently.

> *What Do You Think?*
> Which problem do you most need to work on: recognizing when to keep silent or recognizing when to speak up?
> *Digging Deeper*
> What is your plan for improvement?

II. Wisdom in Exceptions
(LUKE 2:39-52)
A. Ordinary Holiday (vv. 39-42)

39. When Joseph and Mary had done everything required by the Law of the Lord, they returned to Galilee to their own town of Nazareth.

This verse picks up just after the small family's journey to Jerusalem to dedicate Jesus to the Lord (Luke 2:22-24). Jesus' parents have been careful to observe all that *the Law* requires for a firstborn child (example: 2:21). In the 12 years since Jesus' birth (2:42, below), Mary and Joseph undoubtedly continued the ordinary rhythms of life. These include raising their firstborn and their other children in *Nazareth* (Matthew 2:23; 13:55, 56; see lesson 7).

40. And the child grew and became strong; he was filled with wisdom, and the grace of God was on him.

Visual for Lesson 6. *While discussing verse 46, point to the visual and brainstorm ways the class can nurture these traits in younger Christians.*

We might compare and contrast Luke's depiction of Jesus' physical and spiritual growth with those of the prophet Samuel and Jesus' own cousin John the Baptist. Both of the latter seem to have developed in ways out of the ordinary (1 Samuel 2:26; Luke 1:80). But their growth in *wisdom* is not highlighted as it is with Jesus (also Luke 2:52, below). Jesus' experience of God's *grace* may compare with Samuel's "favor with the Lord" (again, 1 Samuel 2:26).

41. Every year Jesus' parents went to Jerusalem for the Festival of the Passover.

As they had faithfully observed the laws regarding Jesus' dedication, *Jesus' parents* do so again throughout his life by traveling *every year* from their home *to Jerusalem* for *Passover*. That is the annual *festival* given to Israel by God to celebrate Israel's deliverance from Egyptian slavery (Exodus 12:1-28). This observance is part of the family's annual experience, along with thousands of other pilgrims. Because the temple was established in Jerusalem, the customary practice is for all faithful Israelites who can do so to go to Jerusalem to cel-

ebrate Passover (Deuteronomy 16:1-8; 2 Chronicles 6:4-6; Luke 22:8).

42. When he was twelve years old, they went up to the festival, according to the custom.

At the age of *twelve*, Jesus is not yet part of the adult world. But he is old enough no longer to be considered just a child. The Jewish custom of the bar mitzvah (meaning "one who is responsible for performing the commandments") to mark the passage to adulthood was not yet developed in Jesus' time. But records from the second century AD, such as the Mishnah, suggest that 13 was generally considered the age when a boy became a man.

B. Disrupted Travel (vv. 43-48)

43. After the festival was over, while his parents were returning home, the boy Jesus stayed behind in Jerusalem, but they were unaware of it.

The Passover consists of an evening feast—the Passover proper—followed by seven *days* of additional celebration—the Festival of Unleavened Bread (Leviticus 23:5, 6). Mary and *Joseph*, doubtless with thousands of other travelers, begin their journey home the next day. But in an extraordinary act for a 12-year-old, *Jesus* stays *behind in Jerusalem*, the center of Israel's devotion to God. Why he has done so is not immediately known (see Luke 2:46, below).

44. Thinking he was in their company, they traveled on for a day. Then they began looking for him among their relatives and friends.

The road north from Jerusalem, crowded with pilgrims going home to Galilee, is likely a chaotic, confusing place. Entire communities travel together, alleviating parents of specific responsibilities for older children because of the safety of their caravan. Mary and Joseph may be traveling with their respective friends, not as a couple or family, thus leaving each to assume that Jesus is with the other.

Only at the end of the day, when they make camp for the night, do the parents discover that their eldest son is not with either of them! Their first thought is that he is with other *relatives and friends*. We can imagine the fear and confusion the parents experience as they ask everyone about Jesus and receive no answers regarding his whereabouts.

45. When they did not find him, they went back to Jerusalem to look for him.

The parents have no choice but to return *to Jerusalem*. Though they surely hurry, the day-long journey back leaves no time before dark to look for the missing boy.

46. After three days they found him in the temple courts, sitting among the teachers, listening to them and asking them questions.

We cannot tell whether the *three days* include the first day of journeying away from Jerusalem. But this time frame does suggest at least two very difficult nights while Joseph and Mary do not know where their son Jesus is. These three days also foreshadow the three days between Jesus' death and resurrection (Luke 24:7).

When they find Jesus, he is *in the temple courts* where Simeon and Anna had identified him 12 years before as God's promised king (Luke 2:25-38). The temple is a magnificent structure, with a huge outer court surrounded by shaded porticoes. There people can meet for teaching and discussion of God's sacred law.

One group this particular day includes Jesus, who interacts with important *teachers* of the Scriptures (see Hebrews 5:12). The reader readily assumes that Jesus is not asking childish *questions*, which can be answered by expert teachers quickly, not requiring lengthy conversation.

> *What Do You Think?*
> Under what circumstances, if any, should you let someone wrestle with an issue for a few days rather than providing immediate relief or help? Why?
>
> *Digging Deeper*
> How do you adjust this approach for children and adults?

47. Everyone who heard him was amazed at his understanding and his answers.

The picture is clearly that of Jesus talking deeply with experts in Israel's Scriptures. A boy of 12 doing such a thing reveals an impressive interest in God's Word. Adult experts engaging the questions from a boy over several days signals the youngster's extraordinary insight.

Many Jewish boys Jesus' age are in the process of learning the text of the law by heart. Consideration of the meaning of the law often comes after this exercise. As a resident of an insignificant town in Galilee and a member of a relatively poor family, Jesus likely doesn't have many resources for his own education. Yet Jesus already has an exceptional *understanding* of the law, as evidenced by his thoughtful, informed *answers*. His grasp of God's Word apparently surpasses greatly his youthfulness. His answers will astound others even more so during his adulthood (see Matthew 7:28).

❧ BOOK SMART ❧

I learned to read at a young age. I remember riding the train at age 7 with my mother as I read an Agatha Christie mystery. A stranger asked my mother if I was actually reading the book, and I heard my mother tell her yes. The stranger pressed, "Does she understand it though?" My mother shrugged and shook her head no. At the time I was offended—of course I understood it!

Looking back, there was much about that novel and others that I didn't understand. The books contained words that I could pronounce but not define. These concealed adult themes I was too young to catch. I just filled in the blanks.

Jesus demonstrated great insight when he was just 12 years old. Though other boys were committing incomprehensible words to memory, Jesus already understood the law and could discuss it intelligently. He didn't have to fill in any blanks. At what stage are you in your Bible study? Do you understand what you're reading, or are you still just filling in blanks?   —P. M.

48. "When his parents saw him, they were astonished. His mother said to him, "Son, why have you treated us like this? Your father and I have been anxiously searching for you."

The parents' amazement at first is not that Jesus is able to talk on an expert level with teachers of the law. Rather, it is that Jesus behaves in such an unconventional way, leaving them in great fear. They have been without their son for three days, not knowing whether they would see him alive again. Jesus' mother can imagine no possible justification for her son's having acted as he has done in causing them the pain they have experienced.

C. Precocious Saying (vv. 49, 50)

49. "Why were you searching for me?" he asked. "Didn't you know I had to be in my Father's house?"

Jesus' response implies that his parents should have known exactly where he was when he was not with them: he was engaged with the things of God. The expression translated *had to be* in this verse is one that Luke often uses to indicate things that occur because of the fulfilling of God's purpose (elsewhere translated "must"; examples: Luke 4:43; 9:22; 13:33). As "a light for revelation to the Gentiles, and the glory of . . . Israel" (2:32), Jesus engages the greatest of his contemporaries to consider the true implications of God's Word. These conversations are a preview of his later disputes with the religious leaders and his final conflict with the temple authorities (22:52–23:25).

> **What Do You Think?**
> How does Luke 2:49 speak to the priorities you need to adopt or adjust?
>
> **Digging Deeper**
> How will you do that in ways other than adjusting your time expenditures?

Notably, Jesus refers to God as his *Father* in response to the implications from his mother's use of the word "father." Though it was not common for Jews in those days to call God "Father," the concept that God is the Father of Israel is important in the Scriptures (example: Deuteronomy 32:6).

Consequently, God can be called "our Father," though generally such an address is considered to be too familiar. Even so, Jesus says *in my Father's house* (compare John 2:16). This expresses Jesus' awareness of his (Jesus') unique, divine identity even at this young age. He undoubtedly knows the Old Testament Scriptures in which God refers to his promised king as his "son" (2 Samuel 7:14;

1 Chronicles 17:13; compare Psalm 2:7). He surely is also aware that the angel Gabriel had told Mary that Jesus would be God's Son (Luke 1:32, 35).

Further, Jesus expresses no surprise that his role in God's plan will cause distress to those who love him. Simeon had warned Jesus' mother that "a sword will pierce your own soul too" (Luke 2:35). Jesus' three day absence from his parents ends in a joyous but perplexing reunion.

This is only the first time that Jesus' vocation will cause his mother grief. Her grief will be all the greater when Jesus surrenders to death (John 19:25). In the wisdom of God, the solution to human brokenness is for the divine Son of God to take the punishment for humanity on himself.

The word *house* translates a phrase that is very broad in the original language. In context, it can refer to anything associated with God. Whatever Jesus does, he does as the work of God (John 5:19). This contradicts the notion that Joseph is the father with whom he should most identify (Luke 3:23; 4:22). Although Jesus is adopted by Joseph and brought up in his house (Matthew 1:25), Jesus' work of his Father does not refer to carpentry (13:55); it refers to salvation.

50. But they did not understand what he was saying to them.

Mary and Joseph know well the angelic and prophetic words spoken to describe their uniquely born son (example: Matthew 1:18-23). Yet the fulfillment of those prophecies must wait, as ordinary life demands attention. To outward appearances, Jesus is a child like any other. We safely assume that his family life mirrors that of most others in first-century Israel. That Jesus should do something so unconventional makes no sense at the time. Thus Jesus' parents cannot understand the significance of what he declares.

This is the first of many occasions when Jesus challenges his listeners with sayings they don't immediately comprehend (examples: Mark 4:1-20; 9:32). In Jesus, God is doing a work unlike anything that people expect (compare Matthew 16:15-23). God's wisdom demands that human values be turned upside down (Matthew 16:24-27; 1 Corinthians 1:18-29). His wisdom requires the almighty Son of God to take on human flesh and suffer a tortuous death to reconcile God with unworthy people (Isaiah 53; Philippians 2:6-11; 1 Peter 2:21-25). Jesus' wisdom and knowledge of God's plans challenge everything that people believe. Every difficult word that Jesus speaks provokes the listener to ponder in order to understand.

> **What Do You Think?**
> What steps can we take to better recognize when a misunderstanding that blocks communication is taking place?
> **Digging Deeper**
> How are the experiences of the disciples instructive for you in this regard (Matthew 16:5-12; John 16:16-18, 25-30; etc.)?

D. Return to Ordinary (vv. 51, 52)

51a. Then he went down to Nazareth with them and was obedient to them.

The whole family now returns to their home in *Nazareth*. The expression *went down* is used because Jerusalem is at the summit of the Judean highlands; all roads leading away from it go down in elevation. Until his ministry begins when he is "about thirty years old" (Luke 3:23), Jesus apparently remains *obedient* to his parents in some sense. This implies not acting in unexpected ways as he has on this occasion.

51b. But his mother treasured all these things in her heart.

Even though Mary does not immediately understand the implications of what has just happened, she remembers this event and ponders its meaning. She reacted the same way regarding the events of Jesus' birth (Luke 2:19). These unexpected, unique episodes can be understood only on the other side of Jesus' death and resurrection, when the wisdom of God revealed in Jesus comes to its unexpected, victorious climax (24:1-7, 25-35, 44-49; etc.). We can imagine that Mary tells these stories over and over to fellow believers in the early years of the church.

52. And Jesus grew in wisdom and stature, and in favor with God and man.

Jesus' growth *in wisdom* is again noted (compare Luke 2:40, above). Human approval is fickle; approval by God endures (3:22; etc.). God's wisdom, on display in the boy Jesus, will have the final word.

Conclusion

A. Defying Expectations

How do we comprehend something that is fundamentally different from every other thing with which we have experience? Ecclesiastes speaks of the regularity of life's cycles, showing the wisdom of understanding circumstances. Luke shows Jesus' uniqueness in how Jesus defied the conventional wisdom of those cycles as he spoke in the temple at age 12. But Jesus' words come to us as the first divine revelation from his lips at the time the uniqueness of his identity began to build.

As people called into fellowship with Jesus, Christians are to follow God's purpose in mundane, daily ways—ways that can give way suddenly to our saying and doing the unexpected. For us to expect to do only and always the unusual is not God's way. Even so, God's will can run counter to conventional expectations on many occasions. Expect the world to scold us for defying its expectations as we continue to follow in the surprising direction of Jesus' footsteps.

B. Prayer

Father, challenge us to grow in your wisdom as Jesus grew. In his name we pray. Amen.

C. Thought to Remember

Being about our heavenly Father's business is our task—no matter what.

HOW TO SAY IT

bar mitzvah (*Hebrew*)	bahr *mihtz*-vaw.
Ecclesiastes	Ik-*leez*-ee-*as*-teez.
Galilee	*Gal*-uh-lee.
Mishnah (*Hebrew*)	*Mihsh*-naw.
Nazareth	*Naz*-uh-reth.
Simeon	*Sim*-ee-un.

INVOLVEMENT LEARNING

Enhance your lesson with NIV Bible Student *(from your curriculum supplier) and the reproducible activity page (at www.standardlesson.com or in the back of the* NIV Standard Lesson Commentary Deluxe Edition*).*

Into the Lesson

Ask the class about a time they were accidentally left behind as a child or accidentally left behind a child or grandchild. Be prepared to give an example of your own if learners are slow to respond. After a few have shared, talk first about how it felt to be left behind. Then discuss how it felt to leave a child behind accidentally. What similarities are there in the two experiences?

Make a transition by saying, "Our experiences as both child and adult in this regard have one thing in common: fear. How Jesus reacted to being left behind in the temple was not one of fear, however. Today's lesson explores why Jesus responded the way he did to this event."

Into the Word

Ask for definitions of the words *identity, calling,* and *mission.* Follow by asking how the concepts relate to one another. Jot responses on the board. After reaching consensus, create three groups (or more for a large class). Assign each group one of those three concepts with regard to how it applied to Jesus; distribute handouts (you create) as follows:

Jesus' Identity Group: Read Ecclesiastes 3:1, 7b; Luke 2:39-52; and others of your own choosing. 1–How does Jesus' perception of God's will inform his true identity? 2–In what ways does his physical growth and favorable perception with God serve as a key to his identity?

Jesus' Calling Group: Read Ecclesiastes 3:1, 7b; Luke 2:39-52; and others of your own choosing. 1–What are Mary and Joseph's roles in helping Jesus fulfill his calling? 2–How does Jesus' intimate connection with his heavenly Father indicate his sense of calling? 3–How does Jesus' priority of being in God's house reveal his calling?

Jesus' Mission Group: Read Ecclesiastes 3:1, 7b; Luke 2:39-52; and others of your own choosing. 1–How does Jesus understand the priority of his mission? 2–How is Jesus' thirst to understand spiritual questions an indication of his sense of his mission? 3–What do Mary and Joseph already understand about Jesus and what do they still need to learn?

After an appropriate time for group processing, reconvene for whole-class discussion. Ask the class what overlaps exist among Jesus' calling, identity, and mission. Explore how are these overlaps similar to and different from the class members' own senses of their calling, identity, and mission. Allow time for discussion.

Alternative. Distribute copies of the "Cycles of Wisdom" exercise from the activity page, which you can download. Form groups of three or four to complete as indicated. Reconvene for whole-class compare-and-contrast of results. Distribute copies of the "Amazement" exercise from the activity page. Repeat the discussion in groups followed by whole-class discussion.

Into Life

Challenge learners in their prayer times this week as you distribute handouts (you create) that feature the following emphases:

Sunday: Focus on thanking God for your identity as his child whom he leads in wisdom.

Monday and Tuesday: Focus on thanking God for calling you to be part of his family and for wisdom you need to do the work he has given you to do in his kingdom.

Wednesday and Thursday: Focus on thanking God for his mission of love in the world and for wisdom to recognize him at work.

Friday and Saturday: Pray for wisdom to live in a right relationship with God, others, and the world.

Close by having learners write a prayer of commitment to choose godly wisdom over secular wisdom at all times.

THE WISDOM
OF JESUS

DEVOTIONAL READING: Mark 7:14-23
BACKGROUND SCRIPTURE: Mark 6:1-6; 7:1-23

MARK 6:1-6

¹ Jesus left there and went to his hometown, accompanied by his disciples. ² When the Sabbath came, he began to teach in the synagogue, and many who heard him were amazed.

"Where did this man get these things?" they asked. "What's this wisdom that has been given him? What are these remarkable miracles he is performing? ³ Isn't this the carpenter? Isn't this Mary's son and the brother of James, Joseph, Judas and Simon? Aren't his sisters here with us?" And they took offense at him.

⁴ Jesus said to them, "A prophet is not without honor except in his own town, among his relatives and in his own home." ⁵ He could not do any miracles there, except lay his hands on a few sick people and heal them. ⁶ He was amazed at their lack of faith. Then Jesus went around teaching from village to village.

KEY VERSES

When the Sabbath came, he began to teach in the synagogue, and many who heard him were amazed. "Where did this man get these things?" they asked. "What's this wisdom that has been given him? What are these remarkable miracles he is performing? Isn't this the carpenter? Isn't this Mary's son and the brother of James, Joseph, Judas and Simon? Aren't his sisters here with us?" And they took offense at him.

—**Mark 6:2, 3**

MANY FACES OF
WISDOM

Unit 2: Wisdom in the Gospels
LESSONS 5–8

LESSON AIMS

After participating in this lesson, each learner will be able to:

1. Identify lack-of-wisdom factors in the rejection of Jesus in Nazareth.

2. Explain Jesus' response to that rejection.

3. Make a plan to identify and change one besetting tendency to reject godly wisdom.

LESSON OUTLINE

Introduction

A. Ordinary and Familiar

"Familiarity breeds contempt" is a very old saying. Over time, we become so accustomed to the things we experience frequently that we lose respect for them. Though outsiders remain in awe, those of us who have experienced a wonder over and over can cease to realize it *is* a wonder. Imagine the children of a great chef. Do they realize how good their family meals are? Extraordinary talent risks being rendered ordinary simply through everyday exposure.

Jesus, though extraordinary, seemed ordinary in many ways. He was born into a poor family from an insignificant village. For most of his life, he received no notice. In what we call his public ministry, he attracted great support as a rabbi and prophet, but also great opposition. In his lifetime, Jesus was known only in his own small part of the world. Worst of all, he died the shameful, tortuous death of a notorious criminal.

Today's text narrates one of the most dramatic instances in which people respond to Jesus out of their familiarity with his ordinariness. We will wonder how anyone could have ignored how exceptional Jesus was, but we will also realize our own tendency to take for granted our Lord who has become so familiar.

B. Lesson Context

Mark's Gospel is the shortest of the four accounts of Jesus' life in the New Testament. Its focus on Jesus' mighty deeds exposes a contrast between the faith of some and the disbelief of others.

Mark begins his Gospel with stories highlighting the joyous excitement of people who are blessed by Jesus' healing (Mark 1:21-34, 40-45). But soon we see religious leaders who object to Jesus' words and deeds (3:1-6). Confronted with danger, the 12 disciples Jesus had appointed (3:13-19) failed in their faith (4:35-41).

In the middle of a very mixed set of responses to his ministry, Jesus tells a parable of seed falling on different kinds of soil (Mark 4:1-9). The varying results represent different responses of faith and unbelief to God's good news (4:10-20). Jesus' experience at home leads us to today's text. (Matthew 13:53-58 and Luke 4:16-30 are parallel.)

I. Homeward Bound
(Mark 6:1)
A. Travel (v. 1a)
1a. Jesus left there and went to his hometown,

Jesus leaves the place near the Sea of Galilee where he had raised a girl from the dead (Mark 5:21, 35-43). From there, he travels about 15 miles west toward *his hometown,* specifically the village of Nazareth. Though Jesus had been born in Bethlehem (Matthew 2:1; Luke 2:4-7), his parents lived in Nazareth and had returned to the town when Jesus was very young (Matthew 2:22, 23; Luke 2:39). Throughout his life, therefore, Jesus is known as "Jesus of Nazareth" (Mark 1:24; 10:47).

Nazareth was a small agricultural village in Jesus' time, in no way famous or influential. Nearby was the prosperous city of Sepphoris, a booming market town. By comparison, Nazareth was a sleepy place with mostly poor farmers and tradespeople in residence.

> **What Do You Think?**
> What preparations might a Christian make to ensure that interactions with hometown folks have the best chance of being taken in a positive way?
> **Digging Deeper**
> Which of those preparations would be appropriate and inappropriate in non-hometown contexts? Why?

B. Companions (v. 1b)
1b. accompanied by his disciples.

Mark draws attention to the *disciples* accompanying Jesus, although they will play no direct role in what is about to happen. Even so, the incident will undoubtedly make a lasting impression on them. Perhaps they will see a connection when Jesus later warns them about sheep among wolves (Matthew 10:16).

II. Neighbors Weigh In
(Mark 6:2, 3)
A. New Information (v. 2)
2a. When the Sabbath came,

The Sabbath is a key observance for the people of Israel. Established in the Law of Moses (Exodus 20:8), its requirement is simple: to rest the entire day, doing no work (20:9, 10).

This day of rest looks back on two of the most important events in God's work: his creation of the world (Exodus 20:11), and his deliverance of Israel from slavery in Egypt (Deuteronomy 5:15).

2b. he began to teach in the synagogue,

The Law of Moses has no requirements for the people of Israel to gather on the Sabbath, only to rest. But during the Babylonian exile, when the people were far from their homeland and the (destroyed) temple (2 Kings 25:8-12), the custom of gathering on the Sabbath began. It became a day to hear the sacred books read aloud and to pray together.

This practice developed and became commonplace over time. It eventually took root in Israel's homeland as the Jewish people returned from exile.

In Jesus' time, *synagogue* services were probably very simple. From what we read in ancient sources, they appeared to include readings from the Law and from the Prophets (Acts 13:15) and a discourse of teaching and exhortation. An example of this is found in Luke's parallel account. In that longer account of the same event, Luke reveals that Jesus reads from and speaks about Isaiah 61:1, 2 (Luke 4:16-22).

Because the gatherings are simple and not prescribed by the law, the opportunity to speak seems to be available to any adult male member of the faith who is present. (Women addressing any public assembly that includes men is seen as inappropriate in the culture of the time.) Praying and singing or chanting is likely also practiced.

Though formal training and expertise are available (example: Acts 22:3), such qualifications are not necessarily expected for a synagogue teacher. For this reason, Jesus is often able to enter a synagogue meeting on a Sabbath and

DON'T DESPISE WISDOM!

Visual for Lesson 7. *While discussing verse 3d, point to this visual as you ask for examples of how rejecting wisdom ultimately harms those who do so.*

offer an address to the people gathered (Mark 1:21, 39; 3:1-6).

2c. and many who heard him were amazed.

People are often *amazed* at Jesus' teaching and mighty acts. But Mark records different kinds of astonishment. Some is from confusion (example: Mark 10:24-26), but more generally it is surprise at the authority of Jesus' teaching and acts (examples: 7:37; 11:18). As this account begins, we are reminded of the amazement at a similar synagogue message in Capernaum (1:21, 22). That incident resulted in faith that God was doing great things in Jesus.

2d. "Where did this man get these things?" they asked. "What's this wisdom that has been given him? What are these remarkable miracles he is performing?

But the nature for the amazement differs in this instance: the people of Nazareth wonder about the source and nature of Jesus' *wisdom*. Though we do not know what Jesus is saying to elicit this response, we can infer from earlier chapters that he speaks about the nearness of God's kingdom (Mark 1:15) as he asserts his own authority within

HOW TO SAY IT

Galilee   *Gal*-uh-lee.
Nazarene   *Naz*-uh-reen.
Nazareth   *Naz*-uh-reth.
Sepphoris   *Sef*-uh-ris.

that kingdom (examples: 2:8-12, 28). In Luke's parallel account, Jesus announces that he is fulfilling the promises of God given to the prophet Isaiah (Luke 4:17-21). Such claims are good news, if they are true. Reasons for the people's skeptical amazement come next.

B. Old Knowledge (v. 3)
3a. "Isn't this the carpenter?

Jesus based his ministry in Capernaum (Matthew 4:13). But for those who had lived alongside Jesus in his hometown of Nazareth, the claims he makes seem incredible. They know him as a common *carpenter*. This is an honorable trade, but a very ordinary one.

> *What Do You Think?*
> What are some good ways to sidestep the question "What do you do for a living?" so that the one asking it doesn't develop misconceptions based on your occupation?
> *Digging Deeper*
> In what circumstances might voicing one's past or present occupational credentials serve to advance the gospel (compare Acts 23:6)?

3b. "Isn't this Mary's son

The skeptics know Jesus' family. This knowledge suggests to them that Jesus should not have any special knowledge beyond his trade. They discount that Jesus might be more than the one whom they knew as he was growing up.

If the skeptics acknowledge that the origin of both his wisdom and mighty works is God, it would answer their question of the previous verse. In Mark's Gospel, neither Jesus' birth nor his adoptive father, Joseph, is ever mentioned directly, and this passage is no exception. Referring to a man as the son of his mother may imply that the father is deceased. However, it also may imply in this culture that the son was born out of wedlock, the father perhaps unknown. Jesus, born of a virgin, doubtless appears at least to some to be the result of an illicit sexual encounter; divine revelation establishes otherwise (Matthew 1:18-25; Luke 1:26-38), but the skeptics may be unaware of this or disbelieve it. So as the skeptics refer to Jesus as

Mary's son, they may be implying that Jesus' conception was dishonorable. Certainly they feel confident that they know of his origin.

3c. "and the brother of James, Joseph, Judas and Simon? Aren't his sisters here with us?"

Beginning sometime in the second century AD, some Christians concluded that Mary remained a virgin her entire life. To explain references to Jesus' siblings, they suggest that these are cousins or other relatives, or perhaps Joseph's children from a prior marriage. However, the New Testament nowhere suggests that Mary remained a virgin after Jesus' birth, only before (Matthew 1:25). It is most reasonable to assume, as did the earliest church fathers, that those named here are Joseph and Mary's natural children, Jesus' younger half siblings.

Jesus' brothers and *sisters* are well known to the townspeople. It seems that Jesus' "mother and brothers" have moved to Capernaum with him by this time (John 2:12). That would leave *his sisters here* in Nazareth. Further, the neighbors may know that Jesus' family—especially his brothers—are not supportive of his ministry. His mother and brothers had sought to bring him home, perhaps thinking that he had lost his mind (Mark 3:21-35).

Jesus' brothers are skeptical of him throughout his earthly ministry (John 7:2-5). But he will appear to at least one of his brothers, *James,* after the resurrection (1 Corinthians 15:5, 7). James becomes not only a believer but a leader in the first-century church (Acts 12:17; 15:13; 21:18). James also writes the epistle that bears his name (see lessons 9-13). *Judas* becomes the author of the New Testament letter of Jude (see Jude 1).

3d. And they took offense at him.

The term translated *offense* occurs about 30 times in the New Testament. It frequently describes someone or something that causes a person to be faithless in some way (examples: Matthew 15:12; Mark 9:42-47; Romans 14:21). The prophet Isaiah referred to God as both a refuge for his people and the cause for them "to stumble" (Isaiah 8:14), the very idea that Mark uses here.

Though Jesus' words and deeds are evidence of his power and love, those who take *offense at him* act faithlessly because they do not understand who Jesus is. Disbelieving the implications of his reported miraculous deeds, the skeptics conclude that one who is as common as they are cannot be inspired by divine wisdom, let alone be wisdom personified (1 Corinthians 1:24). They have forgotten that God likes to use seemingly insignificant people in his work: Abram, an elderly man with no children (Genesis 15:2-5; 18:10, 11); Moses, who spoke poorly (Exodus 4:10); Ruth, a poor widow (Ruth 1:3-5; 2:2); David, an insignificant shepherd boy (1 Samuel 16:11-13); etc.

Generation after generation, God's wisdom is divisive, bringing blessing to those who believe but confirming unbelievers in their stubbornness and consequent judgment. Jesus' appearance becomes the supreme example of that pattern.

> ### What Do You Think?
> What are some good ways to sidestep the question "Where are you from?" so that the one asking it doesn't develop misconceptions based on where you grew up?
> ### Digging Deeper
> On the other hand, in what circumstances might proclaiming the place of one's origin serve to advance the gospel (compare Acts 21:39)?

❧ GROWING UP AND AWAY ❧

I did not travel far from home for college. The short distance made it tempting to go back home often, but I resisted the urge. Over time whenever I did visit home, I began to get a real sense of how I was changing. My growth did not happen just because of what I was studying, but also because of interactions with a diverse group of peers. Being away opened my eyes to other cultures, perspectives, and lifestyles. On visits home, conversations around the dinner table would highlight how I was changing. Home was not a simple fit the way it had been before I left.

Jesus had been away from his hometown. When he returned, neighbors sensed a change in him. As Christ's followers, you too will face times when what is familiar no longer feels like home. As you grow in the Lord, those close to you may no longer understand you. Do not be discouraged when that happens. Jesus understands exactly what you are going through.   —L. H-P.

III. Jesus Impeded
(MARK 6:4-6)
A. Like a Prophet (v. 4)

4. Jesus said to them, "A prophet is not without honor except in his own town, among his relatives and in his own home."

This saying is attested in other ancient Jewish and Greek texts. As the proverb well describes Israel's history of persecuting God's messengers, so *Jesus* now applies it to himself. He will apply it again as a reaction to the rejection that he will experience (Luke 13:33-35).

Jews in Jesus' day are certainly aware of the harsh treatment of prophets in their history. But whether they feel any responsibility for those martyred prophets (or are on guard against repeating that treatment regarding contemporary prophets) is unknown. The evidence in the New Testament suggests that neither concern is foremost in the social conscience; but treatment of prophets is and will be on Jesus' mind (Luke 11:47-51; etc.). Through the prophets, God had spoken to the people's forebears, but they had refused to heed the message. This was sometimes accompanied by violent treatment of God's messengers (Matthew 5:12; 23:29-31, 34).

Jesus' experience in his hometown is another instance of such rejection. It points forward to those who will conspire and call to have Jesus put to death (John 19:4-7). But in the present moment, the people's rejection of Jesus should be seen against a larger backdrop. Not everyone rejects Jesus as those *in his own town* do; outside Nazareth, large crowds follow him (Mark 2:4, 13; 3:9, 20, 32; 4:1, 36; 5:21, 24, 27). And although not everyone in those crowds is a faithful disciple, certainly some are or will be. Those who are offended by Jesus can reverse course and come to believe him. Jesus' own *relatives,* especially his brothers, will prove to be prime examples (see on Mark 6:3c, above).

B. Without Opportunity (v. 5)

5. He could not do any miracles there, except lay his hands on a few sick people and heal them.

This remark is challenging to understand. Our first inclination is to see the Nazarenes' unbelief or lack of faith in and of itself as preventing Jesus from doing *miracles* (compare Matthew 13:58). But in the preceding episode, Jesus raised a girl from the dead when the mourners around her lacked faith (Mark 5:35-43). It is more likely therefore that the Nazarenes' faithless response is followed by action that results in Jesus' leaving the village before ministering for very long. In Luke's account, we read of their attempt to throw Jesus off a cliff to his death (Luke 4:28, 29).

Due to the hostility in the town, Jesus does not attend to the sick for an extended time (Mark 1:21-34). Yet in the time he has, he still heals *a few.* Fierce rejection cannot put a stop to what God is doing in Jesus.

> *What Do You Think?*
> Under what circumstances, if any, will you be prepared to quote Mark 6:4 in reference to how hometown folks react to your witness?
> *Digging Deeper*
> What pushback must you be prepared to neutralize in doing so?

C. Without Boundaries (v. 6)

6a. He was amazed at their lack of faith.

At the beginning of the story, the people of Nazareth are astonished at Jesus' teaching and wisdom, leading to their rejection of someone they believe they know well. Jesus similarly marvels at *their lack of faith.* Though he knows the history of rejecting prophets, it is still a rude awakening to experience the same dismissal in his hometown among people he knows well and loves.

6b. Then Jesus went around teaching from village to village.

This disappointing rejection does not deter Jesus. He continues to travel *from village to village,* among people just as poor and insignificant as his former neighbors. He will be met with both enthusiasm and violent opposition. But Jesus continues forward, steadfast to complete the work that God the Father has given him.

> *What Do You Think?*
> When finding yourself in a hostile environment, how will you know whether you should stay put or move on?
>
> *Digging Deeper*
> What passages in addition to Matthew 7:6; Mark 6:11; Acts 8:1b; 16:36, 37; and 18:9-11 can help inform your answer?

❧ *REJECTION IS NOT THE END* ❧

I once had a job raising money for a nonprofit. In the beginning, I called only prospective donors. I usually received more nos than yeses. Some prospective donors were outright rude when they refused. These calls were demoralizing, but how I dealt with them affected future calls. I had to learn that just because someone had rejected my request harshly did not mean the next person would. To be successful, I had to move on from the bad calls into the next call with a positive attitude, expecting a positive outcome.

It is hard to imagine what would have happened if Jesus had allowed his hometown's rejection to stop him. There would have been no cross, no resurrection, no redemption. Thanks be to God for Christ's perseverance! Likewise, we must not consider experiences of rejection as permission to give up God's mission.   —L. H-P.

Conclusion

A. Normal Wisdom

The text leaves us to ask: Do we accept Jesus as he is? Or do we think he ought to be someone else? As we weigh the great questions of faith and unbelief, perhaps the most astonishing idea is that God did his saving work in one from a town as ordinary as Nazareth. We expect God's work to be grand. Yet in Jesus it was humble.

Far from yearning to be humble, we often long to be grand. But wanting to be extraordinary can be especially problematic for Christians. This is how God's wisdom challenges us to our core. The good news of Jesus teaches us that God's goodness is usually manifested in the lives of ordinary believers and in the fellowship of ordinary churches. The gracious goodness of God surrounds us constantly. If we expect to experience it only in grandiose ways, we will overlook his "ordinary" work in our lives.

Prosperity, victory, status, security—these do not happen in a village like Nazareth visited by a carpenter who used to live there. Such aspirations and outcomes certainly do not look like willing surrender to one's enemies and submission to an unjust execution! Yet in Jesus' humility, God's wisdom was fully expressed.

God's wisdom is similarly expressed today. It is expressed in an ordinary church witnessing to the gospel in a community, in a circle of friends who study Scripture and pray together, in the often unnoticed acts of service rendered to others in the name of Jesus, in sacrificial gifts that provide sustenance of body and spirit for those in need.

Often those who do not know the true God hold such matters in contempt. They cannot believe that people of ordinary intelligence, of limited means, and having little of what the world counts as power can be doing what God desires. Their outlook tragically reflects that of the people in Nazareth who did not believe Jesus.

But the door is not yet closed on such people of today. No place, no group, no person is ever beyond the possibility of repentance. And God always welcomes the repentant.

God still embodies his wisdom in people who appear utterly ordinary. When we feel stuck in our own ordinariness and lowliness, we can take heart that God continues to do the work of his kingdom in people like us.

B. Prayer

Almighty God, we ask you to open our eyes to see clearly the work you are doing around us, in us, and through us. In Jesus' name we pray. Amen.

C. Thought to Remember

God uses ordinary people to do extraordinary things.

INVOLVEMENT LEARNING

Enhance your lesson with NIV Bible Student *(from your curriculum supplier) and the reproducible activity page (at www.standardlesson.com or in the back of the* NIV Standard Lesson Commentary Deluxe Edition*).*

Into the Lesson

Before class, do an internet search for someone who could be described as a hometown hero. Share the information you found with the class and ask for examples they have from their own hometowns. Discuss what is required for someone to be designated that way.

Ask how stereotypes about the neighborhood or place where the hometown hero grew up shape his or her reputation one way or the other with regard to "hero" status. For example, if the area is rural, would people from urban areas acknowledge that what the person did merits "hero" status? Ask how such preconceptions add to or detract from a given person's story of achievement.

Alternative. Distribute copies of the "Wisdom Sayings" exercise from the activity page, which you can download. Have learners work in pairs to complete as indicated.

Lead into Bible study by saying, "We often limit our expectations of others based on where they come from. It was no different in Jesus' day. Let's see how he handled it."

Into the Word

Divide the class into thirds. Designate the thirds as **Neighbors' Perspective, Family's Perspective,** and **Disciples' Perspective.** Give each group a handout (you create) with the following same assignment:

Read Mark 6:1-6 from the point of view of your group name. Then fill in the blanks for these statements: Before Jesus came back to town, I thought I knew _____ about him, but I didn't. While Jesus was speaking, I was surprised to hear him say or watch him do _____. After Jesus finished speaking, my opinion had changed in the following ways: _____.
Inform groups that they are allowed to use their "sanctified imaginations" in making reasonable

entries based on what is consistent with the text of Mark 6:1-6.

After groups have had time to create entries, reconvene for whole-class discussion. Have each group summarize its perspectives. When all three sections have done so, ask the class to compare and contrast the perspectives, pointing out similarities and differences in the opinions and reactions among Jesus' neighbors, his family, and his disciples. Write answers in a simple chart on the board as they are given. Then read Mark 3:21-35 aloud and ask if that text causes any responses to be enhanced.

Into Life

Connect the Into the Word segment with Into Life by asking learners how their responses to the former suggest overlaps with the various experiences of Christians today. This question may result in dead silence and confused looks, but don't relieve any resulting silence for at least 15 seconds.

If no response is forthcoming after that amount of time, ask what any overlap suggests about potential pitfalls of knowing Jesus for a long time (*possible response:* in a mild version of the old saying "familiarity breeds contempt," a person who has been a Christian for many years may assume that he or she knows everything to know about Jesus, resulting in an overly casual approach to him). Brainstorm ways to avoid mentioned pitfalls. Jot ideas on the board.

Allow critiques of ideas only after brainstorming concludes. Go over the ideas one by one, asking learners to cite Scripture support for each. After all ideas are critiqued, call for one minute of silence for learners to identify privately in their thoughts one besetting tendency to replace godly wisdom with secular wisdom.

Option. Distribute copies of the "Follow Godly Wisdom" exercise from the activity page as a take-home.

WISDOM TO FOLLOW

DEVOTIONAL READING: Proverbs 3:13-18
BACKGROUND SCRIPTURE: Proverbs 3:17; 8:32-36; John 14:1-14

JOHN 14:1-14

[1] "Do not let your hearts be troubled. You believe in God; believe also in me. [2] My Father's house has many rooms; if that were not so, would I have told you that I am going there to prepare a place for you? [3] And if I go and prepare a place for you, I will come back and take you to be with me that you also may be where I am. [4] You know the way to the place where I am going."

[5] Thomas said to him, "Lord, we don't know where you are going, so how can we know the way?"

[6] Jesus answered, "I am the way and the truth and the life. No one comes to the Father except through me. [7] If you really know me, you will know my Father as well. From now on, you do know him and have seen him."

[8] Philip said, "Lord, show us the Father and that will be enough for us."

[9] Jesus answered: "Don't you know me, Philip, even after I have been among you such a long time? Anyone who has seen me has seen the Father. How can you say, 'Show us the Father'? [10] Don't you believe that I am in the Father, and that the Father is in me? The words I say to you I do not speak on my own authority. Rather, it is the Father, living in me, who is doing his work. [11] Believe me when I say that I am in the Father and the Father is in me; or at least believe on the evidence of the works themselves. [12] Very truly I tell you, whoever believes in me will do the works I have been doing, and they will do even greater things than these, because I am going to the Father. [13] And I will do whatever you ask in my name, so that the Father may be glorified in the Son. [14] You may ask me for anything in my name, and I will do it."

KEY VERSE

Jesus answered, "I am the way and the truth and the life. No one comes to the Father except through me."
—**John 14:6**

Many Faces of
Wisdom

Unit 2: Wisdom in the Gospels
Lessons 5–8

Lesson Aims

After participating in this lesson, each learner will be able to:

1. State an unwise reaction to Jesus' declarations.

2. Contrast that unwise reaction with Jesus' wise response.

3. Identify one way better to commit to following Jesus in a culture driven by social media.

Lesson Outline

Introduction
A. What Does God Look Like?

"What does God look like?" This is a classic question—asked by children and adults, believers and skeptics alike. It is a theme of celebrated novels and popular movies.

Deep inside we often think God looks like us—perhaps due to our reading Genesis 1:26 a certain way—but older and wiser. On the other hand, when we realize that "God is spirit" (John 4:24), it means he is invisible (1 Timothy 1:17; Colossians 1:15). He may allow created beings to see manifestations of himself at times (Exodus 24:9-11; Revelation 22:3, 4; etc.), but we cannot see his true essence (1 Timothy 6:16). To ask the question "What does God look like?" is therefore not legitimate.

Since that question shouldn't be asked, what about the question "Would you like to see God?" You might answer no because nobody can see God's face and live (Exodus 33:20). Or you might answer yes because when Christ returns, "we shall see him as he is" (1 John 3:2). Jesus' interaction with one of his disciples helps us sort through this yes-and-no desire.

B. Lesson Context

Of the four New Testament's four Gospels, John's is the most distinctive. All four agree that Jesus is the Son of God, the Messiah. When telling the gospel story, Matthew, Mark, and Luke narrate many of the same episodes, usually with very similar words. John's Gospel shares much less material with the other three and offers many teachings that are not found elsewhere. He tells of extended conversations between Jesus and his opponents, as well as between Jesus and his followers. These provide perspective on Jesus' identity and mission as the divine Son of God who became human.

John connects these conversations to Jesus' miracles, which John calls "signs" (John 4:48; 20:30; etc.) to emphasize that they point to Jesus' identity and mission. Like the other Gospels, John arranges his material to focus on Jesus' death and resurrection, in which we see Jesus' mission come to its amazing fulfillment.

Our lesson text comes near the beginning of the chapters in John's Gospel that focus on Jesus' words and actions on the night before his crucifixion (John 13–18). Much of this material is Jesus' private teaching to his followers.

Hanging over the discourse is the shadow of Jesus' looming crucifixion (John 13:1). By what seems to be Satan's defeat of Jesus (13:21-27; 19:16-30), is actually Jesus' defeat of Satan. Though Jesus would no longer be present as he had been, his followers would not be alone, for Jesus promised to send God's Holy Spirit (14:16, 17, 26). By the Spirit's power, they would continue the work that God had begun in Jesus (16:7-14).

This section of John begins as Jesus washed his disciples' feet. This was to show them, in part, that in his death he, their Lord, would be serving them (John 13:1-17). As Jesus brought his teaching to a close, he prayed for his followers, asking the Father especially that they be unified as he and the Father are unified (17:6-26). As Jesus was arrested in the Garden of Gethsemane, he was willingly surrendering to a death that would free his disciples from the guilt of sin (18:2-9).

I. The Way Introduced
(JOHN 14:1-4)
A. Believe (v. 1)

1. **"Do not let your hearts be troubled. You believe in God; believe also in me.**

When the disciples see events unfold that lead to Jesus' death, their natural reaction will be to lose heart (compare John 14:27). Jesus anticipates this reaction with a call to belief. He connects belief in God with belief in himself.

What Do You Think?
What techniques can you adopt to replace worry with trust?
Digging Deeper
Without giving directive advice, how would you use Matthew 6:25-34 to counsel a chronic worrier who says, "I'm not worried. I'm concerned."? How would you use Luke 11:24-26, if at all, to stress the replacement aspect?

In the original language, the verb translated believe, used twice, can be understood in at least two ways. One way sees Jesus as making two statements of fact: "You believe in God and you believe in me." On the other hand, some students propose that the second phrase should be seen as an imperative. Therefore Jesus is saying, "Since you believe in God, you must also believe in me." In this understanding, Jesus is urging the disciples to exercise reliant trust in himself as a logical extension of trusting the Father (compare John 3:15, 16).

Either way, Jesus is clearly defining faith in himself on the same level as faith in God. For the faithful people of Israel, there was no greater truth than that God is one (Deuteronomy 6:4). There can be no other implication: Jesus asserts that he is divine, that he is God. Faith in God and in Jesus is more than just affirming a truth. To place trust in Jesus is to place trust in God.

B. Follow the Son (vv. 2-4)
2a. "My Father's house has many rooms;

In the Old Testament, expressions about one's *house* can refer to all the members of a family or tribe (example: 2 Samuel 7:16); the word can also refer to the temple (examples: 7:6, 7, 13), the place where God's people stand in his presence. Because God is enthroned in Heaven (Deuteronomy 26:15), we can understand God's house to refer to Heaven as well.

It is not certain which way(s) Jesus intends the expression, but the end result is essentially the same. The Father has planned for his people to live forever in his caring presence. Jesus' assurance is that in God's family and in God's presence, there is a place for all his people.

Rooms translates a word that refers to a dwelling place (compare John 14:23, where the same word is translated "home"). Jesus' point here is not that Heaven is a grand place, though it certainly is, but that God has provided room for all members of his kingdom.

2b. "if that were not so, would I have told you that I am going there to prepare a place for you?

In the trials that lie ahead, the disciples will have to rely on God's faithfulness. Jesus' statement suggests that his preparing *a place for* the disciples is an important promise of God's ongoing care. They have many reasons to put their trust in God's provision. Every stage of Israel's history has demonstrated God's faithfulness. The greatest demonstration of God's faithfulness, namely Jesus' resurrection, is only a few days away.

3a. "And if I go and prepare a place for you,

We may wonder if Jesus is referring to his death or to his ascension. Both are necessary for Jesus to *prepare* an eternal *place* for his followers: Jesus' death will pay sin's price for admission into Heaven, while his ascension will result in the gift of the indwelling Holy Spirit to empower and teach his followers (John 14:26; 15:26). All that he has done and all that he is about to do is for the good of those who follow him.

❧ *DUAL PREPARATIONS* ❧

When my family moved across the country, my wife and I had a plan: she would travel to our destination a few weeks before our move date to prepare for the arrival of the rest of us. She had several tasks to perform in that regard, including meeting with her new employer. Her most important task, however, was to ensure that things were on track for our family's move into our new home. On my end, I was to pack and coordinate the move while coping with the difficulty of caring for our 4-month-old daughter by myself.

When we finally moved, we were both thankful for each other's work on the two ends. While my wife was preparing for the arrival, I was preparing for the departure. The work we both put in was necessary and complementary.

Christ has gone ahead to prepare a place for us. But this place is only for those who are preparing themselves to be there. We prepare through faith in Jesus. Exercising such faith is an everyday task that requires intentional effort. How is your preparation coming along?   —L. H-P.

3b. "I will come back and take you to be with me that you also may be where I am.

Jesus' pending departure will not be permanent. He is not abandoning the disciples, even temporarily (also John 14:18). He leaves to act on their behalf and *will come back* to complete that work.

Jesus' declaration bears some similarity to God's statement to Moses of his intent to deliver the Israelites from their captivity in Egypt (Exodus 3:8). In broad terms, God's aim throughout Scripture is that his people *be where he is*. This is a reversal of Genesis 3:23, 24. Compare Revelation 21:3:

> I heard a loud voice from the throne saying, "Look! God's dwelling place is now among the people, and he will dwell with them. They will be his people, and God himself will be with them and be their God."

Jesus takes on himself the divine role of the one to rescue and gather God's people.

4. "You know the way to the place where I am going."

Based on Jesus' ministry and teaching to this point, the disciples should understand who Jesus is and what is about to happen to him. They should realize that Heaven is both his origin and destination *(where I am going)* and that he must die *(the way)* in order that they might be admitted to their heavenly home. But "should understand" isn't the reality, as the next verse reveals.

II. The Way Revealed
(JOHN 14:5-7)
A. Thomas's Question (v. 5)

5. Thomas said to him, "Lord, we don't know where you are going, so how can we know the way?"

Thomas is one of the original apostles (see Matthew 10:2-4; Mark 3:16-19; Luke 6:13-16; Acts 1:13). When hearing his name, most Christians probably think of him primarily in terms of the unflattering designation Doubting Thomas, given his statement in John 20:25.

But two other texts also reveal his character and/or mental state. One is John 11:16, where Thomas speaks with great courage. The other is the verse before us, where he reveals that he does not understand Jesus' teaching, even though Jesus expects that the disciples already know what he is saying. Thomas is not alone in being what today we might call clueless; Jesus' disciples constantly struggle to understand his teaching (see Matthew 15:15-20; 16:5-12; Mark 4:13; 7:17, 18; John 16:25-30). Full clarity must wait until after the resurrection. Thomas won't completely grasp things until he sees the risen Lord.

B. "I Am" the Answer (vv. 6, 7)

6a. Jesus answered,

Jesus answers Thomas with what is now one of the most well-known sayings of Jesus in the New Testament.

6b. "I am the way

The word *way* translates an ordinary word that commonly refers to a pathway of some sort. This can be either a physical one (such as a highway; Matthew 22:9, 10) or a figurative—but no less real—one (example: "the way of God"; 22:16). Jesus describes himself in terms of the latter (compare John 10:9; Hebrews 10:19-22).

6c. "and the truth

God is the source of all that is true. Those who worship God must do so in truth (John 4:24). In Jesus the truth of God is supremely manifest (1:1-5, 14). There is no better or higher truth than he. All that is true comes to its focus in him.

6d. "and the life. No one comes to the Father except through me.

As God is the source of all that lives, so God's *life* is fully in Jesus (John 1:4; 5:26). To belong to Jesus is to have life (10:10), the life of eternity that transforms the present and the never-ending future (3:16). To be apart from Jesus is to be separated from life, as our first parents were separated from Eden's tree of life in their sin (Genesis 2:9; 3:22-24). There are not many ways to God—only one, and Jesus is that one (Ephesians 2:13-18).

What Do You Think?
Other than memorizing this passage, how can we guard ourselves against the false idea that there's more than one route to salvation?
Digging Deeper
How would you respond to the declaration that the "one route" view is narrow-minded?

7a. "If you really know me, you will know my Father as well.

This is a rebuke. Having followed Jesus throughout his ministry, the disciples believe that they know him. But in knowing him, they ought to know his *Father as well*. The Father is the one of whom Jesus has taught, whom he has served, to whom he has prayed, with whom he is fully united (John 1:18; 10:30; 1 John 2:23). But Thomas's words had revealed a lack of understanding.

7b. "From now on, you do know him and have seen him."

The rebuke gives way to a promise, however. From now on, the disciples do indeed *know* the Father. Jesus' resurrection will enable them to realize this even more fully. Seeing Jesus, they see God the Son, who is completely one with God the Father. Hearing this discourse of Jesus will enable the disciples to reach a new realization about the Father and the Son following resurrection morning.

❧ LIKE FATHER, LIKE SON ❧

My maternal grandfather died before I was born. I learned about him through family stories and old family albums. But hearing stories and seeing old pictures are not the same thing as making my own memories with him.

One day when I told my mother of how I wished I'd known her father, she tried to comfort me with more stories about him. Then she shared how much her eldest brother was like her father: in their facial features, their laugh and sense of humor, and their handiness.

From that day forward, I tried to spend more time with my uncle. Getting to know him seemed to be as close as I could get to knowing my grandfather.

My uncle may have been a close reflection of my grandfather, but Jesus is the *exact* image of God the Father. We can know God better by reflecting on the life and words of Jesus Christ in Scripture. Jesus reveals the very nature of God.   —L. H-P.

HOW TO SAY IT

Gethsemane   Geth-*sem*-uh-nee (*G* as in *get*).
Nazareth   *Naz*-uh-reth.

III. The Way Explained

(John 14:8-14)

A. Philip's Desire (v. 8)

8. Philip said, "Lord, show us the Father and that will be enough for us."

The apostle *Philip* has appeared three times thus far in John's Gospel: twice bringing someone to Jesus (John 1:43-48; 12:20-22) and once offering a weak answer to a probing question (6:5-7). Prompted by Jesus' words about *the Father*, here Philip expresses both a longing to see God and a failure to understand Jesus' teaching.

Philip's request reminds us of Moses when he asked to be shown God's glory (Exodus 33:18). God answered by allowing Moses only a partial vision (33:19-23).

B. God's Oneness (vv. 9, 10)

9. Jesus answered: "Don't you know me, Philip, even after I have been among you such a long time? Anyone who has seen me has seen the Father. How can you say, 'Show us the Father'?

Exasperated, Jesus points out to *Philip* what he has missed throughout Jesus' ministry: that Jesus is in complete unity with God *the Father,* expressing the divine nature fully in all that Jesus has done. God is one, so to see God the Son is to see God the Father (2 Corinthians 4:4). The Son and the Father share the same divine nature (Hebrews 1:3).

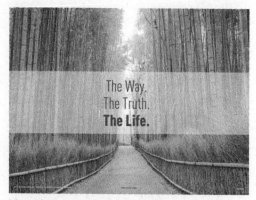

The Way.
The Truth.
The Life.

Visual for Lesson 8. *Ask the class to meditate for one minute on Jesus' words found on this visual before you close the class in prayer.*

What Do You Think?
  Using only the example of Jesus, how would
  you describe God the Father to an unbeliever?
Digging Deeper
  What are some things we are able to teach
  about God only because of Jesus?

This remarkable, paradoxical realization has led Christians who have reflected on the gospel to formulate an understanding of God called the Trinity. There is but one God. But the Father and the Son are distinct divine persons, and the Holy Spirit is also. God is one in nature but three in persons, giving and receiving perfect love without beginning or end. In this divine mystery, God is unlike any created being. Only he is both one and three in this way.

10a. "Don't you believe that I am in the Father and that the Father is in me? The words I say to you I do not speak on my own authority.

Though he is responding to Philip specifically, Jesus' question is for all the disciples to answer. He asks in such a way that expects an affirmative response. Everything that the disciples have heard and witnessed demonstrates the utter unity of God *the Father* and Jesus the Son (John 10:37, 38). Jesus fulfills the will of God. Everything that God has done has its focus and climax in Jesus.

10b. "Rather, it is the Father, living in me, who is doing his work.

The *work* to which Jesus refers includes miracles, sometimes called "signs" (compare John 2:1-11; 4:46-54; 5:1-15; 6:1-21; 9:1-12; 11:1-44). These works are from *the Father.* Miracles clearly indicate the work of God.

C. Jesus' Works (v. 11)

11a. "Believe me when I say that I am in the Father and the Father is in me;

The disciples have followed Jesus as their master, eager to receive his teaching. They should put their confidence in him now, given their previous trust, even when he challenges their very ideas of who God is.

11b. "or at least believe on the evidence in the works themselves.

Jesus' claims regarding his identity are proven by his mighty *works* (John 5:36; 10:38). The disciples have witnessed deeds that God alone can do. They can rely on what those reveal about Jesus' unity with the Father.

> **What Do You Think?**
> What spiritual guardrails can you erect to stay focused on the evidence that proves the truth of Christianity?
>
> *Digging Deeper*
> In addition to books and videos by J. Warner Wallace, what resources can you use to help you keep that focus?

D. Believers' Greater Things (vv. 12-14)

12. "Very truly I tell you, whoever believes in me will do the works I have been doing, and they will do even greater things than these, because I am going to the Father.

Very truly signals the beginning of an important assertion (examples: John 3:3; 5:19; 16:23). The challenge Jesus presents is for the disciples to imagine that what he has done will be surpassed by their own *works* (compare Matthew 21:21).

Jesus' work is the decisive inauguration of God's kingdom. But that work continues and grows in Jesus' followers. Empowered by the Holy Spirit, who will be given after Jesus' resurrection (John 15:26), the disciples are to share the good news in doing Jesus' work. By faith in their Lord, they will be able to see how God is fulfilling through them his promise to gather a people to himself.

13. "And I will do whatever you ask in my name, so that the Father may be glorified in the Son.

The followers of Jesus accomplish even greater things because they are empowered by their Lord, by the Spirit, and in answer to their prayers. To *ask* in Jesus' *name* is not merely a formula that we say at the end of a prayer. It is that we ask while believing that he has the divine authority to answer; but we are also submitting to his will and purpose. We cannot ask under Jesus' authority for that which Jesus does not want to give us. So Jesus gives here not a blank check to cash as we wish. Rather, he gives the assurance that *whatever* we need to do his work of even greater things, he will supply (Matthew 7:7-11). By this means *the Father* will *be glorified* as the world sees and hears who the Father truly is.

14. "You may ask me for anything in my name, and I will do it.

Believers have full assurance that Jesus will supply our every need. To drive the point home, Jesus repeats it.

> **What Do You Think?**
> What red flags would cause you to conclude that a certain request is of a type for which the name of Jesus should never be invoked?
>
> *Digging Deeper*
> What types of things might or might not be prayed for depending on the motives of the one who is doing the asking (James 4:3)?

Conclusion

A. To Know God, Know Jesus

In Jesus of Nazareth, we indeed see God! Fully human and fully divine, Jesus spoke and acted with authority that belongs to God alone. For this reason, his followers came to understand that God was personally present in Jesus.

The God who is incarnate in Jesus is patient, as Jesus was patient with his disciples. He is just, as Jesus was just with the mighty and the lowly. He is gracious, generous, and merciful beyond comparison, as Jesus willingly gave his life for the unworthy, even for his enemies. To know Jesus is to know God. To reject Jesus is to reject God. To follow God's path of wisdom is to follow in the path of Jesus, to love and serve as he did.

B. Prayer

Heavenly Father, as you are revealed to us in Jesus, empower us by the Holy Spirit to live according to the pattern you set forth so others see you in us. In Jesus' name we pray. Amen!

C. Thought to Remember

To know the Son is to know the Father.

INVOLVEMENT LEARNING

Enhance your lesson with NIV Bible Student *(from your curriculum supplier) and the reproducible activity page (at www.standardlesson.com or in the back of the* NIV Standard Lesson Commentary Deluxe Edition*).*

Into the Lesson

Ask the class to name popular social networking outlets. Jot responses on the board as they are mentioned. (*Responses* can include, but are not limited to, Facebook, YouTube, Instagram, Twitter, Pinterest, LinkedIn, and Tumblr.) Tally by shows of hands the outlets your learners make postings to or otherwise maintain profiles in.

Contrast your learners' ordinary uses of social media to that of someone who seeks to become a social media influencer, one of which you have researched in advance as an example. (To avoid politicizing the discussion, do not pick a politician as your example.)

Ask learners how that person's use of social media differs from their own use. If no one mentions it, state that would-be influencers attempt to have others embrace their viewpoints by building a following by leading others to click on social media's various *Like, Follow,* and *Share* buttons.

Alternative. Distribute copies of the "Building a Following" exercise from the activity page, which you can download. Have learners work in pairs to complete as indicated.

After either activity, say, "We live in a world where we constantly encounter someone saying, 'trust me.' Today's lesson will consider Jesus' invitation to do just that."

Into the Word

Ask a volunteer to read only John 14:1-4 of the lesson text. Then pose this question: What difference does it make that Jesus was speaking privately to his disciples and not at this time to large crowds—the social media of his day?

If learners are slow to respond, do not break the silence for at least 15 seconds. Puzzled looks indicate thinking; allow learners the time to process the question. Jot responses on the board. Keep your own responses to a minimum until you revisit this activity in Into Life.

Form multiples of the two following groups: The **Thomas Group** to consider John 14:5-7 and The **Philip Group** to consider John 14:8-11. Ask learners to make an "about me" profile for their respective groups' namesakes. If learners lack smartphones for research, provide Bible dictionaries or other resources as necessary.

Allow groups time to share their profiles. After they do so, draw a 10-point linear scale on the board. Label the left end *1–Unimportant* and the right end *10–Vitally Important.* Then pose this question to each group in turn: How important is today's text in establishing your namesake's profile relative to all the other texts about him? Enter results on the scale; probe for disagreements.

Discuss John 14:12-14 as a class. Launch the discussion by asking, "In what ways do these verses respond to the questions Philip and Thomas had for Jesus?" (Expect varied responses.) When learners attempt to come to grips with John 14:12, focus the class's attention on that verse. Use the commentary to clear up misconceptions. Invite examples of what the "greater things" might be.

Option. Distribute copies of the "Contrast Jesus' Statement" exercise from the activity page. Have learners complete in pairs or small groups as indicated.

Into Life

Reopen the discussion of John 14:1-4 by posing this scenario: "Suppose that tomorrow you had a private heartfelt discussion in the morning with someone regarding John 14:1-4. Then that afternoon you copy-and-pasted the text of those four verses onto a social media update stream. Which witness is likely to yield better results?"

Option. Create visual appeal of the discussion by drawing two columns headed *Advantages* and *Disadvantages* that are intersected by two rows labeled *Private* and *Social Media.* Jot responses within the resulting grid.

Faith and Wisdom

DEVOTIONAL READING: Isaiah 40:1-8
BACKGROUND SCRIPTURE: James 1:1-11

JAMES 1:1-11

[1] James, a servant of God and of the Lord Jesus Christ,

To the twelve tribes scattered among the nations:

Greetings.

[2] Consider it pure joy, my brothers and sisters, whenever you face trials of many kinds, [3] because you know that the testing of your faith produces perseverance. [4] Let perseverance finish its work so that you may be mature and complete, not lacking anything. [5] If any of you lacks wisdom, you should ask God, who gives generously to all without finding fault, and it will be given to you. [6] But when you ask, you must believe and not doubt, because the one who doubts is like a wave of the sea, blown and tossed by the wind. [7] That person should not expect to receive anything from the Lord. [8] Such a person is double-minded and unstable in all they do.

[9] Believers in humble circumstances ought to take pride in their high position. [10] But the rich should take pride in their humiliation—since they will pass away like a wild flower. [11] For the sun rises with scorching heat and withers the plant; its blossom falls and its beauty is destroyed. In the same way, the rich will fade away even while they go about their business.

KEY VERSE

If any of you lacks wisdom, you should ask God, who gives generously to all without finding fault, and it will be given to you. —**James 1:5**

Many Faces of Wisdom

Unit 3: Faith and Wisdom in James

LESSON AIMS

After participating in this lesson, each learner will be able to:

1. Identify double-mindedness as a hindrance to receiving wisdom from God.

2. Explain the connection between lacking wisdom and being "double minded" and "unstable" (James 1:8).

3. Write a prayer requesting God's wisdom while confessing the sin of double-mindedness that hinders receiving such wisdom.

LESSON OUTLINE

Introduction

A. More Informed, Less Wise

In case you hadn't heard, this is the Information Age. Everything, or so it seems, can be accessed online. From medical records to legal opinions, from academic scholarship to celebrity gossip—all is available with a simple search on your computer or phone. Countless libraries' worth of information is now publicly accessible through the internet.

But while we are glutted with information, it is right to ask exactly what we are doing with all of it. In spite of all the generalized and specialized information at our fingertips, are we any wiser as a society? This month's study—five lessons drawn from the letter of James—helps us evaluate that question.

B. Lesson Context: James the Man

There may be as many as five men by the name of James in the New Testament, so we take care not to mix them up (see Mark 1:19; 3:18; 6:3; 15:40; Luke 6:16). Tradition has taken the author of the book of James to refer to James who was the half-brother of Jesus (Galatians 1:19).

Jesus and James grew up in a large family (see Mark 6:3, lesson 7). Along with the other brothers of Jesus, James did not believe in Jesus during Jesus' lifetime (John 7:3-5). But when the Day of Pentecost arrived after Jesus' resurrection, they had come around (Acts 1:14). Paul indicates that James himself had been a witness of the risen Christ (1 Corinthians 15:3-7).

The chronology is not entirely clear, but perhaps by the mid-40s in the first century, James had become a leader in the Jerusalem church. His exact role is not specified, but Paul associates him with the apostles on at least one occasion (Galatians 1:19). Paul also lists James among the "pillars" of the church (2:9); James was a leader in a group that included apostles and elders (Acts 15).

The significance of this is heightened when we consider the centrality of Jerusalem in the thinking of the earliest Christians, who were of Jewish background. The Jerusalem church was more than just one congregation among many; it was the mother church. What happened there mattered to the entire church (example: Acts 15:4, 22-29). We see James's impact on the first-century church in the account of what is called the Jerusalem Council as he gave the final, decisive word on the matter at hand (15:13-21). That was about AD 51.

We have corroborating evidence outside the New Testament as well. According to the Jewish historian Josephus (AD 37–100),

> Caesar, upon hearing the death of Festus, sent Albinus into Judea, as procurator. . . . Albinus was but upon the road; so [the high priest Ananus] assembled the sanhedrin of judges, and brought before them the brother of Jesus, who was called Christ, whose name was James, and some others; and when he had formed an accusation against them as breakers of the law, he delivered them to be stoned (*Antiquities of the Jews*, book 20, chapter 9).

That martyrdom occurred in AD 62.

C. Lesson Context: James the Epistle

The letter of James therefore had to have been written prior to James's death in AD 62. Given the other details of his life, a reasonable supposition is that the letter was written in the 50s, making it one of the earliest of the New Testament documents. Very likely it was written from Jerusalem, given the status of the writer there (see above).

Structurally, the epistle lacks many of the features of an ancient letter, features that we see throughout Paul's letters. It opens with the standard opening features of sender, recipients, and greeting. Beyond that, however, it lacks a thanksgiving (characteristic of Paul's letters; example: Romans 1:8-10), a standard letter body, and a closing (example: Romans 16).

HOW TO SAY IT

Albinus	Al-*bay*-nuhs.
Diaspora	Dee-*as*-puh-ruh.
Festus	*Fes*-tus.
Josephus	Jo-*see*-fus.
Mediterranean	*Med*-uh-tuh-**ray**-nee-un.
Messiah	Meh-*sigh*-uh.
Pentecost	*Pent*-ih-kost.
Sanhedrin	San-huh-drun or San-*heed*-run.

The letter proceeds loosely from subject to subject, repeatedly returning to a handful of prominent topics. Those include trials (example: James 1:2-4, below), wisdom (example: 1:5-8, below), and wealth (example: 1:9-11, below).

The letter approaches Christian living from the obvious backdrop of Judaism. This is evident in the author's use of the Old Testament: he quotes from it five times (in James 2:8, 11 [twice], 23; 4:6) and alludes to it at least that many more times (see 1:10; 2:1, 21, 25; 5:11, 17, 18).

I. Enduring Trials
(JAMES 1:1-4)
A. Greeting (v. 1)

1a. James, a servant of God and of the Lord Jesus Christ,

The opening verses are seen by many as establishing the thematic foundation of the letter. At the outset, we might wonder why *James* does not refer to himself as the Lord's brother (see Lesson Context). Among other considerations, his addressees already know who he is. More importantly, by omitting his familial relationship with the Lord, James may be deliberately refraining from leveraging that status for power.

That he calls himself *a servant of God and of the Lord Jesus Christ* places him in a long and venerable tradition, which includes Moses (1 Kings 8:53), David (2 Samuel 3:18), and various prophets (Jeremiah 7:25; Daniel 9:10; Amos 3:7). James is not shying away from the authority that comes with his role as a leader in the Jerusalem church. Instead, he is laying claim to an ancient means of expressing his authority to speak on behalf of God.

> **What Do You Think?**
> What are some ways church leaders can exercise their God-given authority without being dictatorial in the process?
> **Digging Deeper**
> How should these ways differ, if at all, between exercising authority in the church and in the home?

Visual for Lessons 3 & 9. *Ask the class to focus on the text of this poster silently as they ponder what they need from God. Then close class in prayer.*

1b. To the twelve tribes scattered among the nations: Greetings.

There has been considerable debate regarding the identity of the recipients of James's letter. We wonder if the addressees are to be understood literally (in terms of ethnic Jews; compare Acts 26:7) or figuratively (in terms of Christians of any descent; compare Romans 9:6-8). Given the presence of significant Old Testament imagery (see Lesson Context: James the Epistle), it seems best to understand the addressees in the straightforward fashion.

James is therefore writing to ethnic Jews who have accepted Jesus as Messiah. They are *scattered* in communities around the Mediterranean, outside Judea. This state of affairs is commonly known as the Diaspora, the Greek word that is behind the translation "scattered" here and in John 7:35 and 1 Peter 1:1.

B. Trying Faith (vv. 2-4)

2. Consider it pure joy, my brothers and sisters, whenever you face trials of many kinds,

The imperative verb *consider* implies a thoughtfulness that not only looks *at* a situation but *through* it to its potential result. That is how it is used in 2 Thessalonians 3:15 (translated "bear in mind" in 2 Peter 3:15). *Whenever you face* is the condition for James's exhortation to *consider it pure joy.* Note the phrasing: *whenever*, not if ever. James assumes that his readers will all be tested

in some way. The only question is how to respond when the time comes. *Face* implies a sudden, unexpected encounter, as the word being translated is "attacked" in Luke 10:30 and "struck" in Acts 27:41.

The *trials* Christians face are not all one kind—Satan likes to change it up, offering a variety of unholy shortcuts (compare Matthew 4:1-10). For James, the different kinds of trials include, at a minimum, those related to personal financial status (James 1:9, 27; 2:15, 16), favoritism (2:1-4, 9), economic injustice (2:5-7), and exploitation (5:1-6). Obviously, these categories overlap to varying degrees.

The concept of facing trials or trying times is related to the idea of undergoing temptations (compare 2 Corinthians 8:2). The advice James gives might initially seem counter intuitive; for most of us, our first reaction when undergoing trials is to do the opposite of rejoicing! James knows this, of course, and he addresses this next.

3. because you know that the testing of your faith produces perseverance.

James wants his readers to realize that there is a bigger picture than the troubles they face in the moment. That bigger picture is a goal toward which all their suffering should point: the increase of *perseverance.*

It is important to understand that the perseverance James encourages is not mere passive endurance or just hunkering down until the storm passes. Rather, the perseverance James advocates is active and confident. This includes continuing to do the right thing at the right time. This kind of perseverance continues to act in love in the face of opposition.

Trials in and of themselves do not result in spiritual maturity (see Matthew 13:5, 6, 20, 21). Rather, insofar as trials call forth perseverance on our part, it is that very perseverance that will result in what James discusses next.

4. Let perseverance finish its work so that you may be mature and complete, not lacking anything.

Here is the desired result of exercising the *perseverance* just discussed. The fact that James wants his readers to *be mature and complete* is troubling to some since there was only one perfect person: Jesus (Matthew 19:21; Romans 12:2; James 1:17).

This problem has drawn at least two suggestions. One is that the maturity James has in mind is something that he sees as attainable. He clearly doesn't think of maturity as sinlessness (see James 3:2). This leaves maturity to be understood as consistent, habitual behavior rather than as a status to be obtained. In other words, the one who is mature is the one who consistently strives to overcome sinful behaviors and attitudes. Such a person, to use the language of the apostle John, "walk[s] in the light" (1 John 1:7).

A second proposal takes into account that Jesus said something similar in Matthew 5:48 (where the same Greek word is translated "perfect"). But he went further by stating that the perfection of the Father is the goal. Thus the proposal is that although we know that it's not possible for us to be perfect in this earthly life, that doesn't mean the standard should be lowered. The Father's perfection is our continuing standard.

Either way, this is how we pass life's tests.

❧ PASSING LIFE'S TESTS ❧

The tests we undergo in school or on the job can cause great anxiety. This anxiety can in turn cause poor performance so that the results of the tests don't indicate one's actual knowledge or skills. The fear of failure can be overwhelming. The result can be a vicious circle: test-anxiety results in failing the test, which in turn yields even greater test-anxiety, etc. Physical, emotional, and/or cognitive problems may be side effects.

Secular culture offers some valuable methods for overcoming anxieties that test our knowledge and skills in various areas of life. But the Bible is the source for the best answers to overcome all tests, trials, and temptations—including those unique to the Christian life.

James encourages his readers to approach our testing with a certain mind-set: remembering that God blesses those who are faithful throughout life's trials. Before testing leaves us emotionally and spiritually exhausted, we do well to look at the end result of joy in the longer-term result of spiritual growth. Try this now: Looking back to

a spiritual challenge you overcame years ago, how did that victory contribute to the spiritual maturity you have today?　　　　—C. R. B.

> **What Do You Think?**
> What are some ways to prepare ourselves for the faith-challenges that inevitably come?
> *Digging Deeper*
> What additional steps can we take to turn those challenges into opportunities for spiritual growth rather than something just to be endured?

II. Seeking Wisdom
(JAMES 1:5-8)
A. God's Gift (v. 5)

5. If any of you lacks wisdom, you should ask God, who gives generously to all without finding fault, and it will be given to you.

The focus of James's exhortation shifts from trials to *wisdom*. On a surface level, there is a verbal connection between James 1:4, 5 in the word *lacks*. But the connection is deeper than that. Wisdom is needed in order to come through the trials of life in a way that leads to spiritual maturity. This wisdom is, above all, divine wisdom—wisdom that comes from God (see Proverbs 2:3-6).

James recognizes that fact as he instructs his readers to *ask God* for wisdom (compare 1 Kings 3:9, 10). This exhortation reminds James's readers of the centrality of prayer, during times of both trial and relative ease. Request is a fundamental part of prayer; it acknowledges our lack and our dependence on God to supply the need. In so doing, it also acknowledges God's nature: he is generous *to all*. More than that, he wants to grace us all with his gifts (see Psalm 145:15-19; Matthew 7:7-11).

B. Doubt's Instability (vv. 6-8)

6. But when you ask, you must believe and not doubt, because the one who doubts is like a wave of the sea, blown and tossed by the wind.

As important as it is to *ask*, it is critical to do so while believing and not doubting (compare

Matthew 21:21; Mark 11:24). James's readers may well find themselves struggling to trust God because of what they suffer. Doubting God is hardly a beneficial quality for someone undergoing severe trials!

James illustrates the danger of doubt by comparing a doubter to *a wave of the sea, blown and tossed by the wind*. The lack of stability depicted is not the characteristic of a wise person! Nor is it associated with God, who can be trusted in all circumstances. Isaiah 57:20 uses the same imagery to illustrate wicked people; Ephesians 4:14 uses wind and wave imagery to illustrate those who are spiritually immature.

> **What Do You Think?**
> What are some ways to encourage a friend who feels that God is not answering his or her prayers because of a lack of faith?
>
> **Digging Deeper**
> What would be proper and improper times to introduce Romans 8:28 into the talk?

❧ A LIFELONG SEARCH ❧

When I was young, I recognized that some "old" people knew more than I did. When I brought my troubles to them, they had words of counsel that calmed my spirit. I thought their answers were based on *knowledge* that I did not possess. Finally, I realized that what I was lacking was not knowledge but, rather, wisdom.

This conclusion created an opening for me to seek wisdom. At some point in my early 50s, I finally realized that I was becoming wise(r)! I saw how principles in God's Word could guide me in resolving issues.

Now, 30 years later, I'm still seeking wisdom. Younger people sometimes thank *me* for a wise response! God has given me wisdom just as I asked him. Are you finding the wisdom and peace that come to single-minded searchers?   —C. R. B.

7, 8. That person should not expect to receive anything from the Lord. Such a person is double-minded and unstable in all they do.

The Old Testament contrasts those having an "undivided loyalty" or practicing "deception" (1 Chronicles 12:33; Psalm 12:2) with those who display singleness of heart. To act with the "all" your "heart" (Psalms 9:1; 111:1; Jeremiah 24:7) is to act with unity of purpose, with absolute devotion to God.

This phrasing is another way of expressing the injunction to "love the Lord your God with all your heart" (Deuteronomy 6:5). Double-mindedness, on the other hand, suggests conflicted loyalties and indecisiveness. It is associated with sin because it implies a lack of total devotion to God.

All of this is in the background of the term *double-minded*. Such a person *is unstable* because of conflicted loyalties. He or she tries to serve both God and the world simultaneously and ends up doing neither very well. James's readers, who are enduring trials and persecution for their faith, face an acute temptation to try simultaneously to serve God and to conform to what the world asks of them. James emphasizes that this is ultimately impossible (see James 4:8).

> **What Do You Think?**
> What should you do when you begin to recognize double-mindedness in yourself?
>
> **Digging Deeper**
> What are some helpful and nonjudgmental ways to confront double-mindedness in others?

III. Handling Wealth
(JAMES 1:9-11)
A. High and Low (vv. 9, 10a)

9. Believers in humble circumstances ought to take pride in their high position.

The focus of James's message shifts again. Economic concerns are a central part of James's message in this letter (see Lesson Context: James the Epistle). The verse at hand brings this into view for the first time. So how does this topic connect to what comes before it? Much depends on how we understand who is being spoken about and what will happen to them.

Believers in humble circumstances are not merely

sad or down in the dumps. They are poor (contrast "the rich" in the next verse). The poor are to *take pride in their high position.* This is a very close restatement of James's exhortation that his readers should "consider it pure joy . . . when [they] face trials of many kinds" (James 1:2). There is a goal, or an end, to the experience of poverty: it can be a transformative experience that draws them closer to God.

This passage echoes the same theme of reversal found in the song that Mary sang when Jesus' birth was announced to her (Luke 1:52, 53). In this way, James celebrates the kingdom of God that Jesus inaugurated, which accomplishes this role reversal (compare Matthew 23:12).

10a. But the rich should take pride in their humiliation—

In direct contrast to the poor man who rejoices in an upturn of his fortunes, *the rich* are to *take pride in their humiliation.* Some commentators point out that James seems to have the language of Jeremiah 9:23, 24 in mind here. But who are the rich? Is James speaking of a believer or a nonbeliever?

James does not refer to a rich "brother" here, but simply to the rich. For him, the rich are those who mistreat the poor and oppress them (see James 2:6, 7; 5:1-6). For such a man to be humiliated entails judgment, of being thrown down from his position of power.

Even so, there is a note of redemption here. The rich man who decides to come to God can very well rejoice in being made low—that is, in taking on the humility of a follower of Christ. But as James's language suggests, it is much more likely that the arrogant rich with whom James's readers have to deal will ultimately face the judgment of God for their actions.

B. Fading Away (vv. 10b, 11)

10b, 11. since they will pass away like a wild flower. For the sun rises with scorching heat and withers the plant; its blossom falls and its beauty is destroyed. In the same way, the rich will fade away even while they go about their business.

James draws on very familiar Old Testament

language of judgment to speak of the fate of the rich (see Psalms 90:3-6; 103:15, 16; Isaiah 40:6-8). The stages in which a *flower* withers, or passes away, illustrates this.

The fact that the *rich will fade away even while they go about their business* indicates that the entirety of a selfishly lavish lifestyle will come under the withering judgment of God. Jesus's illustration about the days of Noah is an additional warning (see Luke 17:26-31).

> *What Do You Think?*
> How would you explain James's observations to a wealthy person in a way that does not condemn wealth in and of itself?
> *Digging Deeper*
> How would your answer differ in talking to wealthy believer vs. an unbeliever, if at all?

Conclusion
A. Faithful and Wise

The opening lines of the book of James set us up for our study of the letter as a whole. In these lines we were introduced to three themes we will see again and again over the next few weeks. These themes are the reality of trials, the need for wisdom, and the reality of economic privation.

The trials we face produce the need to ask God for wisdom and can involve economic considerations. Above all, James impresses on us our need for God's wisdom and our inability to live faithful lives apart from it.

Only by seeking God wholeheartedly will we continue to be formed into the kind of people he desires us to be.

B. Prayer

Father, in the midst of the trials that this life presents, teach us to seek wisdom and guidance from you, the only true source of all that is good. In Jesus' name we pray. Amen.

C. Thought to Remember

In every aspect of life,
God invites us to seek his wisdom.

INVOLVEMENT LEARNING

Enhance your lesson with NIV Bible Student (from your curriculum supplier) and the reproducible activity page (at www.standardlesson.com or in the back of the NIV Standard Lesson Commentary Deluxe Edition).

Into the Lesson

Distribute handouts (you create) with all the following statements. After you read each one aloud, call for *agree* or *disagree* by shows of hands; tally results on the board.

1–Most of the truly wise people I know are older and more experienced than I am.

2–Satan uses tough times to push us away from God.

3–It's easy to condemn the wealthy, but it's difficult not to yearn for financial security.

4–The lives of some smart people show how foolish they can be.

5–I've seen how terrible problems or devastating disappointments have brought some people closer to God.

6–Poverty in our community would be eradicated if poor people simply became practicing Christians.

7–Wisdom is difficult to achieve, but it's possible for those who will study and work at it.

8–In difficult times, it's natural to wonder whether God has abandoned us.

9–Poverty is a scourge of Satan; God's favor is usually accompanied by material blessing.

If you have time, ask volunteers to explain why they chose as they did for one or two of the statements.

Say, "Each statement reflects a concern addressed by the book of James, both in this week's passage and throughout the book."

Into the Word

Ask learners what they know about the author of the book of James; jot responses on the board. Then ask learners what they know about the book that bears his name. Add comments from the Lesson Context to complete or correct their understanding in both areas.

Inform the class that today's study introduces us to three major themes in the book of James. Then form three groups (or multiples of three for larger classes), designating them **Wisdom Group, Trials Group,** and **Poverty Group.** Challenge them to listen for instruction from the text on their assigned theme as a volunteer reads James 1:1-11 aloud.

Following the reading of the text, ask groups to make a list of teachings on their assigned topic, with verse references. After discussion winds down, reconvene for a whole-class discussion and for groups to report their findings.

Send students back to their small groups to discuss how the statements from the beginning of the class session compare and/or contrast with the teaching of today's text. After five minutes, reconvene for whole-class discussion to seek consensus on the findings (*expected responses:* wisdom–1, 4, and 7; trials–2, 5, and 8; poverty–3, 6, and 9).

Point to verse 8 and ask for an explanation of what it means to be "double minded." Make a transition to Into Life by asking, "In what ways does being double-minded hinder the Christian's ability to obey the teaching of today's text?"

Into Life

Ask learners to take no more than one minute to write a prayer that requests God's wisdom in a specific area. The prayer should also confess the sin of double-mindedness that hinders receiving wisdom in that area. Assure learners that you won't put them on the spot by asking them to reveal their prayers to the class but that you will invite volunteers to do so. Be prepared to read your own prayer in this regard.

Option. As time allows and the needs of your class dictate, distribute copies of one or more of the three exercises on the activity page, which can be downloaded to be completed by study pairs. If given as take-home work instead, encourage completion by stressing that the activity or activities will be the first matter the class will discuss during next week's lesson.

HEARING AND DOING

DEVOTIONAL READING: 1 Corinthians 1:26-31
BACKGROUND SCRIPTURE: James 1:19-27

JAMES 1:19-27

¹⁹ My dear brothers and sisters, take note of this: Everyone should be quick to listen, slow to speak and slow to become angry, ²⁰ because human anger does not produce the righteousness that God desires. ²¹ Therefore, get rid of all moral filth and the evil that is so prevalent and humbly accept the word planted in you, which can save you.

²² Do not merely listen to the word, and so deceive yourselves. Do what it says. ²³ Anyone who listens to the word but does not do what it says is like someone who looks at his face in a mirror ²⁴ and, after looking at himself, goes away and immediately forgets what he looks like. ²⁵ But whoever looks intently into the perfect law that gives freedom, and continues in it—not forgetting what they have heard, but doing it—they will be blessed in what they do.

²⁶ Those who consider themselves religious and yet do not keep a tight rein on their tongues deceive themselves, and their religion is worthless. ²⁷ Religion that God our Father accepts as pure and faultless is this: to look after orphans and widows in their distress and to keep oneself from being polluted by the world.

KEY VERSE

Do not merely listen to the word, and so deceive yourselves. Do what it says. —**James 1:22**

MANY FACES OF
WISDOM

Unit 3: Faith and Wisdom in James
LESSONS 9–13

LESSON AIMS

After participating in this lesson, each learner will be able to:

1. Identify what negates pure religion.

2. Explain the part wisdom plays in hearing, speaking, and doing.

3. Prepare an action plan of specific steps to take regarding conduct that is grounded in godly wisdom.

LESSON OUTLINE

Introduction

A. Disconnected

The title of today's lesson gets at what is really a fundamental human problem: the disconnect in our hearts and minds between hearing and doing. The problem is not really a lack of information but rather what we do or don't do with it. Consider: we know so much about what we should or should not be eating, yet we find it difficult to adhere to healthy dietary guidelines.

Some have pointed to the problem of an "attention economy." Our attention is scarce, the argument goes, and is therefore valuable. Advertisers, tech companies, and social media platforms recognize this and capitalize on it. Advertising is everywhere. Even gas stations have pumps fitted with display screens in order to advertise while we fill our tanks.

In the midst of all this noise, we learn quickly how to tune *out* calls to action. We become so practiced in this that it can be difficult to tune *in* to the calls that are truly important. Today's lesson has something valuable to teach us in that regard.

B. Lesson Context

Amid all that the Creator provided Adam and Eve in the garden—amid all the evidence of God's goodness—the first humans heard the command not to eat of the tree in the middle of the garden. But they failed to do what God commanded (Genesis 3) when they failed to tune out a contradictory voice. The disconnect between hearing and doing was and is at the heart of sin.

This is also the story of Israel. Even after clear evidence of God's presence during the exodus, the Israelites failed to obey, instead creating an idol to worship (Exodus 32). During the time of the judges, the Israelites went through relentless cycles of oppression, deliverance, and relapse. They never seemed to make the connection between their actions and the results. This pattern was fundamentally a problem of the heart (see Proverbs 4:23).

The power of speech is likewise a thread that can be traced through Scripture, beginning in

Genesis 3. As we study, we remember the context of James's audience: economic oppression, some infighting, and persecution (see lesson 9 Lesson Context: James the Epistle; also see James 2:1-7; 3:13–4:12; 5:1-6).

I. Faithful Speech
(JAMES 1:19-21)
A. Swift and Slow (v. 19)

19. My dear brothers and sisters, take note of this: Everyone should be quick to listen, slow to speak and slow to become angry,

James has just reminded his readers that they are called to be "a kind of firstfruits of all [God] created" (James 1:18). In light of this goal, the instructions of the present verse become all the more necessary.

The three commands in the verse before us are straightforward. They are commands that are already familiar to James's Christian readers of Jewish background, being well established in the Jewish wisdom tradition. An admonishment of similar wording is found in the nonbiblical Sirach 5:11-13, which is part of Jewish literature written in the time between the Old and New Testaments:

Be swift to hear; and let thy life be sincere; and with patience give answer. If thou hast understanding, answer thy neighbour; if not, lay thy hand upon thy mouth. Honour and shame is in talk: and the tongue of man is his fall.

These instructions are about how members of the community interact with one another and, to some extent, how they interact with outsiders. *Quick to listen, slow to speak and slow to become angry* is not so much about casual conversation— although it can certainly apply in that setting— as it is about how they should conduct themselves in verbal interactions that hold the potential to become aggressively confrontational.

B. Wrath and Righteousness (vv. 20, 21)

20. because human anger does not produce the righteousness that God desires.

James now gives the reason for the previous command. *Human anger* is a reference especially

to our tendency to lash out. At such times, we often feel that our fury and the rash actions we take as a result of it are good and positive, or at least justified. This is a situation that all of us have experienced at one time or another: we fall into the trap of thinking that we know better than *God* what is needed in a given situation.

Anger that results in rashly violent behavior or hasty speech cannot bring about God's desired *righteousness*, justice, or salvation. It should probably be said that James is not calling for passivity or for sitting on our hands. Instead, this is a call to the right kind of speech and action: wise, patient, and discerning.

❧ SYMBOLIC SPEECH ❧

I recently renewed my driver's license. This required taking the written test again. Before going to the Department of Motor Vehicles, I read the latest edition of the California Driver Handbook and noticed some changes.

The handbook had quite a bit to say about how to avoid road rage incidents. No matter how bad you think other drivers are, the handbook warns against "speaking" to them by swerving, flashing your high beams, or making obscene gestures. That is, don't use actions as symbolic speech that might incite other drivers into even more aggressive behavior.

What we show by our speech, whether verbally or in actions that are a type of speech, reflects what is going on inside our hearts and minds. How often do you express wrath in ungodly behavior that can provoke others into one-upping your questionable actions? It's not just in heavy traffic that this question is relevant!
—C. R. B.

> **What Do You Think?**
> How does James 1:20 change your view of anger when compared and contrasted with the anger of Jesus in Mark 3:1-6; 11:15-17?
> **Digging Deeper**
> Without giving directive advice, how would you counsel a fellow believer who was prone to anger and fits of rage?

Visual for Lesson 10. *While discussing verse 22, point to this visual as you ask, "Which are we more in need of: bigger ears or bigger hands? Why?"*

1:18), "the perfect law" (1:25), and "the royal law" (2:8).

We cannot be fully certain, but it seems that James envisions a close, almost inseparable, relationship between the *word* and the Holy Spirit (Ephesians 1:13). At any rate, the *humility* with which it is to be received refers not to timidity or weakness, but to restraint.

Consider the pressure that these believers are under to lash out against their oppressors and persecutors. They need the humility that grows out of wisdom and obedience to the Word.

II. Faithful Action
(JAMES 1:22-25)
A. Hearing the Word (vv. 22-24)

22. Do not merely listen to the word, and so deceive yourselves. Do what it says.

We move into a new section of the text with an emphasis on action. There are two kinds of hearing in the Bible. There is the hearing that understands and leads to obedience, and there is the hearing that goes "in one ear and out the other"; this results in no change on the part of the hearer. To put it another way, the Scriptures make a distinction between "hearing only" and "hearing *and* doing" (compare Isaiah 6:9, 10, quoted in Matthew 13:14, 15; Mark 4:10-12; and Acts 28:25-27).

The engrafted Word of God will yield fruit in changed behavior (Matthew 7:15-20). If the behavior has not changed, then the Word has been uprooted or never engrafted in the first place. Our actions are the best indicators of the reality of our hearts.

James is firmly in line here with the overall testimony of Scripture. The thought he expresses is very similar to one found in the Sermon on the Mount: "Not everyone who says to me, 'Lord, Lord,' will enter the kingdom of heaven, but only the one who does the will of my Father who is in heaven" (Matthew 7:21).

Those who fail to act *deceive* themselves (see James 2:14-26). The reality of such self-deception is found in Scripture repeatedly. Horrible to say, when we go down that path decisively, God

21a. Therefore, get rid of all moral filth and the evil that is so prevalent

James's readers know how to communicate, and they know on some level that their anger works contrary to God's desires and plans. But where do they begin the cure? How do they put away the sins that are at the heart of the problem? The word *therefore* in the verse before us introduces the solution.

The phrase *all moral filth* casts a wide net, covering a great many sins, as does the phrase *the evil that is so prevalent. Evil*, of course, should always been shunned, even though it is everywhere. Its presence in a believer's life is not to be tolerated.

> ### What Do You Think?
> What are some things Christians should do to implement the imperative of James 1:21a?
> *Digging Deeper*
> In what ways can Luke 11:24-26 and Ephesians 4:22-29 help you do so yourself?

21b. and humbly accept the word planted in you, which can save you.

It's not enough merely to get rid of the bad; it must be replaced with the good (see Matthew 12:43-45). The agricultural imagery in the verse before us refers to the action of God in the heart of the believer. The phrase *the word planted in you* seems to be synonymous with other terms in the surrounding text: "the word of truth" (James allows it (see Jeremiah 44:24-28; Romans 1:24, 28; 2 Thessalonians 2:10-12). This makes James's imperative here all the more important.

❧ GIVING LIP SERVICE ❧

My second wife, Barbara, and I both suffered the death of our first spouses. Before Barbara and I married, we were invited to be part of a marriage enhancement group. Our married friends hoped we would be able to provide helpful insights to the engaged couples, gleaned from our collective 100 years of married life.

We were dismayed by the baggage some of them were bringing to their anticipated marriages. One couple seemed to be "in love with being in love." They obviously had not seriously confronted some significant issues. This turned out to be true of the married couple leading the group as well. They gave lip service to the workshop material, but a few months after the group finished meeting, they divorced.

James says we must practice what we know if we are to be faithful to Christ. Otherwise, we are only deceiving ourselves.   —C. R. B.

23. Anyone who listens to the word but does not do what it says is like someone who looks at his face in a mirror

James now describes the self-deception of the person who does not act on the Word of God. In the world of the New Testament, people were just as concerned about their appearance as we are today. So mirrors were rather common. But being made of polished metal, they were not entirely like ours. Even so, these ancient mirrors allowed people to check their appearance.

Of course, the purpose of looking *in a mirror* is to be able to do just that. That is the situation James is describing: one who is examining *his face*—that is, the person's physical face—is doing so to get a close, deliberate look. The person takes note of the image in order to make adjustments to improve his or her appearance.

HOW TO SAY IT

Sirach   *Sigh*-rak.

24. and, after looking at himself, goes away and immediately forgets what he looks like.

Looking in the mirror involves being honest about how we look and then remembering as a reference point for the next time we look in that mirror. How foolish to go away from the mirror and remember something false: "Yes, I have a full head of hair!" "No wrinkles—great!" or "Why, I look the same as I did when I was a teenager!"

So it is with the person who hears God's Word and does not put it into practice. God's Word reveals our true selves, "warts and all" as the old saying goes. It shows us what is wrong and puts us on the path to make it right. Not putting the Word into practice is akin to the foolish self-deception of looking in a mirror and pretending our real appearance is different. Like the mirror and the camera, God's Word shows our true selves.

B. Doing the Word (v. 25)

25. But whoever looks intently into the perfect law that gives freedom, and continues in it—not forgetting what they have heard, but doing it—they will be blessed in what they do.

James presses his analogy of God's Word as a mirror that reveals one's true self. He speaks of *law*, but that word is not limited to the books of Law in the Old Testament. God's Word in all its parts is the sure and only guide to right understanding and right living. Although James's readers do not have the full New Testament, they recognize that Jesus came in fulfillment of God's Word. He is the climax of God's all-important instruction of his people.

We tend to think of law as restrictive, but James affirms that God's law gives *freedom*. This is a key theme of Scripture. The God who gave freedom to the Israelite slaves (Exodus 20:2) is the God who gives the commandments that instruct his people in the way of true freedom. Paul reminds us that the ultimate slavery is slavery to sin (Romans 6:15-23).

To enjoy this freedom, we have to do with God's Word what the wise person does with a mirror: pay attention to what it reveals and live accordingly. It is a matter of hearing and doing, not forgetting. What God's Word reveals about us may not be pleasant, but it is true. What's more, God's Word gives the answer to what it reveals about us, the solution to our essential problem.

So James says that the person who acknowledges what God's Word reveals and acts on the Word is the one who *will be blessed* (compare Deuteronomy 30:16). This is the way to receive God's favor, to experience life as God designed it to be experienced.

> **What Do You Think?**
> What are some ways to recognize and enjoy the freedom, or liberty, we have in Christ?
> *Digging Deeper*
> How do we ensure that the exercise of that freedom doesn't cross boundaries noted in Romans 14:1-9; 1 Corinthians 8:9; Jude 4; etc.?

III. Faithful Religion
(JAMES 1:26, 27)
A. Vanity (v. 26)

26. Those who consider themselves religious and yet do not keep a tight rein on their tongues deceive themselves, and their religion is worthless.

The shift of subject in these last two verses is a natural extension of what has come before. From James's praise of the one who does what was heard (James 1:25), he moves to address what that work entails.

Of critical importance for our understanding of these verses is James's use of the word *religious* (a derivative of *religion*). The Greek noun behind this word is found in only two other places in the New Testament: Acts 26:5 and, translated "worship," Colossians 2:18. In some circles the very word religion has taken on a negative connotation. Consider, for example, a 2013 best-selling book titled *Jesus > Religion*, the mathematical symbol ">" signifying that "Jesus is greater than religion."

Or ponder the phenomenon that has emerged in recent years of people who describe themselves as "spiritual but not religious." The misdeeds of world religions has justified for these people not affiliating themselves with any particular faith tradition

In both cases, the distinction being made would likely have struck James as odd, at the very least. For James, religion can be true or it can be *worthless*. In either case, it is not a category to be rejected out of hand.

For the occasion of this letter, a critical determinant of one's religion is one's ability and willingness to bridle the tongue. That does not mean that pagans who control their *tongues* well have a valid religion. To control one's tongue is necessary for one's religion to be valid religion, but such control is not sufficient in and of itself. So having considered the negative of vain religion, James moves to observations about the positive of pure religion, next.

> **What Do You Think?**
> What guardrails can you erect to help you control your tongue in difficult situations?
> *Digging Deeper*
> Which of those guardrails could be useful to everyone? Which are unique to your personality traits? Why is this distinction important?

B. Purity (v. 27)

27. Religion that God our Father accepts as pure and faultless is this: to look after orphans and widows in their distress and to keep oneself from being polluted by the world.

The distinction between *religion that is pure* and religion that is worthless is defined by the contents of each. James underlines that content as including a series of actions.

To look after involves knowing a situation well enough to recognize what constitutes appropriate aid and doing so. *Orphans and widows* are frequently mentioned together in the Old Testament as two of the most vulnerable people groups (example: Isaiah 1:17). God is their best and only hope for help in their state of helplessness, but often he expects his work to be done through our hands (6:8). When no one is willing to do so, bad things happen (Ezekiel 22:29, 30). Those who know the true God will reflect that fact in their response to the needs of the most vulnerable (Isaiah 1:17).

James's example of the orphans and widows might envision a situation in which a deceased father leaves behind a wife and one or more children who need the care of the Christian community (compare Acts 6:1-6; 1 Timothy 5:3-5). The phrase *in their distress* likely envisions financial problems in addition to the grief that accompanies the loss of a loved one.

> **What Do You Think?**
> How does Acts 6:1-7 help you understand the role God expects you to have as your church implements the imperative of James 1:27a?
> **Digging Deeper**
> In what ways can the intent of 2 Thessalonians 3:10 be honored in your church's efforts to help those in need?

Another significant point here is James's link between social and personal holiness. The definition of *pure religion* for James is twofold: caring for others (social or interpersonal dimension) and keeping *oneself from being polluted by the world* (personal dimension). He does not see one as more important than the other. Each is necessary, but neither is sufficient by itself.

It is important to emphasize this to ensure that we do not separate the two or elevate one over the other. Stop and try to imagine a person who excels at helping the poor, but whose personal life is a shamble of unholiness; then compare that person to 1 Peter 1:13-16. Flipped around, imagine a person who focuses only on personal piety, ignoring the needy around him. The condemnation of Mark 12:38-40 may very well await that individual.

Conclusion

A. Why Do You Speak?

From the time we can first utter individual words like "Mama" or "Daddy," we like to talk. As we grow up, our speech helps to form our identity and to distinguish ourselves from others. Talking is, by and large, extremely beneficial. It helps us work through problems, ask for help, comfort others, unburden ourselves, and so forth.

On the other hand, sometimes we just like to hear ourselves talk. It appeals to our pride, makes us feel smart, and can make us feel superior to those around us. James understands this about human nature. He understands that often our words are not as beneficial—either to us or to those around us—as we may like to think. What is best, rather, is when our thoughtfully slow words result in or are accompanied by action.

This is especially true when it comes to our posture toward our fellow believers who are most vulnerable and in need. Consider the thoughts of the apostle John on this subject:

> If anyone has material possessions and sees a brother or sister in need but has not pity on them, how can the love of God be in that person? Dear children, let us not love with words or speech but with actions and in truth. (1 John 3:17, 18).

Openness to what God has to say is the starting point for faithful speech and for the action that accompanies or follows it.

The principles of today's first-century text can be brought readily into the twenty-first century. Do we not deal with the same problems of words in relation to action? In one respect or another, God's Word reveals in all of us our stubborn tendency to run our lives on our terms—to value words and actions (or lack of either) in ways that God does not. If we do so after we have confessed that God's way is the only way, then it is time to allow God's Word to assess ourselves anew.

B. Prayer

Heavenly Father, strengthen our resolve to discipline our speech so that it may result in action rather than attitude. May we not be content with mere words as we minister to others in the name of your Son, Jesus. In his name we pray. Amen.

C. Thought to Remember
Faithful actions must accompany
faithful speech.

INVOLVEMENT LEARNING

Enhance your lesson with NIV Bible Student *(from your curriculum supplier) and the reproducible activity page (at www.standardlesson.com or in the back of the* NIV Standard Lesson Commentary Deluxe Edition*).*

Into the Lesson

Write the following scrambled sentences on the board before class members arrive:

> *begins knowledge end doesn't obedience with there but*

> *person action is seen not a the character best of words in*

> *do you something is love*

Ask class members to unscramble the three sentences. They may do this alone, with a partner, or as a whole group. After all three sentences are successfully unscrambled, read them aloud again: *Obedience begins with knowledge but doesn't end there. / The character of a person is best seen in action, not words. / Love is something you do.*

Ask class members to share illustrations of how they've seen the truth of one or more of the sentences. Inform the class that today's text is just one example of how the book of James is about combining action with our faith.

Into the Word

Distribute handouts (you prepare) on which is printed *only* the three headers from the chart below. Then read aloud James 1:19-27 while class members listen for phrases and verse references to enter under the headings. Do this a second time. Then form study pairs or triads of learners to discover whether anyone has missed anything.

While pairs or triads are engaged in discussion, write the headers on the board. Call time after six to eight minutes to transition to a whole-class discussion of the results. Work toward consensus as you talk through the entries together. Expect the finished chart to look similar to the one below.

Option. Distribute copies of the "Freedom or Frustration?" exercise from the activity page, which you can download. Have small groups complete as indicated (caution: may be very time consuming).

Into Life

Have learners return to study pairs or triads. For each item in the first two columns of their completed handouts, have them discuss and note specific steps to take to act on the biblical commands. If time is short, assign a few items per group instead of asking groups to consider every item. After several minutes, ask volunteers to share action plans, but don't put anyone on the spot. Compare and contrast differences.

Option. Distribute copies of the "What Will You Do?" exercise on the activity page. Because of the highly personal nature of this assignment, it should be a take-home exercise. To encourage its completion, say that you will invite learners to volunteer responses next week.

Close with a prayer seeking God's help to obey. *Alternative.* Have participants in their groups pray for one another about their decisions.

Do These	Avoid These	Reasons Why
more listening, slow to speak (v. 19)	*quick anger (v. 19)*	*anger doesn't produce righteousness (v. 20)*
	moral filth (v. 21)	*make room for the Word (v. 21)*
accept the Word (v. 21)		*the Word can save (v. 21)*
	merely listen to the Word (v. 22)	*self-deception (v. 22)*
do what the Word says (v. 22)		*to be blessed (vv. 23-25)*
	uncontrolled tongue (v. 26)	*vain religion (v. 26)*
take care of those in need (v. 27)		*pure religion pleases God (v. 27)*

LIVING
FAITH

DEVOTIONAL READING: Matthew 18:23-35
BACKGROUND SCRIPTURE: James 2:14-26

JAMES 2:14-26

¹⁴ What good is it, my brothers and sisters, if someone claims to have faith but has no deeds? Can such faith save them? ¹⁵ Suppose a brother or a sister is without clothes and daily food. ¹⁶ If one of you says to them, "Go in peace; keep warm and well fed," but does nothing about their physical needs, what good is it? ¹⁷ In the same way, faith by itself, if it is not accompanied by action, is dead.

¹⁸ But someone will say, "You have faith; I have deeds."

Show me your faith without deeds, and I will show you my faith by my deeds. ¹⁹ You believe that there is one God. Good! Even the demons believe that—and shudder.

²⁰ You foolish person, do you want evidence that faith without deeds is useless? ²¹ Was not our father Abraham considered righteous for what he did when he offered his son Isaac on the altar? ²² You see that his faith and his actions were working together, and his faith was made complete by what he did. ²³ And the scripture was fulfilled that says, "Abraham believed God, and it was credited to him as righteousness," and he was called God's friend.

²⁴ You see that a person is considered righteous by what they do and not by faith alone.

²⁵ In the same way, was not even Rahab the prostitute considered righteous for what she did when she gave lodging to the spies and sent them off in a different direction? ²⁶ As the body without the spirit is dead, so faith without deeds is dead.

KEY VERSE

As the body without the spirit is dead, so faith without deeds is dead. —**James 2:26**

MANY FACES OF WISDOM

Unit 3: Faith and Wisdom in James

LESSONS 9–13

LESSON AIMS

After participating in this lesson, each learner will be able to:

1. Describe workless faith.

2. Give examples of the proper relationship between faith and works.

3. Develop a list of ways to demonstrate faith through action, and choose one to initiate personally in the week ahead.

LESSON OUTLINE

Introduction

A. "A Right Strawy Epistle"

On October 31, 1517, Martin Luther nailed a list of 95 points of disagreement with medieval Roman Catholic doctrine to the door of the Castle Church in Wittenberg, Germany. He had come to see that Catholicism's position on the role of works in salvation did not match the apostle Paul's emphasis on justification by faith.

As debates heated up, the letter of James became more and more a source of frustration for Luther. Representatives of the pope kept quoting it to him in reply to his assertions about justification by faith. By the time Luther published his German translation of the New Testament in the 1520s, he had come to view the letter of James as a "right strawy epistle . . . [that] has nothing of the nature of the gospel about it."

Luther believed he was justified in this conclusion for three reasons: (1) James seems to contradict Paul, (2) James makes no mention of Jesus' death or resurrection, and (3) James himself wasn't of the same caliber as Paul and other apostles. Consequently, Luther moved James, Hebrews, Jude, and Revelation from their positions in the Bible at the time and placed them in a separate section at the end of the New Testament.

Luther's attitude about James eventually mellowed. But many Christians still have a hard time reconciling James with Paul on the role of works. Today's lesson revisits this issue in a limited way.

B. Lesson Context

The Lesson Context of lessons 9 and 10 apply here as well, so that information need not be repeated. But before we move into today's text, it will be helpful to consider the larger context of the central idea of today's lesson.

For all the controversy that James 2 has generated on the role of works over the centuries, it can come as a surprise to see how often works are related to salvation elsewhere in Scripture. Consider the scene Jesus paints in Matthew 25:31-46. In the judgment, individual believers are judged on the basis of what they have done or not done—their works.

Also a pointed statement is Revelation 20:12, 13, where the apostle John says he

saw the dead, great and small, standing before the throne, and books were opened. Another book was opened, which is the book of life. The dead were judged according to what they had done as recorded in the books. The sea gave up the dead that were in it, and death and Hades gave up the dead that were in them, and each person was judged according to what they had done.

As important as that issue is, it's easy to allow it to overshadow something else James stresses: the specific economic needs—the reality of life for so many in the ancient world—that drives much of his thoughts in James 2. The first half of the chapter (verses 1-13) warns against discriminating against the poor in favor of the rich; economic need also is an integral part of his argument regarding faith and works in the second half—today's text.

I. Saving Faith
(JAMES 2:14-17)

A. Speech or Action (vv. 14-16)

14. What good is it, my brothers and sisters, if someone claims to have faith but has no deeds? Can such faith save them?

The tone of today's text is somewhat combative—James is blunt. He is not a dispassionate scholar who pontificates from an ivory tower on theories of the relationship between faith and works. The phrase *what good is it* intends to discover what benefit can come about, based on the conditions James is about to discuss.

Faith, as James is using the term here, is a kind of confessional faith. It is belief or mental assent to the notion that God exists. Faith in its fullness involves a belief and trust that assume the action of a life lived in obedience to the law of Christ (compare Matthew 7:26; James 1:22-25). For the purposes of James's discussion, though, he's using the word *faith* in a more truncated sense that some of his addressees seem to have adopted.

15. Suppose a brother or a sister is without clothes and daily food.

Some commentators have seen this example as comic in its exaggeration. "Surely," we might say,

"no one would be in a position of having no clothing or food whatsoever." But James may be using overstatement (hyperbole) for effect.

Another possibility is that the word being translated *without clothes* is intended to signify inadequate clothing or a lack of proper clothing. The same word is used to describe Peter's clothed status before he donned his "outer garment" in John 21:7 (compare Matthew 25:36). *Daily food,* for its part, echoes the need noted in Matthew 6:11 and 25:35.

16. If one of you says to them, "Go in peace; keep warm and well fed," but does nothing about their physical needs, what good is it?

The callousness of the words spoken here comes through clearly. But it is possible that the words are even stronger than the English translation indicates. Commentators disagree about which of two possible interpretations of the verbs *keep warm* and *[be] well fed* is the correct one. Seen one way, the actions they suggest put the responsibility for finding shelter and food on the poverty-stricken person in the scenario, as in "Go get yourself warmed up and fed."

Seen another way, these verbs may be an example of what is sometimes called the "divine passive," in which God is the implied source of the action. In other words, the intent would be "May God warm you and fill you up."

Either way, the one speaking avoids personal responsibility to act to meet the need (contrast Luke 3:11). Under the second of the two interpretations, he or she goes so far as to provide religious cover for inaction (contrast 1 John 3:17, 18).

> **What Do You Think?**
> In what ways can you help someone receive needed clothing, food, etc., this week?
> *Digging Deeper*
> How do texts such as Acts 4:32-35; 6:1-6; 2 Thessalonians 3:10-12; 1 Timothy 5:3-16; 1 John 3:17, 18; etc., help frame both what you give and how you give it?

B. Alive or Dead (v. 17)

17. In the same way, faith by itself, if it is not accompanied by action, is dead.

James draws a conclusion that reiterates and strengthens his original point. The phrase *by itself* reminds us that we are dealing with a definition of *faith* that James is opposing: mere intellectual acknowledgment or mental assent to certain truths about God (contrast Galatians 5:6).

❧ VICE AND VIRTUE ❧

When I was young, our church fellowship gave lip service to saving faith. We were wary of practicing dead faith, so we tended to focus on doing things that we thought would show our true faith.

Looking back on those days, though, I can see that to prove our faith we often focused not on things to *do* but on things *not* to do! We were expected to avoid certain vices because those were behaviors that indicated we did not have saving faith. Yet I can't remember hearing many sermons on developing virtues instead. We were *against* many practices, but it wasn't always easy to identify what we were *for*.

In retrospect, our focus seemed to be more on ourselves than on others. It could be argued that we were negating the teachings of both James and Jesus by releasing ourselves of responsibility to others. How do you live out your "for" faith?

—C. R. B.

II. Vain Faith
(JAMES 2:18, 19)
A. Demonstrated Belief (v. 18)

18a. But someone will say, "You have faith; I have deeds."

In the second part of his current line of argument, James describes a hypothetical conversation. A challenge is posed to James's assertion that "faith by itself, if it is not accompanied by action, is dead," just stated. The first conversationalist seems intent on putting *faith* and *deeds* into categories that do not relate to one another. The person is, in effect, arguing that faith and deeds can be separated without damage to either.

18b. Show me your faith without deeds, and I will show you my faith by my deeds.

There is no demonstrating of *faith without deeds* since faith is invisible in and of itself. But the deeds of which James is speaking are the necessary products of valid faith. Actions really do speak louder than words. The person who claims faith without deeds makes an absurd, empty claim.

It's possible that James is also opposing here a line of thought that contends that an emphasis on faith by itself is just as acceptable as an emphasis on faith coupled with deeds. James disagrees: these two options are not equally acceptable since faith and deeds are fundamentally inseparable (compare Hebrews 11). There is no saving faith that does not manifest itself in deeds.

B. Bare Belief (v. 19)

19. You believe that there is one God. Good! Even the demons believe that—and shudder.

James presses his point by referring to what is called the Shema: "Hear, O Israel: The Lord our God, the Lord is one" (Deuteronomy 6:4; the word *Shema* is the transliteration of the first three Hebrew letters of this verse). This is important as we recall that James is writing to Christians of Jewish background. Observant Jews of the time recited the Shema three times daily. Its teaching is still understood to be central to the Law of Moses. Jesus agreed with that assessment when he affirmed it to be the commandment that is above all others (Mark 12:28, 29). But what of the person who simply makes this confession and does nothing more?

James affirms that the confession is correct. But then he points out that *the demons believe* the same thing! They know who God is; they recognized Jesus' identity. Early in Mark's Gospel, Jesus encountered a man with an unclean spirit in a synagogue. When the man saw Jesus, the demons within him cried out, "What do you want with us, Jesus of Nazareth? Have you come to destroy us? I know who you are—the Holy One of God!" (Mark 1:24).

Indeed, there is no confusion among the forces of Satan about who God is and the extent of his power. Because they recognize him, they *shudder.* The person who claims faith without deeds is less responsive to God than a demon!

We might sum up James's point with the common saying "Talk is cheap." Claiming to have faith is of no significance at all if we do not act in faith. If demons can at least tremble, should not those who claim to belong to God act in ways that please him?

III. Exemplars of Faith
(JAMES 2:20-26)
A. Abraham (vv. 20-24)

20. You foolish person, do you want evidence that faith without deeds is useless?

In characterizing those who oppose his view as *foolish,* James is calling them "empty," which is how the same word is translated in Luke 1:53. This is strong language, but we have to remember that James is living in a time that sees no problem with strong moral denunciation of those who are, in fact, in the wrong. Behind the uselessness

HOW TO SAY IT

Abraham	*Ay*-bruh-ham.
Deuteronomy	Due-ter-*ahn*-uh-me.
Josephus	Jo-*see*-fus.
Moriah	Mo-*rye*-uh.
Rahab	*Ray*-hab.
Shema	*She*-muh.

or emptiness of those who cling to a deedless faith lies the attempt to think that God accepts people merely on the basis that they acknowledge his existence. Were that the case, then logic would dictate that demons would be saved!

But James seems to realize that arguments from logic might not convince those who oppose his view. So he proceeds to offer concrete evidence from Jewish history.

21a. Was not our father Abraham considered righteous for what he did

Recalling again that James is writing to an audience of Christians of Jewish background (James 1:1), it is quite proper for him to appeal to an example involving *our father Abraham* (compare Paul's similar appeal in Romans 4:11, 12, 16; Galatians 3:7, 8, 29.) As we remember that Abraham was *considered righteous for what he did,* we keep in mind the context of James's remarks of having just said that "faith without deeds is useless." James asks the question we see here (continued below) in such a way that it assumes agreement. Of course Abraham was justified by his works! Had he had no faith, there would have been no deeds.

21b. when he offered his son Isaac on the altar?

It is also noteworthy that, even though James speaks of Abraham's deeds, he specifically has this one very particular deed in mind. The story of the sacrifice of Isaac is told only once in the Old Testament (Genesis 22:1-19), but it had taken on great significance in the Jewish tradition by the first century AD. Rather than, for example, pointing to Abraham's obedience to God's initial call (12:1-5) or some other event, the rabbis constantly point to this particular act as the preeminent example of Abraham's faithfulness. James, who in many ways is safely assumed to be an observant first-century Jew, is certainly familiar with this tradition. So he draws on it here.

22a. You see that his faith and his actions were working together,

When James says Abraham's *faith and his actions were working together,* he is saying that the man's faith functioned in tandem with his actions (see Hebrews 11:17). Again, the kernel of James's argument in this section is that faith and actions are inseparable. They commingle in such a way that Paul speaks of the "work produced by faith" (1 Thessalonians 1:3; 2 Thessalonians 1:11).

22b. and his faith was made complete by what he did.

James goes further: it is *by what he did* that Abraham's *faith was made complete*. Faith itself is brought to its full realization, its final form, its God-intended purpose when it is working (compare Galatians 5:6). This does not imply flawlessness; instead, it means it is sufficient to do what God desires.

23. And the scripture was fulfilled that says, "Abraham believed God, and it was credited to him as righteousness," and he was called God's friend.

The scripture was fulfilled because the faith noted in Genesis 15:6 (the verse quoted) was made visible by the action of Genesis 22:1-10. The importance of Genesis 15:6 is seen in its being quoted four times in the New Testament (here plus Romans 4:3, 22; and Galatians 3:6).

Abraham's obedience to the command of God on Mount Moriah placed him in the class of individuals who are counted righteous, who conform to the standard that God had set forth. For Abraham to be *called God's friend* (also 2 Chronicles 20:7; Isaiah 41:8) reinforces what James has already said about the nature of justification.

24. You see that a person is considered righteous by what they do and not by faith alone.

Is *faith alone*, a faith that produces no action, a valid option? James says no. Abraham's great deed of faith was a long time in coming, but it demonstrated what God had foreseen: genuine trust in God's promise, trust that Abraham later put on the line. To be counted *righteous* like Abraham, one needs the kind of faith that leads to action. James generalizes from the example of Abraham to reinforce his point.

B. Rahab (vv. 25, 26)

25. In the same way, was not even Rahab the prostitute considered righteous for what she did when she gave lodging to the spies and sent them off in a different direction?

We might think it scandalous—or strange, at the least—that James appeals to the example of *Rahab* to make his point. It was already the case in the first century that some had qualms with what Joshua 2 has to say about this woman. (The Jewish historian Josephus, for example, argued that she was not a prostitute, but an innkeeper.) James, however, gives no evidence that he has reservations about appealing to the example of Rahab, even mentioning that she was *the prostitute* (compare Hebrews 11:31) when he could have left that part out.

Justification is not about sinless perfection on the part of the one who is considered *righteous*. Consider, for example, how Abraham himself tried to rush the fulfillment of God's promise by fathering a child with Hagar, Sarah's slave (Genesis 16). Abraham's faith faltered at other times as well; these showed up in his actions. Though he willingly left his home for the land God was to show him, he twice revealed a lack of trust in God when he lied to protect himself (12:11-13; 20:1, 2).

Rahab, like Abraham, was considered righteous on the basis of her faithful deeds—the singular act of harboring the Israelite spies who had entered the city of Jericho. In her hospitality, she provided for Israelites who were in need. In so doing, she set an example of what James calls on his readers to do.

> **What Do You Think?**
> In what situations might you use the example of Rahab as a point of counseling with a fellow believer? Why?
> **Digging Deeper**
> What potential dangers or backfires should you consider before doing so? Why?

❧ ANTIHEROES ❧

An antihero is a character who doesn't display classic heroic traits but is nevertheless the protagonist and unlikely hero. Antiheroes have a significant place in history, sometimes playing an evil or good role, but more often an ambiguous one.

Robin Hood and his "band of merry men"

are a great example. Most heroes don't steal from *anyone*, rich or poor. And in the original stories, Robin Hood didn't just steal—he killed! The story was later sanitized, with Robin Hood outwitting the wealthy to steal their excess and nobly giving his loot to the poor.

Then there is the prostitute Rahab. She was one of the Bible's many antiheroes, mentioned by James as an example of faith that works. Rahab's story shows us how the Bible tells it like it is. She is an example of the fact that God uses flawed people to accomplish his work. That gives hope to all of us potential antiheroes doesn't it?   —C. R. B.

26. As the body without the spirit is dead, so faith without deeds is dead.

James concludes this portion of his letter with an analogy. The comparison assumes that *the spirit* is the animating, life-giving force in the human body. This concept is found throughout the Old Testament (example: Psalm 31:5), as well as in the New Testament (Luke 8:55; 23:46). The analogy is new in the course of James's argument, but the point is the same as before: faith that makes one righteous cannot be separated from deeds that proceed from it. *Faith without* attendant *deeds* is no faith at all.

> **What Do You Think?**
> What are some ways to stay alert to the danger of what has been called "compassion fatigue" as we help meet the needs of others (compare Galatians 6:9)?
> **Digging Deeper**
> Which of those ways would work best for you personally? Why?

Conclusion

A. In Word and Deed

In popular usage, faith often equates to mere belief, an intellectual acknowledgment of the existence of God. James shows us that true, saving faith goes much deeper than this: it touches every aspect of our lives and guides our every action. The examples that James uses—Abraham and Rahab—highlight these points. Consider that

PEOPLE ARE WATCHING YOUR EXAMPLE!

Visual for Lesson 11. *Point to this visual as you ask what conclusions people will reach while watching your learners' actions or inactions.*

it was not Abraham's mere acknowledgment of God's promise that justified him. Rather, it was his action on the basis of that promise that justified him. Likewise, it was not mere verbal acknowledgment of the Israelites' God that justified Rahab (Joshua 2:8, 9). That acknowledgment went hand in hand with her actions in sheltering Israelite spies from certain death (2:2-4). She undoubtedly risked her own life in doing so.

Certainly, we are saved through faith, not by works (Ephesians 2:8, 9); we cannot earn salvation by our works (Romans 3:27; 9:32; Galatians 2:16). But what type of faith saves? The type that works. A profession of faith must be accompanied by action; otherwise it is no faith at all. A profession of faith that is unaccompanied by the works God intends we do brings disrepute on the faith we claim to have. Unless the Word is changing us inside and out—in heart and mind to speak *and* act—our faith will be no faith at all.

B. Prayer

Father, may our faith in you not be limited to a mere affirmation of your existence. Instead, may it be manifested in the way we live, including the way we extend help to those in need. In Jesus' name we pray. Amen.

C. Thought to Remember
Faith with no works
is no faith at all.

INVOLVEMENT LEARNING

Enhance your lesson with NIV Bible Student *(from your curriculum supplier) and the reproducible activity page (at www.standardlesson.com or in the back of the* NIV Standard Lesson Commentary Deluxe Edition*).*

Into the Lesson

Option. Begin by allowing volunteers to share their results of completing last week's take-home activity. Then divide your class into three groups, giving each group one of the following incomplete sentences. Encourage every group member to offer a completion for the group's assigned sentence.

1–*You know I love my spouse when you see me doing this:* _____.

2–*Because I love my children, you'll see me doing this:* _____.

3–*You know how I feel about my job when you see me doing this:* _____.

After a few minutes, call for volunteers to share their completed sentences. Choose a few examples, and ask the class questions like this one: "If [insert name] told you he loves his wife but then did just the opposite of what he mentioned here, what would you conclude?"

Say, "The connection between words and actions is important. Today's Bible study offers us insight on this issue."

Into the Word

Distribute handouts (you prepare) of the lesson text. As you read the text slowly, listeners should do the following (which you will have printed on the handout): 1–Underline every command. 2–Mark illustrations that clarify commands with ≈ symbol. 3–Mark sections that seem particularly important with * symbol. 4–Mark surprising sections with ! symbol. 5–Mark anything you don't understand with ? symbol.

Read the text aloud twice to give class members ample opportunity to absorb what it is saying as they perform the above. Then call for volunteers to point out the verses they underlined and marked with ≈. After discussing disagreements, ask for volunteers to tell what sections they marked with other symbols and tell why. As questions come up,

toss them back to the class by asking, "Who has an insight for that question?" Use the commentary to clarify.

Option. Distribute copies of the "Reconsider the Stories" exercise from the activity page, which you can download, for deeper study. Ask learners to complete this activity in pairs or triads before you have volunteers share what they've discussed.

Brainstorming. Ask half the class to voice reasons why connecting faith with works is difficult; jot responses on the board as they are called out. After two minutes, invite the other half of the class to voice reasons why connecting faith with works is reasonable. Again, take two minutes to jot responses on the board.

During the whole-class discussion that follows, point out that the two lists don't necessarily contradict each other; rather, they actually are mutually supporting at certain points. Ask learners to point out examples of that fact from the two lists. Be prepared to do so yourself.

Option. Distribute copies of the "Finish the Thoughts" exercise from the activity page for learners to complete individually as a post-test. Allow only one minute.

Into Life

Write on the board the phrases *I Believe* and *I Do* as headers to two lists. Ask class members to name tenets of the Christian faith for you to write in the first column. After a suitable list is created, ask learners to suggest specific actions for the *I Do* list that would demonstrate Christian faith for each entry in the *I Believe* listing (example: the statement *I believe Jesus is the only way to God* could draw the response *Therefore I participate in my congregation's efforts to evangelize*).

Challenge students to choose one of the listed actions to initiate personally. Close with prayer for students' faith to be combined with dynamic new works for Christ.

TAMING THE TONGUE

DEVOTIONAL READING: Isaiah 50:4-11
BACKGROUND SCRIPTURE: James 3:1-12

JAMES 3:1-12

¹ Not many of you should become teachers, my fellow believers, because you know that we who teach will be judged more strictly. ² We all stumble in many ways. Anyone who is never at fault in what they say is perfect, able to keep their whole body in check.

³ When we put bits into the mouths of horses to make them obey us, we can turn the whole animal. ⁴ Or take ships as an example. Although they are so large and are driven by strong winds, they are steered by a very small rudder wherever the pilot wants to go. ⁵ Likewise, the tongue is a small part of the body, but it makes great boasts. Consider what a great forest is set on fire by a small spark. ⁶ The tongue also is a fire, a world of evil among the parts of the body. It corrupts the whole body, sets the whole course of one's life on fire, and is itself set on fire by hell.

⁷ All kinds of animals, birds, reptiles and sea creatures are being tamed and have been tamed by mankind, ⁸ but no human being can tame the tongue. It is a restless evil, full of deadly poison.

⁹ With the tongue we praise our Lord and Father, and with it we curse human beings, who have been made in God's likeness. ¹⁰ Out of the same mouth come praise and cursing. My brothers and sisters, this should not be. ¹¹ Can both fresh water and salt water flow from the same spring? ¹² My brothers and sisters, can a fig tree bear olives, or a grapevine bear figs? Neither can a salt spring produce fresh water.

KEY VERSE

The tongue is a small part of the body, but it makes great boasts. Consider what a great forest is set on fire by a small spark. —**James 3:5**

MANY FACES OF WISDOM

Unit 3: Faith and Wisdom in James

LESSONS 9–13

LESSON AIMS

After participating in this lesson, each learner will be able to:

1. List several consequences of speaking with an untamed tongue.

2. Explain the relationship between lack of wisdom and an untamed tongue.

3. Role-play modern situations in which the tongue is used for good or for evil.

LESSON OUTLINE

Introduction
  A. The Power of Words
  B. Lesson Context
  I. Warning to Teachers (JAMES 3:1, 2)
  A. Future Consequences (v. 1)
  B. Present Reality (v. 2)
  II. Power of the Tongue (JAMES 3:3-8)
  A. Like Horses (v. 3)
  B. Like Ships (vv. 4, 5a)
    It's a Learning Process
  C. Like Fire (vv. 5b, 6)
  D. Unlike Tamed Creatures (vv. 7, 8)
  III. Image of God (JAMES 3:9-12)
  A. Blessings and Curses (vv. 9, 10)
    Speaking with a Forked Tongue?
  B. Water and Fruit (vv. 11, 12)
Conclusion
  A. Consider Your Words
  B. Prayer
  C. Thought to Remember

Introduction

A. The Power of Words

The longer we live, the more acutely we are aware of the power of the tongue to destroy. From the days when we hurled schoolyard taunts or insults (or were on the receiving end of those), we realized the power of words to hurt or damage.

Every generation seems to learn this lesson the hard way. Consider, for example, the impact of social media in the world in general and in the church in particular. With fingers typing as an extension of the tongue, Christians argue sharply with each other about faith, politics, etc., in publicly visible Facebook threads. Prominent ministers and authors quarrel with one another on Twitter; relationships are strained or broken on ill-considered tweets of 280 characters or fewer. What would the Bible writers say about such practices?

B. Lesson Context

As we saw in previous lessons, some practices of James's audience ran counter to what they voiced in speech. Up to the point of today's passage, James has written about negative modes of speech, such as the self-justifying claim that one is tempted by God (James 1:13), the flattering speech that reveals partiality toward the rich and shames the poor (2:3-6), the careless speech of those who wish the poor well but do not help them (2:16; see lesson 11), and the superficial speech of the one claiming to have faith but lacking deeds (2:18; see lesson 11).

Other examples of improper speech occurring later include those of judging and slandering (James 4:11), boasting (4:13-16), and grumbling (5:9; see lesson 13). Sandwiched in between is today's text.

Since today's lesson draws heavily on figures of speech, some background information in that regard is in order. Figurative language adds interest and excitement to writing; chief among figures of speech are metaphors. A metaphor takes an idea and imposes it on an unrelated but familiar idea to help explain the qualities of the original.

One easy example is the phrase "Joseph is a fruitful vine" (Genesis 49:22). This does not mean that this particular son of Jacob was literally a grapevine or other vegetation. It means, rather, that he was productive in some way.

James's use of metaphor in speaking of the tongue reflects how other biblical writers use metaphor in speaking of the heart. Indeed, *heart* and *tongue* are used in poetic passages to stand parallel to one another.

> The tongue of the righteous is choice silver,
>   but the heart of the wicked is of little value.
> —Proverbs 10:20

> Therefore my heart is glad and my tongue rejoices;
>   my body also will rest in hope.   —Acts 2:26

Biblical writers use the imagery of the heart to speak of what defines and reveals our true, inner nature. In the same way, the tongue is more than just a part of the body. The tongue is equated with speech, of course. But James's insight extends beyond that. How one uses the tongue reveals the nature of the heart as motives are connected with speech and actions.

I. Warning to Teachers
(JAMES 3:1, 2)
A. Future Consequences (v. 1)

1a. Not many of you should become teachers, my fellow believers,

James opens this portion of his letter with a warning to those who want to become *teachers*. The Greek word being translated is equivalent to the Aramaic word *Rabbi* or *Rabboni*, referring to a respected teacher (see John 20:16; compare 3:2; the same word in the original language is trans-

HOW TO SAY IT

Aramaic	Air-uh-*may*-ik.
Corinthians	Ko-*rin*-thee-unz (*th* as in *thin*).
Jude	Jood.
Nez Percé	Nehz *Purse.*
Rabbi	*Rab*-eye.
Rabboni	Rab-*o*-nye.
Thessalonians	*Thess*-uh-*lo*-nee-unz (th as in thin).

lated "teachers" in Acts 13:1; 1 Corinthians 12:28; etc.). In some cases, people who are not teachers should become teachers (see Hebrews 5:12). In other cases, people who are or desire to be teachers should not be. The latter problem is the issue in the verse before us.

Part of the problem that James may be addressing here is that many desire to become teachers because of the importance it gives them in the church. An unholy desire to be a teacher is likely grounded in a desire for status (Matthew 23:1-7). Rabbis are not necessarily better off financially than others, but they are accorded honor.

1b. because you know that we who teach will be judged more strictly.

James sounds a warning for those who are or desire to be teachers—and he writes as one who is a teacher himself. James has already discussed the problem of discrimination based on wealth and social standing (see James 2:1-13). So the warning against seeking to teach can be seen to continue to address the desire for standing while moving into the discussion of use of the tongue.

It may also be that some teachers are being careless with the words they speak. This could stem from a desire for the honor that the teaching role brings at the expense of the content of what is taught. *Being judged more strictly* calls to mind the words of Jesus:

> Everyone will have to give account on the day of judgment for every empty word they have spoken. For by your words you will be acquitted, and by your words you will be condemned (Matthew 12:36, 37).

To teach carelessly, falsely, with flattering speech, etc., marks one who is not faithfully exerting self-control (compare Romans 16:17, 18; 1 Thessalonians 2:3-5; Jude 16).

There are two primary schools of thought about how James 3:1 relates to what follows. Some see it as introducing the general topic of speech by referring to a particular circumstance of speech. Others see the reverse, saying that this verse introduces material especially important for teachers themselves (see also lesson 13). This commentary will consider the text as instruction specifically for teachers and those who desire to be teachers. Even so, the analogies James uses and the direct points he makes are certainly applicable in an extended sense to all Christians.

B. Present Reality (v. 2)

2. We all stumble in many ways. Anyone who is never at fault in what they say is perfect, able to keep their whole body in check.

The word translated *stumble* begins a word picture of careless uses of the tongue (*what they say*). All of us are guilty of tripping up in various ways. To be wary of how one's words are taken is particularly important for the teacher who is charged with communicating Christian doctrine to new believers. Teachers who fail in this area will speak in ways that are harmful to the church body. Habits of speech are, therefore, particularly important as the teacher gives direction to the community.

Even so, the person who is never guilty of verbal miscues does not exist. The hypothetical person who achieves perfection in speech would, by extension, be able to control every aspect of his or her life; that is, be able *to keep their whole body in check.* Older versions of the Bible use the translation *bridle* instead of *check.* In that sense, James is using a word picture of a horse that is under control. This is reinforced in James 1:26 where the same word is translated "keep a tight rein."

If the teacher can control the tongue in teaching, then the result will be to impart the truth of the faith. Consider all that teachers are responsible for: they must pass along biblical truth accurately and thoroughly. They are responsible for interpretation and application. They guide Christian believers in many aspects of life—spiritually, intellectually, and morally.

Chapter 3 is pivotal as James explicitly connects speech to control of the body. To control the tongue means that one can control one's entire self. Teaching, then, is not limited to speech. It also comes about through the actions of the teacher. Truthful teaching does not simply mean that the teacher says the correct words to explain the Christian faith. Truthful teaching includes consistency: words spoken by the teacher are consistent with the teacher's life. The walk matches the talk.

II. Power of the Tongue
(JAMES 3:3-8)
A. Like Horses (v. 3)

3. When we put bits into the mouths of horses to make them obey us, we can turn the whole animal.

A bridle usually includes a bit, which is a metal device inserted into the mouth of a horse. The bit results in discomfort, causing the horse to respond to the pressure of the reins attached to the bridle. If the rider pulls back on both reins, the horse will slow until the pressure from the reins is released. If the rider pulls the right rein, the trained horse will turn right until the pressure from the bit is relieved. Just as the bit guides the horse, so the tongue of the teacher guides the church and has a similar large impact on its course.

B. Like Ships (vv. 4, 5a)

4. Or take ships as an example. Although they are so large and are driven by strong winds, they are steered by a very small rudder wherever the pilot wants to go.

With a second analogy, James extends his discussion of the impact of the teacher's words on the church. The analogy involves contrasting the size of a ship's steering mechanism with the size of the ship itself. Two forces are at work: (1) *strong winds* on the ship as a whole and (2) the ship's *pilot* at the helm. So much depends on the one steering the ship!

❧ IT'S A LEARNING PROCESS ❧

I learned to ride a bicycle when I was 7 years old. Thirty years later, I bought my first motorcycle. The transition was an easy one because the principles of balance and steering apply to both. At 82, I'm still occasionally asked, "Have you ever had an accident?" My answer is always, "Never a fatal one." I'm still learning as I become a better rider. Steering a boat is similar. Practice makes a skilled helmsman.

Controlling our tongues also takes practice. It can take a lifetime to learn how to use our tongues to help and not to hurt. How practiced are you in the steering of others by means of your tongue?

—C. R. B.

5a. Likewise, the tongue is a small part of the body, but it makes great boasts.

Before James moves to his third analogy, he pauses to ensure that his readers do not miss the point of the first two: *the tongue* has an outsized importance relative to its *small* size.

What Do You Think?
What are some safeguards Christians can adopt to prevent boasting?
Digging Deeper
How do passages such as Psalms 44:8; 94:4; Romans 3:25-27; 2 Corinthians 10:7-18; 11:10-21; and 2 Timothy 3:1-5 influence your conclusions?

C. Like Fire (vv. 5b, 6)

5b. Consider what a great forest is set on fire by a small spark.

Whether we have experienced a forest fire personally or not, all of us are aware of the devastating impact that an uncontrolled blaze can have. Often, these fires are caused by something very *small*—a dropped match or a campfire not adequately snuffed out. The second half of verse 5 leads into verse 6.

6a. The tongue also is a fire, a world of evil among the parts of the body.

Similar phrasing is found in Proverbs 16:27 and Isaiah 30:27.

6b. It corrupts the whole body, sets the whole course of one's life on fire, and is itself set on fire by hell.

Though the tongue is only one piece of *the whole body,* it has an outsized effect.

Three results of an unchecked tongue are noted. The first (*corrupts the whole body*) is that a person is made unholy. The second (*sets the whole course of one's life on fire*) involves a Greek word referring to birth or lineage (see also in Matthew 1:1, 18; Luke 1:14); the tongue can upset the natural cycle of life in very short order. The third (*is itself set on fire by hell*) offers insight regarding the source of abuses inflicted by the tongue (compare Matthew 5:22).

What Do You Think?
What "emergency" tongue-control procedures would you propose for Christians when a conversation starts to shed more heat than light?
Digging Deeper
Under what circumstances, if any, should you merely walk away from such an occurrence rather than trying to help cool things down?

D. Unlike Tamed Creatures (vv. 7, 8)

7. All kinds of animals, birds, reptiles and sea creatures are being tamed and have been tamed by mankind,

James now begins a comparison from another setting: that of humanity's taming of various creatures. By *tamed* James does not mean that humans have made pets or farm animals out of all these creatures (compare Job 41:1-5). The idea of taming is closer to the command of Genesis 1:28 for humankind to "rule over" all creatures. There is no creature that humans have not been able to dominate. Humans have the proven ability to exercise dominion over all earthly creatures, whether for good or bad.

8. but no human being can tame the tongue. It is a restless evil, full of deadly poison.

Animals can be tamed, but can *the tongue*? No one truly brings his or her tongue into full submission.

As we ponder this fact, we should be careful not to take this verse out of context. It would be wrong to conclude, "James says no one can tame the tongue, so why even try? It is a futile waste of time."

Those who accept that argument should read the previous verses again. Although no one is able to keep his or her tongue perfectly controlled, we must make the effort since uncontrolled speech destroys. James's word picture of *deadly poison* brings to mind Psalm 140:3: "[The violent] make their tongues as sharp as a serpent's; the poison of vipers is on their lips" (compare Romans 3:13).

> **What Do You Think?**
> What is the single most important thing you can do this week to tame your tongue better?
> **Digging Deeper**
> What problems have you seen in this regard concerning words "spoken" on social media? What Scripture passage can you keep near your keyboard to restrain your impulse?

III. Image of God
(JAMES 3:9-12)
A. Blessings and Curses (vv. 9, 10)

9. With the tongue we praise our Lord and Father, and with it we curse human beings, who have been made in God's likeness.

Throughout his letter, James is concerned with the divided hearts of his audience (James 1:8; lesson 9). A divided heart most clearly reveals itself in divided speech (see Lesson Context). Divided speech is heard when the tongue speaks blessing in the worship of *God* and then curses those *who have been made in God's likeness* (Genesis 1:26, 27).

Divided speech is shaped by the attitude of the speaker. As the speaker badmouths those who are created in God's image, something negative is revealed about the speaker's attitude toward God.

This point is so important that it bears stressing again from a slightly different angle: if the tongue is blessing God in worship one minute only to turn around and curse those made in God's image in the next, then corrective action is called for. A corrective action of keeping silent will be a start but only a start; the deeper problem to solve is one of heart attitude.

Some students detect echoes of this problem in Israel's deficient practices of worship as those practices were condemned by God: "These people come near to me with their mouth and honor me with their lips, but their hearts are far from me" (Isaiah 29:13).

⁂ SPEAKING WITH A FORKED TONGUE? ⁂

In 1855, the US government told the chief of the Nez Percé tribe that his people would be allowed to keep millions of acres of tribal lands in the Pacific Northwest. A treaty was signed. But a few years later, the government forced a new treaty on the tribe due to the discovery of gold on tribal land.

When the chief died, his son and successor fought to recover the land that had been promised earlier. Some of the Nez Percé were slaughtered; survivors were forced to live on a small fraction of their ancestral lands.

Historical events such as this provide the backdrop for movies of the "Old West" type, featuring Indians concluding that the white man "speaks with a forked tongue," or variations of that phrase. Whether or not Native Americans ever actually said that, we speak with forked tongue when we say we revere God as our heavenly Father but then do harm in word or deed to our fellow humans, who are made in his image. How does our speech bear witness to our God for good or for ill?

—C. R. B.

10. Out of the same mouth come praise and cursing. My brothers and sisters, this should not be.

A modern illustration of this problem is inconsistent use of social media. Think of a hypothetical believer who posts positive messages of witness for Christ one minute, then turns around and posts personal attacks the next! (See the Lesson Introduction.)

The bottom line is that this double life is unacceptable to God. Words that flow from our hearts—whether uttered by *mouth* or typed by fingers—should be consistently holy.

B. Water and Fruit (vv. 11, 12)

11. Can both fresh water and salt water flow from the same spring?

The questions that James asks here and in the next verse are meant to stir reflection in the hearts of teachers and potential teachers. The questions are rhetorical, with answers obvious as they concern clear incompatibilities. Of course *a spring* cannot produce both *fresh water and salt water.*

The application is impossible to miss: teachers in the church are called to speak consistently in truth and love. Those whose hearts are right will find it impossible to mix blessing and cursing.

12. My brothers and sisters, can a fig tree bear olives or a grapevine bear figs? Neither can a salt spring produce fresh water.

The products mentioned are common to the agricultural economy of the day. James draws on this fact to craft another rhetorical question, reinforcing the point just made (see Matthew 7:16).

Conclusion

A. Consider Your Words

Today's lesson concerns the destructive power of the tongue. Specifically, it deals with the words spoken by those who were recognized as teachers in the first-century church (and perhaps those who aspired to that role). Their words were of special concern to James because they involved matters that have an eternal import. All of us can think of ways in which words spoken by teachers have had beneficial or damaging effects on the lives of their hearers. Words should be a source of spiritual growth and sustenance.

But how many of us have seen church splits that resulted from ill-advised words? How many of us

Has your tongue gone wild?

Visual for Lesson 12. *While discussing verse 2, pose the question on this visual, then fall silent to allow time for thoughtful responses.*

have seen men and women leave the faith because of spiritually damaging utterances? These concerns lie at the heart of today's text.

James's description of the tongue may lead us to conclude that attempting to control it is hopeless. Admittedly, the tongue *is* extremely difficult to control, as we know all too well. All of us have said things that we came to regret.

What is more, the work of taming the tongue is a lifelong task. While today's text directly addressed teachers, it calls on all Christians to examine themselves. Are we faithfully using our powers of speech daily? Do we speak words of truth and grace consistently at home, on the job, and in church? Are our critiques healing or destructive?

These are questions for everyone, no matter what position or stage of life. In effect, we are all teachers on some level, by our tongues as well as the examples we set.

B. Prayer

Lord God, as we come to see more clearly the destructive power of the tongue, we pray for strength to bridle and to restrain our tongues from all forms of evil speech. Transform our words so that they bring glory to your name. In Jesus' name we pray. Amen.

C. Thought to Remember

The tongue must be controlled.

INVOLVEMENT LEARNING

Enhance your lesson with NIV Bible Student *(from your curriculum supplier) and the reproducible activity page (at www.standardlesson.com or in the back of the* NIV Standard Lesson Commentary Deluxe Edition*).*

Into the Lesson

Distribute handouts (you prepare) on which are printed the three scenarios below, but just one scenario per handout. Form small groups or study pairs; give each a handout of one scenario. Allow a few minutes for each group or pair to answer this question: Given the facts of the scenario, what action should be taken (or should have been taken), if any?

1– My third-grade teacher in the public elementary school once called me "air-headed" when I didn't have the right response to a question.

2–When a math teacher at our college couldn't get a quadratic equation to compute, a student had to point out that he was trying to take the square root of a negative number! Such incompetence!!

3–One professor at the local college really knows how to teach economics! The students hang on his every word. But from what I know of his life outside the college classroom, the man is a racist.

After a few minutes, have groups present their conclusions for class discussion. Make a transition by putting learners back in their same groups and change the scenarios as follows: (1) instead of a public school teacher it was a Sunday school teacher, (2) instead of math course at college it is a church class in basic doctrine taught by an elder, (3) the professor in economics is also a deacon at your church, and he excels at teaching Bible. After another round of group and whole-class discussion, say, "Let's see if James has some thoughts that can help us with solutions."

Into the Word

Recruit in advance one or more volunteers having artistic skills to come to class with very large sketches they have made of the images in today's lesson text (figs, bit, etc.). Furnish large sections of poster board for the task. Put the sketches on display just before you read the lesson text aloud. Gesture toward them as visual reinforcements at appropriate times during the lesson.

After reading the lesson text aloud, pose the following questions for discussion. 1–Which comparison gives you the greatest insight into problems with the tongue? 2–Which comparison reminds you most of an issue you've seen but not experienced personally? 3–Which comparison illustrates most sharply a difficult situation you have had to face?

Option. For extended discussion, distribute copies of the "Positive Pointers" exercise on the activity page, which you can download. Have learners work in study pairs to complete as indicated.

Into Life

Distribute four slips of paper on which you have printed the following situations, one per slip. Form learners into pairs and give a slip to each pair.

1–You overhear a teacher at church talking at length about how upset he is with your minister.

2–A friend describes the terrible housekeeping habits of a mutual friend.

3–An snippy acquaintance asks you if you got your outfit at a thrift store.

4–A friend gripes about behavior of someone's child.

Ask pairs to develop and enact a role play before the class the situation on the pair's slip of paper. Instruct that the role play should demonstrate a Christian response. Allow each pair two minutes to prepare and two minutes to role-play. After each, encourage reactions in open discussion.

Option. Distribute copies of the "Situational Suggestions" exercise from the activity page. Due to its personal nature and need for possibly lengthy reflection, it should be a take-home exercise. To encourage completion, promise to ask for volunteers to disclose results at the beginning of next week's class.

Close with sentence prayers from learners. Wrap up with your own prayer that asks for God's for help in controlling the tongue.

TWO KINDS OF WISDOM

DEVOTIONAL READING: Psalm 32:1-11
BACKGROUND SCRIPTURE: James 3:13-18; 5:7-12

JAMES 3:13-18

¹³ Who is wise and understanding among you? Let them show it by their good life, by deeds done in the humility that comes from wisdom. ¹⁴ But if you harbor bitter envy and selfish ambition in your hearts, do not boast about it or deny the truth. ¹⁵ Such "wisdom" does not come down from heaven but is earthly, unspiritual, demonic. ¹⁶ For where you have envy and selfish ambition, there you find disorder and every evil practice.

¹⁷ But the wisdom that comes from heaven is first of all pure; then peace-loving, considerate, submissive, full of mercy and good fruit, impartial and sincere. ¹⁸ Peacemakers who sow in peace reap a harvest of righteousness.

JAMES 5:7-12

⁷ Be patient, then, brothers and sisters, until the Lord's coming. See how the farmer waits for the land to yield its valuable crop, patiently waiting for the autumn and spring rains. ⁸ You too, be patient and stand firm, because the Lord's coming is near. ⁹ Don't grumble against one another, brothers and sisters, or you will be judged. The Judge is standing at the door!

¹⁰ Brothers and sisters, as an example of patience in the face of suffering, take the prophets who spoke in the name of the Lord. ¹¹ As you know, we count as blessed those who have persevered. You have heard of Job's perseverance and have seen what the Lord finally brought about. The Lord is full of compassion and mercy.

¹² Above all, my brothers and sisters, do not swear—not by heaven or by earth or by anything else. All you need to say is a simple "Yes" or "No." Otherwise you will be condemned.

KEY VERSE

The wisdom that is from above is first pure, then peaceable, gentle, and easy to be intreated, full of mercy and good fruits, without partiality, and without hypocrisy. —**James 3:17**

MANY FACES OF
WISDOM

Unit 3: Faith and Wisdom in James
LESSONS 9–13

LESSON AIMS

After participating in this lesson, each learner will be able to:

1. State the answer to the question posed in James 3:13a.

2. Contrast the sources, characteristics, and results of the two kinds of wisdom.

3. Create a plan for improvement regarding the one behavior of James 3:17 that he or she lacks most.

LESSON OUTLINE

Introduction
A. How to Suffer

It has been said that all of life is suffering. This idea is not all that shocking, of course. It has been articulated in many contexts around the world. As Christians, we understand that the suffering we experience is a result of sin in general.

Some try to downplay the reality of suffering. But suffering—especially in the form of persecution—is part of the Christian life. In James's day, the limited scope of Christianity shaped the types of persecution. Today, when Christianity is a global faith, persecution differs from culture to culture. In certain African nations, Muslim populations have severely persecuted Christian neighbors. In other locations, official government policy hinders Christian meetings and the formation of churches.

In the West, the matter is not quite so clear-cut. What constitutes persecution? While we are not being thrown to the lions in the Roman Colosseum or burned at the stake, subtle forms of persecution do indeed exist. These include social ostracism, which is part of the life experience of many Christians. How should we handle this kind of persecution when we encounter it?

B. Lesson Context

At the beginning of our studies in James, we noted a few themes that run throughout the letter. These themes unite the disparate topics that James addresses. Wisdom is one such theme. Recall, for example, that at the outset of his letter James encouraged his readers to have perseverance in the midst of temptations or trials (James 1:2-4; lesson 9). This they could do by actively seeking God's wisdom (1:5). In today's text, James addresses two very different situations, both of which demand wisdom on the part of believers.

I. In Education
(JAMES 3:13-18)

James 3:1-12, last week's lesson, introduced an address to teachers and potential teachers among first-century churches specifically. Even so, we proposed extended application to all Christians. We wonder, however, if the remainder of James 3 is also addressed specifically to teachers and potential teachers since James does not use the words *teachers* in these six verses. Ultimately, though, such a question is only hypothetical; it's impossible to imagine these verses applying only to teachers and not to anyone else!

A. Good Teachers (v. 13)

13. Who is wise and understanding among you? Let them show it by their good life, by deeds done in the humility that comes from wisdom.

By speaking of the one *who is wise and understanding*, James likely continues to have the teachers in mind. He introduces the issue in a confrontational way: "So you think you're wise and understanding?" he seems to ask. "Then prove it by living *a good life*." The word in the original language refers to one's entire way of life or lifestyle. This word occurs in a dozen other New Testament passages.

The teacher's pattern of life must manifest good *deeds*; a teacher must put into practice personally what is taught. We see this idea of matching talk with way of life repeatedly in the New Testament: the truth of Christian teaching is verified by the way of life of those who teach it.

The apostle Peter seems equally concerned with the relationship between good deeds and one's lifestyle (1 Peter 2:12). A teacher's understanding—or claims of having understanding—must be backed up with evidence (see James 2:18; lesson 11). There is a word for those who say one thing but do another. That word is *hypocrite*.

The word translated *humility* carries much overlap in meaning with the word *gentleness*.

HOW TO SAY IT

Corinthians	Ko-*rin*-thee-unz (*th* as in *thin*).
Deuteronomy	Due-ter-*ahn*-uh-me.
Galatians	Guh-*lay*-shunz.
Philemon	Fih-*lee*-mun or Fye-*lee*-mun.
Philippians	Fih-*lip*-ee-unz.
Titus	*Ty*-tus.

Paul connects the two Greek words that way in 2 Corinthians 10:1 and Titus 3:2 (there translated "considerate" and "gentle").

❧ WHAT MINISTERS MUST KNOW ❧

In the confidence of youth, many preachers and teachers who are fresh out of Bible college or seminary are tempted to trust in their recently acquired knowledge. That was true of me when I first entered ministry. It took some difficult relationships with critical church members to convince me that knowing all the right answers to doctrinal questions wasn't the sole qualification for having a blessed ministry.

Yet God blessed me with one or more wise elders in every one of those churches. Their years of life had taught them some things about ministry that I had not learned in the classroom. I had knowledge that they didn't have; but they had wisdom that I didn't have.

James doesn't make wisdom and knowledge mutually exclusive. The good teacher will have both! Do you?   —C. R. B.

B. Earthly Wisdom (vv. 14-16)

14. But if you harbor bitter envy and selfish ambition in your hearts, do not boast about it or deny the truth.

Envy translates a word that can also be rendered "zeal," as it is in John 2:17—that's zeal in a good sense. The lesson verse before us portrays zeal in a bad sense, as an attitude that crosses over into inappropriate jealousy (Romans 13:13; etc.). That such envy is *bitter* suggests that it manifests itself in anger and harsh speaking.

It is conceivable in this context that teachers might harbor envy of each other's gifts. This would result in strife, as it had in Corinth (compare 1 Corinthians 1:10-13; 11:18). If this is the case, there is no reason for any of James's readers to *boast about* their understanding or their (so-called) wisdom. Such behavior will seem from the outside to prove that their teaching is a lie. Thus it brings disrepute to *the truth* of the gospel they proclaim.

15. Such "wisdom" does not come down from heaven but is earthly, unspiritual, demonic.

James has articulated the standard: lives must match words. But the reality is that at least some among James's readership do not meet this standard. They adhere to their own *wisdom,* a wisdom that *does not come down from heaven,* meaning that it is not from God (contrast James 1:17). All one has to do is consider its fruits in 3:14 to see this! We might say that *earthly* wisdom is "worldly." The idea is the same: it does not originate from God.

Unspiritual is the very opposite of spiritual (see also Jude 19)—devoid of the Spirit of God. The condemnation *demonic* reinforces the identity of its source (compare 1 Timothy 4:1).

> **What Do You Think?**
> How should we handle wisdom principles that seem to be at odds with one another? (Example: Proverbs 26:4 in contrast to 26:5?)
>
> *Digging Deeper*
> How should your reaction differ, if at all, when someone quotes folk wisdom as advice? (Example: *Look before you leap* versus *He who hesitates is lost.*

16. For where you have envy and selfish ambition, there you find disorder and every evil practice.

All of this should be no surprise: worldly wisdom leads to bad outcomes. In this case, it leads to *disorder and every evil practice* (compare Galatians 5:19-21). The communal impact of this "wisdom" is damaging in the extreme. It threatens the very integrity of the churches.

C. Heavenly Wisdom (vv. 17, 18)

17. But the wisdom that comes from heaven is first of all pure; then peace-loving, consider-

ate, submissive, full of mercy and good fruit, impartial and sincere.

There is a better choice! The adjectives that James applies to *the wisdom that comes from heaven,* from God, call to mind Paul's list of the fruit of the Spirit (Galatians 5:22, 23). Most of these terms are clear because they are used in a manner that is consistent with the other writers of the New Testament.

Submissive means something like "willing to yield" or "open to reason." To be *impartial* goes hand in hand with having sincerity (compare James 1:22, 26; 2:1-4, 9).

❧ A PEACEFUL APPROACH ❧

As my late wife, Pat, declined in health, we bought a "lift chair" for her. It both reclined and boosted her into a semi-standing position. Within a week the chair quit working. I called the furniture store to demand an immediate repair. I was told that a repairman would be out in a week. At my insistence, he came the next day. But the defective part would take weeks to arrive. I then demanded a new chair. My insistence was met with refusal.

But soon Judy arrived. I expressed my frustration, and she volunteered to help. I listened as she sweetly explained the situation. Within a few minutes, Judy received the promise that a new chair would be delivered the next day.

Judy's approach to the problem was a perfect example of wisdom. Her gentleness contrasted with my brashness; her peaceful approach countered my anger. Judy showed me how to practice what James said. Are you a Judy, or do you *need* a Judy?
                                                    —C. R. B.

18. Peacemakers who sow in peace reap a harvest of righteousness.

The desired goal of one who seeks true wisdom is peace. Heretofore, the teachers may have been fostering (or at least haven't tried to stop) conflicts among themselves (James 4:1). Those who are *peacemakers,* however, are said to *sow in peace* (compare Matthew 5:9; Romans 14:19). *A harvest of righteousness* can be both what is sown and what is harvested as a cycle of peace begins. Righteousness is inclusive of one's words and one's works (compare Philippians 1:11).

Is your wisdom FROM ABOVE?

Visual for Lesson 13. *While discussing 3:17, ask the class to prayerfully consider their answer to the question on this visual for one minute or less.*

II. In Persecution

(JAMES 5:7-12)

In order best to understand James's directives in 5:7-12, next, we have to understand that these are in response to the first six verses of the chapter. A strong argument can be made that 5:1-6 is spoken against landlords who are unbelievers. We notice that they are not called to repent but to "weep and wail" in light of the coming judgment (James 5:1; contrast 4:7-10).

Such landowners come from the handful of rich outsiders who make life miserable for many of their tenant farmers and/or day laborers. It is unlikely that such landlords ever hear or read these words themselves. Instead, the accusations are written for the benefit of impoverished Christians of Jewish background to whom the letter as a whole is addressed (note the 14 uses of the phrase "brothers and sisters"; James 1:2, 16, 19; 2:1; etc.).

A. Be Patient (vv. 7-11)

7. Be patient, then brothers and sisters, until the Lord's coming. See how the farmer waits for the land to yield its valuable crop, patiently waiting for the autumn and spring rains.

James is writing to a group of believers who have cause to be angry and despondent. The phrase *brothers and sisters* indicates that James's words are not intended for the rich landlord unbelievers of James 5:1-6 (see above), but for Christians who suffer at their hands.

James points the oppressed believers to *the Lord's coming* as the ultimate solution. This might seem like a cop-out to some modern readers who are used to enacting change through the democratic process. But we have to remember that the world of the first century AD has no such process. Appeal for change might be made to the consciences of those who have the power to make a change (see Philemon 8-17). But hope for change ultimately resides in taking the long view, which looks to the return of Christ.

The patience this requires is illustrated by an analogy of a *farmer*. To await Jesus' return requires *patiently waiting* on the part of believers (compare Galatians 6:9). Just as the farmer waits patiently for his crop, the poor, oppressed believers are to wait patiently for the coming of God's judgment. Because God can be trusted to send a harvest in its time (Deuteronomy 11:14; Jeremiah 5:24; Joel 2:23), Jesus can also be trusted to return as he has promised.

The seasons of rain mentioned may not be similar to our experience. In Israel it is quite rare for rain to fall between May 1 and October 15. Thus *the autumn and spring rains* refers to rain that comes during the rest of the year (compare Song of Songs 2:11). Since James's addressees are "scattered among the nations" (James 1:1), their experience will differ by location. But they probably know of the crop and weather cycles of the land of Israel, at least from what Scripture tells them about it.

8. You too, be patient and stand firm, because the Lord's coming is near.

Just like the farmer of verse 7, James's audience is to be *patient*. This no less applies to us today. The counsel to *stand firm*, or be strengthened, speaks to one's inner resolve. Christians must be resolute and courageous in earthly circumstances while awaiting *the Lord's coming*. Such resolve will involve rejecting the negative views of skeptics (2 Peter 3:3-15; etc.).

> *What Do You Think?*
> ▶ Without giving directive adivce, how would you counsel someone who comes to you admitting a problem with impatience?
> *Digging Deeper*
> How would your approach differ for someone who obviously displays impatience, but seems unaware of the problem?

9a. Don't grumble against one another, brothers and sisters, or you will be judged.

Why would James's addressees be holding grudges *against one another*? Based on what James has said about their oppressors, we could certainly understand how many in James's audience might be tempted to hold grudges against those who have mistreated them. But that is not what James deals with in this verse.

One possibility is that those to whom James writes are taking out their frustrations with their rich oppressors on each another. Perhaps they disagree about how to handle the situation. Perhaps their oppressive situations are unequal, resulting in covetousness of a fellow believer's assets or circumstances. Regardless, they are in danger of being *judged* unless they stop holding grudges (compare James 4:11, 12). It would be tragic indeed if the judgment that God has prepared for their oppressors also comes on some of them because of failure in this regard.

9b. The Judge is standing at the door!

This warning implies the imminent return of the Lord (see on James 5:8, above). That he is *standing at the door* can mean "expected very soon" or "can happen at any time." Either understanding is cause for repentance! Sin must be put aside

immediately. When Christians harbor bitterness toward one another, they lose their witness.

10. Brothers and sisters, as an example of patience in the face of suffering, take the prophets who spoke in the name of the Lord.

Because of the strong opposition they faced, *the prophets* are examples to James's readers (and to all future generations of believers) *of patience in the face of suffering*. They endured so much (Matthew 5:12). As Hebrews 11:33, 37, 38 says, these were men

who through faith conquered kingdoms, administered justice, and gained what was promised; who shut the mouths of lions. . . . They were put to death by stoning; they were sawed in two; they were killed by the sword. They went about in sheepskins and goatskins, destitute, persecuted and mistreated— he world was not worthy of them. They wandered in deserts and mountains, living in caves and in holes in the ground.

The prophets are thus examples to all Christians of all eras in their faith-based manner of life. They did not merely speak the words of God; rather, they lived out their faith and trusted in him by action.

But above all, the prophets were patient. The nations of Israel and Judah heard the words of the prophets and ignored them. We know that this was frustrating for the men who were called to prophetic ministry. It required a great deal of patience for them to keep preaching God's message of repentance to people who would not listen and would not obey—to their own destruction.

> *What Do You Think?*
> ▶ Which of the prophets best serves as an example for you to emulate personally with regard to patience? Why?
> *Digging Deeper*
> Which kind of earthly suffering seems to vex Christians the most? Why do you say that?

11a. As you know, we count as blessed those who have persevered.

This phrase speaks of the prophets as those *who have persevered*. The language is reminiscent of the blessing found in the Sermon on the Mount at Matthew 5:11, 12:

Blessed are you when people insult you, persecute you and falsely say all kinds of evil against you because of me. Rejoice and be glad, because great is your reward in heaven, for in the same way they persecuted the prophets who were before you.

11b. You have heard of Job's perseverance and have seen what the Lord finally brought about. The Lord is full of compassion and mercy.

This leads James to another example of *perseverance* and patience: that of *Job* (see Job 1:20-22; 2:10). *What the Lord finally brought about* refers to the Lord's purpose in allowing Job to suffer as he did (compare Hebrews 10:36).

Consider the outcomes of *Job's* suffering (see Job 42:10, 12-17). Those outcomes cause us to see the grace of the Lord, that he is *full of . . . mercy* (see Exodus 34:6; Numbers 14:18; Psalm 103:8).

B. Do Not Swear (v. 12)

12. Above all, my brothers and sisters, do not swear—not by heaven or by earth or by anything else. All you need to say is a simple "Yes" or "No." Otherwise you will be condemned.

Jesus appears by name only twice in this letter (James 1:1; 2:1). Even so, James regularly alludes to his teachings, particularly as recorded in Matthew and Luke, and frequently from the Sermon on the Mount. The verse before us offers the clearest connection in that regard, which features a direct quotation from Matthew 5:34-37. Elsewhere the teachings of Jesus bubble just below the surface of James's discussions of wealth and poverty, suffering, wisdom, the control of the tongue, and much more.

The verse at hand caps off this section of James' letter. The phrase *above all* implies that the swearing of oaths is the most egregious sin that the original readers are engaged in. Some commentators argue that oath-swearing is the most serious because a broken oath directly involves God in a lie. We can envision situations in which poor Christians are tempted to swear oaths in order to obtain credit for food, all the while knowing they might not be able to pay the bill when it is due. In other words, the swearing of an oath involves them in behavior that does not glorify God—quite the opposite! We note the negative outcomes of oaths in Matthew 14:6-12; 23:16-22; and elsewhere.

Conclusion
A. From Above

Today's lesson brings two disparate passages together under one unifying theme: the supremacy of the wisdom from above, and the need for it in a variety of situations. Teachers, then as now, can wreak great spiritual damage through the spoken word among those they teach. Ordinary believers, suffering greatly under economic oppression, negate the gospel and its power by harboring bitterness against fellow Christians. Both circumstances damage Christian witness to others.

The solution is for Christians to seek "the wisdom that comes from heaven" (James 3:17). When armed with it, we can put suffering into a larger perspective and be empowered with perseverance to endure until Jesus returns.

We all face challenges over the course of our lives. The real question is how we will react when those times come. Will we pause to seek wisdom from above? Or will we rely on earthly wisdom in our response?

The need for wisdom from above and perseverance go hand in hand as our discipline and resolve are tested. All this has a very real bearing on our spiritual well-being in this life; continual rejection of God's wisdom has eternal implications. As we heed James's call to seek wisdom from above, we will experience a harvest of righteousness.

Guaranteed.

B. Prayer

Heavenly Father, by the power of your Holy Spirit this day, help us to focus our hearts and minds on the wisdom that is from above—your wisdom. We ask this in the name of the wisest person who ever lived: Jesus. Amen.

C. Thought to Remember
Choose God's wisdom.

INVOLVEMENT LEARNING

Enhance your lesson with NIV Bible Student *(from your curriculum supplier) and the reproducible activity page (at www.standardlesson.com or in the back of the* NIV Standard Lesson Commentary Deluxe Edition*).*

Into the Lesson

Acrostic. Write the word *WISDOM* vertically down the center of the board. After you remind learners that wisdom has been the theme in the past several studies, ask, "What are some single-word descriptions of wisdom that have one of that word's letters in common?" As learners suggest words, write them on the board, making sure that each description intersects with one of the letters of the word *WISDOM.* After you have six words to complete the acrostic, ask which one is most accurate. Discuss.

Make a transition by saying, "Today we consider more of what James has to say about wisdom as we look at two passages from his letter."

Into the Word

Point out that James 3:13 both asks a question and implies the answer. Ask half the class to read the question out loud in unison and the other half to respond in unison with the second half of the verse. Then distribute handouts (you prepare) featuring two blank columns, one headed *Godly Wisdom* and the other headed *Worldly Wisdom.* As you read today's text aloud, ask students to note behavior that belongs under either heading. Have study pairs or triads discuss and resolve differences or omissions in entries.

After several minutes, reconvene for a whole-class discussion. Compare the lists and discuss differences. Ask, "What can you do to contribute godly wisdom to the church today?"

Option. Distribute copies of the "Commentary from Scripture" exercise from the activity page, which you can download. Let half of the class, in pairs or triads, consider the first passage noted as the other half considers the second. Call for whole-class sharing after several minutes.

Point the class to Galatians 5:22, 23, and ask a volunteer to read it aloud. Ask, "Which items from this list are also in James's list in 3:17?" Wait for responses, then ask, "What does this tell us about how to achieve the wisdom that James describes here?" (*Expected response*: we need the help of the Holy Spirit in order to demonstrate godly wisdom.)

Option. Distribute copies of the "Wisdom of the Sages" exercise from the activity page. Allow one minute for learners to complete Part 1 with quick first impressions. Then put learners into groups of three or four to complete Part 2.

Into Life

Ask students to conduct a search in contemporary sources for examples of godly wisdom and worldly wisdom. Do this in one of two ways:

- *Newspapers and/or magazines.* Bring an assortment of these for students to use for searches.
- *Internet.* Ask students to use smartphones or tablets to search for examples from news items of the last seven days.

With either approach, ask students to complete the activity in the same pairs or triads formed earlier for Bible study. Allow at least eight minutes to work in groups before calling the class together to share discoveries.

Discuss: "Which kind of wisdom was easier to find, and why?" Ask the class to decide on the best example of worldly wisdom and the best example of godly wisdom they found.

Point students again to James 3:17. Ask class members to decide which of the qualities listed there is the biggest challenge to them personally. Have volunteers suggest one particular action step they could take to manifest their chosen attribute of wisdom.

Distribute paper and ask learners to complete the following sentence: "I can demonstrate godly wisdom this week by _____." Close with sentence prayers, asking that God will give wisdom to those who seek it.